AF655261

Production and Operations Management

ANAND SHARMA
B.E. (Mech.), Osmania Univ.
M.Tech. (Industrial Engg.) - IIT Delhi
Fellow, Indian Institution of Industrial Engineering

Himalaya Publishing House

MUMBAI • NEW DELHI • NAGPUR • BENGALURU • HYDERABAD • CHENNAI • PUNE
LUCKNOW • AHMEDABAD • ERNAKULAM • BHUBANESWAR • INDORE • KOLKATA • GUWAHATI

© Author
No part of this publication may be reproduced, stored in a retrieval system, or transmitted in any form or by any means, electronic, mechanical, photocopying, recording and/or otherwise without the prior written permission of the publishers.

First Edition : 2014

Published by : Mrs. Meena Pandey for **Himalaya Publishing House Pvt. Ltd.,** "Ramdoot", Dr. Bhalerao Marg, Girgaon, **Mumbai - 400 004.** Phone: 022-23860170/23863863, Fax: 022-23877178 **E-mail: himpub@vsnl.com; Website: www.himpub.com**

Branch Offices :

New Delhi : "Pooja Apartments", 4-B, Murari Lal Street, Ansari Road, Darya Ganj, New Delhi - 110 002. Phone: 011-23270392, 23278631; Fax: 011-23256286

Nagpur : Kundanlal Chandak Industrial Estate, Ghat Road, Nagpur - 440 018. Phone: 0712-2738731, 3296733; Telefax: 0712-2721216

Bengaluru : No. 16/1 (Old 12/1), 1st Floor, Next to Hotel Highlands, Madhava Nagar, Race Course Road, Bengaluru - 560 001. Phone: 080-22286611, 22385461, 4113 8821, 22281541

Hyderabad : No. 3-4-184, Lingampally, Besides Raghavendra Swamy Matham, Kachiguda, Hyderabad - 500 027. Phone: 040-27560041, 27550139

Chennai : 8/2 Madley 2nd street, T. Nagar, Chennai - 600 017. Mobile: 09320490962

Pune : First Floor, "Laksha" Apartment, No. 527, Mehunpura, Shaniwarpeth (Near Prabhat Theatre), Pune - 411 030. Phone: 020-24496323/24496333; Mobile: 09370579333

Lucknow : House No 731, Shekhupura Colony, Near B.D. Convent School, Aliganj, Lucknow - 226 022. Phone: 0522-4012353; Mobile: 09307501549

Ahmedabad : 114, "SHAIL", 1st Floor, Opp. Madhu Sudan House, C.G. Road, Navrang Pura, Ahmedabad - 380 009. Phone: 079-26560126; Mobile: 09377088847

Ernakulam : 39/176 (New No: 60/251) 1st Floor, Karikkamuri Road, Ernakulam, Kochi – 682011. Phone: 0484-2378012, 2378016; Mobile: 09387122121

Bhubaneswar : 5 Station Square, Bhubaneswar - 751 001 (Odisha). Phone: 0674-2532129, Mobile: 09338746007

Indore : Kesardeep Avenue Extension, 73, Narayan Bagh, Flat No. 302, IIIrd Floor, Near Humpty Dumpty School, Indore - 452 007 (M.P.). Mobile: 09303399304

Kolkata : 108/4, Beliaghata Main Road, Near ID Hospital, Opp. SBI Bank, Kolkata - 700 010, Phone: 033-32449649, Mobile: 7439040301

Guwahati : House No. 15, Behind Pragjyotish College, Near Sharma Printing Press, P.O. Bharalumukh, Guwahati - 781009, (Assam). Mobile: 09883055590, 08486355289, 7439040301

DTP by : Elite-Art, New Delhi.

Printed at : M/S Sri Sai Art Printer Hyderabad. On behalf of HPH.

Preface

To ensure a rapid economic growth of the country and then to sustain it at the level required to meet the future needs of its people, a substantial healthy industry plays a major role. The recent trends of thinking in terms of globalised operations and wide-ranging needs of variety of customers has resulted in many changes in the industry policies of all the countries. The resources are scarce, the unprecented population explosion is creating really unmanageable demands in all walks of life. The industry, therefore, has to be highly-waste conscious. Productivity increase along with variety production has necessitated newer and newer methods of production with newer and newer technology as an inescapable imperative. For this purpose, in an environment of 24 × 7 innovation needs, very competent business managers and highly skilled workforce has also become a daily necessity. The business managers in all functional areas need to work with incorporation of kaizen and concurrent engineering concepts.

The Scope of Production and Operations Management is vast and varies from strategic planning, extensive managerial development, the economic studies, the facilities development planning, establishment and operations with due care for workers safety, the maintenance management and quality control of men, machines and materials. These area need embodiment of various quantitative techniques for quick and sound decision. The utmost importance of operating very lean and agile organisations with latest technology incorporation, thus, bring in the applications of many useful techniques developed and tried out by many industry leaders. The concept of "Lean Supply Chains – domestic as well as global" has brought in a revolutionary change in the business operating systems. The extensive use of internet in Business-to-Business (B2B) e-business transactions between companies is also a method universally employed today.

Over the years, I have been teaching the subject "Production and Operations Management. The close interactions with a widely varied background students (Very few technicals), brought in the idea to change the so-conceived technical subject to a management subject. A very large number (over 95%) of my students had major maths reservations and it was very challenging task to teach the amalgamation of production techniques relevance to the operations Research techniques. With this effort, it was possible for me to take students near to the ground problems through many daily life examples to familiarise the students with the relevant association of production techniques in all walks of life on day-to-day basis. Hence I started this book with an idea to put it across to all new and old business managers as to how operations management is important to all managers, to know how various production systems work and are maintained at cost effective level, and how to assimilate the state-of-the-art technology in daily operations. The enhancement of decision making effectiveness with the help of simple techniques and heuristics of operations Research was emphasised especially for the global competitive necessity.

To make the book comprehensive and easy to follow, I have integrated various sub-systems of the production management in a graduated manner one leading to the other and their inter-synthesis established closely. A very large emphasis has been given to the Global Business environment to understand customers, the skill and social development of the main industrial asset i.e., human elements, Supply Chain Management integrating the whole business into one single value chain and the Quality Engineering and Control (TQM and SQC combined).

The book has therefore, been divided into seven major sections, sequentially connected :

Section I – Global Environment and Operations Strategy

Section II – Production and operations Systems

Section III – Design of Facilities and jobs

Section IV – Strategic Resources Planning

Section V – Managing the Value Chain

Section VI – Quality Engineering

Section VII – Managing Operations through Project Management Techniques

At the end of the book, I have appended three special cases in the following areas:

Appendix A – Manufacturing Sector – Toyota Production System

Appendix B – Service Sector – Southwest Airline operations

Appendix C – Boeing 787, The Dreamliner

The book also contains a large number of solved numerical problems pertaining to a particular subject under discussion. At the end of the book, two annexures contain simple practical problems as follow :

Annexure A – Decision Points

Annexure B – Decision Analysis

To enhance the utility of the techniques of operations Research, various useful tables have been appended for ready reference.

During the course of teaching the subject to students and healthy discussion with learned industry managers at various levels, I had prepared my notes from various sources, converted them into "Power-point" presentations and brought these into the book in the form of tables and graphs etc for easy comprehension. This information has been collected from various sources, for which, it is difficult to identify and acknowledge individually. I, therefore, express my gratitude to all concerned for their kind support to make this compilation a success. I shall, always, be indebted to all my colleges, students and industry managers for their valuable suggestions during time-to-time discussions.

I also, thank my family, not only for their constant endurance but also effective intervention by my two sons (both as industry consultants for Business Strategy and Business Analysis). I also thanks for the untiring efforts of all the staff of my publisher to make this compilation, a reality, in good time.

— Author

This book is dedicated

to

"Customers"

INTERNAL – EXTERNAL

DOMESTIC & GLOBAL

"Happiness Hides in Life's Small Details.
If You'r not looking, it becomes invisible."

—Joyce Brothers

It can be improved as :

"Happiness hides in life's small details.
If you'r not looking, someone else does."
and
hence your competitor takes the lead

—Author

Book Layout

Section I
Global Environment and Operations Strategies

Section II
Production and Operation Systems

Section IV
Strategic Resources Management

Section V
Managing the value Chain

Section VI
Quality Engineering

Section VII

Managing Operations through Project Management

Section I
GLOBAL ENVIRONMENT AND OPERATIONS STRATEGIES

Chapter 1

Production Systems and Operations Management

Main issues:

1. Importance of Production Management.
2. Evolution of Production Management.
3. Production Model.
4. Production for Competitive Advantage.

1.1 Production Management - Utility in Life

The concept "Production System" or "Production Management" is primarily derived from the word 'Product', which is the basic need of any living being. The products may be tangible goods, intangible services or a combination. Most organisations can be described as production systems, because production means conversion of a set of inputs such as materials, labour, equipments etc., into one or more outputs, such as computers, toys, automobiles, education, legal services, healthcare services or electricity etc.

Since 'Production' is defined as the process of conversion of inputs into outputs, useful for the customers, any subsystems of life can be catagorised into this form. *Production is a combination of performance of many activities and these set of activities are called operations*. Thus operation management is a discipline or profession involving process of planning, designing and operating production systems and subsystems to achieve the goal of the organisation.

It is evident that anything and everything being done in life is meant for customers, humans or non-humans and thus all activities performed in life are to be termed as operations. Hence, the subject 'Production Management' is useful to all of us in one form or the other and the techniques, concepts and methods described under this subject is fully utilised to advantage by all of us at all times for any activity performed by us.

While recognising the fact that production is a larger umbrella, it is a major function in any organisation, whatever be the level. The production system would have to have a prominant place in the corporate plan of the organisation, supported by all staff functions such as marketing, design, materials, purchasing, financing and distribution networks etc.

It is quite a challenging task for any production manager to operate, when the resources availability is limited and operating targets are stiff. To top it all, the customers are becoming more and more demanding bringing in more challenge for any production manager to balance quality, cost and volume of production at the same time.

1.2 Evolution of Production Management

Historical Background

Production management in the present modern form has come a long way through history of mankind. What has impacted its development is the constant change in the customers requirement. Production has been useful even as early as the evolution of human beings and has been in existence from stone-age to the present level of civilisation. Rather than going back into long journey, let us examine few important developments, which have been instrumental in the fast track sharpening of tools and techniques to achieve present level of facilities and volumes. The main pillars considered here are the industrial revolution, the civil war period and after, scientific management, human relations and behaviouralism, the operations research era after the second world war, the service revolution and present technology revolution.

The Industrial Revolution

As described earlier, the production systems in some form have been in existence since the evolution of mankind and and roads of Roman empire, the great China wall, Egyptian Pyramids, Bridges during chola kings regime and quite a few other examples exist to indicate that people had devised their own unique production system to achieve these marvels. But todays systems catering for a large number of customers with very varied requirements have to be different. Old cottage systems *i.e.*, products produced in homes, have undergone a drastic change with the industrial revolution during 1700's in England. A concept was evolved with a large proportion of substitution of human efforts with the machine power. Steam engine and other production machines became available. Due to these machines, a large workforce was required in one place and hence the necessity of organising them into logical utilisation for production work arose. The requirement of scheduling and rescheduling of the resources also arose as a result of this revolution. Concept of division of labour or specialisation of labour were developed so that total complex work could be divided into easily manageable tasks and manpower could easily be managed, thus the concept of planning and controlling the work. As known, possibly the first factory system came into being in the textile industry, where handlooms were converted into power looms and hence innovations in spinning and weaving became possible.

This revolution then spread from England to United States and other European countries. In 1790, a concept of interchangeable parts was developed by Eli Whitney. Infact Eli whitney used steam Engine in 1793 in his Cotton factory, used for removing the seeds from cotton and in 1798, he signed a contract with the US congress to make 10,000 identical muskets at very low price and hence his concept helped in producing rifles for the US government on assembly time. This was a change from old production system of sorting out fitting parts or modification of parts so that it should fit wherever required.

Then came the war of 1812, when New England had almost 200 textile mills. Gasoline engine was developed due to war necessity. For supporting the war efforts, quite a few other factories emerged and by mid-1800's a large factory network had been established. Because of technology advances and changed scale of operations, the size of the markets and manpower control became possible.

The post civil war period

The changed circumstances and release of money from the war efforts to the development sector started a chain reaction of great expansion of production capacity to meet the present demand of the century. Large labour force released from slave camps and immigrants rushing to find work were available for rapid development of industry. Steam and electric power running machine tools produced better products. Large amount of money was available from capitalists and financiers and this saw building up of large industrial empires. These entrepreneurs created production capacity of huge proportions. The variety in the production systems became a necessity due to variety of products demand by the immigrants and settlers. This also necessitated building of roads and rail system to ensure fast and cost effective distribution of products over larger territories. By the end of the 19th century, an effective and economical transport network was in place. Obvious extension of this requirement was great explosion of production capacity during early twentieth century.

Scientific Management

During the second half of the Ninetienth century, there were some very useful discoveries in the field of astronomy, physics, chemistry and biology firming up the belief that the universe was being governed by some definite system of natural laws. These natural laws discovered became the basis of scientific management. Like these natural laws, production laws were formulated and used to work out the best way to perform any job required to make a product. It resulted in the publication of the books, such as Fredric Smith's workshop management (1878) and Henry Metcalf's cost of manufactures (1885).

This research work was utilised to formulate methods and philosophy for large scale production to satisfy massive markets. With this as a groundwork, Frederick W. Taylor (1856-1915) developed the concept of scientific management and hence he is known as the Father of Scientific Management. He studied the factory problems of his time scientifically and advocated the concept of efficiency *i.e.,* getting the desired result with the least waste of time, effort and material.

What was advocated by Taylor, had come due to his long experience and involvement in the industry, right from his days as an apprentice to his elevation to the level of Chief Engineer at Midvale Steel Company in Pennsylvania. During this period, he developed interest in using scientific investigation and experimentation to improve manufacturing operations by improving workers efficiency.

Taylor's shop system, a systematic approach to improving worker's efficiency, was based on the following principles:

- **Right person for the right job:** Scientifically, observe every person of the workforce, find his strength, train him for the skill and level of proficiency and match his work with skill, strength and learning ability.
- **Job design and methods:** Involve worker for his job design, explaining him the logic and provide appropriate incentive. The job design would be to his liking which he is likely to perform to the of his best ability and will help him in following a method most suitable for the job and then set the standards of performance, governed by scientifically evolved techniques.
- **Appropriate supervision:** This is a very specific responsibility and should be separately planned for. Create a staff group of managers at various levels (supervisor is a general term, manager at any level can be termed as supervisor), who specialize in developing production processes, designing jobs and work methods, establishing wage policy, selection and training of workers and planning, organising and co-ordinating workers efforts.
- **Incentives and self-motivation:** A worker should be involved in his work so as to perform as a self-motivated individual. Even then an appropriate incentive should be so designed that a supervisor is relieved of their responsibility of breathing on the neck of workers (or driving the workers).

The analysts following above principles of Taylor came to be known as efficiency experts or efficiency engineers and later as **industrial engineers**. The contribution of other persons deeply involved in formulating and fine-tuning the concepts of scientific management can be summarised as follows:

- Frank B. Gilbreth (1868-1934) - Motion and methods study and therbligs.
- Lilian M. Gilbreth (1878-1973) - Fatique studies, employee selection and training.
- Henry L. Gantt (1861-1919) - Gantt charts, incentive systems, training.
- Carl G. Barth (1860-1939) - Mathematical analysis, feeds and speed studies.
- Harrinton Emerson (1885-1931) - Principles of efficiency and methods of control.
- MorrisL. Cook (1872-1960) - Scientific management for education system.

Thus it can be seen that the emphasis of scientific management was on lower level improvements in an organisation, because it can easily be understood that efficiency belongs to "The Man behind the Gun". And it was required to integrate mass-production with efficiency.

Human Relations and Behaviouralism

The concept of scientific management developed and advocated by Taylor was to ensure enhancement of worker's efficiency through proper job design and method, training incentives for efficient working and just about enough supervision.

So far, the type of workers used in the industrial units were uneducated, unskilled and possibly undisciplined. It was, therefore, thought that given these tools, they will work harder or can be made to work harder so as to avoid their otherwise starvation levels. But during the period between the two world wars, it was felt that if the workers were treated as human beings, given their due dignity, they would work more willingly. A philosophy started emerging that social and psychological aspects of work, better work environment, social group pressures and improved worker-management relationships can work better for increase in the worker's efficiency. The famous studies for the purpose are known as **Hawthorne studies,** because these were carried out at the Hawthrone plant of Western Electric Company in 1927, and ran for over 10 years. These studies were aimed at determining the optimal level of lighting to get the most production from the workers. Initial results did not produce conclusive relationship between working environment and the working efficiency. Hence sociological and phychological factors were added to study human motivation and attitude towards production. These Hawthorne studies may not have produced the intended results, but these started a stream of research on social psychology and workers performances. Few important works that can be quoted in this context are the writings of Abraham Maslow, Frederick Herzberg, Doughlas Mc Gregor and Peter Drucker etc. The behaviour lists added the fuel to the fire by suggesting how managers should treat their workers with dignity to achieve better results. Introduction of moving lien concept for the manufacture of FORD cars (1913) was a large technological innovation in this field.

Operations Research

During world war II, an enourmous amount of manpower, supplies, materials, weapons, planes, ships and other resources were required and used. Complexity of work condition is not difficult to comprehend. It was not only the quantum of resources, but also their variety for different sectors of war having much varied design and quantities at short notices. Then there was a necessity to redeploy forces quickly in some other sector with totally different climate and psychological conditions. The effort, therefore, was required to be a total system, with interdisciplinary approach and use of complex mathematical techniques to avoid voids and chaotic conditions. This environment taught very big lessons to the military operations researchers. These experiences then found way to various educational institutions, government agencies and resulted in the form of "Operations Research (OR)". The OR societies were formed and post war period saw some very useful mathematical and heuristic techniques such as linear programming, PERT/CPM network and forecasting methods. Presently, there are large number of quantitative techniques availables for optimal solutions to large number of production problems. As a sum up, operations research techniques have replaced the intuitive methods with definite inputs for solving large complex problems in a scientific manner, with flexibility available in the form of alternatives through analysis. Today these techniques help improving the decision making process in various fields like personnel and production scheduling, transport routing and logistics, facilities location and planning, capacity planning and facility design, resources planning, queuing and statistical quality control, areas of marketing, finances, engineering and accounting etc. Use of computers in this field has added efficiency to their usage.

The Service Revolution

As a result of creation of service organisations during the world war II to support the war effort for many fronts, there has been a tremendous growth of services sector after the war. Today the service sector dominates almost to the level of two-third of the Gross Domestic Product (GDP). There is a huge trade involvement in services and the sector is growing everyday.

The impact of this service explosion for the operations management has been very large. We have areas of services extending from airlines, commercial banks, Rail and road-heads, food and entertainment, health care, hotels, casinos and resorts, trucking, publishing, printing, packaging, delivery, telecommunications, utility services, insurance and diversified financials, general merchandisers to wholesalers, waste management to computer and data processing services to name a few.

Technology Revolution

Development of computer communication technologies including internet has changed the concept of control of operations completely. Various softwares developed for various fields of operations have enabled the managers to move very fast, thereby changing the concept of time management drastically. Easy access to information and more and more real time information has given the advantage of better control of operations. OR models can be used quickly and deliberately. Better machine control, automation for better quality and larger production quantities, co-ordination of material flow, monitoring tool settings, instant customer orders and inventory controls are some of the important areas to increase productivity. For example, use and operation of a very popular software called Enterprise Resources Planning (ERP) has enabled the organisations to ensure instant control over the entire business all at one time, *i.e.*, from customer to marketing to production to quality control to procurement to vendors to distribution network and instant feedback for any change in product design or service design etc. Due to these new technologies, the organisations are being forced to change their way of working, from the conventional method to highly integrated way, thereby a new challenge everyday for the operations managers in various fields. Some of the important concepts changing the POM impact are Robotics with numerical control, CAD (Computer Aided Design), process control, lean manufacturing, Benchmarking, process re-engineering, outsourcing, supply chain management and virtual organisation, which are great help in our global operations.

1.3 Journey for Production Management

We now travel through the journey of the production management in brief. During eighteenth century the name of the subject was manufacturing management when the concept of breaking the total job into smaller performable tasks was thought of and for each task, specialisation of trade efficiency was advocated for workers.

During 1933 to 1950's, the term was changed to production management, when Taylors principle of shop system, described in earlier paragraph, forced managers to develop techniques for economic efficiency in the manufacturing. The cost effective concept of production brought this term into prominance.

During 1970's, the approach was changed to emphasis on the service sector along with manufacturing. Prominance in service system brought the name as operations management. This was also due to the changed ideas from analysis to synthesis in management practices.

Hence today, the operations function is also undergoing a change as a strategic element, with organisation's objectives more pronounced and focussed. Thus today the operations system is supported by sub systems like finance, marketing, accounting, personnel, engineering, purchasing and the distribution network. Hence it can be now safety called as 'operation system'. Global operations and the necessity of classical, behavioural and modeling techniques as of todays requirement justifies the name much more.

1.4 Definition and Scope of Production Management

Production management has been described by the management expert Peter F. Drucker as follows:

"Production is not the application of tools to materials, but is the application of logic to work".

Basically, production means a system used to convert a sets of inputs such as labour, materials and equipment into one or more outputs, such as products or services. Products are tangible assets, which can be seen, and felt or touched, hence is easy to comprehend the involvement of inputs, whereas the services are intangible, difficult to perceive and hence there may be large variations in possible inputs to achieve variety of services.

In short, we can define production management in the following words:

Production Management is a multi-disciplinary approach, which integrates the knowledge of science, technology, engineering and management in order to produce a product in a cost effective manner to meet customers requirements and achieve organisational objective.

In order to produce goods, the production system is often referred to as manufacturing system and hence the production of goods is called manufacturing. Some of the tangible goods can be aeroplanes, computers, automobiles, medicines, steel, soft drinks etc., (the list is endless due to large variations in customer's preferences and requirements). Services, on the other hand, are intangible products that are required to meet customers needs (may be even at the phychological level) including the enhancement of goods utility. Such production systems are called service systems. Few examples can be financial and accounting services, educational needs and legal services etc., (list can be endless again). The services enhance the utility of function to meet the need of the customer and can not generally be stored.

Products can also be a combination of goods and services. It can be in the form of repair of an automobile, producing and serving the restaurants's produce, the cleaning and creation of congenial atmosphere for work, loans for producing products such as house or vehicle loans, installation, training and maintenance of computers delivered to a customer etc.

Production Model

Since operations can be defined as a set of activities, the operations management is a discipline involving process of planning, design and physical operation of the production and sale systems to achieve organisational goals. This brings in clearly an understanding that operation management deals with the process such as production schedules, quality assurance, materials procurement and utilisation and maintenance of equipment and machinery. The production model can be drawn as follows:

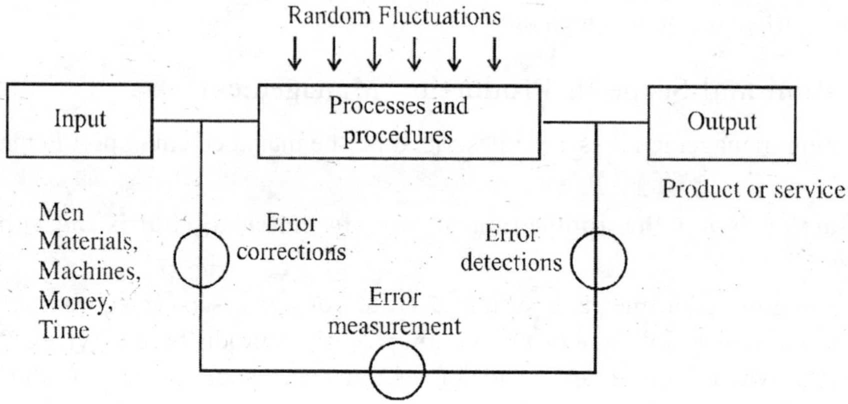

Fig. 1.1: Production model

The production model drawn in fig 1.1 has following important units:

Input unit: Since production is the conversion method, we have to have helping inputs for the production process. The main inputs are 5 Ms as given under:

- Men - skill, quantity and attitude
- Machine - Type, size and quantity
- Materials - Variety and quantity
- Money - Finances required to support the above three inputs
- Moments/Minutes (Time): This is schedule for conversion of other four above mentioned inputs. It will depend on the availability and quantum of work load.

The deliberate calculations, planning and organising is required to have right inputs at the right place at right time to help production.

Process and procedures: It is the method of conversion of material into the end product or service with the help of men and machines (or plants) supported by constant flow of consumables and finances.

Once process is decided (*i.e.,* the method of conversion e.g., casting, welding, etc.,) we have to lay down the procedure for operating that process. An ergonomically designed method and an elaborate clear cut plan to perform as per desired sequence is to be laid down in 'check list' form.

Activities as Random fluctuations: While operating the production system, whatever amount of care is taken in designing a foolproof method, laying down its procedure in transparent way and ensuring all the inputs organised to be available where and when required, there can still be a considerable amount of uncertainty in inputs as well as process to create variation in the resultant product/service, changing its physical or quality standards. The uncertainties can result in the following manner:

- Manpower: Skill deficiency, disinterest of the worker, sickness or absentism etc.
- Materials: Quality of material received, or non availability of materials.
- Machines: Physical condition due to ageing, maintenance deficiency, repair requirements, breakdowns or voltage fluctuations etc.
- Finance: Sudden problems of cash flows for payment for men and materials or for buying maintenance consumables for the machines.
- Time: Wastage of time due to sudden accidents, strikes or labour non-availability etc.

Feedback Mechanism: Another important element of production model is the feedback system to control the results of random fluctuations described above. If product quality has been affected due to any fluctuation, it has to be corrected to ensure good quality product/service reaching the customer.

For this purpose, we incorporate inspection or quality assurance facility *i.e.,* feedback mechanism consisting of three important elements:

- Error detection: Through manual, mechanical or electronic sensors to understand that an error has occurred in the production.
- Error measurement: The detected error has to be measured to ensure that it is rectified fully. This is done with the help of calibrated instrument systems depending on the parameter of error to be measured. Voltmeters, weights, thermometers etc., can be few normal instruments used. Training of the measurement team and proper calibration of the testing equipment is important for error measurement.
- Error correction: Based on the error measurement, the corrective measures are taken to ensure that the production is 'back on rails'. Thus the control mechanism has to have a sensor, a comparator, a memory and an activator.

In this system, named as BURGER MODEL (used by lady Martha Thompson for burger manufacture and making fast food popular across America), the operating systems need to have monitoring and control mechanism strong enough to ensure that no error of known level are allowed unnoticed or uncorrected.

Scope of operations management

We can now summarise various activities under operations management:

Planning activities

- Operations strategy
- Strategic planning and forecasting
- Product/process selection
- Capacity planning
- Facility location planning and layout
- Scheduling strategies

Organising activities

- Job design
- Methods and procedures
- Work measurement
- Setting company standards

Controlling activities

- Manpower planning and control
- Material planning and control
- Production planning and control
- Lean production and Optimised Production Technology.
- Project management
- Quality control

1.5 Value of Human Involvement and Innovations

Due to the challenges for effective global operations, the competitive edge in global market has to be obtained through intelligent use of resources, ensuring waste management and cost containment along with quality assurance.

To use this competitive weapon, the human involvement at appropriate level is not only necessary, but the work force is to be selected, trained, motivated and then utilised through proper monitoring and control. The mental level of the human resources at all levels, right from the worker to the senior-most manager is required to be very high so that the whole team works as self-motivated cohesine force. Infact, in todays environment even this is not enough. Due to constant upgradation of customer's requirements, all the human force has to be highly innovative in their approach to work and it is a 24 × 7 job for everyone *i.e.,* each and every member of the team has to be constantly thinking and applying him/herself towards improvements at all times of the day. Innovative thinking and application would add further value, if it is in anticipation of customers demand for tomorrow.

Discussing the specific responsibilities of the operations manager, with challenges large and taxing, the gravity of problems vary. Division of the responsibilities into two major areas are product design and design of the production system and sub-systems and the area of actual operation of the production system. Both these areas need a high degree of innovation. A constant upgradation of the product design not only from its functional angle, but also with reference to the choice of new technologies and process design, methods of operations and enhancement of quality and safety standards have to be thought of. Again a close watch on materials, machines, production planning, scheduling of resources, their procurement and organising, maintenance of equipment etc., have be in tune. with the latest in the field. Constant upgradation of distribution system network goes a long way to achieve improved services for the customer. All this will be possible only if the work force operating these systems are efficient and motivated.

1.6 Production for Competitive Advantage

To achieve advantage over the competitors and to gain a large share of the market, it is important to ensure the following:

- Product/service differentiation
- Cost optimisation
- Innovation for delight

Product and Services Differentiation

Both the factors are equally important to stay ahead of your competitors. The product designed and positioned in the market must be viewed and perceived by the customer as different from others. The case of plastic water tanks can be viewed in the light of the above statement. In India, we were used to overhead water tanks made of bricks/concrete. But when Syntex brought the plastic tanks to the market, it was a different concept. These were light in weight, tough, easy to erect and easy to service. This totally revolutionalised concept gained acceptance in quick time. It must have been a very aggressive marketing effort (to get the change accepted in so orthodox a country) but because of product/service differentiation, it found its place in the market very quickly.

Cost Optimisation

The second factor *i.e.,* cost optimisation is equally important because the product quality, performance and cost go together for market acceptance. Customer weighs his quality standard visa-vis the price he pays for it. If the product and service quality and performance is perceived to be good and different, the customer is ready to pay even more due to convenience of availability and the long term gain.

Innovation for Delight: With reference to the Product differentiation and cost optimisation the product features, quality and variety requires constant change. This change becomes the delight for the customer if the innovation capability of the organisation is high. The availability of product to the customer to day's requirement is necessary but if the organisation is capable to bringing a new product as per the future requirement, the customer feels very happy. The need for innovative thinking emerges from:

- Organisation vision
- Motivation
- Attitude for excellence
- Creative mind
- Peristance

The contribution of **Jobs** for Apple innovations is a very good example.

For ensuring innovation culture in the organisation, following tools are required:

- Individual Innovation
  - — Motivation
  - — Technical application

— Creativety of the workers and managers

— Analysis and application of results.

- Innovative teams
- Innovative organisation

Few companies known for their innovative approaches are listed below:

- Apple
- Google
- United Health Group
- Proctor and Gamble (P & G)
- Walt Disney
- Fedex
- Genetech
- Nike
- Advance Micro Device (AMD) and
- Target etc.

Operations Management

Operations management provides such a philosophy to achieve the above aim of facing competition.

It strategiges the management of change in the organisation. A close linking and integration of various functions to achieve the aim of competitive edge is essential. Manufacturing has, thus, gained a prominant place in this management system. Various problems in this area to provide effective support to the service function are to be resolved. For the manufacturing competitiveness, overall strategic management of operations is required. Japanese and various Asian countries like China and Korea have grasped the importance of manufacturing as the engine for the economic growth and are doing well.

The integration of various operational concepts can be brought out by describing the achievements of Toyota Motors, in a plant of General Motors. When they formed a joint venture with GM, they did not really transform the technology, they merely managed it well. The concept of workers empowerment and participation produced wonderful results (Human Asset Angle). They also modified the product design for easy manufacturing and assembly (DFMA, described later in this book) and the reorganisation of production layout to ensure better product flows. Inventory levels were practically reduced to Nil. The sharing of quality concerns with the workers created an atmosphere of mutual trust and goodwill. The same old workers (large workforce was reemployed by Toyota) brought in a aggressively loyal attitude in production. It is this integration of resources (duty backed by marketing, finance and purchasing etc.,) that transformed the old California assembly plant of GM into a very efficient factory.

The nature of competition, market share and competitors strategies do place the load on the production. The differentiation, in fact, should be the watchword for all the functions of the organisation to achieve the competitive edge over others.

Hence operations must be viewed as a total system, not as fragmented subsystem approach.

1.7 Career prospects in Production Management

From the above description, it transpires that production management would have people and functions involved in all walks of life. Hence there is practically no limit of career prospects in this field. Even at the smallest job level, there are bound to be persons involved. Their training and job proficiency, their outputs fixation and co-ordination of efforts are important human management responsibilities. At a complex organisations levels, these responsibilities become manyfold and challenging. Since in production and services both, there may be variety of machines involved, the integration in terms of their capabilities, operations, maintenance, outputs and scheduling would be required, for which the knowledge at various levels would be handy. Financial and time management would be of utmost importance in all our daily functions in co-ordinating materials, machines and human beings involved in the system.

For achieving success in life, each one of us has to be a phychologist and a manager within our ambit of responsibility. The quality of decision making for all our functions will depend on the quantum of knowledge and quantity and quality of information utilised for our decision making process in everyday life. Since product and service both are integral parts of production, the knowledge of production management will be very handy.

Thus we can summerise the importance of the production and operations management bringing in the areas of work suitable for career path and enhanced prospects:

- Modern approaches to operations management can be and are applied in all business areas and hence it has a unique position in business education.
- Operations management offers a systematic way of working in life and in all fields of business.
- Operations management results in corporate competitiveness due to its applicability in reducing wastes and increase in productivity.
- The decision making capability of managers through the use of Operations Research (OR) or Management Science (MS) techniques, helps in shaping the corporate operations strategies.

—●—

Chapter 2

Global Business Environment and Operation Challanges

Main issues:

1. Global Business Environment.
2. Customer Requirements and Global Competition.
3. Innovative Strategies such as MOT, TQM, TPM, JIT, EI, BPR etc.
4. Corporate Transformation and Social Responsibility.

2.1 The Business Philosophy

Business philosophy can be understood from a quote of Sir Edmund Hillary, a very tough Mountaineer. It says ***"The ladder to the top is long to climb. The climb is long and ordous. The obtacles are many. Only those who have grit and the stamina, those who are prepared to learn and re-learn from their mistakes and improve constantly and continue to grind can remain in the forefront and ultimately reach the top."***

The massage defines the rigours of the business in the present global environment. The grit and stamina has recently been shown by our steelman Laxmi Mittal in case of clinching the deal for the merger of Arcelor with his own large steel empire. He believed in the philosophy of ''Keep on and win the game "to reach the top".

The business is meant for customer, who is the sole aim and beneficiary of total business operations. Mahatma Gandhi has shown the path of total customer orientation in his famous statement, quoted below.

"A customer is the most important visitor on our premises. He is not dependent on us. We are dependent on him. He is not an interruption of our work. He is the purpose of it. He is not an outsider to our business. He is part of it. We are not doing him a favour by serving him. He is doing us a favour by giving us the opportunity to do so."

2.2 Global Business

The international trade has resulted in global economy leading to a concept of global village, whose geographical boundaries have become redundant for business operations. Today companies need to become international, so that they can buy, produce and sell anywhere in the world markets.

To achieve competitive advantage in this environment of Globalisation, companies have to strategise to exploit global business opportunities in terms of technology, market access, production capability or pooling of financial capital and human resources. In the words of Peter Drucker, **"Production sharing means that a product may be designed and financed by one partner, marketing network to be provided by another partner, the material procurement to be done by someone else and possibly the distribution network of yet another company to be used to advantage."**

Product quality and customer service should be the predominant factor for strategic alliance and production sharing. It brings out the importance of service quality for a long-run relationship with the customer, with a dynamic role of production to be integrated with total dynamism in the service function, so that ever changing expectation of the customers can be taken care of. Innovation and quick response in both the areas is an absolute necessity today. Sharing the advanced technologies is yet another area for joint ventures to achieve the above-quoted requirement of the customer. Advance technologies may result in high initial cost, but the fruits of low labour cost, increased product/service quality, reduced wastages and faster responses to the customer needs offset these high investments. Producing large volumes also reduces the overhead costs per unit of product. Hence automation is heading towards Computer-Integrated-Manufacturing (CIM), wherein large number of companies are taking long term competitive advantage of CIM and ERP in the form of strategic alliances and production sharing.

These concepts are all the more useful under the constraint of scarcity of operational resources. Capital, employees, raw materials and other natural resources lead to the concept of strategic allocation of resources. In addition, the companies have to take care of environmental issues such as ozone depletion, global warming, acid rain, petroleum and chemical spills or radio-active waste disposal etc. Energy is becoming scarce. Hence waste reduction must play prominant role in design, production and distribution to enhance productivity of the operations of the organisation.

2.3 Area Specific Requirements

Though the world market is now open to all, there is still a very large challenge due to specific area peculiarities. Political and economic developments (both very uncertain due to frequent changes at the political level) have resulted in many foreign markets becoming attractive. Due to constant shift in economic policies either as per area market forces or shift in priorities of various governments, formation of blocks such as European union (EU), North Atlantic Free Trade Agreement (NAFTA), South Asian Association For Regional Cooperation (SAARC) etc., place special emphasis on local market requirement. Restrictions and openings of markets due to General Agreements of Tariffs and Trade (GATT) and World Trade Organisation (WTO) provisions applicability.

Fluctuation in International Financial conditions *viz.*, fluctuating currency rates, volatile interest rates, position of stock markets and debt pressure of many nations create large economic inbalances and dictate flexible policy to cater for these changes. "The new emphasis (or reemphasis) is traceable to the increased competition in quality" is adding to the complexity of operations.

2.4 Global Competition

Today the world has changed in its outlook towards business, with WTO provision in place. Open global economy has thrown a number of unique challanges. While formulating the operating strategies of business, the companies face high level of uncertainty in various markets due to frequent changes in political and cultural fields, resulting from fast growing social diversities arising out of financial conditions in domestic as well as international customer base.

The competitive environment of business changes most of the operations to be much faster today than ever before. This has created an increased uncertianty in business for everyone. The buzz word is "either perform or perish" under today's trying conditions.

Information technology has enhanced the exposure and awareness levels of the customers to unprecedented high expectations. Due to globalisation effect, the customer market has become practically unlimited not only due to geographical or cultural reasons, even in the same area, wide variations in produce specifications. In fact, mass customisation is now becoming thing of the past and we are heading almost to the area of individual customisation.

The organisations have to be flexible and be able to respond very quickly to changes in the business environment and changes in customer demands. In order to gain competitive advantage in the global markets, the business managers have to be innovative and flexible at all point of time. Domestic competition is forcing companies to enter into export market and hence face competition from all available players. Communications, transportation and present global trade policies enable companies to operate in the global environment, where in the cost and quality constraints are very large.

Global competition described above gives rise to a very important ingradient of operations management called "productivity". It is related to production and service both. In todays environment, only those companies will prosper who can provide best value to its customers. The best value is determined by what the customer at the other end gets in terms of product function, quality and timeliness related to the price they pay. Hence the company is forced to produce the product, which is perceived by the customer to be different with functional value added with optimum level of cost and the product quality and reliability. The customer is required to be convinced about the utility of the product for long period of usage.

Indian Production Scenario

With the controlled economy, the production sector was possibly at a disadvantage of poor competition. India, with its very large population, could consume whatever was produced.

It is not so any more. With Liberlisation, Privatisation and Globalisation (LPG), the scenario has completely changed. The change, obviously, has brought a large level of uncertainty and with it, the enormous challenge. When you face challenge, and you want to succeed, the options for survival and excellence are to be searched. This search is on and we know, we Indians are improving our manufacturing, service and business image. The present surveys and consumer confidence indicate that India is a long-term gainer. We have to enter the world market with confidence and when we find our niche, we side-place someone else. This is going to identify the competition to retain the market share gained.

Today Indian economy is in a resilient mode for growth, inflation and balance of payment and we are sure to move up the lodder due to Indian vision of all-round development *i.e.*, both the manufacturing as well as service sector. It is not only IT industry, that we think of as a mode of our economic transport, we are into large scale investments and development through a strategic fit as well as creative thinking in manpower development and enhancement of employment potential in agriculture, textile, food processing and large many service sector facilities too. The thrust into agricultural diversification (the real back bone of Indian economy), development and strengthening of agricultural marketing infrastructure, repair, renovation and restoration of water resources, flood management and erosion control, promoting micro irrigation technology, increased rural credit, improved insurance covers etc., are some very positive initiatives in rural sector, in addition to a large scale thrust in big and small industries all-the-way around.

India has a great advantage in its young work force (a study report by Goldman Sachs). We are predicted to be third largest economy, with China and USA leading. In the years to come by, WTO is playing a major role in terms of opening new world markets, non-discrimination and global competition in the world trade scenario. We are moving high in service sector also globally, in addition to improving our manufacturing capability. We are heading towards becoming a manufacturing hub. Lot many multinationals are shifting their manufacturing bases to India due to cost-effectiveness and high quality workforce. Mc Kinsey has identified three skill-intensive sectors, namely electricals and electronics, auto-components and speciality chemicals to make India globally competitive. The apparel and textiles have also achieved a huge market share. IT outsourcing has been a large gain for India and we have a large software market in our pocket. Due to our IT-strength, the automation in manufacturing as well as in service sector is becoming economically-viable businesses. Very significant imperative for focusing on manufacturing is the contribution of world trade to economic development The manufacturing, therefore, has to develop into the engine of our economic growth due to large role in product areas as well as in support of service area. The chances of our economy boom by 2025 seem to be very bright, if we stay on track in terms of long-term policies.

2.5 The Challenges

Customer is supreme in total business strategy and with business shifting its focus from domestic to global arena the challenges to succeed in business have multiplied. The three major challenges for business managers for the 21st century can be listed as follows:

- Managing Customers
- Managing Uncertainty
- Managing Globalisation

Not that these challenges did not exist for businesses of yester-years, these have become very intense due to global competition and there is no respite from continuous increase in this direction. Either we perform (better than competitors) or we perish. The business, therefore, has to be done differently today keeping eyes and ears open to the global customers and global competitors.

Managing Customers. Business manager has to understand his customers in totality *i.e.*, technical, functional, aesthetical, psychological and societal angles. If he does not, his business would not prosper. The issue is very complicated. The customer of today is better exposed, better informed and hence more demanding. Due to the very exposure, he takes no time to shift his loyalty. This exposure can be half-baked truth. Most of the time, customer really does not understand what he wants. May be, he is clear (to a large extent) as to what performance to.be expected from the product or service that he is looking for. How, when and at what quality and cost, are not easily answered questions. Business managers have to obtain it from the customers with due deliberation. For this purpose, a very detailed and elaborate market research, analysis, study, innovations and pro-active actions will be required.

This is only one angle of customer management. After the relevant (so believed complete) information is collected and transformed into the end result *i.e.*, Product or service, this has to satisfy the need of the customer. The marketing and sales team have to be aggressive enough to place the item in the market in such a way that the customer understands it, accept it and can use it fearlessly. It must perform well over a period of time so that a perception of "good and suitable" is developed in the mind of the customer. This aspect is called "customer perception".

The third important parameter for customer management is the after-sales service *i.e.*, the responsiveness and reliability to be established to develop faith of the customer in the organisational ability to match his requirement of product function. The contact, behaviour and preferably "one window or one person redressal" system are good methods to ensure this, A step further called "Proactive service" *i.e.*, reach a customer before he needs you can be very helpful. Psychologically it makes a large difference in customer management.

Managing Uncertainty. Uncertainty is a way of life. It is available to every living being at all points of time. The best part of uncertainty is that the past history or experience can help you very little to predict the future happening. The uncertainty in the customer's mind is, therefore, the most difficult aspect of business to be tackled. Even the best of psychologists find it difficult to reach the mind of his subjects. The socialists, social-scientists, behaviourialists and so many others have tried their minds, but very few can lay hands on the right nerve reaction.

As if this uncertainty was not enough, the addition of dimensions come from the variations in cultures and national economies. Such matrices are difficult to obtain. Hence the requirements of one item (product/service) for an American customer are different from those of an English customer, also are different for a customer from Japan, Nigeria, China or Zimbabwe. We can not standardise even an item of food for their widely different cultures and economies, other requirements multiply exponentially. Is it not only, therefore, a very large challenge across the nations, but even in our own domestic consumption pattern. Therefore, for the similar requirement of product, say mode of transportation for self use, we have to offer either a bicycle or a bus or a car to a customer based on his choice of time, quality, and the drain on his pocket. Similarly a cup of tea would need a variety of cups and varieties of tea leaves for different customers from different part of the country for different status of living.

The third level of uncertainty is felt in terms of a constant change in the customers requirement. This is due to change in social indicators, per capita income, exposure, or functional requirement itself. Changes due to natural forces or due to peers pressures also make the requirements uncertain. This change can be termed as "customers progressive preference"[1], and can be quite telling on business strategy. Business managers, therefore, need to be proactive and innovative all the time to cater for this progression.

Managing Globalisation. To top the above-mentioned uncertainty, a change in the area of business has altered the operational strategies totally during last two decades or so. This aspect has grown tremendously and all national boundaries have fallen apart due to global operations. Economic or Business Blocks such as European Union or North Atlantic Free Trade Association (NAFTA), ASEAN AND APEC or the global agreements in place like World Trade Organisation (WTO) have further enhanced the concept of business into "Global village" business administration. This has resulted in an intense competition. The effect is that the wheels of liberalisation has been set in motion and we can operate no more under 'closed economy' conditions. Imports and Exports have became almost a free business, with quota regime having vanished. Financial liberties, technology transfers, availability of unlimited quantity and variety of materials have thrown open a large number of opportunities with practically level ground for operations for all. To cater for this intense need, new technologies, new methods, capacity maximisation, efficiency increase and optimisation of resources have become a constant research area. Management has developed into an important area for research and study. Production and sales concepts have undergone drastic changes. Outsourcing for resource optimisation is becoming an effective tool in large number of areas. Globalisation has not only increased competition, it has also helped business in term of scale of economies. The products manufacture can be highly cost effective due to large volumes but challenge lies in the variety of the products. The major thrust of globalisation has been in expansion of business across the boundaries of the nations. Today, since we live in a global market place, it is virtually the sale of the same products around the world to varied customers. Another advantage of globalisation has been in the strategy of production in some advantageous location (country) with technology from another country, with raw materials or components from some other country, packaging in another place and distribution in and around the globe by a strategic partner (firm) in some other Country. This has resulted in the use of the best of cost effective resources of various kinds to put into the product. The quality of the products have improved **(a definite gain for the customers)** due to intense competition in markets when the companies strive hard for market share and profitability. Thus the ability to make products available to a constantly changing markets requirement on time, at desired locations to level of the customers paying capacity may make the difference to the graph of success both in terms of product acceptance, market share and the financial returns. This is where efficient production and efficient distribution can help to a large extent for meeting delivery schedules.

2.6 Customer Preference

Quality, technology and competitiveness are much too interrelated and inter-dependent elements. Quality and cost requirements also have a bearing on the trade operation because quality requirements of various markets are largely varying. Based on the national economic condition, products of varying cost and quality needs to be planned for specific markets. Availability and utilisation of some advanced technologies also would depend on how much an economy can afford. Cost, availability and skill of labour. ethics, societal pressure and labour laws also have bearing on financial health of the industry.

In addition to the financial angle of quality and price, the business has to take care of ground reality with references to the customer needs of various areas.

The total Business chain is illustrated in Figure 2.1 below:

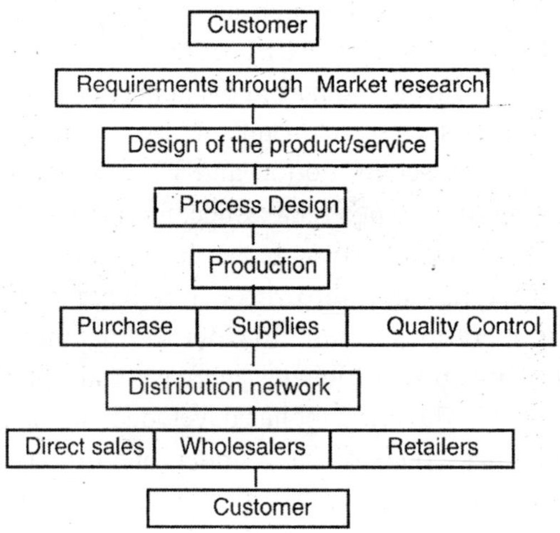

FIG. 2.1. Business Areas of Importance

Areas of Customer Focus

Customer's focus on requirement should be studied from the following angles:

• Functional • Technical	Core needs
• Aesthetical • Financial	Value addition
• Psychological • Societal	Delight

The above aspects, therefore, vary the product in the following manner:

- Production features
- Product quality
- Price
- Product Variety
- Customisation
- Place and Schedule of delivery

For customer satisfaction and loyalty focus, the company has to consider the following important factors:

- Customisation
- Short Product life cycle
- Quality of the product
- Cost/price
- Delivery schedules.
- After Sales Services

Customisation: Customisation would need the following emphasis:
Customer behaviour,
Customer preference,
Mass and individual customisation

Customer Behaviour: Today's customers impose their own will on the type of products required by them. Customers have, not only become very demanding in term of quality and cost, but also in terms of their immediate fulfilment of changing demands. The world market is open to large variety of customers with the use of internet and media exposures. The exposure enhances the mental upliftment of the customers. Constant change in the needs and wants of the customer is 'in thing' today, which means that anticipation or forecasting of demand is bcoming very difficult day-by-day. What is required by the customer is no more dependent on the operational efficiency of the supply system, but on the positioning of brand and its variety. It is a large supply chain challenge. Upgradation of information on the customer behaviour is, thus, very relevant and critical today, before supply chain is designed.

The second important variation in customer behaviour comes from living standards. There is a large difference between the requirements of urban and rural customers and even between metros and other urban customers. For example, the behaviour of people changes while staying under stressed and busy conditions of metro cities resulting in their daily requirements in the form of casual clothes, different eating requirements and even different entertainment services. which may not be so intense in other urban population. Rural requirement of even basic products like clothing, food, housing and entertainment are totally different.

The third type of customer behaviour change occurs due to education levels or cultural and religious beliefs. There are regional variations noticed in persons from one area to another and hence the type of bus service facilities are different in Mumbai than those in Delhi and Kolkata.

When this aspect of regional imbalances is taken to the global platform, behaviour differences amongst nations multiply manyfold. The out-going and weekend recreational habits of Americans are different from those of Japanese and hance the product difference varies from SUVs (sports utility vehicles) for outings in America to bicycles in Japan. Similarly, the comfort conditions for Americans, Indians and Nigerians are different, resulting in variety of products for high-wage Americans to low-wage Nigerians.

Thus we can sum up the variety of products due to various behavioral aspects:

Gender, Age, Race and Income differentiation

Attitudes toward life, career, social status or political influence.

Product warmth due to excitement, social approval or self respect etc.

Customer Preferences: Today the customers show preference towards colourful, many featured, small, trendy cell phone sets and hence companies has to be alive 24 hours a day to produce something different from yesterday. The constant change in such behaviours put pressure on the research and development and marketing facilities, requiring support from all other partners of the supply chain. Constantly changing preferences at faster speed lay emphasis on new items, for which the cost effective business (earning reasonable profit) can be obtained through effective R&D, product sales and acceptance and hence increased marketing efforts. Sometimes, the marketing can help in changing customer preference, when a new product, much different from the so-far-traditional product, is brought to the customer. Plastic tank for overhead water storage can be cited as a good example. Constant change in speed of Personal Computers (PCs) has brought a change in customer thinking with increased usage of PCs in large many areas.

Customer preferences are also important from the variability point of view. The customer may prefer red colour today, black tomorrow and white day after. Such variations become even large, when we consider customers across the globe. Price, quality, utility, availability and responsiveness to the time of delivery of the product, therefore, have to be taken into consideration while deciding on the operational strategy of the organisation. If a particular product is required by the customer. Say in 48 hours or any other time schedule and due to constraint of the market such as availability of raw material, labour skill, manufacturing capability or technical capability, an organisation is not able to meet this demand, this demand is lost. Hence customer preferences have to be weighted with reference to the organisational capability, before deciding the operational strategy.

Mass and Individual Customisation: Due to the state of exposure and knowledge base enlargement of the customer, he is no more willing to buy whatever is made available to him.

Today he needs products and service to his taste, even in the area of colour, size and shape. This taste is forced on the manufacturers and hence they are required to produce a tooth paste in gel category and also white paste with grey and red lines. The car colour has to be black, maroon or silver grey etc. to cater for the taste of different groups of customers. Some customers prefer daily provisions to be delivered to their place (both, the husband and wife may be office going people) and hence free home delivery of milk, bread and chopped vegetables or even ready-to-cook products is an example of customisation.

Customers also have started demanding a particular material to be used in a product or the exact features to be built into the product. A very specifically featured PC, a particular battery for the inverter or car, a shirt of a particular colour (whether wrinkle free cotton shirt or a synthetic material shirt for easy maintenance), a particular size of packaging, like small soaps, small 10 millilitre shampoo etc. are number of examples of customisations required. It is the strategic decision as to how to produce such wide variety of products to satisfy customers needs. Real Estate industry has started constructing condominiums of specific range, different interiors (even to the particular customer taste) and provision of facilities to suit a group of people. The electronics and electrical products have a large variety of products in the market with continuous improvement on regular basis.

It is not possible to produce products to every customer's taste and hence the grouping or customer segmentation is a must, putting major features in each group of products and then working on customisation even in that group, say by putting a particular type of seats in a car with choice shade or adding memory level to a PC based on customer order and so on.

This requirement does not create flexibility in manufacturing only, but adds flexible dimension to the supply chain also. The manufacturing facility would need the support from other partner like supply of varied raw materials, packagings for a set of product or even different modes of distribution channels so as to ensure timely delivery at a place and time desired. Choice of cargo planes has come into existence instead of cargo ships for certain types of products for quick delivery schedules. This also calls for keeping a bank of suppliers to supply specific materials and components as per time requirement. This may increase the inventory levels of varied products. But Vendor Managed Inventory (VMI) concept can help in this direction. Thus customisation (a strong market force) has introduced 24 × 7 innovation as a reality. Lost customers or Turnaway customers can be a great loss to business, even to the extent of loss of corporate credibility. The onus falls on to Supply Chain Management for such failure. Close interactions among manufacturers, suppliers, supply chain operators and the marketing outfit is essential for success of the business due to high customer satisfaction level.

Short Product Life Cycle: What has been discussed in the preceeding paragraphs is an indication of the age of products. The customer starts expecting an improved or a different product as he has used the present one for a certain period of time. This is the second challenge of this century termed as "Managing uncertainty" Uncertainty of market demand due to constant change in customers behaviour and preference, curtails the life of a product. Maroon or white may be a preferred colour fot a short time, soon changing to silver or black. This is a very big challenge for the manufacturers and in turn for the supply chain managers. Under the intense pressure of competition, the innovation has become a way of like for business managers.

The major problem is as to how to calculate or predict the most reasonable life cycle for a product. This can normally be judged from actual sales figures, which can indicate the peak and decline period. The moods, changing tastes and resulting preferences will indicate the direction of business. Armed with this information, the Company may apply statistical methods to forecast future course. The decision is more important to time the launch of the new product to replace the declining product. Do we have to notice the declining sales and then only we start taking action for its replacement ? It may be too late, because the company may be out of business, if the product acceptability vanishes at quick speed, may be due to competitors strength of product. Who-so-ever is ahead in this race, survives the market better. Hence the normal way to deal with the problem is the launch of a new product in such a way that the combined sales are practically maintained at the same level. Thus when the present product is on the rise, simultaneously new product is designed, produced and brought to the market before the peak of the first product occurs. In case the life of the first product is larger, the company will get the benefit of better Return on Investment (RoI). If the decline is faster, the second product is pushed up to fill the gap, (thus maintaining the market share) in such a way that the peak of the second product occurs as the first product declines.

It may be the strategic decision from the point of view of marketing and financial outputs. But this enhances pressure on manufacturing outputs (additional capacity for the second product) and on supply chain system (dealing with the first product, and at the some time, catering for the second product simultaneously, may be at different load factor). The additional capacity in manufacturing and in supply chain has to be intelligently planned so that it can merge into next product requirement easily. In supply chain management, it may be a carefully crafted level of outsourcing capacity. The strategy has been illustrated in Fig. 2.2 below.

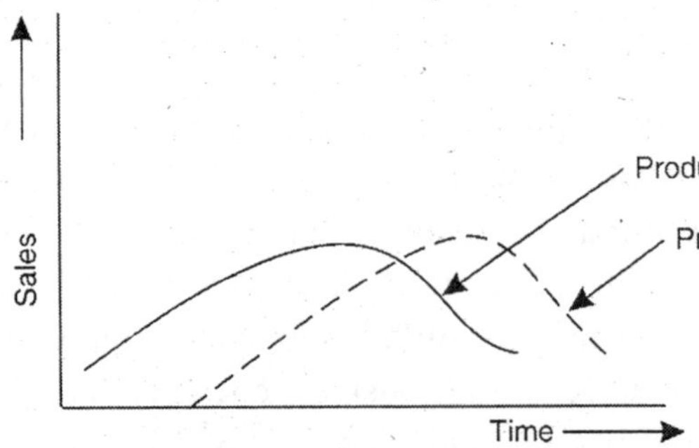

FIG. 2.2. Strategy for Short Product Cycle Products

Quality of product/service : The discussion on customer focus, so far, has hovered around the type and variety of product for customisation. Another important area needing attention is quality of the product. As per Juran, "Quality is fitness for use". In the words of Dr. Deming, "Do it right the first time and every time". These two definitions of quality specify the uncertainty of the customers requirement from quality angle. For fitness for use, quality varies with the use and hence with every customers usage. If we take the trivial example of drinking a cup of tea, one person may accept a cup with tea spilling over to indicate his acceptance of quality of service, whereas another person may even have tea in a chipped cup, it being even lower service level quality. But if the person refuses the cup in both these conditions, his service will be upgraded to a decent well washed cup with good tea, possibly with a saucer underneath. These are three different levels of quality of services expected by these customers. Thus it is evident that quality is as wide-ranging as the number of customers. Quality can be judged on different parameters. Product quality will depend on its physical, performance, aesthetic or even shape and colour parameters. All these parameters are widely different for customer of different tastes, attitudes, cultures or even different regional background.

In case of service, quality is more uncertain for quantification. It many be just the smile of service provider or sweet talk, that may satisfy a customer. Hence the quality of service depends on intangible parameters also and is generally subjectively determined.

All these variations in quality are difficult to cope up with. But the most important factor is the price that a customer pays for a product or service. Very demanding customer would like to have the best of product/service at the lowest price. But if he wants a high quality product/ services, he may be willing to pay for it, provided he perceives the high quality level. Therefore, the quality variations for customisation are to be built in with the design, production as well as in the distribution system flexibility.

Quality in Design and production must satisfy the customers requirement of the performance, shade and shape of the product/service. But for the distribution system, quality is the delivery of the right product at right place at right time and at right price, which the supply chain configuration has to cater for with the right product mix and selection of the right mode of delivery as per customers schedule. If the company delivers the dented product due to inappropriate mode of transport, customer will reject the product. If it is not delivered in time, he may buy some other product. If it is not priced as per his quality cost perception, he shifts his loyalty to the product of the company's competitor. Thus even the sales strategy can make the difference due to sales service or after sales service quality.

Cost/price: The company has to introduce the concept of value of the product/service to the customer. Hence the discussion on supply chain should include the dicussion on the value chain. The customer percieves the value of the product/service in terms of its cost/price. Let us take an example of serving the healthy food to a customer. For a customer needing healthy food, it may be a highly valued item, but if the food is not tasty (sensory aspect of the product), its price perception for the customer will be low. He may not be willing to pay for such a food. Thus the value of the product must keep the balance between the cost and quality of the product.

Cost effectiveness of the products also have a large role to play in operational strategy. The detailed analysis of the input costs will be helpful, in addition to 'what if' analysis and the appropriate technology and waste management aspects of the production. Customers look for a product with a total functional utility at the least price. The organisation, therefore, must concentrate on such products which can fulfill this condition of the customer in that segment of society. Competition study also will be a great help to remain competitive. Corporate social responsibility of producing a product of at right quality, right price, considering the competition in the market have to be balanced to create a distinguishing product for the market. For flexibility of product range (constantly changing customer of product range, quality and price) and customisation, innovation (uniqueness of the products and speed of product development) would be the keyword. An organisation, therefore, has to decide on its market competitiveness based on its financial resourcing, geographical and customer oriented distribution network, technological capability and the competance of human resources to ensure optimum results.

Value chain: Customer's focus extends to the value chain, which means extension of the chain from demand to the delivery end. The value chain would include the addition of value to all the links of the supply chain. It is connected with quality and efficiency of all operations, so as to reach the level of least possible total cost for the end user. It is optimisation of inputs, conversion and distribution. Then only the right perception builds up in the mind of the customer on the product and the service level of the organisation. The optimisation of internal as well as the external linkages is crucial for cost/price perception and hence for business.

In this discussion, few important and desirable outputs of the value-chain can be used for better understanding of the cost/price relatioship. These are namely

- Firstly, the value chain should be based on the understanding of the customer with reference to performance, aesthetics and service quality.
- Secondly, it should cater for "every time" concept of quality *i.e.*, should support the business in continuously changing environment.
- Thirdly, it should cater for optmisation and integration of various linkages through proper information flow from customer to production to sales to distribution.
- Fourthly, information flow should build up the product change capability, so as to stabilise the market share through improved products and services.
- Fifthly, IT-enabling of the chain should ensure co-ordination of efforts of the organisation, so as to avoid wastes at every stage.
- Sixthly, it covers the area of waste management, disposal of scraps or surpluses and that of reverse logistics so as not to impede the flow of product/service.
- Seventhly, the constant interaction of all the stages/linkages of supply chain will enhance anticipating and forecasting capability of the organisation.

- Lastly and finally, the value chain ensures the capability of the supply chain for dealing with the uncertainties, thereby helping in growth of the business with better monitoring and control system.

Delivery Schedules: This is the service end of the supply chain. A customer focus in this area means that the product/service must be made available to him as and when he needs it. He can not be expected to wait (unless there is no alternative available to him). Till few years back, a customer would accept a delay in his car delivery, as we had only few limited options. Intially Maruti had the the strategy of waiting period. But the strategy does not hold water any more, when, due to change in government policy, there are larger number of options available to the customer. Sometimes it could be a deliberate attempt of the market to let the customer wait for product, (to create hunger for the product), but today, if the product of company A is not available when and where it is required, the customer may be immediately shifting over to the next alternative. Even government organisations have to be competitive in the market (no more monopoly) because of the availability of private players (each trying to get a better foothold in the area of their operation). Even in the service sector, there are large number of operators offering better and better services and obviously, old thinking of "buy only Swedeshi or Binaca" is no more valid.

This behaviour of present day customer has forced the companies to think aggressively and innovatingly in the areas of production, distribution as well in service. Inspite of the strong wish of the companies to operate very lean, the inventory levels are to be raised to decouple the stocks and ensure product/service availability even in case of sudden changes in demand in the market. Lean manufacturing and resultant supply chains are to be synchronised with customer's need of delivery schedules and hence certain compromises are to be made. The pressure on supply chain efficiency, therefore, is very large. Turnaway customers are more damaging to business than enhanced level of inventories, because it is not only the loss of business today, there is further loss due to the chain reaction of other perspective customers following this information of such experiences. It may even cost a company its reputation and credibility and hence the loss really can be high and non-quantifiable.

In this regard, the information flow system right from customers to suppliers to internal organisational elements, to the market and end users needs to be established. This is very important method to deal with uncertainties of ever changing customer's preferences, buying habits, buying powers and buying schedules. Seasonal variations also must be captured in time due to any significant change in the population pattern in any market aimed it. Inventory placement in strategically important pockets can help to serve the customer of certain specific tastes or cultures/religious etc.

Hence the information flow for Business can be depicted as follows :

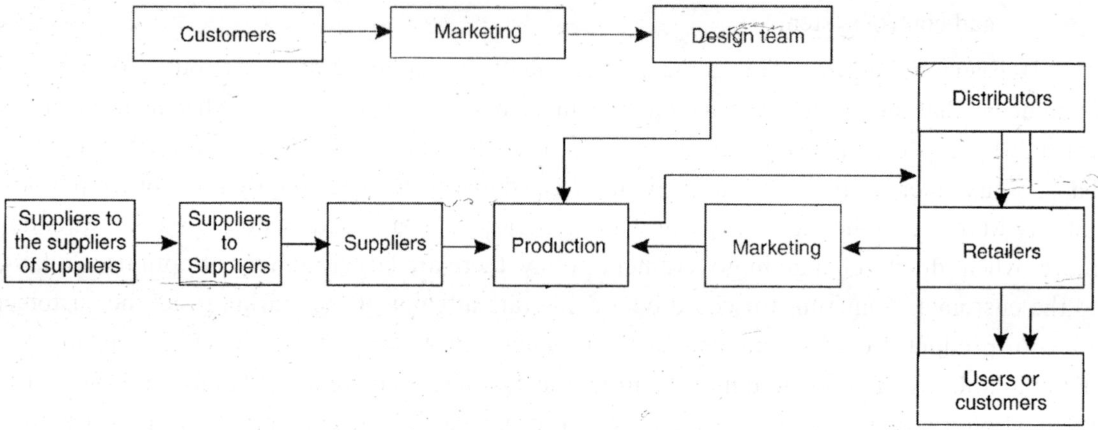

FIG. 2.3. Information Flow for Business

After Sales Service: Delivery of product or Service is not enough to satisfy a customer. It is also important to ensure that the product/Services is useful and its functional value is fully available to him. For this purpose, a strong relationship through after-sales-service is to be established so as to keep his loyalty towards the organisation. Proactive visits help in this direction.

Customer Relations Management (CRM)

Of late, a new term has emerged in the business market, known as Customer Relation Management (CRM). The innovations in product development result in bringing out and launching a new improved product much before the old product starts becoming unacceptable. Constantly changing requirement of the customer, in any case, is forcing products being of short life cycle. Thus the business of looking after customer is becoming more challenging and acutely intense.

Even with the best efforts, it may still be the case of missing on customer because of globalised market and availability of number of products in the same range of utility and cost. A study shows that every year, there is a loss of about 50 per cent of customers on every product and it is a world wide phenomenon. The challenge, therefore, shifts towards retaining customers rather than adding customers to the kitty. Fifty per cent loss of customers is a vast loss of business and opportunity to improve both the product and market share. Old customers feedback can come very handy to improve the features of the product and therefore forecasting of the demand becomes slightly easier.

It is, therefore, obvious that the companies need to concentrate on customer retention strategies in an organised analytical way. This thinking has resulted in the concept of Customer Relationship Management (CRM). When we talk about the relationship management, the social scientists have to be involved because the psychology and behaviour of customer has to be studied constantly and ever charging customer needs to be kept under scanner at all times.

Due to large number of intangible parameters involved in this study, help of many experts in various field is required. The inputs are obtained from the Marketing and sales teams, purchase team and vendors, distribution and retailers and equally importantly, from the human resources team. Information through focussed study by field experts *i.e.*, psychologists, social-scientists and social behaviouralits is collected, sifted and analysed before being used in the matrix, co-ordinating all important factors and parameters responssible for the change. These data would require simulation trials so as to authenticate the data and validate the model so formulated. Because of large variation and complications, even after software solutions, the superimposition of managers experience helps in arriving at a worthwhile solution. More innovative the business managers are on human behaviour, better business they should be able to manage. Customer Relations Management would, therefore, need a deliberate software solution, campatible with ERP software, so that integration produces better results.

The aim of the CRM strategy is to understand the need of the existing customers and to increase the customer base of new entries. Customer service, therefore, is no more an inward looking operation. It has became a total focus of the organisational business. To serve the customer better, company should develop a 'Single window operation', where a customer entering the system should be able to perform multiple functions for his needs through easy procedures. The latest concept in India in this direction is creating 'Malls', for serving the customer at one place through number of products under one roof. such as clothing, toys, vegetables, watches, sports goods, shoes, paintings, and even health and entertainment products. The business, thus, is aligned and designed from customers point of view, bringing in Customer-Managed Relationship. The major help factors are accessibility of all relevant information to the customer, much before he is tempted to visit the business location. The total system of business is to be transparent to the customer to let him feel free to choose' and confident that he is the 'King' of business.

Internal Customer Integration: Only one angle of customer relation has been projected above. During organisational working, inter-departmental cohesion is as important to succeed in the overall goal of customer satisfaction. Internal and external customers, who help or use the services are, therefore, as vital to consider.

In any chain of organisational hierarchy, each department acts as internal customer to another connected department. If we consider the marketing orientation as the key philosophy of the business, its effect can be seen on the whole organisation. As mentioned earlier, even to obtain customer needs, marketing, sales, purchase, and distribution teams have much to offer. These interactions are very valuable for defining the marketing orientation of the business and integration efforts bringing desired results. It will help in organising the flow of information and marketing intelligence across the functional areas.

Generally, inter-departmental rivalry and resistance to change in the minds of people are big limitations, but goal orientation should be able to bring everyone in line, and with proper monitoring and control system in place, orientation should be possible to interact harmoniously to pursue the overall corporate objectives of profitability by maintaining better customer relations.

External customer interactions: Internal focus can be useful only it the information flow from external sources is equally smooth and effective. Our suppliers and retailers are constantly in touch with the customers and deal with their requirements on daily basis. Due to constant interaction, they have better understanding of their psychology. Retailers have much brighter chance to offer feedback on the behavioural aspect of the product in terms of psychological and aesthetic view of the customer. Through this information, the company will be able to help establish better customer relationship.

Structure and Performance: For achieving better businesses results, each internal and external customer must be satisfied with the feedback and delivery of service of connected departmental customer. Similarly, treating vendors and retailers as part of the family is a must to establish better customer relationship from operational angle. Help, trust and sharing of vital information among these internal and external customers will make business a success.

2.7 Innovative Strategies and Continuous Growth

Need for innovation

To ensure competitive edge in the market, various innovative techniques and strategies have been developed over a period of time. Some of the modern concepts and innovative strategies adopted in USA, Western European countries and some of the eastern countries like Japan and Korea etc., are listed below:

- Management of technology (MOT)
- Variety reduction and standardisation
- Short product life cycles
- Flexible production and assembly lines
- Just-in-time (JIT) manufacturing
- Total quality management (TQM)
- Total productive maintenance (TPM)
- Computerised scheduling and rescheduling
- Employee involvement (EI) and multiple skill development
- Business process Re-engineering (BPR) and corporate restructuring
- Vertical de-integration
- Outsourcing and strategic partnership.

Production Strategties

Various elements of production strategy are summerised in Figure 2.4:

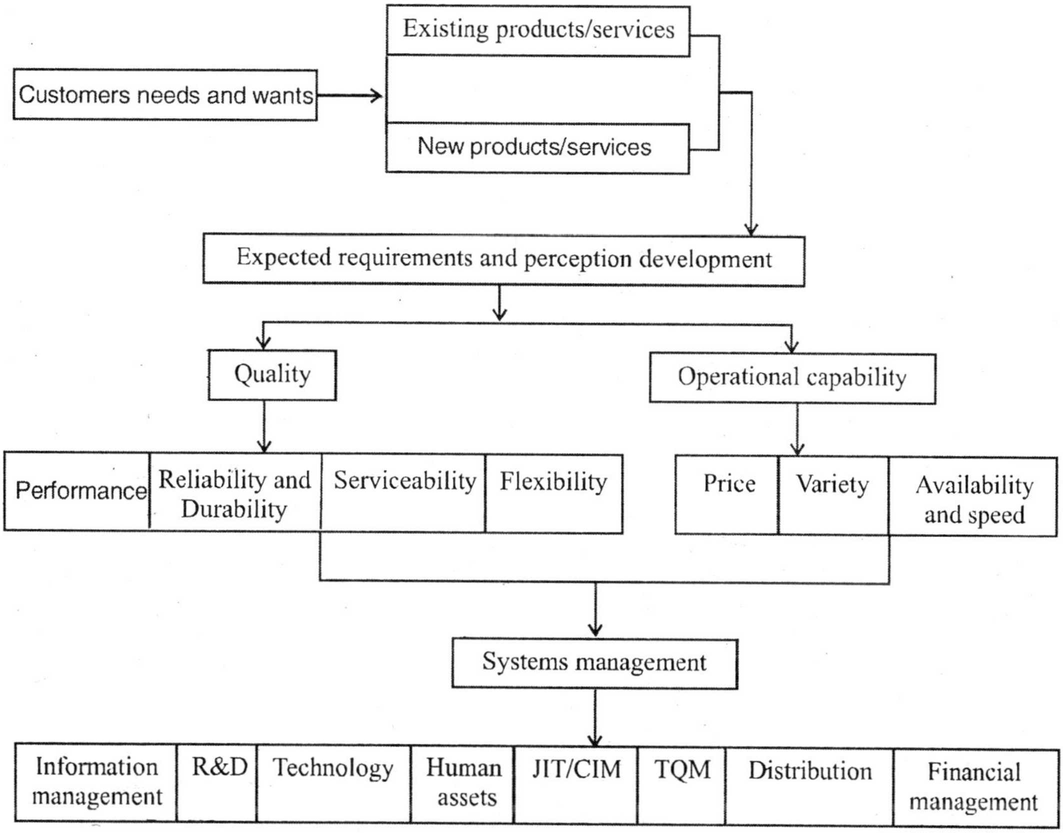

FIG. 2.4: Production strategy elements

The above-mentioned strategies help in flexibility and waste reduction not only in operating decisions, but also in strategic decisions for devising better control methodology. The ultimate aim is to create dynamic equilibrium in our operation management system in all fields such as operations, personnel, engineering, marketing, finance, materials, maintenance and distribution network etc. to gain maximum benefit from available business opportunities. The growth of the organisation and business follows as a result of the above strategies. This is true for optimum strategies in service sector also, with minor modifications.

2.8 Corporate Transformation

When an organisation decides to operate globally, it has to focus on larger segments of customers over wide area coverage across the globe. Hence it has to achieve the optimal fit between the aspiration of the customer segments aimed at, their culture and the requirement of change necessiated due to constant exposure and continuous development balanced with reference to the organisation goals and apiration and needs of own people. **Michael Porter** has identified four constituents of a globally successful organisation, (*i*) the factors of production (skill, technology, infrastructure and the constant upgraduation), (*ii*) demand conditions (variety, quality, cost), (*iii*) domestic rivalry (internal benchmark in market share, quality, operation and costs and level innovations) and (*iv*) the servicing the products (after-sales support and regular interaction with users).

During the discussion on the innovative strategies, it has been emphasised that there are changes due to continuous variation in the perception and demands of the customer. These changes are further aggrevated due to globalisation, wherein organisations have to change due to global inbalances. Todays necessity of acquisition and mergers, joint ventures and collaborations has resulted out of this compulsion.

There is a very famous saying "only thing constant in this world is CHANGE". This has been a fact since the inception of human civilisation and is a natural phenomenon. It has been carried forward from the natural process to operations management. In business, the changes occur due to constant integration of technology, process and procedures, the resultant organisational structure and the human beings.The organisations have to be ready to absorb all these changes and maintain a **"Dynamic Equilibrium"** in their operations.

The above environment makes it incumbent on any organisation to be receptive to change and hence ready to change itself to suit the day's requirement. Flexibility in the organisational structures, therefore, is of utmost importance. This is termed as corporate transformation, for creating strategic vision. Some of the steps suggested for dynamic equilibrium in a vibrant organisation are as under.

- Appreciate and understand that change is inevitable and this must perculate down to the lowest level of the organisational structure, thus change in the mind set of all personnel for effective implementation.
- Laydown the strategy for change *i.e.*, specific transparent projects in each area of working be specified and explained to people so that it becomes easier to implement.
- Layout a time schedule for all change projects and ensure 'change masters' help in following this schedule. Change masters are people to help and monitor change implementation.
- Based on departmental change projects, each department must laydown action plans for implementation, manage resources for the project and draw time schedule for such an action plan. A strong project management with built in monitoring and control procedures will ensure smooth implementation.
- Make people receptive and personally responsible for their specific activities. This personalisation should become motivator and change can be easily made a reality. Job design and job title, technical and financial responsibility, work method and procedure and belief towards better customer focus will help in the process. This will ensure participation by all those involved *i.e.*, every member of the organisation.
- Draw a measuring parameter chart and identify transparent system of result measuring. Performance index will be a great help as an additional helping tool.
- Motivation through training, skill development, mentoring, congenial work environment and incentives etc., is necessary for personnel involvement.

- Adopt the change projects as per ground realities and keep working in phases. Continuous renewed efforts are required, even if there are setbacks.

For these implementations, constant review of the organisational structure will be necessary. Various techniques like Business Process Re-engineering (BPR), Total Quality Management (TQM), Statistical Process Control Methods (SPC), Kaizen (Continuous improvement), Benchmarking (BM) and implementation of ISO9000 procedures are helpful in the corporate transformation, as and when the changes are to be implemented. The aim of all these techniques is quality and cost control through re-utilisation, opportunity driven excellence, and striving for customer focus.

In the sphere of corporate transformation and restructuring, the organisation has to start at the top leadership level. The culture of the organisation should be based on 'Employee' rather than 'respected president'. When everyone is expected to be creative, then all be treated at the respectable platform. 'Open culture' based structure works better, though heirarchy levels have to be defined for monitoring and control systems. This requires an attitudinal change even at the senior most level, not only a 'mindset change' at the workers level. Things would automatically change and get controlled at the operations end.

2.9 Corporate Social Responsibility (CSR)

Business leaders have been thinking, talking and implementing their business plans according to customer's changes. Others follow strategies in term of cost and quality because of legal restrictions of the land.

In the present context, these two perceptions of the corporate units have to change. **"Customer is the reason for our existance"** is not only a sentence to be spoken, but to be practised, more so today because of his awareness and the resultant demands. The corporate world, therefore, is developing positive attitude towards doing things 'what is right' rather than 'what is legally right'. The organisations are thinking and practicing the concept of "corporate social responsibility". Few of the reasons are:

- ***Consumer satisfaction***: Putting more and more pressure for a right product for right price with right quality, has been the changed attitude of the consumer groups. These sentiments are being presented at the stockholder meetings, product liability suits through consumer preferences and through political lobbying activities.
- ***Government regulations***: Due to above pressures, state and union governments have been formulating various laws and regulations to protect customer through legislation bindings, such as ISI marked brands and various safety laws. Even on the environment front, organisations are being forced to implement environmental protection systems through ISO 14000 standards implementation.
- ***Self-interest***: Organisations internely using long term advantages of social interactions, through which they try and pull the customer towards them, by maintaining some social systems like drinkling water supply and health clinic etc. They are winning the hearts of the poor and hence more and more customers become inclined to associate with their

business due to this social interaction. This may result in long term loyalty of such customers towards them.

Thus we can refer that it is basically the socio-economic sample of the business in addition to the profit maximisation as the responsibility of the corporate organisation.

The other side of the coin also must be seen and understood to draw a balance. The social work (either the expenditure for social activities or loss of profit due to price reduction) expenses can be substantial as social obligations are practically never ending process, or otherwise it is loss of face. Similarly, if organisation does not care for the social angle, it may result in loss of broad support from the public *i.e.*, customers, who are responsible for the profits of the organisation. The organisations, therefore, cannot afford to be aloof from their social commitments. They owe it to the customer and therefore must act rationally and responsibly, because the profit is generated only due to the patronage of the customers.

2.10 Value of Human Involvement for Innovation

While listing out the challenges for effective global operations, it has been brought out that competitive edge in global market has to be obtained through intelligent use of resources, ensuring waste management and cost containment along with quality assurance.

To use this competitive weapon, the human involvement at appropriate level is necessary. The work force is to be selected, trained, motivated and then utilised through proper monitoring and control. The mental level of the human resources at all levels, right from the worker to the senior-most manager is required to be very high so that the whole team works as self-motivated cohesine force. Infact, in todays environment, even this is not enough. Due to constant upgraduation of customer's requirements, all the human force has to be highly innovative in their approach to work and it is a 24 × 7 job for everyone *i.e.*, each and every member of the team has to be constantly thinking and applying himself/herself towards improvements at all times of the day. Innovative thinking and application would add further value, if it is in anticipation of customers demand for tomorrow.

Discussing the specific responsibility of the operations manager, the challenges here are large and taxing, may be the gravity of problems vary. Dividing the responsibilities into two major areas such as product design and design of the production system and sub-system and the area of actual operation of the production system requires cohesive thinking. Both these areas need a high degree of innovation. A constant upgradation of the product design not only from its functional angle, but also on the basis of the choice of new technologies and process design, methods of operations and enhancement of quality and safety standards have to be thought of. A close watch on materials, machines, production planning, scheduling of resources, their procurement and organising, maintenance of equipment etc., have be in tune with the latest in the field. Constant upgradation of distribution system and network goes a long way to achieve improved services for the customer. At this will be possible only if the work force operating these systems are efficient and motivated.

—●—

Section II
PRODUCTION AND OPERATION SYSTEMS

Chapter 3

Product and Service Design

Main issues:

1. **Product Life Cycle and Product Design.**
2. **Distinction between Products and Services**
3. **Product Design Tools such as DFMA, CE, VE, QFD etc.**
4. **Design for Continuous Improvement and Environmental Effects.**
5. **Computers in Design System.**

3.1 Product Life Cycle

Any product passes through primarily four important stages, known as the product life cycle. These stages are

- Introduction or infant stage
- Growth
- Maturity
- Decline

The concept of the product life cycle indicating above stages is depicted in figure 3.1 given below :

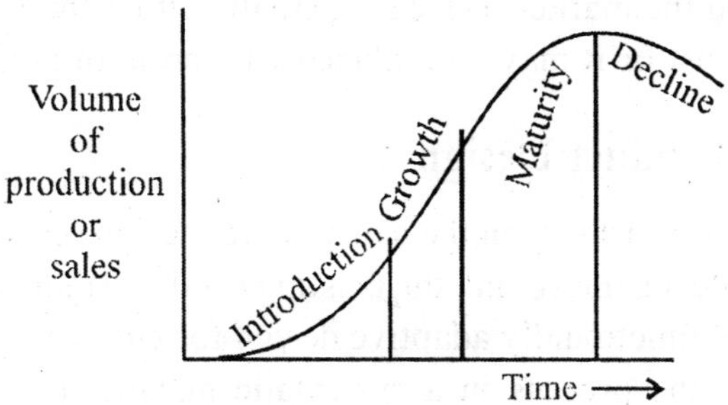

FIG. 3.1. Product life cycle

The very beginning of any production system and the requirement of operations management emerges from the product itself. The rest of the activities have to be coordinated with reference to the design of the product and its forecasted demand indicating the design of the capacity of the production system. Hence a business strategy is to be developed for product/services through the design, development and introduction of the product/service. The strategy formulated for operations management involves obtaining detailed information of the customer needs, converting it into a suitable product through proper design and then an appropriate production system devised based on available/required resources in terms of manpower, machines, materials and the capital investment capability of the organisation.

- With the product design, the detailed specification of a product become clear to fulfill customers requirements.
- Based on the design characteristics, the method of its production can be formulated.
- Based on the method of production, the production system can be designed for quality and value.
- The specifications for manpower, machines, materials and processes can be clearly defined thereafter.

Introduction stage : The initial stage when the product is designed and developed, is called as introduction stage of its life cycle for a new product. For an old product, this stage will involve major changes envisaged in the basic characteristics of the product as the change of function necessitated.

Growth stage : Product having been designed and developed now is available to the consumer and the acceptability or otherwise will determine the growth pattern. The sales will grow dramatically, if the product has found its acceptance with the customer. Marketing efforts need intensifying to push the initial thrust further. With increase in demand, production facilities expansion has to be concentrated upon for meeting the market demand.

Maturity stage : Next stage after growth is that of maturity, when product becomes standardised. Production capacity needs a look for high-volume production. High quality of the product to be taken care of for sustaining and increasing the market share. High level efforts in increased sales would result in high profits.

Decline stage : Finally the product enters the decline stage, when sales decrease either due to change in the customers perception and preference or a new product with better specifications has entered the market. Hence eventually either the product may be completely dropped from marketing list or it may be replaced with an improved version of the products.

Pre-stage Work For Product Design

Whether a company embarks upon the new product design (cost, complexity and balances may be the reasons) or intends improving the existing product (more comprehensive and useful method for cost effective, functionally adaptive design for customer's satisfaction), there is no short cut to run through the process in a systematic manner. For technical, functional and economical design, the designer uses the knowledge obtained through research and development sources. It is a very vast field, requiring sustained efforts over a period of time. To clarify these specific areas of pre-stage work, the following things need active consideration :

- Research may be defined as the preliminary investigative work, leading to various inventions, discovery of natural laws, novel techniques etc., through basic or applied research utilised in product development.
- Development is the effort contributing to the improvement in the existing level of available information by the way of improved ideas, systems and techniques etc for mulated as a result of the research work.
- Design is the conversion of research and developmental activity into an idea resulting in a product suitable for use after its manufacture.

Reasons for Product Development

The main aim of creating a product is for meeting customer needs. It is a difficult task as most of the time, a customer may be able to throw very hazy requirement, possibly indicating only the functional basis of his idea. But what constitutes a good design for such a product is again not easy to comprehend. The three main ingredients of a good design could be functional soundness, economic viability and aesthetical acceptability.

The neccessity for product development can be summarised as follows.

Utilisation of idle resources: Generally an odd idea is germinated due to the necessity of a person having idle resources such as money, machines or manpower and he wants to put these to good use. He can get an idea looking at things around him, during discussion with his people or friends, reading some magazine or periodicals etc. It is just an accidental occurrence developing into necessity to take the idea to a logical conclusion in the form of a product or service.

Incomplete range of products: Some products are designed to fill in the gap amongst the available range of the products.

Supplement the range: When the products are available in wide range but a company wants to offer a totally new product as an innovation. This results in widening the range. Such products may be designed in advance to fill in the gap at the time of existing products reaching maturing and declining stage.

Risk coverage: While dealing with few products, there is a risk of total market eclipse due to sudden change in customer preference or change in technology. Companies, therefore, may introduce a new product as per latest trend, in order to stay afloat in the market.

The above reasons are applicable not only for new products, but also in improving existing product line through the use of new technology or achieving diversity in product range. Product life cycle may also force the issue suddenly.

3.2 Stages for product Design

Whatever be the product life, the design process passes through the following steps :

- **Needs identification:** This is a initial step in product development, in which we establish the need of the customer and then conversion of the functional need into a useful product. The ideas may came from many sources namely, Customers, managers, marketing, production, or engineering teams, etc. When an organisation can afford it, a formal market research and development department should take on this job. It can be a combination of basic research (where there is only scientific knowledge available with no commercial use established), or applied research (scientific knowledge having commercial uses) and then forming an idea as to what an product could be, to satisfy the customers needs.
- **Advance product planning:** This step involves collection of relevant scientific relationships useful for product design as per the rough conception. It includes preliminary market analysis and creating alternatives for product concepts, operational requirements, design criteria and logistics etc.
- **Advance design:** Once the information regarding various natural rules and concepts have been obtained, these need to be meshed together to obtain an approximate design and shape of the product. This is a stage, when a designer identifies the product either as a bicycle, or a bus or a motor car, based on function, quality and cost requirement of the customer. The technical and economic feasibility is conducted at this stage to ensure that the product will be worth the effort for its development.
- **Detailed engineering design:** Having identified the product completely and arriving at the conclusion that product could be worth further efforts, the design team undertakes the actual engineering design, working out shapes, lengths, width and various other dimensions of the product. The concepts of design for manufacturing and assembly (DFMA) and design with reference to available or recommended material must be kept in mind by the designer. The available resources should also be kept in view. In case the product design needs a new, available technology, process design aspect also has to be taken into account.
- **Conceptualisation:** From the detailed engineering design, the designer produces its product shape (known as isometric design of the product) which can be conceptualised as to how the product would look like after manufacturing. This could be shown to the customers to obtain any modification in order to fine-tune the design of the product (as acceptable to the customer).
- **Acceptance:** The designed product with its detailed specifications is then passed down to the process design team, so as to compare the compatibility of the design with the available resources *i.e.* the capability of workers and machines, finances and technology

if need be. When compatibility has been established, it can now be released for actual manufacturing, matching with available or would be available resources.

- **Execution:** This is a step where the design details are converted into an actual product as a pilot sample. Pilot sample is a full scale product manufactured out of design details, so that its actual functional performance can be tested.
- **Product evolution:** A customer will be more concerned about the functional utility of the product, much less about the shape of the product. For this function capability, the pilot sample undergoes the performance tests of various kind, depending on the important functional parameters, the product is required to satisfy. There can be number of parameters chosen and product tested for.
- **Product clearance for production:** The pilot sample having been satisfactorily tested for its performance, the design can be cleared for production. Any drawbacks found on performance evaluation can be taken care of by suitable design or process change. The note of the pilot sample testing authority with their dated signatures is a must for actual production work to commence.
- **Process Design:** Based on the final design, the process design is then finalised for quality, cost, technology and volume considerations.

3.3 Product Design System

In order to obtain a reasonably good product, the above mentioned steps are followed in two different ways. One such approach is called the traditional approach and the other one as integrated approach.

Traditional approach: When each team operates in its own areas of responsibility without much interaction with the other team, it is called a traditional approach. The drawback of this approach is the failure of co-ordination and hence even a minor change in product specification because of any limitations of a team, could result into a very different product than that is intended.

Integrated approach: When all the teams are brought to the same platform to discuss any limitations, a concerted joint effort generally emerges into a product very near to the customer's requirement. All team members are within the company and hence could be made to participate. The involvement of the customer could be ensured either through the group members of the team acting as customers or else the product being discussed with customers with the help of computer facility available (laptops can be taken anywhere now and product specifications and shapes shown.)

Various teams responsible for ensuring the production of a product/service are listed out in Fig. 3.2.

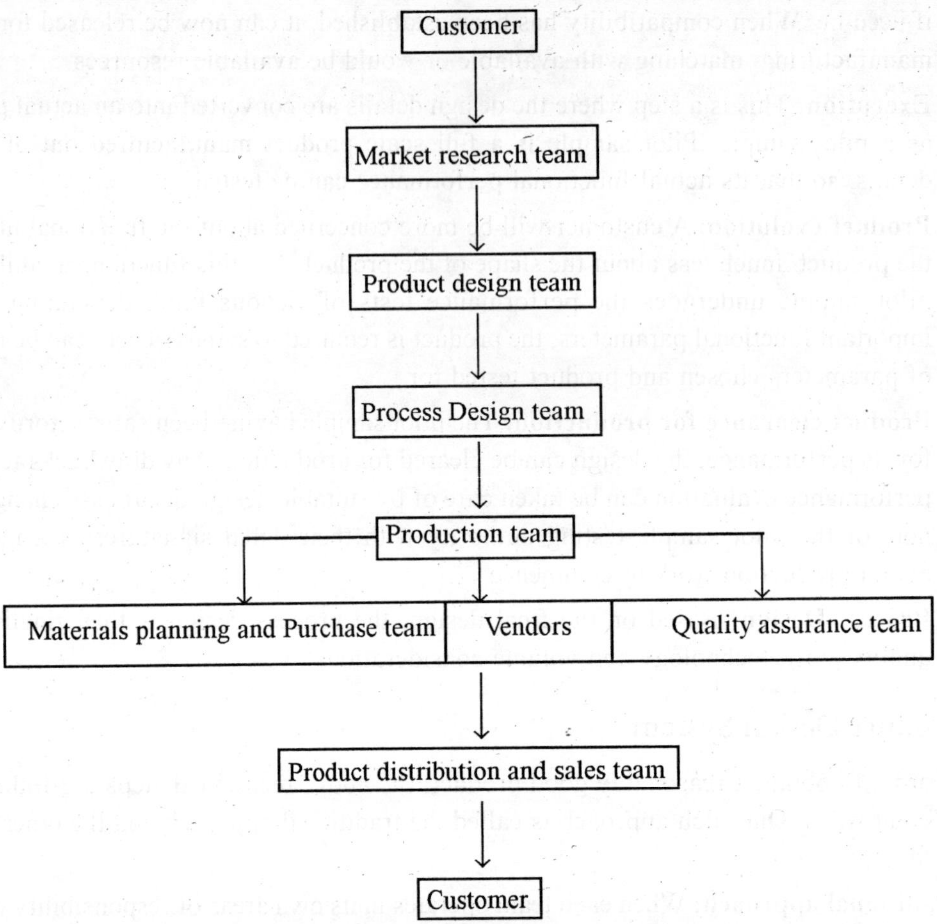

FIG 3.2. Chain of product movement

By following the integrated approach of product design, most of the companies have benefitted through reducing costs, decreasing product development time and improved product quality by changing their product design process based on continued interaction by :

- Following the concept of 'design for production'.
- Fine-tuning the design for manufacturing and assembly (DFMA).
- Working out the concurrent design of product and production process (Method is called Concurrent Engineering or CE).
- Close interaction with vendors and customers.
- Exploring the necessity of business process engineering (BPR) and design for six sigma (DFSS) so as to achieve defect free production.

Design for production: When designer keeps in mind the effective production process as to how this product will be produced, major problems faced during production are taken care of at the design stage itself.

Design for Manufacturing and Assembly (DFMA): As the name suggests, there is a system or software available today, where co-ordination between design, manufacturability and assembly can be done all at one time. This is very helpful design approach to save time at a later date during after-sales-service.

Concurrent Engineering: When the design engineers and the production people develop the actual production system together, it is called concurrent engineering (CE). These people also evaluate how the design characteristics match the existing and proposed production resources, human and equipment capabilities and the product mix. For complicated products, simulation approach (*i.e.*, simulation of production system before the actual system is put in use) has been found to be very useful. Thus CE emphasises cross-functional integration and concurrent development of the product/service. This is done through programme management teams, technical teams and support teams working together.

- *Multi-disciplinary teams:* Normal designs can be prepared by the design team or design engineers on their own. But when operations personnel are also involved at an early stage of design, coordination results from manufacturability view point. It is also worthwhile to include personnel from marketing, sales, engineering and purchase etc for better co-ordination.
- *Customer and vendor involvement:* Involvement of customers during the design stage helps in simplifying product by building in all desirable requirements of the customer. Many companies are using the "test customer's" concept *i.e.*, use of computer softwares to evaluate the products for cost effectiveness along with requirement fulfillment. Similarly using vendors as helping tools, a large number of material and other potential problems can be minimised. It can be very cost-effective activity due to right choice of material substitutes and different tool design for improving quality of the product.

Business Process Re-Engineering (BPR): When the demand of the product changes drastically either due to market forces and Competition, or the intention of the organisation to enter the market in an aggressive manner, there arises the necessity for total transformation of the existing facilities and bring in the dramatic change in the resources level, (men, machines, product, technology or any other area), the design of the product has to undergo a total change from the existing. BPR, therefore, has to be a deliberate decision due to heavy involvement of efferts and capital investment along with the will to re-oganise.

Design for Six-Sigma (DFSS): Six-Sigma efforts are enforced when the organisation cares for the quality as its uppermost focus. No-defect or zero-defect production would need a simple design along with 'Poke-yoke' technique embedied in the work of the entire organisation. The design would need very careful thought and thorough CE approach.

- Product design/redesign and its development increases the amount spent on research and development and design activities.
- The necessity of a flexible, preferably computerised, production system is increasing. Frequent changes should be possible in flexible production system be as to cater for redesigned product quickly.

- The requirement of flexible and faster method of design plays an important role in business strategy. Hence there have been developments of computer-aided design (CAD) and computer aided manufacturing (CAM). Type of manufacturing systems undergoes a tremendous change under such compulsions.

3.4 Design Principles for Products

In order to make product useful and cost-effective, there are some guiding principles for the product design. In addition to taking the benefit of integrated approach, concurrent engineering and use of multi-disciplinary teams, the use of these design principles channelise the thought process of designers. Simplicity of design will solve a large number of problems of production as well as maintenance. Few principles of product and process design are:

- Minimise the number of components.
- Standardise the components and tools.
- Use common components and processes.
- Use modularity for variety production.
- Simplify assembly operations by using simple fasteners and process orientation for assembly.
- Design products as 'fail-safe'.
- Keep specifications and tolerances reasonable.
- Design robust products.

Minimise the Number of Components: When the product design is simple with very few components, the average time spent on components is reduced minimising the component coding effort. The buying and holding effort and cost of Inspection time and preservation efforts are also minimised. If we are in a position to reduce the mobile components, the wear and tear is reduced and the product functional reliability increased.

But reduced components cannot be a thumb-rule. When the product is complicated and large, it may be worth-while to make the product design simple by increasing the number of components of comparative simplicity. The guiding factor, therefore, is the use of systematic design evaluation techniques such as value engineering and value analysis to ensure easy manufacture and maintenance.

Standardise the components and tools: By developing standard components, it is easier to manufacture and assemble large number of products using similarly produced components. It can result in better quality and lower price. Whereas against this, specialised or unusual product components will take more time, money and working efficiency, thereby resulting into a costilier product. The process design for the standardised components is easier as the method of mass production for such components can be adopted, for which less number of resettings will be required.

Use common components and processes: When the company adopts a number of standard components, these can be used across many products or used to serve several processes. The variety in product mix is easily possible using such components. If a product has been designed using new components, these have to be produced by a special process design method, using different tools and fixtures, different machines, possibly by specially trained workers resulting in extra cost at every step, whereas common components can be purchased off-the-shelf and used without wasting time and efforts. Common components would also introduce better quality standard due to experience mechanics in producing high volume of similar component. The mistake in assembly of products also would be reduced.

Use modularity for variety production: The requirement of large variety of customers needing different configurations of products can be easily met with by first producing standard assemblies or standard subassemblies and then by adding and subtracting components for customised products. Various function modules to suit different configuration can be used satisfying the range of customers. The variety of products is achieved without using different processes or reset or changeover thereby having variety at low costs. A high level of customisation is possible by this method. Added advantage is to have an alternate version of a module packed and connected in easy way, with no components specially designed. Assembly process will be easy and interchangeability possibility makes it simpler. Combining several functions into a single module makes testing easier resulting in reduction of quality assurance costs.

Simple fasteners and orientation: While adding one component to another, various types of fasteners are used such as bolts and nuts, screws or snaps etc. If these fasteners are designed to be simple, the much needed time for assembly of the product can be reduced to a great extent. Simple and linear fasteners can be used with the help of robots. It justifies even a costlier fastener at times, if the operation cost can be reduced, offsetting its initial cost. Similarly, for some products, the sequence of assembly and orientation of components may be very crucial such as assembly of toys, furniture or computers etc. If alignments of parts are difficult to achieve, the time taken for positioning and fastening will be more. By careful planning, this can be simplified.

Fail-safe design for assembly: This is called "Poke-Yoke" by Japanese. Fail-safing of design means having design for ensuring the assembly without any mistake, even if it is intentional. A minor design of bolt fitting only at one position of the assembly and not in any position will ensure its correct assembly. Let us take a example of a product, whose last assembly component is a closing window. The alignment and physical contact of two knobs or points to have the whole product operating is crucial and it is possible only if this closing window is fitted is one position only (otherwise alignment and necessary contact will not be possible and the whole product becomes worthless).

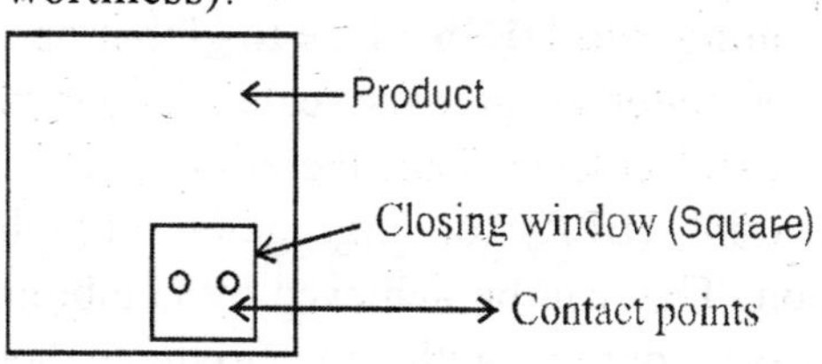

FIG. 3.3. Fail safe design

If this window part is square, it can be fitted in any direction. To ensure its fitting in one desired position only we have to design it either as 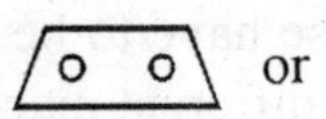 or 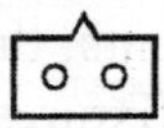.

By these design change, the closing window assembly has become fail-safe. It can be fitted in one position only, ensuring the point contacts certain.

Reasonable Specifications and Tolerances : It is an established fact that if the specifications of a product are demanding and rigid, it requires longer working and hence becomes costlier. The persons achieving those demanding specifications have to be highly skilled. Normally for this reason, a very effective value analysis must be done so that for each function of the product, just the right specifications are worked out. Physical properties of the product, therefore, should be just enough to pass functional and performance test. The selection of material should just serve the purpose. For light function, light weight material can be used, but even for higher strength, steel should not be used if aluminium can serve the purpose.

The second consideration should be given to tolerance and quality of the product. With respect to the resources available, the laid down tolerance should be possible to achieve, be it because of the proficiency of the manpower, capability of the machine or the quality of material itself. If the technological capability is only for producing ± 0.01 centimeter variation, then ± 0.001 cm accuracy will be hard to achieve, requiring 100 percent inspections, sorting out and reworking, thereby costing enormously high. If the tolerance required can be reduced (from functional angle), then achievable level is beneficial, or else the product to be redesigned having carried out value analysis effectively. Expecting high tolerance on the fangs of tilling harrow is too much to ask for, functionally nor required, whereas a computer component would need closer tolerance from the fit point of view.

Robust Product Design: Whatever be the attention paid to design and the best available production process, there is bound to be variations in materials, wear and tear on the equipment and even in the human efficiency due to stress with passage of time. Some random fluctuations such as weight, length, strength or the alignment of the product will also create variations. The variations will affect the quality of the product. Robustness of design should reduce the effect of various variations on product quality and functional capability.

By proper analysis (as recommended by Taguchi), the product and process should be designed in such a way that their characteristics minimise the effect of variations. Similarly other characteristics should be studied for reducing effect on the product performance. It will improve quality of the product and also will reduce the cost. Product reliability will also increase due to robust design.

Zero-Defect Programming and DFSS : Due to global operations, competition is tough and the productivity has to be better to cater for scale of economies. There is a need to design the products/services for zero-defect level. This, therefore, intelligent business sense to consider Business Process Reengineering (BPR) for large gains through the product/process design with high quality production. This can be achieved by combining the concept of Design for Six-Sigma (CDSS) *i.e.*, fail-safe designs with appropriate method of production via., BPR. A deliberate Failure Mode and Effect Analysis (FMEA) helps the possibility of premature or short time failures, if the design of product and process can ensure a very large MTBF (mean time between failures). Robust design with reasonable tolerances can result in very cost effective production.

3.5 Methods of Product Design

While discussing product design process, it was argued that due to market challenge in the global environment, the products and processes have to satisfy following important conditions from the customers point of view:

- Functional utility
- Quality and reliability and
- Optimum cost

In order to meet all these requirements of the consumer, following important tools and methods have been developed over a period of time, out of necessity, to ensure high product quality at low cost.

- Value Engineering and Value Analysis (VE and VA)
- The Taguchi Method of Robust Design
- Computer Aided Design (CAD)
- Design for Manufacturability and Assembly (DFMA)
- Quality Function Deployment (QFD)
- Concurrent Engineering (CE) and Prototyping

Value Engineering and Value Analysis : An ever-enquiring human mind assumes that anything and everything can be improved. This gives rise to the concept of value engineering, (VE).

The purpose of value engineering approach is well served when the user is able to define and segregate the unnecessary from the necessary in order to develop alternative to accomplish necessary **lowest total cost**. The total cost is the sum of all efforts and expenditures incurred for development, production and application of the product. It consists of the following:

Development cost - Research/development, design and prototype testing.

Production cost - Labour, material and machine running cost.

Application cost - Sales, marketing and distribution of product.

Reasons for Unnceccessary Cost.

While working out lowest total cost, there is a necessity of removing the elements and reasons for the unnecessary cost. These may be:

- Mental setting improper - Information, beliefs, habits and ignorance.
- Single solution fixation - Mental road block or unprogressive approach such as fear of failure.
- Faulty communication - Background, education and training etc.

Having identified the unnecessary, we can now define VE. **"Value engineering is the systematic application of recognised techniques, which identify the function of a product or service, establish a monetary value for that function and provide only the necessary function at the lowest total cost. Hence it is provision of cost for a necessary function not to degrade a function or product to get to the lowest cost."** The concept of VE can be applied in the areas of change in design, technology, material or appearance.

Before we describe the value engineering application and analysis, the organisation has to define the term "value" in their operational system. Value is the functional performance for a given cost and this may vary from customer to customer and hence organisation to organisation. The basic value may be supplemented with prestige or aesthetic value, where costs are added due to the changed function perception of the targeted customer. Hence the VE is best performed by asking question about ***why***, ***what***, ***where***, ***when***, ***how*** and ***who***. These questions are asked for all aspects related to the function of the product. A function can be defined simply as to what can make an item work or sell. For example,

A refrigerator - to preserve food

A heater - to provide heat

A stop - to restrict movement

or A golden clip - to fasten objects and to enhance appearance.

Use of VE/VA in Problem Solving

The purpose of problem solving is best served if we adopt a system of team approach. The best team is the heterogenous group of experts from various fields *i.e.*, representing a cross-section of all skills used for product development, also from the areas not directly connected with the product. It is important that all the members have enough expertise. Agenda for discussion by the team must be laid down to keep the track right, but discussion on those agenda points should be frank, open and energetic. Then only true worth of value analysis will be achieved. The team processes the value analysis projects through the following phases:

- General phase
- Information phase
- Function phase
- Creativity phase
- Evaluation phase
- Investigating phase
- Recommendation phase

***General phase*:** This is the preparatory stage of the VE exercise, wherein the ground is prepared for further progress. Few important tasks performed during this phase are :

- Use good human relations
- Inspire team work

- Workout specifics
- Overcome road blocks
- Apply good business judgement-decision on impartiality.

• **Information phase:** This phase is used to collect all essential and relevant information for the project under study. For the product, the design details and other specifications such as weight, manufacturing process, materials, parts, details of suppliers and various relevant costs etc., are useful and collected in advance. The team, then, specifies the scope of the study, the level of approach, the time schedule and the cost of the study. The scope also must specify the aimed benefit to be achieved, so as to ensure that study undertaken has been worth the effort and result.

In general, the scope of this phase can be summarised as follows:

- Secure the facts
- Determine costs of sub-systems
- Identity cost on specifications and requirements
- Projection selection

  Economic return (ABC analysis)

  Expertise required about a particular problem

  Segregate simple and then difficult tasks so as to form the sequence of operations.

  Detail out the stiff competition level

  Select complex assembly, which offers better opportunity for simplification.

Function phase: In this phase, The function of the product *i.e.*, the primary function for the functional value and secondary function for the prestige or aesthetic value is identified. The product is, then, segregated into components, sub-assemblies and assemblies so that their involvement and utility for primary or secondary function can be listed out. The function cost relationship chart is prepared, with functions listed out in the descending order of their relative importance, in following manner.

Function	Relative weightage	Cost

***Creativity phase*:** This is called the brain storming phase, wherein a creative mood is allowed to prevail. The team leader should caution the team not to worry about the absurdity or the usefulness of the ideas, nor they should worry about any fear of redicule. All members are treated at the same level. All ideas, however trivial, small or absurd it may look at this stage, must be recorded. Hence important aspects of the creativity phase can be summarised as

- Establish positive thinking - no arbitrary constraint
- Develop creative ideas - judicial thinking should be turned off - no preconceived ideas should prevail or no pre-audit of these idea be allowed.

Evaluation phase: During this phase, the ideas are assessed and analysed one by one along with their associated cost worked out under information phase. Then the team should start analysing good or bad features, necessary and unnecessary aspects beginning with the lowest cost idea. The team them lists out the ideas generating the best value in terms of utility, quality and cost and evaluate the best value ideas for further development. The summary of this phase can be prepared as follows:

- Evaluate, refine and combine ideas.
- Develop function alternatives through cost matrix.
- Evaluate by comparison and arrive at

  Basic workable solution based on cost, quality and reliability.

  Prepare decision matrix.

Investigating phase: In addition to the analysis of facts, ideas generated and inter-relationships of functions, components and assemblies with the cost, the team should further evaluate the decision matrix by superimposing additional outside source information along with the internal resource compatibility. The team prepares the feasible solutions to the problems. Various specialists, consultants and vendors can be consulted for refining the idea-interaction to arrive at better solution. This is done primarily to seek any further improvement in the value-addition. All possible viable ideas are amalgamated into positive improvements and a firm decision taken for all useful alternatives.

The investigating phase can be summarised as under :

- Use company and industrial standards to arrive at feasible value-added solutions.
- Consult vendors and specialists for further refining the solution.
- Use special products, processes and procedures to get higher value product.

***Recommendation phase*:** This is a stage when the value engineering team presents its project report to the higher management. The recommendations should be coherent, methodical, worth implementation and should project the benefits to be acrued due to this solution being implemented. At this stage, it is important that the study report is accepted by the higher management for implementation based on cost benefit analysis or value addition analysis. Physical execution of the solution and its monitoring for success is later part of this phase. In case of any difficulty in execution, these must be attended to immediately by revisiting the evaluation phase. Cost, quality and value of the product must be proved worth the efforts undertaken to produce the study result and its effective implementation. The phase action can be summarised as under:

- Present facts
- Present costs
- Motivate positive actions *i.e.*, implementation procedure and schedule
- Follow up action to ensure physical results and improvements achieved.

Methods Developed through VA

There are two important methods used for the purpose, namely **DARSIRI** method and **FAST** method.

DARSIRI method has seven important stages to be performed in that order. There are,

D = Data collection

A = Analysis

R = Record Ideas

S = Speculation

I = Investigation

R = Recommendation

I = Implementation

Whereas **FAST** method is Function Analysis System Techniques, which also can be used for the same purpose.

The TAGUCHI Method

Very popular method used for robust design of products suggested by TAGUCHI underlines three basic principles:

- When there is a variation in the value of the product attribute from the target value, the cost to the producers and in turn, to the consumers increases at a higher rate than the increase in the value.
- The design features of the product and the process indicate the amount of change in the product attribute.
- The design features of the product and the processes can be identified through experimentation or simulation so that change in the characteristics can be incorporated in the product design which reduces these variations as compared to the normal production variation.

The method can be used for change in the product characteristics such as weight, shape or length etc. It can be used even for study of relationships between various process characteristics such as speed and heat effects or heat and surface finish characteristics etc. Refer Figure 3.4 below:

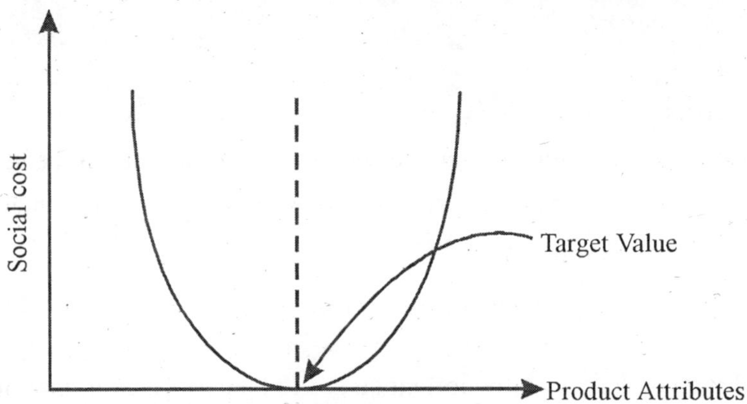

Cost of deviation from target value

FIG. 3.4. Cost of deviation from target value

As suggested by TAGUCHI, the requirements of characteristics comparisons are large due to the fact that there are several product and process design features, each having several alternatives and hence the evaluation experimentation process is very large, almost prohibitive. But Taguchi suggested various statistical experimental design techniques to obtain maximum information about several design features with much reduced number of experiments.

Computer Aided Design (CAD)

While applying the VE method and the TAGUCHI method for several components, several cost variations and functionality relationships, there is a very large computation effort involved. It is also very time consuming, which an organisation in present global environment can ill-afford. Hence a very popular tool for product design is being preferred by the companies. It is a software based technique called computer-aided-design (CAD).

To gain the benefit of computer characteristics such as storage of large information and its amenability to quick alterations/changes, the companies adopt this method. The CAD systems are computer-programmes that allow a user to produce and easily modify the product design on the screen of the monitor. The technology advancement is adding to the utility of CAD everyday.

Benefits of the CAD System

- *Graphics display*: The end result of many parameter interactions into the form of the product is available to the design engineer on the screen and he can have view of various cross-sections, including the three-dimensional perception. Because of this capability of the computer hardware and the software, it is possible to make proportional changes in the design scale or change the angle of a particular arc or line very easily just by the click on a computer mouse. The need of entire redraw has vanished due to this computer capability of faster corrections.
- *Design storage and retrieval:* Similar to the capability and huge capacity of the computer memory for storage of large information in data base, it also has the capability of

strong design characteristics of existing products and components. Just by entering the base input information about the product, the design can be retrieved on the screen of the monitor. The available design helps in two ways. Firstly, the existing design indicates that this design can be used for improvement and no large re-designing effort is required for this product. Secondly, the available design can be the starting point for designing an improved product which has nearly similar specifications. This saves time and helps in maintaining common component inventory.

- *Automatic evaluation of specifications:* If there is a need for a new design, the time consumed is quite large in working out major configurational values such as length, strength, heat resistance etc. But in CAD system, the additional variations can be fed to the computer and at any time, a new design can be obtained quickly without going through the total design efforts. The performance characteristics can be recalculated and compared with the product requirements.

The concept is called Computer Aided Engineering (CAE). By carefully operating the CAD software, we can quickly alter the design for new products (variety production), also may obtain design options for further optimum product selection. The systems have further been advanced into CAD/CAM software (computer aided design and computer assisted manufacturing), thus saving time for converting design drawings into manufacturing equipment system.

Design for Manufacturability and Assembly (DFMA)

This is very useful methodology, where the information guideline procedures, checklists, charts, diagrams and graphs etc., help the designer to develop a plan for components, sub-assemblies and assemblies, evaluating the production improvements and the resultant production costs. This ensures a close co-ordination of design with its amenability for manufacturing as well as for assembly and disassembly ease during maintenance. This methodology not only focuses on machining and handling due to various shapes, dimensions, clearances or orientation, but also takes care of their implication in assembly operations. The design of assembly robots can be easily affected as a result of the information from DFMA softwares.

A similar approach has been used to design service facilities. It is called Design for Service (DFS), which helps designers make the product easier for service operations by co-ordinating critical components at appropriate places.

Quality Function Deployment (QFD)

This method of product design takes care of customer's requirements of quality. The method has the capability of identifying customers preferences of product specifications and integrating these requirements into technical design. Hence it is called Quality Function Deployment (QFD). It help in eliminating wasteful product features and activities not contributing to the value-addition for customers requirement. Various matrices of different related requirements are constructed into one comprehensive matrix, called the **House of**

Quality.

The basic QFD relationship matrix relates the customer's requirements to the technical attributes of the product. QFD is a formal system for identifying customers perception of quality and hence eliminating unnecessary product features (not required by the customers) and activities not contributing towards quality.

A detailed market research is carried out to obtain specific features of functional performance (since customers can easily relate functional requirement of the product with its quality expectation). These expectations or requirements are listed out and then broken into more and more product features, such as length, weight, width or shape to functional characteristics. These requirements, then, are related to production requirements such as type of machine or production process, material to be used etc. This interactive relationship then becomes QFD matrix based on which the most economical design is obtained by using right combination of features and process capabilities. The QFD process is repeated until optimisation of customers needs and wants is obtained.

Thus QFD is based on completion of a number of metrices and then combining them into a comprehensive large matrix known as House of Quality drawn as Figure 3.5 given on next page.

Concurrent Engineering (CE) and Prototyping

As described in paragraph 3.3 under the traditional approach, the design of the products and the suitable design of processes have been treated as two separate activities. By designing the product in isolation and then trying to find the best method of producing it has obvious drawbacks of going back and forth either requiring a new method, buying new machines and training manpower for it, or going back to modify the design with reference to the available production resources. It takes a long time to bring the product to the market and involves unnecessary costs. The integrated approach, on the other hand, can solve the compatibility problem of design and process resources by various teams working together. All the teams working simultaneously or concurrently will produce a reasonable design, and compatible process. This method is therefore, called Concurrent Engineering. This concept has considerably compressed the time and effort of design, production and introduction cycle, because it promotes efficient and high-quality product design with simultaneous production process at the time of design itself. All functional finance, marketing, purchase, engineering and distribution and sales teams, get involved in this process.

Prototyping is a method for customer collaboration during product finalisations. A full scale model is manufactured, shown to the customers and tested for performance. It achieves acceptance of the product by the customer, aesthetically as well as functionally.

Design for Continuous Improvement

There is a neccessity of progressive improvement in the design of any product due to constant change in the customers requirements. Therefore the product design should cater for

Technical attributes

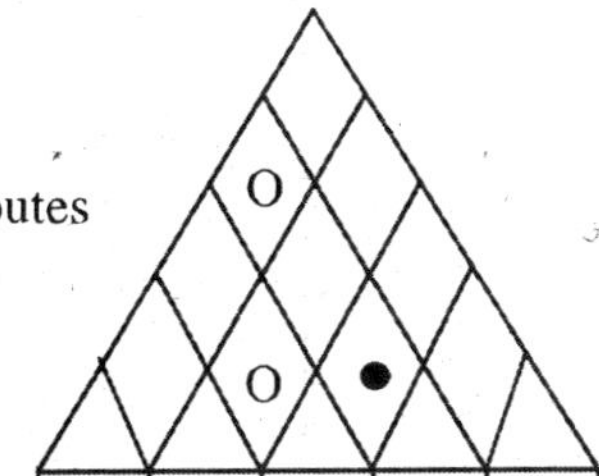

O Strongly positive
● Positive
× Negative

Customer Requirements	Weightage	Battery type	RAM capacity	Hard drive	Keyboard	Case material	Customer Evaluation: Own	Competitor 1	Competitor 2	Competitor 3	Target	Ratio=Target/own
Light weight	3	O	●	●	●	●	3	3	3	2	3	1
Small size	2	O	●	●	O		2	2	3	2	3	1.5
Battery charging	3	O					3	2	2	3	3	1
Durable	2	●		●	●	O	2	3	3	3	2	1
Speed of processing	3		O	O			3	3	3	3	3	1

Measurable Performance	Battery type	RAM capacity	Hard drive	Keyboard	Case material	Total
Own	2	3	3	3	2	
Competitor 1	3	3	3	2	3	
Competitor 2	2	3	2	3	3	
Competitor 3	3	2	1	3	2	
Raw importance						271
Percent importance						100

Strong 3
Medium 2
Weak 1

FIG. 3.5. House of Quality

these additions/reduction. in features/dimension, if feasible. Modular design serves the purpose better to enhance the probability of improvement of the product. Progressive improvement in Golf ball surface is a good example, wherein the aerodynamic design has been continuously improved by creating more and more cuts an its outer surface.

3.6 Designing and Developing Services

There are some important differences between production of goods and services-

- Goods need raw materials, whereas the services may not (though virtual service is changing this concept).
- Goods can be stored and transported whereas the services generally may not do so.
- Direct involvement of customers in the production of goods is generally not required except specifying the goods requirements of its function, whereas services require close interaction of the customer to specify the requirement as to what level it is required and when.

In order to differentiate good and services, the table 3.1 can be referred.

Table 3.1

Goods	Services
1. Tangible	1. Intangible
2. Fixed design	2. Heterogeneous
3. Can be stored/inventoried	3. Desirable and short lead time
4. Customers involvement for specifications	4. Close interaction with customer
5. Capital intensive	5. Labour intensive/multiple skills
6. Transportation possible	6. Generally cannot be transported
7. Offered to the customer in manufacturted form.	7. Generally designed and carried out as per customers requirement of time and cost
	8. Output cannot be inventoried
	9. Quality subjectivity determined.

Since services are intangible and may or may not need the help of products, their design is different from that of the product. In services, customers are routinely involved to make it highly customised. In hospitals, banks and restaurants etc., customers enter the production system very deeply, as service is provided as per the customer's specific demand to the extent required. Service can be designed on general requirement basis, but actual service provision is customised as asked for. Services offered could be standard or customer specific. Other type of services could be mixture type *i.e.*, number of services possible as demanded such as repairs, maintenance, rental or sales etc.

Generally we catagorise schemes for producing and delivering services as under:

- ***Goods dominant services:*** In this case, the goods are manufactured on standard basis through either product based or process-based production. Goods may be produced with practically no customer involvement. All large stores selling products come under this category, as products only available are offered to the customer as choice. Food in a restaurant with fixed menu laid down is another such an example.
- ***Customer participation dominant services:*** A large number of services are designed to be available to customer as he needs and a high degree of involvement of customer is necessary. Automated gas stations, automated teller machines, salad or coffee bars

etc., provide such a service, where the service is available as per the choice of the customer including variety.

- ***Customised product service:*** Services provided in medical clinics or hair cutting saloons are such examples, where the service is totally customised and is provided through personal involvement of the customer.

The customers requirement, therefore, is to be obtained in advance and system designed accordingly. Simulation Techniques (Monte Cardo Simulation) is an important method for design of services, wherein the past data is used to decide the facilities and level of service that can be provided. Later modifications are usually introduced on the basis of customer demands either in terms of volume or diversity and variety. The general design principles such as simplicity, concurrent engineering and protyping etc., apply to design services also. However some additional considerations can be summed up for service design :

- Short lead time to be specified *i.e.*, how fast the service can be provided or required?
- What variety of service can or will be provided?
- In area of variety also, what customisation can be offered?
- The type of customers the service to be aimed at including the geographical area peculiarity.
- Customer involvement level to be specified.

Simulation Technique for Service Design

In case of services, the relationships between various variables of the system are, generally, not specific and hence formulation of mathematical models is not very easy. Computer simulations can be used for such a purpose, wherein it is often possible to simulate or imitate the problem by developing a model of some real life phenomenon and then the optimal solution reached at through trial and error processes on the given system. Large number of real life experiments are carried out with some basic assumptions and then the sensitivity analysis carried out for perceived variations.

Thus "simulation" is the process of designing a model of a real system and conducting experiments with the model for the purpose of understanding the behaviour (within the assumptions and limitations imposed) for the operation of the system.

Though simulation can be gainfully used in a large number of situations, few important uses are given below :

- Business training games
- Design of maintenance/service status
- Plant and warehousing locations
- Waiting line or queuing situations
- Inventory management
- Financial management including risk management
- Weather forecasting situations
- Flight training and operations situations

These models are developed on the theory of random numbers, because of the randomness of the situations occurring in real life systems. A Random Number table has been provided at the end of this book for ready reference and use.

Monte Carlo Simulation

This is the most commonly used simulation technique. It includes probability factors guided by the random sampling for probability of events occurring. The technique consists of following steps:

- Setting up a probability distribution for the variables.
- Assign an appropriate set of random numbers (RNs) to represent the values of the variables.
- Conduct a simulation experiment by random sampling.
- Repeat the above step till required number of simulation runs have been generated.
- Design and implement the decision and maintain control.
- For any modification, re-run the simulation model.

As can be understood from the above description, a pattern of happenings in a given situation is assumed to follow some probability distribution and is correlated to the sampling from this theoretical population of data by means of random numbers. Thus we generate the simulation statistics by picking up a random number and relating it to the standard probability distribution function to obtain random variable. Random numbers can also be generated from computer process. The procedure of simulation has been demonstrated through the following problem 3.1.

Problem 3.1

In a service station, the customers arrive randomly and their services requirements are also random. The data collected over a period of time has been tabulated below:

Arrival Pattern of customers:

Time between arrivals (minutes)	Frequency of arrival
0.5	2
1.0	9
1.5	10
2.0	20
2.5	10
3.0	14
3.5	10
4.0	14
4.5	9
5.0	2

Service requirement pattern

Service time (minutes)	Frequency
0.5	12
1.0	21
1.5	40
2.0	10
2.5	15
3.0	2

Workout the simulated pattern for service design of the service station and comment on the results for any modifications.

Solution :

Step 1. Based on the arrival and service requirement patterns, we first develop the associated random number table as follows:

Table of random numbers of arrival pattern

Time between arrivals (minutes)	Frequency	Cumulative Frequency	Cumulative Probability	Random numbers Associated
0.5	2	2	0.02	00 - 01
1.0	9	11	0.11	02 - 10
1.5	10	21	0.21	11 - 20
2.0	20	41	0.41	21 - 40
2.5	10	51	0.51	41 - 50
3.0	14	65	0.65	51 - 64
3.5	10	75	0.75	65 - 74
4.0	14	89	0.89	75 - 88
4.5	9	98	0.98	89 - 97
5.0	2	100	1.00	98 - 99

Table of random number for service pattern.

Service time (minutes)	Frequency	Cumulative Frequency	Cumulative Probability	Random numbers Associated
0.5	12	12	0.12	00 - 11
1.0	21	33	0.33	12 - 32
1.5	40	73	0.73	33 - 72
2.0	10	83	0.83	73 - 82
2.5	15	98	0.98	83 - 97
3.0	2	100	1.00	98 - 99

Step 2. Develop the simulated service design system for 20 customer arrivals, as follows. (Random numbers to be picked up from the random number tables given at the end of the book).

Simulated System

Arrival Number	Associated RN	Time between arrival	Time of arrival	RN for service	Time of service	Start of service	End of service	Waiting time	
								C	S
1	91	4.5	4.5	37	1.5	4.5	6.0	–	4.5
2	55	3.0	7.5	28	1.0	7.5	8.5	–	1.5
3	46	2.5	10.0	20	1.0	10.0	11.0	–	1.5
4	43	2.5	12.5	58	1.5	12.5	14.0	–	1.5
5	62	3.0	15.5	95	2.5	15.5	18.0	–	1.5
6	22	2.0	17.5	76	2.0	18.0	20.0	–	–
7	96	4.5	22.0	29	1.0	22.0	23.0	–	2.0
8	32	2.0	24.0	02	0.5	24.0	24.5	–	1.0
9	88	4.0	28.0	58	1.5	28.0	29.5	–	3.5
10	28	2.0	30.0	57	1.5	30.0	31.5	–	0.5
11	18	1.5	31.5	12	1.0	31.5	32.5	–	–
12	99	5.0	36.5	58	1.5	36.5	38.0	–	4.0
13	54	3.0	39.5	24	1.0	39.5	40.5	–	1.5
14	63	3.0	42.5	02	0.5	42.5	43.0	–	2.0
15	64	3.5	46.0	84	2.5	46.0	48.5	–	3.5
16	99	5.0	51.0	08	0.5	51.0	51.5	–	2.5
17	38	2.0	53.0	35	1.5	53.0	54.5	–	1.5
18	86	4.0	57.0	87	2.5	57.0	59.5	–	2.5
19	39	2.0	59.0	48	1.5	59.5	61.0	–	–
20	18	1.5	60.5	44	1.5	61.0	62.5	–	0.5

Step 3. From the simulated table above, it is observed that

Waiting time for customer (C) = Nil

Waiting time for service (S) = 35.5 minutes

Total elapsed time of operation = 62.5 minutes (end of service)

Hence proportion of customer waiting = Nil

$$\text{and proportion of service waiting} = \frac{35.5}{62.5} = 57\%$$

Step 4. Comments: In this case, the service facility is waiting almost half the total operation time, which is very large and not cost-effective. Hence service can be redesigned by reducing service facility (manpower/machines), so as to reduce the waiting time for services. In this situation customers are highly satisfied as they donot wait for their jobs at all and are attended to very promptly.

3.7 Environmental Effect on Design

Today we are living with large number of environmental concerns. To address the issue, a set of international standards (ISO14000 series) have been formulated. The pressure is mounting everyday to cleanse up our surroundings so that all living and non-livings can lead a good life. This pressure, obviously, passes down to products and services. These concerns have to be addressed at the design, manufacture and service stages. Some companies across the Globe have become environmentally sensitive on their own, whereas others have been focussing on it due to regulations and resultant penalties for non-conformance. If planned properly, design and manufacturing can be done in such a way that environmentally hazardous materials and products can be eliminated and cost benefits obtained. The treatment of finish by coating of cadmium or a cyanide bath solution for plating have been eliminated just by reducing number of coats for finish. The savings have been large in some cases.

Pollution control and waste minimisation during manufacturing are the areas to be addressed. Some companies have even built facilities to recycle wastes. Others have changed materials to reduce toxic emissions during or after manufacturing. Various ways can be adopted for enhancing positive environmental effect on design of products and services:

- Reduce or eliminate toxic or hazardous materials.
- Recycle materials of waste to reduce toxic emissions.
- Design for optimum use of materials, thus eliminating wastes.
- Make product bio-degrading or green as best as can be done *i.e.*, use environmentally friendly materials.

3.8 Use of Computers in Design Systems

Design activity can be very time consuming. Complexity of product/service further aggravates the problem. The present environment of global competition, short product life cycle and large variety have necessitated rethinking on our traditional methods of design. With the advancement of information technology, use of computers in design have became almost mendatory. The softwares are being developed everyday. Hardwares are being improved to be compatible. The use of computers in design, in the form of CAD/CAM softwares has become almost part of design life. The advantages of computer utilisation can be summarised as follows:

- A large storage of data in database is a great help.
- The interaction of relevant information for product design is much easier and faster.
- The retrieval and usage of data have became very quick.

- Time spent in design has been curtailed drastically due to speed of the computers and compatible softwares.

The time of design can be minimised further by buying readymade designs from following sources:

- Research associations.
- Government research organisations.
- Educational institutions/establishments.
- Private design organisations.
- Through licences to operate/manufacture.

3.9 Periodical Review of Designs

The "Change Management" as a reason for corporate transformation has resulted in the impact of change on operations strategies. Operations strategies, therefore, must include plans for flexible production system due to a continuous changing set of competitive priorities, with a production technology to bring about these required changes. Arranging necessary capital and acquisition production technology amenable to support these changes through dynamic equilibrium has, therefore, become a necessity for discussion of such strategies.

The changes in the product specifications, functional or technical, largely occur either due to organisations own research and development efforts or the production and material managers feedback. Both these can be called proactive changes, being offered to the consumer as a future thinking. The information of change may also result from the customer demand either through the sales/marketing team during their continuous survey or through vendors . It is this aspect of change, which requires immediate modification in product and service design and manufacturing or process/product design and service design. In either case, the optimal benefit can be accrued to the system only if there is continuous marrying up of the production team with the marketing team.

Various elements of operations strategy are the product positioning strategies, product design and production plans, outsourcing plans, process and technology plans, allocation or resources and facility planning (for product as well as for service operations) and these are to be carefully linked. The product positioning strategies must be very closely linked with the marketing strategies.

Thus there is a definite necessity to establishe close interaction between the marketing and the production system. The reason for such realtionship is constant update of product and its customisation to ensure highest customer satisfaction. For this interaction, the requirement of the customer has to be built into the product design, so that it can be appropriately placed in the market. Concurrent Engineering (CE) is the method of involving all interested functions together right from the product conception to production to delivery to the market and to the customers end. It is also for a constant upgradation of the product with dynamic customer need that production and markets are interlinked very closely and at all times. Improve in product features, quality and distribution system can then be ensured to reach customer with greater confidence.

The nature of relationship between production and marketing can be shown as under:

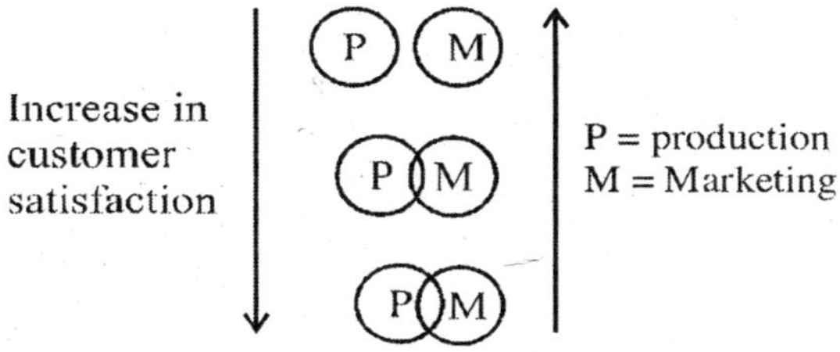

FIG. 3.6. Production/marketing relationship

—•—

Chapter 4

Strategic Planning and Demand Forecasting

Main issues:

1. Strategic Planning by organisations.
2. Environmental Factors for Business.
3. Forecasting of Demand (Short Range and Long Range).
4. Computer Softwares for Forecasting.

4.1 Strategic Planning by Organisations

Strategic planning is a process of understanding the mission of the organisation under the present industrial environment of operations and to prepare the future guidelines for the foreseeable future so that tomorrow's decisions can be directed towards the decided aim. Hence, based on the future industrial conditions (as can be intelligently visualised), the process of evolving a working philosophy can provide future business linkage within the organisation.

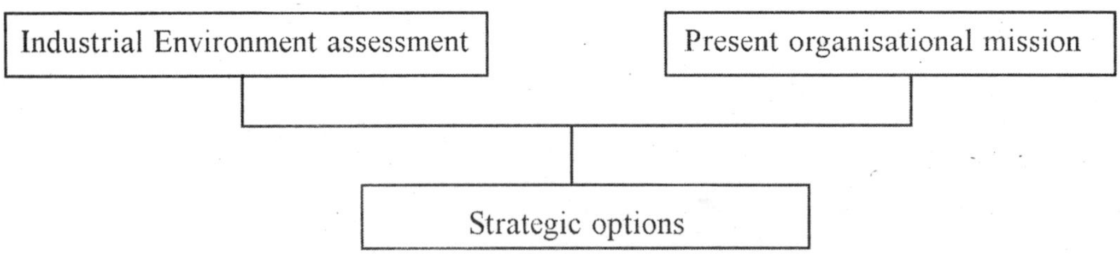

FIG. 4.1. Strategic Planning Base

Planning is an essential part of our life. A business manager plans the product mix, materials, processes and workers training. Any planning work would constitute the following steps:

- Aim of the planning activity.
- Action plan (Selected out of various alternatives)
- Resources plan for selected coarse of action
- Monitoring techniques

In business, planning is a basic function. Here a manager has to decide for business activity based on the aim, vision and mission of the organisation. This would emerge from the gap identification *i.e.*, the requirement emerging from the difference of present level activity to the desired level of activity based on the market force and the customer segment planned to be served by the organisation. For deciding down the aim of the business activities, the company has to analyse its present position, strength, weaknesses and the market competition. This would identify the "Gap" which will help in setting up the aim of the organisation (objective in business term).

The next deciding step is formulating the strategy to accomplish this objective. It would be worked out in the form of deciding on of an action plan. The aim or objective is to be divided in large number of activities, which can be independently performed. This is called Work Breakdown Structure (WBS) and detailed action sequence has to be designed for each of these activities. Various alternative can be studied to select the most appropriate coarse of action, leading to a cost effective plan.

The third step for achieving success of business plan is to workout various resources required for each activity. It requires working out the skill and strength of the task force, the time schedule for completion of the activity, the type and number of machines and materials required and the financial resources to make the dream come true.

The planning should include detailing out specific responsibilities of each person and the organisation of the task as a whole, and laying down policies, procedures and programmes to complete all the tasks dovetailing resources and time schedules.

4.2 Scope of Strategic Plan

In order to ensure success, the future developments in terms of environmental happenings such as technology and market competition also needs to be taken into account while preparing the plan. Future forecasting of events would need the conceptual skill and experience of a business manager with the highest level of commitment, to produce a worthwhile plan for success. This plan can be given the following names:

- Corporate Plan
- Strategic Plan
- Aggregate Plan
- Business Plan
- Integrated Plan

The Strategic Plan should contain the following:

- Mission and objectives of the organisation

- Past experience and background information
- Organisational structure
- Technology details and appropriate selection
- Manufacturing strategies, plans and product mix
- Marketing planning
- Manpower strategies and planning
- Financial strategies and planning

It is an integrated plan involving all the departments of the organisation *i.e.*, marketing, sales, production, human resources, purchasing and materials, engineering, finances and the distribution systems, so that an optimal strategy plan is evolved which, then is broken into departmental plans for co-ordinated efforts to produce aimed results of success, excellence and market supremacy. Any organisation has to concentrate on the following:

- Proper product mix, appropriate process and technology.
- Coherent planning to ensure optimum utilisation of resources.
- Professional management and conceptual skills, foresight and effective monitoring support.

Forethought and detailed look into present and future markets would result in proper production plan, based on technology plan, engineering plan and the quality plan. Producing a right product at the right time at cost effective level, supported by engineering, technology, scientific and management plans will see the organisation rise and stay the market leader. To ensure the effective implementation of the business plan, the mile-stones for monitoring and the transparent method of measurement with monitoring techniques has to be specified in the plan itself.

We can now summarise the strategic view point of the operations management in the given schematic diagram. (Refer Fig. 4.2)

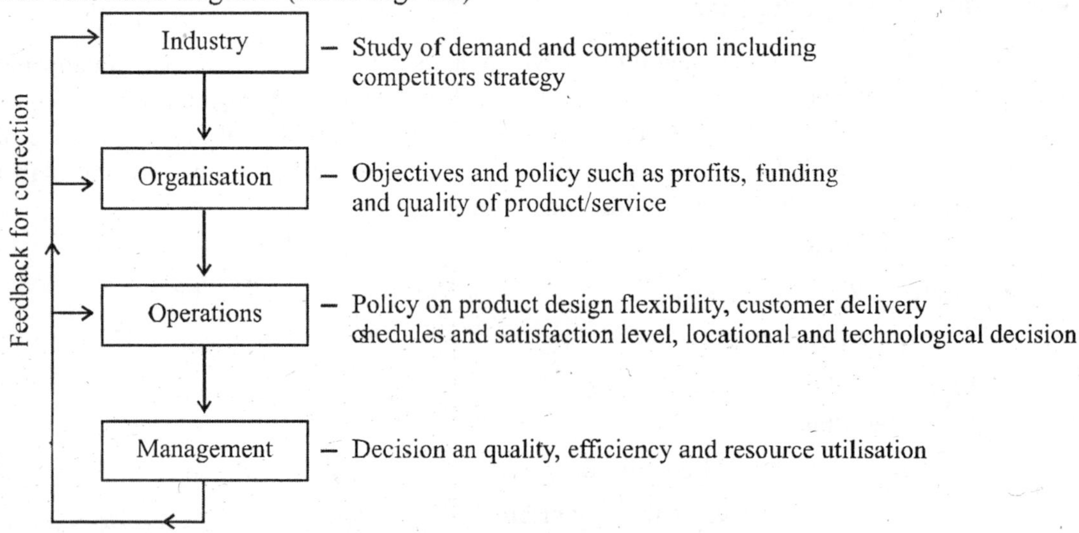

FIG. 4.2. Strategic balance of operations

4.3 Evaluation of Operational Strategies

The various factors on which the operational strategies can be evaluated are as under:

- Cost and delivery lead time
- Quality
- Profitability
- Consistency
- Flexibility

4.4 Environmental Factors for Business

When an organisation plans to write a success story, it looks around at the business environment in which it has to prosper and compete. For any manufacturing organisation, the major functions are marketing and sales, technology, engineering, materials and purchase, production system, maintenance of assets and production planning and control (PPC). In order to perform well in these functions, a manufacturing organisation will need deep insight into the following areas:

- Demand, production and resultant sales
- Processes and technology available
- Fiscal policy of the government
- Availability of resources - manpower, machines, materials and finances
- Customer preferences
- Competitors strategies
- Social and political environment

Any major variations in any of the areas will affect the corporate plan and the resultant production plan, as these changes will have direct or indirect bearing on corporate function.

It is also an established fact that changes are inevilable. The nature, controlling the universe, itself is probabilistic.

"Future is probabilistic, but look into the future with confidence". Hence forecasting in various areas in imperative.

Now the question arises as to how-to look into the future. In the words of Edmond Burke-

"You can never plan the future but by the past"

Whereas Patrick Henry Says **"I know of no way of judging the future, but by the past"**. The importance of a close look into present and then an intelligent peep into the near future will bring in coherence in our business plans.

4.5 Factors Leading to Forecasting of Product Demand

After the selection and design of the product, the company has to decide on the possible future demand, so that necessary planning for these volumes can be done and resources planned out to achieve it. First step in operations management is the sales forecast *i.e.*, estimation of future demand for products and services. For an organisation, forecast of product demand is not just a simple calculation. As discussed earlier, even for product demand, forecastings of technology, fiscal policies, customers preferences and competitors strategies have to be understood. Therefore forecasts are obtained for some important parameters such as interest rates, market share and future trend of pricing before a forecast for the product is ventured into. The time horizon, for which forecast is also to be obtained, is also important due to continuous change in customers preferences, the requirement of small volumes of variety products and change in the technology. Even with these changes keeping in mind, an operations manager needs long-range forecast for his strategic decisions about products and facilities. It is not practically feasible to make frequent changes in the facilities system, hence strategic planning should ensure utilisation of the resources with flexible method of operations. Short term forecasts are helpful in planning day to day work, so that the demand does not go unfulfilled, nor there is unnecessary stocks accumulated, whereas long term strategy will ensure opimum utilisation of resources for long period.

Trends in the Forecasting Pattern

For arriving at the approximate forecast of demand, the changes in the data obtained are to be incorporated as the time progresses. This is called the variation in the time series models for such forecasts. These variations may be due to a number of factors affecting the value over a period of time and can be grouped under the following categories:

- Secular trend
- Cyclic fluctuation
- Seasonal variation
- Irregular variation

Secular trend

When the value of the dependent variable tends to increase or decrease over a longer horizon, the variation is termed as "secular trend". Increase in population, sales of the products, increase or decrease in the price index or variation in per capita income are some of such examples. It can be shown as follows:

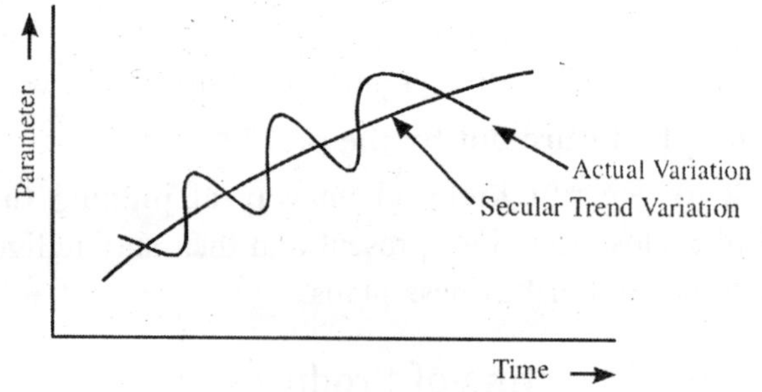

Fig. 4.3 Secular Trend

Cyclic Fluctuation

If the variations is in the form of peaks and lows in a business tend, these can be called cyclic fluctuation. If the variations are almost uniform over a given period, these period can be different for different businesses, may be, one year or five years. This need not follow a regular pattern, as shown below:

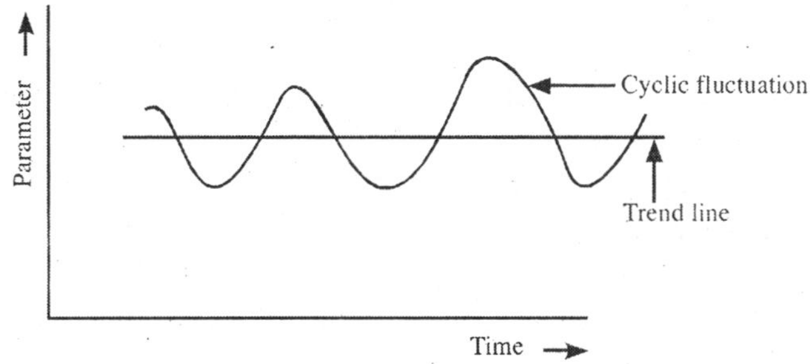

Fig. 4.4 Cyclic Fluctuation

Seasonal Variation

The type of change occurs due to changing seasons in terms of the variation pattern observed during the year itself, such as sales of airconditioners or heaters, following a seasonal variation, peaking during April/May or October/November.

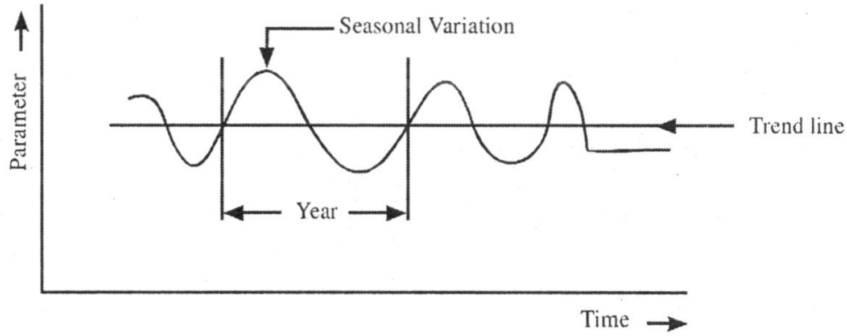

Fig. 4.5 Seasonal Variation

Irregular variation

This type of change in the demand of a product shows no definite pattern. It is completely unpredictable and changes occur in a very random manner, such as follows.

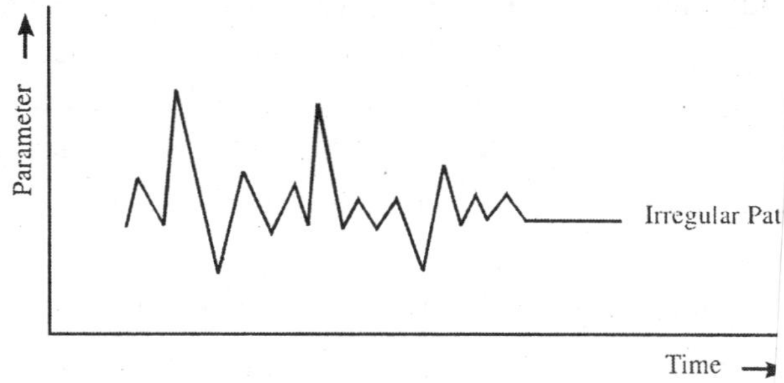

Fig. 4.6 Irregular Variation

4.6 Types of Forecasts:

Due to the variations described above, the types of forecasts required are:

- Long term forecasts - for about one year or little more
- Medium range forecast - generally for a month
- Short term forecasts - Weekly or even daily.

In case of operations management, we can collect data and then forecast for planning new facilities to be installed or the data can help in monthly production plans along with adjustments on weekly basis (based on sales feedback). The forecast is also very helpful in workforce scheduling, because getting suitable manpower at short notice may not be feasible. Due to variation in volumes, the manpower is also required to be scheduled and rescheduled, which is a tough job for any operations manager.

To summarise, the organisation has to decide on the following aspects of forecast, before committing resources to obtain it:

- Purpose of the forecast
- Lead time of the forecast
- Parameter to be forecasted
- Information available
- Factors affecting the parameter
- Accuracy required in forecast

4.7 Methods of Demand Forecasting

Two methods can be adopted for arriving as a reasonable level of forecast for product demand:

- Qualitative Methods
- Quantitative Methods.

Qualitative Methods of Forecasting

The qualitative methods of forecasting are based of judgement and previous experience. May be the previous years sales month-wise could help in deciding the demand for current year depending on the trend of increase of product sales. The company can also use the opinion of some experts of the relevant field as to how the market is likely to behave. An addition, the company can decide on demand based on the market and sales push it wants to adopt for gaining the higher market share. These methods can be formalised under following names:

Manager's experience and guess: This method is adopted when only one person uses his r her best judgement. It may be due to the past experience or hunch or intuition of the market litions. Obviously such a simple method has it own short comings (may be highly subjective, bias can be strong) and hence can be adopted for short term forecasts, so that even if level is high, cost effect may not be large. But in the absence of any scientific forecasting, this could be the best bet, when time span for making the demand decision is extremely small.

Nominal group consensus: In this case, few experienced and knowledgeable excecutives or departmental managers from all the departments can be asked to produce their own opinion. It may be in the form of selecting a specified committee entrusted with the job of sales forecast. Since the number of inputs have increased, compared to single managers experience, the human bias can be reduced and a better forecast is likely to emerge. These forecasts, obviously, will be compromised forecasts, with an advantage of experience of managers in various fields and then averaging of the variations.

Delphi method: This method is a further improvement over the first two methods described above. It was developed to obtain the group information but with reduced human bias. The method starts with the selection of a panel of experts, preferably from different fields of experience, so that a wide range of opinion can be obtained. The names of panel members are not disclosed to anyone in the group. It is known only to the panel co-ordinator or the group leader or facilitator (as he is called). These panel members are reguested to send a relevant forecast along with supporting arguments. Information can be obtained through a list of questionnaire specifying the data or input required. The information so obtained is then compiled, summerised, analysed and sent back to the panel members, without disclosing the identity of others for fine-tuning. There may be a revised questionnaire, more refined, if required to obtain improved information on forecast. The process is repeated till consensus or near convergence is arrived at.

Survey of the Sales Force and Customers: The sales force submits their survey as per the actual sales achieved and the attitude of the customers noted during the process of sales. This estimate can be, then, realistically adopted for all regions as per the average obtained.

Market Research: White using various methods of market research for obtaining customers requirements, the trend can be analysed for each segment of customers. This information can be statistically extrapolated for demand forecast, with due hypothesis testing procedure.

Quantitative Method of Forecasting

Quantitative methods of forecasting are based on the mathematical models developed from past historical data. Trends can be extended to form some idea about the future. Due to high probabilistic pattern of development, it may not be very good information to bank on, but it is atleast the starting point for future reference. If the environmental factors are superimposed on historical data, a fairly good estimate can be obtained on this basis. Forecast accuracy refers to the extent to which, the forecasts are related to the actual happening.

Short Range Quantitative Methods: These methods are used to provide estimates of future parametric values spanning our a short time horizon, say from few days to few weeks. Due to short duration forecasts, the effects of season, trend or cycles may not be high. These are useful, when random fluctuations are frequent and cannot be planned for a long period due to embedded uncertainty like sick worker, sudden strike, rejection of material or a sudden machine failure etc.

Some of the methods used for this purpose are:

- Cumulative average method
- Moving average method
- Weighted moving average method
- Exponential smoothing method

Cumulative Average Method

This is a very simple technique, when the past data shows very low variation in the sales. If the sales per month indicate almost the same levels such as 1500, 1530, 1480, 1510, 1500, 1490, 1520 etc., it means that the product is acceptable in the market, but the customers using or buying are few or their requirements are not undergoing major changes. In that case, the production can be catered for the average value of these sales. It can be obtained by adding all individual values, say sales for the month and then dividing by the number of values used (*i.e.*, numbers of months).

$$\therefore \quad \text{Average forecast} = \frac{1500 + 1530 + 1480 + 1510 + 1500 + 1490 + 1520}{7} = 1504$$

Thus it can be seen that the average demand of the product is around 1504 (average works out to 1504) which is not significantly different from 1500. Hence the demand forecast on the average basis can be taken as 1500 only.

Mathematical model for this method will be

$$\overline{x} = \frac{x_1 + x_2 + x_3 + \ldots + x_n}{n}$$

where $\overline{x}$ = average value of the parameter or variation

$x_1, x_2 \ldots x_n$ = actual values of variable observed during the period

n = number of observations used for forecast

Moving Average Method

The difference over the previous (average) method is that in this case, we use variable values progressively for obtaining average value, rather than using all the values together. This method is useful, when the demand is varying, but the variation may not be uniform. A possible case could be seasonal variation.

For example, the sales of air-conditioners (a seasonal product) are not uniform throughout the year. It will start picking up just before the onset of summer and will decline as the summer progresses into winter. Therefore, the sales values for the month of January and February (only season discounts sales possibly) are really no indication for sales for March, April and onwards. Hence averaging the sales value for January to October may not be realistic. We should adopt the sales of March and April for forecasting for May and April-May together for getting the average sales for June and so on. Since we are using the sales values progressively this is called Moving average method. Thus

$$\text{Forecast for May} = \frac{\text{Sales for March and April}}{2}$$

and $$\text{Forecast for June} = \frac{\text{Sales for April and May}}{2}$$

Mathematically, the moving average model can be written as follows:

$$F_t = \frac{S(t-2) + S(t-1)}{2}$$

where F_t = Forecast for time t

S (t – 1) = Sales of period t – 1

S (t – 2) = Sales for period t – 2

The general expression for moving average model can be written as

$$F_1 = \frac{x_1 + x_2 + \ldots\ldots x_n}{n}$$

and $$F_2 = \frac{x_2 + x_3 + \ldots\ldots x_{n+1}}{n} \text{ etc.}$$

Weighted Moving Average Method

In this method, we donot treat all the values at the same level of importance. If we take the case of sales of airconditioners once again, the sales during the month of march is more related to the sales for April, rather than the sales for February. Thus we allot less importance to the sales of February and more to the sales during March. Similar argument can be carried forward for successive months. The importance of a value (relevance to the forecast required) is called weightage and hence the mathematical model for weighted Moving Average method can be written as follows

$$F_1 = \frac{w_1 x_1 + w_2 x_2 + \ldots\ldots w_n x_n}{w_1 + w_2 + \ldots\ldots w_n}$$

where F = forecast required

w_s = weightage for successive values of variables

x_s = variables with reference to the relevant forecast

Problem 4.1

From the actual sales indicated below, work out the forecasts for future months of the year, using moving average and weighted moving average methods.

Months	Jan	Feb	Mar	Apr	May	June	July	Aug	Sep	Oct	Nov	Dec
Sales (000's)	2.0	1.4	1.9	1.9	3.1	1.8	1.5	1.3	2.2	2.7	2.0	1.3

Solution:

The solution has been worked out in the given table:

(Assuming weightages of 3: 2 and 7: 2: 1 for 2 months and 3 month forecast respectively)

Months	Actual Sales (000's)	Last Month Sales	Average last 2 months	Weighted average last 2 months	Average last 3 months	Weighted Average last 3 months
Jan	2.0	—	—	—	—	—
Feb	1.4	2.0	—	—	—	—
March	1.9	1.4	$\frac{1.4+2.0}{2} = 1.7$	$\frac{1}{5}(3\times1.4 + 2\times2.0)$ = 1.64	—	—
April	1.9	1.9	1.65	1.70	$\frac{1}{3}(2.0+1.9+1.4)$ = 1.77	$\frac{1}{10}(7\times1.9+2\times$ 1.4 + 2.0) = 1.01
May	3.1	1.9	1.9	1.9	1.73	1.85
June	1.8	3.1	2.5	2.62	2.30	2.74
July	1.5	1.8	2.45	2.32	2.27	2.07
Aug	1.3	1.5	1.65	1.62	2.13	1.72
Sep	2.2	1.3	1.4	1.38	1.53	1.30
Oct	2.7	2.2	1.75	1.84	1.67	1.31
Nov	2.0	2.7	2.45	2.50	2.07	2.4
Dec	1.3	2.0	2.35	2.28	2.30	2.16

Exponential Smoothing Method

This is a refined and modified method of weighted moving average. In this case, the importance or weightages are allotted to the most recent forecast obtained and the actual sales during the recent past period. This gives better results of forecast, because it smooths out the variation of forecast with the help of physical achievement through the last period sales. The mathematical model for this method can be written as

$$F_t = \alpha . S_{(t-1)} + (1 - \alpha) F_{(t-1)}$$

where F_t = Forecast for the time t

α = Smoothing constant

$S_{(t-1)}$ = Most recent sales volume [for time $(t - 1)$]

$F_{(t-1)}$ = Most recent forecast [for time $(t - 1)$]

α, the smoothing constant, is used to smooth out the variation in the actual sales and the corresponding forecast. α really is the weight or importance attached to sales and obviously $(1 - \alpha)$ to the corresponding forecast. The value of smoothing constant α varies as.

$$1 \leq \alpha \geq 0$$

By allotting higher value of α ie 0.5 onward, a manager is likely to obtain better forecast, because of higher level of faith in the achievement of his sales force.

Problem 4.2

From the given data in problem 4.1 workout the relevant future forecast by exponential smoothing method, using smoothing constant $\alpha = 0.7$.

Solution:

Exponential Smoothing Table

Months	Actual sales	Last Month	Forecast (a = 0.7)
January	2.0	-	-
February	1.4	2.0	3.0 (assumed)
March	1.9	1.4	$(0.7 \times 2.0 + 0.3 \times 3.0) = 2.30$
April	1.9	1.9	$(0.7 \times 1.4 + 0.3 \times 2.30) = 1.67$
May	3.1	1.9	1.83
June	1.8	3.1	1.88
July	1.5	1.8	2.73
August	1.3	1.5	2.08
September	2.2	1.3	1.67
October	2.7	2.2	1.41
November	2.0	2.7	1.96
December	1.3	2.0	2.48

Problem 4.3

Use exponential smoothing technique to workout forecast for the following series data under two situations, when smoothing constant is 0.3 and when smoothing constant is 0.7. Which forecast will you accept and why?

Period	1	2	3	4	5	6	7	8	9	10
Observations	27	30	32	31	28	27	30	33	33	31

Solution:

In order to compare two forecasts, we will workout the variance of observations from the worked out forecasts using the given relationship of exponential smoothing.

For ease of calculation, the first previous forecasts is assumed as 27 *i.e.*, the observation for the first period itself

Table for $\alpha = 0.3$

Period	Observation x	error ($e_t = x - F_t$)	$\alpha_1 e_t$	F_t	e_t^2
1	27	(27 – 27) = 0	0.3 × 0 = 0	27	0
2	30	(30 – 27) = 3	0.3 × 3 = 0.9	27 + 0.9 = 27.9	9
3	32	(32 – 27.9) = 4.1	0.3 × 4.1 = 1.23	29.1	16.8
4	31	1.9	0.57	29.7	3.61
5	28	–1.7	–0.51	29.2	2.89
6	27	–2.2	–0.66	28.5	4.84
7	30	1.5	0.45	29.0	2.25
8	33	4.0	1.20	30.2	16.0
9	33	2.8	0.84	31.04	7.84
10	31	0	0	31	0
					$\Sigma e_t^2 = 63.27$

Now we draw a similar table for $\alpha_2 = 0.7$

Period	x_t	$e_t = x - F_t$	$\alpha_2 e_t$	F_t	e_t^2
1	27	0	0	27	0
2	30	3.0	2.1	29.1	9.0
3	32	2.9	2.01	31.1	8.41
4	31	– 0.1	– 0.07	31.0	0.01
5	28	– 3.0	– 2.1	28.9	9.0
6	27	– 1.9	– 1.33	27.6	3.61
7	30	2.4	1.68	29.3	5.76
8	33	3.7	2.59	31.9	13.69
9	33	1.1	0.77	32.7	1.21
10	31	– 1.7	– 1.19	31.5	2.89
					$\Sigma e_t^2 = 53.58$

Working out Variance for α_1, $V_1 = \dfrac{63.23}{9} = 7.02$

Variance for α_2, $V_2 = \dfrac{53.58}{9} = 5.95$

Since variance for $\alpha = 0.7$ is less, the forecast obtained with this value of the smoothing constant will be preferred.

4.8 Long Range Quantitative Methods

Long range mathematical models are applied when estimations are to be done for a longer duration, say, more than a year. These models help to make strategic decisions for long term planning for production facilities set up based on the forecasts. These facilities cannot be uprooted or changed on monthly or even annual basis. The planning of product mix, processes, technologies and resultant ground facilities will have to be based on these long term forecasts. These may need minor modifications, due to time-to-time changes in demand.

The Variations in the demand have been discussed already. And hence the production facilities have to be flexible to cater for these variations. Flexibility is, generally, adjusted within the established facilities.

The long term methods applied to forecasting are linear Regression model and Correlation, interpolation and extrapolation and time series models.

These forecasting models establish relationship between two variables, one called the dependent variable (in case of product demand forecast, it will be the parameter of the forecast) and the other an independent variable because the variability in the demand pattern occurs with reference to this variable change.

The independent variable in case of time series is time, during which the changes occurs.

Linear Regression Model

Simple linear regression model is used where there exists a linear relationship between the dependent and the independent variable such as the forecast of sales volume as the time progresses. The linear regression model can be written as follows.

$$y = a + bx$$

where y = dependent variable (say sales or demand)

x = independent variable (say time)

a, b = relationship constants to be determined to identify the rate and level of growth

When the data of the past sales is utilised, a linear line representing the trend in demand growth can be used once the initial state point value (a = y-intercept of the straight line) and the slope of the line (b = slope) have been determined. The value of a and b can be calculated from the following relationships:

$$b = \frac{\Sigma x^2 \Sigma y - \Sigma x \Sigma xy}{n\Sigma x^2 - (\Sigma x)^2} \text{ and } a = \frac{\Sigma x^2 \Sigma y - \Sigma x \Sigma xy}{n\Sigma x^2 - (\Sigma x)^2}$$

$$\text{or else; } b = \frac{\Sigma dx \, \Sigma dy}{\Sigma dx^2} \text{ where } dx = x - \bar{x} \text{ and } dy = y - \bar{y}$$

Problem 4.4

The following table shows the number of motor registrations in a certain territory for a term of 5 years and the sales of motor tyres by a firm in that territory for the same period.

Year	Motor registrations	No. of tyres sold
1	600	1,250
2	630	1,100
3	720	1,300
4	750	1,350
5	800	1,500

Find the regression equation to estimate the sales of tyres, when the motor registration is known. Estimate sales of tyres, when registration is 850.

(Bombay University, B.Com., April 1978)

Solution:

In this case the sales of tyres are to be calculated (forecasted) as against motor registrations. Hence the independent variable (x) is identified as motor registrations, whereas the dependent variable (y) is number of tyres. To obtain the regression equation of y on x, the table below is prepared.

Table for regression calculations

x	y	$x - \bar{x} = dx$ ($\bar{x} = 700$)	$y - \bar{y} = dy$ ($\bar{y} = 1{,}300$)	dx^2	$dx\,dy$
600	1,250	– 100	– 50	10,000	5,000
630	1,100	– 70	– 200	4,900	14,000
720	1,300	20	0	400	0
750	1,350	50	50	2,500	2,500
800	1,500	100	200	10,000	20,000
$\Sigma x = 3{,}500$	$\Sigma y = 6{,}500$	$\Sigma dx = 0$	$\Sigma dy = 0$	$\Sigma dx^2 = 27{,}800$	$\Sigma dxdy = 41{,}500$

Since $$\bar{x} = \frac{\Sigma x}{n} = \frac{3500}{5} = 700$$

and $$\bar{y} = \frac{\Sigma y}{n} = \frac{6500}{5} = 1300$$

These values of $\bar{x}, \bar{y}$ have been used for dx, dy calculations. Calculating the slope of the regression line,

$$b_{yx} = \frac{\Sigma dx\,\Sigma dy}{\Sigma dx^2}$$

$$= \frac{41{,}500}{27{,}000} = 1.49$$

Substituting this value of b_{yx}, we get the regression equation as under

$$y - \bar{y} = b_{yx}(x - \bar{x})$$

or $$y - 1{,}300 = 1.49\ (x - 700)$$

or $$y = 1.49x - 1{,}043 + 1{,}300 = 1.49x + 257$$

This is the regression equation for forecasting the sales of tyres.

when $x = 850$ (given as no of registrations)

$y = 1.49 \times 850 + 257 = 1{,}524$ tyres.

Problem 4.5

From the data given, find the average increase in the salary on annual basis.

Year	1	2	3	4	5	6	7	8	9	10
Monthly Salary (in hundreds)	52.5	58.7	65.0	70.2	75.4	81.1	87.2	95.5	102.2	108.4

Solution:

Since the salary is increasing in a gradual manner, the regression method can be applied to work out the trend of increase. Regression calculation are given below:

The Regression Table

Year (x)	Salary in hundreds (y)	x^2	xy
1	52.5	1	52.5
2	58.7	4	117.4
3	65.0	9	195.0
4	70.2	16	280.8
5	75.4	25	377.0
6	81.1	36	486.6
7	87.2	49	610.4
8	95.5	64	769.0
9	102.2	81	919.8
10	108.4	100	1089.0
$\Sigma x = 35$	$\Sigma y = 796.2$	$\Sigma x^2 = 385$	$\Sigma xy = 4887.5$

From the given data, the slope (b) of the regression line $y = a + bx$ can be calculated as follows:

$$b = \frac{n\Sigma xy - (\Sigma x\, \Sigma y)}{n\Sigma x^2 - (\Sigma x)^2}$$

$$= \frac{10 \times 4887.5 - 55 \times 796.3}{10 \times 385 - (55)^2} = 6.16$$

and
$$a = \frac{(\Sigma x^2 \Sigma y) - (\Sigma x \Sigma y)}{n\Sigma x^2 - (\Sigma x)^2}$$

$$= \frac{(385 \times 796.5) - (55 \times 4887.5)}{10 \times 385 - (55)^2} = 45.73$$

The salary increase trend is now established as the slope of the regression line *i.e.*, 6.16 times every year. And the respective salaries can be calculated from these value of a and b.

The regression line established is y = 45.73 + 6.16x

Problem 4.6

By using the following data, find out two lines of regression:

$\Sigma x = 250$, $\Sigma y = 300$, $\Sigma xy = 7{,}900$, $\Sigma x^2 = 6{,}500$, $\Sigma y^2 = 10{,}000$, n = 10

(Delhi University B.Com., (Hon) 1984)

Solution:

From the given data,

$$\bar{x} = \frac{\Sigma x}{n} = \frac{250}{10} = 25$$

$$\bar{y} = \frac{\Sigma y}{n} = \frac{300}{10} = 30$$

b_{yx} = regression slope of y on x

$$= \frac{n\Sigma xy - (\Sigma x \Sigma y)}{n\Sigma x^2 - (\Sigma x)^2}$$

$$= \frac{10 \times 7{,}900 - 250 \times 300}{10 \times 6{,}500 - (250)^2} = 1.6$$

Similarly
$$b_{xy} = \frac{n\Sigma xy - \Sigma x \Sigma y}{n\Sigma y^2 - (\Sigma y)^2}$$

$$= \frac{10 \times 7{,}900 - 250 \times 300}{10 \times 10{,}000 - (300)^2} = 0.4$$

Hence the two lines of regression would be

$$y - \bar{y} = b_{yx}(x - \bar{x})$$

or $y - 30 = 1.6(x - 25)$

or $y = 1.6x - 10$ (*i*)

and $x - \bar{x} = b_{xy}(y - \bar{y})$

or $x - 25 = 0.4(y - 30)$

or $x = 0.4y + 13$ (*ii*)

Correlation

The coefficient of correlation (r) is the relative importance of relationship between dependent and independent variable. Thus correlation analysis is the statistical tool, which can be used to describe the degree to which one variable is linearly related to the other. The value of correlation coefficient (r) varies between -1 and $+1$ indicating either a negative or positive correlation between those variables. Minus 1 (-1) indicates perfect negative relationship *i.e.*, two variable are related and moving totally in opposite direction, where as plus 1($+1$) means that x and y go up in the same proportion. Zero (0) would mean no relationships existing at all. Correlation coefficient, therefore indicates the accuracy of the forecast.

Correlation coefficient can be worked out from the following relationship.

$$r = \frac{\Sigma(x-\bar{x}) \cdot \Sigma(y-\bar{y})}{\sigma_x \sigma_y} = \frac{\text{Cov}(x, y)}{\sigma_x \sigma_y}$$

where r = Correlation coefficient

cov (x, y) = Co-variance between x and y

σ_x = Standard deviation of x-series data

σ_y = Standard deviation of y-series data

Also $r^2 = b_{yx} \cdot b_{xy}$

Also
$$r_{(xy)} = \frac{\Sigma(x-\bar{x})\Sigma(y-\bar{y})}{\sqrt{[\Sigma(x-\bar{x})^2 \Sigma(y-\bar{y})^2]}}$$

where $\bar{x}$ = mean value of all x variables

$\bar{y}$ = mean value of all y variables

This Correlation Coefficient is called **Karl Pearson** Coefficient of Correlation.

Since the value of r remains unchanged due to any change in origin of scale where u, v are changed parameters,

$$\therefore \quad r_{xy} = r_{uv}$$

Based on these relationships, the correlation coefficient can be easily calculated.

Problem 4.7

Find the relationship between sales and expenses in terms of Karl Pearson's coefficient of correlation for the data collected from ten firms during market research.

Firm	1	2	3	4	5	6	7	8	9	10
Sales (000' units)	50	50	55	60	60	65	65	60	60	50
Expenses (000' Rs)	11	13	14	16	16	15	15	14	13	13

Solution:

The problem can be solved by changing the scale and origin of the data by putting $u = \dfrac{x-60}{5}$ and $v = y - 14$. The computation table is worked out as follows.

Firm	Sales (000's) (x)	Expenses (000's) (y)	$u = \dfrac{x-60}{5}$	$v = y - 14$	u^2	v^2	uv
1	50	11	– 2	– 3	4	9	6
2	50	13	– 2	– 1	4	1	2
3	55	14	– 1	0	1	0	0
4	60	16	0	2	0	4	0
5	60	16	0	2	0	4	0
6	65	15	1	1	1	1	1
7	65	15	1	1	1	1	1
8	60	14	0	0	0	0	0
9	60	13	0	– 1	0	1	0
10	50	13	– 2	– 1	4	1	2
			$\Sigma u = -5$	$\Sigma v = 0$	$\Sigma u^2 = 15$	$\Sigma v^2 = 22$	$\Sigma uv = 12$

These computed values can now be used in the relationship

$$r_{xy} = r_{uv} = \frac{n\Sigma uv - \Sigma u \Sigma v}{\sqrt{[n\Sigma u^2 - (\Sigma u)^2][n\Sigma v^2 - (\Sigma u)^2]}}$$

$$= \frac{10 \times 12 - (-5) \times 0}{\sqrt{[10 \times 15 = (-5)^2][10 \times 22 - 0^2]}}$$

$$= \frac{120}{(125)(220)} = 0.73$$

Hence the two parameters are ordinarily correlated.

Problem 4.8

(a) Compute the correlation coefficient between the corresponding values of x and y in the following table:

x	2	4	5	6	8	11
y	18	12	10	8	7	5

(b) Multiply each x value by 2 and add 6. Also multiply each value of y by 3 and subtract 15. Find the correlation coefficient between new values of the variables. Show whether the result in both the cases is same and why?

Solution:

(a) for computation of Karl Pearsons' coefficient , we have

x	y	$x-\bar{x}$ $= x-6$	$y-\bar{y}$ $= y-10$	$(x-\bar{x})^2$	$(y-\bar{y})^2$	$(x-\bar{x})(y-\bar{y})$
2	18	– 4	8	16	64	– 32
4	12	– 2	2	4	4	– 4
5	10	– 1	0	1	0	0
6	8	0	– 2	0	4	0
8	7	2	– 3	4	9	– 6
11	5	5	– 5	25	25	– 5
$\Sigma x = 36$	$\Sigma y = 60$	$\Sigma(x-\bar{x})=0$	$\Sigma(y-\bar{y})=0$	$\Sigma(x-\bar{x})^2=50$	$\Sigma(y-\bar{y})^2=106$	$\Sigma(x-\bar{x})(y-\bar{y})=-67$

From the data, $\bar{x} = \dfrac{\Sigma x}{n} = \dfrac{36}{6} = 6$

and $\bar{y} = \dfrac{\Sigma y}{n} = \dfrac{60}{6} = 10$

These values have been used for computation

$$\therefore \quad r_{xy} = \frac{\Sigma(x-\bar{x})\Sigma(y-\bar{y})}{\sqrt{[\Sigma(x-\bar{x})^2\Sigma(y-\bar{y})^2]}}$$

$$= \frac{-67}{\sqrt{(50\times 106)}} = -0.92 \quad \text{(high negative correlation)}$$

(b) Replacing new values of the variables as $u = 2x + 6$ and $v = 3y - 15$

x	y	$u = 2x + 6$	$v = 3y - 15$	u^2	v^2	$u.v$
2	18	10	39	100	1521	390
4	12	14	21	196	441	294
5	10	16	15	256	225	240
6	8	18	9	324	81	162
8	7	22	6	484	36	132
11	5	28	0	784	0	0
		$\Sigma u = 108$	$\Sigma v = 90$	$\Sigma u^2 = 2144$	$\Sigma v^2 = 2304$	$\Sigma uv = 1218$

$$\therefore \quad r_{uv} = \frac{n\Sigma uv - \Sigma u\Sigma v}{\sqrt{[n\Sigma u^2 - (\Sigma u)^2][n\Sigma v^2 - (\Sigma u)^2]}}$$

$$= \frac{6 \times 1218 - 108 \times 90}{\sqrt{[6 \times 2144 - (108)^2][6 \times 2304 - (90)^2]}} = -0.92$$

The value of coefficient is same, as there is no effect due to shift of origin or scale.

Interpolation and Extrapolation

Interpolation is a technique of obtaining / estimating the value of the dependent variable for any intermediatory value of the independent variable. Hence this method is used for forecasting any demand for any period based on certain data (as to what it would have been). This is useful for planning purposes for periods where the data is not easily available.

Similarly, extrapolation is defined as the technique of forecasting most likely future value of the dependent variable against a given independent variable value. Future forecasting is obtained by this method by the extension of trend data for the near foreseeable future.

The values of the independent variable are termed as arguments and the corresponding values of the dependent variable are known as entries.

In order to use these data to obtain a near realistic estimate, following assumptions are utilised for the forecasts being useful. These are

- No sudden peaks or falls. Random fluctuations such as natural calamity etc to be avoided.
- In the absence of evidence to the contrary, there should be regularity in fluctuations for rate of change to be uniform.

Methods of Forecasting (Finite Differences)

There are generally two methods adopted for the purpose of estimation through interpolation/extrapolation.

- Graphical Method
- Algebraic Method

Graphical Method

The available data can be plotted on a graph indicating the relationship of the independent and dependent variable. Then a smooth curve is drawn through the points so obtained and for a desired period, the interpolation / extrapolation is carried out by projecting the period onto the trend curve.

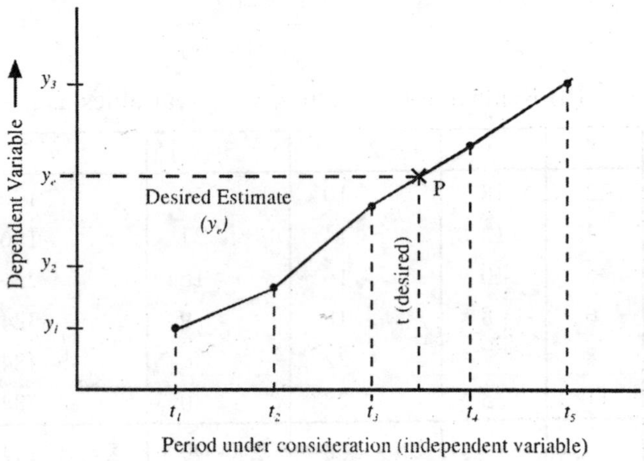

FIG 4.7.

Algebraic Method

We can use either the method of curve fitting for any polynomial relationship or the method of finite differences

For polynomial $y = ax^n + bx^{n-1} + ...$, various equations such as for regression analysis can be solved for obtaining the desired estimate.

The Method of finite differences

(i) Through operator Δ:

The calculus of finite differences is quite a convenient tool for interpolating data when the arguments are of equal interval. The equidistant values of the independent variable x can be taken as $a, a + h, a + 2h, ... a + nh$ etc and corresponding values of the dependent variable y can be $f(a), f(a + h), f(a + 2h), ... f(a + nh)$,

Then operator Δ, *i.e.* the differential operator can be written as

$$\Delta f(x) = f(x + h) - f(x)$$

where $a = a, a + h, a + 2h$, etc

$$\Delta f(a) = f(a + h) - f(a)$$

and $\Delta f(a + h) = f(a + h + h) - f(a + h)$ and so on

These are first degree differences

Similarly $\Delta^2 f(a) = \Delta [\Delta f(a)] = \Delta[f(a + h) - f(a)]$

$$= \Delta f(a + h) - \Delta f(a)$$

$$= [f(a + 2h) - f(a + h)] - [f(a + h) - f(a)]$$

We can thus obtain the second and higher order differences etc and these can be expressed in the table known as "The table of Finite Forward Differences", as under

Argument	Entry $yf(x)$	First difference $\Delta f(x)$	Second difference $\Delta^2 f(x)$
a	$f(a)$		
		$f(a + h) - f(a) = \Delta f(a)$	$\Delta f(a + h) - \Delta f(a) = \Delta^2 f(a)$
$a + h$	$f(a + h)$		
		$f(a + 2h) - f(a + h) = \Delta f(a + h)$	
$a + 2h$	$f(a + 2h)$		
		$f(a + 3h) - f(a + 2h) = \Delta f(a + 2h)$	$\Delta f(a + 2h) - \Delta f(a + h) = \Delta^2 f(a + h)$
$a + 3h$	$f(a + 3h)$		
		etc.	etc.

This is called as Table of Diagonal Differences. By using a variable $u = \left(\frac{x-a}{h}\right)$, we can write the Newton's formula for forward differences as under

$$f(x) = f(a) + u \Delta f(a) + \frac{u(u-1)}{2'} \Delta^2 f(a) + \frac{u(u-1)(u-2)}{3'} \Delta^3 f(a) + ...$$

which can be used to obtain the estimated value.

(ii) Through operator ∇:

A similar formula known as Newton's Backward differences formula can be obtained by using.

$$\nabla f(x + h) = f(x + h) - f(x) = \Delta f(x)$$

The corresponding Bachward difference table can be written as under

Argument	Entry $yf(x)$	First difference $\nabla f(x)$	Second difference $\nabla^2 f(x)$
a	$f(a)$		
		$f(a + h) - f(a) = \nabla f(a + h)$	$\Delta f(a + 2h) - \nabla f(a+h) = \nabla^2 f(a+2h)$
$a + h$	$f(a + h)$		
$a + 2h$	$f(a + 2h)$	$f(a + 2h) - f(a + h) = \nabla f(a + 2h)$	
$a + 3h$	$f(a + 3h)$	$f(a + 3h) - f(a + 2h) = \nabla f(a + 3h)$	$\Delta f(a + 3h) - \Delta f(a + 2h) = \nabla^2 f(a + 2h)$
		etc.	*etc.*

Then the relationship based on Bachward differences can be written as under

$$f(x) = f(a + nh) + u \nabla f(a + nh) + \frac{u(u-1)}{2'} \nabla^2 f(a + nh)$$

Where $$u = \frac{x-(a+nh)}{h}$$

(iii) Through operator E:

When arguments are at regular equal intervals, the operator E is defined as

$$Ef(x) = f(x + h)$$

and $$E^2 f(x) = E[Ef(n)] = E[f(x + h) = f(x + 2h)$$

In general $$E^n f(x) = f(x + h)$$

Hence $$E = 1 + \Delta$$

Interpolation with Arguments at unequal intervals

We can use two methods for such calculations.

- Newtons Divided Differences Formula
- Lagrange's Formula

Newton's Divided Differences Formula (Through Operator Δ)

If we have the unequal intervals arguments, these can be written as a_0, a_1, a_2 ..... etc and corresponding values of the entries as $f(a_0)$, $f(a_1)$, $f(a_2)$, ... etc.

Then we define

$$f(a_0, a_1) = \text{Divided differences of y with arguments } a_0, a_1$$

$$= \frac{f(a_1) - f(a_0)}{(a_1 - a_0)} = \Delta f(a_0)$$

Then tabular form for successive divided differences can be drawn as under

Argument	Entry $y=f(x)$	$f(a_0, a_1)$	$f(a_0, a_1, a_2)$	$f(a_0, a_1, a_2, a_3)$
a_0	$f(a_0)$			
a_1	$f(a_1)$			
a_2	$f(a_2)$	$\frac{f(a_1)-f(a_0)}{(a_1-a_0)} = \Delta f(a_0)$	$\frac{\Delta f(a_1)-\Delta f(a_0)}{(a_2-a_0)} = \Delta f(a_0)$	
a_3	$f(a_3)$	$\frac{f(a_2)-f(a_1)}{(a_2-a_1)} = \Delta f(a_1)$	$\frac{\Delta f(a_2)-\Delta f(a_1)}{(a_3-a_0)} = \Delta^2 f(a_0)$	$\frac{\Delta^2 f(a_1)-\Delta^2 f(a_0)}{(a_2-a_0)} = \Delta^3 f(a_3 - a_0)$
		$\frac{f(a_3)-f(a_2)}{(a_3-a_2)} = \Delta f(a_2)$		

Now, Newton's divided differences formula can be written as

$$f(x) = f(a_0) + (x - a_0)\, \Delta f(a_0) + (x - a_0)(x - a_1)\, \Delta^2 f(a_0) + \ldots\ldots\ldots$$

Lagrange's Formula

This formula can be written as follows

$$f(x) = \frac{(x-a_1)(x-a_2).....(x-a_n)}{(a_0-a_1)(a_0-a_2)....(a_0-a_n)} f(a_0) + \frac{(x-a_0)(x-a_2).....(x-a_n)}{(a_1-a_0)(a_1-a_2)....(a_1-a_n)}$$

$$f(a_1) + \ldots\ldots + \frac{(x-a_0)(x-a_1).....(x-a_n)}{(a_n-a_0)(a_n-a_1)....(a_n-a_{n-1})}$$

These formulae can be conveniently used to obtain estimates under above mentioned data conditions. The problems are now solved to show the actual use of these formulae under practical situations.

Problem 4.9

Interpolate the index number for 1970 from the following data

Year	1968	1969	1971	1973
Index Number	100	107	157	212

Solution:

If we donot specify any method to be followed, the easiest course is to use the graphical representation of data and use the straight lines between various points to interpolate the required data. Thus the graph is drawn between year and index number.

From the graph, the value of index for 1970 can be obtained as 124.

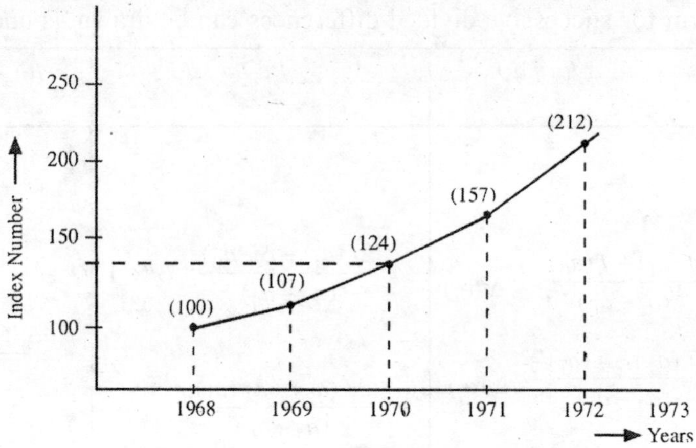

FIG 4.8.

Problem 4.10

Find $f(x)$; given the $f(0) = 3$, $f(1) = 6$, $f(2) = 8$ and $f(3) = 12$ and Find $f(6)$.

Solution:

Let the function be defined as

$$y = ax^3 + bx^2 + cx + d$$

Putting the value of x, *i.e.* $x = 0, 1, 2$ and 3

$$f(0) = d = -3$$

$$f(1) = a + b + c + d = 6$$

$$f(2) = 8a + 9b + 2c + d = 8$$

and $$f(3) = 27a + 9b + 3c + d = 12$$

Solving these equation for a, b, c and d we get

$$a = \frac{3}{2},\ b = -8,\ c = \frac{31}{2} \text{ and } d = -3$$

Now we can obtain the polynomial function as

$$f(x) = \frac{3}{2}x^3 - 8x^2 + \frac{31}{2}x - 3$$

To get $f(6)$, we have $x = 6$

$$f(6) = \frac{3}{2}(6)^3 - 8(6)^2 + \frac{31}{2}(6) - 3$$

$$= 126 \text{ (estimated value of } x = 6)$$

Problem 4.11

The following table shows the value of the function for different ages:

Age (in yrs.)	20	30	40	50
Function Value $f(x)$	5	7	11	15

Interpolate the function value for the age at 27.

Solution:

Since the age intervals are equal, we can use Newton's formula of forward differences.

Here $$u = \frac{x-a}{h}$$

$$= \frac{27-20}{10} = 0.7$$

Drawing the table for the forward differences, we have:

x	$f(x)$	$\Delta f(x)$	$\Delta^2 f(x)$	$\Delta^3 f(x)$
20	5			
		7 – 5 = 2		
30	7		4 – 2 = 2	
		11 – 7 = 4		0 – 2 = 2
40	11		4 – 4 = 0	
		15 – 11 = 4		
50	15			

Hence by Newtons formula for forward differences,

$$y_{(27)} = y_0 + u\, f(x) + \frac{u(u-1)}{2'} \Delta^2 f(x) + \frac{u(u-1)(u-2)}{3'} \Delta^3 f(x)$$

$$= 5 + 0.7 \times 2 + \frac{(0.7)(0.7-1)}{2} \times 2 + \frac{(0.7)(0.7-1)(0.7-2)}{3\times 2} \times (-2)$$

$$= 5 + 1.4 - 0.21 - 0.09$$

$= 6.1$ (*i.e.*, function value for age at 27)

Problem 4.12

The following table indicates the quantity of air conditioners sold by a shopkeeper each year. Find the missing term by using a suitable method of interpolation.

Year	1995	1996	1997	1998	1999	2000
No. of airconditioners	44	95	155	?	240	350

Solution:

(a) If we use the base year as 1995, then we can take the help of finite differences (having 5 entries)

$\therefore \quad \Delta_5 (y_n) = 0 \quad$ for all values of x.

or $\quad (E^{-1})5\, y_0 = 0$

or $(E^5 - 5E^4 + 10E^3 - 10E^2 + 5E^{-1})y_0 = 0$

or $y_5 - 5y_n + 10y_3 - 10y_2 + 5y_1 - y_0 = 0$

using the values for the data sheet,

$350 - 5 \times 240 + 10y_3 - 10 \times 155 + 5 \times 95 - 44 = 0$

$\therefore \quad y_3 = 193$

Hence the shop keeper sold 193 airconditioners in 1998.

(b) If we use 2000 as the base year, we can take help of theorem (formula) of backward differences

The table for Backward Differences is written as under:

x	$f(x)$	$\Delta f(x)$	$\nabla^2 f(x)$	$\nabla^3 f(x)$	$\nabla^4 f(x)$	$\nabla^5 f(x)$
0	44					
		51				
1	95		9			
		60		a – 224		
2	155		a – 215		834 – 4a	
		a – 155		610 – 3a		10a – 1969
3	a		395 – 2a		6a – 1135	
		240 – a		3a – 525		
4	240		a – 130			
		110				
5	350					

Since there are 5 entries, the polynomial of 4th degree is to be considered. From theorem of finite differences.

$$\Delta_5 (y_n) = 0$$

$$\therefore \quad 10a - 1969 = 0$$

$$\therefore \quad a = 196.9 \approx 197$$

Hence the missing data is 197

(There is a minor variation in the values through two methods)

Problem 4.13

Given the following data, find the corresponding value of *f(x)* by applying Newton's Divided difference formula.

x	1	3	5	7	8	10
$f(x)$	15	18	22	27	30	35

Solution:

Due to non-equidistant arguments, we use Newton's Divided Differences Formula. The table drawn for Divided Differences is as follows:

x	$f(x)$	$\Delta f(x)$	$\nabla^2 f(x)$	$\nabla^3 f(x)$	$\nabla^4 f(x)$	$\nabla^5 f(x)$
1	15					
		$\frac{18-15}{3-1}=1.5$				
3	18		$\frac{2-1.5}{3-1}$=0.25			
		$\frac{22-18}{5-3}=2$		0		
5	22		$\frac{2.5-2}{5-3}$=0.25		0	
		$\frac{27-22}{7-5}$=2.5		0		– 0.004
7	27		$\frac{3-2.5}{7-5}$=0.25		– 0.04	
		$\frac{30-27}{8-7}$=3		– 0.25		
8	30		$\frac{2.5-3}{8-7}$=0.5			
		$\frac{35-30}{10-8}$=2.5				
10	35					

Using Newtons Divided Differences Formula

$$f(x) = 15 + (x-1)\,\Delta f(1) + (x-1)(x-3)\,\Delta^2 f(1) - (x-1)(x-3)(x-5)\,\Delta^3 f(1)$$

$$+ (x-1)(x-3)(x-5)(x-7)\,\Delta^4 f(1) + (x-1)(x-3)(x-5)(x-7)(x-8)\,\Delta^5 f(1)$$

$$= 15 + [(6-1)](1.5) + [(6-1)(6-3)](0.25) + [(6-1)(6-3)(6-5](0)$$

$$+ [(6-1)(6-3)(6-5)(6-7)](0) + [(6-1)(6-3)(6-5)(6-7)(6-8)](-0.004)$$

$$= 26.74$$

Problem 4.14

Using Lagranges Formula for $f(0) = 2$, $f(1) = 3$, $f(2) = 12$ and $f(3) = 35$, Find $f(5)$

Solution:

Since it is a case of non-equidistant arguments, we can use Lagranges formula,

$$f(x) = \frac{(x-1)(x-2)(x-3)}{(0-1)(0-2)(0-3)}f(0) + \frac{(x-0)(x-2)(x-3)}{(1-0)(1-2)(1-3)}f(1) + \frac{(x-0)(x-1)(x-3)}{(2-0)(2-1)(2-3)}f(2)$$

$$+ \frac{(x-0)(x-1)(x-3)}{(3-0)(3-1)(3-2)}f(3)$$

$$= -\frac{1}{3}(x^3 - 6x^2 + 11x - 6) + \frac{3}{2}(x^3 - 5x^2 + 6x) - 6(x^3 - 4x^2 + 3x) + \frac{35}{6}(x^3 - 3x^2 + 2x)$$

$$= x^3 - x^2 - x + 2$$

$$\therefore f(5) = 5^3 + 5^2 - 5 + 2 = 147$$

Time Series and Causal Models

These are also statistical forecasting models. In case of time series models, the future value of the dependent variable is forecasted, using only the previously available values in terns of time. The causal models assume that the value of the dependent variable is related to the values of the other variable known in the time schedule form.

There are, basically, five major components of the time series models, namely a permanent component (D), a trend component (T), seasonal component (S), a cyclic component (C) and a random component (E_t). Normally the time series models donot include all the five components. These components have been described under forecasting variations, in the chapter.

A particular model may be of the type

$$Y_t = (P + T) + S + E_t$$

or, $$Y_t = (P + T) \times S + E_t$$

Where Y_t = Forecast at time t.

It practice, a small number of general function relationships are used for the time series modelling generally suitable for short-range forecasts.

4.9 Selection of a forecasting system

The selection of an appropriate forecasting model, wherein the available past data can be used to advantage, requires careful study of the data and the process used it for. Some of the important factors considered for model selections are:

- Cost
- Accuracy
- Data Trend

- Time horizon
- Nature of the product of service

During the discussion of various methods, it was described that mostly the trend shown by the data with reference to time can be a very good guess about the suitability of mathematical model for the future forecasting. When the variations are very small, Cumulative Average Method can be safely applied, whereas in cyclic or seasonal variation, moving average method or weighted moving average method can be applied. But this is only for short term horizon. Data requirement for exponential smoothing is quite different and it could be very good model, when the sales are varying and confidence of the manager is high or low in this sales teams. But what is underlying importance for a forecast is that the results should be fairly accurate and match with the market sales. For this purpose, whatever method can give better result should be preferred, but if there is a choice, obvious parameter for selection is **least cost of forecast**.

Cost and Accuracy: Cost and accuracy go hand in hand for forecast. If a higher accuracy is required, the data required has to be large. To obtain this data, more time and effort will be required. For effective use of large data, the statistical methods will be more useful and it will become costly to design, implement and operate the system. Even judgemental or qualitative methods can be costly depending upon the time and effort spent on them. It is equally easier to understand that because of different conditions and levels of business, the same method or model may not be useful and cost effective for different organisations.

Data Trend: It is a two way weapon. If the accuracy requirement is very high, the amount of data and the nature of data collected are different. On the other side, the data availability and the use of model using it could determine the accuracy achieved as data is not easy to come by. In case of data collection procedure through market research, the marketing team goes to the customers to obtain their preferences about a product. If product is such that there is better relevance for design for the attitude and the intention of the customer and team collects the data regarding price levels and the time schedule of the product (these could be treated as attitude and intentions), then the data collected could be meant for short range product rather than for a long term forecast.

However, If we are trying to forecast for a new product, the methodology to go to the customers may become costly. Instead we could use historical data and analogy, or the Nominal group method, which will be cheaper and faster. Data trend, with respect to time, will give a better indication for use of a suitable method.

Time Horizon: The choice of the forecasting model will be governed by the nature of the product parameter. For example, forecast of workers cash requirements, materials and machine schedules are short term in nature and can be forecasted by short term models like moving average or exponential smoothing methods. On the other hand, capacity requirement planning (CRP) or capital funds requirements are long term strategic decisions and hence would need models like regression, market research or extrapolation methods.

Nature of product or Service: An appropriate method can be selected depending on whether a product is high volume and high cost or high volume and low cost, also whether it is a manufactured product or high volume ready product required for service. If products show seasonal variation of growth and decline, the forecasting method has to have short term implications.

4.10 Monitoring and Control of Forecasting Model

For accurate forecasts, deviation occurred between the forecasted value and the actual value of the relevant parameter of the forecast is required to be small. Large differences would indicate that either the underlying assumptions for the model have not been selected properly or the model selection itself has been wrong. Following techniques can be used for monitoring:

Mean Error

To arrive at the validity of the model for accurate forecast, we compute the Mean Error (ME), which is defined as

$$\text{ME} = \sum_{i=1}^{N}\left(d_{a_i} - d_{f_i}\right)$$

where ME = Mean error or forecast bias

d_f = forecasted value of demand

d_a = actual value of demand

N = Number of time periods over which the experiment has been conducted

Tracking signal

A forecast model can be monitored and controlled by laying down the upper and lower limit of variation permitted for the forecast, after which range, the parameter of the forecast needs a change. One such method for model control is called tracking signal and is defined as under:

$$\text{Tracking signal} = \frac{\sum_{i}^{N}(d_a - d_f)}{MAD}$$

where MAD = Mean Absolute Deviation

$$= \frac{\Sigma\left|d_a - d_f\right|}{N}$$

Thus it can be assumed that if the value of MAD is small, the actual data closely follow the forecast and the model assumptions and type both are good. Model of forecast, therefore, can be closely monitored by the principle of Mean Error (ME) and Mean Absolute Deviation (MAD). If the model has been performing well, the tracking signal should be around zero. Also the upper and lower limits of variations should be carefully selected as a close range would necessitate change of parameter often, whereas for a longer range, the parameter will not be changed often enough and the accuracy of the forecast will suffer.

Standard Error

A still better method of expressing range of the forecast is called Standard Error of the forecast, denoted by S_{yx} and the relationship for calculation of S_{yx} is

$$S_{y_x} = \sqrt{\frac{\Sigma y^2 - a\Sigma y - b\Sigma xy}{n-2}}$$

It is a measure to indicate as to how closely the historical data points have been spread about the trend line. If S_{yx} is small, it shows that upper and lower limit of variation of forecast are close and that the assumptions of the model are well satisfied.

When the forecast errors are normally distributed, the value of MAD and S_{yx} are related as follows:

$$S_{yx} = 1.25 \text{ (MAD)}$$

In a typical case, if the calculated value of sum of errors is 1000 units and MAD for the same period is calculated as 200 units

$$\text{Then the tracking signal} = \frac{\text{Sum of Errors}}{\text{MAD}} = \frac{1000}{200} = 5$$

This is very high value

This is also called Standard deviation (SD)

Hence, SD = 1.25 (MAD)

Similarly, if the sum of error is negative, tracking signal will be negative. For the forecasting model being operating satisfactorily, the tracking signal should be around zero. Hence the direction of the tracking signal would indicate the direction of forecasting error, indicating whether forecasts should be increased or decreased. Thus the tracking signal would move towards the new parameter value of the model correcting the model performance.

4.11 Computer Software for Forecasting

When information technology has advanced so much, there is no shortage of relevant softwares in all fields of operations, along with compatible hardware to run these softwares. The speed of operation of computers and the data base memory have also become phenomenal. Even in the forecasting field, most of the computation is now done on computers with the help of readily available softwares. Some of the important and effective softwares for forecasting are:

- Forecast Pro
- Autobox
- Smart forecasts for Windows

There are other softwares available in the market for general and specific purpose usage and can be selected for forecasting. Some long service softwares are SAS, SPSS with the latest as ERP. In fact it is only a small list of universally used softwares. There are a large number of captive softwares developed and used by many organisaions to suit their own operations.

4.12 Forecasting in Small Businesses

Small businesses have some peculiar problems in their day to day and strategic applications. Some of the major problems of small businesses are:

- Small space
- Small capital base
- Limited Speciality skills
- Lack of data
- Small infrastructure to obtain and use data
- Shortage of time to develop new product

These factors, however, do not restrict their operations. All organisations, big or small, operate with effective forecasting technique to help them through market analysis. There is a ready– made help available to them through Government Agencies and large number of publications from Government and Private bodies listing out quite exhaustive and authentic data, that can be made use of. Quite a few research organisation operate in some specialised fields and their services can be quite cost effective, instead of consuming time, money and physical efforts for data collection, their analysis and the resultant forecasts. Some of these organisations offer much cheaper services to small businesses. For new products or for start up organisations, Consultants in various fields can help these small organisations.

4.13 Forecasting in Services

Services are highly uncertain and intangible. Hence the forecasting for service function is the most difficult operation. Market Research Method can be followed to gather data for analysis and help in service design, but there is likelihood of wide variation in ground reality. As the time progresses, the requirement keeps changing. Yet, there has to be some firmness in data to forecast the service requirement. One method is judgemental *i.e.*, manager's own experience of the past, coupled with the geographic and locational peculiarity. In fact, it is one of the best method to start with. Published past data can be taken for trend analysis, or else physical data collection (after initial planning and setting up) will help better. It is time consuming but more reliable.

—●—

Chapter 5

Process Planning and Design

Main issues:

1. Process Planning and Design
2. Product Mix and Types of Process Design
3. Economic Evaluation
4. Process Planning for Services

5.1 Process Planning and Design

After the design of the product, it is imperative to decide as to how to produce the designed product on the shop floor. In fact, the product and process design are so interlinked that both need a deliberate discussion based on the market demand and the money available for such a project. The design of the product would largely depend on the type of technology and the level of manpower available or that can be made available. Similarly the process has to be based on the type of product demanded by the market.

Process decisions are strategic in nature, due to the fact that resources once procured and established in the production centre can not be easily or conveniently uprooted or changed.

The decisions have to be in line with the organisational competitive goals. These decisions would emerge from the business focus of competitive priority in terms of quality, flexibility, time and cost. Initial investment level plays a major role in such a strategic decision. But process management is really not one-time decision. With the technology advancement and competing market forces for a constant change, the decisions need constant review and redesign.

There are four major process management decisions, namely process structure, customer's involvement, resources flexibility as well as capital intensity and the type of production processes to be selected. These have to match the operations strategy of the organisation. Since design of products and that of the production processes are closely interrelated, the concept of Concurrent Engineering (CE) or Simultaneous Engineering (SE) is a useful tool for effective results.

Soon after the decisions on process planning, the fundamental structure and character of the operations function is established. For such decisions, therefore, several departments such as design engineering, marketing, production, manufacturing engineering, industrial engineering and materials management are involved to ensure that no bottlenecks arise during production.

5.2 Major Factors for Process Planning

In the previous chapters, production management has been defined as a management of resources for converting inputs or raw materials into products/services, through a conversion process in order to satisfy customer needs and to achieve organisational objectives. As a first step, the product identification and design has been discussed. Based on the detailed specifications finalised for the product/service, the production method, input and conversion process and procedures are to be decided for its effective implementations. The forecasting methods have also been described to know the volumes of this designed product/service to be produced based on the volumes, the type and number of manpower and machines, the quantum of materials required and the necessary finances to be organised, are to be decided. Designing the process for the conversion operations for the product / services is therefore, the next logical step.

The type of process to be selected will depends on the operations strategy discussed in the last chapter. The conversion processes can be listed out as follows :

- Casting and Moulding process
- Metal Removal Process
- Forming and Finishing process
- Extrusion Process
- Chemical Process

During the process planning, it is advisable to follow the multi-disciplinary or concurrent engineering approach so that the overall co-ordination of product design, technology and process design can be achieved. Major factors to be considered for the process design are listed out below :

- Product Demand
- Volume flexibility
- Degree of automation - technology level
- Degree of Vertical Integration
- Quality requirements

Product Demand

The design of the production process has to match the product specifications and demand. But to lay facilities for the present demand is not enough as the demand keeps varying and the capacity, therefore, has to be developed for this flexibility so as to keep the pace with the actual sales pattern. The flexibility must cater for the increase or decrease of demand. Some processes lend themselves easily to this flexibility, some with difficulty. Therefore the choice of the production process will depend on the future forecast and its trend. The choice of price and hence that of the choice of the production process must be co-related.

Degree of Vertical Integration

Due to perpetual variability in the market demand, the firm may not be able to muster all the resources to produce the desired volume. The vertical integration is the volume of production and length of distribution system a company would like to bring under its own production control. Based on this decision, the facilities to be installed can be planned and designed. Capital investment can pose a serious restriction on the production capacity planning. In todays competitive atmosphere, strategic outsourcing is a common and useful trend. This helps in quick reaction to changes in customers preference or those due to competitors challenges. Change in the technology also may be a factor forcing it to outsourcing rather than making capital investments, which may not be very lucrative due to sudden change in technology in short span of time.

Volume Flexibility

Requirement of variety of products and fast change in attitude of customers to demand new product at short notice is becoming a common phenomenon. Even own innovations of the company can result in producing new products is not uncommon. This can result in increase of market share through new products and aggressive marketing strategy. This flexibility, therefore, would be of two types namely, volume flexibility and product variety. The production process should cater for both *i.e.*, should be responsive for quick change from one product to another and also for producing larger volume of a particular or few products becoming popular and having higher demand. Higher capital investment will be required for installing high production capacity and hence a very deliberate design is adopted for peak level of demand. For optimal product mix calculations by the manager, linear programming is a good helping tool.

Product Mix and Manufacturing Challenges

Problem 5.1

A firm makes two products X and Y and has a total production capacity of 9 tonnes per day, X and Y requiring the same production capacity. The firm has a permanent contract to supply atleast 2 tonnes of X and atleast 3 tonnes of Y per day to another company. Each tonne of X requires 20 machine hours production time and each tonne of Y requires 50 machine hours production time; the daily maximum possible number of machine hours is 360. All the firm's output can be sold and the profit made is Rs. 80 per tonne of X and Rs. 120 per tonne of Y. It is required to determine the production schedule for maximum profit and to calculate this profit.

[*Delhi University MBA (1983)*]

Solution :

Step : 1 Formulating the problem into an LP model *i.e.*, mathematical form,

Maximising profit (Max Z) $= 80\,x_1 + 120\,x_2$

where x_1 = Quantity (in tonnes) of X produced

x_2 = Quantity (in tonnes) of Y produced

And the constraints are,

$x_1 + x_2 \leq 9$ Production capacity constraint

$x_1 \geq 2$ Fixed supply constraint

$x_2 \geq 3$ Fixed supply constraint

$20x_1 + 50x_2 \leq 360$ Production machine constraint

and $x_1, x_2 \geq 0$ Non-negative constraint

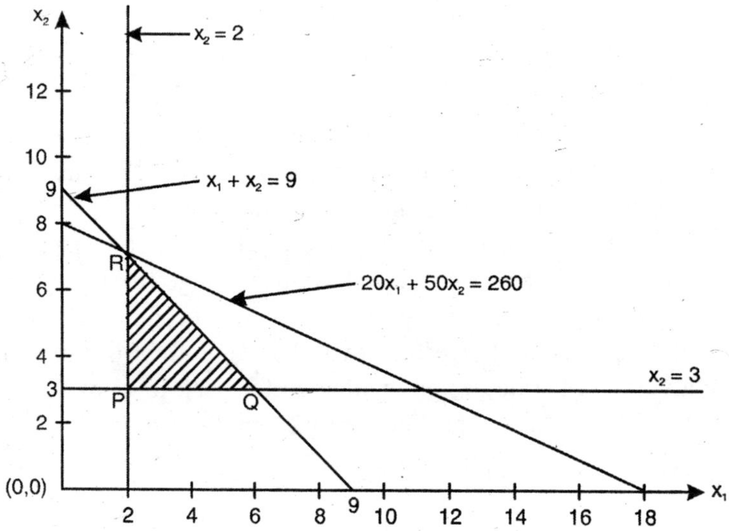

FIG. 5.1. Graph for Maximisation case LPP

Step 2 The lines drawn treat inequalities as equalities. Now superimpose inequality as per the problem statement

Step 3 The feasible region satisfying all the given inequalities is marked as PQR (shaded for easy recognition)

Step 4 Due to the concept of convex set, the extreme points PQR and S are the solution points.

Step 5 Calculating the value of profit (Z) from all these extreme points.

Point	Grid Points reference	Z = objective functions
P	(2, 3)	$Z_P = 520$

Q	(6.2, 3)	$Z_Q = 856$
R	(2, 7)	$Z_R = 1{,}000$

The maximum profit value of Rs. 1,000 occurs at point Q (2, 7)

Step 6 Hence optimal production schedule for maximum profit should be

Quantity of X = x_1 = 2 tonnes

Quantity of Y = x_2 = 7 tonnes

And Max profit = Rs. 1,000 per day

Problem 5.2

A marketing manager wishes to allocate his annual advertising budget of Rs. 20,000 to two media A and B. The unit cost of insertion in medium A is Rs. 1000 and that in B it is Rs. 1500. The medium A is a monthly magazine and not more than one insertion is desired in one issue. At least 5 messages should appear in medium B. The expected effected audience for unit message in A is 40,000, whereas in B, it is 55,000

(a) Develop a linear programming model

(b) Solve it for optimising the insertions in A and B, so as the maximise the audience exposure

Solution :

Step 1 The linear programming model can be formulated as under

Max Z = $40{,}000\, x_1 + 55{,}000\, x_2$

where x_1 = number of insertions in medium A

and x_2 = number of insertions in medium B

subject to, $1{,}000x_1 + 1{,}500\, x_2 \leq 20{,}000$ (one in each month)

$x_1 \leq 12$ (once monthly)

$x_2 \geq 5$ (minimum for B)

and $x_1, x_2 \geq 0$

The standard simplex statement can be written as

Max Z = $40{,}000x_1 + 55{,}000\, x_2 + O.S_1 + O.S_2 + O.S_3$

Subject to, $1{,}000x_1 + 1{,}500\, x_2 + S_1 = 20{,}000$

$x_1 + S_2 = 12$

$-x_2 + S_3 = -5$

and $x_1, x_2, S_1, S_2, S_3 \geq 0$

where S_1, S_2, S_3, are slack variables added

Step 2 For initial solution, we put $x_1 = x_2 = 0$ and write simplex table

Zj	Cj	40,000	55,000	0	0	0	Quantity	Ratio
	Variables	x_1	x_2	S_1	S_2	S_3	bi	bi/aij
0	S_1	1,000	1,500	1	0	0	20,000	40/3
0	S_2	1	0	0	1	0	12	∞
0	S_3	0	–1	0	0	1	–5	5 →
$\Delta_j = C_j - Z_j$		40,000	55,000 ↑	0	0	0		

Here x_2 is entering variable and S_3 the leaving variable.

Step 3 Since it is not an optimal solution, we prepare simplex table II

Zj	Cj	40,000	55,000	0	0	0	Quantity	Ratio
	Variables	x_1	x_2	S_1	S_2	S_3	bi	bi/aij
0	S_1	1,000	0	1	0	1,500	12,500	25/3 →
0	S_2	1	0	0	1	0	12	∞
55,000	x_2	0	1	0	0	–1	5	–5
$\Delta_j = C_j - Z_j$		40,000	0	0	0	55,000 ↑		

It is still not the optimal solution. Hence S_3 is the incoming variable and S_1, the outgoing variable.

Step 4 Drawing simplex table III, we have

Zj	Cj	40,000	55,000	0	0	0	Quantity	Ratio
	Variables	x_1	x_2	S_1	S_2	S_3	bi	bi/aij
0	S_3	2/3	0	1/1,500	0	1	25/3	25/2
0	S_2	1	0	0	1	0	12	12 →
55,000	x_2	2/3	1	1/1,500	0	0	40/3	20
$\Delta_j = C_j - Z_j$		10,000/3 ↑	0	–110/3	0	0		

The solution still not being optimal, the incoming variable is x_1, whereas the outgoing variable is S_2

Step 5 Writing simplex table IV, we get

Zj	Cj	40,000	55,000	0	0	0	Quantity
	Variables	x_1	x_2	S_1	S_2	S_3	bi
0	S_3	0	0	1/1,500	–2/3	1	1/3
40,000	x_1	1	0	0	1	0	12
55,000	x_2	0	1	1/1,500	–2/3	0	16/3
$\Delta_j = C_j - Z_j$		0	0	–110/3	–10,000/3	0	

Since all the values of Δj are either zero or negative, we have achieved the optimal solution to the problem.

Thus $x_1 = 12$
and $x_2 = 16/3$ } The corresponding Values of bi for the variable
and $Z = 20{,}000/3$

Quantity $S_3 = 1/3$ indicates unutilised capacity of B.

Problem 5.3. (Product Mix — Simplex Method of LP)

A manufacturing unit has 100 kg of raw material A, 180 kg of material B and 120 kg of material C available as daily stock for shop floor, whereas material D is available aplenty. There are three products P,Q and R on the Master production Schedule for the month of January. The costs of the raw materials are as follows.

Raw Material A	Rs. 80 per kg.
Raw Material B	Rs. 30 per kg.
Raw Material C	Rs. 50 per kg.
Raw Material D	Rs. 20 per kg.

Proportion of raw material required per unit of production

Product P	A = 5%	B = 10%,	C = 5%,	D = 80%
Product Q	A = 5%	B = 5%,	C = 10%	D = 80%
Product R	A = 20%	B = 5%,	C = 10%	D = 65%

The selling price of product P, Q and R are Rs. 40.5, Rs. 43 and Rs. 45 respectively. If product P can be sold only 30 kg per day, determine how much of each product must be produced per day to earn maximum profit during January.

Solution:

Calculating the cost of each product per kg. of produce,

$$\text{Cost of product P} = 80 \times \frac{5}{100} + 30 \times \frac{10}{100} + 50 \times \frac{5}{100} + 20 \times \frac{80}{100}$$
$$= \text{Rs. } 24.50 \text{ per kg.}$$

$$\text{Cost of Product Q} = 80 \times \frac{5}{100} + 30 \times \frac{5}{100} + 50 \times \frac{10}{100} + 20 \times \frac{80}{100}$$
$$= \text{Rs. } 26 \text{ per kg.}$$

$$\text{Cost of Product R} = 80 \times \frac{20}{100} + 30 \times \frac{5}{100} + 50 \times \frac{10}{100} + 20 \times \frac{65}{100}$$
$$= \text{Rs. } 35 \text{ per kg.}$$

For calculating the product mix for daily production based on maximum profit, let these quantities be x_1, x_2 and x_3 respectively for product P, Q and R.

For formulation of the problem.

Objective function is

$$\text{Max Profit (z)} = \text{Rs. } (40.50 - 24.50)\, x_1 + (43 - 26)\, x_2 + (45 - 35)\, x_3$$
$$= 16x_1 + 17x_2 + 10x_3$$

The constraints are

$$x_1 \left(\frac{5}{100}\right) + x_2 \left(\frac{5}{100}\right) + x_3 \left(\frac{20}{100}\right) \leq 100 \quad (i)$$

$$x_1 \left(\frac{10}{100}\right) + x_2 \left(\frac{5}{100}\right) + x_3 \left(\frac{5}{100}\right) \leq 180 \quad (ii)$$

$$x_1 \left(\frac{5}{100}\right) + x_2 \left(\frac{10}{100}\right) + x_3 \left(\frac{10}{100}\right) \leq 120 \quad (iii)$$

and $x_1 \leq 30$ $\quad (v)$

$x_1, x_2, x_3 \geq 0$. (Non-negative)

These equations can be written in standard form for using simplex Method.

$$\text{Max Z} = 16x_1\ 17x_2 + 10x_3 + 0.S_1 + 0.S_2 + 0.S_3 + 0.S_4$$

Subject to,

$$x_1 + x_2 + 4x_3 + S_1 = 2000$$
$$2x_1 + x_2 + x_3 + S_2 = 3600$$
$$x_1 + 2x_2 + 2\,x_3 + S_3 = 2400$$
$$x_1 + S_4 = 30$$

and $x_1, x_2, x_3, S_1, S_2, S_3, S_4 \geq 0$.

Initial simplex table is written with $x_1 = x_2 = x_3 = 0$.

We get $S_1 = 2000$, $S_2 = 3600$, $S_3 = 2400$, $S_4 = 30$

Variable	C_j / Z_j	16 x_1	17 x_2	10 x_3	0 s_1	0 s_2	0 s_3	0 s_4	qty. bi	Ratio b_i/a_{ij}
S_1	0	1	1	4	1	0	0	0	2000	2000/1 = 2000
S_2	0	2	1	1	0	1	0	0	3600	3600/1 = 3600
S_3	0	1	(2)	2	0	0	1	0	2400	2400/2 = 1200 →
S_4	0	1	0	0	0	0	0	1	30	$\frac{30}{0} = \infty$
Z_j		0	0	0	0	0	0	0		
C_j-Z_j		16	17 ↑	10	0	0	0	0		

Max value of $C_j - Z_j = 17$, corresponding to x_2, which becomes the entering variable and from lowest ratio, 1200, S_3 becomes the leaving variable. Hence table II will be

Variable	C_j / Z_j	16 x_1	17 x_2	10 x_3	0 S_1	0 S_2	0 S_3	0 S_4	Qty b_i	Ratio b_i/a_{ij}
S_1	0	$\frac{1}{2}$	0	3	1	0	$-\frac{1}{2}$	0	800	$800 \times \frac{2}{1} = 1600$
S_2	0	$\frac{3}{2}$	0	0	0	1	$-\frac{1}{2}$	0	2400	$\frac{2400 \times 2}{3} = 1600$
x_2	17	$\frac{1}{2}$	1	1	0	0	$\frac{1}{2}$	0	1200	$\frac{1200 \times 2}{1} = 2400$
S_4	0	1	0	0	0	0	0	1	30	$\frac{30}{1} = 30$ →
	Z_j	$\frac{17}{2}$	$\frac{17}{2}$	0	0	$\frac{17}{2}$	0	0		
	$C_j - Z_j$	$\frac{15}{2}$ ↑	0	− 7	0	0	$\frac{-17}{2}$	0		

Max $C_j - Z_j = \frac{15}{2}$ pertains to x_1, which becomes enering variable and min ratio = 30 pertaining to S_4. Thus S_4 becomes the leaving variable. Hence the simplex table III is as under

Variable	C_j / Z_j	16	17	10	0	0	0	0	Qty.
		x_1	x_2	x_3	S_1	S_2	S_3	S_4	bi
S_1	0	0	0	3	1	0	$-\frac{1}{2}$	$-\frac{1}{2}$	785
S_2	0	0	0	0	0	1	$-\frac{1}{2}$	$-\frac{3}{2}$	2355
x_2	17	0	1	1	0	0	$\frac{1}{2}$	$-\frac{1}{2}$	1185
x_1	16	1	0	0	0	0	0	1	30
	Z_j	16	17	17	0	0	$\frac{17}{2}$	$\frac{15}{2}$	
	$C_j - Z_j$	0	0	-7	0	0	$\frac{-17}{2}$	$\frac{-15}{2}$	

Since all the value of $C_j - Z_j$ are either zero or negative, we have reached the optimal solution. No further increase in profit is possible.

Thus the optimal product mix will be

Product P = 30 kg per day

Q = 1185 kg per day

R = 0 (x_3 does not figure in the solution)

The actual production as per customer requirement can be varied within these weekly limits and product R can not be produced and supplied.

Software use : The same problem can be solved using Microsoft (Excel spread sheet) using linear option. It will be faster method.

5.3 Degrees of Automation Technology

The flexibility requirement discussed above can be partially met with by having automated production process, wherein the change can be affected quickly. But automation is very expensive system and integration of automated production process with the existing mechanical system is not easy. Though automation can save drastically on running cost and labour, the initial investment may not always be justified as offset may not be cost effective. Another advantage of automation is improvement in product quality along with volume flexibility. Hence if it is found to be cost effective in the long run (based on the cost benefit analysis for a larger period of time), automation must be planned for. It is a deliberate decision based on corporate operational strategy. With the advancement in technology, automation is becoming affordable to competitive designs.

Quality Requirement

Competition in the global operations drives the organisation hard to improve quality of the products and services. In days gone by, the highest quality was produced by selective processes and small volumes. But today's global market requirements dictate large volume of variety of products to cater for diverse customers in many geographical areas, where tastes, costs, quality standards and economic conditions may be so different. Hence today mass-production processes, with a very high level of quality are adopted. The change in the process design, therefore, is necessitated due to global quality standards with the design of process leading to automated machines for quality and uniformity.

5.4 Types of Process Design

The following can be the reasons for variations in process design:

The product design and the volumes: When the volumes are large, one particular production system may be totally dedicated to this product only.

Variety in products: When there are no major changes in the specifications but in the product mix.

Flexibility in Volumes for Variety in the same product: When the basic specifications are not much different, but there is a requirement of batch production for variety in the same basic product line. Types of process design, therefore, can be as follows:

- Product focussed
- Process focussed
- Group or Cellular manufacturing

Product - Focussed

For this production process, organisation establishes the production department arranged for a type of product / service. Based on number of operations to be performed for a product, various machines required are arranged in a particular sequence, in which these operations are to be performed on the product from the beginning to the finish. This process design is suitable for the product, which is fixed and produced in larger volumes.

This type of process arrangement is, therefore, called a production line, to carryout continuous operation for the same product regularly. The product, in this case, follows a linear path (called as Product layout) The production is carried out with the entire process design dedicated to one product/service only. The raw materials, components, sub assemblies as well as assemblies follow the same linear path and the end of the line produces the product in question. Depending on the minor variations in specifications, product batches may be produced on the same line, provided the facilities are reset (re-organised) according to another similar product, if technically feasible.

Product focussed process system is also used for assembly operations, where a large number of components are assembled to complete a product at the end of this line. A good example of this assembly line is assembly of automobiles, where one type of car can be assembled on one line, but minor variation in the same car can also be done as in case of batch production. Similarly continuous operations are performed in case of process industry, where screening, grinding, cooking, mixing, separating, blending, cracking, fermenting, evaporating, reducing and distilling etc. are different operations required to be performed almost non-stop and in that sequence continuously. Such operations are performed in chemical plants, fertiliser plants, petroleum refineries, plastics or paper industry. But due to a large number of facilities to be placed in sequence (may be repeated in case of necessity), this is a costly design, suitable for low cost, high volume and better controlled production.

Process Focussed

In this case, similar operations are grouped together with one group of machines for one type of operation. Thus similar technological processes are kept together to cater for the need of any product needing that process. All welding or painting operations are done in one place only and therefore operations are not continuous, but intermittent (*i.e..*, start when required or when machine is available and stop when operations over or where a required machine in a particular process group is not available). Such process-focussed systems are called job shops. Only one type of job is performed in one shop (or area). The products move from one department to another in batches, depending on the time availability of the machines.

Some examples of this system are hospitals, repair shops for various products and some manufacturing plants. The system has a great level of flexibility and requires less capital investment. The machines are scheduled to offer maximum utilisation. On the other hand, these systems require better coordination and effective scheduling, with trained workers and effective supervision. Monitoring and control requirement is large in operating such systems.

Group or Cellular Manufacturing

This method of manufacturing is different from the above two methods *i.e.*, product focussed and process focussed. The concept of Group Technology has been developed only around 1940's during the World war II period in Russia. After the war, it became very popular. The technology has been refined over a period of time. The concept is very simple and is being used effectively for variety manufacturing.

Group Technology is applied in the form a code for the product indicating various manufacturing specifications. Cellular manufacturing is sub-set of the broader group technology concept. The coded specifications have simplified the manufacturing activities. Few of the advantages are :

- Code of the product specifies the product route or the sequence of operations. Therefore it is easy to identify various processes and their sequences.

- The design of many parts/components can be simplified if we group together the components with similar basic design characteristics and specifications. Computer helps in identifying similar parts/ components through the code system.
- The grouping of similar parts helps in their manufacturing at one work station and provides the advantage of mass production in generating these similar grouped specifications.
- Similar family groups are assigned facilities for manufacturing. Hence the organisation of the production facilities used in this way is called cellular manufacturing.

In order to highlight the features of cellular manufacturing, we have to start with identification of parts with similar basic specifications. Let us take the case of manufacturing of a brass screw of the shape given in fig. 5.2 below.

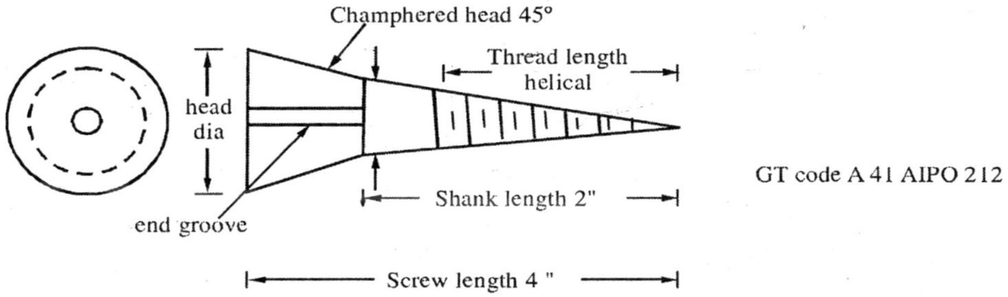

FIG. 5.2 Specifications of a Screw (Brass 4″)

Interpretation of GT Code :

Field/Position	1	2	3	4	5	6	7	8	9	10
GT Code	A	4	1	A	1	P	0	2	1	2

Let us define the GT code for manufacturing ease.

Each letter or digit written in the code has a specific meaning based on its place in the code. Computer would have the legend and would recognise the part easily. Let us assume that the code specifications are described as under :

Place	Description	Place	Description
1.	A Screw	6.	P helical threads
	B Bolt		Q straight threads
2.	1. Iron	7.	0 1½ inches threaded
	2. Aluminium		1 1¼ inches threaded
	3. Copper		2 1 inch threaded
	4. Brass		
3.	1. 4 inche length	8.	1 Straight head
	2. 3 inches length		2 Champhered head (45°)
	3. 2 inches length		3 Champhered head (30°)

4.	A 2" shank length	9.	1 3/4 inch dia of head
	B 1½" shank length		2 ½ inch dia of head
	C 1" shank length		3 5/16 inch dia head
5.	1 ½ inch shank diameter		4 ¼ inch dia head
	2 3/8 inch shank diameter	10.	1 without end groove
			2 with end groove

Various dimensions have been transferred to the figure of screw drawn. As per code, it is a Brass Screw of 4 inches total length, identified through place 1, 2 and 3 of the code. The other operations of the product can be read from legend code.

For manufacture of a Brass screw of 4 inches length, we use a bar of Brass having slightly more than 4 inches length, out of which 4" can be cut off. The maximum diameter in the design is 3/4 inch, Hence the bar stock has to be about 1 inch diameter. Hence the GT Code of the product has been specified as A41A IPO 212 indicated next to the figure 5.2

For manufacturing, the Brass bar has to be first reduced to 3/4 inch dia and then create the head by champhering it at 45°, till we read the end diameter of the shank achieved as ½ inch as marked. Now the next operation can be putting the groove through the head.

Now we start reducing the shank to reach a pointed edge at the end for a total length of 2 inches. Having done it, we prepare the reduced bar to make helical threads to a length of 1½ inches. This completes the manufacture of a Brass screw of 4 inches length, as desired.

Now we discuss the grouping of operations

Group 1 (Cell 1)	–	Turning operations of bar to 3/4 inch diameter
	–	Turning champhered 45° for head formation
	–	Cutting the end groove
Group 2 (Cell 2)	–	Turning the bar from shank end diameter to the end of it making it tapering to zero.
	–	Cutting the total shank length to 2 inches
Group 3 (Cell 3)	–	Threading of the tapered bar with helical threads for a length of 1½ inches.

This simple product can be manufactured through these three cells by organising machines, man power, materials and tools according to the cell operation requirement.

Since screws and bolts are similar products made from similar materials, needing similar machines for turning, threading, cutting etc., a variety of products can be obtained by cellular manufacturing method as follow.

If we wish to manufacture a Brass Screw of 3 inches or 2 inches lengths, the code is to be modified as A42 or A43 in the first three places. The computer will direct the product accordingly. Similarly, other dimensions can be changed by using straight heed of different dia or threads of different length. This can be now done through separate cells as explained below.

Since the coding legend indicates variety of specifications for a similar basic product, the cell manufacturing can be used to product variety of a basic product by performing production work in different suitably laid out cells. Let us manufacture screw. Since group 1 or cell 1 need basically turing and cutting operation, same set of machines can be used for screw or bolt manufacturing. Then the variation of screw in terms of total length and material can be affected by using bar of appropriate material and length. So in cell 1 itself, we can manufacture following variety of products

1. Screw Iron or Aluminium or Brass or Copper
2. Screw with 4 in 3 in and 2 in lengths

Further variation can take place in the head shape production Hence we can have

Cell 1 A – Screw with straight head

Cell 1 B – Screw with Champhered head

After this change, now each of these products from Cell 1 A and B can be sent to different cells to produce the following products :

Cell 2A – Turning the shank portion

Cell 2A (a) – helical threads

Cell 2A (b) – straight threads

Any screw of any material with any length can be sent to these specialists cells for a particular process to be performed and the end result of basic product will be number of permutation and combinations into products for different use.

If we start 10,000 bars of Brass with 1 inch diameter, we can have different numbers of screws of different specifications that is say 5000 screws 4" straight head with groove having 1½ helical thread, 2000 screws 4 inches champhered head with groove 1½ inc. helical threads and another 3000 screws 4" inches with champhered heed without groove with 1 inch straight threads to be manufacture in different cells. Diagrammatically, it can be illustrate as under.

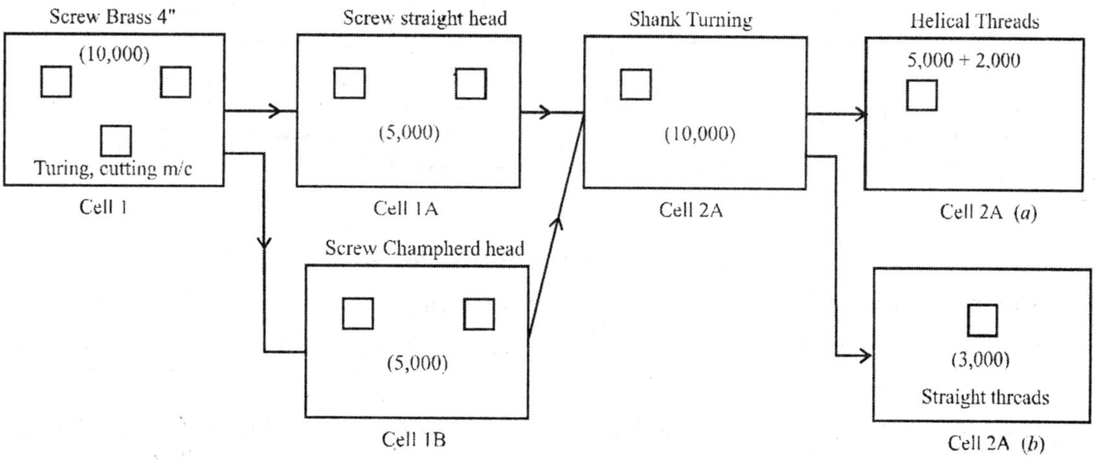

FIG. 5.3. Cells layout for Variety Production

It can be seen that each cell has its own peculiar production process installed and will be used for that operation. When basic product dimension change, then only a machine setting may be required to change, but not the process. Hence in each cell it is mass production for a particular product at one time and we still get batches (variety of products) thus gaing the advantage of batch production through mass production.

Another arrangement that can be used for cellular manufacturing is the route selected out of the process layout as given below:

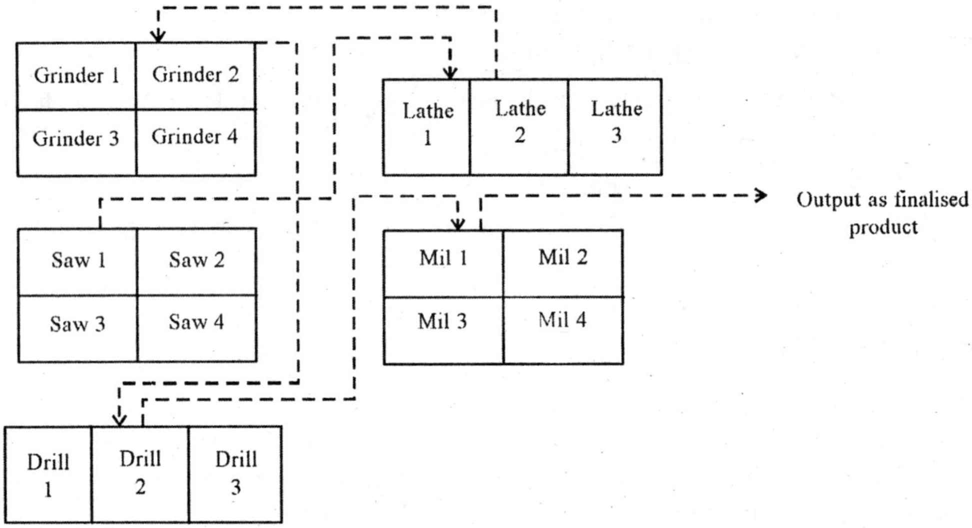

FIG. 5.4. Cellular Manufacturing

Thus the cell structure for this product can be shown as follows :

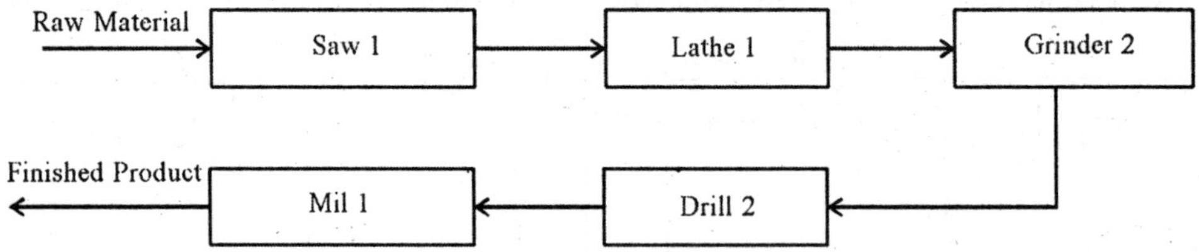

FIG. 5.5. Cellular Layout for a Product

Major advantages of group / cellular manufacturing

- Resetting of machines are simplified, thereby reducing idle time and increasing production volumes.
- Variability in a cell is reduced dramatically. Variations due to the performance of the same job repeatedly.
- It is a straight line manufacturing. Material handling can be better planned.

- Less parts variability and practically same work in each cell produces the advantage of batch productions (variety of end products) through mass productions manufacturing in each cell.

5.5 Marrying up Product/Process Design and Inventory Management

According to the product and process design, the inventory is also required to be planned. In IT - enabled system, it is easier to control. For a product, the design will be available in the data base. In case of a repeat order, computer will pick up the design and its related process design and the delivery of the product can be easily predicted. Thus the inventory problem in customer focus production can be reduced to minimum. For large volumes of the product, inventory management needs careful look so that inventory levels are kept low and for a short duration. Production of a particular product can be planned based on sales and required process system can be planned out for some other important product in case of spare capacity. Scheduling and Rescheduling of resources, in any case, is a regular exercise to be undertaken by the production manger in consultation with other departmental managers.

5.6 Pre-planning Analysis

The pre-plaining analysis of production system is important because of production and distribution of products in required quantity at competitive price. The pre-planning analysis, hence, starts right from the product planning stage, going into process design and inventories. Following precautions are important at preplanning stage:

- Accurate evaluation of customer preference, market conditions and the sales forecasts.
- Research and Development efforts with extensive value analysis helps in economic design.
- Extensive use of technological knowledge and other environmental conditions to ensure quick decision.
- Appropriate corporate planning, evaluation and organisation of resources.
- Material analysis, planning and vendor analysis.
- Quantum of investment and profitability.

5.7 Economic Evaluation for Capital Investment

Creating assets is a long term commitment and once started, cannot be easily disposed off when capital is required on a long term basis. Hence it is important to carryout economic analysis of capital investment for generating profit. It has a direct bearing on the future operating cost of the organisation. Unnecessary locking up of the capital in unproductive or slow earning assets should, therefore, be avoided, be it equipment or material stocks. The financial forecast sales and technology forecasts have to be done together as part of the capital budgeting. Cost benefit analysis on long term projects must be carried out with due care. Along with this, even short term planning is as important, because it creates cumulative effect on long term budget plans. Decision Tree analysis technique is an effective method for financial planning.

Consideration for Capital Budget control (Long Range and Short Range)

- Innovative thinking and SWOT analysis
- Looking for better investment opportunities
- Effective cash flow planning
- Detailed economic analysis of projects
- Auditing of Financial outlays
- Management information system (MIS) and its Effective Implementation and Control.

Problem 5.4

A manufacturing company is to decide on capital investment for a capacity creation for a desired process. There are two alternatives available.

Cost of a larger facility = Rs. 300 lakhs

Cost of a smaller facility = Rs. 120 lakhs

The capacity is to be created taking a time horizon of 5 years during which the demand probabilities are as under

High demand = 0.4

Medium demand = 0.4

Low demand = 0.2

The estimated returns from statistical methods have been obtained as follows.

	High demand (Prob. 0.4)	Medium demand (Prob. 0.4)	Low demand (Prob. 0.2)
Large facility	150 lakhs	120 lakhs	30 lakhs
Small facility	70 lakhs	30 lakhs	(–) 5 lakhs

Suggest, in what facility should the company invest.

Solution :

We prepare a decision tree based on the information available.

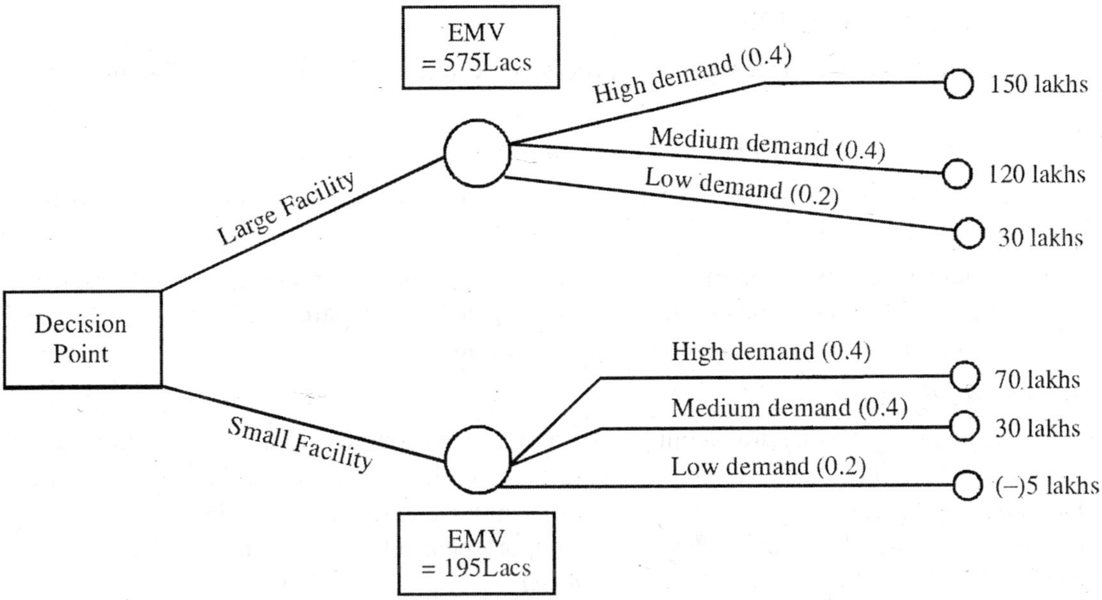

FIG. 5.6. Decision Tree for Capital Investment

For large facility

Expected value earned due to high demand = 0.4 × 150 × 5 = 300 lakhs (for 5 years)
due to medium demand = 0.4 × 120 × 5 = 240 lakhs (for 5 years)
due to low demand = 0.2 × 30 × 5 = 30 lakhs (for 5 years)
Total expected earning for large facility = 300 + 240 + 30 = 570 lakhs (for 5 years)

For small facility

Expected value earned due to high demand = 0.4 × 70 × 5 = 140 lakhs (for 5 years)
due to medium demand = 0.4 × 30 × 5 = 60 lakhs (for 5 years)
due to low demand = 0.2 × (–5) × 5 = –5 lakhs (for 5 years)
Total expected earning for smaller facility = 140 + 60 – 5 = 195 lakhs (for 5 years)

Capital Investment analysis

For larger facility, Earnings = 570 lakhs
Investment = 300 lakhs
Net Saving = 270 lakhs

For smaller facility Earnings = 195 lakhs
Investment = 120 lakhs
Net savings = 75 lakhs

Hence for a period of 5 years investment, larger facility must be invested in and installed.

Process of Capital Budgeting

Based on the above discussion, the process of capital budgeting can be summed up as under :

- Drawing forecasts for the future expenditure
- Proper selection of projects, their cost benefit analysis and time schedule for physical and financial control.
- Periodical review through proper audit and rescheduling of assets and resources utilisation. Capital expenditure procedure must be transparent, clearly spelt out and rigidly followed as per the authorisation control.

Economic Analysis

Strategic plans must be drawn out based on thorough economic analysis. Resulting capital commitments as well as regular periodical operating cash flow pattern control must be exercised. There should be different heads of accounts of capital budgeting and each should have the procedure of control laid down. Few of the important heads of accounts suggested are as follows (Time horizon to be specified for budget):

- **Strategic investment :** long term benefit and opportune investment.
- **New projects investments :** detailed economic analysis bringing out earning capacity and payback periods.
- **Expansion investments :** It is meant to follow the allocations with the growth of the organisation. Increased income and profits with the growth of the operations are clear indications and targets must be laid out and controlled.
- **Replacement investments :** For growth to be effective, constant review of increased facilities should have provision for, in the capital budget. Improved system should be catered for to achieve better returns.
- **Tactical investment :** Day to day cash flows also should be in beneficial area.

Methods for Economic Evaluation

The aim of economic evaluation is to ensure optimum return from various operations and projects. For this purpose, following simple methods can be adopted.

Pay back Period Approach

Payback period is the length of time required to achieve return of cash earning by the investment equal to the original cash outlay.

$$\text{Thus pay back period} = \frac{\text{Original investment}}{\text{Annual Cash Flow}}$$

Problem 5.5 (uniform rate of return) :

If Rs. 25 lakhs have been spent in a project and a uniform rate of return of Rs. 5 lakhs every year is expected, work out the payback period.

Solution :

$$\text{Payback period} = \frac{\text{Rs. 25 lakhs}}{\text{Rs. 5 lakhs}} = 5 \text{ years.}$$

Problem 5.6 (Non-uniform rate of return)

When the returns are not uniform every year, compute the actual payback period based on the following information, if the project investment is 25 lakhs.

Year	Annual Cash Flow	Cumulative Cash Flow
1	3,50,000	3,50,000
2	4,50,000	8,00,000
3	5,50,000	13,50,000
4	8,00,000	21,50,000 →
5	10,00,000	31,50,000

Solution :

It can be seen that the payback period is 4½ years against 25 lakhs investments. It is very popular, easy to adopt and hence widely used approach.

Discounted Cash Flow Method

Under this method, two approaches are popular:

(*a*) Net Present Value (NPV) Approach

(*b*) Internal Rate of Return (IRR) Approach

Net Present Value (NPV) Approach

In this approach, the minimum rate of return is assumed and then computations are done to make use of the present value amount. It is compared with the original investment to workout profitability. It works on the principle that other things being equal, the present value of cash flow discounted at a specified rate of return (assumed) equals the amount of the investment required so that the investment proposal is acceptable. The simple methods of calculations are :

(*i*) Simple Interest applicable

$$I = \frac{P \times r \times t}{100}$$

where I = Interest occurred

P = Principal amount invested

r = rate of interest (simple) in percentage

t = time period of investment

(*ii*) Compound Interest applicable

$$S = P\left(1+\frac{r}{100}\right)^t$$

where S = Sum of money at a specified future period, other notations being the same as in case of Simple interest

(*iii*) Simple Payment Compound Amount Factor (SPCAF)

The SDCAF is given by the following relationship

$$SPCAF = \left(1+\frac{r}{100}\right)^t$$

So that S = P (SPCAF)

(*iv*) Sinking Fund Deposit Factor (SFDF)

If R is the accumulated amount after t payments at a compound interest rate of r %, then

$$S = \frac{R\left[\left(1+\frac{r}{100}\right)^t - 1\right]}{(r/100)}$$

Then R = S(SFDF)

$$\text{where} \quad SFDF = \frac{(r/100)}{\left[\left(1+\frac{r}{100}\right)^t - 1\right]}$$

(*v*) Uniform Present Work Factor (UPWDF)

P = R (UPWDF)

(*vi*) ***Annuity Tables :*** Readymade tables are available in the standard form so that detailed calculations can be avoided. There are separate tables for SPCAF, SFDF etc. produced at the end of this book.

Problem 5.7

Based on the data given below, suggest better system, assuming annual rate of interest at 10%.

Proposal I - Investment Rs. 30,00,000 Annual return Rs. 6,50,000 for 7 years

Proposal II - Investment Rs. 25,00,000 Annual return Rs. 6,00,000 for 7 years

Solution :

A. (*a*) Uniform Present Work Factor Analysis (Proposal I)

As per relationship given above .

$$P = R(UPWDF)$$

$$\text{calculating UPWDF} = \frac{\left[1-\left(1+\frac{r}{100}\right)^{t}\right]}{(r/100)}$$

$$= \frac{\left[1-\left(1+\frac{10}{100}\right)^{-7}\right]}{(10/100)} = 5.13$$

$$\therefore \quad P = 6,50,000 \times 5.13 = 33,34500$$

$$\therefore \quad NPV = 33,34500 - 30,00,000 = \text{Rs. } 3,34,500$$

(*b*) Uniform Present Work Factor Analysis (Proposal II)

$$P = 6,00,000 \times (UPWDF)$$

$$= 6,00,000 \times 5.13 = 30,78,000$$

$$\therefore \quad NPV = 30,78,000 - 25,00,000 = 5,78,000$$

Hence the proposal II is better and to be adopted

B.Cost Analysis

Proposal I : Total cash after 7 years = R (USCAF)

$$= 6{,}50{,}000 \times \frac{\left(1+\frac{r}{100}\right)^{t}-1}{(r/100)}$$

$$= 6{,}50{,}000 \times \frac{1.949-1}{0.1} = 6,50,000 \times 9.49$$

$$= \text{Rs. } 61,68,500$$

Proposal II : Total cash after 7 years = Rs. 6,00,000 × 9.49

= Rs. 56,94,000

Hence Proposal I is better

Internal Rate of Return Approach (IRR)

In the previous method of Net Present Value (NPV), the rate of earning is already decided. But in this method, the earning rate is decided by hit and trial method. We arrive at the earning rate by equating the present value of earning to the amount of investment.

Mathematically, IRR is the rate of discounted cash flow r, at which the present value p of the uniform series at the end of the period payment R will become exactly equal to the present investment C.

$$C = P$$

and $$NPV = P - C = 0$$

But $$R = P(CRF)$$

$$\therefore \quad CRF = \frac{\left(1+\frac{r}{100}\right)^t}{\left[\left(1+\frac{r}{100}\right)^t - 1\right]}$$

By getting the value of r in this case, we get IRR = r.

Analytical Methods of Analysis

There are some well defined computing methods (statistical or heuristic), which can be used for economical analysis.

These investment analysis methods are :

- Linear Programming Method
- Simulation Method
- Decision Tree Method
- Cost estimates using network analysis (CPM / PERT) etc

Linear Programming and Decision Tree methods have been discussed in chapter 5 and the method of simulation in Chapter 3 Network analysis is available in the last chapter of this book titled. "Project panning and scheduling".

Thus linear programming method (simplex method) can be used for product mix analysis and the simulation method for service design.

Problem 5.8

The data presented in the given table indicate the probability of profits (investment utilisation) under different conditions of sales in various companies :

	Outcomes	
	High Sales	Low Sales
Probability	(0.4)	(0.6)
Company A	+ 45,000	– 10,000
B	+ 80,000	– 25,000
C	+ 30,000	+ 5,000

Suggest as to which company should be preferred for investment by the investor.

Solution :

The decision tree for the given data can be drawn as follows:

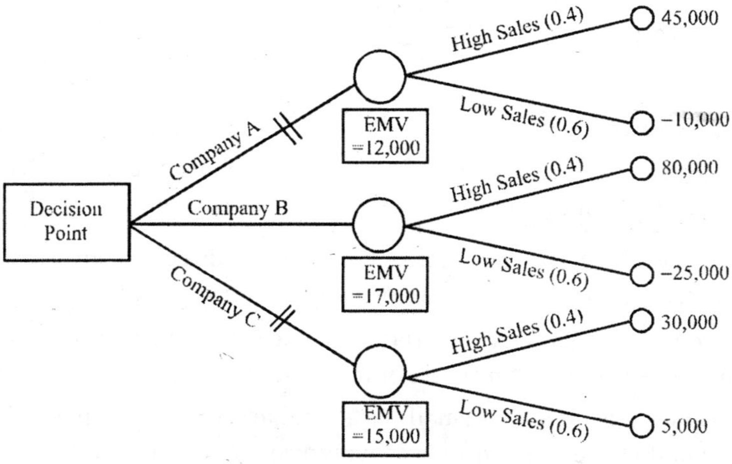

FIG. 5.7. Decision Tree

Since Expected Monitory Value (EMV) = Σ pi Oi

where pi = probability of occurrence

Oi = outcome of the event

Hence,

$$\text{EMV (A)} = (0.4)(45{,}000) + (0.6)(-10{,}000) = 12{,}000$$

$$\text{EMV (B)} = (0.4)(80{,}000) + (0.6)(-25{,}000) = 17{,}000$$

and

$$\text{EMV (C)} = (0.4)(30{,}000) + (0.6)(5{,}000) = 15{,}000$$

It is evident that the maximum expected benefits accrue through an invėstment in company B, Hence company B is preferred by the investory for his investment choice. [Note : The corresponding EMVs have been marked on the decision nodes, as can be seen and the two choices not preferred by the investor are crossed out]

Profitability Ratios

Some of elementary relationships are indicated below:

- Operating Profit Ratio $= \dfrac{\text{Sales} - \text{Cost of Production}}{\text{Sales}}$
- Net Profit Ratio $= \dfrac{\text{Net Profit}}{\text{Sales}}$
- Return on Investment (ROI) $= \dfrac{\text{Profit before Tax}}{\text{Capital Cost}}$

- Capital Turnover Ratio (CTR) $= \dfrac{\text{Sales}}{\text{Capital}}$

- Earning Power Ratio $= \dfrac{\text{Net Profit}}{\text{Capital lost}}$

5.8 Process Selection Analysis

It is a strategic decision to select a type of process for actual production. There are various types of processes, out of which the appropriate selection can be made.

Conversion Process : In this process, a raw material is directly converted into a product like manufacture of steel sheets from iron ore or making atta out of grain.

Fabrication Process : When raw material is changed into a specific form or shape like manufacture of water coolers out of tin sheets or manufacture of a car fender from sheet metal.

Assembly Process : When various small parts / subassemblies are put together for make a full product like manufacture of a car on a moving production or assembly line.

Testing Process : When a product / service is tested for its performance, the process is called testing. It is a necessary process to ensure defect free product / service availability to the customer.

Hence based on the requirement, a specific process or a combination of processes can be chosen to obtain a cost effective product / service. It may be through a job shop, (small batches of number of products) an assembly line or a continuous flow operation which can be used for efficient production.

Break Even Analysis

There are occasions, when the production can be achieved in number of ways *i.e.*, through more than one process. For selecting a cost effective process, the method of Break Even Analysis can be applied as follows :

Let us assume that in Process I,

Fixed Cost $= FC_1$

Variable Cost $= VC_1$

Total Cost $= TC_1$

Similarly for Process II (Second and alternate Process)

Fixed Cost $= FC_2$

Variable Cost $= VC_2$

Total Cost $= TC_2$

Drawing the cost / volume relationship for both the processes,

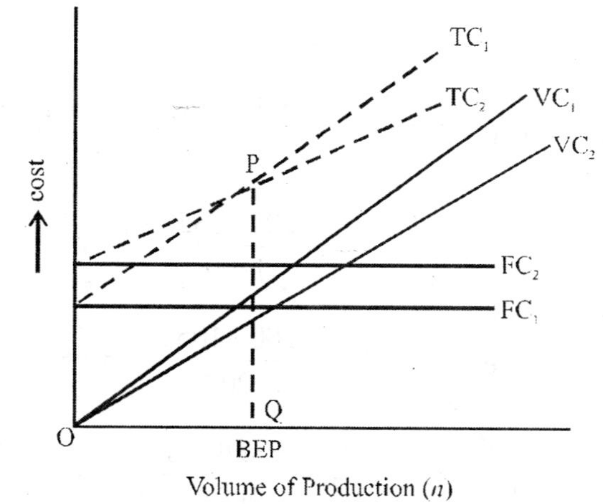

FIG. 5.8. Break-Even Analysis

The lines representing Total Costs for Process I and II *i.e.*, line TC_1 and TC_2 intersect at point P, where both the process are equally costly. This is called the Break-Even Point (BEP) and the volume of production at Q is the quantity of product, which can be produced by either process at the same cost.

The selection of process will be based on the forccaste demand. If the demand ie., manufacturing volume is less than BEP ie., to the left of Q on the graph, Process I works out to be cheaper. If the product is such that even after prolonged sustained efforts, the volume is not likely to exceed OQ, then facilities for process I should be bought and installed. But if the volume of the product is likely to exceed the BEP *i.e.*, more than Q, even if the initial take off volumes are low, process II facilities should be installed, so as to make full use in due course of time.

Problem 5.9

A company manufactures two products A and B. Following data has been collected for analysis :

Description		Product	
		A	B
Number of units produced		1200	1800
Sales price per unit		Rs. 1500	Rs. 1200
Input Costs :	Raw material / unit	Rs. 1000	Rs. 800
	Labour cost / unit	Rs. 200	Rs. 150
	Other expenses / unit	Rs. 150	Rs. 100
Fixed Cost		Rs. 25,000	Rs. 30,000

(*a*) What is the profit volume ratio for each product?

(*b*) Workout BEP for Product A and Product B separately.

Solution :

(*a*) Profit volume ratio for Product A $= \dfrac{\text{Selling price} - \text{Input cost}}{\text{Sales Revenue}}$

$$= \frac{1500 - 1350}{1500} = 10\%$$

Profit volume ratio for Product B $= \dfrac{1200 - 1050}{1200} = 12.5\%$

(*b*) BEP for Product A $= \dfrac{\text{Fixed cost}}{\text{profit for unit}} = \dfrac{25{,}000}{150} = 167$ units

BEP for Product B $= \dfrac{30{,}000}{150} = 200$ units

5.9 Selection of Machines / Plants

It is quite evident from the preceding discussion that process design is finalised based on production total cost. For the decided process, appropriate machines are required to be selected, bought and installed. Few factors considered for machine selection are :

- Capital investment
- Detailed specifications of the machines required
- Capacity of machine required
- Appropriate Technology as per process selected
- Flexibility of operations and life expectancy
- Maintainability and Reliability

Based on the above factors, appropriate length, width, speed, height, production output capacity etc can be compared with cost for different machines and only technically suitable and economically viable machines should be selected. Number of machines of each type would depend on the space available and the volume of production to be achieved. Work stations ie., group of machines for some specific operations can then be designed and planned for installation and commissioning.

The selection of machines/plants will also depened on the type of process choosen for production, when there are alternate processes available for the product is question, the cost analysis can be good guide. The concept of **Break-Even Point (BEP)** has already been discussed in this book. It has been brough out that if the anticipated demand is less than the BEP, one process could be cost-effective and cheaper. The machines for this proces,, therefore, will be procured and insfalled. When the demand of product is expected to be rising soon going above the BEP level, the other process is to be selected, machine procured and installed.

The quantity of machines for a particular set up can be calculated from the following relationship :

$$N = \frac{Q_1 ti}{nT(1-pi)}$$

where N = no of machine

Q = Annual capacity of the plant

t_i = Processtime of ith operations by the machine

n = efficiency of the machine (in decimal)

T = Total number of working hours available for the machine per year

p_i = Anticipated scrap unit (in decimal).

5.10 Process Planning for Services

The design procedure for the services should be the same as that for products. But it is not so, because of characteristics differential in two systems. The services are intangible, customer oriented and heterogeneous in nature. Customers involvement levels also may be different.

Thus the service design will differ with respect of degree of the customer contact resulting in necessity of standardistation of service or otherwise and the ratio of product goods and intangible service.

Customer demands are different (heterogeneity) and hence production flexibility is important part of service planning and design. Degree of automation will also result from standardisation levels possible, because automation should be able to deal with flexible demands along with standardisation of design. The design of service has to vary according to the above-mentioned factors and hence can be achieved in the following ways :

- Product or process focussed production, standardised goods and hence offering standardised services with little or no customer involvement in production such as variety of consumer goods in a departmental store or fast-food outlets.
- Services standardised, but increases customer involvement such as drawing money from Automated Teller Machines (ATMs), self-filling petrol stations, automated coffee machines on Airports etc.

The service design can be done based on customer demand only. Some highly customised services like medical clinics, beauty clinics or hair cutting saloons etc, require high personal attention to the customers. In such facilities, special attention is therefore, required for reception, holding, service and customer release such as car service stations, where even pick and drop facilities need be designed to woo customers to the service. Provision of waiting air conditioned halls, arrangements of Televisions, Newspapers and Coffee Vending machine are part of service facilities design in some cases.

Steps for Service Design : The design of services can be done through the following steps:

- Identify service requirement and select appropriate process.
- Ensure fail-safing of the system like service reminders to the car owner, queue formation for intakes, proper sign posting with service facility identification etc
- Establish and monitor time frame for services to ensure that the customers are not unduly harassed through long waiting period.
- Level of service to be provided to achieve high customer satisfaction and good profitability to the organisation.

Hence, for service design, the following procedure can be adopted:

- Draw process flow chart to assess optimum facility requirement. Carryout value analysis for each area.
- Process flow diagram and flow chart should result in preparing a service blue print i.e, action plan with resources planning.
- Carryout fail-safe analysis for value additions and better design.
- Obtain past data to design initial service levels and then improve with time experience.
- Use simulation technique for designing the initial service levels for optimum customer satisfaction. This has been described under "Service Design" in Chapter 3.

—●—

Section III
DESIGN OF FACILITIES AND JOBS

Chapter 6

Capacity and Aggregate Planning

Main issues:

1. Concept of capacity and Aggregate Planning
2. Resources assessment and capacity estimation
3. Capacity Expansion Strategies
4. Production Plans

6.1 Necessity of Aggregate Planning

In the previous two chapters, we have discussed the product and service design and for producing these facilities, we had a long discussion on the Process Planning *i.e.,* integrating the type of pruduction facility with the type of production to be carried out. Having worked out the forecasts for the demand of the designed product and service, the stage is now set to plan actual operation. We have to plan out as how we carry out the production work for meeting the demand of the product/service, which would mean planning the type and number of machines and allied facilities, the type and quantity of material needed and how many workers of what skill will be needed for finishing the work in time to satisfy the customer demand as and when it occurs. This planning is called production planning. When we plan for all relevant resources for a certain period of time, it is termed as Aggregate Planning.

If we plan the work in advance, the execution and implementation of these plans are likely to result in desired production in right quantity of right quality at right time.

An aggregate plan is a subset of the corporate plan of the organisation, which is drawn out based on the vision and mission of the organisation. It is primarily worked out to achieve the operational aims of the organisation.

The company has to identify the answers to three basic questions:

- Where are we Now ?
- Where do we want to Go ?
- How do we Go there ?

These answers will establish the gap of operations as per the aim of the organisation with the present level of operations. Once this has been identified, the corporate plan has to be drawn out as an integrated plan to indicate the following:

- Mission and the aim of the organisation
- Audit for past results (due reasons for short falls)
- Technology planned
- Manufacturing strategies – Product mix and Processes
- Marketing plans
- Financial strengths and plans
- Manpower strategies – Recruitment/Training

Now, the company is at a stage to establish its production capacity with reference to its future plans. The aggregate plan would emerge out of the manufacturing strategy keeping technology, Marketing and financial balances in view.

6.2 Planning Horizon

The aggregate plans are generally not the long range plans, due to the fact that the production capability has to cater for the changing customers requirements and possible expected volume changes. Hence generally the company plans for 6-18 month period and even then, have review updating and flexible manufacturing ready to be implemented as and when demanded. Generally long term plans are prepared and then medium range plans in updated basket are implemented. We have our National Plans for a 5-year duration, even then, we keep updating it to suit the day to day variations in economical, political and social fields. In industry for a product specific plan, the horizon obviously should be very small.

The long term plans for the industry can be drawn only to indentify the range of product or the type of service we could plan for in near future. This will help in strategic planning of capital resources *i.e.*, the type of plants, their present and future locations, major vendor policy and development of reliable vendor base along with the strategic technological planning like future trend of technology and type of possible automation that need be adopted for future demands. Strategic plans for distribution network also needs long range thinking. But out of this visionary planning, the organisation has to extract what is termed as 'Aggregate Plan' for say 6-18 months period and exact nature of machines, modifications for this period, the materials and supply arrangements, organisation set up, recruitment and training, outsourcing and material inventories for the production levels in question are detailed out.

At this stage, the company decides on the plan for a specific product mix, for a specified period say a month, their volume of production, machine planning, material planning and schedules and quality control standards. This is called Short Range Planning.

Aggregate Planning:

As discussed above, it is worked out to find

- Facilities, capacities, production method and cost effective production techniques.
- Planning of the expected bracket (present and near future demand) during the plan period
- 'What if' analysis to ensure no looking over the shoulder, when things donot work the way they should. Hence monitoring system has to match these changes and systematic variation in the production capacity to be planned for.
- No wastages or least amount of wastages to ensure full utilisation of available resources, which are generally scarce. Financial aspects needs tighter control.

6.3 Aggregate Production Capacity

Production capacity means the rate at which a company produces its output or at what rate it can produce its output.

Based on this definition, we can deduce that the production capacity can be divided into two types, namely:

- Input capacity
- Output capacity

Input capacity is the existing or planned capacity which can be installed. To make it clear, the number of seats in an aircraft is called as the input capacity available. Similarly, the number of hotel rooms available (beds) is the input capacity of the hotel.

Output capacity is the output obtained from an existing facility such as fertiliser plant, produces, say, 430tonnes per day, though installed capacity may be more.

Similarly, tons of paper produced per day by a paper mill is its output capacity.

Next obvious question to be answered is as to why input and output capacities are likely to be different and what happens to this difference.

Input capacity is the capacity created for a product or service. But when the system is operated physically, the rated output of facilities may not generally be at the manufacturers declared level due to following reasons:

- Working environmental conditions different from ideal conditions, at which equipment is tested for its output.
- Climatic conditions change the working efficiency of men, machines and material and hence output achieved is the result of the outcome at the derated capacity.

- In case demand does not justify the operational level at full capacity, actual output is deliberately obtained at reduced level.
- Ageing of manpower and equipment. In such cases, the difference is accounted for under the concept of capacity utilisation, *i.e.*, how much output is obtained out of the installed input capacity.

If an aircraft has 250 seats and only 198 passangers are travelling, the capacity utilisation is $\frac{198}{250} = 79.2\%$

Similarly, a hotel having 570 beds strength with occupation only as 90 beds, the capacity utilisation is 68.4%.

In production capacity, if the plant can produce 420 tonnes per day, but due to some variations (absentism, bad material or machine breakdown) we get only 360 tonnes of output of the product, then the plant is said to be operating at $\frac{360}{420} = 85.7\%$ efficiency (capacity utilised).

It brings out that the random fluctuations described as part of the Production model earlier, produce day to day variations. The manpower efficiency variation such as sickness, late coming, agitated state of mind, worry about accidents and training level all can contribute towards low output. Similarly either difficult working climatic conditions such as heat, sand, dust, humidity etc or ageing of the machines can make a substantial difference to the output achieved. It may not only affect the quantity, it also can bring down quality of the product or service. Material delivery delay beyond the lead time or partial rejection of the output are also the reasons of reduced capacity.

Therefore, while deciding on the capacity planning, the company planners must take the ground realites into account and not to decide the level of production based on rated outputs. This can be called "the sustainable actual capacity". The same concept should be tried out at the service planning stage.

The aggregate capacity is different from the output of a specific product, because due to diversity of the product mix in any production system, it is the output rates of various products converted to a common unit of output rate. Thus the production capacity should not be defined for each single product, but for a family of products and this capacity should be brought to the same measuring level. Aggregate Planning, thus, is normally prepared at the facility level. This plan is then merged into the corporate plan to ensure compatibility with the overall aim of the organisation.

The production capacity, can be expressed as a unit manufacturing 500 units of pumps in a month or 3,000 refrigerators in a month. The variable for planning can either be the work force (measured as 50,000 manhours or labour hours) or machines (expressed as machine hours). Similarly the consumption of materials can be written as the litres of paint consumed in one week (family of paints).

To create a capacity plan, we have to identity the product mix, their forecasted demand and process design to produce these products. Manpower planning and material planning is then done based on Master Production Schedule (MPS) prepared for the purpose for a certain period of time.

Accurate forecaste (discussed in earlier chapter) are essential for Aggregate Capacity Plan to be successful.

6.4 Long Range Capacity Planning Strategy

The aggregate plans and capacity plans are subsets of the corporate plan of the organisation. When we support a corporate plan, the strategic plans have to have the same vision, mission and aim reflection in the short term plans drawn for day to day working. Hence we have to decide the requirements on long term basis, in the following fields:

- Manpower planning including hiring/firing policy
- Make or buy decisions or outsourcing levels
- Inventory policy and vendor policy
- Production Supporting Marketing plans and sales support strategy
- Financial outlays, loan structures etc.
- 'What if' and trade off decisions for alternatives in case of difficulties

Based on these basic decisions, the production capacities have to be arrived at. The capacity strategies should be based on the following factors:

- What is the strategic and short range forecast for demand for a specified product mix ?
- What are the resources available with company at this present time *i.e.*, available manpower and machines ?
- Based on resources constraints, how much production capacity is available ?
- What is the capacity gap and where are the bottleneck in operations for a given product mix ?
- What is the cost to upgrade or bring down the existing capacity as per demand plan ?

In order to get the answers to these questions, the policies in the above mentioned planning areas are to be formulated in the following manner:

- If there is shortage of appropriate skilled labour, hiring and training is resorted to. Such action plans should be part of the production plan.
- If the demand level is not very certain or low during the initial stage of the product introduction, casual labour or part time labour of suitable skill can be engaged. The analysis of local labour market should be part of the plan so that timely action can be taken to support the capacity required.

- If shortage of manpower is to be covered through internal means only, overtime planning can be included.
- During strategic planning for materials, due consideration on selection and ratings of the vendor must be done to avoid any mid-way stoppages. Outsourcing can be part of planning at this stage.

For taking the decision on the capacity on the long-term basis, it is important to decide as to what and how much to manufacture within own resources and what all and how much can be outsourced. For this analysis, Linear Programming Model can be used for Product Mix. For strategic decision, Decision tree theory can be adopted.

Problem 6.1

Ashok Manufacturing have developed a new product. During the process planning stage, the management found that the investment for the manufacturing facilities should be optimised and hence carried out the analysis in the following manner:

(a) The entire production volume can be manufactured. The total cost for the building and other facilities is estimated to be Rs. 2,00,000 and will be a total loss if the product fails. In case the product is successful it will fetch Rs. 8,00,000. The chances of failure being 0.75, if the course chosen without any study.

(b) If proper study is resorted to, it is estimated that the product will find favourable market with 50 percent success. In case, the manufacture is resorted to, the chance of success is 0.4 with Rs. 5,50,000 gain but with failure, it will result in the profit of Rs. 2,50,000 only.

(c) If the market is unfavourable, the manufactured product is estimated to be a secure only 10 per cent with an outcome of Rs. 5,00,000 and failure possibility giving only Rs. 2,50,000 loss.

(d) If the product is outsourced to another manufacturer already hairing manufacturing facility, it will fetch only Rs. 40,000. But this amount will be only Rs. 50,000 in Rs. 40,000. But this amount will be only Rs. 50,000 in case of riser selling after study with favourable market and loss of Rs. 5,000 under unfavourable market conditions. Study of the proposal costs only Rs. 20,000.

Suggest an appropriate strategy for Ashok Manufacturers out of the choices described above.

Solution:

Based on the data given above, the decision tree for all the three alternatives can be seen in figure 6.1.

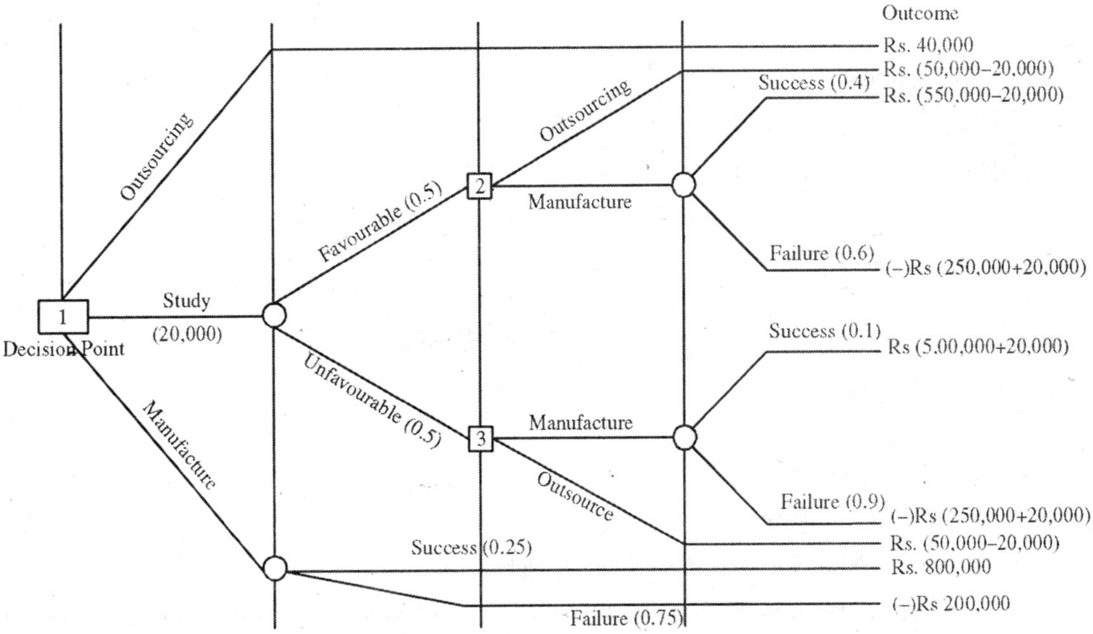

FIG. 6.1. Decision Tree for Investment strategy

Calculating EMVs at various Decision Points (1), (2) and (3):

Decision Point (2) Action after study (under favourable market)

- Outsourcing Rs. 30,000
- Manufacturer (0.4 × 5,30,000) + (0.6 × (–) 2,70,000)
  = (2,12,000 – 1,62,000)
  = 50,000
- Net EMV under favourable market
  = 0.5 (30,000 + 50,000)
  = Rs. 40,000

Decision Point (3) Action after study (under unfavourable market)

- Out sourcing Rs. (–) 15,000
- Manufacture (0.1 × 4,80,000) + (0.9 × (–) 2,70,000)
  = 48,000 – 2,43,000
  = (–) 1,95,000
- Net EMV under unfavourable market = 0.5 (–15,000 – 1,95,000)
  = (–) 1,10,000

  Outcome as per study = 40,000 – 1,10,000 – 20,000
  = (–) 90,000

Decision Point (1)

- Outsourcing Rs. 40,000
- Study Rs. (–) 90,000
- Manufacture $(0.25 \times 8,00,000) + (0.75 \times (-2,00,000))$
  = Rs. 50,000

Hence they should adopt the strategy of Manufacturing.

Main considerations for capacity Planning Strategies

- Product Design
- Forecasting of demand
- Process Design
- Product Mix Decision
- Quality of products as per Customers Level
- Scheduling of resources for optimum utilisation of existing facilities and decision on outsourcing/new resourcing provisioning
- Materials and Vendor Management and Inventory Levels desired
- Manpower arrangement and job design as per method selected.

6.5 Forecasting Capacity Demand

After the product design, the major hurdle to plan production is the accuracy to which the product demand is established. Quite a few methods have been discussed, but some environmental factors will still keep the uncertainity at a higher level. Hence use of quantitative methods of demand forecasting is to be superimposed by intutive or judgemental methods to build-in the intengibles or non-quantifiable parameters.

Another dimension of the capacity demand is the constant variation needed to cater for market situation and product acceptance level as the time goes by. Slowly as the production increases, there is likely to be an increase in the output rate of the manpower due to Pearing curve effect but decrease in the output rates of the machines due to ageing. The experience effects, therefore, are needed to be built in during these plans for capacity.

A peculiarity in the geographical area can make the difference in the type and quantity of products. Certain variations are also encountered. Hence close watch in demand for capacity should be kept and timely action taken.

6.6 Economies of Scale

While deciding the planned capacity, it is worth considering as to what basis the capacity is to be planned on. When we are on product based system, layout for a product or products should be finalised and capacity should be built in for the volumes of these individual products. When we plan on the process based system, each process facility can dictate how many machine hours of a facility are available and can be made use of. The third system can be based on the volumes of certain specific products in some specific geographic area. Either way, the question to be answered is as to how we can make optimum use of existing capacity or how we can place optimum level of facility for the quantum of job at hand.

Economics of the production would be best served by manufacturing product mix as per facility utilisation and the market consumptions. The economies of scale can be determined with the help of linear programming models (Simplex Method), so as to obtain the optimum use of materials and money for optimum production through the capacity available.

6.7 Capacity Requirement Planning and Expansion Strategy

Initial capacity placement or utilisation depends on the starting demand of the product. When the product is new, just designed and produced, it will take time for the market acceptance. If the product is liked by the customers instantly, the demand surges ahead and production capacity has to match on a faster rate. In case of slow acceptance, the change in the production volumes are also slow and deliberate. Even for older products, the demand may not be increasing at the same old rate, because the customers may be looking for some better product or a different product altogether. This aspect has been discussed during the product life cycle discussion. Either way, there is a considerable possibility of uncertanity of demand and even if we can maintain long range demand pattern at a certain level for quite some time, the short-range pattern may not be uniform. It can be highly unpredicable.

Because of the above reasons, the production capacity has to be monitored to match the demand and as a corrective action; the decrease or increase in the production capacity has to be affected to match the market demand.

Short-term demand variation: When the demand is varying in small intervals of time, the capacity of producing can be increased or decreased in the following manner:

- Overtime work
- Outsourcing/additional market
- reduction in capacity utilisation *i.e.*, reduction in machine production hours or by reducing number of shifts

Long term Demand Variation: Generally the production capacity for long range demand variation can be added in large increaments such as adding machines, adding working shifts, increasing building sizes or by adding new processing units. This capacity change for different situations has to be carefully deliberated upon, planned and then installed. Strategies for such situations are discussed below:

Strategy for Excess Capacity: This is a deliberate strategy to be adopted when the product is conceived to be good and is expected to be received well in the market. The customer liking the product would need enhanced capacity so that the spurt in demand or faster rate of consuption can be taken care of.

For this purpose, the initial capacity is planned to be higher than the initial of demand and the capacity is expanded well before the inventory is exhasted. This is to ensure a ready availability of the product for customer. This can be shown diagramatically as illustrated in fig. 6.2.

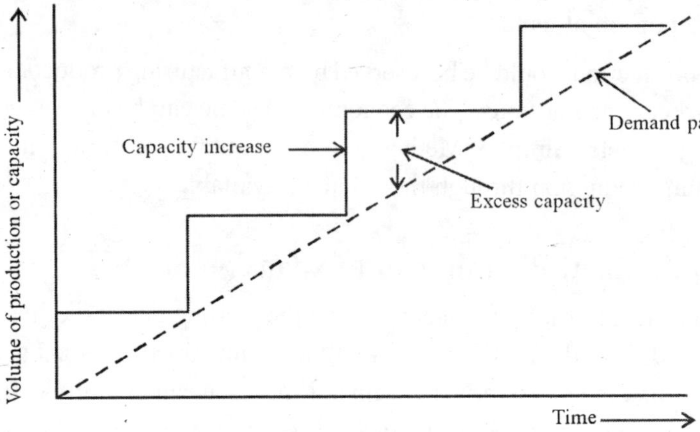

FIG. 6.2. Excess Capacity Planning

By allowing excess inventory build up, the sudden demand can be met out of excess capacity available (as marked above). It may be worthwhile to mention here that there has to be a judicious decision as to how much excess inventory has to be kept, because excess inventory means capital tied up and hence cost involved. Excess capacity here, may mean that there exists capability of facilities to produce products on as required basis, but does not signify actual use of it unless required. If inventory level is decided to be kept low, the production can be achieved through overtime in case of demand. Faster response to the customer demand is a definite advantage.

Thus this strategy can be adopted under following situations:

- Product is low cost and inventory cost is low
- When sudden demand increase is expected
- When company had resources available to follow the strategy through deliberate use of excess capacity through overtime or additional use of manpower and machines.
- When company deliberately decides to push the product through aggressive marketing and sales efforts.
- When company deliberately decides on a higher level of customer satisfaction. But there can be a disadvantage of high inventory cost or high cost of maintaining the unused excess capacity.
- When production disruptions are expected due to volatile situation either political or unionised.

Strategy for Balance Capacity: This is normal logical strategy when the market is reasonably uniform and working conditions are also expected to be normal. When there is a reasonably established pattern in product acceptance and customer preference and hence demand is likely to progress at a steady slow rate, it is the best strategy to follow.

As can be seen from the fig 6.3 below, the company starts using capacity slightly higher than the initial demand and build up inventory to a reasonable level so that gradual increase in demand can be met with. When the inventory levels come down, increase the capacity at a reasonable average level can be decided.

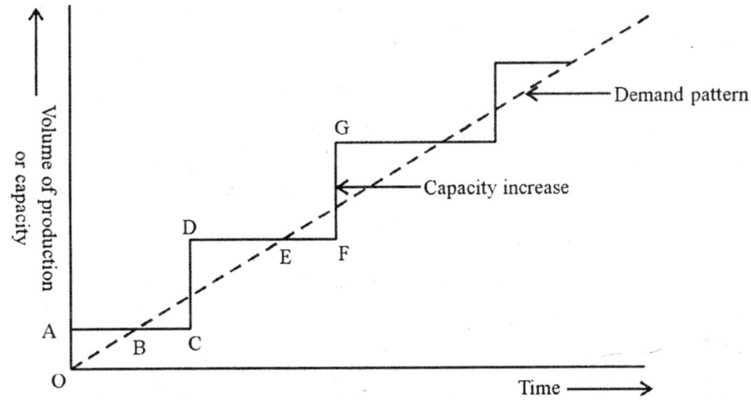

FIG. 6.3. Balanced Capacity Strategy

From the above figure, it is seen that during the initial stage when demand has grown from O to B, we operate the production system at a level of OA unformly till C. During the period AB, an inventory build up can be noticed as OAB (excess). This is then neutralised during the period BC, where the demand is at a higher level than the production and the shortage of production during this period is served through the inventory build up during the period AB.

When the inventory usage reaches a level of almost neutralisation, the capacity is enhanced as CD (beyond the demand at this time) and this capacity is used till the time F *i.e.*, DF is uniform capacity following the same principle of initial build up through DE and neutralisation through EF.

By following this strategy of Capacity matching the demand pattern, we get the following advantages:

- Uniform utilisation of resources over a reasonably long period
- Inventory costs are optimised by building and neutralising the inventory during short intervals
- Reliable supply but also quick response when demand increases.
- Planning of resources done at regular intervals, but not very often, cutting down the cost of planning. Organising resources will be easier in such a case.

The disadvantage of the strategy is the its failure in case of inaccurate demand or when demands are relatively fluctuating.

Strategy of deliberate low capacity: This is just the opposite strategy to the excess capacity strategy. In this case, the capacity is kept lower than the demand to ensure no unnecessary inventory build up or the case of non-utilisation of existing resources when demand uncertainty becomes larger. At times, it is a deliberate policy of the organisation to keep the demand hungry of the product just to gain psychological advantage of a very strong perception of good product, high sales and hence the shortage. This, at times, is a deliberate marketing strategy so that customer waits in anticipation of getting a good product at reasonable price at a later date. This is diagramatically shown below in fig. 6.4.

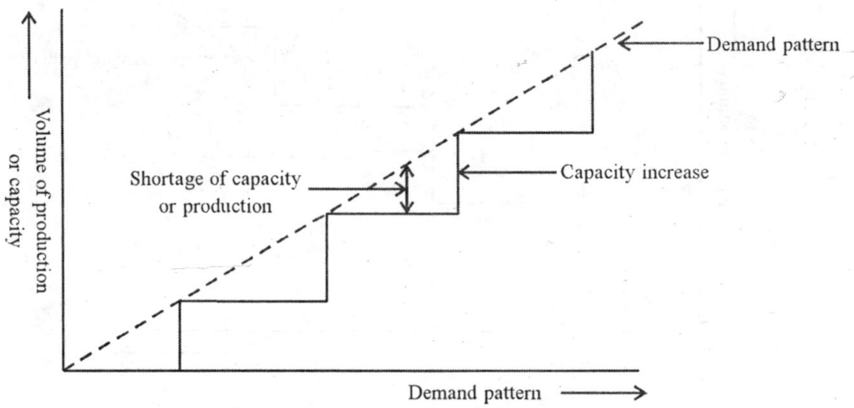

FIG. 6.4. Low Capacity Strategy

The circumstances under which the company can adopt such a strategy are:

- Minimum level of equipment or low resources cost
- Product of high cost and hence inventory cost may be very high
- Deliberately keeping the demand hungry to gain psychological advantage
- Uncertainty of demand high
- Capital investment high and financial burden not feasible or risk not acceptable.

The obvious disadvantage of the strategy is not meeting the demand and may need high overtime or costly outsourcing in case of urgent need.

6.8 Type of Production Plans

The demands are generally uncertain and the actual sales differ even on day-to-day basis and month-to-month basis. But these uncertainties can not be a reason for not deciding a reasonable level of capacity provision. Minor variations are taken care of under the concept of capacity utilisation on ground. The installation and commissioning of production facilities has to be firm, at a definite level with provisions for future expansions in the form of additional manpower to use enhanced capacity or even expanding capacity (*i.e.*, adding machines only at the time of capacity expansion requirement) as and when really needed. To cater for such situations, it is recommeded to follow either of the production plans discussed below. Generally, the industry follows three types of production plans

- Fixed Production Plan
- Chase Production Plan
- Intermediate Production Plan

It is to be done on the basis of man-machine combination. The optimum output of the worker is to match with the optimum output of the machine he is using. Any constraints of working hours, or material availability have to be taken into consideration while deciding on daily production.

Manpower output

For planning the output of men, two methods are generally adopted:

Actual experimentation: Every organisation should fix up realistic output levels in the form of standard time of an activity. For this purpose, actual activity is to be performed by certain number of workers of the organisation (may be carried out at more than one location where the company operates its production lines). The averages time taken by the people is worked out and then average of these averages on the basis of number of experiments can be calculated. This is called average operation time of the acitivity. The operating allowances are then added to this time to obtain the standard output time (This is discussed in details in another chapter). This standard time can be taken as the basis of planning for manpower output.

ILO Standards: The output standards published by the International labour organisation for various zones can be used as planning standard for the production.

PMTS (Pre-determined Motion Time Systems) Standards: This method is based on standard industrial engineering tables for predetermined timings for various motions of an activity, (motions are like grasp, lift, move, release etc,). We can then add all the motion timings to get the activity time, used for planning purposes.

Machine output

- For fixing realistic machine output, we can use the method of a standard capacity worker operating a machine and the output achieved can be used as planning standard machine output.
- We can use the manufacturers declared output as the basis and then apply operating corrections to bring the output level to the actual working conditions. This is called the derating of machine output, applying the corrections for ageing, climatic conditions, maintenance levels, maintenance policies and any other important influence on the output.

Fixed Production Plan

In this production Plan, the production level is kept fixed or constant throughout the period of planning (Generally for one year). The volume of production has to be planned on daily basis because the production takes place during physical eight hour shift. Planning can be done for one two or three shifts depending on the demand and the capital investment made to buy certain number of machines. Due consideration is given to maintenance of machines in case it is decided to operate two or threé shifts. Before discussing the individual plans, let us consider as to how the volume of actual production can be decided.

The output per day is fixed based on actual capacity available with referrence to man-machine optimum output as discussed above. In this plan, we first calculate the likely production for each day (mathematical calculation) and then actual is corrected to actual of outputs expected as per man-machine output.

Let us take the demand pattern as given in the following example:

Table for Fixed Production Plan

Month	*Demand (units)*	*No. of Working days*	*Output per day*	*Monthly output*	*Inventory*		
					Initial	*Add on*	*End month*
April	10,000	24	800	19,200	—	9,200	9,200
May	11,000	25	800	20,000	9,200	9,000	18,200
June	12,000	25	800	20,000	18,200	8,000	26,200
July	13,500	26	800	20,800	33,500	5,800	39,300
August	15,000	26	800	20,800	26,200	7,300	33,500
September	16,000	24	800	19,200	39,300	3,200	42,500
October	18,000	24	800	19,200	42,500	1,200	43,700
November	21,000	23	8,00	18,400	43,700	(4,600)	39,100
December	24,000	25	800	20,000	39,100	(4,000)	35,100
January	26,500	25	800	20,000	35,100	(6,500)	28,600
February	28,000	24	800	19,200	28,600	(8,800)	19,800
March	30,000	25	800	20,000	19,800	(10,000)	9,800
Total	2,25,000	296					

Total Demand for the year = 2,25,000 units

Total number of working days = 296

$$\therefore \text{ Output desired per day} = \frac{2,25,000}{296} = 760 \text{ per day}$$

Mathematically calculated output per day is 760 units.

Now, we superimpose capacity restriction on it. If we have two machines which can give us 400 units per day each, we can use this capacity of production as

400 + 400 = 800 units per day (Slightly higher than desired output)

Hence, we use the output per day = 800 in the appropriate column above, throughout the year (Fixed production for the year)

As can be seen from the calculation table, the monthly output is calculated by multiplying daily output (800) with number of working days possible during a particular month.

Having known the monthly output from the production system, we can meet the demand from this production volume with the remaining quantity becoming the inventory. To get better picture on inventory, three columns, namely initial inventory, add on during the month and the end month inventory indicate true picture of the inventory levels.

In certain cases, say, during the month of November, the output is less, whereas the demand is more. This difference is met out of the existing inventory. The shortfall of the units have, therefore, been given in the bracket. (Inventory cannot be negative since it is a physical asset). All the calculations can now be followed easily.

***Interpretation of the plan*:** As can be seen with reference to the capacity contraint, we have to produce extra 40 units (800 – 760) per day throughout the year and hence an inventory of 9,800 units at the end of the year is indicated.

Second important issue is the level of inventory during various months. Since we have taken output per day as the average of the annual total demand, initially inventory build up has to be accepted to be high. As demand slowly increases, the inventory levels come down as can be seen during later part of the year (November ownwards) till it is reduced to 9,800 at the end of the year.

Advantages of the plan

- It is fixed level of production, hence planning of manpower remains the same througout the year and no additional effort is required for replanning/additions.
- Machines used are same throughout the year and no addition planning for rescheduling etc required.
- Production level being the same every day. Vendor can keep supplying the same quantity at regular intervals, no recalculation of inventories required during the year.
- Maintenance efforts in terms of the machines, manpower and maintenance consumables remain the same throughout the year.
- Planning of cash flow is standardised.

Disadvantage of the Plan

For major period of the year the inventory levels are high and hence higher inventory costs.

Chase Plan

In the chase plan, rest of the planning remains the same, except for the output figures per day. As the name suggests, the production volumes per month are kept just enough to meet the demand of the month (production chasing the demand), the output per day changes every month, thereby changing all the inputs on monthly basis. The number of machines, manpower, materials and financial outlay becomes different every month and hence needs calculations and provisionary corrections every month. This can be shown in the table given below:

Table for Chase Plan

Month	*Demand*	*No. of working days*	*output per month*	*Monthly output*	*Inventory*		
					Initial	*add on*	*End month*
April	10,000	24	400	9,600	—	(400)	—
May	11,000	25	440	11,000	—	—	—
June	12,000	25	480	12,000	—	—	—
July	13,500	26	520	13,520	—	20	20
August	15,000	26	580	15,080	20	80	100
September	16,000	24	670	16,080	100	80	180

Just to show the typical calculations for the chase plan, only a six monthly period has been shown with demand levels and number of working days.

Since it is chase plan, we have taken an average output based on the demand for that month only. Since one machine can give us 400 units per day (See the fixed plan assumption), we can use only one machine during April and a short fall of 400 units can be allowed as demand unfulfilled. In case required, we could plan this quantity through **overtime** on the same machine.

Similarly, the outputs of 440, 480, 520, 580 and 670 are to be adjusted through the following ways:

- over time
- Buying decision/out sourcing

In this case, we can observe that the inventory levels have came down drastically in comparison with fixed production plan. Hence inventory costs have been reduced dramatically.

Advantages of the plan

- Very low inventory holding

Disadvantages

- The continuous variation in the manpower. The people for the overtime have to be located and used. In case of large production, constant hiring/firing needs to be done in case of output varying and it is not an easy task due to labour laws inforce.
- Continuous variations in Materials and Supply schedules – Vendor may fail the system.
- The changes required every month in the maintenance schedules, manpower and consumable costs.
- Cash flow calculations and organising finances to support flexible operations needs careful planning and continuous monitoring, needing extra efforts.

Intermediate Production Plan

Since the two plans discussed above are extreme plans, not very suitable one way or the other, it is preferred to follow intermediate plan, wherein the change in the output pattern is brought above on quaterly basis, *i.e.*, we decide output based on moving quarterly demand, thus controlling inventories on the quarter basis, and arranging machines, manpower and money on three monthly basis. Thus it is economic plan from all angles, as overall perspective.

The calculations for the intermediate Production Plan are apended below:

Table for Intermediate Plan

Month	*Demand*	*No. of working days*	*output per month*	*Monthly output*	*Inventory Initial*	*Inventory add on*	*Inventory End month*
April	10,000	24	450	10,800	—	800	800
May	11,000	25	450	11,250	800	250	1,050
June	12,000	25	450	11,250	1,050	(750)	300
July	13,500	26	600	15,600	300	1,900	2,200
August	15,000	26	600	15,600	2,200	600	2,800
September	16,000	24	600	14,400	2,800	(1,600)	1,200

Here the quantity 450 can be produced ovetime through buying from outside source. A quantity of 600 (against 585 calculated output) can be produced by working a machine of 400 units a day for another 4 hours for meeting the target.

It can be observed that the inventory levels are almost neutralising on quarterly basis and hence very economical.

Other disadvantages of manpower, machine material and financials are easy to handle quarterly basis.

Hence, generally, this plan is adopted by most of the manufacturing organisations.

Chapter 7

Facilities Locations and Layouts

Main issues:

1. Strategic issues in Facility Location
2. Service Location Characteristics
3. Methods of Plant and Service Location
4. Layouts and Line Balancing

7.1 Strategic issues in Facility location

Facilities locations can not be decided in hurry. These decisions have to be very deliberate because of the fact that change due to any hasty decision would involve cost and time efforts putting a heavy burdent on the financial health of the organisation.

These decisions involve deliberate extensive studies for collecting factual information from various sites under consideration. These studies should include all tangible as well as non-tangible factors. Though there may be no clear-cut best location, an optimal advantage can be arrived at by considering serveral good locations and then selecting the best location on major advantage basis. The strengths and weaknesses of various short-listed locations would, therefore, need study. Then only a trade-off decision can be made.

Selecting a facility location involves a sequences of decisions, involving some strategic as well as tectical local decisions. These decisions would have to include international, domestic or local considerations.

One of the major strategic issue for facility location involved pertains to the decision makers choice of risk-level.

- Is the decisions-maker ready to risk the capital for an international or domestic operation ?
- Is the decision-maker ready to face the brunt of the union atmosphere in a particular area ?
- Is the decision-maker socially committed person ready to look after his own region or people for enhancement of local social indicators ?
- Is the decision-maker ready to think environmentally positive for general public advantage? Is the decision based on available facilities or for developing new infrastructure in terms of manpower, material, suppliers local availability, incentives available from the local or national government etc ?

These strategic issues carry a major weight in the process of short-listing eligible locations for a particular facility for the type of service it is expected to deliver to the society at large.

7.2 Factors for Plant Location Selection

Having designed the products/services and decided on the volume of requirement, there arises the necessity to decide on the location of various facilities so as to make their optimum use for cost effective production. This problem is termed as Facility Location or Plant Location.

Plant location may be necessited due to the following reasons:

- New venture / plant establishment
- Expansion of the existing facility or diversification of product line.
- Significant change in demand concentration
- Change in climatic conditions.
- Political / economic conditions and government policy.
- Major changes in resources such as cost and availability of labour, raw materials or infrastructure etc.
- Merger with another company with resultant readjustments.

The decision on the facilities location is very important strategic decision due to the fact that once decided, the facilities are not easily relocatable without incurring heavy cost. In addition, a substantial amount of effort and costs go into taking the decision on locations, because an extensive market research will have to be carried out to collect authentic, on ground information for various relevant factors that affect the selection of the location.

In the initial stage, it is imperative to decide what factors are important for product manufacture. Generally no single location can be ideal or superior. On the basis of major factors such as geographical preference, cheaper land, or suitable government regulations etc., some short listing of locations is required to be done, so as to take a trade-off decision based on authentic information about various relevant factors. After initial short listing of important locations based on some major considerations, a meticulous market research for all short listed locations must be undertaken.

A not very exhaustive list of factors is given below for manufacturing and services separately due to some distinguishing features:

Factors at Regional Level

- Land availability and cost
- Availability of market with information on demand density
- Availability of labour - number, skill, attitude, aptitude and union response.
- Availability of raw materials-natural and synthetic
- Availability of utilities such as power, water, roads, railheads, communication facilities and banking etc.
- Government policy and national thrust of development
- Political and social environment
- Availability of community facilities such as schools, accommodation and hospitals etc.
- Related industry proximity (Compatible industry)
- Future expansion possibilities
- Environmental regulations.

Factors at Local Level

- Local government incentives and tax structure
- Community attitude
- Local Union attitude
- Transportation Facilities
- Security concerns
- Climatic conditions such as rains, temperature, humidity, water table etc.

Factors at International Level

- Currency exchange rates / transfer of profits regulations
- Tax structures and cost advantage
- Labour sanctions or any other legal restriction
- Industry policy and Technology Transfer rules
- Economies of scale
- Risk of business through joint ventures/collaborations.

Based on the above factors, the plant location has to be decided on their combined effect An over-riding factor such as Government Policy or Political environment may be an important reason for a particular location.

7.3 Services Location Analysis

For product, the analysis may be simple due to verifyable facts available; but for service location, this is slightly difficult decision because of the intangibility aspect.

Most important factor for services is proximity of the customers and the concentration of demand. If service facility has to be really cost effective (may not always be so, due to critical requirement of loads being low). Health and emergency services are some important facilities, which have to be located in close proximity of customers. In addition, traffic pattern and availability of transport facilities to suit customers requirement is equally important.

In addition, since it is highly customer - oriented facility, the location must be known to the customers and they should be able to reach the place easily, hence exposure and accessibility become important. Compatible industry also help the service facility such as availability of type of spares, manpower and tea shops etc. near the automobile repair service facility. Some important factors for service industry can be summarised as follows:

- Exposure
- Accessibility
- Compatible industry / Facilities

7.4 Factors for Site Selection

Once a suitable location has been identified, the next step is to select the site for the plant or facility. Some of the important factors for site selections are:

- Size of the plot including expansion requirement (normally 50 percent for expansion)
- Type of the building - horizontal or vertical (local byelaws)
- Water, power, sewage, roads, telephone and other facilities
- Closeness of Transport Facilities
- Any special restriction like safety funnel of aircraft landing, hazardous material or process restriction or a specific Government regulation like establishing similar facilities together such as the software zones, electronic parks or automobile hub etc.

7.5 Methods for Plant Location Selection

All the factors considered for location selection may not be lending themselves to easy analysis as some of the factors will be beneficial towards cost of the plants, other may have intangible advantages. Some of the factors are tangible, which can be quantified and produce better analysis but other non-tangible factors can be viewed differently by different managers. Some factors may become predominant due to strong political or social consideration and hence may override all other technical as well as non-technical factors. It is therefore, necessary to take care of all factors to produce coherent decision, For this purpose following method are available:

- Factor Rating Method
- Weightage Rating Method
- Bridgeman Method
- Centre of Gravity (CG) Method
- Linear Programming Method

Factor Rating Method

Since detailed survey would have been performed on the short-listed possible locations, the table can be worked out allotting a suitable rating for each factor against each location. The ratings are recommended to be based on cost (since we intend deciding the most cost effective location) on a scale of 1 to 10. To be producing a balanced situation, we can decide ratings as

1 – Least Cost Factor

10 – Highest Cost Factor

A representative table is drawn below for making decision on the suitable location:

Table 7.1. Factor Rating Method

Sl.	*Factor*		*Ratings for*	
		Location A	*Location B*	*Location C*
1.	Land Cost	8	7	4
2.	Market Proximity	5	7	8
3.	Labour Availability	8	5	3
4.	Labour Attitude	4	3	4
5.	Power Cost	7	5	5
6.	Transport Facilities	5	4	8
7.	Community Services	6	5	5
8.	Raw Material	7	3	8
9.	Union Attitude	8	3	5
10.	Political Environment	5	5	5

The list of factors is decided based on their relevance on the type of production facility being decided on. These ratings are then added for each location as follows:

$\Sigma A = 63$, $\Sigma B = 47$, $\Sigma C = 55$ since minimum total belongs to location B, it is considered to be least cost location and hence preferred over the other two.

Weightage Rating Method

In factor rating method, only the cost of provision of facility was considered but all the factors may not have the same bearing on the location. Some factors may have a higher importance than other. Hence in this method, we allot the weightages to various factors, based on their importance, such as union interference in the negative direction may become very important factor for a plant, where there is large involvement of unskilled worker. Similarly, socially a project may not be liked by some community, hence will gain prominence. Political influence of an MLA or an MP for a project may be overriding factor for a particular facility, hence importance of various factors can be considered in the following manner:

1 or 0.1 - lowest importance

10 or 1.0 - highest importance

The factors are then relatively weighed in the range of 1 to 10 or 0.1 to 1.0. The weightages allotted are mentioned against each factor. Multiplying the factor ratings with the respective factor weightage, the sum of these products (Rating × Weightage) against each location are then compared. The lowest total would indicate the most preferred location.This has been illustrated in the tables 7.2 and 7.3:

Table 7.2 Data for Various Locations

Sl.	*Factor*		*Ratings for*		
		Location A	*Location B*	*Location C*	*Weightages*
1.	Land Cost	8	7	4	0.9
2.	Market Proximity	5	7	8	0.4
3.	Labour Availability	8	5	3	0.6
4.	Labour Attitude	4	3	4	0.2
5.	Power Cost	7	5	5	0.7
6.	Transport Facility	5	4	8	0.5
7.	Community Services	6	5	5	0.5
8.	Raw Material	7	3	8	0.6
9.	Union Attitude	8	3	5	0.4
10.	Political Environment	5	5	5	0.3

The revised table of the locations is given below, with the multiplication result of the ratings with the weightages.

Table 7.3 Weighted Factor Rating Method

Sl. No.	Location A	Ratings for Location B	Location C
1.	7.20 (8 × 0.9)	6.30 (7 × 0.9)	3.60 (4 × 0.9)
2.	2.00	2.80	3.20
3.	4.80	3.00	1.80
4.	0.80	0.60	0.80
5.	4.90	3.50	3.50
6.	2.50	2.00	4.00
7.	3.00	2.50	2.50
8.	4.20	1.80	4.80
9.	3.20	1.20	2.00
10.	1.50	1.50	1.50
Total	ΣA = 34.10	ΣB = 25.20	ΣC = 27.70

After comparison of the sum total, location B becomes the most preferred location due to its lowest cost consideration and relative importance of relevant factors.

Bridgeman's Method

In first two methods, there is a high level of subjectivity while allotting either the ratings or the weightages. Hence an improved method (logical and technically sound) must be evolved. Further improvement in the accuracy of the result can be achieved by tangible factors written as their absolute value due to possible quantifiable value, Whereas all intangible or non-qualifiable factors can retain their ratings.

The method makes use of absolute values as well as ratings, thereby reducing the subjectivity to quite an extent.

For working out the preferred location based on Bridgemen's Method, the relationship is as follows

$$\frac{\text{Demerit of Location A}}{\text{Demerit of Location B}} = \left(\frac{OA_1}{OB_1}\right)^{w_1} \times \left(\frac{OA_2}{OB_2}\right)^{w_2} \times \ldots\ldots\ldots\ldots \left(\frac{OA_n}{OB_n}\right)^{w_n}$$

where OA_1 = The value of factor 1 (absolute or rating) for location A

OB_1 = The value of factor 1 for location B

w_1 = The weightage of the factor 1

Similarly all the factors (any number 1 to n) are listed out and the ratios between location A and B are calculated.

As can be seen, the expressions for each factor produces a fraction. All fractions multiplied will also result in a fraction. This fraction can now be used for location preference.

$$\text{If } \frac{\text{Demerit of Location A}}{\text{Demerit of Location B}} > 1, \quad \text{location B is preferred}$$

$$\text{If } \frac{\text{Demerit of Location A}}{\text{Demerit of Location B}} < 1, \quad \text{location is A is preferred}$$

$$\text{If } \frac{\text{Demerit of Location A}}{\text{Demerit of Location B}} = 1, \quad \text{both locations considered equally good}$$

Point to Note: Only two locations can be compared by this method at one time, hence when number of locations to be compared are more than two, we have to increase our computation as comparison of $\frac{\text{loc A}}{\text{loc B}}, \frac{\text{loc B}}{\text{loc C}}$ or $\frac{\text{loc C}}{\text{loc A}}$ etc.

Problem 7.1

Given the following data, compare and suggest better location for a factory, (use Bridgeman's method) :

		Values / Ratings		
Sl.	*Factor*	*Location A*	*Location B*	*Weightages*
1.	Land Cost	230 lakhs	180 lakhs	8
2.	Market Proximity	5	7	4
3.	Labour Availability	30 lakhs	28 lakhs	6
4.	Labour Attitude	4	3	2
5.	Power Cost	70 lakhs	82 lakhs	7
6.	Transport Facility	60 lakhs	70 lakhs	5
7.	Community Services	65 lakhs	60 lakhs	5
8.	Raw Material	110 lakhs	115 lakhs	6
9.	Union Attitude	8	3	4
10.	Political Environment	5	5	3

Solution:

Using Bridgeman's relationship

$$\frac{\text{Demerit of Location A}}{\text{Demerit of Location B}} = \left(\frac{OA_1}{OB_1}\right)^{w_1} \times \left(\frac{OA_2}{OB_2}\right)^{w_2} \times \ldots\ldots\ldots\ldots \left(\frac{OA_n}{OB_n}\right)^{w_n}$$

$$= \left(\frac{230}{180}\right)^8 \times \left(\frac{5}{7}\right)^4 \times \left(\frac{30}{28}\right)^6 \times \left(\frac{4}{3}\right)^2 \times \left(\frac{70}{82}\right)^7 \times \left(\frac{60}{70}\right)^5 \times \left(\frac{110}{115}\right)^6$$

$$\times \left(\frac{8}{3}\right)^4 \times \left(\frac{5}{5}\right)^3$$

$$= 7.11 \times 0.260 \times 1.51 \times 1.76 \times 0.33 \times 0.46 \times 1.49 \times 0.76 \times 50.56 \times 1.00$$

$$= 42.70$$

Since $\frac{\text{Demerit of Location A}}{\text{Demerit of Location B}} > 1$, location B is preferred over A

Centre of Gravity Method

This method is applicable for multi location problem, where a preferred location is worked out with reference to some already existing facilities. Few such situations are given below:

- Establishing a Central warehouse for all existing production facilities.
- Establishing the Corporate Headquarters as central location to existing facilities.
- Establishing a packaging unit, where the individual assemblies produced in various locations are brought to a packaging unit plant, where assembly, packaging and transportation are carried out as a cost effective facility.

It can be understood from the following configuration of existing facilities.

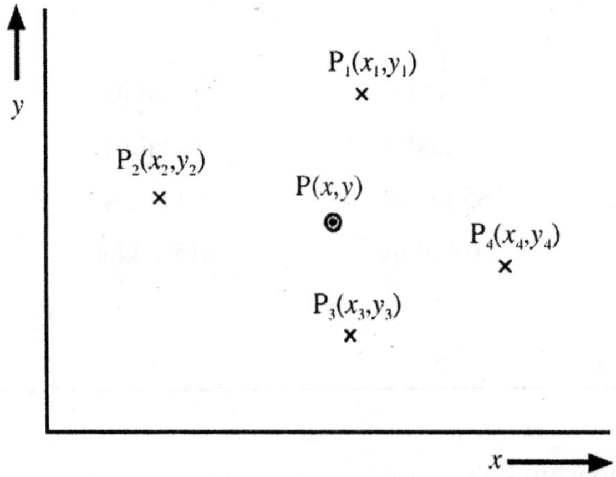

FIG. 7.1. Existing and desired location of facility

Let P_1, P_2, P_3 and P_4 be the existing facilities where as the central locations reference is denoted as P.

Let C_1, C_2, C_3 and C_4 be the unit cost of transportation per unit distance.

The location grids of the existing facilities are

P_1 as (x_1, y_1) P_3 as (x_3, y_3)

P_2 as (x_2, y_2) P_4 as (x_4, y_4)

If the central location of the facility to be established with reference to these existing facilities is represented as P (x, y).

Then, we can compute

$$x = \frac{c_1x_1 + c_2x_2 + c_3x_3 + c_4x_4}{c_1 + c_2 + c_3 + c_4}$$

and

$$y = \frac{c_1y_1 + c_2y_2 + c_3y_3 + c_4y_4}{c_1 + c_2 + c_3 + c_4}$$

The location P (x, y) thus obtained mathematically from the principle of centre of gravity can then be adjusted by the concerned manager to an appropriate location nearby with reference to some compatible or desirable service existing.

The same method can be used for any number of existing facilities, such as

$$x = \frac{c_1x_1 + c_2x_2 + \dots\dots\dots + c_nx_n}{c_1 + c_2 + \dots\dots\dots + c_n}$$

and

$$y = \frac{c_1y_1 + c_2y_2 + \dots\dots\dots + c_ny_n}{c_1 + c_2 + \dots\dots\dots + c_n}$$

Problem 7.2

The locations of the raw material sources are given as P_1 and P_2 and the warehouse location as P_3 and P_4 where the finished goods are shipped to. These locations are P_1 (20, 40), P_2 (10, 30), P_3 (30, 50) and P_4 (40, 60). Calculate the location of the new plant P so as to minimise total transportation cost for the network of facilities, given the unit cost of transportation per unit distance as follows.

Location P_1, Cost C_1 = Rs. 200 per unit distance

Location P_2, Cost C_2 = Rs. 250 per unit distance

Location P_3, Cost C_3 = Rs. 250 per unit distance

Location P_4, Cost C_4 = Rs. 300 per unit distance

Solution:

Let us draw the network diagram to get a clear picture of distances moved (refer fig. 7.2)

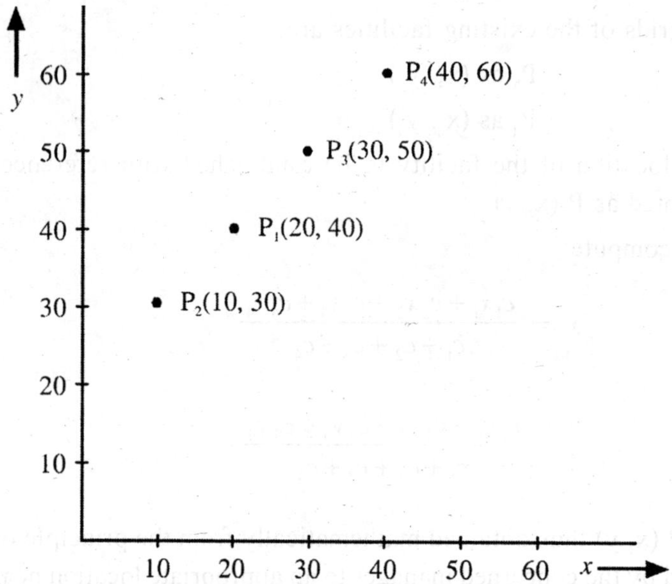

FIG. 7.2. Centre of Capacity Method

If the location of the new plant is taken as P (x_0, y_0), then

$$x_0 = \frac{c_1x_1 + c_2x_2 + c_3x_3 + c_4x_4}{c_1 + c_2 + c_3 + c_4}$$

$$= \frac{200\times20 + 250\times10 + 250\times30 + 300\times40}{200+250+250+300} = 26$$

and
$$y_0 = \frac{c_1y_1 + c_2y_2 + c_3y_3 + c_4y_4}{c_1 + c_2 + c_3 + c_4}$$

$$= \frac{200\times40 + 250\times30 + 250\times50 + 300\times60}{200+250+250+300} = 46$$

Hence the location of the new plant will be (26, 46). Due to administrative reason (infrastructural facilities availability), we can locate the plant at (25, 45), on a higher capacity road, which can be used to advantage to ship the products.

Now we calculate the optimal cost of transportation for this location

$$\text{Total cost of transportation} = c_1[(x_1 - x_0)] + c_2[(x_2 - x_0)] + c_3[(x_3 - x_0)] + c_4[(x_4 - x_0)]$$

$$= c_1[(y_1 - y_0)] + c_2[(y_2 - y_0)] + c_3[(y_3 - y_0)] + c_4[(y_4 - y_0)]$$

$$= [200(25 - 20)] + [250(25 - 10)] + [250(30 - 25)]$$

$$+ [300(40 - 25)] + [200(45 - 40)] + [250(45 - 30)] +$$
$$[250(50 - 45)] + [300(60 - 45)]$$
$$= \text{Rs. } 24{,}000 \text{ for year.}$$

In case, different loads are moved, then the cost calculation will be done on the basis of Ci × Li etc where Li are load moved from i location to new plant (x_0, y_0) with C_i as the unit cost of transportation.

Linear Programming Method

For selection of optimal location, the transportation model can be used to ensure optimal transportation cost of movement. This method is applied when there are number of alternate locations (short listed) available. We can workout the cost of transportation, if some locations are fixed and another optimal is to be chosen. (Assuming that all locations are equally eligible to be the new location)

Problem 7.3

The data on cost and loads are given below. Work out the preferred location for sourcing out of S_3 amd S_4.

Source	*Destination*				*Shipment available*
	D_1	D_2	D_3	D_4	
S_1	200	300	400	450	200
S_2	100	200	100	200	400
S_3	300	200	200	300	300
or, S_4	100	300	400	300	300
Shipment needed	200	200	300	200	

Solution:

If location S_3 is selected as the third source, the allocation of shipment is done with respect to the minimum cost.

Source	D_1	D_2	D_3	D_4	*Availability*
S_1	200	300	400	450 200	200
S_2	100	200	100 200	200	400
S_3	300	200 200	200 100	300	300
Demand	200	200	300	200	

The shipment from S_2 to D_1 is at minimum cost of Rs. 100 and hence total demand of 200 is shipped from here. Similarly the other shipments (as per availability) are S_3 to D_2, S_2 to D_3 and S_1 to D_4.

If we take S_4 as the third source instead of S_3, then the cost will work out to,

Source	D_1	D_2	D_3	D_4	Availability
S_1	200	300 / 200	400	450	200
S_2	100 / 200	200	100 / 200	200	400
S_4	100	300	400 / 100	300 / 200	300
Demand	200	200	300	200	

Hence the transportation cost obtained is

$$= 100 \times 200 + 300 \times 200 + 100 \times 200 + 400 \times 100 + 300 \times 200$$

$$= \text{Rs. } 2{,}00{,}000, \text{ which is more than that from } S_3.$$

Hence S_3 is better location for sourcing.

Due to this allocation at minimal costs, total cost of transportation works out to

$$C = 100 \times 200 + 200 \times 200 + 100 \times 200 + 200 \times 100 + 450 \times 200$$

$$= \text{Rs. } 1{,}90{,}000$$

7.6 Layout Planning

For any business activity, each facility would need a layout for facilitating operations. The facility should gain maximum advantage out of physical movements of various materials needed for any activity or operation. The handling cost minimisation would be possible, if there is a smooth operation across all the activities. This should also enhance the worker productivity. The optimum use of the space available dictates, how well the layout should be planned to facilitate safe working and smooth flow.

The physical arrangement of various facilities should emerge out of the following important considerations:

- What all should be planned for a work centre, so as to maximise productivity ?
- How much space should be earmaked for smooth flow of the materials for the activity planned ?
- How should the space be organised to ensure inter-facility interaction ?

- Where exactly each work centre be located to ensure avoidance of back tracking and distance travelling to reduce cost of handling ?

Hence for the strategic advantage to be obtained from a good layout, the following priorities should be considered:

- Increased customer satisfaction.
- Easy flow of materials and information.
- Efficient utilisation of space.
- Increased productivity of labour and equipment.
- Enhanced safety and improved morale of the workers.
- Improved communications.

Characteristics of a good layout

Based on the strength of the above factors, for any effective layout, following principles can be followed:

- Planned activity inter-relationship.
- Planned straight line material flow.
- Minimum back-tracking
- Minimum handling between operations.
- Planned Material handling methods.
- Layout adaptable to changing operations.
- Adequate storage space and density.
- Minimum walking by production operators.
- Adequate employee service functions.
- Planned control of noise, dirt, fumes and humidity etc.
- Not to impede material flow.
- Planned scrap removal.
- Receiving and shipping in logical locations.
- Maximum flexibility and visibility for safety.

These major characteristics or principles are to be kept in mind while designing any facility layout, be it small enterprise, or in a very large complicated layout (macro level as well as at micro level).

The layout decisions involve the position of various departments as per the operations to be performed. The aim of these placements is to enable a department or a work group to function smoothly without unnecessary loss of efforts / time.

Inputs to the layout decisions:

- Objectives and the criteria for space design.
- Estimate of the demand resulting in the requirements of facilities and their inter-relationships.
- Design of the processes indicating the number of operations, the flow intensity and the pattern of the operations.
- Restriction of the space availability such as area of the plot or building configurations (if already existing).

7.7 Manufacturing Facilities Layouts

The size of the plot or site is derived from the type and numbers of machines and other facilities requirement. This information emerges from capacity requirement planning (CRP) as discussed in the previous chapter. Exact specification of machines, their sizes, alon with the ventilation or movement area, also the information of other supporting facilities like office, canteens, toilets, generator rooms, etc is to be obtained. 50% space for future expansion is also to be added for the size of the plot. The plot is now organised for its filling up with all necessary facilities. The layouts are planned in two stages:

- Macro Level Stage
- Micro Level Stage

In Macro Level Stage, the relative location of various departments is decided whereas at micro level, internal adjustment of machines and other equipment is planned out.

Layout, in general can be defined as

"The locations and relative positioning of all utilities (departments and machines including place for human working and movement, service area and material stores etc.) are arranged for accident free working and cost - effective streamlined production." An extensive planning for macro level as well as micro level positioning of facilities for cost effective production is necessary. Circumstances to necessitate a layout can be as follows:

- Initial setting up of facilities.
- Expansion or diversification of existing product line.
- Change in technology.
- Existing layout proving to be poor, resulting in health hazards.

Macro Level Layout Planning

For developing a macro-level layout, it is essential that the area of each department is worked out with any length or breadth restriction. Therefore, to start any planning on the macro level work, the complete detailed microlevel layout has to be finalised for each department. The foreseeable future expansion in the department is also to be visulised so that necessary space can be earmarked with due integration with the existing facilities. Having known the areas of the departments and the flow process for the entire work, the planning for placing various department can commence. This planning can be adopted in two different ways:

- System Layout Planning (SLP)
- Computerised Layout Planning (CLP)

Systematic Layout Planning

This method is used when number of department are limited and few and it is feasible to handle the layout by manual planning. The SLP has following major steps involved:

Step 1. Identify various departments and enter their respective areas against each.

Step 2. Draw an activity relationship chart (relative location of department in the layout). This chart is called REL-Chart.

Step 3. Place various departments on the layout chart at random locations and transfer the inter-departmental relationship from the REL-chart to this department placing.

Step 4. Re-organise the departments according to closeness rating of the departments, by readjusting places of very close relationship departments together and increasing the distances of open or undesirable relationships. This is called an approximate diagram of the layout.

Step 5. Superimpose the areas of various departments on their respective locations. It may need further readjustment to locations keeping the best of relationships intact. There may be few sacrifices desirable at this stage. The resultant layout is called **Block Diagram** of the layout.

Step 6. Due to various adjustments involved, there are likely to be few alternate layouts possible. These layouts are to be evaluated for optimum advantage and to be finally approved at the highest level of the management.

Various steps described above can be shown as under:

Step 1 and 2 (REL-Chart for departments)

Srl.	Name of the department	Area (M^2)
1.	Office	100
2.	Shop Floor	450
3.	Generator Room	50
4.	Canteens	50
5.	Change Room	25
6.	Toilets	25
7.	Parking Area	150
8.	Stores	200

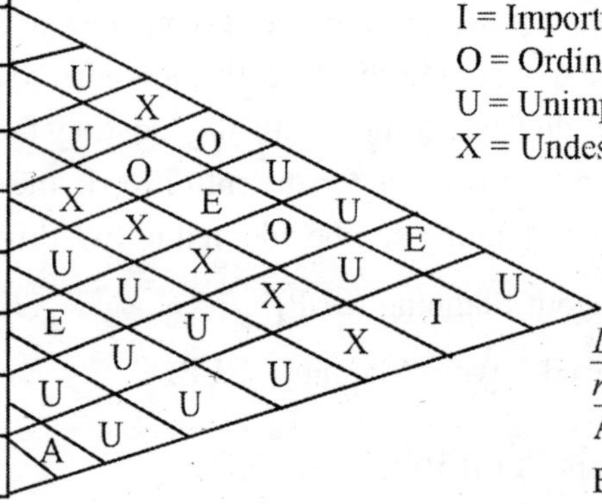

Legend of relationship

A = Absolutely close
E = Essential close
I = Important
O = Ordinarily important
U = Unimportant
X = Undesirable

Legend for drawing relationships

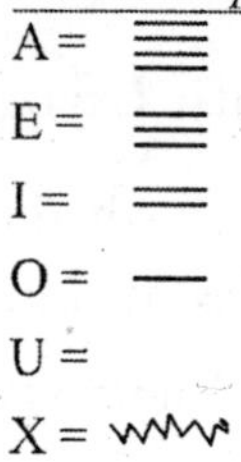

FIG. 7.3. Relationship Chart (REL - Chart)

Step 3

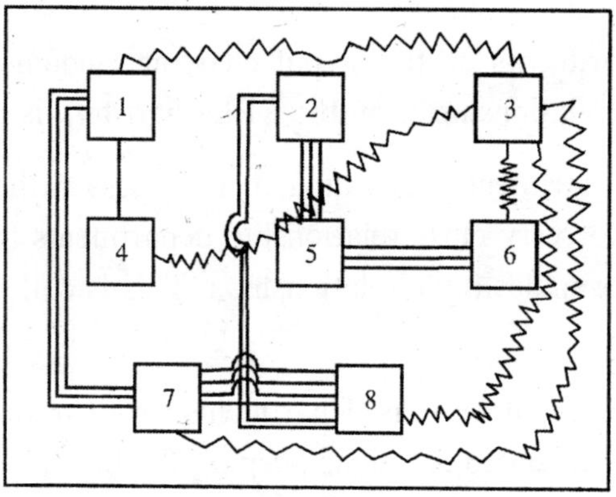

FIG. 7.4 . Relationship of departments drawn

Step 4

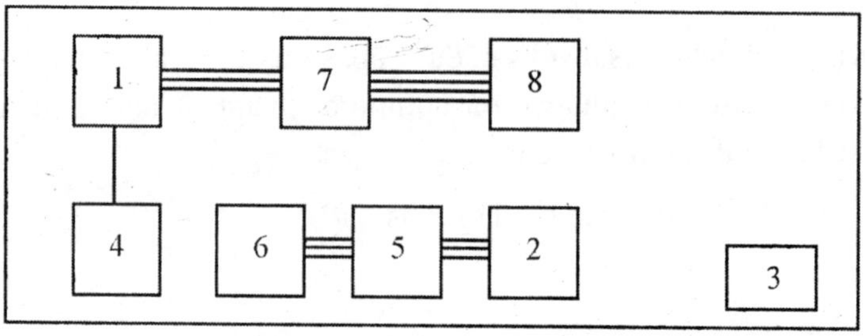

FIG. 7.5. Departments readjusted

Step 5

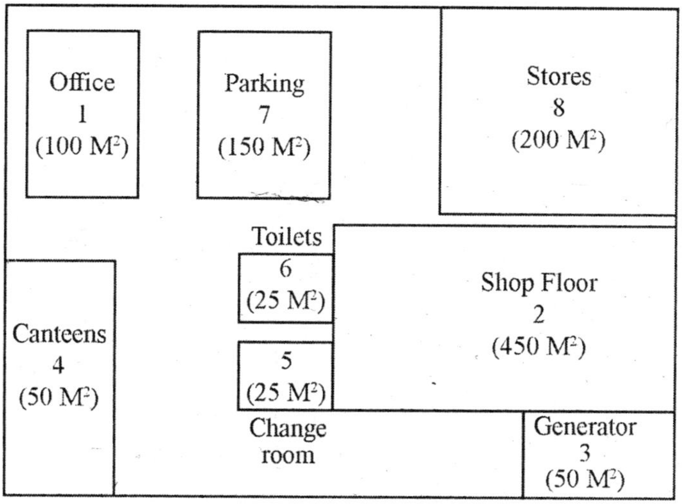

FIG. 7.6. Areas superimposed on Departmental locations (Block Layout)

Step 6

The readjustment of departments 4, 5 and 6 will create alternate layout and can then be weighed for better planning on the ground. Also future expansion areas need be proportionately divided while drawing isles and corridors for smooth material / job flow.

Computerised Layout Planning

In case of Systematic Layout Planning (SLP), the main criterion for layout development has been the activity or departmental relationships and even with this constraint, we could handle only limited number of departments. When the number of activity centres or departments increase, say even 15-20, the layout development becomes complicated and hence the necessity to use computers for the purpose.

For making full use of softwares developed for the purpose, some authentic input data are required to be collected. Few important information matrices are given below:

- ***Travel or Flow Matrix:*** This is a modified chart as compared to REL - chart. Here the relationship is connected to the total cost of movement of facilities from one department to another and the total cost incurred will depend on the total distance covered during such inter-departmental move. The intensity of traffic play an equally important role. Hence it is essential to develop the travel chart or flow chart of the departments. One such chart is drawn below:

Table 7.5 Frequency of Movements (Flow Matrix)

	Departments									
	1	2	3	4	5	6	7	8	9	10
1	–	15	20	25	0	70	65	5	15	35
2	–	–	10	30	25	5	10	25	10	40
3	–	–	–	0	20	60	0	50	45	95
4	–	–	–	–	45	75	50	0	5	10
5	–	–	–	–	–	0	5	10	15	60
6	–	–	–	–	–	–	30	80	5	0
7	–	–	–	–	–	–	–	55	0	0
8	–	–	–	–	–	–	–	–	40	30
9	–	–	–	–	–	–	–	–	–	20
10	–	–	–	–	–	–	–	–	–	–

- ***Flow - Cost Matrix:*** Similarly a flow-cost chart or matrix is to be prepared to act as input to the computer programme. In this chart, we reflect the total-cost of flow or movement of material or any facility from one department to another. It is to be done in term of cost per fixed unit distance (say 20 meters) standardised for all departments) This flow cost chart takes care the unit cost of travel, which may be different from one place to another, depending on type of transportation available. A sample flow cost matrix is drawn below:

Table 7.6 Total Cost of Movement (Flow Cost Matrix)

	Departments							
	1	2	3	4	5	6	7	8
1	–	110	120	70	65	0	80	70
2	–	–	50	0	60	70	50	10
3	–	–	–	45	75	25	0	80
4	–	–	–	–	50	60	70	0
5	–	–	–	–	–	15	25	75
6	–	–	–	–	–	–	45	120
7	–	–	–	—	–	–	–	100
8	–	–	–	–	–	–	–	–

Reflecting

$C_{ij} = c_{ij} \times d_{ij} \times n_{ij}$

where

C_{ij} = Total cost

c_{ij} = unit cost

d_{ij} = distance travel

n_{ij} = flow intensity

There are number of softwares used for layout purposes. There are basically two types of software heuristics developed for layouts over a period of time:

- Improvement algorithm
- Construction algorithm

Improvement Algorithm

This algorithm can be used for improving an already existing layout, but not for developing a layout. The software developed by Armour and Buffa (published in Management Science 1963) was named as CRAFT. It is described below:

CRAFT (Computerised Relative Allocation of Facilities Technique)

It was initially developed to handle upto 40 departments

Basic Inputs

- Travel chart.
- Initial or existing or any layout.
- Distances taken from the centroids of the departments.
- Area and number of departments.
- Flow and cost data or flow cost matrix
- Any restricted area.

Procedure for iterations. It is an iterative heuristic and is a well-directed search technique based on steepest descend. The working principle is shortest descent pairwise inter-change (SDPI), in which the departments in the existing layout are interchaged (only one pair at a time) and process of pairwise interchange continuous till the resultant cost benefit becomes negative.

This means that if the cost is reduced due to interchange of any two departments at a time, it is treated as an improved layout. If cost increases, this change is rejected for creating inefficient layout.

A typical improvement in layout is shown below:

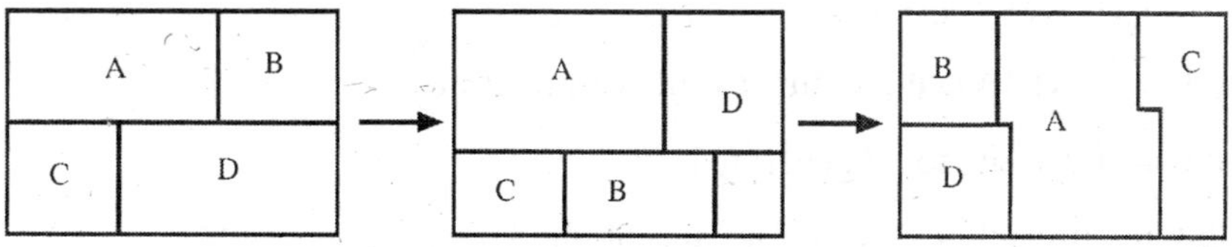

FIG. 7.7. Progressive improvements in layout

It is important to note that the distances for travelling of material from one department to another is taken as eucledeon distance and not straight line distance. The departmental centroids are identified and distances between centroids accordingly marked.

Limitations of CRAFT

- Material handling is the sole objective used in layout planning. The departmental inter-relationships are not considered.

- Non-production departments cannot be included in the layout improvement unless the concept of material handling is altered, such as cost of paper/files movement in case of office.
- Undesirable location relationship not taken into account.
- It uses encledeon distances between centroids.
- The efficiency of final layout will depend on the initial layout. If initial layout is very inefficient, improvement may not be optimal desired.

Since it was only a layout improvement heuristic, with so many limitations, there were other layout (construction or development) softwares developed later.

Large Construction Algorithm

During 1967, the very early stage of computer technology development, two construction algorithms were developed, namely:

- ALDEP (Automated Layout Design Program)
- CORE LAP (Computerised Relationship Layout Planning)

ALDEP

This algorithm was developed by seeh of and Evans and the work was published in the Journal of Industrial Engineering December 1967. Due to limited computer capability at that time, this program could be used for developing layout involving only upto 63 departments and a three - story building configuration. In this algorithm, the evaluation capability has been added, so that improvement in the layout design can be affected and evaluated.

Basic inputs:

- Length, width and area of each floor (building outline plan)
- Scale of the layout print out
- Number of departments in the layout with their areas
- Number of layouts to be generated
- Minimum allowable score for an acceptable layout
- Minimum departmental preference, A , E etc
- REL - chart
- Location and size of any restricted area for each floor.

Procedure for Layout Development

- The total area of the plot to be divided into a number of bays, each of appropriate width (considering width of the departments)

- Select the first department for placement in the layout randomly out of total number of departments and place it in the north-west corner of the plot in the first bay. Width being fixed, area is to be adjusted in length through this bay. Department placed in the layout is called a WINNER.
- The second department to be placed next to the above winner is to be chosen as VICTOR based on the highest departmental closeness rating or preference, by scanning through the REL - chart fed as an input. While scanning through the REL chart for the highest relationship with the already placed department, computer selects the highest relationship for the Victor with the Winner,. but not below the rating as per input condition indicated above. The Victor is picked up and placed right next to the winner in the same bay as per the vertical scanning pattern. As soon as the placement is done, this department will act as winner for the next victor.
- In case, computer is unable to locate a victor for the last winner due to absence of highest relationship desired, then the victor is chosen randomly and placed next to the last winner, adjusting its area in the bay space.
- When there is a problem of clear selection of victor due to more than one victor possible with the same relationship (say 3 departments have same rating E with the last winner) then, the victor selection is random out of the departments in tie of relationship. (ie., any one randomly out of these three departments each with E rating with the last winner).
- The selection and placement of successive victors continues till the last department in the first bay has been placed. The next victor, then, is placed right next to the last winner, but in the next adjacent bay and the process continues for all the bays in the similar manner. The placement pattern flows as per the arrows indicated in Fig. 7.8 belows:

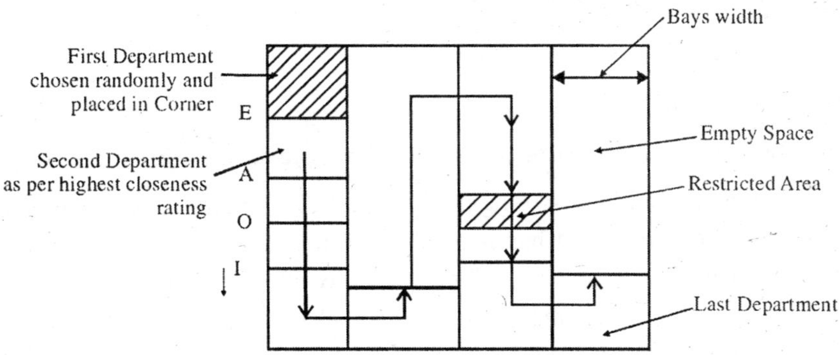

FIG. 7.8. Scanning Pattern in ALDEP

- Wherever a restricted area (as marked above in Fig. 7.8) comes in the way of placing any victor, the victor will be placed next to the restricted area as marked.
- The empty space will be available only after the last victor has been placed in position.
- The scoring is used as the evaluation technique for the layout. For the score, the successive relationships *i.e.*, A, E, I, O, U, or X between departments placed in the layout are added as per the numerical values of these relationships.

These numerical values are:

$A = 4^3 = 64$

$E = 4^2 = 16$

$I = 4^1 = 4$

$O = 4^0 = 1$

$U = 0$

$X = (-4)^5 = -1024$

Hence the score will be worked out as follows

Score = E + A + O + I + A + E + U + X + ... etc.

= 16 + 64 + 1 + 4 + 64 + 16 + 0 – 1024 + ... etc.

- For evaluation to stop, we have to assign any positive value say 328 (any negative score layout is rejected by the computer for print out). Then based on input data, only limited number of layouts as per condition are printed by the computer, having a score either equal to or more than the minimum allowable score specified (say in this case 328), Minimum score that can be specified is zero.
- For selection of best layout, the printed layouts are arranged in the order of descending score pattern and then superimposing any pressing constraint to pick up the suitable list of alternate layouts.

Drawbacks

Following are obvious limitations of this software algorithm:

- Random selection of departments.
- Wide fluctuation in relationship valuation.
- Placement or scanning pattern.
- No restriction on X-rated departments (*i.e.*, undesirable departments can be placed together)
- Due to scanning pattern and scoring method, best or optimum layout may not be printed. For example, if the last deptt has X-rating with the earlier winner, the score, per force, may become negative. Hence even a very good layout of 123 score will not be printed as the total score will then become 1023 – 1024 = –1 (negative)

CORELAP (Computerised Relationship Layout Planning)

This is an improved version over ALDEP with the drawbacks of ALDEP taken care of. This Algorithm was developed by Lee and Moore, during 1967.

This algorithm could take care of the layout of not more than 45 departments, when developed and is described below:

Basic inputs

- REL chart
- Number and areas of the departments
- Length and width ratio of departments
- Other inputs as in case of ALDEP

Procedure of Layout Development

- Initially the computer works out the total closeness rating of all the departments based on REL chart information. Total closeness rating of department is the sum total of ratings of all other departments with any department. Hence $TCR_{(i)} = \sum_{1}^{n} R_{ij}$ for ith department. Where R_{ij} denotes the rating of department *i* and *j*.
- The numerical values of the relationships are applied in the modified way (as distinct from ALDEP) as A = 6, E = 5, I = 4, O = 3, U = 2, X = 1 (these are much better stepped with no negative values for X)
- Computer selects the first department for placing in the layout based on the highest TCR.
- The first department so chosen is placed in the middle of the layout (called the winner).
- The victor for this winner is chosen based on the highest departmental rating is A, E etc and placed next to the winner.
- The successive victors are placed around the earlier winner in succession. It is either in the clockwise or anticlockwise direction as marked in the scanning pattern.

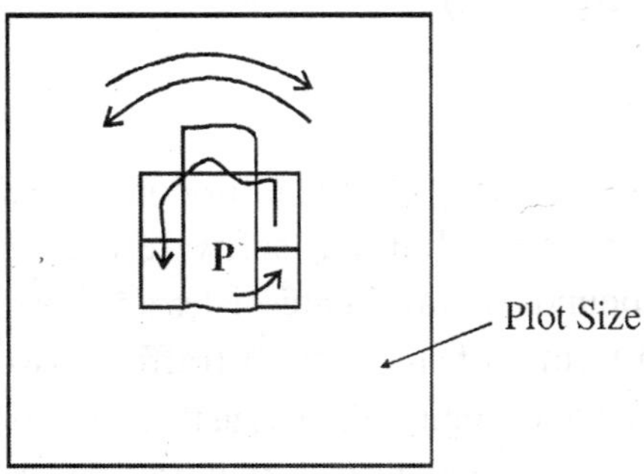

FIG. 7.9. Scanning Pattern of CORELAP (First Deptt P placed in the middle)

- In case of a tie for the victor amongst similarly related departments, the selection is based on the highest TCR from amongst the tie departments.
- In case of no suitable department found as per minimum departmental preference ie., no A or E etc, then Victor is chosen based on the highest TCR again.

Evaluation Criterion

The highest value score layouts in the descending order will be preferred for consideration.

Advantages Over ALDEP

- No random selection of departments.
- TCR is the criterion for closer placement.
- No negative rating for X-rated departments.
- No wide variation in closeness ratings.
- Start point of layout is centre of the plot

Other Important Softwares

Some other softwares developed for layout purposes are:

- LAYOPT - General Purpose Layout Optimising Programme
- PLANET - Plant layout Analysis and Evaluation Technique
- PREP - Plant Relayout and Evaluation Package
- COFAD - Computerised Facilities Design
- CAN - Q - (Computer Analysis of Network of Queues)

In fact, with the present level of IT - development, a large number of captive Softwares for facilities layout even for improved version of manufacturing and services are being developed. One such forceful software "MAYNARD" has been developed by the firm of the same name (based in Pittsberg, USA)

7.8 Present Status of Softwares

With the advancement of technology, the utility of the system has become large with cost of the layout as a major criterion. Today a software can develop total architecture of the manufacturing facility like boundary walls, gates, isles and corridors etc and departments placed show their relationships in terms of intensity of traffic between them. This is shown on the screen as bands (thicker the band, higher the intensity). If two departments of higher intensity are to be brought together to reduce material handling cost, the menu-based system enables it and as per result of readjusted layout total, cost is reflected on the screen. It can help in taking a decision if the layout has improved due to cost reduction.

With the help of Systematic Layout Planning (SLP) or Computer Layout Planning (CLP), the evaluation of the existing layout can result in the improvement of the layout and strealinng achieved as follows: (Refer Fig. 7.10)

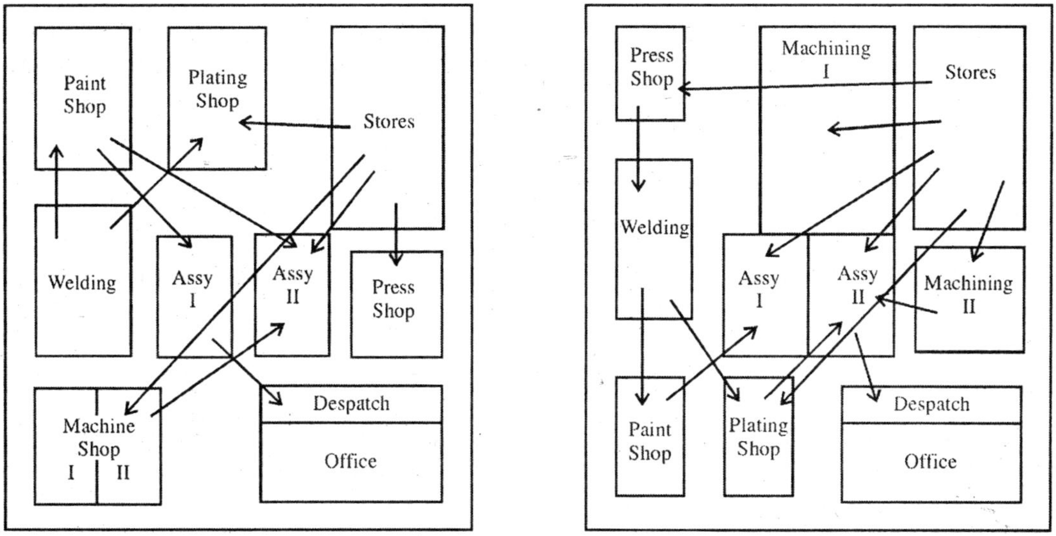

FIG. 7.10. Improvement in Layout

Problem 7.4

In an organisation, there are ten departments, getting the materials from the stores. As per the layout, the stores can be located either at position A or at B. The number of loads for each department are mentioned in the figure. Each group can be taken as unit distance apart. Workout, which position of stores is better suited.

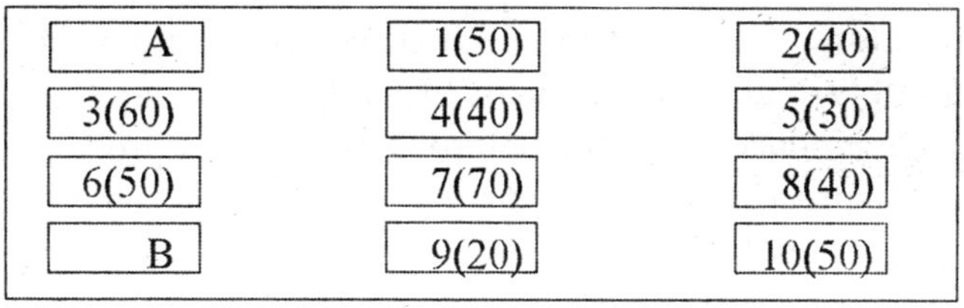

Solution:

The load distance chart can be prepared as follows

For Location A				*For Location B*			
Area	*Distance*	*Loads*	*Load Distance result*	*Area*	*Distance*	*Loads*	*Load Distrance result*
1	1	50	50	1	4	50	200
2	2	40	80	2	5	40	200
3	1	60	60	3	2	60	120
4	2	40	80	4	3	40	120
5	3	30	90	5	4	30	120
6	2	50	100	6	1	50	50
7	3	70	210	7	2	70	140
8	4	40	160	8	3	40	120
9	4	20	80	9	1	20	20
10	5	50	250	10	2	50	100
		Total	1160			Total	1170

The basis of efficient layout, in this case, is takent as cost. The cost per unit distance inside the factory are assumed to be uniform, so that the material handling cost minimisation produces better layout.

As can be seen from the table above, the load distance results are as under:

Stores at A Load distance result = 1160 units

Stores at B Load distance result = 1170 units

Since stores A location results in less cost (less load-distance), it is preferred to place the store at location A.

7.9 Microlevel Layout Planning

The micro level layout is also called "Plant Layout" or "Facility Design". The Layout design depends on the type of production planned to establish the facilities on the ground to ensure cost-effective production system. There are two types of production systems:

- Intermittent Production
- Continuous Production

Intermittent Production: In this type of production, the process of manufacture can be started and stopped depending on the type or stage of the job. There can be either job shop production, wherein individual and different jobs are undertaken, as and when demanded or it could also be a Batch production activity, where smaller volumes of the same product are manufactured and activity comes to a halt as soon as these jobs are over.

Continuous Production: This type of production involves a specialised continuous manufacture of a large quantity of identical products. In mass-production, a large number of similar (standardised) products are produced, preferable through automated product lines. Another type of continuous productions is process type industry products, where the intermediate stoppage can be very costly. In such jobs, the output of one workcentre is the input to the next work centre and process has to be continuous, so as not to loose the workdone of one centre to the other centre. Manufacture of medicines, fertilisers and paper etc fall under this catagory.

Types of Micro-layouts

The choice of layout depends on the process selected and the type of activities required to be performed so as to produce the product for the entire requirement and to the satisfaction of the customer.

There are following types of layouts adopted for any particular job:

- Process layout or Flexible-flow layout
- Product layout or Line-flow layout
- Fixed position layout
- Mixed layout
- Hybrid or Cellular layout

Process layout or Flexible-flow layout: This layout is created for a situation when a number of products need a workcentre but it is primarily low-volume, high customisation situation. In this case, we create shops of similar process machines laid out for use by any product at any time, provided an appropriate machine is available for such a use. For example, all drilling machines, all milling or painting machines are located in one area, therby organising the reasources as per the function, not for any specific product. The advantage of such a layout is better utilisation of available resources, reduction in idle time of men and machines, reduced initial capital investment for not buying many machines of similar type, which could be the necessity if resources are dedicated for any specific product only. A major challenge for designing such a layout is the relative position of work centres for avoiding any confusion in apparent chaos of divergent process with flexible work flow.

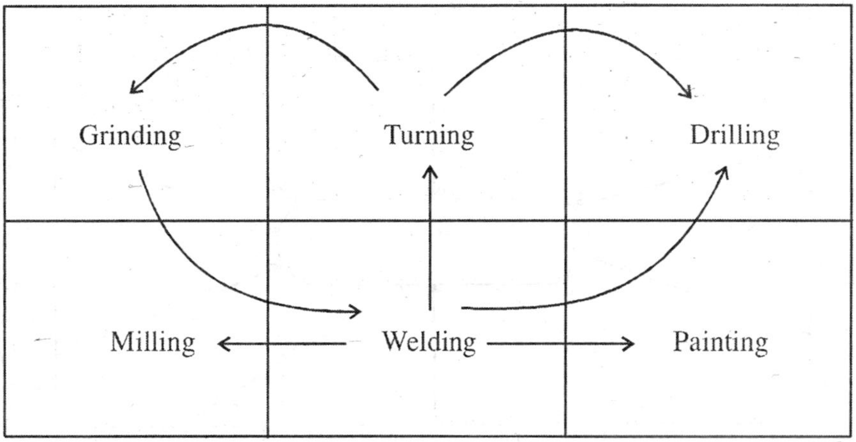

Fig. 7.11. Process layout

Product or line-flow layout: This layout is adopted on a linear flow pattern for repetitive type of jobs. In this case all facilities are arranged in a linear fashion as per the sequence of operation of the product, for which the layout is designed. It tranpires that each product would need a line or product layout for itself and hence duplication of similar machines cannot be avoided. The chances of few machines (of lesses or operation time) remaining idle are large. It is a conitnous flow uniform rate production layout and hence would need a better balancing of intermediate work centres.

The production volumes are high, but it is for a standardised product. It has the inherent advantage of smooth and logical flow lines (as per sequence of operations for a product) and reduced material handling. The design, planning and control of the flow lines are easy, but balancing various work centres is tough task (The balancing of such production lines is being discussed in the next part of the chapter). It is capital intensive resource layout.

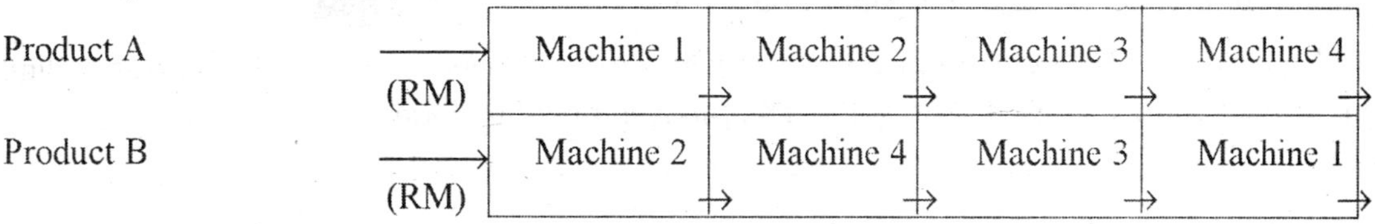

FIG. 7.12. Product Layout

Fixed Layout: In this arrangement, the manufacturing product is fixed in place and other resources such as manpower and their equipment converge to the facility site. This layout is suitable when the product is particularly heavy and difficult to move. Ship-building, air-craft assembly, locomotive assembly, construction of a house or a dam etc. are few important examples for this catagory of the layout. This layout is useful for uniform rate work, but it is expensive and time-consuming. Though process design and scheduling is comparatively easy, the resource-utilisation level is low.

The typical fixed layout for ship-building is illustrated in Fig. 7.13.

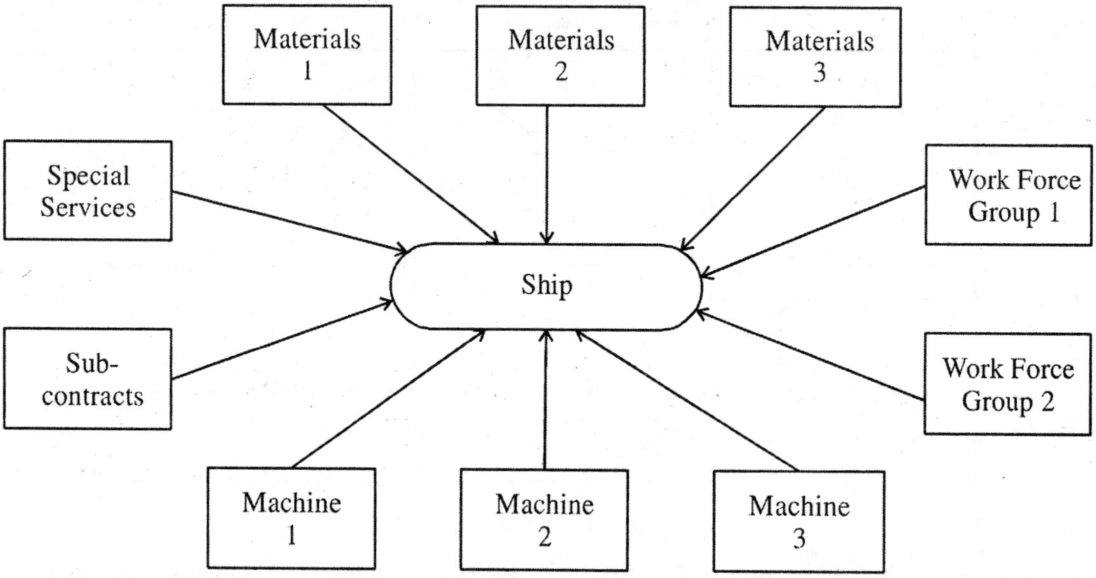

FIG. 7.13. Fixed amount

Mixed Layout: In this type of layout, generally, the company organises both basic layout namely Product and Process Layout to get advantage of both, at the same time. The manufacture of product/ assemblies/ components is done through "Process Layout", ensuring cost-effective work through better resource-utilisation and then adopting "Product Layout" for the Product Assembly operations.

Hybrid Cellular Layout: To take the advantage of both the basic labouts, the companies use combined elements of a flexible-flow or process labout and that of a line flow or product layout.

These layouts are created when the volumes are not very large and when production and assembly of product are to be done under one roof.

A typical hybrid layout is given in Fig. 7.14 wherein the machine centres are arranged according to Processes and the product passes through centres in flow-line form.

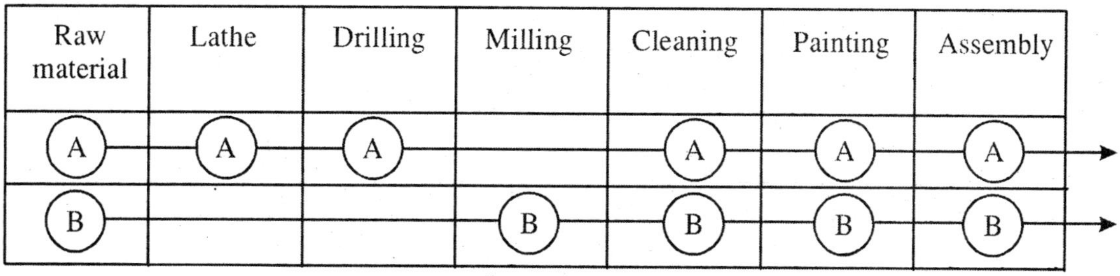

FIG. 7.14. Hybrid Layout

The 'hybrid layout' can be created in two different ways:

- One-worker, multiple machine operations.
- Multiple machine of different type with set of worker operating these in a small group for a specific product. This is called "Group Technology" cell system.

One Worker, Multiple-Machine (OWMM) Cells: When the job volume is not very high the line-manager or the production manager can decide alloting few machines to a worker to be operated simultaneously to achieve a line-flow. One worker can also be given the responsibility of operating a number of similar machines. Both the arrangements, obviously, need different types of skilled operators. It is more useful when the machines are automatic and need less attention, compared to semi-automatic or mechanical machines.

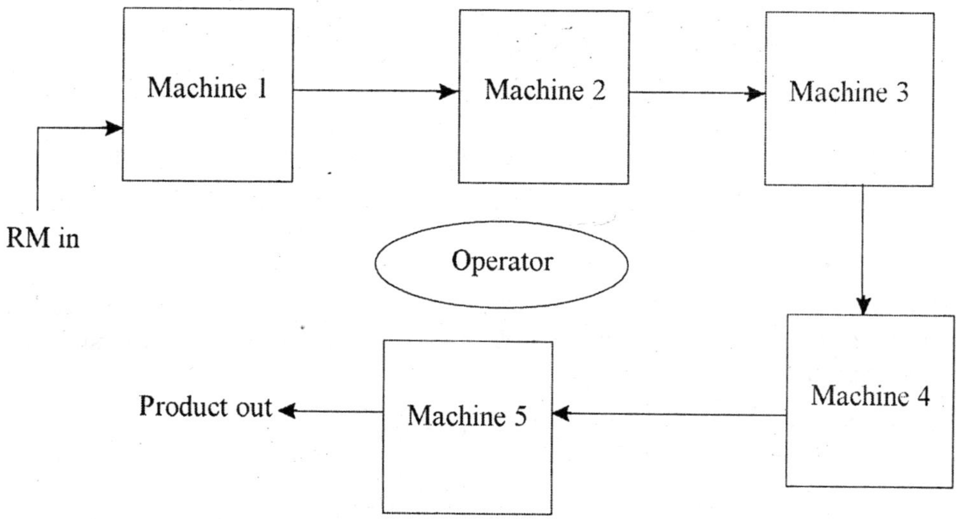

FIG. 7.15. One Man, Multiple-Machine Cell

Group Technology (GT): This is also an option of layout when the volume of production is low, but variety of similar basic product is desired. In this case the operation cells are created for a group of machine (each cell as Product Layout) with set of workers to operate them. It is a unique way of selecting a work (or part products) to be done by a cell. Thus, group parts or whole products with similar characterstics are catagorised into a "family" and groups of machines and operators are allocated for their production. These families are based on size, shapes and manufacturing requirements, for example, bolts of different types/ sizes can be grouped as a "family". A typical Group Technology (GT) Layout is given in Figure 7.16 below.

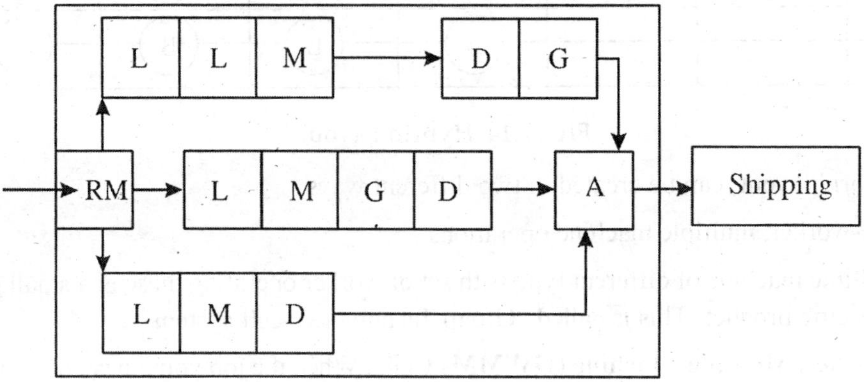

FIG. 7.16. GT Cells

where in L = Lathe Machines
M = Milling Machines
G = Grinding Machines
D = Drilling Machines
A = Assembly Area
RM = Raw Material

The detailed discussion on the GT cell system has already been done in chapter 9.

Flexible Manufacturing System (FMS): Another similar layout is used in case of Flexible Manufacturing System, wherein the operations manager create a hybrid layout, introducing cells and flexible automation. This is primarily a computer-controlled production system. A cell has two or more dissimlar work-stations located close, through which a number of parts are changing the route of one cell product to different cells. With varied capacity, the variety of similar family products can be produced.

This system has also been discussed under chapter 11.

7.10 Line Balancing Situations in Product Layout

The production planning in a mass production system or assembling operations amounts to establishing facilities in such a way that we can maintain a definite rate of production and to achieve that production rate with optimal workforce level. While the production rate is indicated as cycle time to produce one unit of the product, the optimum utilisation of work force depends on the basis of output norms. The actual output of the individual may be different from the output norms. The time to operate the system, hence, keeps varying. It is, therefore, necessary to group certain activities to workstations to the tune of maximum of cycle time at each work station. The assembly line, then, needs balancing so that there is minimum waiting of the line due to different operation time at each workstation. The sequencing is, therefore, not only allocation of men and machines to operating activities, but also optimal utilisation of facilities by proper balancing of the assembly line.

The line balancing involves the following:

- Listing of all elemental activities and estimate their individual operation time.
- Writing down the sequencial requirement (technical or technological sequencing/priority) in the form of a precedence diagram.

We can use visual or heuristic methods to balance the lines.

Visual Method of Balancing

Problem 7.5

Let us consider the flooowing tasks, whose elements are marked on the precedence network below:

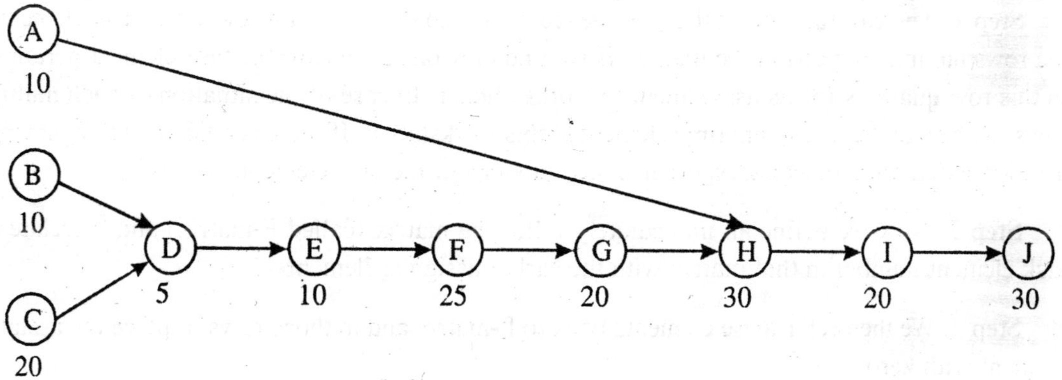

FIG. 7.17. Process Flow Diagram

The figure on each element A, B, C etc. marked are the operation time for each activity. If the output of this line is 60 minutes as cycle time, workout the sequencing of various workstation and clubbing of activities at each workstation.

Solution:

Total operation time of the product

$$= 10 + 10 + 20 + 5 + 10 + 25 + 20 + 30 + 20 + 30\text{min} = 180 \text{ minutes}$$

Cycle time of the line = 60 minutes

To balance the line, the sequencing of the activities can be done as follows. (Taking into account the technical sequence as per precedence diagram and cycle time for the line).

Workstation	*Groupin 1*	*Workstation Time*	*Grouping II*	*Workstation Time*
I	ABCDE	55	BCDE	45
II	FG	45	FG	45
III	HI	50	AHI	60
IV	J	30	J	30

This type of grouping is achieved by visual method.

Moodie and Young's Heuristic

This is a systematic heuristic method for assembly line balancing for proper sequencing of activities.

First of all, a precedence matrix, listing out immediately preceding activities, (P-matrix) and immediately following activities (F-matrix). The heuristic method involves following steps–

Step 1. The careful look at the precedence matrix so drawn would reveal the task element of the rows having all zeros in the matrix. If we find only one such row, the task element pertaining to this row qualifies for its assignment to workstation 1. In case of the situation of such multiple rows, we assign the maximum time element to this workstation. If there is a tie, then assignment is decided based on manager's experience, *i.e.*, any one of the task element.

Step 2. Now we define an immediately following matrix (called F-matrix) and correlate the task element number in that matrix with the earlier assigned element.

Step 3. We then refer these elements back to P-matrix and in those rows, replace the assigned element with zero.

Step 4. We again assign the next work element based on step 1 and keep repeating step 1, 2 and 3 for further assignments. The process of such assignments would continue till such time the total workstation time is either equal to or less than the cycle time.

Step 5. Now we start assigning to workstation 2 and follow similar procedure.

The heuristic method has been illustrated with the help of a problem 7.6.

Problem 7.6

Work out assigning workstations to work element defined in the table with cycle time as 60 minutes.

Work Element	*Time of each work element (min)*	*Precedence (Immediate predecessor element)*
A	10	—
B	10	—
C	20	—
D	5	B, C
E	10	D
F	25	E
G	20	F
H	30	G, A
I	20	H
J	30	I

Solution:

Let us first prepare P and F-matrices out of the table given in the problem.

Work	*Element number*	*P-matrix*			*F-matrix*		
A	1	0	0	0	8	0	0
B	2	0	0	0	4	0	0
C	3	0	0	0	4	0	0
D	4	2	3	0	5	0	0
E	5	4	0	0	6	0	0
F	6	5	0	0	7	0	0
G	7	6	0	0	8	0	0
H	8	1	7	0	9	0	0
I	9	8	0	0	10	0	0
J	10	9	0	0	0	0	0

Workstation 1

Step 1. In the P-matrix, we find three rows with all zeros and hence we assign based on the element time. Work element 3(C) has largest time and hence is first to be assigned to workstation number 1.

Step 2. Against work element 3 so assigned to workstation 1, we notice work element4 in F-matrix.

Step 3. This element is assigned zero in the P-matrix against element 3(C). This leaves row 4 as 2, 0, 0 and is not all-zero's row.

Step 4. Now we are left with rows for element 1(A) and 2(B), with all zeros and since time of both the element is same, we assign any, say element 1(A) to workstation 1.

Total workstation time row = 20 (element 6) + 10 (Element A)] = 30 minutes

Unutilised cycle time = 60 – 30 = 30 minutes

We notice work element 8 against element 1(A) in the F-matrix and if we replace zero against element 1(A) in the P-matrix for the row of work element 8, we get row as 0, 7, 0. It is not a all-zero row, hence does not qualify for assignment consideration.

Now, we have only one row having all zeros in P-matrix and that is work element 2(B). Since its element time is 10, less than the unutilised time of the workstation 1, it can be assigned to workstation 1.

Total unutilised time of WS 1 = 30 – 10 = 20 minutes

We have assigned element 2(B), we read row against this in the F-matrix, and it is found to be 4. By replacing 2 with a zero against element 4 in P-matrix, we get modified row 4 as 0, 0, 0 which is the only all-zero row. Hence element 4(D) qualifies next for assignment to workstation 1. Time for element 4(D) is less than the remaining unutilised time of workstation 1.

Now, unutilised time for WS 1 = 20 – 5 = 15 minutes.

Having assigned work element 4(D), we notice element 5 against it in F-matrix.

Substitute zero against element 4 in the row for element 5.

By this process, we get only one row 3 for element number 5 as all zero row and hence qualifies for next assignment. The time for element 5(E) is 10 min., which is still less than the remaining unutilised time of workstation 1. Element 5 is, therefore, assigned to this workstation.

Remaining unutilised time for WS 1 = 15 – 10 = 5 minutes.

Since there is no more element with time less than 5 min, we close assignments to workstation 1. We then concentrate on workstation 2.

Workstation 2

The last work element assigned is element 5(E). Having replaced 5 with zero in P-matrix against element 6 (from F-matrix for last assignment element 5), we get row for element 6 as 0, 0, 0 and it qualifies for assigning to WS 2. Following the same procedure, we now replaced 6 in P-matrix against element 7, we get all zero row and hence element 7(E) is also assigned to WS 2. Total allocated time for WS 2 is 25 + 20 = 45 min.

Unutilised time for WS 2 = 60 – 45 = 15 min

We do not have any work element left with equal or less than 15 min. Hence no more assignments to workstation 2.

Workstation 3

Last assigned element to WS 2 was 7(G). Replacing 7 by zero in P-matrix, we get element 8 as 0, 0, 0 row. Thus, element 8(H) is next to be assigned to WS 3.

We have element 9(I) in F-matrix against element 8, we replace element 9 with a zero in P-matrix and get last row (element 10) as all-zero row. Thus element 10(J) is next to be assigned.

Unutilised time after assigning element 8 and 9

= 60 – (30 + 20) = 10 min.

Since time left for WS 3 is less than for element 10, it cannot be assigned to WS 3.

Workstation 4

The only element left for assignment is 10(J) and hence is allocated to WS 4.

Thus the work element allocations to various workstations are:

Workstation	*Element assigned*	*Work station time*
WS 1	3, 1, 2, 4, 5 (ABCDE)	55 min
WS 2	6, 7 (FG)	45 min
WS 3	8, 9 (HI)	50 min
WS 4	10 (J)	30 min

Rank-Position Weight (RPW) Method of line Balancing

This is yet another method of balancing the assembly line (Primarily a Product Layout). In this case, the Rank-Position Weight (RPW) is calculated for each activity or operation based on their respective processing time and sequence in the operation.

RPW for an activity is calculated as under:

$RPW_{(i)}$ = ti + processing time for all the activities following activity *i*.

Where ti = processing time for the activity i.

For the purpose of calculating the PRW for each activity, the relation ship or precedence diagram is drawn so that the preceeding/ following activities can be easily identified.

In order to design the work centres with best possible balancing, the following steps are to be followed:

Step 1: Break down the total work into number of smaller operations/ activities (called the WBS) which can be seprepated and performed independently on various work centres.

Step 2: Draw the precedence diagram or Activity-relationship network based on WBS given above.

Step 3: Mark the processing time of each activity on the network.

Step 4: Calculated the RPWs for all activities as suggested above.

Step 5: Rearrange the activities in the descending order of their RPWs and mark the processing time against each activity in this table.

Step 6: Work out the cycle time of the product based on the demand/ production requirement.

Step 7: Work out the total time requirment for the entire work (or product) by adding individual times of activities and calculate approximate number of workstations by dividing the total product time by the cycle time.

Step 8: Now, start assigning various activities to work centres based on the RPW sequence table, by following the sequence as given below:

(*a*) Highest RPW

(*b*) Sequence priority of the activity.

(*c*) Cycle time/ unutilised cycle time for a work centre.

The proceduce has been illustrated through Problem 7.7 given below:

Problem 7.7

A company is setting up an assembly line to produce 192 units during a day (8-hrs shift). Various work elements with their respective processing times and their inter-relations are given below:

Work element	*Processing Time (Seconds)*	*Innediate Predecessor*
A	40	None
B	70	A
C	30	D, E, F
D	40	B
E	50	B
F	30	B
G	20	A
H	120	G
I	130	H
J	110	C, I

Using RPW method Decide on the assignment of the work elements to various workstation for the best balance.

Solution:

Step 1: The activities have been segregated as A to J and their processing times have been mentioned in the problem.

Step 2: The procedure matrix has been drawn indicating the preceeding activities. The precedence diagram or relationship network is drawn as follows:

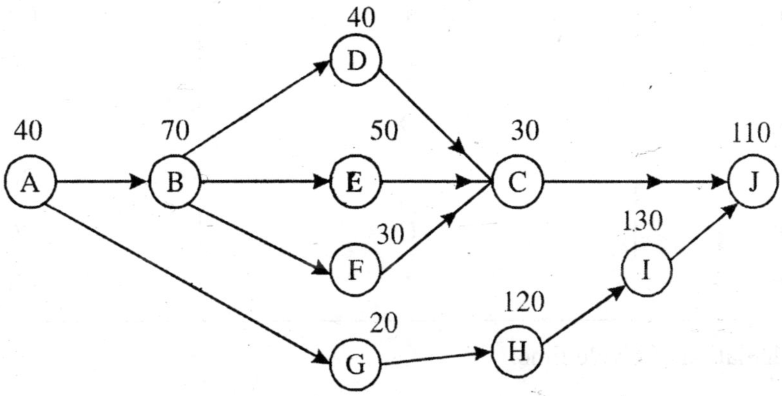

Step 3: The processing times of individual activities have been marked on the above network itself in seconds.

Step 4: From the above network, the relationship of the activities clearly bring out the activities following a particular activity. Hence we calculate the RPW for each activity as follows:

(*i*) $RPW_{(A)} = 40 + 70 + 20 + 40 + 50 + 30 + 120 + 30 + 120 + 110 = 330$ Seconds

(*ii*) $RPW_{(B)} = 70 + 40 + 50 + 30 + 30 + 110 = 330$ Seconds

(*iii*) $RPW_{(C)} = 30 + 110 = 140$ Seconds

(*iv*) $RPW_{(D)} = 40 + 30 + 110 = 180$ Seconds

(*v*) $RPW_{(E)} = 50 + 30 + 110 = 190$ Seconds

(*vi*) $RPW_{(F)} = 30 + 30 + 110 = 170$ Seconds

(*vii*) $RPW_{(G)} = 20 + 120 + 130 + 110 = 380$ Seconds

(*viii*) $RPW_{(H)} = 120 + 130 + 110 = 360$ Seconds

(*ix*) $RPW_{(I)} = 130 + 110 = 240$ Seconds

(*x*) $RPW_{(J)} = 110 = 110$ Seconds

Step 5: Rearranging the activities in the descending order of their RPWs.

RPW	*Activity*	*Processing time*
640	A	40
380	G	20
360	H	120
330	B	70
240	I	130
190	E	50
180	D	40
170	F	30
140	C	30
110	J	110

Step 6: Calculation of Cycle time:

Number of units produced = 192

Time available for production = 8 hours

= 28,800 Seconds

$$\therefore \text{ Cycle time} = \frac{28,800}{192}$$

= 150 Seconds.

Step 7: Total time of all activities = 40 + 70 + 40 + 50 + 30 + 20 + 120 + 30 + 130 + 110

= 640 Seconds

$$\therefore \text{ Approximate Number of Work Stations} = \frac{\text{Total Time}}{\text{Cycle Time}} = \frac{640}{150}$$

= 4.3 or Say 5 workstations.

Step 8: Assignment of activities to various workstations is done in the table below: (as per sequence for step 8)

RPW	*Activity*	*Processing Time*	*Proceeding Activity*	*Assignment*	*Residual Cycle Time*
640	A	40	–	WS I (A)	150 – 40 = 110
380	G	20	A	(G)	110 – 20 = 90
360	H	120	A	X	time not available
330	B	70	A	(B)	90 – 70 = 20
360	H	120	A	WS II (H)	150 – 120 = 30
240	I	130	H	X	Time not available
190	E	50	B	X	Time not available
240	I	130	H	WS III (I)	150 – 130 = 20
190	E	50	B	X	Time not available
180	D	40	B	X	Time not available
190	E	50	B	WS IV (E)	150 – 50 = 100
180	D	40	B	(D)	100 – 40 = 60
170	F	30	B	(F)	60 – 30 = 30
140	C	30	D, E, F	(C)	30 – 30 = 0
110	J	110	C, I	WS V (J)	150 – 110 = 40

Step 9: All activities have been assigned under 5 workstations, as follows:

Workstation I, Activity A, B, G

Workstation II, Activity H

Workstation III, Activity I

Workstation IV, Activity C, D, E, F

Workstation V, Activity J

Schematically it can be drawn as follows:

Workstation I	Workstation II	Workstation III	Workstation IV	Workstation V
A, B, G	H	I	C, D, E, F	J
130 Sec	120 Sec	130 Sec	150 Sec	110 Sec

It is fairly well-balanced process line or assembly line. Last activity J occupies only 110 Sec, but being the last activity on line, does not hold any immediate activity to create inefficiency.

Chapter 8

Manufacturing Operations and Scheduling

Main issues:

1. Production Planning and Control
2. Production Methods and Procedures
3. Personnel and Machines Scheduling
4. Optimum Resources Utilisation Methods

8.1 Production Planning and Control

In the previous chapters, we have discussed the aggregate plans and the production plans, deciding on the capacity of the production facilities for their optimum utilisation. Now our aim is to ensure its organising, monitoring and control for maximum advantage.

The production planning activity is very large, complex and time consuming, needing utmost attention. It is because there are large number of activities performed having direct or indirect influence on the product quantity and quality. It would need all the skill, imagination, experience and innovation of the planning manager, because production planning and its control dictates how efficiently these are in a position to achieve their production targets. For this purpose, the companies may be adopting different methods, working philosophy or even the managerial leadership but the basis of control remains almost unchanged.

The aim and objectives of production control can be listed as follows:

- To ensure on-time production target
- To achieve quality of production as per company standards
- To maintain the production facilities for optimium output

- To ensure no slippages or delays in delivery schedules
- To optimise the input resources like manpower, materials and money
- To minimise the work-in-process (WIP) inventory
- To minimise the cost of production through value Analysis, planning of machines and avoidance of wastages.
- To improve customer satisfaction level.
- To avoid production delays due to accidents, backlogs or bottlenecks etc by intervening at the right time and place.
- To ensure actual MIS to the higher management for future/further planning.

Having decided on the production plans, we have the pleasent but difficult job of analysing production facilities in terms of of manpower and machines and arrange them in such an order so as to achieve the maximum output from the available facilities.

This brings us to the next logical dicussion on machine scheduling. The machine scheduling can be effectively done if we have reliable input on the following factors:

- Product design, with complete specifications
- The volume of production based on the demand forecast and its constant updating
- The technology to be used
- Process design for the product
- Production method and procedure for implementing it
- Number and type of machines available and their actual optimum outputs
- Availability of input materials such as raw materials or components etc.
- The type, skill and the number of workers and supervisory staff available and their output norm (*i.e.*, the standard time fixed by the company)
- Quality standards, machining tolerances, testing methods and facilities
- Planning of distribution, after sales services and the maintenance support

8.2 Production Methods and Procedures

With the authentic, reliable and updated information available on the above-mentioned activities, planning for utilisation of machines and manpower can now be taken up.

The machines available can be used for two different purposes:

- job shop orders
- Mass production orders or flow process orders

The type of work in producing job shop orders is slightly different from that of mass production. Whereas in mass production system, the product is made with the same type of processing in the same sequence but the job shop orders require different processes in different sequences. The selection of the process depends on the continuity of process and the volume of production.

Job Shop Production

In case of job shop orders, the type of production required is low volume requiring the variety of processes. For this purpose we need the layout, generally, of the process type, so that the operations can be performed in any department depending on the availability of machines,

In job shops, we generally get non-standard jobs and hence the worker skill required in such situations has to be high. The allotment of an operation for a particular work centre and its subsequent completion within the stipulated time with stepulated quality has to be ensured. Preplanning, routing of the order jobs and ensuring materials as per schedule are of high priority.

This type of work also needs good documentation such as job cards, process flow diagram, process charts and material requisitions etc. Quality control documentation also is of high importance because in such type of work, a large number of customers will get the results of production and each job needs to be done well in order to expect any repeat order for future good business. Consumption documents for future planning also need be kept meticulously so that corrective action on material consumption and man-machine output norms can be taken.

Job Production Progress Review

For job shop orders, the shop supervisor often displays progress charts for each production lot or product. These progress charts should have physical progress displayed in such away that the worker also understands it to compare whether he is progressing as per schedule or not. These charts help in the following manner:

- Actual physical progress in schematic form against planned progress.
- Approximate percentage progress or progress against time schedule to ensure corrective action.
- Locations of the bottleneck easy.
- Each work centre schedule clearly visible.
- Facilitate additional loading in case of early finish of the job.
- Improves dissemination of information to concerned managers.
- Reduces unnecessary paper work or mismatch of actual work versus planned work

Batch Production Work

This is almost similar production work like job shop orders, but with a difference in terms of number of similar products to be produced. Batch production can be planned and scheduled easily because their production method is fixed and streamlined and does not required rescheduling very often, except, when the product line has changed. The supervisor and inspectors function can be reduced as it can be achieved now based on the sample system, rather than being careful possibly for each product.

The scheduling and quality control needs to be planned more meticulously, so as to ensure higher customer satisfaction.

Method adopted for a batch of product must be carefully planned and facility organised accordingly. The procedure to be adopted for its implementation must be simple and transparent, displayed for the benefit of the woker and it should be easily undertstood by him to feel confident and safe.

Mass Production or Flow Process Production

In the continuous flow production system, generally, the product layout should be adopted with very good balanced production/assembly line. The method is standardised for each product and hence co-ordination, material procurement , scheduling, quality assurance and production controls are easy.

In case of flow process or mass production system, the production process is divided into various feasible tasks to be performed at distinct work stations. These work stations are arranged sequentially so as to progress the work flow smoothly as per sequence of the process.

The flow process production can be either continuous (such as in process industry) or repetitive (discrete) for general type of products. Many products, where any disruption of work causes total breakdown of product line due to specific process requirement such as temperature or the speed etc, are produced by continuous flow process such as paper, fertilisers and bulk foods etc. On the other hand the repetitive flow process production system is used for generally one type of product in the same sequencial order. Various workstations are well synchronised, the products are discrete and can be divided into distinctive tasks to be performed at different work stations. The difference for intermittent type is that various workstations can stop or start works without demaging the work of the previous workstations in later case.

8.3 Master Production Scheduling

A very important and useful helping tool for achieving production on cost effective level is Master production schedule (MPS). This is a step of production planning through which the systematic, organised and controlled operations can be conducted. Master production scheduling is the laying out sequence and time of activities for production for each product to be completed on each machine. This sequencing will result in preparing the schedule (*i.e.*, the time in and time out) of a product on a machine. The schedule obviously takes into account the time required for each unit of the product on a machine and the number of units to be manufactured during one run. Thus we set the quantity of each and every unit to be manufactured through sequence of machines on a short range basis, say week or a month.

The master production schedule normally should be drawn on weekly basis, but can be extended as monthly planning due to the requirement of constant weekly review of the customers preference, forecasted demand, number of orders received or sales achieved, the inventory levels resulting during the weeks, or else how much of capacity has been utilised during the period under review.

Based on this information, future schedules can be corrected. Infact, now there are softwares available, where these frequent changes in production volume can be implemented through Master Production Schedule (MPS) so that wastges are minimised. One such method is being discussed under "Resources Planning" known as Material Requirement Planning (MRP).

To summerise the aim of drawing out an MPS, we can state that,

- we can schedule the quantity and time horizon of a product to be available to the customer as per his stated or expected schedule. This ensures high customer satisfaction.
- balancing the production facility (*i.e.*, capacity control, no under loading, no over loading) so as to utilise the system efficiently and cost-effectively.
- better planning, organising and utilisation of resources (manpower, machine and materials) to avoid any form of wastages.
- ensuring proper maintenance of production facilities for optimum and timely utilisation.

Dynamics of MPS Planning

It has been discussed above that there is a need for constant review of the production planning due to expected or anticipated changes, which is a constant process and hence the flexibility is to be inbuilt into MPS. For this purpose, MPS planning has to be dynamic.

MPS is normally drawn out for few weeks to few months dividing into following time horizons:

First few weeks (Say maximum of one month): It is a firm commitment made for the shop floor and normally no change should be permitted in this plan, otherwise the production resources might be wasted out. It is required to be changed under extraordinary circumstances, (when demand has changed suddenly and drastically such as the product design change needing specific authorisation. Thus part of the MPS can be changed only through the authorisation from the highest level of management. Production resources planning and provisioning has its own lead time and hence any change at quick pace is likely to be costly. If change of schedule of one product is allowed over the other, customer satisfaction level is likely to suffer.

Next few weeks: This period also has to be planned based on short term demand forcast and hence should have a firm MPS designed. But due to availability of time to manage changes, certain variations can be accepted and planning revised. There should be sufficient time permitted for these change to procure material, reorganise various product lines and to ensure re-structured cash flow for the change occuring.

When planners have already loaded the production capacity fully, any change is likely to affect production cost to some extent. If can be managed without any major change in the availability of resources with minimum cost implication and without any major effect on other products. This would also require proper authorisation from higher ups.

Next few weeks: Though this period is also expected to be having full capacity utilisation, If there are gaps or space available, re-orientation of schedule can be made. Time availability for such change makes it easier for perceived change in the quantity, quality or type of the product.

MPS Planning Method

As mentioned above, the requirement of orders can be listed out against these time horizons as given in fig 8.1 below:

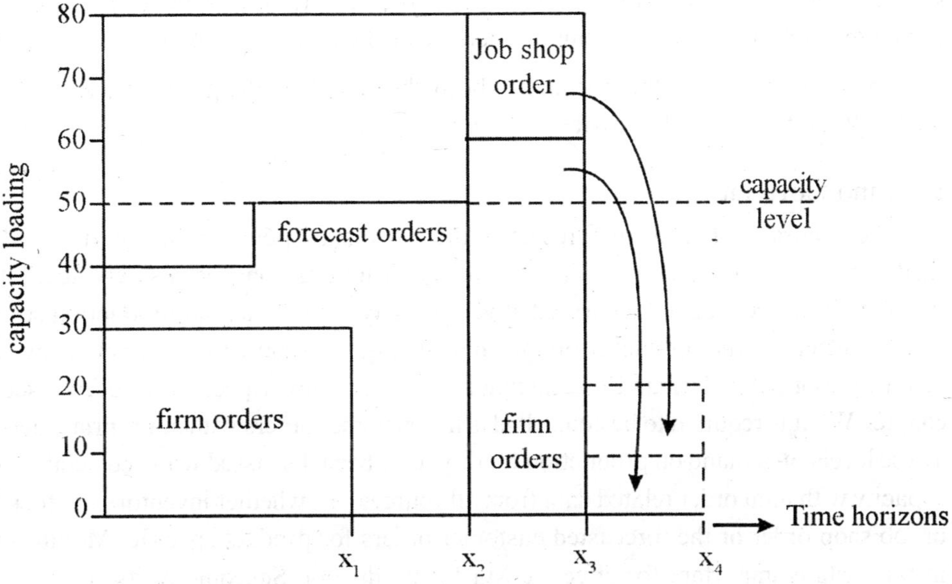

FIG 8.1. MPS Planning and Capacity Adjustment

As can be seen above, x_1, x_2, x_3, x_4 are different time horizons. During o to x_1, the company has few firm orders, with the time horizon indicated. It also has the anticipated demand (shown as forecast orders). The total load is well within the loading capacity of the production system. From o to x_2, the forecast orders are increasing till it has all the load of future forecast only (say x_1 to x_2). This load is still matching the facility capacity. As we plan the third horizon *i.e.*, period x_2 to x_3, the total orders have exceeded the capacity of production and hence MPS has to change this additional production during the period x_3 to x_4 units of time. This is how MPS planning has to be affected.

The same information can be tabulated for a firm schedule specifying exact period of production as follows:

Demand for Product (from all sources)

	Weekly demand (Units of production)				
Source of demand	1	2	3	4	5
Internal orders	10	10	–	10	–
Branches orders	20	20	–	10	–
Customers orders	10	20	50	40	(10)
Job shop orders	–	–	–	20	(20)

This shows that 10 units from customers requirements have been shifted from week 4 to 5 as the capacity of product is 50 units and the system is overloaded.

Similarly the additional job shop orders of 20 units exceed the production capacity, hence shifted to period 5. The shifting has been marked in bracket as the orders have been procured during the period fourth week, but are being executed during week 5.

The underloading of the system has been shown during the period week 1 *i.e.*, when the total load is 40 units against the capacity of 50 units.

Demand Correlation

The accuracy of demand forecast is the basic start point of any production planning. The facilities can be planned only when the resultant load is comprehensively accurate. Demand of product, therefore, has to be correlated very closely with the actual production so that neither the market suffers of the product shortages nor the organisation with the load of inventory cost as a result of poor sales. Demand forecasting and its accuracy aspects have been discussed in earlier chapter. What is required to be controlled is the customer orders with appropriate delivery promises. These levels of demand on production facility have been discussed while correlating the production capacity with total order related data from all sources *i.e.*, whether inventory or stock based demand or job shop order or the forecasted customer orders for product specific. Monitoring the changes in forecasts is important for effective Master Production Schedule or its constant updating. The most uncertain data decided in the MPS is that for service requirement, which is very difficult prediction. When we add repair or warranty requirement in the production capacity, it is all the more difficult data to obtain.

In addition, there is no shortcut to monitoring and updating the demand data on the weekly basis and so is the necessity to update and upgrade the MPS on the weekly basis. The short fall or inventory building of the previous week has to become an integral part of the review and update system for the MPS for the coming weeks.

It is for better control of production that dynamics of MPS is treated in the form of a computerised MPS, the software through which the variations can be taken care of very economically. One such system is IBM's "Communications Oriented Production Information and Control System (COPICS), which itself is being constantly updated. The major ingradients of this system are:

- Customer order servicing
- Forecasting and projection
- MPS planning
- Inventory management
- Manufacturing Activity Planning
- Order releasing

- Purchasing and receiving
- Plant monitoring and control method including the material control
- Engineering Production Data Control
- Cost Planning and Control
- Plant Maintenance schedules

Problem 8.1

Demands of two products A and B are as follows:

Demand for product A

Weeks	1	2	3	4	5	6
Total demand	20	20	50	50	30	30

Demand for Product B

Weeks	1	2	3	4	5	6
Total demand	30	30	40	40	40	30.

The safety stock for product A is being planned as 30 units and for B, it is 40 units. The lot size for product A is 50 and for B, it is 60. It is also noticed that the initial inventory is 70 units for product A and 50 units for product B. Workout the appropriate production schedule.

Solution:

The MPS (Master Production Schedule) is as follows

Product A

Weeks	1	2	3	4	5	6
Total demand	20	20	50	50	30	30
Initial inventory	70	50	30	30	30	50
Production Need	—	—	50	50	50	50
End Inventory	50	30	30	30	50	70

Product B

Total demand	30	30	40	40	50	30
Initial inventory	50	80	50	70	90	50
Production need	60	–	60	60	–	60
End inventory	80	50	70	90	50	80

8.4 Types of Production Control Systems

The master production schedule (MPS) has since been discussed and the production department is now in know of the number of products and their quantities to be despatched to the market to make these available to the customer. The resources planning for this production work as per MPS has to be maticulously done to avoid any bottlenecks and if any, necessary control system to be built in. But this will vary with the type of control planned or decided so that the production plans, facilities earmarked, materials procured and other necessary supports such as money and marketing efforts are fully utilised.

There are following types of production planning and control systems that can be employed to cater for different situations:

- Pond Draining System
- Push System
- Pull System
- Bottleneck System

Pond Draining System

The system is symbolic of holding resources at three levels *i.e.*, raw materials, work in Process and finished goods inventories. This is treated as equivalent to three ponds holding these inventories. The raw materials are supplied by the vendor as per the demand from the purchase department of the producer. The information system from the customer to marketing and to production team may be sketchy and products are manufactured based as producers priority. Raw materials are converted into end products through the work in process stages, where components, subassemblies and assemblies are obtained and assembled. The finished goods inventory 'pond' is drained out due to products being supplied to the customer. This deficiency is made up by assembly space of WIP (components and assemblies) as per the requirement. When WIP Pond supplies these products, it is called draining out of the WIP Pond. To make up for these drained out products, the load on the raw material Pond increases and it supplies part of it to the WIP stage, to head for end product stage.

When Raw material Pond gets drained out, the supply valves are opened from the vendors. As a result, the orders are placed on the suppliers for this purpose. This system can be operated on the basis of stocks or customer orders *i.e.*, either produce to stock basis or produce to order basis. Either way, the necessary draining out has to suit the requirement of the production system. It may look very simple system, but is very useful, amenable to use of IT-enabled facilities in the present day technology compatibility.

If we obtain reliable and authentic information about the customer needs, the system can be operated very scientifically using the most sophisticated tools. Information about supplies, suppliers and production facility can be used to advantage for production planning and control. It can be used for produce to order, produce to stock, product focussed and process focussed manufacturing system. If information flow is slow, the system can lead to excessive finished goods inventories, possibly not suitable to satisfy customer. The system has been shown in Fig. 8.2 below:

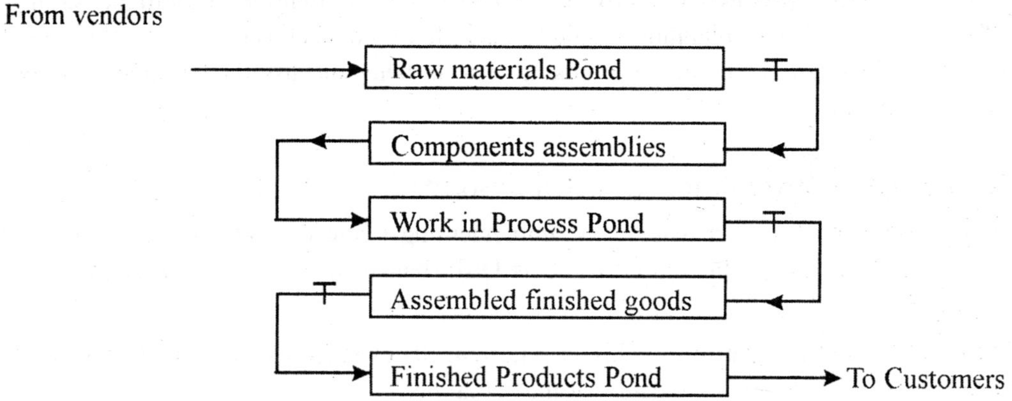

FIG 8.2. Pond Draining System

Push System

In push system of production control, the organisation needs an effective flow of information about the customers demands and great efforts to be made about its accuracy. Based on what the customer would need and when, the lead time analysis for the level of production helps in planning. The planning of raw materials, sub assembles and assemblies is done and procurement ordered as per lead time analysis results. These raw materials and assemblies are then pushed into the system, forcing WIP to move forward and produce the finished good inventory just about when and how much is needed. This is why the contol system is called a Push System.

The supplies are ordered on the lot size basis and the batches of materials are then pushed across the production facility on this basis. The flow of raw materials and assembled units are planned and controlled as per the production schedule drawn for batch production.

The system is useful when the company aims at a high level of customer satisfaction and wants to supply products as per the promises offered. But to make it effective, the accuracy, the speed and the lead time are the informations needed for help in system effeciency. By proper control, the large savings in inventory costs can be achieved due to reduction in raw materials, as well as in finish good inventories.

Pull System

In this case, the emphasis shifts to what to produce next. Hence inventory controls at all stages must be exercised. Company should order raw materials only for next immediate production and then produce and supply. Thus the end products are pulled towards the customers. WIP and raw materials are pulled through the production system as per the production schedule. This system can be named as just in time (JIT) manufacturing or lean manufacturing. These concepts are being discussed in chapters to follow.

Bottleneck system

There are bound to be bottlenecks in the production system whatever be the level, gravity or the reason there of. When production control system focusses its attention on bottlenecks, it is called Bottleneck system. Hence planning should be such that bottleneck is taken care of before it stops work. This is done through innovative thinking. This is being discussed later under. "Theory of constraint" by Goldratt.

8.5 Disturbances in Production Control Systems

There are some problems that arise while implementing planned production planning and control (PPC) system. These problem are treated as Disturbances to PPC, since these affect the control system.

- **Seasonal demand variation** – This is a normal disturbance expected and known and hence PPC must be flexible enough to cater for the actual need.

- **Variations in customer preferences**–These can be predicted only to a limited extent. Generally Market research, sample survey, sales team interaction with customers and retailers bring it out. But if there is a huge unsold inventory, there is a reason for worry and production must be corrected.

- **Use of computers**–This is a device now extensively used in practically all industries. If properly used, it is a great help, otherwise wrong interpretation can lead to erroneous planning effecting the business control in the long run. No half-hearted efforts should be tried.

8.6 Personnel Scheduling

Services are generally labour intensive, hence we need large number of multiskilled workforce. Specific skills are required for manufacturing also. Personnel schedulings, therefore, is an ever-present management problem. When a worker does not show up for work, someone else has to take his place to offset the production delays or stoppages. In services like hospitals, retail stores, hair cutting saloons or for fire fighting and police duties, the operational scheduling has to be matched with personnel scheduling.

For streamlined process industry operation, the personnel scheduling may be easier because the schedule of duty hours can be fixed and required number of personnel then deputed for the job. The same schedule can continue over a long period.

But when the demand pattern is fluctuating on day to day or even hour to hour basis, this scheduling of manpower can became slightly complicated. The situation becomes acute, when the personnel element of a service is predominantly higher and hence cost consuming. Added complication is the off-duty hours or off-days during the week.

For this purpose, manual scheduling can be adopted, when number of operations are limited. But when the scheduling operations are larger and total job has complex routings, the help of the computer can be taken. Even heuristic methods are found useful for such situations. Linear programing methods such as Assignment models are available for personel scheduling. Added variables like off days or only 5 days work schedule can be built into the mathematical models.

Such methods have been extensively used and are common tools in services like airline scheduling, retail store or health care facilities. The optimum utilisation resulting in just reasonable costs can be ensured by using these methods with proper constraints considered.

The personnel scheduling under different situations has been shown through various examples given below.

Problem 8.2

An Airline Company has drawn up a new flight schedule involving 5 flights. To assist in allocating 5 pilots to these flights it has asked them to state their preference by giving each flight a number out of 10. The higher the number, the greater is the preference. Certain of these flights are unsuitable to some pilots due to domestic reasons. These have been marked as M. The matrix below lists out these preferential scores, based on which the airline wishes to allocate flights to meet as high a preference as possible. Show the allocations to various pilots.

Pilots ***Score for flights***

	I	*II*	*III*	*IV*	*V*
A	8	2	M	5	4
B	10	9	2	8	4
C	5	4	9	6	M
D	3	6	2	8	7
E	5	6	10	4	3

Solution:

Since it is a case of maximisation of preferential scores for flight allocation, we, first, convert the matrix to standard minimisation matrix, so that Hungarian Assignment Method (HAM) can be used for assigning flights to pilots. The resultant minimisation matrix is obtained by subtracting all elements from the highest preferential score of 10. The resultant matrix is as under

	I	*II*	*III*	*IV*	*V*
A	2	8	M	5	6
B	0	1	8	2	6
C	5	6	1	4	M
D	7	4	8	2	3
E	5	4	0	6	7

Now using HAM heuristics for optimisation,

Step 1. Subtract minimum element of each row from all the element of that row, we get revised matrix as

0	6	M	3	4
0	1	8	2	6
4	5	0	3	M
5	2	6	0	1
5	4	0	6	7

Step 2. Subtracting minimum element of each column from all elements of that column in the revised matrix above, we get

0	5	M	3	3
0	0	8	2	5
4	4	0	3	M
5	1	6	0	0
5	3	0	6	6

Step 3. Drawing minimum number of horizontal/vertical lines to cover all zero, we get

0	5	M	3	3
0	0	8	2	5
4	4	0	3	M
5	1	6	0	0
5	3	0	6	6

Since we draw only 4 lines ≠ Size of the matrix *i.e.*, 5, we go to step 4.

Step 4. Locating minimum uncovered element *i.e.*, 2 subtracting it from all uncovered elements and adding the same to the elements at the intersection of the lines above, we get

0	5	M	1	1
0	0	8	0	3
4	4	0	1	M
7	3	8	0	0
5	3	0	4	4

Step 5. Repeat step 4 and 3, we first get minimum number of lines drawn through all zeros.

0	5	M	1	1
0	0	8	0	3
4	4	0	1	M
7	3	8	0	0
5	3	0	4	4

Since we still get 4 lines ≠ size of the matrix *i.e.*, 5, repeat step 4 and 3.

Step 4.

0	4	M	0	0
1	0	9	0	3
4	3	0	0	M
8	3	9	0	0
5	2	0	3	3

Minimum uncovered element now is 1.

Step 5. Repeat step 3, drawing minimum lines across all zeros

0	4	M	0	0
1	0	9	0	3
4	3	0	0	M
8	3	9	0	0
5	2	0	3	3

It is now seen that the number of lines drawn through all zero, are 5 *i.e.*, equal to the size of the matrix. Thus the optimal solution has been obtained. We can now proceed to step 6.

Step 6. Making allocations on unique zeros.

[0]	4	M	~~0~~	~~0~~
1	[0]	9	~~0~~	3
4	3	~~0~~	0	M
8	3	9	~~0~~	[0]
5	2	[0]	3	3

Allocation as per minimisation matrix have been achieved. Now superimposing these allocations from the original matrix, we have

	1	2	3	4	5
A	[8]				
B		[9]			
C				[6]	
D					[7]
E			[10]		

Thus flight assignment with maximum preferential scores are as follows:

Flight Pilot	Flight	Score
A	1	8
B	2	9
C	4	6
D	5	7
E	3	10

Maximum Score achieved = 40

Problem 8.3

An Airline, operating all seven days a week, has a time-table shown below:

Flight	**Delhi**	**Calcutta**	**Flight**	**Calcutta**	**Delhi**
1	7 am	9 am	101	9 am	11 am
2	9 am	11 am	102	10 am	12 noon
3	1-30 pm	3-30 pm	103	3-30 pm	5-30 pm
4	7-30 pm	9.30 pm	104	8 pm	10 pm

It is decided that crew must have a minimum layover of 6 hours between flights. Obtain the pairing of flights that minimises the layover time away from home and also mention the town where the crew must be based for cost effective scheduling.

Solution:

Keeping the minimum layover of 6 hours *i.e.*, 360 minutes between the flights pairing, we first formulate the time matrix for crew based at Delhi (figures indicate minutes).

Flights	**101**	**102**	**103**	**104**
1	1440	1500	390	660
2	1320	1380	1710	540
3	1050	1110	1440	1710
4	690	750	1080	1350

Similarly, we draw a matrix of flights pairing for crews based at calcutta

Flights	**101**	**102**	**103**	**104**
1	1200	1140	810	540
2	1320	1260	930	660
3	1590	1530	1200	930
4	510	450	1560	1290

To cater for cost effective operation, we now draw a matrix of minimum layover from any location between flights pairings

Flights	101	102	103	104
1	[1200]	[1140]	390	[540]
2	1320	[1260]	[930]	540
3	1050	1110	[1200]	[930]
4	[510]	[450]	1080	[1290]

The rectangles drawn are showing the minimum layovers for crews based at Calcutta, whereas the open figures are for crews based of Delhi:

It is a minimisation time matrix, hence HAM can be used.

Step 1. Substracting smallest element of each row from all elements of that row, we get the following reduced matrix.

Flights	101	102	103	104
1	[810]	[750]	0	[150]
2	780	[720]	[390]	0
3	120	180	[270]	0
4	[60]	[0]	630	[840]

Still retaining calcutta crew timings in rectangles.

Step 2, 3 Substracting minimum element of a column from all element of the column, we get next reduced matrix and then draw minimum H/V lines across all zeros.

Flights	101	102	103	104
1	[750]	[750]	0	[150]
2	720	[720]	[390]	0
3	60	180	[270]	0
4	[0]	[0]	630	[840]

Only 3 lines cover all zeros, hence not an optimal solution

Step 4, 3 Subtracting smallest uncovered element *i.e.*, 60 from all uncovered elements and adding the same to the elements at the intersection of lines, and drawing minimum lines across all zeros, we get

Flights	101	102	103	104
1	[690]	[690]	0	[150]
2	660	[660]	[390]	0
3	0	120	[270]	0
4	[0]	[0]	690	[900]

Now, number of lines drawn = size of the matrix = 4

Hence it is an optimal solution. Proceed to step 6.

Step 6. Making allocations on unique zeros, we get

Flights	101	102	103	104
1			[0]	
2				[0]
3	[0]			⊠
4	⊠	[0]		

Hence the optimal assignments are:

Pair of flights	**Crew based at**
1-103	Delhi
2-104	Delhi
3-101	Delhi
4-102	Calcutta

Total layover time = 390 + 540 + 1050 + 450 = 2430 minuts or 40 hours 30 minutes

Problem 8.4

In a job shop, the quantum of work has been estimated based on previous experience and it has been found that the general level of manpower required on various weekdays is as follows

Mondays	**Tuesdays**	**Wednesdays**	**Thursdays**	**Fridays**	**Saturdays**	**Sundays**
6	6	6	6	10	10	10

Work out the work-shift schedule by adopting 5 day a week policy and ensuring two consecutive days off for a worker.

Solution:

Total manpower requirements per week = 6 + 6 + 6 + 6 + 10 + 10 + 10

= 54 persons

Since number of work shifts per week per worker is 5 (five days policy), average number of workers required per day = $\frac{54}{5}$ = 11.

We have to develop the workshift schedule for 11 workers for all the sevendays a week, offering two consecutive days off for every worker. We select any two consecutive days off for every worker. In case of a tie, we can use random selection methods. The planning is reflected in the table below

Number of workers per shift							
Worker	**Monday**	**Tuesday**	**Wednesday**	**Thursday**	**Friday**	**Saturday**	**Sunday**
1	6	6	6	6	10	10	10
2	6	6	5	5	9	9	9
3	5	5	5	5	9	9	8
4	5	5	4	4	7	7	7
5	4	4	4	4	6	6	6
6	4	4	3	3	5	5	5
7	3	3	2	2	4	4	4
8	3	3	2	2	3	3	3
9	2	2	2	2	2	2	2
10	2	2	1	1	1	1	1
11	1	1	1	1	0	0	0

The days marked against a worker as rectangle are his off-days.

8.7 Job Shop Manufacturing

Job shop manufacturing is a function of the production organisation, where the orders received have wide variation in their method of production and the volumes are generally low, even as low as a single or a few products. These orders may be needing the services of various process departments such as turning, welding, grinding, driling, milling, plaining, soldering, forging or even heat treatment. Hence the layout followed for such manufacturing is process type, where various process facilities are grouped together for similar production process in a particular area. Different processes have their own bays or departments. Carrying out work on a single customer order may not be economical. Hence batch type manufacturing is adopted, where a number of products or job orders needing a similar process are taken up at one time and are processed through a specific production route. The production facilities, grouped together, are called work centres. The movement of the order is through these work centres.

The capacity requirement planning (CRP) is meticulously carried out so that wastage of capacity is minimised. MPS in such cases is also not easy, but batch routing and scheduling can reduce the wastage rate considerably.

Material Requirement Planning (MRP), which has been discussed later under the chapter with the same nomenclature, becomes important in these type of productions due to large variety of materials to be organised. Material handling system design is alse an important consideration. Thus the job shop scheduling involves the following elements and route:

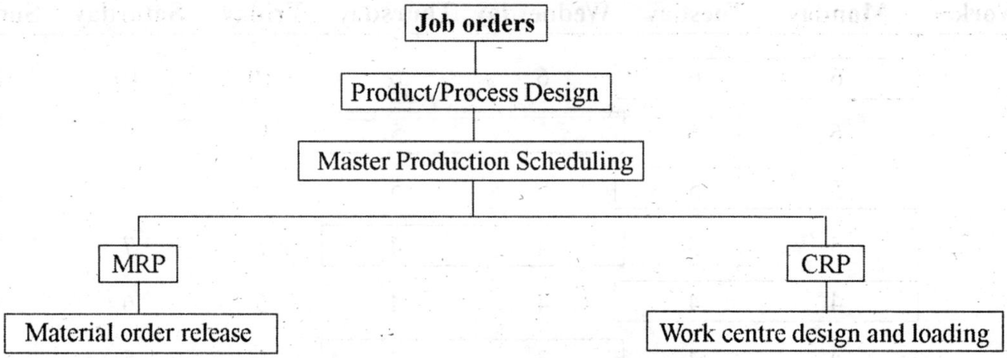

FIG 8.4. Job Shop Manufacturing

Since the jobs or orders are diverse in nature, even if we group similar products together, their manufacturing sequences may not be the same. Work centre design, therefore, could vary largely and the routing and scheduling may be difficult to coordinate. It may result in WIP being high at certain work centres and interruption in the manufacturing cannot be ruled out. Hence job shops scheduling is not very easy job. It needs working on the principle of flexibility. In fact , flexibility is required to be used as a helping tool in organising the workers and machines with quick shift planning for the material handling equipment and high level of flexibility in material procurement and physical handling so that various orders can be assigned and reassigned/unassigned as per the requirement. Higher worker skill and use of MRP software (as given above) for quick flexible change order is an assets in the planning of production schedules.

Shop-Floor Activities – The above discussion may sound very complicated for job shop scheduling, but by following a laid down procedure, it can become quite manageable. Product/Process design, priority and routing becomes important in such planning.

On the job-shop floor, following activities can be planned:

- Allotting priorities to various job orders so that these can be planned for production sequencially.
- New work centres designed to undertake specific process are loaded with appropriate job orders (based on the production capacity) and then following routing of the products (as per sequence of operations), the manufacturing plan can be prepared.

- Loading and routing are to be planned keeping the WIP in mind because there should be no crowding up of WIPs on few work centres
- Planning the output control, which is again an important activity so that the production smoothness is ensured.
- Monitoring and control should raise the level of work centre efficiency, but a definite system of its measurement must be laid down.

These activities of loading, routing and scheduling can be represented by the Gantt/Bar chart. These are being discussed seprately under Sequencing/Scheduling Methods.

8.8 Scheduling of Operations

Important Terminology in Scheduling

Loading – For production purpose, the number of jobs alloted to a machine or a group of machines is called loading. When we have ten jobs at hand and with respect to the work content requirement, only 4 can be allocated to a machine, it is called its loading. Loading must be related to the capacity of machine or work centre, depending on the output expected of it. It is also called shop loading or machine loading.

Routing – It is the order in which a job moves from one facility (or a work centre) to another facility for further processing. When we have a job to be processed on three different machines, the sequence of these machines is decided on the basis of sequence of operations required for the product. In short, routing is the processing stages required to manufacture a product on different machines.

Sequencing – When more than one job is loaded on a machine or a work centre, the sequence in which these jobs are to be processed through production centres is called sequencing. This decision can be taken on the basis of urgency of the job or cost effectiveness of the use of production facilities. Thus it is the priority for a job in the queue on a work centre, where the job has been loaded.

Scheduling – Having achieved loading and sequencing (the routing is fixed for each product or job) the decision to allot time space *i.e.* the start time and finish time of job on each machine is called its scheduling. It is very important decision to ensure its implementation and hence the resources allocation for all the processing on all machines must be made and ensured according to the schedule of a product on a machine.

Monitoring and Control – It is not enough to lay down the schedules. Its smooth implementation is more important. Hence the production manager has to ensure all possible resources to be made available at appropriate schedule *i.e.*, manpower, machines, materials etc and develop a system to ensure that these resources are used to advantage within the time space alloted to complete the desired job. This is called monitoring. Things may still go wrong such as sudden illness, machine failure or shortage of materials etc. In these situations, timely action to remove these bottlenecks and ensure production process back on rails is called the control function of the manager. This is also called expenditing because of tracking the progress and timely corrective action.

Finite loading – As brought out under the definition of loading, the total working capacity of the machine or the work centre should be considered while loading the jobs. When the loading of jobs is restricted to a maximum of the production capacity of the machine or the work centre, it is called finite loading. It is illustrated below. Refer Figure 8.5 below.

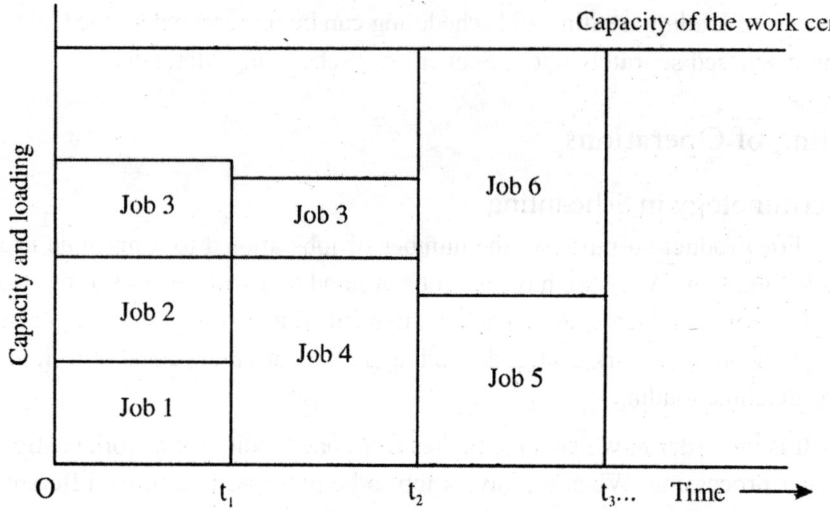

FIG 8.5. Finite Loading

• ***Infinite loading*** – When loading of jobs are done irrespective of the capacity consideration of the production facility, it is called Infinite loading. In such cases, scheduling and rescheduling should be a constant process to ensure timely completion of jobs as per sequence and schedule. This may result in long queues at the work centres. Refer Figure 8.6 below.

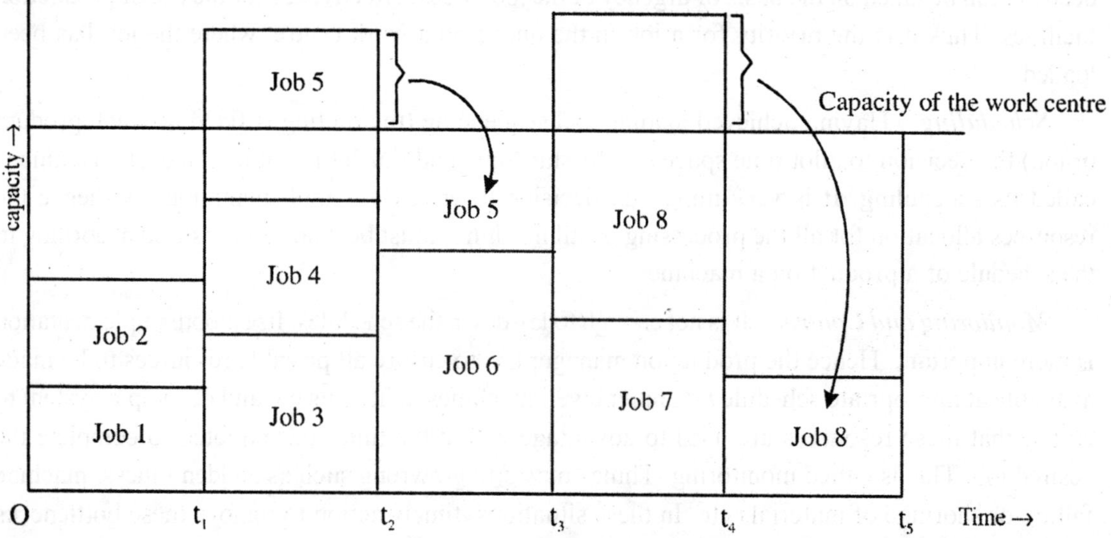

FIG 8.6. Infinite loading

Forward scheduling – While allocating time and resources to jobs, we can follow two methods. When the jobs are assigned or allocated to the earliest unallocated time slot on a work centre, it is called forward scheduling. This is done when customers are very eager to get their jobs at the earliest. It may result in excessive work-in-process inventories for facilities to be free to take up further work in queue. It can be understood from Figure 8.7 given below:

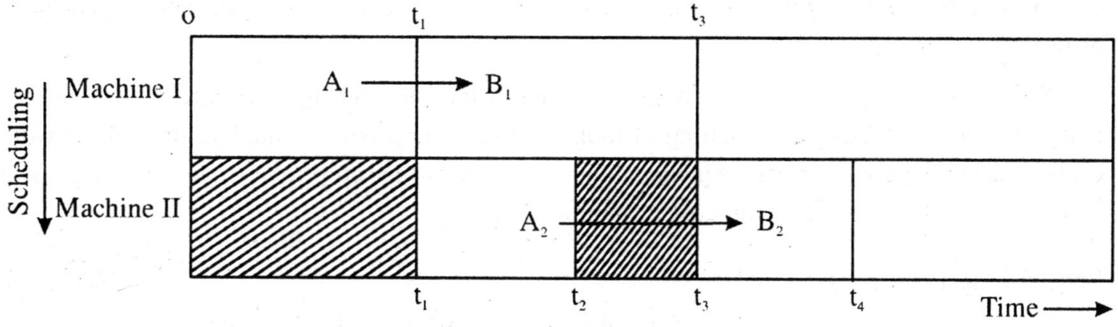

FIG 8.7. Forward Scheduling

Backward Scheduling – The situation is complicated when a particular specific job is to be completed on priority due to customer surgency or else it may be necessary with respect to its dovetail with some other work at a specified time. In this case, therefore, the manager plans it in such a way that its schedule can be ascertained by working backwards from end to start on each production facility. Hence it is called Backward Scheduling. It normally reduces work in process inventories because jobs are likely to be completed just when these are required. Refer Figure 8.8 for easy understanding :

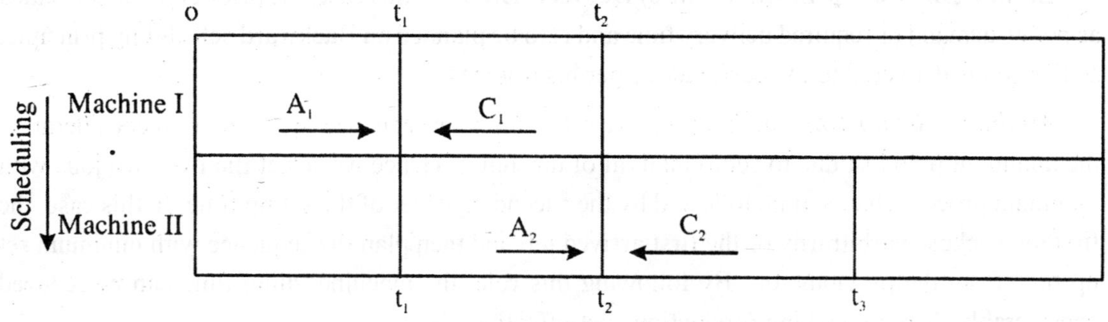

FIG 8.8. Backward Scheduling Planning

Here Job C is required by time t_3 and hence its operation on machine II (the later operation) is planned out from t_2 to t_3 back words. It can became on machine I so as finishly t_2 hence adjusted backward from t_1 to t_2.

8.9 Order Sequencing Rules

Order Sequencing – Deciding the order in which various jobs loaded to a machine or work centre are to be undertaken for processing.

The sequencing can be decided based on following principles:

Average flow time – The average amount of aggregate time of jobs spent on the shop floor.

Average number of jobs on the floor – Is the number of jobs on the average to stay in the shopfloor during a certain given period.

Average tardiness of jobs – The average time of job conpletion delayed beyond its scheduled or promised delivery date.

Set up or change over cost – While changing a machine set up from one job to another, readjustment of machine and resetting of tools take time. This is unproductive time of the work centre. Hence the manager can sequence the jobs such that the setup time (time for change over from job A to B) and its resultant cost is minimised.

Sequencing Priorities

Based on the above principle, following sequencing rules can be followed:

First Come First Served (FCFS). Under this rule, we undertake the jobs for processing in this same order as they arrive on the shop floor.

Shortest Processing Time (SPT) or Minimum Process Time (MPT). This order helps in cost effective processing, when smaller duration jobs are undertaken on priority. The jobs with the shortest processing time are undertaken first and others in their ascending order of the processing time. This will ensure a number of smaller jobs clearing the shop floor faster. It helps in satisfying large number of small job customers faster.

Earliest Due Date or Earliest Date of Delivery (EDD). In this case, the priority job is scheduled as per its demand or required delivery time and is to be planned on Backward scheduling principle, so that job is delivered to the customer as per his urgency.

Minimum Set up Time. In this case, we select the jobs sequence by taking into consideration the minimum time lost due to setup interval of machines. Hence we select the first two jobs with minimum process change time followed by the ascending order of the set up time. In this case, the first job is chosen arbitrarily or the first arrived job and then plan the sequence with minimum set up time from the previous job. By following this rule, the machine idling time can be reduced considerably there by making production cost-effective.

Critical Ratio (CR). Under this rule, the next job to be processed is selected to be the one with the least time to due date dividing by total remaining production time (called the critical ratio)

Selection Criterion for Right Sequencing Rule

There are many sequencing rules or priorities available as described above and the operation manager is always in difficult situation due to uncertain environmental requirements such as customers pressure, organisational benefit or availability of machines etc. Some major creteria, that can be used by the manager, are as follows (Selection as per available situation):

- Idle time
- Average number of jobs.waiting for processing
- Set up time and costs
- Inventory levels (in-process inventory costs)
- Number of jobs delayed (due to inherent uncertainity)
- Average number of jobs delayed
- Average time to complete a job
- Standard derivation of time for jobs delayed
- Standard derivation of time for jobs completion.

The manager, ultimately, is concerned about maximisation of his resources utilisation as well as customer satesfaction. In the bargain, he should be able to balance the load for maximising profitability for the organisation.

Problem 8.5 (Scheduling 2 jobs through 2 machines)

The processing times of two jobs to be produced through two machines are given below. If the sequence of operation is Machine 1 to Machine 2 (M_1—M_2), work out the most time effective scheduling of jobs.

Jobs	Processing time on machines (minutes)	
	M_1	M_2
J_1	15	20
J_2	22	12

Solution:

Since the job routing has been indicated as M_1—M_2, we can draw the bar chart as follows

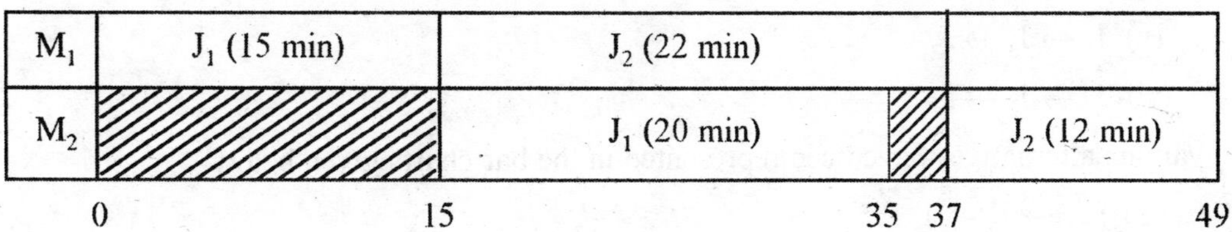

The time taken for both the jobs would be 49 minutes if we schedule job J_1 prior to J_2. The shaded area is indicates the idling time of machine 2. (15 + 2 = 17 min)

If we decide to take up Job J_2 first, than the resultant bar chart for scheduling would be

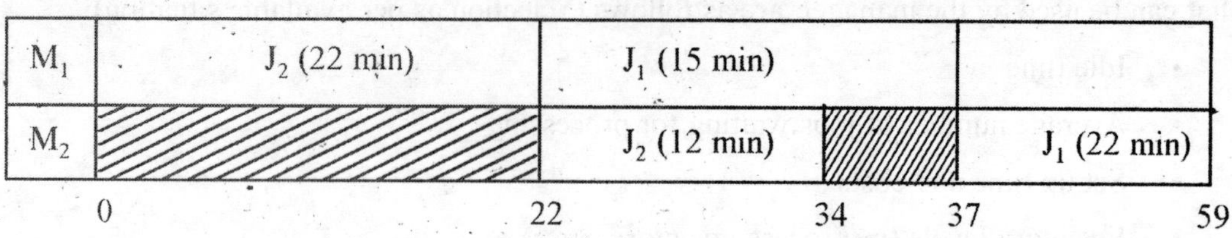

In this case, the total time taken to finish both the jobs has increased to 59 minutes. It is not cost effective (idling of machine 2 = 22 + 3 = 25 minutes)

Hence the sequencing of jobs should be $J_1 \rightarrow J_2$

Problem 8.6 (Scheduling 3 jobs on 2 machines)

The processing times of three jobs J_1, J_2 and J_3 on two machines M_1 and M_2 are given in the table below:

Jobs	*Processing time* M_1	*(minutes)* M_2
J_1	4	8
J_2	5	6
J_3	2	8

Work out the most time effective schedule of the shop, given the routing as $M_1 \rightarrow M_2$.

Solution:

For time effective Scheduling, we work on various alternatives of job sequencis *i.e.*,

(i) $J_1 \rightarrow J_2 \rightarrow J_3$

(ii) $J_2 \rightarrow J_1 \rightarrow J_3$

(iii) $J_3 \rightarrow J_1 \rightarrow J_2$

(iv) $J_2 \rightarrow J_3 \rightarrow J_1$

(v) $J_1 \rightarrow J_3 \rightarrow J_2$

(vi) $J_3 \rightarrow J_2 \rightarrow J_1$

Various alternatives have been represented in the bar charts given below:

Case (i) $J_1 \rightarrow J_2 \rightarrow J_3$

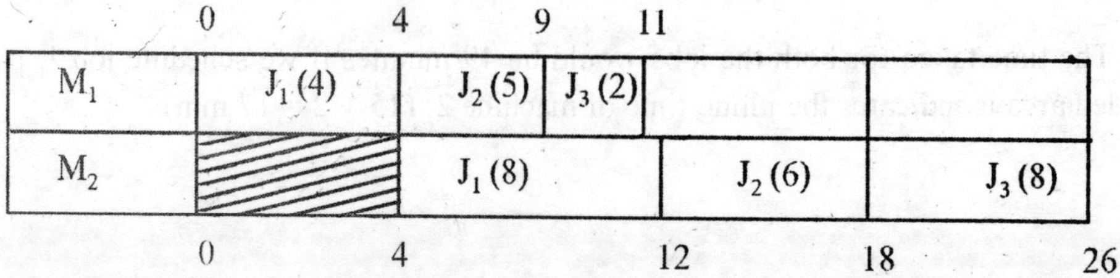

Total Elapsed Time (TET) = 26 minutes

Case (ii) $J_2 \rightarrow J_1 \rightarrow J_3$

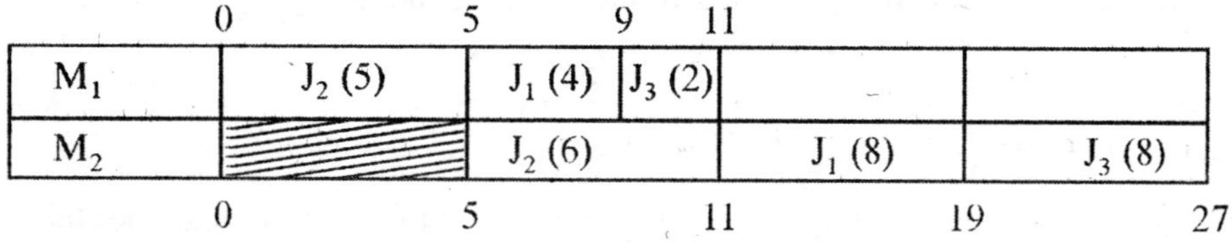

TET = 27 minutes

Case (iii) $J_3 \rightarrow J_1 \rightarrow J_2$

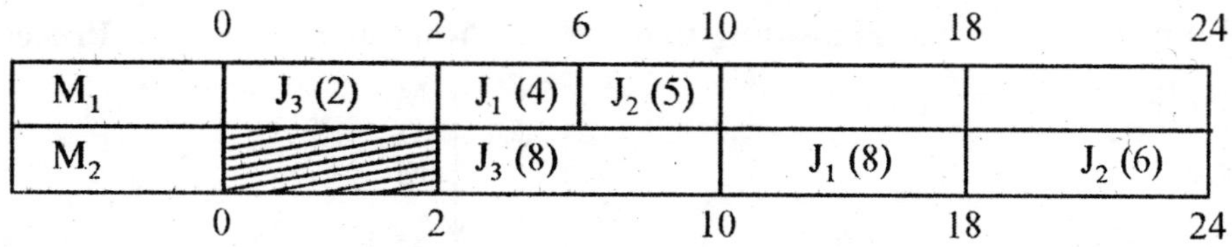

TET = 24 minutes

Case (iv) $J_2 \rightarrow J_3 \rightarrow J_1$

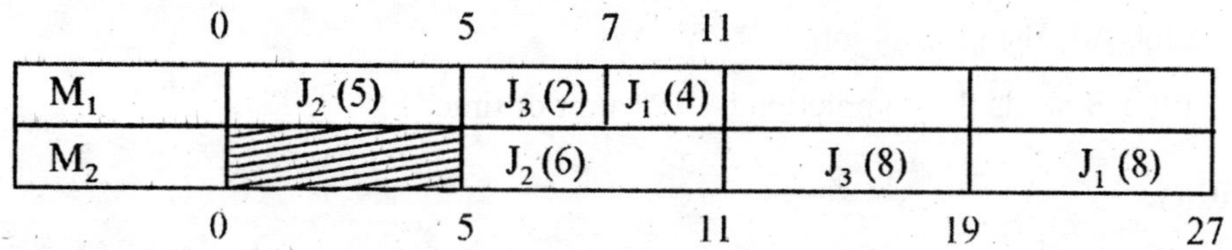

TET = 27 minutes

Case (v) $J_1 \rightarrow J_2 \rightarrow J_1$

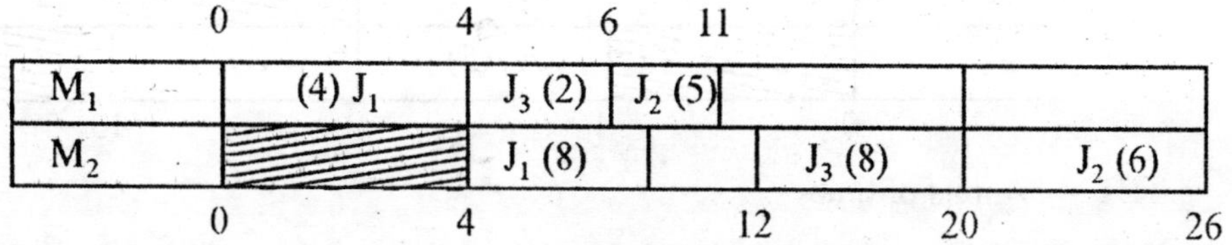

TET = 26 minutes

Case (vi) $J_3 \rightarrow J_2 \rightarrow J_1$

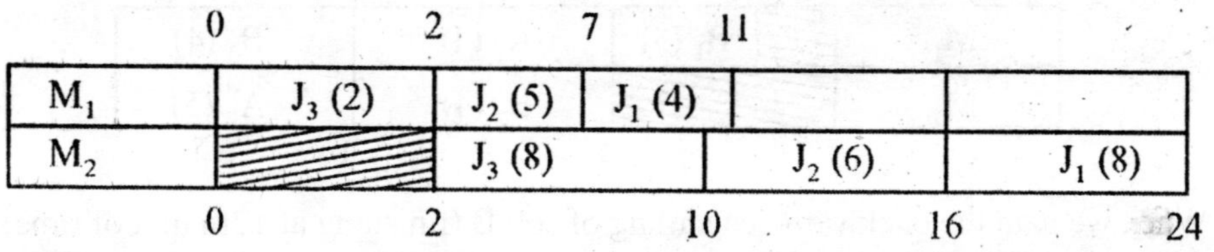

TET = 24 minutes

From the above bar charts, it is evident that alternatives (iii) and (vi) are equally effecient, taking total time of 24 minutes and machine waiting time as 2 minutes.

Hence the most time effective scheduling can be either $J_3 \rightarrow J_1 \rightarrow J_2$

or $J_3 \rightarrow J_2 \rightarrow J_1$

Problem 8.7 (EDD Case)

The job sequencing and the processing times of two jobs on two machines have been reflected in the table below:

Job A

Routing	Presenting time
M_1	4
↓ M_2	5

Job B

Routing	Processing time
M_1	3
M_2	4
↓ M_1	4

It is given that Job B needs the completion by 12th unit of time. Work out the scheduling and the total elapsed time (TET) when

(a) Job A is the priority job.

(b) Job B needs the completion by 12th unit of time.

Solution:

(a) When job A is a priority job, it is to be scheduled earlier than B and hence the bar chart scheduling **(forward scheduling)** is as under:

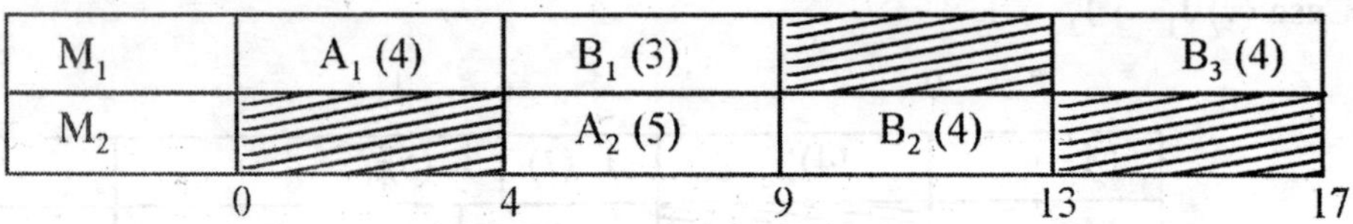

TET = 17 units of time

(b) When job B is required to be handed over by 12th unit of time (as against 17th as per above plan, the backward scheduling is drawn as under:

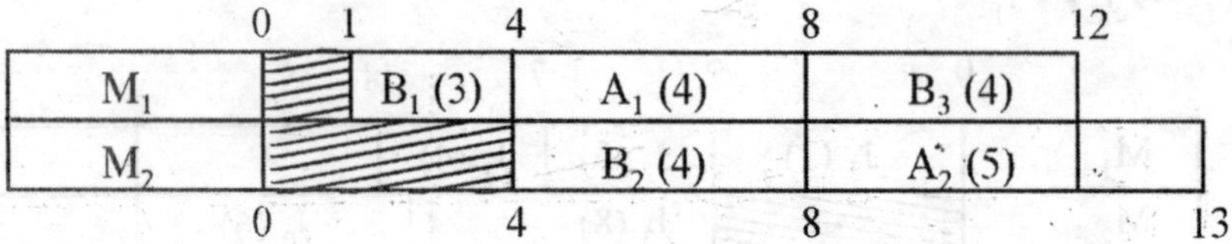

When we plan the backward scheduling of Job B (finishing at 12th unit of time) the job has to start at time 1. This leaves machine 1 idling from time 0 to 1, which is undesirable due to waste time.

Instead of this plan, if we start job B at the beginning of the schedule *i.e.*, at time 0 at machine 1, then the job B will be finishing at time 11 (ahead of desired Schedule, hence Safer and the schedule of job A will be readjusted to be finishing at time 12 only (instead of time 13 arrived at above). Hence the backward schedule of job B is adjusted as follows:

0 3 11

M_1	B_1 (3)	A_1 (4)	B_3 (4)	
M_2		B_2 (4)	A_2 (5)	

3 7 12

Problem 8.8

The processing or operating time for five jobs on a work centre are indicated in the table below. Carryout the scheduling of jobs under the given priorities and compare.

(a) FCFS priority rule

(b) SPT priority rule

Jobs	*Processing time*	*Due date*
A	5	7
B	7	15
C	19	24
D	14	21
E	6	16

Solutions:

(a) Priority Rule-FCFS. Since the priority has been kept as FCFS, the loading of all five jobs on the work centre will be dealt with by forward scheduling as follows –

$$A \rightarrow B \rightarrow C \rightarrow D \rightarrow E$$

The Bar chart showing scheduling is as under:

0 5 12 31 45 51

A	B	C	D	E
(5)	(7)	(19)	(14)	(16)

The total Elapsed Time (TET) works out to 51 units of time.

(b) Priority rule SPT. By using SPT rule, the sequencing of jobs changes to

$$A \rightarrow E \rightarrow B \rightarrow D \rightarrow C$$

This scheduling can be drawn as follows

0	5	11	18	32	51
A (5)	E (6)	B (7)	D (14)	C (19)	

Since there is only one machine involved, scheduling is easy to achieve as can be seen above. To compare, we compute the following:

(i) Total completion time

(ii) Average completion time

(iii) Average number of jobs

(iv) Average tardiness

Job sequence	*No of jobs in the system*	*Processing Time*	*Flow Time*		*Due date*	*Tardiness or delivery*	
			FCFS	*SPT*		*FCFS*	*SPT*
A	5	5	5	5	7	–	–
B	4	7	12	18	15	–	3
C	3	19	31	51	24	7	27
D	2	14	45	32	21	24	11
E	1	6	51	11	16	–	–
	Total	51	144	117		31	41

To tabulate these results:

Criterion	*FCFS*	*SPT*
Total Completion Time	51	51
Average Completion time	$\frac{144}{5} = 2.9$	$\frac{117}{5} = 2.3$
Average tardiness	$\frac{31}{5} = 6.2$	$\frac{41}{5} = 8.2$

While comparing the two sequencing rules, it is noticed that on the completion time criterion and Average number of jobs in the system, FCFS values are higher and hence SPT rule is more efficient avoiding shop floor congestion and average consumption time. But the tardiness is more under SPT rule. Hence no definite genralisation can be made.

Problem 8.9

Following table indicates the time for set up required between various jobs. Work out the sequencing of jobs and compare the time lost if there is more than one sequence possible.

Job	Set up time				
	A	B	C	D	E
A	–	5	12	7	3
B	10	–	5	10	7
C	10	7	–	8	10
D	12	8	12	–	5
E	6	10	7	8	–

Solution:

If job A is planned to be processed first, the sequence based on minimum set up time is as follows:

To start with job A, the minimum set up time from A, is 3 and it belongs to job E, being minimum of 5, 12, 7 and 3.

After job E, the minimum set up time is for C (*i.e.*, 7 as compared to 10 and 8). In this case 6 has not been considered because A has already been placed in the sequence. Hence the third job in sequence is C.

The next job after C will be B due to set time 7 (minimum of 10, 7, 8 and 10).

Last job to be processed remains D and hence placed last in the sequence.

There is no alternative to this sequence, hence, we follow the sequence as A → E → C → B → D.

8.10 Sequencing/Scheduling Methods

Bellman Johnson's Rule for Sequencing

This algorithm is a sequencing method useful only when two machines are available and many jobs are loaded on this work centre. The sequencing is done with an aim to minimise the total throughput time (or, Total Elapsed Time TET). This rule has following steps for sequencing the jobs:

Step 1. From the matrix of processing times of various jobs on both the machines, locate the minimum processing time (MPT) for any job on any machine.

Step 2. If this minimum processing time (MPT) is associated with machine 1, the concerned job is placed at the earliest available position in the job sequence. If MPT pertains to machine 2, the related job will be assigned to the last available slot in the sequence. Eliminate the assigned job from the list of consideration.

Step 3. Out of the remaining jobs, repeat step 1 and 2 and start placing the jobs in the sequence.

Step 4. Repeat step 3, till all the jobs have been sequenced.

This method, has been illustrated with the help of an example.

Problem 8.10

There are six books available in a shop and these are to be processed through two machines in the order M_1 to M_2 (the sequence of operation). The relative processing times of the jobs on two machines are as given in the table below:

Books:	1	2	3	4	5	6
Printing (M_1) (hrs):	30	120	50	20	90	100
Binding (M_2) (hrs):	80	100	90	60	30	10

Determine the order in which these books should be processed in order to minimise total time required for all the books.

Solution:

Since it is a case of sequencing 6 jobs through 2 machines, Johnson's algorithm can be used as follows:

Step 1. Minimum Processing Time for any book on any machine is 10 hours (from the table above)

Step 2. This time 10 hours belongs to machine M_2 *i.e.*, Binding against Job 6. Hence job 6 has to be assigned in the last place in sequence. The initial sequence is as follows

	6

Step 3. Neglecting job 6, the next MPT for remaining jobs is 20 and pertains to job 4 on machine M_1. Hence Job 4 will be the first job in the sequence

4		6

Step 4. Repeating step 3 for the remaining jobs, the final sequencing obtained is as follows

4	1	3	2	5	6

Scheduling: After sequencing, the bar chart for scheduling is drawn below:

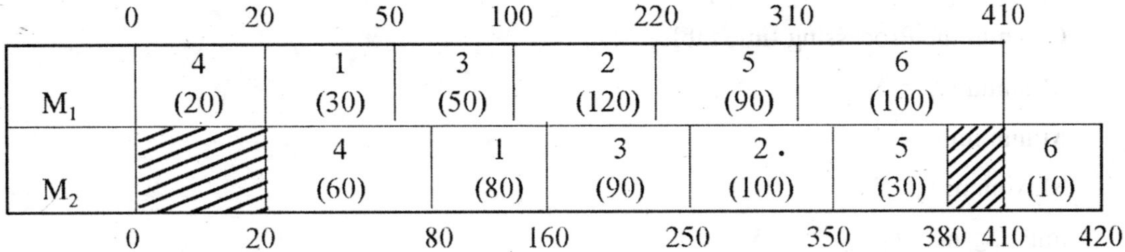

Hence TET = 420 hours

Scheduling n jobs through 3 machines.

Though Johnson's rule (algorithm) can be applied to sequence jobs on two machines only, the problem of sequencing on three machines can be tackled by slight modification to the above algorithm, by redesign, the work centres in such a way that these machines can be treated as two work centres *i.e.*, modified $M_1 = M_1 + M_2$ and modified $M_2 = M_2 + M_3$

Maintaining the same sequence of operations, under certain conditions, johnson's rule can be applied for modified M_1 and M_2 by combining their processing times as given above. These conditions to be satisfied are:

- Minimum of $ti_1 \geq$ Maximum of ti_2;
- Minimum of $ti_3 \geq$ Maximum of ti_2

Where t_{ij} = processing time of job i on machine j.

Then notionally,

$$\text{New } t_{i(a)} = t_{i1} + t_{i2}$$

and $$\text{New } t_{i(b)} = t_{i2} + t_{i3}$$

Johnson's rule now can be applied for new set of work centres a and b. The following illustration will clarify the procedure.

Problem 8.11

Find the sequence that minimises the total elapsed time (in hours) required to complete the following jobs on the machines in the order $M_1 \rightarrow M_2 \rightarrow M_3$.

Machines	*Jobs*				
	A	*B*	*C*	*D*	*E*
M_1	5	7	6	9	5
M_2	2	1	4	5	3
M_3 ↓	3	7	5	6	7

[*Delhi University, M. Com., 1975*]

Solution: It is a case of 5 jobs sequencing on 3 machines. We can use modified Johnson's rule, if it satisfies the conditions specified for the purpose.

Given in the Processing time table

Minimum $t_{i1} = 5$

Minimum $t_{i3} = 3$

Maximum $t_{i2} = 5$

min $t_{i1} \geq$ max t_{i2}. *i.e.*, $5 = 5$

and min $t_{i3} \geq$ max t_{i2} *i.e.*, $3 > 5$.

Since necessary conditions have been satisfied, Johnson rule can be applied in the modified form,

for $M_{(a)} = M_1 + M_2$

and $M_{(b)} = M_2 + M_3$

For these modified work centres *a* and *b*,

$t_{A(a)} = 5 + 2 = 7$

$t_{A(b)} = 2 + 3 = 5$

$t_{B(a)} = 7 + 1 = 8$

$t_{B(b)} = 1 + 7 = 8$

$t_{C(a)} = 6 + 4 = 10$

$t_{C(b)} = 4 + 5 = 9$

$t_{D(a)} = 9 + 5 = 14$

$t_{D(b)} = 5 + 6 = 11$

$t_{E(a)} = 5 + 3 = 8$

$t_{E(b)} = 3 + 7 = 10$

Hence the modified processing time table works out to

	A	B	C	D	E
Machine (a)	7	8	10	14	8
Machine (b)	5	8	9	11	10

Now applying the Johnson's rule, we get the sequence as:

B	E	D	C	A

or

E	D	C	B	A

The bar chart for scheduling can now be drawn considering routing $M_1 \rightarrow M_2 \rightarrow M_3$.

Assigning *n* jobs to n machines

This specific case of scheduling n jobs to n machines or n work centre can be discussed under the following conditions.

- Number of jobs are equal to number of workcentres.
- Each work centre gets only one job loaded
- Each work centre can handle any job independently
- Assignments can be based either on operations time or operation cost or profit earning basis.

Hence in case of such problems, a linear programming Method called "Hungarian Assignment Method (HAM) can be used to advantage.

Hungarian Assignment Method (HAM)

This is a heuristic model to help assigning n jobs to n machines or n persons to n jobs etc. The steps for the optimal solution are as under (based on cost or time matrix for the problem for **minimisation** case).

Step 1. Locate the smallest element of each row and subtract it from all the elements of that row.

Step 2. From the matrix obtained from Step 1, locate the smallest element of each column and subtract it from all the elements of that column. Thus we create number of zeros in the reduced matrix.

Step 3. Draw minimum number of horizontal or vertical lines through all zeros of the matrix obtained in step 2.

If the number of lines so drawn are equal to the size of the matrix (*i.e.*, number of the rows/colums), the optimality of the solution has been reached. Then proceed to step 6. If not, proceed to step 4.

Step 4. Select the smallest of all uncovered elements in the matrix after step 3 and subtract it from all uncovered elements of the matrix. Also add the same to all the elements at the intersaction of the lines.

Step 5. Repeat step 3 and 4 till optimality reaches *i.e.*, number of lines drawn = Size of the matrix.

Step 6. Make feasible assignments on unique zeros.

In case of maximisation problem, the matrix is first reduced to minimisation matrix by subtracting all elements from highest element of the matrix and then using HAM.

Problem 8.12

While revising the layout of a shop, four new machines to be assigned to the appropriate locations, with five places vacant. Due to the restriction of sequence of operations, machines M_2

cannot be placed at location C and machine M_3 cannot be installed at locations A. The matrix given below is the cost matrix for such placements. Workout optimal locations of machines.

Machines	*Cost of Placement at Places*				
	A	*B*	*C*	*D*	*E*
M_1	9	11	15	10	11
M_2	12	9	–	10	9
M_3	–	11	14	11	7
M_4	14	8	12	7	8

[Delhi University, MBA; April 1989]

Solution:

Initial check

(a) Is it a minimisation case – Yes.

(b) Is it a balanced problem – No.

Then we add an additional row M_5 to balance the matrix (with all elements as zeros).

(c) Also assign M (Very large number) at the places of restricted placement.

Thus the matrix would became:

	A	*B*	*C*	*D*	*E*
M_1	9	11	15	10	11
M_2	12	9	M	10	9
M_3	M	11	14	11	7
M_4	14	8	12	7	8
M_5	0	0	0	0	0

HAM is used to obtain optimal assignments.

Step 1. The lowest value element of each row to be subtracted from all the elements of the row. The reduced matrix will be as under

0	2	6	1	2
3	0	M	1	0
M	4	7	4	0
7	1	5	0	1
0	0	0	0	0

Step 2. The smallest element of each column of the reduced matrix (above) is to be subtracted from each element of the column. The resultant matrix will be

0	2	6	1	2
3	0	M	1	0
M	4	7	4	0
7	1	5	0	1
0	0	0	0	0

Step 3. Drawing minimum number of horizontal/vertical lines covering all zeros, we get

0	2	6	1	2
3	0	M	1	0
M	4	7	4	0
7	1	5	0	1
0	0	0	0	0

Since the lines drawn = Size of the matrix = 5, we have reached the optimal solution.

Hence proceed to step 6.

Step 6. Make assignment on unique zero elements

	A	B	C	D	E
M_1	[0]	2	6	1	2
M_2	3	[0]	M	1	~~0~~
M_3	M	4	7	4	[0]
M_4	7	1	5	[0]	1
M_5	~~0~~	~~0~~	[0]	~~0~~	~~0~~

Procedure: (i) under column C, these is a single unique zero at M_5. Hence first assignment is made at M_5 C. Cross all other zeros in the respective row. Hence all zero under A, B, D and E are crossed out.

(ii) Under Column D, there is a unique zero left at M_4 and hence assigned.

(iii) Under row M_1, there is a unique zero at A, hence assingned.

(iv) Similarly in Column B, now there is only one zero left at M_2, hence assigned and zero at M_2E crossed out.

(v) Under Row M_3 there is only one zero, hence assigned.

Hence the placement of machines has been finalised as under:

Machine M_1 to location A

M_2 to location B

M_3 to location E

M_4 to location D

M_5 being imaginary machine, the place C will remain vacant.

Problem 8.13 (Job Assignment — Hungarian Assignment Model)

ABC Airlines has drawn up a new flight schedule for five flights. On asking the flight preferences from the pilots, each pilot indicated a preference score (out of 10), *i.e.* the higher the score, better the preference. Some of these flight combinations were not considered suitable for pilots due to technical reasons. These have been marked as X in the preference matrix given below:

Flights

Pilots	1	2	3	4	5
A	8	2	x	5	4
B	10	9	2	8	4
C	5	4	9	6	x
D	3	6	2	8	7
E	5	6	10	4	3

Score matrix

Assign pilots to various flights so as to accomodate their preferences as much as possible.

Solution:

Since it is based on the preference score, we have to maximise these preference combinations. Hungarian Method of assignment can be applied to a minimisation problem and hence this maximisation matrix has to be reduced to a minimisation matrix before proceeding to find optimal assignment. (We subtract each score from the highest preference score of 10 and rewrite the matrix.

The minimisation matrix so obtained is as under (alloting M for prohibitive route)

	1	2	3	4	5
A	2	8	M	5	6
B	0	1	8	2	6
C	5	6	1	4	M
D	7	4	8	2	3
E	5	4	0	6	7

Checking precondition: Number of rows equals columns, (the problem is balanced)

Now using Hungarian Assignment Method (HAM), we start

Step 1. Locate the smallest element of each row and subtract it from all the elements of that row. The resultant reduced matrix works out to

(Row minimas are $R_1 = 2, R_2 = 0$ $R_3 = 1, R_4 = 2$, $R_5 = 0$)

0	6	*M*	3	7
0	1	8	2	6
4	5	0	3	M
5	2	6	0	1
5	4	0	6	7

Step 2. Locate the Smallest element of each column and subtract it from each element of the column to get the revised matrix, (smallest elements of columns $c_1 = 0$, $c_2 = 1$, $c_3 = 0$, $c_4 = 0$, and $c_5 = 1$)

0	5	*M*	3	6
0	0	8	2	5
4	4	0	3	M
5	1	6	0	0
5	3	0	6	6

Step 3. Draw minimum number of horizontal/vertical lines to cover all zeros,

0	5	*M*	3	6
0	0	8	2	5
4	4	0	3	M
5	1	6	0	0
5	3	0	6	6

The number of lines obtained = 4, which is less than the number of rows/columns *i.e.* 5. Hence we proceed to step 4. (Solution is not optimal)

Step 4. Locate the smallest element of all uncovered elements and subtract it from all uncovered elements and add the same at the point of intersection of lines. We get a new matrix. (Min uncovered element = 2)

0	5	M	1	4
0	0	8	0	3
4	4	0	1	M
7	3	8	0	0
5	3	0	4	4

Step 5. Repeat step 3 (draw minimum horizontal/vertical lines through all zeros).

0	5	M	1	4
0	0	8	0	3
4	4	0	1	M
7	3	8	0	0
5	3	0	4	4

There are still 4 lines drawn, which are less than 5 (Solution is not optimal). Hence repeat step 3 and 4. (Min uncovered element = 1).

Step 3, 4. (Repeat)

0	4	M	0	3
1	0	9	0	3
4	3	0	0	M
8	3	8	0	0
5	2	0	3	3

Step 5. (Repeat)

[0]	4	M	✗	3
1	[0]	9	✗	3
4	3	✗	[0]	M
8	3	8	✗	[0]
5	2	[0]	3	3

Now, the number of lines drawn = 5 (hence optimal solution). Proceed to Step 6.

Step 6. The assignment of pilots to the flights are marked on unique zeros, as superimposed on the table above. The assignments are as follows:

Pilot	A	to flight 1
Pilot	B	to flight 2
Pilot	C	to flight 4
Pilot	D	to flight 5
Pilot	E	to flight 3

8.11 Scheduling Product Layout Manufacturing

In the product layout manufacturing we have discussed two types of manufacturing *i.e.*, batch production and mass production. A variety of standardised jobs with low volumes can be manufactured under Batch production system. But when there is requirement of producing large volume of the same standard product, we call it as mass production.

Scheduling of such operation is generally simple. Two types of problems are faced under such situations:

- When variety of products are manufactured on the same production line, lot sizing has to be ensured to be cost effective or else the jobs are scheduled for minimising the set up time for change over of jobs.
- When a specific date of delivery is to be adhered to, the EDD job (described under sequencing above) is planned into the total schedule so as to ensure its production just in time for delivery (not early to result in long inventory, not later just in case a last minute failure of some kind, discrupting the delivery schedule).

In order to achieve this scheduling, the resources allocation and availability has to be ensured. For Batch production, the Economic order Quantity (EOQ) for the batch lot size is to be planned and procurement accordingly carried out. Various mathematical models have been discussed in chapter 12 under varying utilisation situations.

8.12 Line of Balance (LOB) Method

This is a case of mass production when it involves large number of components, assemblies and sub-essemblies and when we have to balance out delivery schedules of many products to customers in the near future time schedule.

The method used is called "Line of Balance (LOB) Method.

To achieve the optimum balance, certain conditions are to be paid attention to as follows:

- Layout used is process or cellular.
- Batch or Mass production.
- Batch of longer duration or larger volumes.
- Delivery schedules *i.e.*, customer's requirements are known.
- Capacity of production line is enough to follow the schedule.
- Processing one product at a time.
- Each batch consisting of the same volume for each product.

Steps adopted for LOB

Step 1. Draw out the cummulalative delivery schedule for all the products.

Step 2. Decide on the time horizon for working out the LOB of resources.

Step 3. Describe a vertical line for each processing step on the bar chart as per time schedule limit to review the progress of manufactured units at that point of time.

Step 4. Evaluate the pie chart to see whether LOB has been successful. If not, the monitoring should identify the bottlenecks and control pushed in with sufficient resources to ensure that LOB is achieved.

This progress chart must be drawn periodically so as to ensure dynamic control over the production situation. Regular interval review will keep the production under control and ensure timely delivery of products to the customers as per their requirements. LOB is beneficial, when product or services are made available to match the delivery schedules specially when the production line has number of steps and production lead time is long. Today, a large number of computer packages are available. Few of these are:

- Win Magi
- Macola
- SAP
- Baan
- People Soft etc.

8.13 Mass Production System Scheduling

While discussing the basic principles of Production planning and control (PPC), it has been brought out that the objectives of PPC even for mass production are the same as that for batch production. The cost effective schedules delivery assurance system and the effeciency of the production lines have been discussed. It was brought out that while a product line manufacturing layout and operation are comparatively easier, the main problem of line balancing has to be tackled to enhance the line efficiency and the achievement of higher production volumes. In case of process line manufacturing, the concept of Line of Balance (LOB) has been discussed to ensure effective resources planning for delivery schedules to be matching with the production schedules.

In case of Mass Production System, a lower Work-in-Process (WIP) inventory is beneficial, though the overall inventory control and efficient material handling system is to be ensured. Computerised packages can be and should be used for higher efficiency production.

The Aggregate Planning and Scheduling methods discussed above are equallly applicable here in mass production also.

Resources levelling, in this case, is easier and hence during aggregate planning, the input resources like manpower, machines and materials consumerate with the overput desired are balanced out. For this purpose, available resources must be weighed against the desired delivery schedules, so that the outsourcing decisions can be made well ahead of time to meet the organisational objectives.

For the purpose of mass production, the linear programming methods for product mix, ingradient mix, transportation and resources assignments etc are used so to optimise the cost of production. Some heuristic methods are also available for the purpose. Use of computers to search quick optimum decisions helps a lot in this direction, because nonlinear relationship can be taken care of for cost optimisation.

Chapter 9

Service Operations–Planning and Scheduling

Main issues:

1. Service operations Planning
2. Major Challenges in service operations
3. Scheduling strategies
4. Customer satisfaction level

9.1 Pecularities of service system

While discussing the design of the outputs *i.e.*, Products as well as services, some of the important differences in the production of product and service have been highlighted. There are few similarities but some distinct differences as well.

The services being intangible, uncertain and highly customer oriented, the major pecularities are to be taken into account while scheduling these operations.

The basic characteristics of services are as follows:

- Intangible outputs
- Need-oriented and customised
- Urgent requirements and hence short lead time
- Labour intensive and hence high cost
- Quality subjectively determined by customer
- Widely diverse in nature and perishable.

It is easy to understand that for customer satisfaction, service operations may need the product or may not. But necessity of service exists at all times. Hence the number of jobs in the service sector are, in fact, exceeding those in the manufacturing sector all over the world and the gap is constantly increasing. There are large corporation which provide one service, few important names being Walmart, Citigroup, BCG, SBC Communications, AT&T, etc., and lot many more consulting organisations. The list of services is also increasing at alarming speed. Few of the important areas are airlines, banking, entertainment, transportation, telephone, mobile communication devices, insurance, health care, real estate and many utility services. To become competitive in the global arena, high automation level services are becoming important for Coat-effectiveness and high customer satisfaction level.

To sum up the above discussion, we can say that service systems are

- highly diverse
- huge or tiny and anywhere
- retail and non-retail.
- well paid option for workers with high skill and training requirement and
- amenable to planning, organising, controlling and mageging at high level in order to survive and grow.

9.2 Major Challenges in Service Operations

There are few major characteristics of service that makes it very challenging for planning and implementation namely:

- Services are customised and delivered by people.
- The demand is wide varying in peaks, highly diverse and non uniform.
- Services are idiosyncratic *i.e.*, same service at one place may be well received, whereas in another place, it may be totally disastrous.
- Quality of service is highly subjective *i.e.*, quality of work may not represent the quality of service (expectations of customers vary largely).
- Management of services needs high level of understanding of the market *i.e.* customers habits and attitudes as well as that of the service force. Contact in services plays a significant role.

9.3 Need for service scheduling

Due to the above characterstics of services, the level of service requires careful consideration *i.e.*, how much to depend on customer and how much service to be provided, whether standard or as asked for, also as to how much should be the product/service relationship, because the services can be made cost effective only if the strategics for service operations are clearly defined and implemented.

Hence we can provide service with customer playing a leading role, a passive role or no role in actual operation. Product costs, technology, physical availability of material and product as backup support, product/services quality and prompt delivery are major issues to be addressed. Therefore a deliberate attempt to schedule these properly would be required.

To illustrate the service variability, let us take a simply case of Hair cutting saloon service. The demand in this service may vary hour to hour. Type of service may be varying from haircutting to messaging to facials or nailcutting etc. the service provider would never know what the customer would demand, when and how much.

Similarly, car tyre puncture happens at random, and while getting it mended, the customer may ask for brake setting or repair of any other component as he arrives at the service station. He may be in tearing hurry, resulting in limited service. Having more time on week-ends could result in high probability of more cars for servicing and other repairs on saturday and sundays. A relaxed customer may reach service station at any time convenient to him, or else he may be planning to get up early and bang the service station very early to have the job done at the fastest pace, when the loading is low. This creates a large randomness of service facility utilisation.

Hence the service strategies can be based on the following factors:

- Customer contact and public relation
- Price of the services
- Speed and the convenience of the service
- Unique skills and multiple skill requirement
- Variety of the service required and without prior notice.

Service Scheduling Challenges

The large variation in service pattern is a very major challenge to adjust the service production capacity to match the idiocyncracies of the customers and the resultant highly changing pattern of demand. Most difficult task is to cater for varying needs of the manpower to this ever-changing requirement. Cost benefit analysis, therefore, is not always easy due to uncertain loading. A high customer satisfaction level remains the key to earn money out of service operations, inspite of all uncertainties.

The erratic demand can be met with by innovation based on past experience. The service levels (design) are created initially to provide some standard services at a pre-set levels and making service facilities as flexible as possible, without sacrificing the cost benefit as well as customisation. Design of service has to be based on some anticipated pattern (collection of past data for similar operations or past experience of the manager) and then design the waiting line system for a certain pre-decided customer satisfaction level.

9.4 Useful strategies adopted

For the satisfaction of customers, their attitude and habits have to be studied, based on which, the following methods can be utilised:

- Fixed schedule service availability.

- Fixed service operation availability.
- Non-peak hour incentives.
- Appointment schedule system of service
- Reservation for certain catagory of customers during suitable hours
- Using casual/part time manpower to cater for peak hour service.
- Out-sourcing or subcontracting part services
- Keeping in-house stand-by facility to make operations flexible.

Fixed Schedule Service – When the service is offered for a certain period of time, it is easy for customer to respond during that period only. It makes demand concentrated during this period. For example, postage stamps are available at the post office from 10 am to 3 pm similarly the payment of Electric bills can be made during 10 am to 4 pm etc. Thus the services are scheduled during fixed hours.

Fixed Service operations – In this strategy, the service provider decides and announces that the service provided is limited to repair of say, electronic gadgets or issue of pollution under control (PUC) certificates. A service station may offer gas filling as well as vehicle washing and lubrications only. This is fixed service provision.

Non-peak hour incentives – In order to spread the demand, the service provider may announce discounts on the service during certain period of time when the demand generally is low, such as servicing of air conditioners during winter months or sale of wollens during late summer months. Discounted airfares during low tourist season or low golf course charges on week days are some examples for such services.

Appointment Schedules – This strategy helps in smoothing out demand over the working hours by calling customers at fixed appointed hours, so that neither the service provider nor the customer has to wait unnecesserily. Doctors and Advocates etc follow this strategy. Even if the prices of such services are different for certain periods, the peaks can still occur. This could be avoided by offering services when the customer wants it. This is true for weekend services for most customers tackled by policy of appointment, leading to more efficient and cost effective services.

Reservation – Whereas in appointment fixed time service, the reservations offer a fixed portion of the capacity to be available during certain specified period such as a doctor may be available for out-patients during the day, while specialists may be busy in important operations. There may be certain seats available on the aircraft for the VIP for urgent travelling or hotel rooms for certain important frequent customers. Strategy has to ensure optimum level of service being reserved, otherwise it may go waste if the customer does not show up. Incentives for timely utilisation with reminder system for reserved service can help.

Part time/casual workers – This is to ensure peak demand service by deliberately keeping some skilled or unskilled persons on call, during the peak demand period. These persons are engaged only when demand occurs. Hence the system is not unnecessarily burdened with their overheads.

Out sourcing/Subcontracting – It is similar to part time engagement except when service is transferred to a facility where extra capacity is available.

Stand-by facilities – When service requires quality, in house facility can be created and used when demanded, if the data suggest their likely use at number of occassions. Some fluctuations are to be caterd for, like sudden sickness, sudden vehicle failure situations (may not always be cost-effective).

9.5 Methods for service scheduling

Two important methods have been found useful to deal with the service scheduling:

- Queuing design and implementation.
- Simulation method for service design and rescheduling

Queuing Design

The Quencing design or the concept of waiting lines for their utility in service operations is an important system for service scheduling. Queuing or waiting line theory is a prediction of the behaviour of the system in terms of its measurement of performance. The information of this behaviour is required by the management for designing or deciding the appropriate level of service based on the customer satisfaction level. The queues formed under different situations can be depicted as under:

(a) Single line facility

(b) Single Queue, parallel facilities

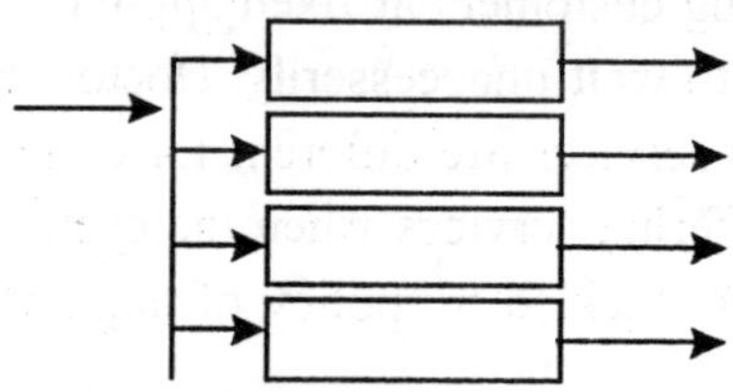

(c) Multiple facilities

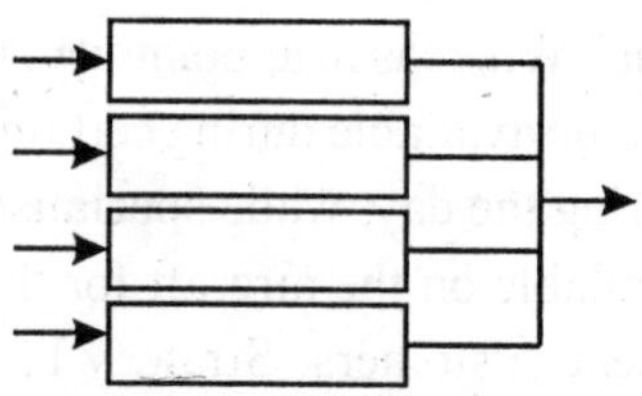

(d) Combination of facilities

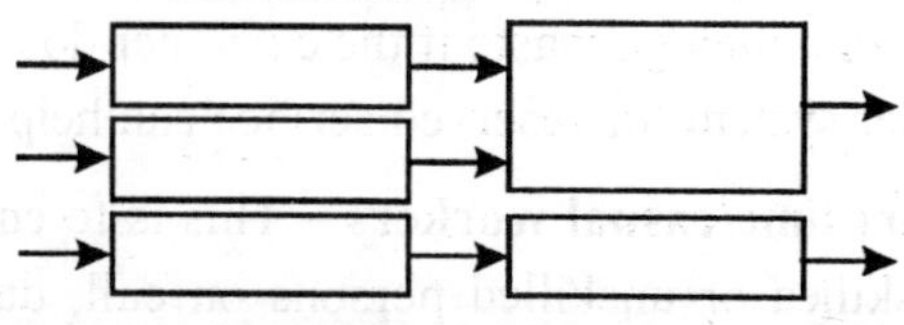

Thus the Queue is formed due to arrival of the customer for the service, when service facility can not undertake the work immediately on their arrival. A quencing system, therefore, would have the following elements:

- Inputs or arrival of customers
- Queue regulations or quene discipline.
- Service mechanism
- Customer behaviour.

Arrival of Customers: The arrival pattern is generally random as customers arrive according to their priority, unless regulated through appointments. The general pattern of arrival follows Poisson distribution.

Queue Discipline: In order to regulate service for better customer satisfaction, following methods can be adopted

- **First Come First Served (FCFS):** Service Provided in the Order of Arrival.
- **Priority**: out of turn service such as children or handicapped person or any other special requirement, (technical or administrative).
- **Emergency:** Important or needy customers may be served on priority such as very sick patient or a VIP needing special attention.
- **Service In Random Order (SIRO):** By random selection of customer, when situation so demands.

Customer Orientation for Excellence in Service

Customers Cheracterstics – The complexity of the queue changes with reference to the customers behaviour. For this pupose, the environment and customer's reaction to it needs to be studied.

Size of the customer population: It depends on the type of the service and hence the population available as customers. Populations can be finite, when it is certainly known what type of customers can be expected. For High-end condiminiums being constructed by a builder, there cannot be very many persons queuing up for such flats costing more than 5 crores of rupees. Knowing general trend of people, it will be easy to handle allotments. On the other hand, if the population is infinite, the number of and types of customer's are also infinite. To handle infinite population queues, mathematical analysis and methods can be used.

Type of customer population: Whether a population would need almost the same type of service or widely varying service, will indicate the type and length of the waiting line. Homogeneous crowds are easy to handle, but hetrogenous population can be handled through seperate but small queue counters, as they may be buying or needing different items.

Arrival Pattern: The general system of customer arrival is highly probabilistic, unless this is streamlined with the reservation or appointment system. In general, therefore, we formulate mathematical models on probabilistic approach. The customer may arrive at 9 o'clock in the morning and there may be many such customers flocking at the same time (early risers and needing faster service). Also there may not be a single customer for next one hour at the car service station (late risers, not in hurry). Then there may be a customer arriving at 11-30 hours, but requesting for top priority service as he has to go to an important engagement, but his car has failed. Thus we can see that the customer arrival pattern is very very uncertain. For such arrivals, probability attached to the inter-arrival time can appear to follow a poisson process or the Poisson Distribution, in which the time between successive arrivals is exponentially distributed. Thus we designate average arrival rate expressed as customer per unit time.

Customer Behaviour: Some customers, by nature, are very well behaved and would like to wait if the service facility is not available immediately. Some customer may walkout only by seeing the large queue, even without understanding the implication of service length and the waiting time. This is called Balking. It is a probabilistic response and it changes with the queue length. There are some customers, who could form the queue, but will leave when they find waiting becoming too long. This behaviour called "Reneging" is also probabilistic.

Thus the arrival and waiting pattern are probabilistic and hence service design must cater for this behaviour. The waiting line characterstics should be accordingly utilised for analysis and design.

Similarly, the service time of various customers is also highly probabilistic because the type or extent of service cannot be predicted in advance and is generally decided at site. Generally service time is treated as experimentally distributed and is denoted as average service time. Service Mechanism *i.e.*, number, type and the configuration of servers will also be important for waiting line analysis.

9.6 Queuing Models

- ***Notations***

Queuing models are generally described as M/M/1, FCFS/∞/∞ ,which means:

M = Arrival pattern (Poisson Distribution)

M = Service pattern (Exponential Distribution)

1 = Single server

FCFS = Queue discipline – First come First serviced.
(It can be PRI for priority)

∞ = Infinite queue length (for finite queue length, if is n)

∞ = Infinite population (for finite population, it is n)

• ***Measurement Parameters (M/M/1 model).***

Since arrival pattern, generally, follows Poisson Distribution, we represent it by (λ) and service pattern following negative exponential distribution is represented by (μ).

Thus, Average waiting time for customer $W = \dfrac{1}{(\mu - \lambda)}$

Average waiting time in the queue $Wq = \dfrac{\lambda}{\mu(\mu - \lambda)}$

Average witing time in the system $Ws = \dfrac{1}{(\mu - \lambda)}$

Average number of waiting customer in system $Ls = \left(\dfrac{\lambda}{\mu - \lambda}\right)$

Average number of waiting customers in the queue $Lq = \dfrac{\lambda}{\mu}\left[\dfrac{\lambda}{\mu - \lambda}\right]$

Probability of empty facility (No waiting) $P(o) = 1 - \dfrac{\lambda}{\mu}$

Probability of busy System $P(w) = 1 - P(o) = \dfrac{\lambda}{\mu}$

Traffice Intensity $(\rho) = \left(\dfrac{\lambda}{\mu}\right)$

• ***Measurement for M/M/K model (K-server model)***

$$\rho = \frac{\lambda}{K\mu}$$

$$W_s = Wq + \frac{1}{\mu}$$

$$W_q = \left(\frac{L_q}{\lambda}\right)$$

$$L_q = \frac{\left(\frac{\lambda}{\mu}\right)^K \rho}{K!(1-\rho)^2} P(o)$$

and
$$P(o) = \left[\sum_{i=0}^{K-1} \frac{\left(\frac{\lambda}{\mu}\right)^i}{i!} + \frac{\left(\frac{\lambda}{\mu}\right)^K}{K!(1-\rho)}\right]^{-1}$$

Problem 9.1

Customers arrive at a single-window Drive-in bank according to poisson distribution with mean 10 per hour. Service time per customer follows the exponential distribution with mean 5 minutes. The space in front of the window including that for the serviced car accomodate a maximum of 3 cars. Other cars can wait outside this space.

(a) What is the probability that an arriving cstomer will have to wait outside the indicated space ?

(b) How long is an arriving customer expected to wait before starting the service ?

Solution:

From the given data,

$$\lambda = 10 \text{ per hour}$$

and
$$\mu = \frac{60}{5} = 12 \text{ per hour}$$

(a) Probability that an arriving customer drive directly to the space provided in front of the window

$$= P(0) + P(1) + P(2)$$

$$= \left(1-\frac{\lambda}{\mu}\right) + \left(1-\frac{\lambda}{\mu}\right)\left(\frac{\lambda}{\mu}\right) + \left(\frac{\lambda}{\mu}\right)^2\left(1-\frac{\lambda}{\mu}\right)$$

$$= \left(1-\frac{\lambda}{\mu}\right)\left(1+\frac{\lambda}{\mu}+\frac{\lambda^2}{\mu^2}\right)$$

$$= \left(1-\frac{10}{12}\right)\left(1+\frac{10}{12}+\frac{100}{144}\right)$$

$$= 0.42$$

(b) Probability that an arriving customer has to wait outside the indicated space

$$= 1 - [P(0) + P(1) + P(2) + P(3)]$$

$$= 1 - 0.42 - \left[\left(\frac{\lambda}{\mu}\right)^3 \left(1 - \frac{\lambda}{\mu}\right)\right]$$

$$= 1 - 0.42 - \left[\left(\frac{10}{12}\right)^3 - \left(1 - \frac{10}{12}\right)\right]$$

$$= 0.48$$

(c) Average waiting time for a customer in the queue,

$$W_q = \frac{\lambda}{\mu} \cdot \left(\frac{1}{\mu - \lambda}\right)$$

$$= \frac{10}{12}\left(\frac{1}{12 - 10}\right)$$

$$= 0.42 \text{ hours.}$$

Problem 9.2

At a service counter of fast-food joint, customers arrive at the average interval of six minutes, whereas the counter clerk takes on an average 5 minutes for preparation of the bill and delivery of the item. Calculate the following

(a) Counter-utilisation level

(b) Average waiting time of the customer at the joint

(c) Expected average waiting time in the line

(d) Average number of customers in the counter area

(e) Average number of customers in the line.

(f) Probability that the clerk is idle.

(g) Probability of finding the clerk busy

(h) Chances that the customer waits more than 30 minutes in the system.

(j) Probability of having 4 customers in the system

(k) Probability of finding more than 3 customer in the system.

Solution:

Given data,

$$\lambda = \frac{60}{6} = 10 \text{ per hour}$$

$$\mu = \frac{60}{5} = 12 \text{ per hour}$$

(a) Counter utilisation level $= \rho = \dfrac{\lambda}{\mu}$

$$= \frac{10}{12} = 0.833$$

(b) Average waiting time at the joint

$$W_s = \left(\frac{1}{\mu - \lambda}\right)$$

$$= \left(\frac{1}{12-10}\right) = \frac{1}{2} \text{ hour} = 30 \text{ minutes}$$

(c) Expected average waiting time in the line

$$Wq = \frac{\lambda}{\mu}\left(\frac{1}{\mu - \lambda}\right)$$

$$= \left(\frac{10}{12}\right)\left(\frac{1}{12-10}\right) = \frac{5}{12} \text{ hours} = 25 \text{ minutes}$$

(d) Average number of customers in the service area

$$L_s = \left(\frac{\lambda}{\mu - \lambda}\right)$$

$$= \left(\frac{10}{12-10}\right) = 5 \text{ customers}$$

(e)Average number of customers in the line

$$Lq = \frac{\lambda}{\mu}\left(\frac{\lambda}{\mu-\lambda}\right)$$

$$= \frac{10}{12}\left(\frac{10}{12-10}\right) = 4 \text{ Customers}$$

(f) Probability that the clerk is idle

$$P(o) = \left(1-\frac{\lambda}{\mu}\right)$$

$$= \left(1-\frac{10}{12}\right) = 0.167$$

(g) Probability that the clerk is busy

$$P(w) = 1 - P(o)$$

$$= 1 - 0.167 = 0.833$$

(h) Chances that customer waits for more than 30 minutes

$$P(T > t)_{t=\frac{1}{2}\text{hr}} = e^{-(\mu-\lambda)^t}$$

$$= e^{-(\mu-\lambda)^t}$$

$$= e^{-1} = 0.368$$

(i) Probability of having 4 customers in the system

$$P(n) = \rho^n (1 - \rho)$$

$$P(4) = \left(\frac{\lambda}{\mu}\right)^4 \left(1-\frac{\lambda}{\mu}\right)$$

$$= (0.833)^4 (1 - 0.833)$$

$$= 0.0804$$

(j) Probability of finding more than 3 customer in the system

$$P(K > 3) = \rho^{(K+1)} = (0.833)^4$$

$$= 0.482$$

Simulation Method:

Simulation Method of design has already been discussed under chapter 3 of this book.

9.7 Customer Satisfaction Level

What follows from the above discussion is as to how all possible efforts are made to keep a customer happy and satisfied so as to keep getting repeat orders as well as addition of service requirements. With the goodwill created, more and more customers can be added. However some of the factors which achieve high customer satisfaction level through services can be summerised as under:

- Customer to be provided service to the level he expects it.
- The types and the value of service provided should meet the customer's requirement.
- The comfort, convenience and the ambience created for showing courtsey to the customer like pick and drop facility, television, water and paper arrangements, a cup of coffee (complimentary from the service provider) help in creating goodwill.
- Friendly behaviour of the personnel in the service system is much welcome by the customers.
- The skill, professional approach and schedule adherance by the service personnel is an asset to create confidence in customer's mind.

—•—

Chapter 10

Just-In-Time Production and Lean Manufacturing

Main issues:

1. Pre-requisites for JIT and its utility in production.
2. JIT concept and Support from Purchasing and Maintenance
3. JIT Implementation
4. Synchromous Production and TOC
5. Optimised Production Technology (OPT)
6. Lean and Agile Manufacturing

10.1 The Just-In-Time (JIT) Revolution

World War II created awareness and necessity across the world that production needs a push in terms of volumes and quantity with minimum inputs. The requirement of the Armies fighting the war, whether American, British, German, Japanese or any other combination, for whatever sector of geographical locations, was so diverse in terms of number of products and the quantities of each product that it taught various lessons of production to the world. In war, another important element is time. Infact, the most important requirement is the delivery of equipment at the appropriate place with right product mix, in just sufficient quantities. This was the beginning of JIT concept. Whereas the over-delivery would have been the burden on logistics, under-delivery could be a cause of defeat even for a small item say short delivery of snow boots, while fighting in Russia during winters.

After the second world war, Japanese were practically at zero level of industry, but by 1980s they become the world leaders. Thus the industrial history of Japan after world war II has become the history of a developing economy through manufacturing.

After Hiroshima and Nagasaki, Japan was practically converted into rubbles concrete, with large scale destruction of cities, manpower, infrustructure and other resources. With limited money, limited manpower and limited raw materials, Japanese started house to house manufacturing, buying just enough material for just enough manufacture for just available demand. This cycle came to be known as Just-In-Time (JIT). They could illafford inventory or wastages due to own financial limitations. Limitation of space was also a big handicap as the house was required by the family for sleeping in the night.

Thus the development of JIT concept due to post-war conditions could be summerised as follows:

1. Japanese ruined economy
2. Scarcity of resources
3. Centralised industrial planning
4. Employee involvement
   (a) Experience in various disciplines
   (b) Small Scale family business
   (c) Space restriction and manpower availability restriction.

The Japanese Government was restructuced by the Allied Powers General Head Quarters with General MacArther as the head. The overall guiding vision for the industry enamated from there and later through Ministry of International Trade and Industry (MITI). This Ministry was responsible for Industrial planning for activities that formulate the industrial policy and pattern of future growth, controlling which industry will grow, and which will decline. Inspite of these odds, Japanese industry has flourished so well and so fast that it became a very strong developing economy in very short time.

The success of Japanese industry is primarily for the reason of their management system. Their managers considered the value of human resources as the most important element of work. Hence their style of life-time employment, constant performance evaluation and training, non-specialised career paths, collective decision making, collective responsibility and deep concern for the employees, was successful and copied by the world in due course of time to write their own success stories.

Open discussion and total employee involvment provided the benefit of floor experience during decision making. Interactions with other departments created multiple skill culture for different corporate disciplines.

In 1970's and 1980's, when the Japanese became an economic power to recon with, its electronics and auto industries became the world leaders and with the help of Dr. Deming, they set the standards of product quality and cost. This was the formalisation of JIT with Quality circle (QC) concept, where "you solve your own problem" was practiced hard and was successful due to total employee involvement that made them part of the total business.

A real look at the concept of JIT indicates that it is very simply doing the work at just about the time it is required, (like fill up petrol in your bike just when it is required), buy your milk or salt or vegetables just when you need them or schedule the work and arrange men, machine and materials just when required to produce a product at just about the time the customer needs it, with just about the quantity required.

Some people call it the little JIT. When the concept is utilised for overall productions work *i.e.*, the organisation of designed work to convert it into end product, specifying the responsibilities assigned to ensure timely and cost-effective production, it is called the Big JIT. Generally, it is really JIT.

10.2 Definition of JIT and Lean Manufacturing

Just-In-Time (JIT): It is a philosophy based on planned elimination of all waste with continuous improvement of productivity. It encompasses the successful execution of all activities required to produce a final product, *i.e.*, from design engineering to delivery. It includes improving quality to zero defects; to reduce lead times by reducing set up times, queue lengths and lot sizes; to incrementally revise the operations themselves; and to accomplish these things at minimum cost. In broad sense, it applies to all operations *i.e.*, – job shop, process as well as repeatitive activities and to many service industries.

Some companies have given their own names to this concept of JIT such as:

Hewlett Packard	– Stockless production
	– The repeatitive production system
General Electric	– Management by sight
IBM	– Continuous flow manufacture
Motorola	– Short cycle Manufacture

In addition, some companies also use the term "Lean Manufacturing,"

Lean Manufacturing: Lean Manufacturing is defined as "A philosophy of production that emphasises the minimisation of the amount of all the resources (including time) used in various activities of the enterprise. It involves identifying and eliminating non-value-adding activities in design, production, supply chain management, and dealing with the customers. Lean producers employ teams of multi-skilled workers at all levels of the organisation and use highly flexible increasingly automated machines to produce volumes of products in potentially enormous variety".

Thus JIT or lean Manufacturing is a set of Methods of manufacturing. It emphasis waste reductions as its main theme.

10.3 The Seven Wastes

These seven forms of wastes were identified and advocated for control/avoidance by Shigeo Shingo, a Toyota Motor Company employee. These are:

- **Waste of over–production:** Eliminating by reduced set up times, process synchronisation and compact layout etc. It means "Produce just what is needed now".
- **Waste of Waiting:** Eliminating non-productive activities by Synchronous work flow and balance of uneven loads by flexibility in use of workers and equipment.
- **Waste of Transportation:** Avoid by establishing proper layout and location of transport facilities and handling the minimum and rationalised operations.

- **Waste of Processing:** Eliminate unwanted and unnecessary products by thinking beyond the economy of scale.
- **Waste of Stocks:** Reduce through short set up times and reduced lead times, synchronise work flow by balancing or smooth out demand fluctuations.
- **Waste of Motion:** Eliminate all unncessary motions through proper method design. It will improve productivity.
- **Waste of making defective products:** Develope stream-line production process and method to prevent defects, thus reducing inspections.

Americans call the avoidance of these wastages as **value-added Manufacturing.**

Problem 10.1

A factory wanted to reduce set up time so that JIT programme can be effective and they wanted an lot size of 20 units (EOQ). The data given to the analyst is as under.

Demand	= 15,000 units per year
Daily Demand rate	= 50 units
Daily production rate	= 150 units
Holding Cost	= Rs 20 per unit per year
Labour rate	= Rs 200 per day

Find the set up time.

Solution:

From EOQ formula

$$\text{EOQ (Q)} = \sqrt{\frac{2DS}{C}\left(\frac{p}{p-d}\right)}$$

Substituting the data, p = 150 and D = 15,000

$$C = \left(\frac{200}{8}\right) = 25,\ d = 50,$$

$$\text{and EOQ} = 20 \text{ units}$$

$$\therefore \quad S = \frac{CQ^2}{2D}\left(\frac{p-d}{p}\right)$$

$$= \frac{200}{8} \times \frac{20^2}{2 \times 15000}\left(\frac{150-50}{150}\right)$$

$$= \frac{200 \times 400}{16 \times 15,000}\left(\frac{100}{150}\right)$$

$$= 0.22$$

$$\therefore \qquad \text{Set up time} = \frac{S}{C}$$

$$= \frac{0.22}{25}$$

$$= 0.008 \text{ hours}$$

$$= 0.53 \text{ minutes}$$

$$= 31.68 \text{ Seconds}$$

10.4 Prerequisites For JIT Manufacturing

JIT manufacturing is just a simple philosophy *i.e.*, drastically reduce raw materials, WIP and finished goods inventory by synchronising the production element. If the flow lines are well co-ordinated, balanced and operated with little delays or no delays, work centres will operate smoothly and it will reduce the manufacturing lead times. WIP is the key element to be taken care of.

JIT is most useful and successful in repectitive manufacturing because of continuous flow lines. Repetitive Manufacturing can be defined as the repeated production of the same discrete products or families of products. Repetitive methology minimises setups, inventory, and manufacturing lead times by using production lines, assembly lines or cells. Work orders are no longer necessary; production scheduling and control is based on production rates. Products may be standard or assembled from modules. Repetition is not a function of speed or volume. In large and complex situation, the design and implementation of the JIT system is not very easy. JIT may be very useful production method, but it requires some changes before actual implementation. Some of the changes required are:

- Stabalise production schedules.
- Increased capacity of work centres.
- Simple design and multiple skill operators.
- Improve production facilities through proper maintenance.
- Develop captive and loyal vendors to ensume no failures due to materials.

Thus well-designed Master Production Schedule (MPS) is key to successful JIT manufacturing.

10.5 JIT Production Systems

JIT system of today is popular because lot many people and organisations have worked on the development and implementation of JIT concepts *i.e.*, improving the design and operation of production systems. Though the start up was with Japanese, it is a world wide accepted system today. In short, JIT system means reduction or elimination of production deviations *i.e.*, getting closer to the following conditions:

- Produce only one type of product or develop JIT system for each product.
- Apply it to a constant demand and hence repetitive production.

- Product available to the customer at the productions end.
- Production input resources are available at the place of production.
- Materials management is superb, in terms of quality, quantity and time, on just-required basis.
- Being repeatitive process, the processing time is almost constant for each unit produced (Fatique allowances and learning should balance it out)
- Arrangement of sequential workcentres is easy to organise.
- Production is defect free.
- Machines are well maintained and never allowed to breakdown (Practice preventive maintenance)
- Employes are committed, always available and follow the production method resulting in no mistakes.

When we design a system described above, it is easy to operate. It may be compared to the assembly work place for a car assembly with workcentres arranged sequentially and all parts/ components and material handling systems available at their respective places when required, so as to produce a customised car when required. But it is not always practical. Probabilities, uncertainties, bottlenecks, breakdowns, shortages and sickness etc. can all be there with no control on their random occurance. Hence to take care of a production system under natural uncertain conditions, we have to find ways and means to incorporate JIT into our life systems and make JIT production feasibly and workable. This is done by changing the design and operation of the system in such a way that uncertainties are avoided even if at slightly higher costs, but level of end result certainty rising.

Hence the JIT production system would be successful if the demand variations, unreliable material deliveries, product defects, machine breakdowns, processing lines variations and the unnecessary wastage in set ups are eliminated to the best of system capability. Though there are no ideal production systems, we can strive to be very close to it. Day is not far when CIM (Computer Integrated Manufacturing) in full accomplishment will prove that JIT production is possible to its uppermost efficiency level. There has to be WILL to ensure such a level. For the system to came up to the desired level of efficiency for JIT production concept, we have to concentrate on all the seven S's:

- Structure
- Strategy
- Systems
- Skills
- Staff
- Subordinate goals
- Style

Japanese firms also have their own variations of JIT. They use the variations of soft S's to advantage based on their management style. Emphasis on systems may be different but aim remains the same *i.e.*, produce what is required, how much is required and when it is required.

Japanese strongly believe in stockless production. It means that production run takes place only against orders and delivery made just when it is ready. The relationship between quantity and quality is strong and is ensured. Wastes are not permitted, thereby using manpower, machines and materials optimaly productive.

To summerise the JIT manufacturing philosophy, it is emphasised that it is an order-to-delivery system which has to be dramatically organised with the key objective to utilise the production capacity fully with few workers and machines and still achieve better volumes and quality. The time schedule for delivery at the customer's end at a time when the product is just needed, can be illustrated as follow:

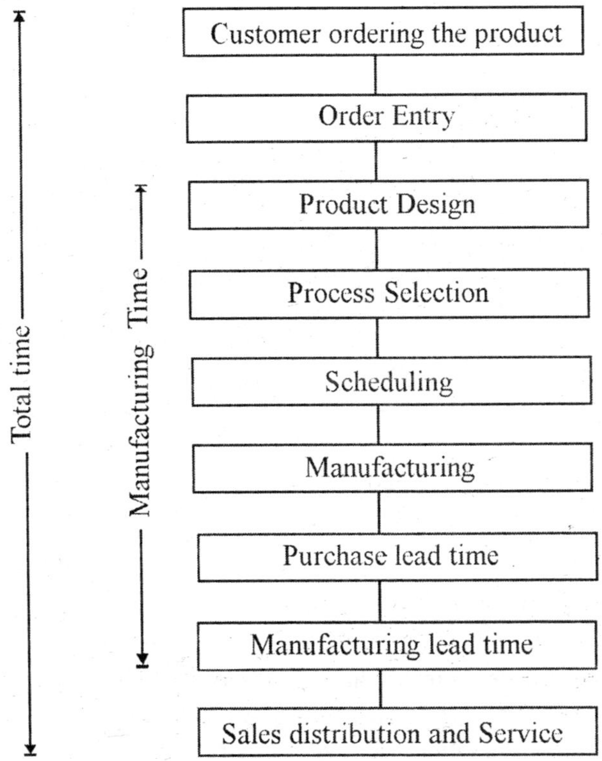

FIG 10.1. ***Ordering to Delivery Time.***

For illustrating this aspect, we can use the waiting line or queuing theory through an example.

Problem 10.2

A manufacturing unit wants to reduce its manufacturing lead time from 15 days to 6 days. Present average level of jobs arrival is 200 units per day and the system can handle 210 units per day. What should be the new productions rate? Calculate the reduction in the WIP inventory with the revised production rate.

Solution:

From the usual notations of queucing theory,

$$\text{Average arrival wait (W)} = \frac{1}{\mu - \lambda}$$

Where μ = average production rate

λ = average arrival rate

$$W = \frac{1}{210 - 200}$$

$$= \frac{1}{10} = 0.10 \text{ days}$$

$$= 6 \text{ minutes}$$

If we change the manufacturing lead time from 15 days to 6 days.

$$6 = \frac{1}{\mu - 200}$$

$$\mu = 201 \text{ units}$$

Hence the production rate goes up by one unit for reducing lead time from 15 to 6 days.

$$Ls_1 = \frac{\lambda}{\mu_1 - \lambda} = \frac{200}{201 - 200} = 200 \text{ units}$$

$$Ls_2 = \frac{\lambda}{\mu_2 - \lambda} = \frac{200}{210 - 200} = 20 \text{ units}$$

Hence WIP reduced from 200 units to 20 units.

Workers Involvement in Kaizen

Whenever there is any problem arising in production, there is a pile up of work-in-process (WIP) inventories. In traditional manufacturing, this is not a major problem because a larger WIP inventories will result in continious production even with the problem at hand. This is to ensure high capacity utilisation in terms of manhours and machine hours. But in JIT production system, it is totally unacceptable, because in this case, we strive to reduce inventories in all areas to a just sufficient level.

When the inventories are reduced, the production problems start coming to notice. In JIT system, these problems are overcome through the interaction of workers and managers just as and when these are noticed. Therefore JIT is a system of enforced problem solving.

Man Behind the Gun. Any business can succeed only when its people want it to happen. JIT can and will happen only with the will and effort of the production workers and the associated teams. People will make it happen, whether it is problem solving, effective operations or continuous improvement to make operations better. It is the dedicated, committed and involved worker with high level of motivation that can make the JIT successful. The training and motivation with confidence of workers for safe operations, can bring in the desired results.

Quality Circles (QC). This technique has been extensively used by Japanese for problem solving. Though quality, quantity, time and place are synchronised in JIT, the problems may still arise and to find the quick solution to it, every one connected should be concerned so as not to impede the flow of production. In Quality circles (QC), all the concerned persons, *i.e.*, the production workers, materials personnel, quality team, design or sales persons etc can sit together to analyse the problem(Composition depends on the type or area of the problem). These people go over the problem, get into its root cause and devise a method to over come it. Due to large involvement and commitment by all concerned, the problem gets resolved fast and managers implement at production level to continue the JIT production. Through this method, the managers reduce the interruptions to production to bare minimum level and WIP can be incrementally reduced. When there is practically no WIP, it indicates that the problems have been resolved.

Another important aspect is the belief that continual improvement in the system is posible and must be tried out at all times. This means that a total vigilance is required to study and identify a potential problem, before it becomes a complecency so that pro action is initiated to avoid its emergence as a production blockade. This system is called Continuous Improvement (CI), which is termed as KAIZEN by the Japanese. There has to be a goal of continuous improvement so as to achieve better results. Workers are encouraged to spot such areas, when either the problem can be anticipated or where improvements can be made for further simplification of the system. It may be in any area, be it product, design or any production technique.

Japanese Manufactureres have used the term SMED (Single Minute Exchange of Dies), a concept signifying just about enough setup time, aiming at less than a minute for this change.

A culture of mutual trust and team work among workers, between workers and management, between management, unions and the workers must be built in any organisation. Quality Circles (QC) was one such concept tried out successfully by the Japanese. It is also called "Participative Management" by some organisations. Team work is the real key to the business success and more so for JIT production. In fact, individual workers shooting off tangentially on their own are discouraged and instead inward-looking team effort must be preferred.

Quality Circles (QC) was seen as the workers participation programme, when workers themselves identified the quality variation and offered suggestions to eliminate them. The potential solutions, as described above, was discussed by a team of employees (called QCs). Japenease train their workers in basic skills of data charting and sampling analysis etc. for this purpose.

Employee Empowerment. Another System tried out is employee empowerement as discussed earlier. The workers are encouraged to think and operate to get good ideas. If they are allowed as team mates in decision making process, they operate better. Initiatives come handy to improve systems, if there is delegation of authority, rather than wait for some one else to take the decision. This should not go outside the team work preview. Quality problem, machine manufacturing or any other safety concern must be attended to immediately not waiting for an accident or defect to occur. Vendors and customers involvement can help achieving effective improvements.

10.6 Quality Management

Total Quality Control : The Total Quality Control (TQC) has been applied by the Japanese for improving quality in every area of business. Quality has been defined by JURAN as "Fitness for use". Thus the product needs to be produced to make it just appropriate for its intended usage. Poor quality is wasteful and if the waste can be avoided, the quality of the product will improve and so will the productivity. The TQC, therefore, is a good tool to achieve better results. Since in JIT, the emphasis is at zero defects level (almost), the quality control has to be inbuilt into JIT production system. The utilisation of TQM (Total Quality Management) Philosophy, therefore, is imperative. TQM will be discussed in details in a later chapter. but here it will suffice to mention that it has to be a cummulative effort of all the personnel of the organisation to do their work deligently and without wastes at any level in any operation. Hence all the departments have to be a constant helping hand to the production process to ensure timely help and quality work. It is total commitment of everyone that can ensure JIT implementation in quality production for timely deliveries to the customers. The main interest of everone has to be customers satisfaction.

For quality improvement, the defects levels have to be brought down. If the defects are noticed through the system of feedback mechanism as described in production model, these can be rectified and product produced according to quality standards. If the defects go unnoticed and reach the customer, customer's reaction is expected. To avoid such situation, the necessary changes in design and production procedures are required to be introduced. This technique is called "poke yoke" by the Japanese. In English, we call it fail-safing or foolproofing. In JIT manufacturing, this is a great help in streamlining the defect elimination.

Kanban System of production Control: In chapter 8 on manufacturing operations and scheduling, the 'pull type' production control system has been discussed, in which the inventory is controlled for the next operation. The raw materials are pulled to what is needed at production and products pulled towards the supply point to the customer. At intermediate stages, there is WIP constantly being pulled for the next stage of production. This is exactly what we do in JIT production. Hence it was mentioned that JIT is the pull system of production planning and control.

In case of JIT manufacturing, the batches of products go directrly without being stored as inventory. Toyota is using JIT system in the form of KANBAN, a Japanese concept. Kanban means a visual record generally referred to be a card. Japanese use this very simple system of planning and controlling the production. There are two type of kanbans in use namely:

(a) A conveyence (or C) kanban

(b) A production (or P) kanban

Conveyence or C-kanban: This card is similar to a requisition permitting the transfer of material from a supply work centre to a utilisation work centre.

Production or P-kanban: This card authorises the production and replacement of earlier transferred material through the C-kanban.

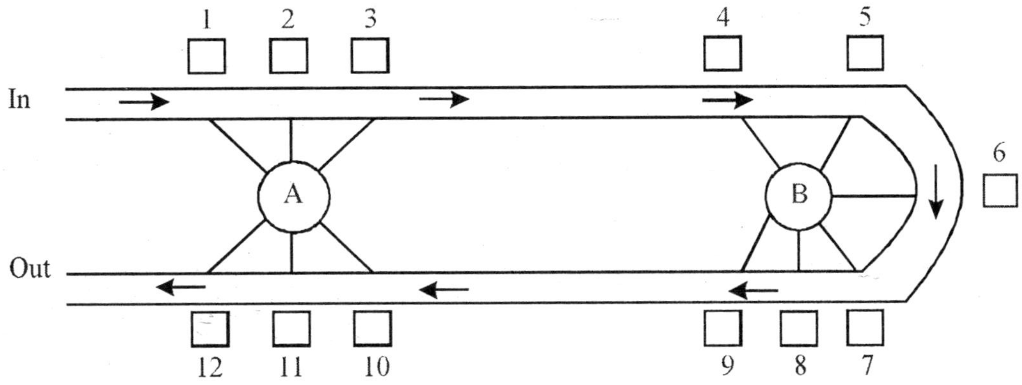

FIG 10.2. Pull type Kanban system

The materials are loaded into bins, which are decided based on the production sequence and the number of items in a bin proportional to the specified number of products to be manufactured. By having decided the number of bins and the quantities prescribed in each bin, the inventories are controlled at the shop floor, without wasting time now in actual counting. When we reduce the number of cards between two work centres, WIP inventories are reduced to zero and components arrive at the use point just in time. This satisfies the JIT demand.

An easy pull system work centre has been described below to show the usefulnees of the kanban system. An assembly system needing 12 different components has been illustrated in the figure. Two workers A and B are the operators for the assembly. Each components has a basket or bin kept for it, where in necessary inventory *i.e.*, number of components required for the assembly of a product are kept. If component 1 is required to be one per product and we have to assemble 25 products, there are just 25 components kept in bin No.1. Similarly, proportional number of components are kept in successive bins.

Assembly starts as the bins are supplied through the material handling system. Operator A picks up components from 1, 2 and 3 bins in sequence and in requisite number from each bin sufficient for the assembly. When assembled, the product moves further on the conveyor belt and part-assembled product reaches operator B. He starts picking up components from bins 4, 5, 6, 7, 8, 9 sequencially one by one and keep assembling. He also picks up requisite number of components from each bin required for completing the assembly. When bins are out of the reach of opearator B, the partly assembled product is sent to operator A, who, by now, has turned back in his chair. He assembles the components from bin 10, 11 and 12 in succession and completes the assembly. The completed product goes out to the stores as finished product.

It is called pull system because the components are pulled from successive bins just to send the products to the next workcentre, and by pulling all the components sequentially, the assembly is completed. When 25th product is being assembled, each bin in quick succession will become empty as the inventory of components kept in the bins was just sufficient for 25 products. By the time, operator A and B return to their original position, they find that old bins have been replaced with new ones authorising assembly of a different product now indicated on the new card or kanban. This is a very good illustration of JIT production system by kanban method of inventory and production control. Here C-kanban has been used for bringing the components and P-kanban for authorising production of products.

Thus it is automatic assembly of requisite number of components of a product. The information available on the card accompanying each bin as illustrated in fig 10.3, helps the operators to perform as per the information and there is no time wasted in counting material or the products.

Conveyence (C) Kanban Card

Part No: to produce	K135C	Part Description:	Motor
Lot size needed :	25	Container type:	Red crate
Card No.	2 to 12	Retrieval storage location :	5W/14K
From work centre:	22	To Work Centre:	135

Production (P) Kanban card

Part No. to produce:	K135C	Part Description:	Motor
Lot size to produce:	25	Containes type:	Red crate
Card No.	4 to 12	Completed storage location:	5w 14K
From work centre:	22	To Work Centre:	35

Materials Required

C 7335 storage location: 5W 17C

K 5432 storage location: 5W 15B

FIG 10.3. Kanban cards

Some companies use only single card kanban system, where the card is progressively moved from bin 1 to bin 2 and so on. Thus the movement of bins to required work centre can be achieved. All bins are to be placed in standard locations as per the work centre requirement. The movement of cards and containers has been illustrated in fig 10.4 below:

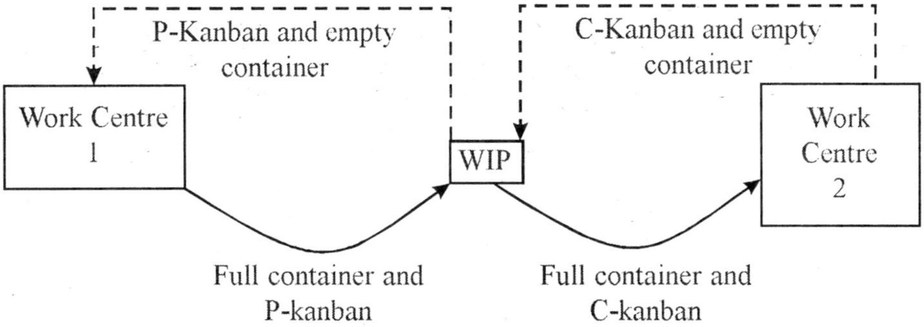

FIG 10.4. Movement of Kanban Cards

For a simple shop floor production control, the use of kanban can be illustrated as follows:

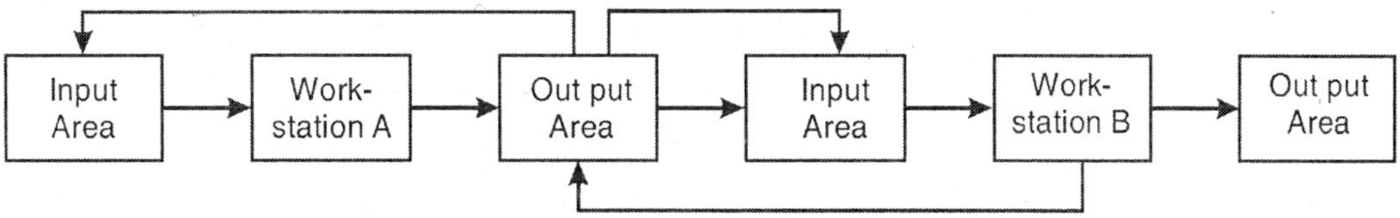

FIG 10.5. Kanban on Shop Floor

Uniform Load Scheduling

In kanban and JIT production, the balancing of the production system make it easy to operate. Thus, to achieve good control over JIT production through kanban method of control, there should be uniform load scheduling, when the product range is more than one. These products must be planned in such a way that the lot sizes are small and the flow time is almost similar. We can reduce the change over or the set up time drastically in such a case.

Support from Purchasing and Maintenance

As discussed earlier in this chapter, for making JIT production system successful, the machines and materials should not fail the system. Hence a constant attention to preventive maintenance of machines and strict control over purchases must be exercised. Captive vendor management (CVM) and quality control are the techniques useful for effective support to operate the JIT manufacturing.

10.7 JIT in Services

The advantages and requisites of the JIT system are equally applicable in services industry. In service operation the savings on time, cost and lead times help in better customer satisfaction. Hence many service organisations have adopted the JIT system to advantage.

Poke-yoke: In service operations the most useful technique is 'Poka yoke' discussed under JIT production. It is, more appropriately called mistake-proofing. The philosophy of poka yoke is redesigning a process so that it is very difficult to make a mistake in the process.

For assembly of a product, where there are a number of parts to be assembled, one system to ensure Poke Yoke is to arrange these parts in a sequence, keep them in different bins (as in case of pull system of kanban) and permit the assembly only through this laid down sequence.

Operation check list: One more simple technique is the "check list". One effective "check-list" to ensure inspection on various subsystems is listed our in Figure 10.6. This check list consists of details of inspections to be carried out is by the inspector. When he ticks in front of each sub-item, full inspection is ensured and he can be held accountable for any failure of a subsystem, if at all. By writing this checklist, chances of him making a mistake are reduced and poka-yoke effectively implemented.

Item to be checked	Checked
1. Dimension	☐
2. Bulb	☐
3. Colour	☐
4. Voltage	☐
5. Noise level	☐

Checked by (Name and Dated Signatures)

FIG 10.6. Inspection check lists

Similarly, when there is repetitive work to be done, a printed templete can be designed so that it acts as a check list. There should be different colour templates designed for variety of products and at one time, only one product cartons should be given to the worker for pasting it.

House Keeping: Another good technique used in services JIT system is good house keeping. House keeping can be defined as the service activity of identifying and maintaining an orderly environment for preventing errors and contamination. There can be large number of such examples. One such example is identifying a fixed place of such keeping house keys. Mistakes are likely to reduce and the house lady does not have to look for the keys either in the toilet or under the pillow in the bed room. In large companies, such as aircraft manufactureres, where there are thousand and thousand parts to be assembled, it will be impossible to locate and sequence them, if the housekeeping has not be planned well.

Japanese call these house keeping rules as 5 processes. These are:

Seiri (sort)

Seiton (straighten)

Seiso (sweep)

Seiketsn (standardise)

Shitske (self-discipline)

These rules are very useful in service operations and are required to make the services more competitive.

EDI and Optical Scanning: In service industry, the useful technologies for JIT implementation are optical scanning and electronic Data Interchange (EDI). With the help of these technologies, a service provider or a retailer can maintain real time information on products and it also allows suppliers to use this information for their production or procurement action in time for shipping the required products as soon as reduction in inventories are noticed. In captive vendor system, there is no waiting even for a formal release order or purchase order for these supplies to be recouped. By this method, we can reduce effective lead time drastically. If the total system is IT-enabled, the sales counter information (sales effected and billed) is enough for a retailer to act immediately, say, every evening, to rush supplies to the sale stores so that the shelves are full again for next day sales.

The two systems of optical scanning and EDI help in fast deliveries for restocking and automatic information conveyence for further production. The risk of stock out is reduced and inventory levels can come down drastically. In case of fast food joints, the small kanban system (smaller lot size preparations) is used to restart the preparation, when a certain pre-decided order point is reached. Thus it helps the fast food provider to satisfy the customer quickly with almost freshly cooked item. JIT system of production and service is, thus, gaining popularity due to obvious cost and lead time advantage and the resultant customer satisfaction.

10.8 Key to successful JIT Implementation

Following steps can help in success story of JIT implementation:

- Stabilise and level the Master Production Schedule (MPS) with uniform load scheduling.
- Reduce or eliminate set up times.
- Reduce lot sizes for production as well as for purchase.
- Reduce lead times for production and delivery.
- Priority to effective Preventive Maintenance.
- Multiple skilling and flexibility in work force.
- Loyal and quality consious vendors and strict quality assurance programme for zero defects.

- Use kanban concept to advantage, use smaller lots. (JIT is required to use kanban system but kanban system is not a must for JIT operations).

10.9 Tools for JIT

Following tools and techniques can be utilised for effective JIT implementation:

- Value Engineering and Value analysis.
- Process flow charting.
- Method study and work measurement.
- Preventive Maintenance – Total Productive Maintenance (TPM)
- Standardised design of products and delivery systems
- Kanban systems
- Failsafing in design and implementation
- Lot size reduction techniques
- Flexible work force.

10.10 JIT II

The JIT II concept was conceived and implemented by the Bose Corporation. This organisation is known for high quality sound system. In the concept, a vendor is engaged to be an active member of the purchasing department of the customer. The concept is also called Captive Vendor Management (CVM) in broader sense. The vendor representative remains with the manufacturing department and is responsible to plan and schedule the replenishment function for the materials. The method adopted is named as "Vendor Managed Inventory (VMI)" through the CVM. The timely issue of purchase orders as per line requirement of materials is the function of this vendor representative. His on-ground availability helps in reducing costs for improved manufacturing. Thus JIT II establishes extremely close interaction of buyer with the vendor. The system offers Win-win situation to both, the buyer as well as the vendor because it provides the organisational structure needed to improve the material supply coordination by scheduling and integrating purchasing, production and logistics together.

10.11 Sychronous Production and Theory of Constraints (TOC)

In order to ensure JIT being effectively followed, there is another approach, which helps in production scheduling and inventory management. Any bottlenecks, naturally, are the sources of disruption in the production schedule and for JIT operations, these are not desirable. Hence if various work centres are planned for foreseeable bottlenecks, the operations will become smoother. Goldratt suggested an approach called Theory of Constraints (TOC). It is also called **Synchronous Production** or the Drum - buffer - rope approach, because this is how Goldratt explained his approach of Theory of Constraints (TOC). The Original software of Goldratt was named as

Optimised Production Technology (OPT). It is still in use duly marketted by Scheduling Technology Group Ltd. Another software available for the same concept is manufacturing 5 by Thru-Put Technologies. While explaining the synchromous production, it can be seen that it is quite similar to JIT production. It also takes care of production balancing and small lot size production. Variation from JIT production is its pull-push approach of scheduling and its focus on efficient management of system imbalances, rather than eliminating them.

Theory of Constraints

The theory of constraints (TOC) was developed by **E. Goldratt** based on the following observations (obvious in actual practice):

(a) All stages of production donot have the same production capacity in a multi-stage production system. There are variations in manpower output or the machine output. Also there are random variations due to lapse of time or change in working conditions/environment..

(b) These variations and their random happenings would affect the production efficiency and capacity.

(c) The method and procedure used in normal classical production generally does not solve these problems, but can amplify.

A perfectly balanced line is not easy to obtain due to random inbalancing. The smallest production capacity of any stage will dictate the maximum rate of production. This rate of production is called the "throughput" while considering a bottleneck of this nature (limiting the production capacity of the system). Any resource that limits this production capacity is called the 'Bottleneck Resource'.

The system with bottlenecks can be depicted as under:

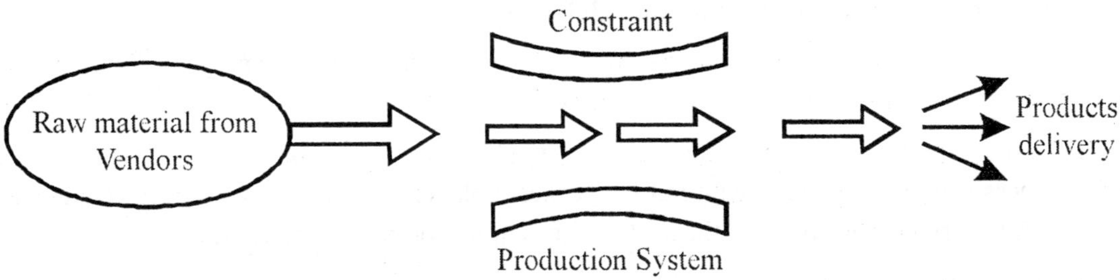

FIG 10.7. Constrained Production System

The system throughput is limited by a bottleneck or constraint. To resolve this problem, 'non-bottleneck resource' having the capacity more than the demand can be used and therefore, would not restrict the "through put" of the system. Such 'over-capacity' cannot and should not be built at all stages or work centres as it will be costly. Instead, a non-constrained resource should be developed, so that it does not become a bottleneck, but operates close to its capacity so as to avoid bottleneck.

This clearly results in capacity imbalance in the production system and would result in the loss of 'through put' for the entire system. This is the main theme of Theory of Constraint (TOC). It states that we should manage the bottlenecks by managing the constrained resources. It is a practical approach to production because bottlenecks would arise or exist and these have to be managed in the best possible way.

The variation in the system due to machine breakdowns, material shortages, production of defective components or the human fatique (we have called these as Random Fluctuations in Production Model), also reduce the maximum effective capacity. This results in increase in the throughout time and higher WIP inventories. Fluctuations would also create bottlenecks even in very efficient and balanced systems. The third type of bottleneck creation is due to machine and material imbalances. Even if the production takes place, demand variation can create bottleneck at the finished goods stages, creating material handling problems. A particular workstation may not have enough materials to keep its full capacity going. These variations and problems of bottleneck arising out of these are taken care of in Synchromous Production.

Hence the Key philosophy of TQC can be summerised as "the continuous improvement of production performance. In this case, we use new measure of **through put** (the rate that cash is generated by the sales), **inventory** (the money" used for inventory upkeep) and the **operating expenses** (the money spent in inventory conversion into throughput), the **method** to establish the production performance.

Goldratt himself stated that

"Before we can deal with the improvement of any section of a system, we must define the system's global goal and the measurements that will enable us to judge the impact of any subsystem and any local decision on this global goal".

Also to quote **Dr. Edwards Deming** – "We learned that optimisation is a process of orchestrating the effects of all components towards achievement of the stated aim".

Both these quotes define the theme behind the TOC. The production system is a chain, whose effectiveness is judged by the strength of its weakest link. Therefore, use of Project Management Technique is very helpful to study the system through its component activities.

Various steps to identify Theory of Constraints are:

- Identify the system constraint.
- Blow up the constraint and innovate to exploit it.
- Constraint decision controls the rest of the system (rhythm set by this decision)
- Find and make resources available to minimise the effect of the constraint.
- If constraint has been taken care of, go to step 1, But this constraint solution should not result in developing another constraint.
- The chain of actions continues for all constrants identified.

Synchronous Production

The basic idea behind synchronous production is getting to the ground reality in terms of output capacity of manpower and machines with type of raw material used in production. Hence Dr. Goldratt recommended in his "Theory of constraints" that working of synchronous production is very valid for balancing the actual working capacity and not the rated capacity. He recommended a mechanism for co-ordinating production so that the actual flow of production is balanced for various work centres to operate smoothly. This scheduling method for Synchronous Production is called the **Drum-Buffer-Rope method**.

The Drum: It is a mechanism for controlling the flow of production (*i.e.*, the rhythm of the Drum beats). This rhythm has to match the final output required in a JIT pull system, so as to adjust the flow according to the customers demand. The drum, therefore, is also Master Production Schedule (MPS) as the flow of production occurs what is inbuilt into the MPS.

We have to take care of the anticipated or available bottlenecks of the system. Thus, in synchronous production system, the drum becomes the bottleneck or constraint resource where the production is pulled from the previous stage and pushed to the next stages, thereby becoming a combination of pull-push system of production control.

The Buffer: The variations in production system are inevitable and hence have to be taken careof. Due to the random variations, the production thru-put will not be as desired. But customer wants the products when he needs them (which is JIT philosophy). To cater for these variations, a BUFFER is to be developed. If bottleneck resource is materials, then the production does not stop due to idle time available at the bottleneck work centre. If the material shortage goes beyond optimum level (being taken care of by idle time), we need building up inventories at the bottleneck operation stage. Thus in synchronomous production, a buffer stock is kept in front of the bottleneck work centre, so as to ensure that bottleneck operation continues uninterrupted. This is true for assembly operation also.

The Rope: Though the rhythm is set by the drum, there may still be random requirements (bottlenecks) to be taken care of. For this purpose, the system must have a communication link to pass information in quick response to the following operations because these operations will be controlled by the amount of resources available with these operations by the bottleneck.

A simple method suggested is to plan for over produce at the work centres preceding the bottleneck. Further work centres, naturally, will be governed by the bottleneck resources. In JIT Scheduling, the Rope is the kanban pull system, so also in synchronous production. The link or communication system is thus, the Rope to control the production using a daily production schedule.

A schematic diagram showing this method is given below (Refer fig 10.8)

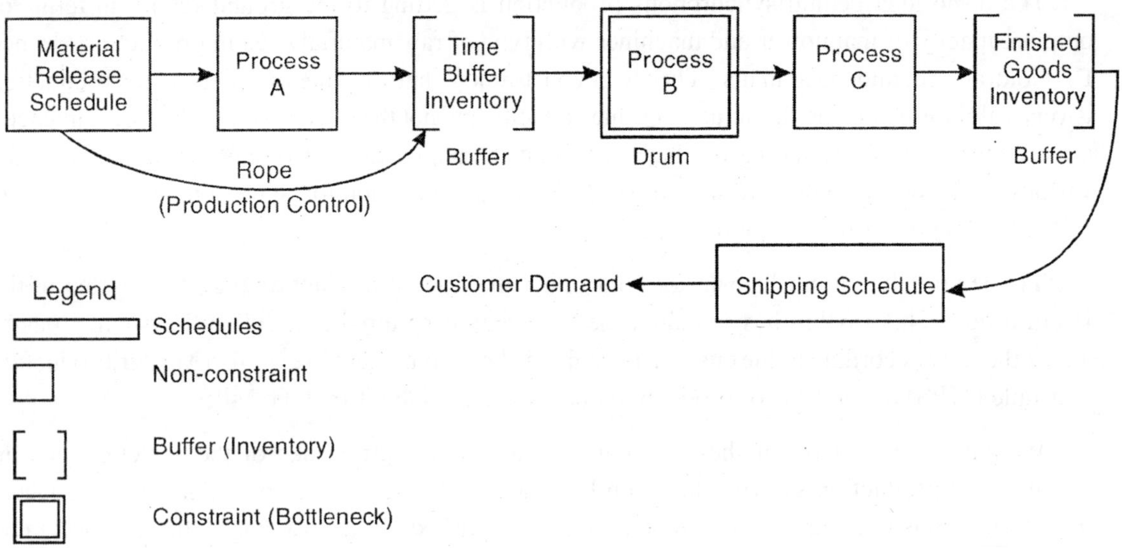

FIG. 10.8. Drum - Buffer - Rope Production Control

The main themes of the synchronous production (The Drum – Buffer – Rope method based on the principle of TOC are:

- The bottleneck establishes the rate of production and hence scheduling has to start with the bottleneck work centre (The Drum) setting the rhythm or the pace of production).
- Buffer inventory in front of the bottleneck work centre must be maintained so as to permit smooth production operation.
- An information communication system (The Rope) to keep the bottleneck operations working at pre-determined pace by conveying the bottleneck to relevant work centres.

Goldratt's Rules for Production Scheduling

E. Goldratt has suggested the following golden rules for production scheduling under constrained system operation:

- Balance the flow lines, not the system capacity.
- The level of utilisation of a bottleneck resource is not determined by its own capability, but by other constraints.
- Utilisation and activation of a resource are not the same.
- An hour lost in the bottleneck is an hour lost for the entire system.
- An hour saved at a bottleneck is a mirage.

- Bottleneck govern both the thru-put as well as inventory in the system.
- Transfer batch may not and many times should not be equal to the process batch.
- A process batch should be variable both along its route and in time.
- Priorities can be set only by examining the systems constraints. Lead time is a derivative of the schedule.

10.12 Value Stream Mapping (VSM)

This is another concept for cost effective production. It is a qualitative tool aimed at eliminating waste (Muda). Because waste levels bring the efficiency of production lower, the value stream mapping proves to be very effective tool to enhance the production efficiency by bringing down the waste level. Through this concept, the production manager creates a visual "map" of every operation involved in the flow of materials and information in a product supply chain.

The concept of map of VSM consists of identification of current state, the desired future state and the implementation plan to enhance this state from present to the future. This is called "walking over the process". The mapping involves all activities of the supply chain *i.e.*, from incoming raw materials to the delivery of the end product to the customer. Thus it is a critical examination of the whole supply chain with a view to eliminate any unnecessary activity, material or information. The process is useful due to its capability of displaying more information than a typical process map or process flow chart with six-sigma process improvement efforts. Thus the VSM follows the stages shown in Fig. 10.9.

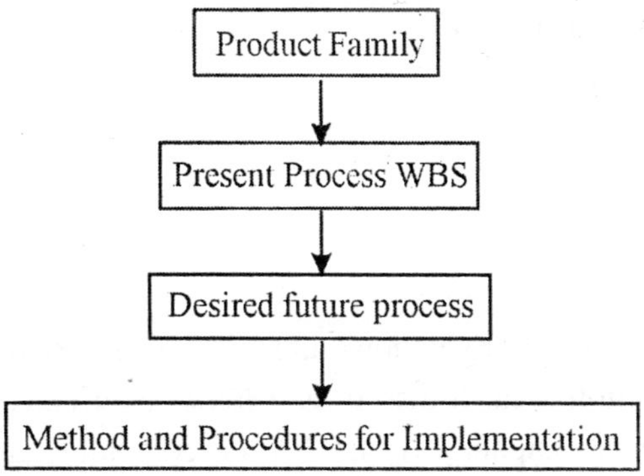

FIG. 10.9. Value Stream Mapping stages

Product Family Selection: The mapping can be started for any important product family, which could result in worth while improvement.

Present Process WBS: The existing process system is, then, studied ensuring that all WBSs are critically examined for locating any Muda (waste) of any kind, be it in materials, information or the activity execution method. Detailed Method study helps in this identification. The examination starts from the customer end for any wasteful feature. Study encompasses the information about efficiency and output of manpower and machines, set up time or change-over time, production batch size, operators number and training levels and product variety, working and standard time, scrap and accident rates etc. Process Analysis, thus, becomes very stingy going over every small detail with a "magnifying glass".

Desired Future Process: Based on the customer requirement (information updated again), the products and processes are modified to approach just the right level for customer satisfaction in term of cost, time and quality. Once the desired level is drawn, the study of various constraints takes priorty for any unnecessary failure at the later date. Unlike the Theory of Constraint (TOC), which accepts the present system bottlenecks and then only work out the maximum throughput under the given constraints, the VSM takes the responsibility of improvement through the comparison of current state and the future desired state, by eliminating the bottlenecks.

The aim of value stream Mapping is to reach the production rate of the entire process closer to the customer desired demand rate. The advantage of applying this tool to waste-elimination process is to ensure reduced lead time and 'work-in-progress' inventories, reduced rework and scrap rates, thereby reduce the indirect labour cost and enhanced productivity.

10.13. The optimised production Technology (OPT)

The optimised production Technology (OPT) is a computer software, which was originally developed by Goldratt for the Drum – Buffer – Rope method. It was designed to implement the synchronous production. Since it is propritory product, the details and algorithm are not known. But it is known that it is a system for planning production, material requirements and resources utilisation. The software has four modules:

- BUILDNET
- SERVE
- SPLIT
- OPT

BUILDNET: Creates the product production route *i.e.*, sequence of operations, materials needed and route through the production area. It also provides the requirement such as set up time, run time and delay schedule along with capacity availability; order quantity and order delivery schedules.

SERVE: Creates a tentative schedule for the waiting jobs.

SPLIT: It distinguishes critical and non-critical resources as per the resources utilisation through SERVE. About 100% or near utilisation are considered bottleneck operations.

OPT : It reschedules the critical operations through forward scheduling method and recycles the non-critical operations through SERVE.

From the description of the software above, it is easy to identify some basic rules of OPT such as:

- Critical resources determine the production for the system.

- Level of utilisation of non-critical resources should reflect the needs of the critical ones.
- Bottlenecks determine thru-puts and inventories.
- Transfer batch size need not equal the process batch size.
- The process batch size should not be fixed over all processes.
- Schedules to be developed on optimised resources levels.

The schematic diagram for the information inputs and outputs for OPT is given below (self-explanatory) Refer Fig. 10.10.

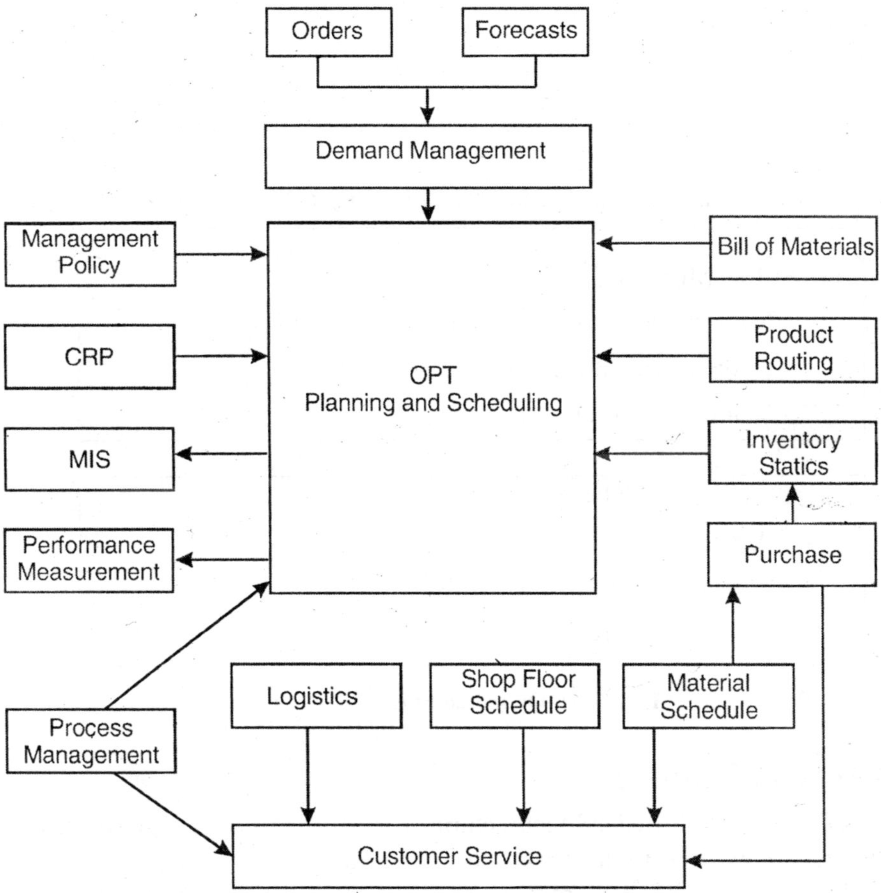

FIG. 10.10. Information Inputs and Outputs for OPT

Thus a simplified outline of OPT can be drawn as follows (Refer Fig 10.11)

Input Data
- Sales Forecast
- Resources available
- Product routings and BOM
- Work patterns

↓

OPT System

↓

BUILDNET MODULE
- Combined BOM, routing and order data

↓

SERVE MODULE

Backward schedule, load profile and **critical resources**

↓

SPLIT MODULE
- Net work of critical and non critical activities
- Optimal critical resources
- Non-critical resources

↓

OUTPUT REPORTS
- Work dispatch data
- Work centre statement
- Material requirement plans

FIG. 10.11. Optimised Production Technology

10.14 Lean Manufacturing

Lean system can be followed in Manufacturing as well as in service. Toyota Production System (TPS) is an effective example of this approach. Toyota has worked on this system for almost 14-15 years, continuously improving their production system. Lean systems can be defined as the operation systems followd for maximising the value addition to all the activities of an organisation. The system involves the production design, the operation strategy, the process design, quality management, layouts, supply chain design, technology and other resources management. Such usage in Manufacturing operations is called "Lean Manufacturing". The wider concept can be terms as Production with optimum waste reduction.

Various charactersties of lean Manufacturing (equally applicable to services system also) can be summerised as follows:

- Work flow - the pull method
- Quality improvement at the source through poka-yoke.
- Small Lot Sizes
- Uniformly loaded work stations.
- Standardised work methods
- Standardised components and modular assembly designs
- Captive Vendor Management (CVM) through Buyer-Vendor partnership.
- Flexible work force with multiskill training
- Automation
- House keeping and 5-s concept
- Total Productive Maintenance (TPM)
- Kanban system, JIT and JIT II system of inventory control
- Value Stream Mapping
- Supply Chain Integration
- Continuous Improvement or Kaizen philosophy

10.15 Agile Manufacturing

Market force, demands the quality, cost and time of delivery to be balanced with customers schedule and hence and pull and push system of market forces would place its demand on the manufacturing system. Accordingly fast market transformation provides an opportunity for quick tangible results. Global markets with global forces of competition would push any organisation to the wall and ensure it agile operation. The rapid pace of technological development (thus technological forecast of utmost help in agile manufacturing) provides tools and techniques to the agile managers. This in real value-innovation.

The term ***Agile Manufacturing*** has emerged due to high level of uncertaity, dynamic business environment and ever changing customer needs for high quality and low cost products. Thus it can be described as a manufacturing system having capacity to meet the fast changing needs of the customer coupled with the proactive management style. This would necessitate effecient and optimum use of human resources (hence the concept of Human Assets Management described earlier) for optimum utilisation of non-human resources in the most cost effective manner and that too very rapidly with assurance of positive changes in products and services to serve the customer of tommorow (better if it is ahead of demand and offered to the customer as a progressive demand satisfaction).

Thus Agile Manufacturing has been aptly defined by Goldman (1995) as **"A comprehensive and strategic response to fundamental and irreversible structural changes that are undermining the economic foundations of mass product based competition."** In the words of

Verndat (1999), it is **"Flexible, responsive and efficient (manufacturing concept), which continuously evolves and adapts to their markets, be innovative and capture new markets"**.

It is, hence, evident that agility creates positive and rapid innovation so as to ensure enhanced competencies and capabilities at all level of functions. Agility encompasses timely availability, responsiveness, customer delighting as well as aesthetical satisfaction. It meets all the expectations of the customers, be it technical utility, economical, aesthetical, social or psychological needs. With the rapid change of business due to LPG (Liberalisation, Privatisation and Globalisation), the intense global competition has forced the pace of operations to be innovative all the time. The necessity has arisen due to the following factors:

- Voice of the Customer (VOC)
- Voice of the Organisation (VOO)
- Voice of the Information (VOI)
- Voice of the Marketplace (VOM)
- Voice of the Globalisation (VOG)
- Voice of the Technology (VOT)

10.16 Re-manufacturing

The present day imperative of cost reduction makes a business manager a 24 × 7 man, thinking and re-thinking as to how the cost of production can be reduced without sacrificing the quality requirement. Few cost-saving techniques has been described in the book at appropriate place. To name only a few concepts, these could be JIT, lean manufacturing, agile manufacturing, or flexible manufacturing etc. Today in the same line of thinking, Re-manufacturing is emerging to be a useful and economic concept. It also helps in environmental management.

Cost-Saving Concept

Re-manufacturing is a concept like Reverse logistics where the utilisation of the logistics in the reverse direction *i.e.*, resources returning to the base station for picking up products for onwards supply becomes cost effective. These returning resources are used either for carrying the packaging materials or the products for the base-place market. In case of re-manufacturing, the process starts with the reclaim of the used durable products. These products can be broken into three types of components.

- good components – reusable-meeting the specification and quality requirements.
- Partially good products – can be re-worked to be made useable in the product assembly.
- Totally demaged products – can be recycled as scrap and the new components manufactured and used in the product.

In any case, the re-manufactured components *i.e.*, reworked or new manufacture have to have the same or similar performance characteristics and the quality standards as new units. The aim is to get product meeting the functional requirement. Such process is also very useful in case of modular design products.

The product so re-assembled is now sent back into the market with a warranty atleast equal to that of a newly manufactured product. The concept is also named as Re-cycling. In fact, in the language of Giuntini and Gaudette (2003), Re-manufacturing, by contrast, is the ultimate form of recycling. It conserves not only the raw material content, but also much of the value added during the process required to manufacture new products". Hence Re-manufacturing is not really a "recycling" process but is different in the form that part of the product is retained or reworked and only unuseable scrap material is recycled and replaced through a newly manufactured component. Thus it adds value to the waste (scrap) materials by converting them into useful component/products. Hence whereas in recycling, the total material is converted into input form, in re-manufacturing, it is partially done, thus effecting saving to the overall production process.

According to the WTO report (2005), "Remanufacturing process has experienced so much business that global trade has already crossed 100 billion US dollars in Re-manufacturing and has established manufacturing facilities in Europe, latin America, Asia, Africa and the United States".

The cost savings, therefore, can be summerised in the following manner:

- Saving of material and labour efforts against the recovered components meeting the dimensional, performance as well as quality requirements. Hence such components are recovered, disassembled, cleaned and maintained to be used as such.
- The re-worked components also save the manufacturing efforts partially, since only part-effort brings such components to the workable standard. This reduces the material cost and labour content partially.
- The newly manufactured components can also reduce the cost, if by now, these can be manufactured out of newly developed easily workable, substitution materials, which can be cost saving as well as eco-friendly.

Environmental Advantage:

All across the globe, environmental pollution is a great concern today. The industrialisation has increased the threat of environmental degradation not only in production, but also in the distribution network utilisation. Deforestation for the sake of industrial development as well for housing necessity has also added to the woes. The increase in the quantity of green-house gases present in the air, has been greatly responsible for the global warming phenomenon. It is also leading to the faster and irrevocable melting of ice-glaciers in Antarctic regions. As per Indian studies conducted by the Ministry of environment and forests, Government of India (2009), India's aggregate and per capita emissions over next two decads will remain quite modest, well below those of the developed countries.

Through Re-manufacturing, Low landfills, solid waste reduction and now product savings are few potential benefits leading to the environmental efficiency. It is primarily because Re-manufacturing. It is primarily because Re-manufacturing, according to WTO, is the process in which a recovered good, or core, is transformed through cleaning, testing and other operations into a product which is tested and certified to meet technical and safety specifications and has a warranty similar to that of new product. Many industries employing this concept of Re-manufacturing have derived the cost and environmental benefits. Some of the industries in this category are "earth-moving equipment, automotive components, medical equipment and infrastructure. A wide range of products are being remanufactured such as automotive parts, locomotives, buses, aircrafts, earth-moving plants, machine tools, engines, electronic equipment and components, photo copiers, mobile phones, computers and many consumer durables."

To sum up, the re-manufacturing can be involved either in reuse, repairs, recondition or recycle components, and parts (for value-addition and cost saving, along with environmental economy). Due to improved material, working may result in energy saving also.

10.17 Business Process Re engineering (BPR)

Business Process Re-engineering has been defined as "The Fundamental rethinking and redical redesign of business processes to achieve dramatic improvements in critical contemporary measure of performance such as cost, quality, service and speed."

The definition clearly lays out the spectrum of line of action for changing today's method of working to a totally new concept so that we can satisfy customers at a relatively faster pace with quality product of totally new design at reduced cost.

It was adopted by some industries which were old and could not cope up with the change required to suit the customers requirement. It is a costly but very deliberate change and may or may not bring proportional results. It may be very difficult to implement due to resistance from workers towards the change. A total redical change, therefore, will be all the more difficult. The retraining is not easy. The organisational and human dynamics may be too complex and multi-dimensional. With the time elapse, this concept is loosing shine. In todays context, the transformation needed is "Technological Innovation".

Hence to bring about change due to BPR, we need to understand that it is beneficial from the points of view of developing new market for a product change, quality change and the resultant cost benefit. It also introduces innovation and creativity to help in resolving the dynamics of the customer requirement. But the limitations also have to be understood. In addition to the basic problem of acceptance of change, it has high cost involvement and in the present context, high IT-operated system development and utilisation and would need integration and good team work with high Technical Capability. The long-term benefits have to be clearly defined. It is not fast result technique. Hence once decided, it has to be ruthlessly implemented with proper monitoring and periodical audit systems in-built. The progress evoluation can satisfy the top management about its efficacy on the longer time period benefit basis.

The strongest voice to enhance competitiveness, thereby forcing the business to be innovative for requirements is quick adaptation. The organisation has to adopt itself to meet the cost, performance, variety and psycological expectations of the customer. Voice of the organisation is predominantly the support system for customer satisfaction. In order to achieve this aim, the vibrant (quickly transforming) organisation would need tools and techniques for agility. Information system plays very significant role in this direction. Vertical, lateral as well as need based quick delivery of information saves efforts and time, thus helping the business to be lean and efficient, due to large scale integration with the help of IT-tools.

Customer is the initiating force for any business and his expectations are to be met with, by aligning the business mission with these expectations. Hence to summerise, we can list out various components of BPR as follows

- Strategic Business Planning – to ascertain and workout, as to what is good for the organisation for beating the market competition.
- Activity Modelling – to ensure no part of the plan is left out of consideration, analysis and resourcing.
- Data Modelling – to make decision-making process easier and mathematically helpful.
- Activity Based Costing – This is to work out the cost-benefit analysis of the re-engineered process making it worthwhile for implementation.
- Economic Analysis – the result of cost benefit should indicate the expected return of profit and market share.

Principle for BPR Implementation

Based on the decision that BPR is worth the effort in terms of technology, cost effective production volumes, quality and delivery schedules to stay floating (if not far ahead) in the market, U→S→A principle for implementation is adopted, where

U (Understand the existing Process) by

- Diagramming
- Story boarding
- Walking,

} the process

S (Simplifying the process by eliminating waste) by

- Rearranging
- Eliminating
- Combining
- Simplifying

} the activities.

A (Automate the process) by

- Electronic Data Interchange
- Enterprise Resource Planning
- Manufacturing Execution System.

—●—

Chapter 11

Advanced Technologies

Main issues:

1. Production Automation for competitive Advantage
2. Advanced Production Systems
3. Cost and Risk Analysis
4. Advancement in Services automation.

11.1 Production Automation

In the traditional methods of production, capital investment is large. Certain advanced methods of production have resulted out of constant search of solutions for present day problems.

These advanced technologies are the application of latest discoveries in the following fields:

- Science
- Engineering
- Technology
- Management

These discoveries are applied in the design and implementation of some unique production system for cost effective operations inspite of wide variety of product requirement. The latest in information technology and automention can be integrated into the production processes.

The capital intensity, therefore, is required to be reduced by bringing down the cost of equipment. Since the capabilities of the technology have been constantly increasing and costs decreasing, many choices are now available to the production managers for improved outputs with reduced unit cost of production.

11.2 Necessity of automations

In the past, automation meant the reduction in human effort and increase in the machine capability for production. The output obtained from machines was far greater resulting in huge savings in addition to the savings achieved due to manpower reduction. In today's concept, automation means use of information technology to enhance utilisation of machine element in production by intergrating all the advancement of technology, latest science and enginering laws into all our operational processes for short term as well as long term benefits, more so in long range planning. Due to these technological advancements, even the quality improvement, production volumes increments and high level of flaxibility have all become feasible and easier.

Basically there are two type of automations namely Fixed and flexible. Whereas the fixed automation produces one type of product as per fixed sequence, the flexible automation can be used for handling various products. The programming of these machines can be changed for different products to meet varied demand of the customers. It could work for small batches or for high volumes. Fixed automation is generally preferred when the demand is large for a fixed product (design being stable) and product life cycle is long. In case of flexible automation, the variety of the product may be large with smaller volumes and the machines can be programmed to alternate between products.

11.3 Issues in automation

Though the necessity of automation has been brought out in the precious paragraph, the level of automation and the cost structure has to be justified. There are some important issues that we need looking into before designing the automation system for production or service.

Few important issues emerge out of necessity for automation as follows :

- utilisation analysis
- flexibility level
- cost benefit analysis
- technology availability
- manpower capability

Utilisation Analysis

Quite a large number of big companies are still using mechanical or manual technologies. Present level of automation with reference to the economies of scale as well as variety of product with short product cycle has to match with the cost and time schedule. Hence the mismatch has to vanish if full utilisation of automation has to be taken advantage of. We have to analyse as to why some companies prosper with manual technology and why some large organisations fail inspite of using very advanced technologies. Important issues are:

- Automatic use of automation is not always successful if it is not managed properly. Defining the level of automation, working out suitable organisational structure, designing products and processes to warrant such an automation are few musts for success. Hence we may not succeed always if integration of systems and their effective management does not get proper attention.

- Automation is a costly process and hence has to be accepted by the organisation from aptitude and attitude point of view. Workers have to accept its utility and managers its productivity, to ensure success.
- Cash benefit analysis of all subparts of automated production system may not result in the same decision. But over all benefit must be established.
- Automation is not always feasible. Some technical problems for some unviable operations need to be taken into consideration.
- All the companies may not justify the automation level at least for initial production work. Flexibility in facility development and pleacement must cater for automation to be integrated as and when justified and found feasible from technical, technological and economic point of view. Production profitability, therefore, is the key word.

Flexibility Level

The ever changing market, quick change in the customers behaviour and preference and global competition are key factors to work out what flexibility has to be ensured in the production system to bring in the automation. Market share improvement through short-life cycle products and variety of products will dictate the flexibility level of the organisation. We need to cater for the following variations:

- Modifications in the production schedules to match customer requirement schedules.
- Quick change of product or many variations of the same product for better customisation
- Innovative approach to bring quick design change in the product and process system.
- Quick changes in the production capacity to respond to quick demand variation.
- Aggressive marketing to present and sell new products satisfying customers needs. This also needs flexible approach and building excess capacity for such changes.

For this concept, use of automated systems in the form of CNC and DNC programmable machines, robots identification and process control systems are adopted to advantage (as described in succeeding paragraphs).

Cost Benefit Analysis

When we bring in the new technology to increase automation level or even shift from manual to mechanical or highly automated systems, the cost factor becomes important. Hence cost benefit analysis has to be done with reference to the capital cost and running cost involved in automition to ensure quality and quantity for quick response to market needs. This is a complex and not easily quantifiable state system but can be adopted through input/output cost analysis *i.e.*, money spent to sales benefits over a period of time (gestation or pay back period). Net Present Value (NPV), internal Rate of Return (IRR) or other capital budget approaches discussed in earlier chapters.

Technology Availability

In Automation implementation, it is important to find, as to what technology level is available across the Globe for the type of product and what can be made use of. Also we have to consider whether the technology under consideration has been used and established its use-efficiency. The next issue involved is how easy it is to obtain the type of technology required legally, economically and technically. It has been experienced that in certain cases, the implementation of the automation project has not been easy and due to complexity and capital involvement, it takes longer than anticipated to implement, throwing cost benefit analysis out of the gear. For an effective implementation, therefore, following things must be kept in mind :

- Strategic plan encompassing all company operations.
- Production technology know-how to be understood by organisation dealing with it.
- Proper time schedule to be worked out for implementation phase.
- Identify automation areas specifically
- Specify and understand the risks associated with the automation implementation.
- Automation has to be accepted by people, aptitude wise and attitude wise. Inevitablity of change must be understood and accepted by all.

Manpower Capability

For any new technology to be absorbed by the organisation, following are necessary:

- Attitudinal capability of people
- Justification of Change
- Technical capability of people matching with the change
- Facilities available for training, retraining, displacements, multiple skill development and constant skill upgradation needed commensurate with change/automation.

It is important from the basic concept point of view that automation replaces people. Hence displacement of people is very big issue. It is not only a technical problem of retraining or multiple skilling, it is also a social problem and will become acute for a developing nation, where unemployment is a major concern and any retrenchment or displacement will cause bigger flutters in the society. Hence unless the country generates alternates in employment, the issue of automation may have to wait or get delayed. Even for training for the new technology, the mental level of the workers can be a big issue.

11.4 Types of Production Automation

Todays automated machines have a very large range of diverse features enabling them to be used for variety production, quality production and volume production and that too with large savings on labour and time. To name a few, today we use numerically controlled machines, robots as material handling systems and automated inspection and control mechanisms, all in perfect synchronisation and coordination.

Based on the above discussion, the types of automated systems of production available are as follows :

- Computer Numerically Controlled (CNC) machines
- and Small attachments.

- Automated quality control systems
- Automated identification systems
- Automated process control systems

Computer Numerical Controlled Machines (CNC machines)

These machines are totally computer controlled. In early days, the numerically controlled machines were evolved with paper punch tapes used for reading instructions for production and later for automatic tools settings and resettings. Now the operations and controls are automatic processes performed by machines with practically no human involvement except for initial settings. There is a constant improvements and addition of features in these machines as the technology advances. Now, there are Direct Numerically Controlled (DNC) machines, where a number of machines are controlled by one computer. This has been possible due to the enormous speed and enhanced features in the present day computers. These machines carry out all operations automatically as per the programmed system. The tools are also accordingly designed so that their automatic operation and settings are possible after having been programmed. The automation level increase is costly but inevitable as per the IT-progress and more and more improvement opportunities being available. Infact, we are heading towards total robotism and computer integrated manufacturing.

Robots and Small Attachments

The use of robots for various functions is becoming increasing popular due to accuracy and human like performance without human bias involved. A large number of jobs are being performed by robots today. Japanese are constantly designing more and more soplisticated robots. The first robot in America was used to unload a die-casting machine in General Motor Company. For development of industrial and domestic robots, USA has the Robotic Institute of America, busy in development and improvements in the utility of robots in large fields of life.

Robot is a programmable, multi-functional device designed to handle materials, tools and components etc for the performance of variety of operations. Through the use of micro-computer functioning as the mind of the robot, it can perform all the functions and tasks programmed for. Due to technological advancement, robatism has gone many steps forward and their field and level of utilisation is really amazing. Quite a few operations like handling of welding guns, arc welding tools, spray painting machines, screw drivers etc can be handled by robots today due to their three–dimentional movements. The holding or grasp Work is done with the help of sensors. The robot can identify the area of its operations through sensors and can operate effectively, efficiently and accurately. The major advantage of robots is that it can operate without human feelings such as loss of interest or efficiency under heat, dust, smoke or darkness conditions. Due to computer controlled acuracy, the quality of task performed is much better when compared to that performed by the best skilled human worker. The robots are accurate, predicable, flexible and capable of performing variety of tasks as per their programming capability. Now, there are advanced version of CNC machines. These advanced machines can automatically select and change tools. These are called Machining Centres performing many tasks. To save human effort, instead of using robots, we can design small, simple, and easy to operate machine attachments. This also can became and has been a method of automation.

The variety of robots today is large and these can perform many types of functions even in human-hostile environment like heat, fumes, dust, darkness or even noise. Due to their capability of movement in horizontal, vertical or even radial directions, these can be used for welding, painting, screwing or any other functions. The precision in operations is very high as the grips at the end of their arms are vaccum, magnetised or even adhesive devices.

Because robots are computer-controlled, it is possible and advantageous to programme or re-programme for variety of tasks and variable volumes. This produces flexibility in operations, which is the requirement of the market these days.

Automated quality control systems

This is yet another automation tool available to ensure product quality. These machines can perform many quality functions like checking physical dimensions of parts, compare with the standards set, as per the tolerance limit permitted, therely completing the inspection for quality acceptance or rejection of lots.

There are number of automatic machines to check electronic circuits or even for testing of softwares for their capacity, capability and feasibility with the present day IT-enabled system, even one hundred percent in special machines are available. These automated quality controllers not only reduce the human bias in measurments but also enhance the accuracy and speed of inspections, therely effecting savings in quality control inspections.

Automated Indentification Systems

These are the technologically advanced machines, where the requisite data is acquired and fed into the computer to identify the data matching product. with the help of Bar codes. Any unique product can be correctly identified. Similarly, inventory items can be identified for their specifications, location of storage and proper shop floor control. Design of material handling machines can be effectively matched with the help of such automated machines.

Atuomated Process Control Systems

These machines use the sensors such as for robots or identification machines in order to obtain some specified measure or parameter of performance of the production process and then compare it with the set standards (which are also available in the database of the computers) with the help of appropriate software. These comparisons can show if the process is in control or not, which means whether the end product satisfies the laid down parameteric value of performance or not. In case of any out-of-control signal, the resetting signal is sent by the computer to ensure error correction at the appropriate place, say tools resettings, chemical composition, mix change or thickness of the brakeshoe etc. Now we are in the age-group of CAD/CAM (Computer Aided Design/Computer Aided Manufacturing). The automated process control can be inbuilt into the production system quite easily and feed back mechanism sensors operate dispassionately to control the process quite effectively. This concept is also available for control of few machines or the group of work centres.

It is emphassed that there has to be a proper integration in design, performance levels and qualitative requirements of various automated systems to take full benefit of automation. It is also important to realise that since human element is reduced through automation. the unpleasant work or less innovative functions should be more suitable for automation. But flexibility available through a committed skilled worker is not available through automated work. Hence if the product design and process design are simplified through new technologies in the area of material handling and scheduling instead of using human elements.

11.5 Advanced Production Systems

Advanced production systems are not only automated systems, (as it is not only the question of getting the best out of every machine), it is also linking machines for multiple tasks and intergrating them in such way that the advantage of production at the optimum level can be achieved inspite of many constraints on the system. When the thinking gets into the innovative mode, the automation goes a step higher to improve the productivity through an alternate route. Variety of new technologies have been evolved in manufacturing as well as in services. Few of these are listed below:

- Group Technology
- Process Automation
- Automated Flow lines
- Automated Assembly lines
- Flexible Manufacturing System
- Software Systems
- Computer-integrated Manufacturing
- Bar Coding/Optical Scanning and Electronic Data Inter-change
- Environmental friendly process technology.

A brief resume of these different advanced production technologies is offered below:

Group Technology

As the name suggests, it is a concept applied on the basis of grouping together certain families or components of products with similar characteristics and generally similar specifications requiring almost similar production process. This concept has already been described under Group layout or cellular layout, where general principle and the method of obtaining variety of products of similar basic design has been discussed.

While using this technoloical concept, components of almost similar design, similar shapes or almost similar dimensions can be manufactured so that these may be branded as family of product identified and where production can be achieved through similar process. For example, some components combined together could have round shapes, some others having linear bar/brick shapes etc. The processes used for producing these components could be obtained as turning on lathes for round shapes, the bent shapes on bending and planing machines and the linear bar/brick shape components either by casting or casting and planning simply by straight edge cutting on shaping machines.

Such groups facilitate the job flow, matetial flow, setting up and the WIP (Work in Process) inventory. The variety production is made cost effective following batch production through mass production in each group or cell. The basic principles of Group Technology can be, thus, summerised as under:

- Components of similar properties and manufacturing requirements are grouped together.
- Capable of being processed through group of machines for certain similar specifications.
- Variety of similar products possible to be produced.

Thus the major Advantages of the group Technology are:

- Reduced set up time
- Reduced production lead time
- Reduced Work in Process (WIP)
- Reduced tooling time
- Optimising variety production
- Reduced delivery schedule

The principle of Group Technology (GT), thus, becomes the stepping stone for some other important technologies such as computer Aided Design (CAD) and cellular Manufacturing, which have been briefly discussed under the chapter "Facilities location and Layouts".

For the purpose of using GT as the production principle, the parts or components are assigned a coded description defining all its design and processing characterstics like its material, general dimesions such as shapes, size or the types of process to be used such as turning, casting, forming, metal removal, polishing or painting etc. This information in coded description is used as an input to the CAD software, where these parameters and characterstics are utilised for designing the product in a simple integrated manner. It also can be used to identify existing components with similar characterstics which can be clubbed together for design and manufacturing. It may also identify any existing components, which can act as a substitute and no new design may be necessary. Part of the design effort can be saved by taking existing design as basis and developing the new product from thereon. The group or cell facilities together for these similar parts, thus, is the basis of cellular manufacturing.

In this case, a particular cell of machine setup may be similar and hence very little time is wated for resetting, even if minor changes are necessary. The training of manpower for similar jobs can be reduced to minimal and then the company can take the benefit of concept of learning curve to make their workers more and more skillful and proficient just by using them for repeatative jobs in a cell manufacturing work.

The improvement in quality due to similar continuous productions is an obvious advantage of the system, in addition to reaping the fruits of mass production concept of each cell producing variety of products through combination of cells as per variety requirement.

Process Automation

Process automation has been defined as a set of procedures followed to replace some human activities to be performed by machines. When we use a machine for automating a manufacturing job, the speed, quality, production volumes and unbiased manufacturing are obvious advantages. Jobs like welding, bending, grinding, drilling and painting etc. can be easily done through automated processes. With the help of IT-automation, large volume of work can be done uninterrupted for a longer period (practically without a mistake) like printing invoices and bills, data storage, inventory control and keeping Master Production Schedule (MPS) updated. Repeated jobs are best done through automated systems, where human-boredom attitude does not come into the job, spoiling it or slowing it down. Numerically control machine (*i.e.*, CNC or DNC) and concept of Machine Centres have already been explained in the chapter. Large use of Robots through appropriate programing in variety of ways is another automated help.

Computer Aided Design and Computer Aided Manufacturing (CAD and CAM) are beneficial tools for products design and production.

Automated Flow Lines

The flow lines are basically a product layout system, when various machines are placed in a linear way as per the sequence of operations of the part or the component. This has been discussed in the chapter on layouts. When such system is operated through automated machines, it is called Automated Flow line, wherein a number of automated machines are designed, procured and installed as per the processing required by the product. In addition to automated processing machines, the material handling systems are also necessarily automated to be compatible with the total manufacturing requirement. The raw material feeders operate as per pre-arranged timing and sequence and carry out work with minimal human involvement. When a machine completes its portion of operation, the work is automatically fed to the next automatic machine through a automated conveyor system and the material handling system brings in the material to this new machine as per the time schedule. Coordination is done with the help of automatic sensors so that there is no delay in the processing on any machine. The component comes out in the final finished product form at the end of the flow line. Thus the automated flow lines are used for producing a component in the repeated manner. Automobile industry is a major user of this concept.

Since it works on the product layout concept, the initial capital investment is high, which can be offset by adjusting high level of production volume. Due to high demand of stardardised components for a longer period, the initial cost will be divided resulting in to low overheads (Smoothed out over large volumes). This system in the present set up is not very popular as most products are becoming short cycle products. Non-Flexibility of the system is a major drawback for todays scenirio. The changes have been brought about in the form of Group Technology (Variety production) or Flexible Manufacturing System or Flexible Assembly System.

Automated Assembly Lines

The automated machines in a flow line are Fixed Automation, (concept used in a manufacturing). When a similar system of automated facilities such as robotes are used for assembly operations for a product, it is called the Automated Assembly line.

In this case, the assembly line (basically a product layout) is the flow process of automated assembly machines (generally robots designed for each work centre). These are progressively linked together with a suitable material handling equipment compatible with the requirement of load and shape of assembly work on a work centre. Materials *i.e.*, the components to be assembled and the connection required for assembly operations like nuts, bolts etc are fed to each automated machine helping the assembly operations. These could be even the welding or painting robots to have the process completed on a work centre.

Each work centre is required to complete only certain specific assembly tasks, after which the semi-completed product is fed to the next work centre (automatically transferred with the help of either a conveyor belt or a suitably designed material handling platform). The process is repeated till the end of the assembly line, when all the assembly operations are complete and the product in the finished shape is available.

The design of assendly lines has to be maticulously done because it may not always be possible to completely duplicate the work of a human being by automated system. For jointing two parts together, cheaper fasteners like nut and bolts can be used by human worker, whereas in the automated system, some easy-to-assembly fastner has to be designed to make robots operation simpler.

Hence to modify the design of product and process amenable to automated assembly, we may have to adopt simple and smaller number of joints and fastner with reduced number of assembly operations. The design of components should be self-aligning to make it easy. The quality of subsequent assembly components must be very good so as to ensure smooth-fit during assembly.

Using these basic concepts, we can have cost effective and quality assemblies achieved. through automated assembly lines. The cordination during product design will play a major role in cost reduction, if we can use same robots for number of products. Product flexibility with suitable material handling system can be a great help in reducing initial capital investments. By this method, we can reduce the cost per unit produced/assembled. Variety of products can be produced by suitable design of products as well as those of robots which can be programmed for a number of components/products.

Flexible Manufacturing Systems (FMS)

Flexible Manufacturing System is a set of automatic machines organised into a sequence for production of variety of products. These are connected and integrated with automated material handling equipment with the help of a computer. Thus it is a computer controlled process technology extensively used for short life cycle products in small batches.

As can be seen in the figure given below, the raw materials and components for a product are loaded on the suitably designed material handling system and the product to be manufactured is identified to the computer in the coded entry specifying complete specification of the product.

According to the programmed sequence, the automated machines operate at a work centre and produce partially finished product. It is then transferred to next work centre for further processing and so on. The machines receive the operating instructions and command from the computer as required at that time for a particular product in the production line. Automatic loading, tool setting and unloading take place as per the sequence required. It is totally computer controlled process, thereby reducing dependence on human operations.

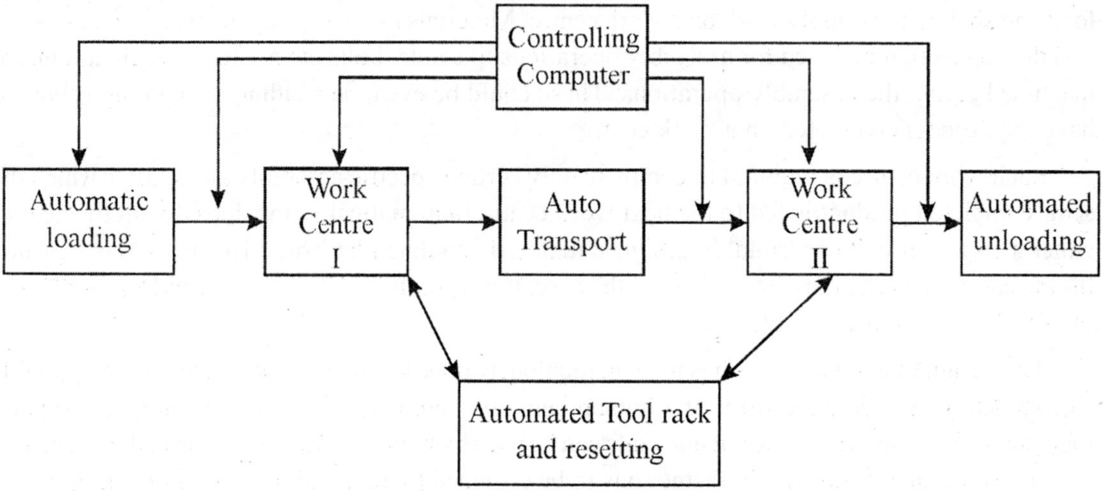

FIG 11.1. Schematic plan of FMS layout

As evident from fig 11.1, the loading of raw material for a production is automated, the movement from loading station to the work centre is through the automated transport. Work to be excecuted at a work centre is commanded by the computer. Its movement from one work centre to another and then to the job unloading station is also automated. The tool rack is totally automated, resulting in tool setting and resetting as per job specification, commanded by the control computer.

This system is called flexible manufacturing system because the instructions from the control computer can be changed at any time *i.e.*, resetting tools and operations on any workcentre for any change in the specification of the product. Thus production of variety of a product can be affected through this procedure. If we are manufacturing a bolt, it can be changed to a screw with changed length and changed thread combination.

Another flexibility available is the number of products out of one set of specifications. Computer instruction can stop a product with as low a volume as one and can be varying to any quantity till instructions alter. Hence we can produce moderate variety of products with moderate volume. Generally, the number of components in a product are also kept moderate to avoid complexity in the production line. Thus we can summerise the goal of the FMS as **"Production of moderate variety of same basic product in moderate flexible volumes"**.

Characterstics of FMS

The basic characterstics of flexible manufacturing system are as under:

- Product Variety of a stable basic design.

- All products have similar components of a family.
- Number of components are moderate (say 2 to 50)
- Volume of production of a batch to be kept moderate (Say 1 to 30,000) and preferably small batches, so as to keep software design as simple as possible.

The Future of the FMS

- FMS should be delivering the products directly into the warehouse by automatic unloading devices.
- The robots design is likely to be more and more sofisticated so as to have vision and sensing achievable.
- One hundred percent inspections should be possible due to accuracy of computerised operations.
- Machine failings easy to identify so as to order repairs on time.
- Customer satisfaction can be high due to better controlled order schedules.
- Net-working between production and marketing and suppliers will reduce inventory problems.
- Finished goods inventories can be brought to practically Nil as customer order can be undertaken when requirred. Intime delivery of a customised product can be easily achieved.
- Machine utilisation can be improved by using apporpricate software.
- Global operations can be easily controlled.

Software Systems

Computer Aided Design and Manufacturing : During the discussion on product design, the necessity of computer Aided Design software was highlighted. This software helps in designing a product faster and is also capable of quick change in the design to cater for variation in the requirement of the maket. Computer Aided Design (CAD) software covers many automated technologies such as computer graphics and Computer Aided Engineering (CAE) so that the engineering characteristics as well as visual aspects of the design are simultaneously viewed and analysed. CAD also includes the technology called Computer Aided Process Planning (CAPP) to help proper instructions to the CNC machines for proper manufacturing. CAD software is also being used for visual on-screen tests so that any necessary modification can be carried out. Computer Aided Manufacturing is a technology that helps in automations of production lines to ensure speedy production, quality production and cost effective production. Now the CAD and CAM can work together as compatible tools for an effective manufacturing. The above description can be sumerised as follows:

CAD: Is the software where interactive engineering design and storage of these designs are easily done. This programme can help in codifying the specifications instead of elaborate drawings. Any layout transformation, projections and visual display of 3-Dimension view of the product are also possible. CAD in the present form is very powerful tool to automate certain design activities, it can help design engineers in reducing their workload and enhancing their design capability. They can standardise product design, the documentations and store a large production data. The latest software release is Auto CAD (2002i) and is in tremendous demand across the globe.

CAM: It is a programme which can direct machines, tools, material handling equipment and control mechanisms to ensure quality product being manufactured out of automated facilities.

CAM automates the planning and control systems for production and hence has the capability of planning production, working out loading, routing and scheduling various activities for CNC or DNC machines. It can also plan and exercise control of the production output and hence is becoming very popular production technology.

The two systems have been combined together to become CAD/CAM. Constant interaction of two operations *i.e.*, design and manufacturing brings in the advantage of their better effectiveness.

This merger has speeded up the process of design to cater for fast changes and simultaneously planning its production as and when required. Stored designs are great help in quick change into variations in products. It leads to increase in productivity, flexibility and product quality at a highly reduced cost.

Automated Manufacturing Planning and Control Systems (MP&CS)

These are computer-based information systems useful for planning, scheduling, monitoring and controlling the manufacturing operations. Through the information flow system, the information regarding materials, work flow and production constraints etc are used to release production and purchase orders, thereby controlling the order entry processing, purchasing, manufacturing controls as well as the cost accounting systems. These systems are effectively used in efficient handling of the supply chain links.

Computer-Integrated Manufacturing (CIM)

In computer-Integrated Manufacturing facilities, all processes are computer controlled with automated information system (digital form). Therefore CIM is the total integration of various computerised production processes such as design (CAD/CAM), process control, quality control, inventory control, group technology, financial budgeting and its reporting system control. All activities of the organisation should be computerised to get full benefit of automation and it is now possible due to introduction of CIM technology. It is not in use fully as yet. But in time to come, it is likely to become very popular due its obvious advantages of speed, quality and cost. With further advancement of computer technology and computer capability, when even thinking is incorporated in computer design, computer-Integrated Manufacturing is possibly the best technology to be available for production. Constant improvement, in any case, is the order of the day and complete CIM is not far. Implementation of CIM would have the following easy steps:

- Preliminary design and analysis of product and processes.
- Identify key areas and obtain detailed design and analysis to concentrate on to the actual requirement.
- System to be installed and commissioned integrating all the subsystems.
- Validate and maintain the system for effective utilisation.

From the above steps, it can be easily interpretted that computer-Integrated Manufacturing (CIM) is a mathematical approach of the organisational heirachy in which the various functions of design, production, quality and inventory etc are mutually rationalised and co-ordinated through suitably designed computer hardware and softwares integrating computer capability with information technologies for optimum results.

Necessity of CIM

Since CAD is already in use for sufficient length of time and computer Aided manufacturing (CIM) has been integrated with CAD, it is an obvious step forward in human quest for constant improvement that greater interaction and integration of all interconnected activities associated with production are sought for and it has resulted in the development of CIM. The Necessity of CIM can be summerised as under:

- Quick design, proactive decision on flexible products and operations and better operational control.
- The change management and productive flexibility is possible.
- CIM offers very simple tools to facilitate the jobs of designers, system analysts and other change masters.
- Due to generic and flexible inbuilt capability of CIM, it protects and reduces capital investments due to involvement of technology in present form.
- It provides mathematically correct checklist for the process implementations and control.

Intergrated Systems

CIM is an integrated combination of the following subsystems of production:

- Computer Aided Design (CAD)
- Computer Aided Engineering (CAE)
- Computer Aided Process Planning (CAPP)
- Computer Aided Manufacture (CAM) and
- Information Process Design (IPD)

The integrated relationships of these subsystems can be understood from the following diagram (Fig. 11.2)

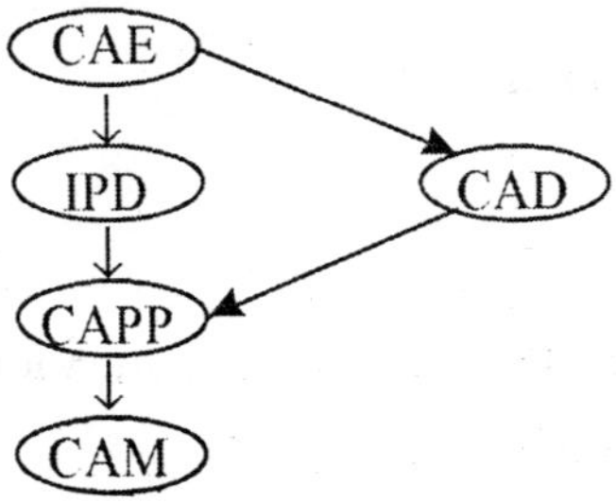

FIG 11.2. Components of CIM

Thus we can summerise the CIM as an integrated technology consisting of both hardware and softwares.

Hardware System: Workstations, DNC/FMS systems, tool handling device, storege device, shop floor data collection, etc. Also CAD/CAM System, work terminals, printers, plotters, moderns etc.

Software Systems: Modules for sales/marketing, Accounts and Finance, Design, Data base management, production control, manufacturing control, inventory control, Process Planning and Monetoring and also the Information Management module.

Various sub systems comprise of the following:

CAD Database

- Design CAD
- Analysis and Simulation
- Documentation

CAM Database

- Assembly
- Inspection and testing
- Material handling

CAPP Data Base

- Shopfloor planning and Control
- Manufacturing Resources Planning
- Resources Scheduling
- Quality assurance
- Inventory control (JIT and Kanban)
- Process related database, such as FMS, GT, Robots, CNC machines and AGV's

Information Process Design

- Software for Manufacturing and Assembly
- Factory Automation
- Marketing and Financial planning
- Strategic Planning

CIM-related Activities

Following important activities of CIM need constant attention. These activities are:

- Customer requirement and orders
- Product design
- Bills of Material

- Procurement
- Inventories – Raw materials, WIP and Finished goods
- Production Scheduling
- Production procedures including quality control systems
- Facility maintenance, breakdowns and tool wear.
- Personnel Scheduling
- Cost Accounting
- Packaging and shipping including distribution network.

Benefits of CIM

Many advantages acrued out of the implementation of CIM are:

- Quicker design and production
- Short product cycle and marketing time
- Productivity enhancement
- Reduced labour cost
- Reduced Scrap and rework, hence reduced wastages
- Reduced Inventories
- Improved quality
- Improved customer service
- Improved flexibility
- Constant improvement at lower capital investment due to simple tools to cater for change management.

Computer Aided Factory Integration and Management System (CAFIMS)

It is an integrated system and software solution for factory management. It is the result of a project by Department of Electronics (GOI). Since Factory Managment involves many functions like facility management, production management, manpower management, materials management, Quality management, services management, Financial management and Distribution management, this software CFAIMS has the capability of operating on PC network using client server architecture and it has practically all productions and supporting systems under integrated control almost like the ERP software.

Bar Coding and Optical Scanning

This technology is already in use. In fact optical scanning and Bar coding has become very common in India, where even a shop keeper or a departmental store with computerised billing system uses it to advantage. This technology is used in manufacturing also. It is a numerical code (obtained from a central clearing house) converted into set of bars and printed on the product packaging. This can be seen on general grocery items and many general products. The bars are so unique that the code identifies the product completely. These bars are then read using an optical scanner with the help of light and converts the bar widths and the number into the numerical code again. In a normal grocery store, when the bar code is read through the scanner, it excutes a number of commands for the computer, such as generating the price on the bill, simultaneously carrying out inventory adjustment in the database indicating whether this particular item is available on the shelf after this sale. It also co-ordinates the information about purchase units, so that inventory tallying work is effectively carried out by the computer. This is very useful information to draw inferences about the acceptance, utility or spurt in demand of a certain product. The information can be used for future strategic decision. The analysis of the information can also be helpful in understanding the efficency of a marketing strategy used for a certain product for certain length of time. It can give out the information whether the product is more popular in certain specific geographical area or whether a large number of credit card holders are buying the product. It also helps in inventory control system knowing whether a product is fast consuming or a non-starter. Accordingly sales strategies can be formulated and productions accordingly adjusted.

The system of Bar coding have been extensively used for tracking movement of materials, through the codes appearing on the packages, parts and work orders etc thereby locate these by simply reading with a hand scanner, fed to the computer. The Airway Bill code can indicate whether your packet has been delivered, when and to whom.

Similarly, the barcoding system used by the Airlines helps them in locating and tracking customer luggage or parcels as done by UPS and Federal Express etc. The production units also extensively use the system for locating orders, components and raw materials. This is a useful tool in operating CIM through integration with the other subsystems of CIM.

The biggest advantage of the system is error reduction and savings in the labour cost. Another advantage is accuracy of data entry as the Bar code eliminates the chance of wrong typing of the call number.

Electornic Data Interchange (EDI)

EDI is another computerised system which the interconnected departments such as production, ordering, suppliers and customers all at the same time. Any of these constituents can transmit and share, on the press of the button, any information available to the receipient. To illustrate, let us take an example of placing an order for material purchase by an organisation. This data typed on the screen of a PC is transmitted electronically to the vender, who does not have to wait or wastes time in physical receipt of the order. He can organise the supplies, completes all the formalities required out of the order and supplies the material as per the lead time allowed. If by chance, there is a breakdown in the production unit and a certain product line gets stranded, the material required for that product should not be immediately received. This information can be amended on the purchase order and it is available to the supplier on line. He therefore, accordingly modifies his supplies and thus an inventory build up is saved in addition to the saving on material transportation.

The same system is used to advantage by retail suppliers to the retail stores. The days inventory is known to the store as well as the suppliers because of updating realtime information of the computer billing system. The supplier would automatically notice the days sales and will recoup only that much quantity unless the retail store amends the figure for his strategic placement. Restocking level strategy can be conveniently controlled through EDI operation.

In addition, EDI system can be used by customers to track their order supplies or even through the production system. The production schedule can be known to customer and he can accordingly plan his business as per the possible delivery schedules.

EDI System also can help modifying the master production schedule (MPS) with the help of information available through sales. If a particular product sales show a considerable variation, the production and material purchase can be suitably controlled by amending lot sizing in purchase as well as in production.

Hence we can summerise the advantage of EDI System as the real time information control with paperless transmission and transfer of information, thereby saving cost. Also real time transfer of information result in quick adjustments in action taken on the information. The use of EDI by WALMART can be quoted as an effective use of the technology, through which a very smooth supply chain is operated by the company inspite of dealing in such large number of products with large varieties of each product. In fact, their inventory and sales control has to have EDI to be cost effective in their operations due to enormity of the transactions in the range of millions every year. They insist that their suppliers also use EDI for smooth operations. Similarly GE has been able to reduce their inventories and prices due to use of EDI.

Some of the EDI softwares in use are:

- ANSIX12
- EDIFACT
- XML
- Rosetta Net
- Flat File Format

Large number of companies are also using the following for controlling their inventories:

(a) GSM (Cellular Phone Technology)

(b) GPS (Global Positioning System)

11.6 Environment Friendly Process Technology.

Global concern on the environmental degredation resulting into the necessity of formulation of ISO 14000 environmental Management Systems, has increased the avareness that product designs should be accordingly correlated in terms of cost, easy to reuse and less harmful to the environment. The so called "Green Revolution is gaining ground all over the globe to produce green products. Hence the environmental concern does not restrict itself only its the product design, it also has to be thought of in processes and the technologies used for manufacturing or producing it. This aspect also takes care of financial benefits (reusable materials) in production methods. The production technology today should be environment friendly, so that the customer needs are fulfilled with the benefit of performance as well as availability of non harmful green product.

For green productions, following care is recommoded:

- Use recyclable material and reduce wastage materials such as solvent bottles.
- Toxic gas production should be reduced if not eliminated. In addition, their treatment to the acceptable harmless level to be incorporated.
- Raclaim and recycle toxic by-products to be profitable.
- Increasing the energy efficiency by using less costly energy sources.

11.7 Cost and Risk Analysis

For selection of a process, we have already discussed the break even analysis. The break-even analysis is used for comparing possible processes for a product. The significance of the break-even point is that below the break even point (volume of production) a certain process is beneficial, (based the fixed cost and variable cost consideration) whereas when the volume of production is expected to be more than the break even point volume, a different process may prove to be cheaper.

The process cost, in this consideration, is not only dependent on the production facilities, it will also vary with respect to the designed capacity of the process as well as the type of technology utilised. For evaluating alternative processes and technologies, normally cost and risk analysis is carried out.

The cost analysis based on Break-even point concept is not enough for selecting a particular technology. A Risk Analysis is necessary for finding out probability of effectiveness of each situation. This analysis is carried out based on Decision theory for analysis or Decision tree. Such an analysis for expected life, capacity or flexibility offered for low or high demands can be built in the decision making process. Thus we should not depend only on the Break even cost analysis for strategic selection of a suitable process for production but we should carry out risk analysis taking uncertain or probabilistic factors into consideration. As it is, forecasting of demand itself is a probability decision. It is worth considering, therefore, a set of options including financial benefits, long term cost benefit and the risk involved in such probabilistic situation.

In carrying out capital investment analysis (Initial Costs), we have to understand that different processes and technologies utilisation can result in different cash flows. Thus, for evaluating the cost of facilities *i.e.*, for technology procurement and cost of equipment, we use the method of Net Present Value (NPV), which has also been discussed else where in the book. A careful analysis, therefore, is required before committing money into procurement process.

Various modern advanced technologies, involving different level automation, can be compared on the basis of the following factors:

- Profitability and cost benefit
- Likely increase in the market share
- Initial investment and risk analysis
- Product quality improvement
- Production flexibility
- Implementation period and its likely acceptance by the workers.

11.8 Advancement in services through automation

Services are the key earners today and better service can help in keeping customers attached and loyal to the organisational products. If the service provided is excellent, the customers may be willing to pay even more for a better service. This advantage could be available through one-to-one contact with the customer making him happy through technical competance, good time scheduling, reliability in service operations and above all, the customer-worker relationship through extremely good behaviour.

A very wide range of services is available today and if a company keeps opportunity-grabbing intentions clear, a large business can be developed. In certain industries such as banking, insurance, airlines, food and beverages, air cargo, real estates, retailing and wholesaling, advertising and broadecasting, health services, entertainment, hotels and restaurants, communications and utility services like electricity, gas supply etc., these opportunities are plentiful.

When service operations are automated, the utility gets enhanced many fold and customer satisfaction rises almost one hundred per cent. Money transfer from USA to India in matter of minutes, messages available on laptop almost instantanesly, computerised bank statements, automatic teller machines (ATMs) operation for instant withdrawal of money from any bank ATM at any place, India or abroad, are the bright example of automated services providing customers requirements practically on the touch of a button. Thus we see that the service industry gains tremendously through automation unlimited thereby reducing the costs.

More and more advanced technologies and integrated systems are available for service operations. It is easy to standardise the service operations and hence initial investments can be easily justified if the enormous standard service is provided with very little running expenditure. There are methods and tools available to bring in a large flexibility in the services provided to the customers. Convenience of customers is another major factor which reduces cost as today a customer sitting home can avail a large number of services at any time convenient to him. Cost of operations are reducing drastically as the level of technologies is rising. Drive in banking, drive in coffee shops, driving in shopping centres and malls are advantageous services. It is agreed that as the automation level goes higher, the customer contact comes down. Initial cost of provision are high, but with the service facility becoming so convenient, the operation cost reduces. Automation for all types of services may not be suitable. In some cases, the customer contact needs to be high such as in fast food joints, where customisation necessity needs high customer involvement. Preparation of food also requires high human involvement. Automation, therefore, should be judicious. The type of services to be provided, their speed and accuracy is coming through the advancement of automation technologies such as internet and intranets. Another good example could be the outsourcing of services through call centres to a country with economic and resources advantage.

—•—

Chapter 12

Maintenance Management

Main issues:

1. Various Systems of Maintenance
2. Objectives and Economy of maintenance
3. Maintenance and Replacement Policies
4. Replacement Models
5. TPM and its implementation

12.1 Reasons for Maintenance

For an efficient, hassle free and cost effective production system, it is necessary that all its components and equipment are kept properly maintained, repaired, caliberated and in good operating condition. It is a pre-requisite for uninterrupted material flow and production flow. But keeping the production operation system in perfect running condition is not the only reason to avoid break of flow and interruptions, it is also to keep the cost, quality and quantity of product under control for timely delivery to the customer so as to keep him happy. Another reason for good maintenance is also to maintain safe working conditions in order to avoid accidents.

Hence, the impact of good maintenance system is felt on various subsystems:

- Production costs
- Production quality
- Production capacity
- Service quality
- Customer and product safety
- Customer satisfaction for timely delivery

The maintenance of all assets is, therefore, an important managerial function. Optimal use of assets only can assure a healthy level of business. Preventive maintenance is essential for day-to-day operations, whereas a long term deliberate maintenance at regular intervals can save the assets from major detercoration and frequent failures. The timely replacement of parts, subassemblies and assemblies can help in total or partial failure of the asset and these replacements can bring the asset to a reasonable level of working efficientcy. Total replacement or part replacement is a matter of company policy.

Maintenance is becoming all the more important because of increased cost of equipment due to automation and enhanced/improved technology. With competition growing tougher and tougher, better utilisation of resources is imperative for any manager and well-maintained plants and equipment is an important step in this direction. It ensures higher productivity and better profitability. As a general rule, maintenance should not be perceived only as repairs or breakdowns, but it should be undertaken periodically not to permit breakdowns as best as it can be helped.

Thus, for maintenance, the company should devise methods and policy in the following manner :

- A planned schedule for daily or periodical inspection of the assets/equipment for day-to-day resettings and minor repairs.
- A schedule for proper lubrication of all moving parts.
- A plan for periodic monitoring of complex, critical and expensive equipment for certain ill-health symptoms such as excessive noise, vibrations, excessive heating, increase in pressure or any noticeable drop in the performance capability.
- A plan for periodic replacement of moving parts as per the life-history predictions, as a deliberate policy before the failure occurs.
- A plan for procurement of certain spare parts for general plant/equipment maintenance.
- A plan for manpower requirement including their skill-upgradation for effective maintenance.
- A plan for periodic shutdown of facilities for thorough checkup and overhauling/repairs to avoid breakdowns.
- Deliberate maintenance policy for all levels of maintenance and repairs.

12.2 Definition of Maintenance

Based on the above plan schedule, we can define maintenance as **"A function of the plant management concerned with day-to-day problems of keeping the assets in healthy operating condition"**. For an effective policy on maintenance, the company can take the help of statistical tools to predict failures and take necessary corrective action. Three important failure distribution functions that can be utilised are:

- Normal Distribution
- Negative Exponential Distribution
- Hyper-exponential Distribution

It is worth bringing out the necessity of failure and maintenance due to the system life operation. We draw a bath-tub curve to explain this necessity (Refer fig. 12.1 below):

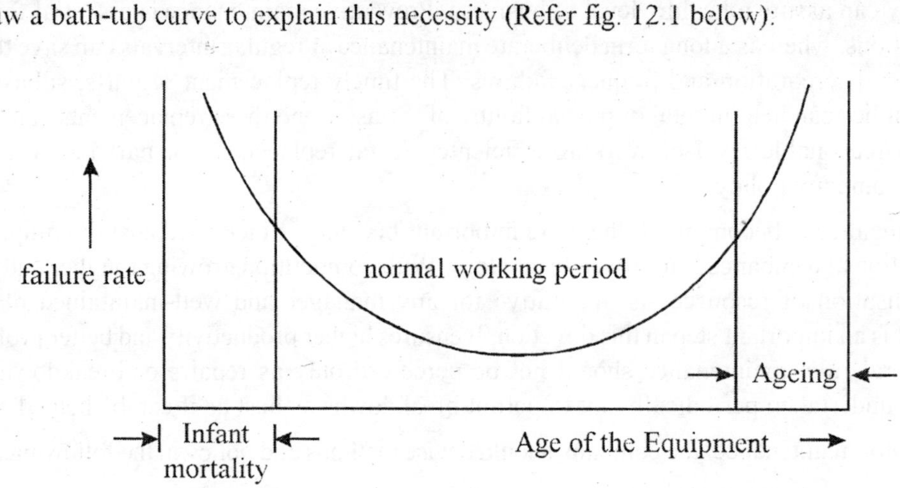

FIG 12.1. Bath tub Curve (Equipment Life Cycle)

12.3 Scope of Maintenance

Maintenance does not only mean the maintenance of machines. We have to consider maintenance of men, buildings and services also. For effective maintenance, the area and scope of maintenance is described as under:

Area of Maintenance:

- Plant and buildings
- Machines
- Supporting facilities/services
- Premises and Surroundings
- Waste disposal
- Pollution control

Scope of maintenance:

- What is to be maintained ?
- Where is it to be done ?
- Who does the maintenance ?
- How the maintenanse is to be carried out ?

12.4 Objectives of Maintenance

Some of the important objectives of maintenance are listed below:

- Minimising the idle time (down time) of plant facilities.
- Minimising the repair time and cost.
- Minimising the production loss due to breakdowns
- Minimising accidents through effective inspection system and resultant maintenance and repairs.
- Minimising inventory carrying cost by proper planning and effective spares management.
- Improving quality of products
- Improving the productivity of production facilities.
- Prolonging life of capital assets.
- Keeping manpower and machines in good operating coditions.
- Maximising economy through optimum use of the facilities.

12.5 Economy of Maintenance

Since maintenance is an essential managerial function to keep the assets useable and healthy, the function has to be performed so that it is cost effective. The economy of maintenance depends on the selection of type maintenance and the efficiency of the maintenance team. For working out the optimal level of maintenance, the cost-curve analysis, as given below, can be used, provided proper records of failures and maintenance are kept.

The company works out an optimum maintenance plan keeping in view the necessity of preventive, predictive and breakdown maintenance. The trade off between repairs or preventive maintenance has to be carefully balanced. Diagramatically, the offsetting of repair cost with the help of preventive maintenance has been shown but these decision are not very simple because a number of uncertain perameters operate such as production capacity, product quality, safety of workers and the customer satisfaction levels. Hence level of and type of maintenance is a delibrate company policy and should be speltout for the information of all concerned. In today's context while adopting FMS (Flexible Manufacturing System) as the method of productions, one machine breaking down can stop the whole process and a similar problem can arise even with cellular manufacturing. Hence the maintenance planning has to match the system suitably. Few suggestions that can work are provision of extra machine capacity, replacing parts early or regular upgraduation of skill of the operators etc. in addition to effective preventive maintenance.

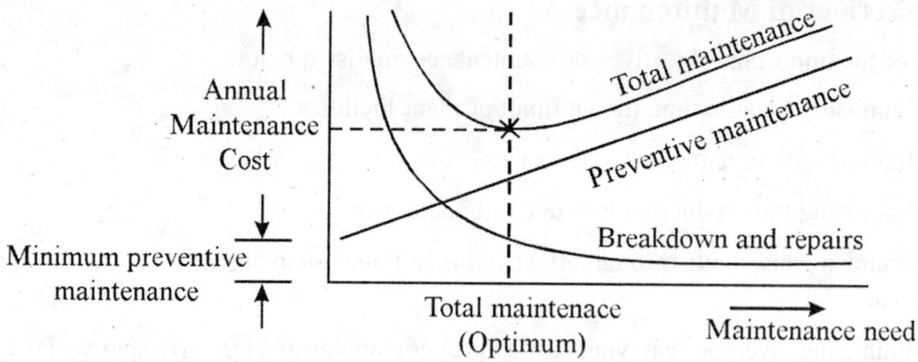

FIG. 12.2. Total Minimum Maintenance Cost

12.6 Types of maintenance

For physical system, the maintenance can be carried out under following stages:

- Corrective maintenance
- Preventive maintenance
- Predictive maintenance
- Breakdown maintenance

Corrective Maintenance: It includes the breakdown maintenance, failure/defect analysis and the resultant conective action. It involves the in-depth analysis of the following aspects:

- Process improvement
- Design improvement
- Analysis and replacement of defective parts
- Analysis and improvement in maintenance operations.

Preventive Maintenance: These are proactive systems which can prevent breakdowns of the equipment and buildings, otherwise it may result in accidents and production loss to the company. The preventive maintenance has to be commensurate with the product specifications, hence decided at the design or production stage. Depending on the type and length of work, the periodic inspections of the assets are important, so as to know where the things can go wrong and preemptive action could be initiated not to allow the assets to reach stage of unuseability. For this purpose, peridicity of inspection and resultant servicing at periodic intervals are planned out. In fact, preventive maintenance schedule is spelt out by the manufacturer, in most cases, based on the general history and specifications of the equipment, such as servicing of a car is planned every 5,000 Kilometers of run (generally). The servicing schedule can be daily, weekly, monthly. quarterly or even annual. Some equipment may have the preventive maintenance schedules, say, every 100 hours of running.

Predictive Maintenance: This method of maintenance is more applicable to equipment and machinery having a number of moving parts. The situation is improving with CNC/DNC and other sophisticated electronic machines coming into operations, the number of moving parts are reducing and hence maintenance theory is undergoing a change. But for any machine or equipment, a periodic inspection drill has to be put in place so that servicing can be predicted and action taken to maintane it in time. Keeping maintenance team and maintenance spares in ready condition is important, so that timely action can be taken in order to reduce the machine downtime. Machine history sheets kept as updated documentation helps in planning predictive maintenance.

It will help in reduction of maintenance inventory to minimum. Appropriate service/maintenance schedule is to be drawn out thereby minimising the maintenance workforce or their better utilisation. More important items to be keept ready, in todays context, are the testing equipment in duly caliberated conditions with maintenance planned in situ. The equipment, most of the time, need not be removed from the line of production. For moving parts, there are vibration detection equipment and hence predicting can be done easily and the electronic equipment can be inspected through the current drawn characteristic. The general policy in predictive maintenance is diagonising and repairing or replacing parts as per condition or the laid down usage time. Corrective or scheduled maintenance are parts of predictive maintenance.

Breakdown Maintenance: Repairs are to be carried out when the machines and other assets like buildings either breakdown or malfunction or are demaged hampering the working operations. Repairs are reactive action and are undertaken only when system has failed fully or partially. Hence it is called "Breakdown Maintenance". Generally, the maintenance crew and the repair shop staff works with the line operaters, so that the actual health of the equipment is known and the operator is simultaneously satisfied with the repair work. He will have better confidence to work on this equipment, if repaired and put back into operation in his presence. In the words of **Robert U. Hall,** workers should be involved in doing their own repairs (or getting actively involved in their machine repairs).

"It creates more pride in the machine and it requires closer observation that the operator merely watches it run. This also helps dispel the propensity for equipment abuse-the feeling that" I can operate it as I please, and some one else will figure out if something is wrong. The company has more than enough money for repairs anyway". Sometimes additional standby machines and spare parts are kept to be put into use, when regular equipment is out for repairs. For example, when a tranformer breaksdown, this equipment is removed from the line and a standby transfomer of matching capacity is installed so as to avoid inconvenience to the users for a long period.

12.7 Maintenance Policies

The selection of maintenance policy depends on the maintenance activity desired to be established for the plant facilities. Better maintained facilities, undoubtedly, would ensure smooth and efficient production at cost effective level. If the maintenance levels are reduced, there is likelihood of frequent breakdowns either due to poor operating conditions or due to natural wear and tear not timely addressed. This may workout to be a costly proposition due to the requirement of frequent replacement of components/assemblies or even machine as a whole. Thus high level of maintenance should be a deliberate management policy.

Causes of Machine Failures

With the necessity of assets maintenance having been established, we now look into the causes as to why machines fail or need constant maintenance. The maintenance policy of the company will be more effective if we carry out the analysis of the causes of failures. Few reasons for machine failure are listed out below:

- Over-utilisation of machines
- Using machines on excessive speeds to increase production,
- Demage due to environmental conditions, such as dust grade wrong grade or oils or use of unwanted chemicals.
- Inadequate preventive maintenance – poor inspection or delayed frequency.
- Incorrect machine setup
- Deliberate or accidental collisions
- Wrong materials used, for which machine and its tools are not designed
- Natural wear and tear.

Important considerations in maintenance policy

While finalising the maintenance policy for the company, few important issues should be taken care of. These important points for active and deliberate considerations are as follows:

- The company may decide to contract out the specialised jobs of repairs and maintenance of assets such as buildings or even some jobs during peak period to cover gaps.
- The company may decide to delay some maintence to slack period, if it does not disturb the balance of operations, *i.e.*, job like major overhauls or painting jobs.
- If the company decides to replace the equipment, machine or manpower at an appropriate optimum time, it should best be done after proper replacements.

Need for Maintenance Policies

There are several replacement policies in force and for selection of appropriate policy, their maintenance cost function serves a good guide for optimality. The data collection should include the failure time, frequency and their cost factors.

Replacement of Defective Equipment

Equipment is replaced essentially for two reasons :

Due to degradation or deterioration: The equipment is subjected to replacement because new equipment offers improved, fasters or cheaper services.

The decisions to be made in this case are the time at which the replacement is to be made and what type of equipment should be used as replacement. The over-riding factors for such replacements are maintenance cost, the salvage value and the technological advancement and innovations.

• ***Due to sudden and Permanent failures:*** When the equipment has failed suddenly and permanently, there is no choice but replacement. In such cases, either the failed components are replaced (called failure removal), or some units replaced even if they are operating satisfactorily. This is done to avoid unscheduled interruptions in the operations or due to incompatibility with the failed unit replacement. This removal is called preventive removal.

Periodicity and Policy for equipment replacement

Once preventive removals has been decided upon and the planned units are isolated, the next stage of decision making is to determine the optimal policy of replacement. *i.e.*, whether block removal, peridical removal of a single component, age-specific removals or removals due to inspection results. Hence there could be several or different policies operating as optimal in different parts of the plant, with the added fact that a policy of preventing removal will usually require the observing and recording of some parameters such as the age, or the state of wear. Thus preventive maintenance is very complex and expensive method of improving the equipment liabilities. While developing the maintenance cost functions for different policies, care must be taken to include all the pertinent cost factors. If due care is not taken, then seemingly optimal policy may actually be costing more than a policy of failure removal. Some of the costs which the preventive removal policy will include are the cost of collecting, recording, analysing and reporting information, the cost of the scheduling and carrying out tests and inspections, additional capital investment in special testing and controlling devices, as well as any increase in spare parts inventory and increased labour cost to handle extra work load imposed by the policy.

Types of Replacement Policies

Some of the typical replacement policies which could be used in a preventive removal programme are as follows:

Policy I - This is to cover the situation when no preventive replacements are performed, only failure removals on failed components are carried out. Let us take Cf as the average cost of performing a failure removal, then the total cost of maintenance during the period T is $\frac{C_f \cdot T}{u_1}$.

Thus the average cost per unit time is denoted by $C_1 = \frac{C_f \cdot T}{u_1}$

Where u_1 = Expected failure time

$$= \int_0^\infty x\, f(x) dx$$

$$= \int_0^\infty x_i \, p(x_i)$$

Where $p(x_i)$ = frequency of failure.

Policy II: This is applicable, when the equipment is removed after some decided hours of operations with no failure occuring *i.e.*, after the predicted component age. When failure occurs, in any case, the replacement is made. Thus if C_p is the average cost of preventive removal, the average cost per unit time is

$$C_2 = \frac{C_f - (C_f - C_p)S(t_0)}{\int_0^{t_0} S(z)\, dz}$$

Where S(*z*) is the survival rate for not failing equipment

and z(*x*) = $\int f_{(z)}\, d_z$

$$= \sum_{xi} p(xi)$$

Policy III: When preventive removals are performed at regular laid down intervals, say, t_p, $2t_p$ etc regardless of the age of the componenet in use. Failure removals are made when needed.

Average cost per unit time $C_3 = \dfrac{C_p + C_p.H(t_p)}{t_p}$

Where $H(t_p)$ is the expected number of replacement made in the time t_p. This policy is preferable if t_p is large.

Policy IV: This policy is adopted when failure may not be immediately removed and the equipment is idling until the next removal is due as per the scheduled time. Let us take the cost of period of idle time, with length t is K + M*t*. If the failure occurs in an interval $[(rt_p - t_d), rt_p]$, then the failure removal is not performed until rt_p; r = 1, 2, 3 etc.

Then the average cost per unit time

$$C_4 = \left(\frac{1}{t_p}\right) C_p + C_f \, . \, H(t_p - t_d) + \int_0^{t_d} (K + M_t)\, h\,(t_p - s_z)\, d_z$$

Where H(*t*) = $\dfrac{dH(t)}{dt}$

The condition which implies that the idle time would be included and $t_d > 0$ *i.e.*, if $C_f > K$.

Policy V: In this case, the inspections are carried out when the wear of the equipment is measured. The particular cost function will depend upon the probabilities of failure, when the equipment is in any of the possible state of wear and on the conditional transitive probabilities, giving the probabilities of the equipment leaving one state and entering another.

If there are two possible states–unsatisfactory called state I and satisfactory called zero (0) and if the probabilities of failure in these states are p(1) and p(0), respectively, and transition probability is W, and all are constants, then

$$C_5 = \frac{C_f \cdot p(1)[W + p(0)]}{W + p(1)} + \frac{W\left(e^{-Wt_1 - p(1)t_1}\right)}{W\left(W + p(1)t_1\right)} \times \frac{C_p - p(1)C_f - p(0)C_f}{W + p(1)} + \frac{C_k}{t_1}$$

Where C_k = average cost of inspection

Policy VI: In this case, there is continuous inspection at an average cost of Cc per unit time. Immediately when the wear has the value 1 (*i.e.*, unsatisfactory state), a preventine removal is performed. Failure removals are performed at the time of equipment future.

$$C_6 = [C_f\, p(0)]\,[C_pW + C_c]$$

Policy VII: This policy is applicable when the unit cost of putting equipment into service in groups is lower than the unit cost of putting equipment into service piece by piece. It is desirable to detemine optimum time interval between group replacements. If C_1 is the unit cost of group replacement, C_2 the cost of individual replacements, then the number of new pieces put into service at the beginning of time and H (t), the expected number of failure removals upto time t, then $C_7 =$

$$\frac{NC_1 + H(t)\,C_2}{t}$$

The decision at the management level is to be taken whether these activities will be done on as scheduled basis or when the equipment just fails. Appropriate Mathematical models can be used accordingly.

12.8 Maintenance Replacement Models

Based on the maintenance policy decided by the top management, few mathematical models can be put to use for optimum decision on the basis of merits of these policies. The maintenance replacement models under different situations will be helpful in this comparison. Three important areas are under consideration:

- Replacement of items deteriorating with time
- Sudden failures without warning
- Gradual replacement of workers diminishing due to retirement, death, retrenchment or deliberate movement etc.

Replacement of items deteriorating with time:

When the item ages due to constant use, its working efficiency gradually reduces, and it may be economical to replace it with the new one (same or improved version). When such a replacement is considered, there may be a number of choices available based an the running cost of the equipment.

Situation 1. When Money Value Remains Constant

In such a situation, the decision to replace the equipment results in the following options:

- If the time is measured continuously, then the average annual cost will be minimised by replacing the equipment when the average cost to date becomes the current maintenance cost.
- When the time is measured in discrete units, then average annual cost will be minimised by replacing the equipment when the next period maintenance cost becomes greater than the current average cost.

Thus mathematically, we can write the policy decision in the form:

(a) ***Time 't' a continuous variable:***

$$R(n) = \frac{1}{n}\ [C - S + \int_0^n R(t)\,dt\ , \text{ when } n \neq 0,$$

or $\quad R(n) = ATCn$

Where $\quad C$ = Purchase cost of new asset

S = Residual or Scrap Value of old equipment at the end of t years

$R_{(t)}$ = Running Cost for the year t

n = Replacement period of the equipment

$R_{(n)}$ = Running cost for the year n

(b) ***When time 't' is a discrete variable:*** The average cost incurred over the period of n year

ATC_n = Average total cost for period n

$$= \frac{1}{n}\ [(C - S) + \int_0^n R(t)\,dt\ ]$$

and $\quad ATC_{n-1} > ATC_n < ATC_{n+1}$

or $\quad ATC_{n-1} - ATC_n > 0$

or
$$ATC_{n+1} = \frac{1}{n+1}\ [C - S + \sum_1^{n+1} R(t)\,dt$$

$$= \frac{1}{n+1}\ ATC_n + \frac{R_{(n+1)}}{(n+1)}$$

Thus $$\frac{R_{(n+1)}}{(n+1)} - \frac{ATC_n}{(n+1)} > 0$$

or $$R_{(n+1)} > ATC_n$$

Problem 12.1

A machine costs Rs. 45,000 and the operating cost estimated to be Rs. 1,000 for the first year. It increases Rs. 10,000 every subsequent year. How fast the machine show be replaced if it is assumed that its resale value is zero?

Solution:

The cost calculations for the machine are as under:

Year of Service (n)	*Running Cost $R_{(n)}$*	*Cumulative Running $\Sigma R_{(n)}$*	*Depreciation Cost (C – S)*	*Total Cost Cost $[C - S + \Sigma R_{(n)}]$*	*Average Total Cost $ATC_{(n)}$*
1	1,000	1,000	45,000	46,000	46,000
2	11,000	12,000	45,000	57,000	$\frac{57,000}{2}$ = 28,500
3	21,000	33,000	45,000	78,000	$\frac{78,000}{3}$ = **26,000**
4	31,000	64,000	45,000	1,09,000	27,250
5	41,000	1,05,000	45,000	1,50,000	30,000
6	51,000	1,56,000	45,000	2,01,000	33,500

Since the Average Total Cost of the machine is the lowest in the third year (so marked on the table), and is Rs. 26,000, the machine should be replaced after every three years.

Problem 12.2

The data collected in running a machine, the cost of which is Rs. 60,000, are given below:

Years	*1*	*2*	*3*	*4*	*5*
Resale Value (Rs.)	42,000	30,000	20,400	14,400	9,650
Cost of spares (Rs.)	4,000	4,270	4,880	5,700	6,800
Cost of Labour (Rs.)	14,000	16,000	18,000	21,000	25,000

Determine the optimum period for replacement of the machine. [*ICWE, June, 1990*]

Solution:

While the Resale Value of the machine is the depreciated value 'S' and cost of spares and labour is the running cost of the machine per year R(n), we can work out the total cost table for the same as follows:

Year of Service (n)	*Running Cost (Rn)*	*Cumulative Running Cost* ΣRn	*Resale Value S*	*Depreciation Cost (C – S)*	*Average Cost* T_C	*Total Case* $ATC_{(n)}$
1	18,000 (4,000 + 14,000)	18,000	42,000	60,000 – 42,000 = 18,000	36,000	36,000
2	20,270 (4,270 + 16,000)	38,270	30,000	30,000	68,270	$\frac{68,270}{2}$ = 34,135
3	22,880	61,150	20,440	39,600	1,00,750	35,583
4	26,700	87,850	14,400	45,600	1,33,450	**33,363**
5	31,800	1,19,650	9,650	50,350	1,70,000	34,000

Since the Average Total Cost of the machine is the lowest during the fourth year (marked above), the machine should be replaced after every fourth year.

Situation 2. When value of money changes at constant rate. When the value of money changes at constant rate r, then we can calculate the depreciation value 'd' as:

$$d = \left(\frac{100}{100+r}\right)^n$$

The machine should be replaced when sum of all discounted costs is minimum.

Problem 12.3

A pipe line is due for repairs. It will cost Rs. 10,000 and last for 3 years. Instead, if a new pipe line is to be laid, the cost will be Rs. 30,000 and will last for 10 years. If the cost of the capital is 10% and salvage value as zero, which alternative should be preferred ?

Solution:

The cost of the capital being 10%, the present value of the money over a period of 1 year will be

$$d = \left(\frac{100}{100+r}\right)^n = \left(\frac{100}{100+10}\right)^1 = 0.91$$

The discounted value of cost for replacement after n years is

$$Dn = c + cd^n + cd^{2n} + \dots\dots\dots$$

$$= c\,(1 + d^n + d^{2n} + \ldots\ldots\ldots) = \left(\frac{C}{1-d^n}\right)$$

where c is the initial cost.

$$D_3 = \frac{1000}{1+(0.91)^3} = \text{Rs. } 4{,}021 \text{ for 3 years}$$

and $$D_{10} = \frac{30{,}000}{1+(0.91)^{10}} = \text{Rs. } 4{,}820 \text{ for 10 years}$$

Since the discounted value of the existing line after 3 years is less, the existing line should be preferred for repair after every 3 years.

Situation 3. Present Worth Factor Criterion:

(i) When the equipment deteriorates over a period of time, its running cost increases monotomically and the value of the money decreases with constant rate. In such a case, PWF = $(1 + r)^{-n}$ where r = rate of interest and PWF is called the present worth factor:

(ii) When money is taken on loan, but is repaid in installments, the replacement of the item is based on PWF. If

C = the purchase cost of the item.

R = annual running cost

n = life of the item in years

S = Scrap value of the item at the end of its life

r = annual interest rate.

Then the present worth of the total cost during n years,

= C + R (PWF for r% interest for n years) – S (PWF for r% interest for n years)

Problem 12.4

A person is considering the options for buying a new machine for his plant. He has received the quotation for the machine with the following details.

	Proposal A	Proposal B	Proposal C
Present Cost	Rs. 10,000	Rs. 12,000	Rs. 15,000
Total annual cost	Rs. 2,000	Rs. 1,500	Rs. 1,200
Life expected	10 years	10 years	10 years
Salvage Value	Rs. 500	Rs. 1,000	Rs. 1,200

If the interest rate of loan is 12%, which proposal should he accept for purchase ? For instalment payments, PWF = 5.650.

Solution:

Calculating the Precent Worth Factor.

$$PWF = (1 + r)^{-n}$$

$$= (1 + 0.12)^{-10} = 0.322 \text{ (Single payment basis)}$$

and PWF = 5.650 for installment basis payment over 10 year period.

The present value calculations for the three proposals is worked out as follows.

Proposal	*Present Value*	*Value at the end of Life*	*Present Value of Salvage Cost*	*Net Cost*
A	10,000	2,000 × 5.65 = 11,300	500 × 0.322 = 161	21,139
B	12,000	1,500 × 5.65 = 8,475	1,000 × 0.322 = 322	**20,153**
C	15,000	1,200 × 5.65 = 6,780	1,200 × 0.322 = 386	21,393

Since proposal B is the least cost proposal, it should be accepted.

Replacement of items failing completely

(i) Situation I. When components fail and can be replaced

This is a situation of high predictability and higher uncertainty. Hence we use the probability distribution of failures. Since the item fails after a period of t years, we should minimise the total cost at the end of t years.

Let us denote

$S(t)$ = Number of components surviving at time t

and $F(t)$ = Fraction of components failed at first failure.

N = Total number of components in the system.

Then, the probability of failure of components during the period (t) and (t – 1) will be

$$P(f) = \frac{S(t-1) - S(t)}{N}$$

Conditional probability that a component survived upto period (t – 1) and then failed will be

$$= \frac{S(t-1) - S(t)}{S(t-1)}$$

Let the cost of replacement after failure = Cf

and cost of preventive replacement = Cp

T = Service life

I = Initial Investment

Then the cost of total replacement

$$= \frac{N F_{(1)}(T) C_f + N\{1 - F_{(1)}(T) C_p\}}{N.I}$$

$$= (C_f - C_p)\left[\frac{F(t)(T) + C_p/(C_f - C_p)}{I}\right]$$

This will be minimum, if factor $(C_p/C_f - C_p)$ is minimum

$$\therefore \qquad I = \int_0^T S(t)\,dt$$

or $$S(t) = \frac{dI}{dt}$$

(ii) Situation 2. When we follow group replacement policy *i.e.*, group replacement at the end of period t.

In this case,

$$F(t) = n\,p(t) + \sum_{x=1}^{t-1} p(t)\,F(t-x)\ ;\ t \le L$$

$$\sum_{x=1}^{L} p(x)\,F(t-x)\ ;\ t > L.$$

and cost of replacement at time t, is

$$C(t) = nC_1 + C_2 \sum_{x=1}^{t-1} F(x)$$

MAPI: This system was developed by George Terborgh of the Machine and Allied Products Institute (MAPI) and therefore, its name. It is very useful technique for high cost item replacements. It can be used for new as well as old machine replacements. For new machines, a concept of Economic life is used and the method is called Depreciated Cost Factor (DCF). Since the total cost is calculated as the sum of the capital cost and the operating cost, the recovery value is worked out on the basis of Capital Recovery Factor (CRF).

$$R = P\ (CRF)$$

where R = End of the period payment

P = Present value

and $$CRF = \frac{r\,(1+r)^n}{(1+r)^n - 1}$$

Where r = rate of interest

Problem 12.5

An automobile bearing failure pattern follows the normal distribution with a mean of 40,00 Kilometers run with standar deviation of 5,000 Kilometers. If there are 300 bearings in operation with the conpany, how many bearings would be expected to fail ?

(a) by 50,000 Kilometers run

(b) between 50,000 to 55,000 Kilometers run.

Solution:

For normal distribution failure pattern.

$$Z = \frac{x - \mu}{\sigma}$$

(a) Given $\mu = 40,000$ Km

$\sigma = 5,000$ Km

$x = 50,000$ Km

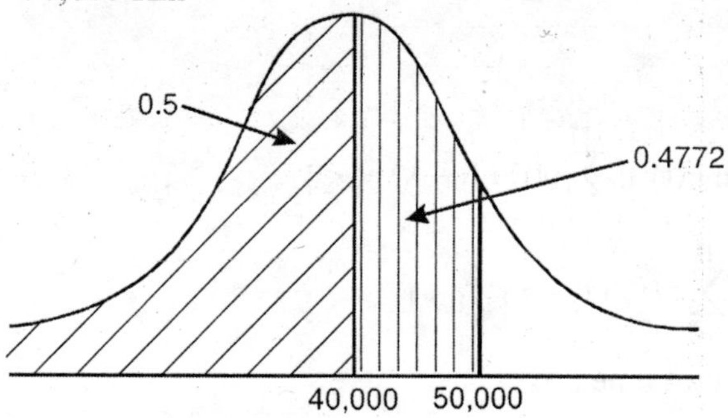

In that case,

$$Z_a = \frac{50,000 - 40,000}{5,000} = 2$$

The corresponding probability of failure = 0.5 + 0.4772

= 0.9772

Total number of bearings failure expected = 0.9772 × 300

= 293 bearings

(b) In the second situation, we have the cases of failures upto 55,000 Km run.

Then $Z_b = \frac{55,000 - 40,000}{5,000}$

$= 3.0$

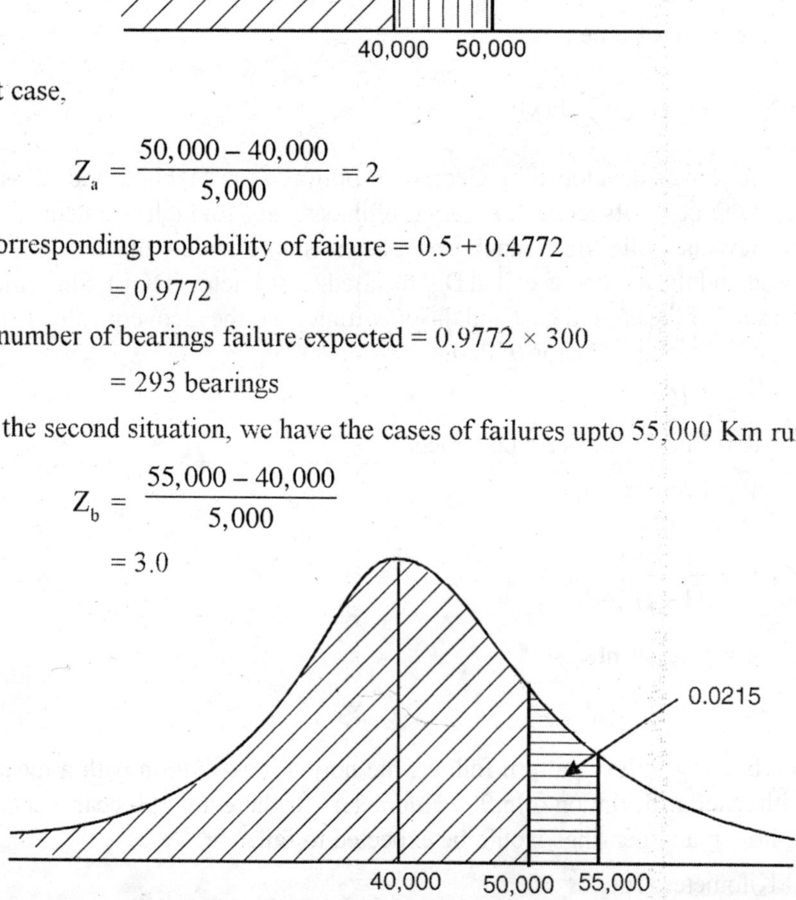

This value of Z would occur with probability = 0.5 + 0.4987

= 0.9987

Thus the probability of failure between 50,000 and 55,000 Km run will be 0.9987 – 0.9772 = 0.0215

This has been marked with seperate shading.

Hence Total number of bearings failing between 50,000 and 55,000 Km run = 0.0215 × 300 = 7 bearings

Problem 12.6

The cost of a new machine is Rs. 50,000. The maintenance cost during nth year is given by $R_n = 5{,}000\ (n - 1)$, with n = 1, 2, 3 .... etc. Suppose the discount rate per year is 0.05, after how many years, it will be economical to replace the machine by a new one?

Solution:

Working out the weighted average costs for each year we prepare the table as follows.

Year (*t*)	*Running cost* *R (t)*	*Discount factor d (t – 1)*	*Discounted maintenance factor d (t – 1)*	*Cumulative Value*	*Cumulative d (t – 1)*	*W(t)* $= \frac{C + \Sigma R\ dt}{d\ (t-1)}$
1	0	1.00	0	50,000	1.00	50,000
2	5,000	0.95	4,970	54,970	1.95	28,190
3	10,000	0.90	9,000	63,970	2.85	22,446
4	15,000	0.85	12,900	78,870	3.71	21,259
5	20,000	0.82	16,400	95,270	4.53	**21,031**
6	25,000	0.78	19,500	1,14,770	5.31	21,614

From the above table, we observe that the minimum value of the weighted average cost occurs at the fifth year (marked so). It is recommended that the economical period of replacement of the machine is at the end of 5th year.

Problem 12.7

A total of 1,000 bulbs have been supplied by a vendor. The cost of individual replacement is Rs. 10 but the bulk replacement cost is only Rs. 2.50 per bulb. The failure pattern is estimated as follows:

Period in months	:	1	2	3	4	5
Failure rate (%)	:	0.1	0.15	0.25	0.3	0.2

Work out the optimum replacement policy.

Solution:

On individual replacement policy, the weighted average life of the bulb = 1 × 0.1 + 2 × 0.15 + 3 × 0.25 + 4 × 0.3 + 5 × 0.2 = 3.35 months.

(i) The cost of individual replacement $= \dfrac{\text{Total cost of replacement}}{\text{average life}}$

$$= \frac{1{,}000 \times 10}{3.35} = \text{Rs. } 2{,}990$$

(ii) Considering the case for bulk replacement, we work out the Replacement interval based on binomial distribution.

Interval (Months)	Number of bulbs replaced	Cost of replacement
1	$N_1 = N_0p_1 = 1{,}000 \times 0.1$	1,000
2	$N_2 = N_0p_2 + N_1p_1 = 160$	1,600
3	$N_3 = N_0p_3 + N_1p_2 + N_2p_3 = 281$	2,810
4	$N_4 = N_0p_4 + N_1p_3 + N_2p_2 + N_3p_1 = 377$	3,770
5	$N_5 = N_0p_5 + \ldots\ldots\ldots + N_4p_1 = 350$	3,500

While considering the bulk replacement, the cost of replacement will be Rs. 2,500 for each interval (*i.e.*, Rs. 2.50 × 1,000 = Rs. 2,500). Thus the total average cost per month will be as under

Interval (Monthly)	Loss of Capital	Operating Cost Monthly	Operating Cost Cumulative	Total Cost	Average Cost
1	2,500	1,000	1,000	3,500	3,500
2	2,500	1,600	2,600	5,100	**2,550**
3	2,500	2,810	5,410	7,910	2,640
4	2,500	3,770	9,180	11,680	2,920
5	2,500	3,500	12,680	15,180	3,040

Minimum average cost of replacement occurs at the end of 2 months. Hence we recommed bulk replacement after 2 months.

12.9 Total Productive Maintenance (TPM)

This very innovative approach to maintenance has been developed and extensively used by the Japanese for their equipment, plants and machinery. It is really a combination of the above-described methods of maintenance namely preventive, predictive as well as breakdown maintenance. Japnese have coined it as Maintenance Prevention (MP), which is the combination of preventive maintenance (PM) and the Predictive Maintenance Action (PMA). Thus the main objective of the TPM is to make the operational system maintenance free and this is called Maintenance Improvement (MI).

As against the concept of breakdown maintenance, wherein the defective components are replaced when the equipment has failed, in TPM, the preventive maintenance is carried out on the selective basis so that chances of breakdown in these areas are reduced considerably. The process is termed as condition-based-maintence *i.e.*, preventive maintenance in a particular selective area based on the condition of machine and parts at the point of time. The second part of TPM *i.e.*, predictive maintenance is utilised to predict the condition of parts being selected for preventive maintenance. The combination leads to what is called as Maintenance Prevention (MP) or its ultimate name as Maintenance Free Service (MFS).

By taking the help of equipment records (History Sheet) we forecast the likely breaking down parts and when. The easy measure of reliability of the machines is Mean Time Between Failures (MTBF), whether breakdown is partial or full. The MTBF analysis for all the parts/components/ sub assemblies/assemblies etc is done statistically and breakdown maintenance is carried out before actual breakdown occurs. Hence it is realty predictive maintenance. This maintenance activity is performed by a small dedicated maintenance team and is called Productive Maintenance (PRM). This team is integral part of the production department only. TPM can be diagramatically shown as under (Refer Fig. 12.3):

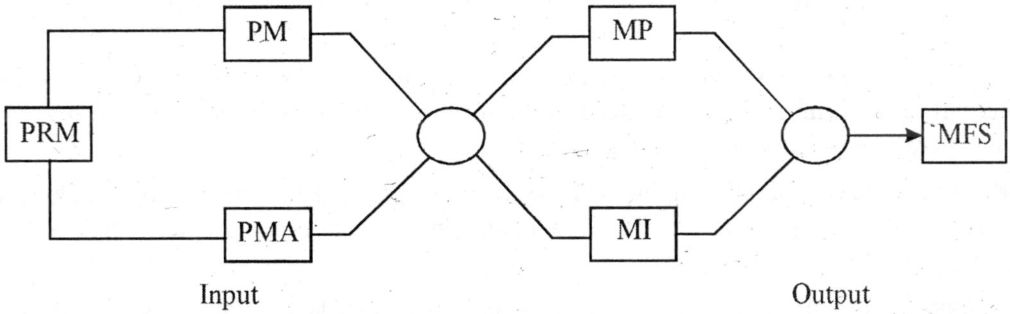

FIG. 12.3. TPM Cycle

Legends PRM = Productive Maintenance
PM = Preventive Maintenance
PMA = Predictive Maintenance Action
MP = Maintenance Prevention
MI = Maintaintibility Improvement
MFS = Maintenance Free Service.

12.10 Total Productivity Management (TPM)

Since productivity can easily be defined as the outcome or output per unit of input, the imperative parameter of high productivity is elimination or minimisation of wastes or losses of the input to achieve the best possible optimum output. In todays business environment of intense worldwide competition, this concept is becoming all the more valid and much pronounced than it had been. The concept of 'Total Productivity Management', is therefore gaining the high place approach to optimise the effectiveness of the production elements in a structured way, hence named as a management concept and is fast becoming the industrial standard. Applicability of the concept is equal in product as well as in service sector.

Total Productivity Management (also called TPM) along with the same abbreviation for Total Productive Maintenance (TPM as used by Japanese) focuses on the improvement of planned loading time, which means that the inputs are effectively planned for a sustained loss-free usage either through appropriate fail-safe design or through fail-safe process system. Hence Total Productive Maintenance becomes a subset of the overall concept of **Total Productivity Management**. The production efficiency can be enhanced through the following improvements:

- Better availability of manpower and machines
- Higher performance levels *i.e.*, enhanced outputs.
- Better quality yield of product/service with minimum wastage *i.e.*, minimum rejects and reworks.

Availability of Manpower: To ensure higher availability of manpower, the manpower maintenance concept is to be introduced and ensured. The physical health, safety, Upkeep and high morale through proper motivation and training are essential areas to be taken care of. Commensurate payment levels and gain-sharing assurance goes a long way to obtain the utmost from the workers at all levels. (Reference can be drawn to the conversion of human resources into human assets described earlier in the book).

Availability of Machines: This can be ensured by reducing breakdowns and setup times (change over period). The savings are then noticed in the form of maximum utilisation of resources by ensuring operations performed for maximum durations.

Proper maintenance of the equipment in use should be planned and ensured to avoid losses of productivity and to avoid situation of the production/operation not taking place, while it should be.

The other aspects of machine maintenance is the loss of speeds or small stops of workstation or available facilities due to improver planning and scheduling or while working on reworks (quality problems), thereby reduction in volume of production/operations.

These above described losses lead to the **Overall Equipment Effectiveness (OEE)** indicator, which is a measure of the effeciency of production (either in terms of quality or quantity). TPM is effectively used to improve OEE.

Minimisation of losses: Through TPM methodology, the identification and quantification of the losses or wastages can be effectively achieved. Once identification and quantification is complete, the necessary priorities should be allotted to important areas of improvement without wasting any time (Job empowerment for workers can be an effective method of achieving it). TPM provides various tools to achieve both the short term as well as long term improvements.

High performance levels: In case of manpower, these can be achieved through effective cultural as well as on job training and improvement in learning curve leading to the improvement in the output. It should be ensured through the concept of "Practice makes a man perfect", provided practice is structured for the optimal performance. Continuous improvement through acceptance of change must be practiced to enhance performance level.

Desired quality yield: Quality cannot really be defined because it is in the eyes of the customer. Since it is customer perception based achievement, the expectations of the customers must be understood so that it can, then, be translated into physical/virtual product/service. If the product/service ensures "the fitness for use" or conformity to the customers requirement', the perception of good quality is achieved, or otherwise, the perception must be created in the mind of the customer so as to encash as his/her psyche for better business performance.

Thus, it is primarily a manufacturing concept which involves people, continuous improvement philosophy and the integration of production and maintenance function for high productivity. It improves equipment effectiveness, achieve appropriate level of upkeep of the equipment at preventive as well as at the repair level. Scheduled plant maintenance and training of all concerned staff is the key factor for such an achievement. Japanese have used the concept to a great advantage.

Advantages of TPM

As a results of above actions, Japanese have achieved the following advantages due to TPM:

- high availability of manpower and plant
- high level of safety and hygiene
- better product quality
- longer equipment life and enhanced MTBF (Mean Time between Failures)
- lower level of demages to the equipment
- greater cost effectiveness.
- focussed and structured maintenance policies
- Skill training for operation and maintenance.

In fact, the maintenance is used to preserve the functions of all physcial assets, be it the human assets, machines, other equipment or buildings and connected facilities and services.

Increase in the efficiency through Productive Maintenance: Through the productive maintence, the assets can be kept in a state of readiness and productive efficiency so as to take as the zero-defect planning *i.e.*, reduced down time and prevention of defects. The Mean Time Between Failures (MTBF) of all human and non-human resources can be enhanced tremendously through regular productive maintenance.

Productive maintenance also helps in elimination or minimisation of accidents, injuries and pollution levels of the working atmosphere. Japanese concept of keeping the workplace as neat and tidy through the practice of 5-S (*i.e.*, **Seiri**-orderliness, **Sieton**-tidiness, **Seiso**-purity, **Seiketsu**-cleanliness and **shitsuke**-self discipline) is an effective concept to help productive efficiency. Thus it aims at improving the attitude and skills of the organisational workforce for improving the productivity *i.e.*, output efficiency. This concept removes the barrier of operator and the maintenance staff as it develops the willingness of all personnel to improve their own place and equipment for better results. In fact, Total Quality Control (TQC) and Total Productive Maintenance (TPM) become almost synonymus except for the fact that TQC is a software oriented concept, whereas the TPM is the hardware oreinted concept *i.e.*, while TQC targets "building quality into product/ service, TPM ensures it achivement through well-maintained system and equipment responsible for ensuring quality. **Thus Total Productive Maintenance (TPM) can be safely called a sub-set of its larger umbrella Total Productivity Management.**

Combining all aspects of productivity enhancement through proper management, it can be summerised as follows:

- *Human Resources:* Standard time, Mean Time Between Failures, accidents, absentism, turnover, suggestions strength etc.

- *Customers*: Requirement, Complaints, delivery schedule and quality adherance, satisfaction index.
- *Production* : use of CAD, CAM, CIM, SPC, process cabability index, machine output, downtime, maintenance cost, volume of production, cost per unit of production etc.
- *Research and Development:* New products, expenditure versus results, cost estimating errors.
- *Suppliers:* Service rating, lead time adherance, quality performance index, billing accuracy, market intelligence, material substitution suggestions etc.
- *Marketing/Sales:* Cost of marketing versus sales, sales expenditure versus revenue, order accuracy, feedback, new customers.
- *Supply chain management:* Product mix, timely Supplies, distribution overheads, logistics versus revenue etc.
- *Administration:* Cost of Poor Quality (COPQ), cost per error, fleet data and utilisation index, payment schedules and manpower training.

—●—

Section IV
STRATEGIC RESOURCES MANAGEMENT

Chapter 13

Human Assets Management and Ergonomics

Main issues:

1. Human beings as Human Assets
2. Learning and Experience Curves
3. Job Design and productivity
4. Methods study and work measurement
5. Production standards
6. Work Compensation and Incentives
7. Worker Unions

13.1 Human Resources as Human Assets

Human beings are resources to be used to gain full advantage of their potential. But to achieve optimal utilisation, human resources need a higher level of competance. In this highly competitive environment, human effectiveness is required to be much higher. The conversion of human resources into human assets is the requirement of the day.

The advancement in science, technology and management have been possible only because human resources have been functioning beyond their normal working capability. Computers would not have come to the level of today from what we saw during 1960s. Internet would not have been invented, if there was no undue quest of human brain to do something drastically better. Innovative ideas of the managers can satisfy the present day customer. A very large number of products and services are possible today only because human beings have put themselves on a very high pedestal of thinking. These are all the examples of human resources converting into human assets. The difference, by now, is easy to understand. If a person works on normal pace, with best of output produced, he feels very happy. But if he works only the way he is told to, he becomes stale. The learning curve concept can increase his output level, but boredone will, probably, bring it down.

Thus there is a definite necessity to make the jobs interesting for a person so that he should be prepared to perform it willingly. The difference is that instead of working on a job because he has been asked to do it, he should be doing it better if he wants to do it. Involvement, commitment and willingness are the parameters changing his working format. This change is termed as **"change from human resource to human asset"**. A person becomes an asset to the organisation, when he undertakes the operation with pride, commitment and involvement by considering it as "his job".

In order to make a person reach this level, it is recommanded to put him through the following stages to help in this conversion. Gradual change in the mind set through deliberate attempt for modification should come about.

These stages of conversion are –

- ***Proper selection, recritment and placement of a person :*** through a deliberately designed Qualitative Requirement (QR) specifying all the qualifications required for a job profile.
- ***Proper training :*** for a person to make him confident of operating the facilities he is to interact with, following training schedules are required :

  (a) cultural training regarding the organisation set up (to feel part of the team).

  (b) technical training for job specific and tools specific.

  (c) psychological training to make him mentally robust to withstand oprational pressure.
- ***Motivation exposure :***

  (a) identifying motivation method or utility value for a person.

  (b) applying motivation system commensurate with the company policy

  (c) concept of gain-sharing.
- ***Job description, job enrichment and job ownership :*** to make him feel part of the job.

By now, he is ready to act as an asset to the company and the personnel policy of the company has to be consistent with the above requirement. The method of assessment through the system of objective performance appraisals with measuring perameters on their Key Result Areas (KRA) helps in keeping the working level high.

13.2 Learning and Experience Curve.

Learning Curve

Based on day-to-day opeations, it is evident that initially when workers are not very familiar with their tasks and the production facilities processes and proceedures, they tend to take longer to perform a given activity and hence production of initial few units will take more time. As the workers go through the procedures every day, their reflex actions become sharper and the output level starts increasing. After a certain period of time, standardised output rate levels-off and further increase in productivity is rather slow. This is based on human nature, psychology and the principle of "Practice makes a man perfect". Various studies carried out for the purpose show definite relationships of production hours with the amount of learning schedules.

The studies show that assembly of a product is reduced by a factor of 0.8 when the production volume is doubled. This means that if the first product takes 10 hours to assembly, the second unit would need about $0.8 \times 10 = 8$ hours and the fourth unit as $0.8 \times 8 = 6.4$ hours and so on. This trend is called the learning curve.

A typical learning curve can be drawn as follows (Refer Fig 13.1 below)

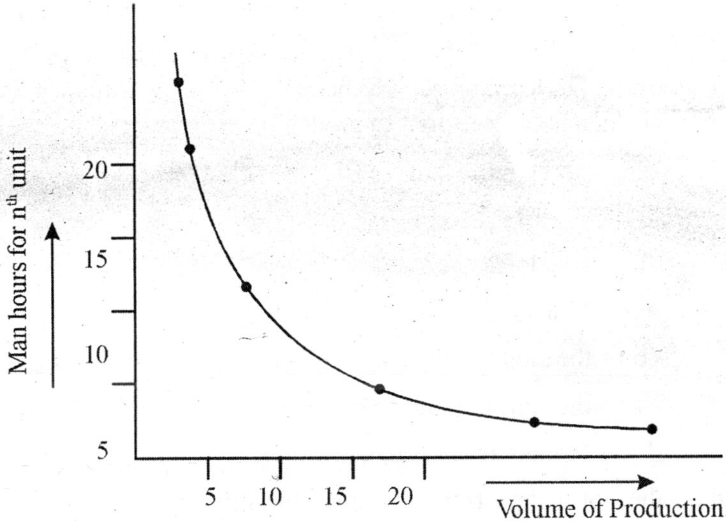

FIG 13.1. The Learning Curve

This curve indicates that when the number of units produced are small, it takes longer for producing the nth unit. But as the production volume increases *i.e.*, when a worker has worked on more number of units, the time of completion comes down, till at a certain volume, this time almost levels off, (curve becoming almost asymptotic to the volume axis).

The variation in the rate of learning depends on the uptake level of the worker *i.e.* his intelligence quotient, his aptitude, reflex actions capability and complexity of the job. Simpler the job, greater the learning. Higher the will to learn, higher the learning rate.

By careful studies, we can obtain information on the following parameters :

- The average number of manhours required for an activity. This is called operation time (OT) of the activity.
- The total number of manhours to complete an activity.
- The exact number of manhours for completion of an activity.

The Analysis

Learning curve analysis based on the above information can be carried out by the following methods :

Arithmatic analysis: If we know the learning rate of a group of average workers, calculations for completion of successive units/activities can be done methamatically. If the learning rate is known as 0.8, when the number of similar activities performed are doubled, the successive activities can be expected to be completed as under :

If, 1st unit production takes	10 hrs	
then, 2nd unit production takes	10×0.8	= 8 hrs
4th unit production takes	8×0.8	= 6.4 hrs
and, 8th unit production takes	6.4×0.8	= 5.1 hrs

By this method, we can get the approximate idea about the time required to produce certain definite number of units.

Logarithmic analysis. The learning curve generally follows logarithmic relationship of number of units produced to the manhours required to produce.

Then the relationship can be written as

$$T_n = T_1 (n^b)$$

and $b = \log r/\log 2$

Where T_1 = Manhours for the first unit

b = the slope of the learning curve

r = the learning rate percentage

and T_n = Manhours for producing n^{th} unit.

By getting the values of b and r from learning tables, the calculation of manhours required to produce n^{th} unit can be done.

A typical learning curve values of b are given below (from the relationship given above as b = logr/log2)

Learning rate percentage (r)	**value of b**
70	– 0.515
75	– 0.415
80	– 0.322
85	– 0.152

Learning Curve Tables. There are standard learning curve table (given at the end of this book) for obtaining learning curve coefficients.

These can be used for comparison of actual manhours taken by our workers for an activity.

Following methods are used to select a particular method for use of these tables:

- One method of selection of learning rate is through the experience of the analyst, coupled with the information published in various relevant journals (based on actual study).
- Second method that can be adopted is through actual experimentation of own workers and operation time (OT) for the specific activity noted on the average basis. The variation in OT for subsequent units is also noted down and the rate of learning can be interpretted as described under Arithmetic method. The industry standards are set on this basis. A further concept known as Standard Time (ST) for an activity is being discussed subsequently.

Experience Curve

From the concept of learning curve, it is derived that more number of units are produced by workers as time progresses and as they gain more insight into the process and procedures. Unit cost of production comes down with the learning of the workers. But it is found that even with the labour turnover, the unit cost of production comes down. This suggests that some other important relevant factors are responsible for this trend of cost reduction. Some possible reasons are the improved equipment and supporting facilities, better method design and simplified procedures and also better management through better information flow. This is known as "Experience Curve". The experience curve would indicate that a production process has a n% of the cost of making the $2n^{th}$ unit of the product. This helps in gaining market share if the cumulative effect of learning curve and experience curve produces a definite advantage of quality, cost and volume of production.

13.3 Job Design

A job is the set of activities, tasks and responsibilities of the human being. To design the normal job, we attach importance to the performance expectation and the working environment that will indicate as to how much work can be undertaken by a human being. The procedure laid down to perform the job is called the job description". While writing down the job description, we have to be as specific and transparent as we can be, to make the job understood by the performer. It is not an easy task, because there are large number of variables and the trade offs are not easy to obtain. The total work to be performed is broken into conceivably small activities or tasks that can be done independenbly (called Work Breakdown Structure or WBS). This can be produced as a CPM or PERT network, wherein various taskes are marked on the relationship diagram. Along with these activities or tasks, the designer has to indicate the resources and tools required to perform each task. The job design should specify skill and training required, the design of the working space the average time required for each task along with the quality specification including dimensional and performance tolerances.

Repeatitive jobs are generally easy to define, wheras job shop tasks are to be written out in concise manner with due care in job content and job specifications. Any specialisation for the job must be defined clearly so that the worker has the confidence of performing the job. These can be divided into two types :

- Normal task with skill variety
- Specialised job

For normal work, the person can be trained easily and one person can be trained for more than one job. Such jobs are to be defined everytime a person is asked to perform. It is "Jack of all, master of none" concept which is tried in such tasks. Multiple skill development comes useful for normal jobs. Such workers are called handymen. Specialised jobs, on the other hand, are the jobs that only few persons can perform and these need higher skill, and concentrated training. Such jobs will be performed by persons specifically trained and assigned for the purpose. With better skill and repeated performance, such persons can become very efficient and their outputs improve. Higher quality jobs should be performed by specialised workers. It is for this reason of repeatitive nature of such jobs that the job becomes monotonous, less satisfying and boring in due course of time. Therefore, tough training and procedure qualifies a worker for better quality product. The quality starts suffering as per passage of time due to worker's growing disinterest. This may result in absenteism or even larger turnover. In such cases, they job content has to be revised to make it interesting and challenging. When there is a conflict between technical and psychological impact of work, something different has to be thought of. Either it is motivation incentive or job variation that can be brought in. In addition it is suggested that longer duration repeatitive job content should be performed by machines, whereas some job with gaps in operations can be allotted to workers. Taylor suggested **"Work study and Scientific Management"** to improve on the job design and job content.

Job Empowerment and Job Ownership

It has been observed that raising productivity is not possible only by work methods, but it has lot to do with the psychological and organisational impact. Both the quality and quantity of output depend on how interesting the job is and how much control workers have on it. Hence for job design, both the aspects must be assimilatated together for proper blending of technical and psychological requirement for its effect on quality and productivity. Even specialised jobs need the variety and repeatitive contents. One method to make the job interesting is job empowerment where some portion of decision making is passed down to the workers and if they 'OWN' the job, they are likely to perform better. Such authorisation to workers to act on their own for their OWN task is a very powerful tool for continuous excellence in production so much needed for global competitiveness.

Job Enlargement/Enrichment

The job of a woker can also be made interesting by allowing him additional responsibility *i.e.*, added tasks, which can reduce his monotony. This addition of tasks is called job enlargement. This is referred to as horizontal job enlargement.

Another way to make the job more interesting is to use job enrichment concept to advantage. In this case, we try and expand the responsibility of the worker needing higher skill. It may be in the form of vertical expansion, *i.e.*, involving the workers in the design of the process. Additionally a worker is allotted a job responsibility for self quality control and handling customers complaints. Such vertical job enlargement helps in utilising creativity, interpersonnel communication and problem solving capabilities of the workers. Workers, while monotoneusly at a level performing their task, will be thinking of improvements and quality control all the time. This makes the job interesting. The same concept can be extended to all areas of work not only for production. For example, a sales person can be given added responsibility of deciding stock levels, product mixes, the display of products and the profit margin variations. Purchasing man can be entrusted the additional responsibility of suggesting design changes, facility layouts and wastage reductions.

These job enrichment methods require integrated functioning of enhanced training and greater motivation including gain sharing, larger knowledge of quality control systems and interaction with tools for higher production.

Job Rotation

Some times changing the place of work even without changing job content can do wonders for job satisfaction. Some organisation make jobs team-oriented and at regular interval, interchange the team on jobs. By bringing in the team competition, the jobs become interesting. But the jobs need be well-defined. Even single workers changing the place of work at the some location or else if the relocations has any special value for the worker (say his own place of residing) can be effective.

Yet another system followed is creating more jobs in a production line. Each job being different, requiring different skills or physical demands, the jobs can be made interesting by relating the persons with challenges attached, so that no worker is attached to a boring or highly repeative jobs for a long time. The unpleasant, boring or physically more demanding jobs can be shared by workers. This has to be carefully planned, so that advantage intended to be gained does not become disincentive for workers. Job rotation for the sake of rotation should never be tried.

All these methods such as "job description", "job empowerment", "job enrichment", "job rotation" or job 'OWNERSHIP' are meant to bring in more interest and cohensiveness in the ranks and file of the workers and manager alike. The basic and the foremost aim of all these thinking ends into customer satisfaction. The main issue, therefore, is customer focus, be it the internel customer or the external customers.

Quality Assurance

This is yet another important component of the job design. The responsibility of quality assurance given to the worker helps in better quality control. Quality control is the responsibility of all. When a worker is involved in the vertical expansion of the job *i.e.*, product design, process design and control responsibility, on the-spot quality correlation if required, is better when the worker works on the principle of job ownership.

Another method of improved quality assurance by worker is his involvement in the maintenance and repair of machines and other facilities. He may not be doing it himself but it may ensure that no time is wasted in these functions as it affects his productivity and quality of the product. Team work system for group of related tasks has been found to be very productive, quality oriented and useful in any field. The change in the organisation structure, delegation of responsibility and authority and degree of training helps if consistently done and properly controlled. By this process, the organisation will be able to achieve better integration of resources, whether in mechanical processing or in automated processing. Local Worker can easily identify the problem on the spot and corrects it before it becomes a major headache, when automation level is higher. The worker or supervisor has more time to think and utilise their skill better to achieve process improvement.

Service Industry

In service industry, this focus becomes more prominant in deciding operational strategies. In case of service, the worker should be empowered to decide what to do, when to do, how to do and how much to do as far as customer service level is concerred. Then he may be able to perform tasks even beyond his normal domain of work. Multi-skilled jobs or Multi-tasking is better done when the worker has the authority/freedom to do the work on heterogenous tasks. Thus 'one window' system makes customers very happy. Similarly the concept of turnkey projects is paying rich dividend, where same set of workers help in packaging, loading, helping house-hold servants in their work to speed up work, wrapping up and helping any disabled person with wheel chair can be very satisfying, in addition to preparing all necessary documentation for his move. Such things are becoming very popular now.

13.4 Employee Productivity

To remain competitive in global operations, it is imperative that the total energy of the organisation is focussed on improvement in productivity in all its areas of operation *i.e.*, productivity in all departments. It should be the national moto if the growth of economy has to be ensured. It applies to both, the short range (tactical) as well as long range (strategic) aim for employee utility enhancement.

Practically all organisations have access to the latest technology (the level and area they look for), the necessary facilities and machines of appropriate capability and the best brains to utilise these resources effectively but the competitive edge emerges out of the utmost utility of its work force. Hence it is the "Man behind the Gun", that playes a major role in creating value with the available resources. Productivity of the organisation, therefore, needs a very careful strategic thinking to plan and achieve.

In essence, all the strategic achievements of any organisation have been and will be possible only through the competitiveness created by the employees and hence the concept of turning human resources into human assets has been emphasised. The employee, therefore, represents an asset of strategic importance well planned, well placed and well controlled. Quality work results only from the quality of these human assets.

Productivity – Productivity can be defined as the measure of resources utilisation *i.e.*, the amount of output (product/service) produced due to a certain level of inputs (of all kinds). Thus, mathematically

$$\text{Productivity} = \frac{\text{Amount of output}}{\text{Amount of input resources used}}$$

Problem 13.1

(a) If a person serves 224 customers during 24 hours working, workout the labour productivity.

(b) When we employ 2 workers for 8 hrs and one worker for 2 hours and they handle 232 customers, what is the labour productivity ?

Solution :

(a) Labour Productivity $= \frac{224}{24} = 9$ Customers served per hour

(b) Labour Productivity $= \dfrac{232}{(2 \times 8) + (1 \times 2)} = 13$ Customers per hour

Productivity enhancement

Based on above definition, the implications of productivity can be understood as follows :

(a) Higher productivity can be achieved by enhancing output for the same amount of resources used.

(b) Higher productivity can be achieved by getting output at the same level but with reduced input resources.

(c) Productivity can also be increased by increasing the input resources for achieving a higher proportion of the output.

Thus, it is evident that we should be able to utilise the input resources (by improving their quality or quantity) in the best possible way and to keep them at the cost effective pedastal.

Though from the formula, the cost or the price of products or services does not come into play, but these aspects have a very important role to play. Organisational level productivity Implications are that when the cost of the resource increases, and if the profits are to be maintained at a certain level through a combination of output/input proportion, the price of the product is to be proportionately increased. This implies that if the cost of input material or the input labour increases, the higher production level must be ensured for each manhour spent. This can be done in the form of higher automation or the improved methods used for production. This change in man–machine mix changes the mix of their costs dramatically. Even then, labour cost reduction through automation is very small element. Other resources such as product quality, costs, inventories, engineering and research and development costs, materials, shipping, training etc are larger costs to be controlled for better productivity. Infact instead of reducing capital investment, more emphasis on reduced inventories, innovative product and process design and improved quality shows the impertance of human competance for improving productivity in all these areas. The contribution of human element in the areas of CAD/CAM, CIM, automated material handling systems, innovations in product design and improved quality systems lead to an improvement in the nature of operations both in manufacturing as well as services, ultimately resulting in higher productivity *i.e.*, smaller the work force, leaner and more productive are the manufacturing and service operations.

Measurement of Productivity

Defining Productivity as the ratio of output to input is simple but not easy to calculate. The units of output and input have to be defined. Let us take the case of productivity in a certain time period against some measures, which can be adopted easily.

- ***Labour Productivity :*** Number of products produced during a given period devided by the cost of direct labour incurred during the period.
- ***Material Productivity :*** Number of products produced during a given period divided by the amount spent on material procurement for this production.

- *Capital Productivity :* Number of products produced out of the assets procured divided by the asset value incurred.

While working out the productivity as given above, there one some factors, which are not inbuilt into the measures. For example, price is not included in the material productivity. There are large number of materials with different accounting units of productions. Hence it may not be a good method to work out productivity. It gives some awareness to the managers about the trend of his spendings. At a certain time, the labour employed may be costly either due to skill, geographical variation or general trend of wage policy. Also, we may be substituting materials by cheaper or costlier version depending on the research effect or the local availability or short supply. Hence the calculations will go haywire. Reduction in workforce due to antomated machines or decision to buy ready assemblies instead of manufacturing all components resulting in less manpower engagement also changes the calculations. In case of old machines being discarded and sold and then replaced by new improved ones make a large difference in calculating the capital productivity. In order to solve these problems in some logical way, we can adopt the method of examining the productivity of multiple factors in assessing the effeciency of a production system. Bureau of labour statistics publishes statistics on multifactor productivity, which is a composite measure of labour, capital, energy and materials resources. This information is available on National basis in the report of GDP per employed person published by the Government.

Working Environment

Since labour is an important resource and labour productivity should be controlled well due to its direct impact on production, we summarise the factors affecting the labour productivity:

Work environment

- Materials
- Machines and automation
- Facility layouts effeciency
- Job design
- Working conditions like light, temperatures, dust, fumes and humidity etc.

Workers Ability

- Altitude towards work and quality
- Aptitude
- Experience
- Education
- Intelligence

Workers Motivation Factors

- Wage policy
- Communication

- Performance appraisal Systems
- Efficiency
- Incentives
- team work and competitiveness
- standardisation and specialisation
- Competance
- Authority, Responsibilities and Accountability
- Union influence
- Safety and psychological need satisfaction
- Physical conditions like Age, robustness and home environment.

It is not easy to predict human behaviour in general or its wide variation from time to time. Only a rough guide can be followed. But, at least three important factors can be identified, which affect worker productively. These are :

- Job Performance Standards
- Technology, machines and work methods
- Product Quality.

Hence for the workers, we should design measureable parametres for their set KRAs (Key Result Areas) and assess at the time of their periodic performance appraisals, so as to obtain general idea of workers productivity. There may be wide variations in the performance abilities, because each individual is so different in terms of general health, mental robustness personalities and interests, ambitions, education level, training and their length and quality of experience. Some levelling off can be obtained through motivation but it is a very complex variable. The values of various parameters for each individual are different and so are his motivational incentives. But these can be used to advantages. Based on the working environment and the behaviour of the worker, the productivity can vary significantly. Another important factor for productivity measure is the learning curve of a person based on his intelligence and learning attitude.

13.5 Workers Health and Safety

Working Conditions

These vary Significantly from one organisation to another depending on the type of product and processes in use. On any working shop floor, the general or special hazards exist. A worker may slip because there is water lying on the floor, he can be hurt due to some partitions coming in way, may fall from a ledder, may be hit by flying pieces from grinding, welding or turning machines, he may have his clothes caught in rotating or moving parts of machines. In addition, fires, electricity, toxic materials like paints, acids fumes, dust or noise can be all harmful to the worker and may effect his health. In order to control such accidents/hazards, enough care should be taken to make the work place safe and healthy.

For a worker to be healthy and safe, working conditions should be good from the following angles :

General Cleanliness. Regular Shopfloor cleaning (including safe layout) to be ensured. Dust, dirt and chemicals spilling to be avoided. Debris and scraps to be removed. Badly designed tools and equipment to be avoided.

Illumination. General lighting as well as job spot lights, where ever required, should be provided. Manufacturing, computer laboratory and assembly would need different lighting arrangements.

Temperature and humidity. As per laid down norms such as 24°c as working temperatures and controlled humidity for normal office work must be provided. For shop floor, forced ventilation or airconditioning may be necessary.

Noise and Sound. These are major distractions, hence need to be within permissible limits, otherwise it can be safety hazards. At times soft music may enhance working capacity. Alarms for various purposes can be helpful in pre-warnings to ensure safe operations.

Workers Health and Safety Laws

There are government regulations and laws for making workplaces safe and hazard free. For better output, there is a growing concern in this area.

Two important sets of laws governing health and safety are :

- Workmen compensation Act and laws
- Occupational Safety and Health Administration Act (OSHA)

Such laws exist in every country and these are binding on all organisations. Because of the growing concern, the environmental protection has been recognised as a major consideration and hence at the international level, the Environmental Management Systems (EMS) in the form of ISO 14000 series guidelines have been issued. Various countries have adopted these system to make environment free of the hazards. In India, we have adopted this standard as IS 14000, which is legal and binding on all organisations. In addition, specific safety laws have been formulated and are in practice for specific industries.

It is a great mental upliftment for the worker if he knows that his organisation cares for his health and safety by adopting various measures. Safe environment of working increases the productivity of the worker. To look after the health, the services of medical attendants and doctors can be provided and regular check up schedules are introduced by companies for the benefit of workers.

Accidents

It is well established fact that unsafe work place can contribute to two major effects for the workers :

- Accidents
- Diseases or chronic occupational disability

The accidents occur due to some deficiency in safeguards. It is a discrete event, which results either in injury or machine breakdown resulting in stoppage of work. Psychologically it is not only the demage to worker or machine at a particular accident place, it also distrubs the area around, where other workers would try and help those involved in accident. Thus the stoppage of work and loss of production is larger than the accident place itself.

The accidents can occur anywhere in the work area, whether due to unsafe working conditions or a careless act by a worker. For example, a moving part of the machine may catch garment of a worker due to guard plate having been demaged or not being provided. Similarly, fast driving is an intentional unsafe act. Use of inproper tools, poor lighting, spilling of water or chemicals on the shop floor or unncessary passages obstructing smooth flow of men or material, poorly maintained tools or machines or equipment (like tyre bursting of an aircraft while taking off or landing is poor maintenance of tyres), exposed electrical wiring, earthing not being connected properly, staircases without hand bars etc can be only few example of causes of accidents.

The important aspect of accidents is that it may be only one-time happening, but demage could be very large (may be loss of life due to a fatal injury). All accidents therefore, must be recorded, investigated, reasons found and necessary precautions implemented. In case of accidents, the root cause investigation is important.

Similarly, unsafe behaviours such a mental tension in worker, alcoholism, rude attitude or unintentional mistake due to work design etc must be taken care of. Bad lighting, poor clothing, poor house keeping, narrow isles or corridors etc must be avoided.

Even when an accident occurs, quick reaction to it is a must. Workmen compensation Act provides a good rescue for heavy demages.

13.6 Work Study And Work Simplification

Due to global competition and pressure on the organisational financial health, the emphasis is shifting to methods of production in order to improve productivity in all fields of operations. There are enormous improvements in technology and the economical development as a result there of. The technology to be used, therefore, must suit the requirement of the work to be produced. Even if the manual and mechanical means of productions are not used, the importance of human involvement cannot be underestimated. It is the most useful and productive resource in production. What ever be the level of automation, the production, installation, commissioning and usage has to be controlled by human workforce and the design and use of electronic hardware and software still remains the function of the human beings.

In order to carry out production, a method of doing work has to be decided and its procedure *i.e.*, sequence of operations has to be listed out. The imperative part is that this should be the 'best method' as advocated by Taylor. The best method has to be evolved by the concerned manager. The concept called 'workstudy' was suggested by Gilbreth. Plenty of work was done during the later part of 19th century and the methods of carrying out work study were fine-tuned. Due to continous work on workstudy, the awareness and significant advancement has resulted in the area of productivity. Some of the stalwerts of workstudy were Gilbreth, Robert owen, Jean Perronet, Charless Baggage, Frederick Habsey, Henry Gantt, Charles Prodaux and Russel Currie.

Definition of Workstudy

According to the British Standards Institute, "Work Study is a generic term for those techniques, particularly "method study" and "work measurement", which are used in the examination of human work in all its contexts and which lead systematically to the investigation of all factors which affect the efficiency and economy of the situation being renewed in order to effect improvement."

A much simpler definition was suggested by Russel Currie as" the systematic, objective and critical examination of all the factors that govern the operational efficiency of any specified activity in order to effect improvement".

An international definition by international labour organisation (ILO) given in its Hand books says ***"work study is a term to embrace the technique of method study and work measurement, which are employed to ensure the best possible use of human and material resources in carrying out a specified activity"***.

Objectives of Works Study

As we proceed to find the work contents in order to have optimum use of resources "(The definitions of work study emphasises) we have to study various factors contributing to overall improvement in productivity. Objectives of the work study are as follows :

- Optimum use of manpower
- Optimum use of machines and materials
- Using these resources only for essential work and no more.
- Convenience for use of resources to avoid any wastages.

Techniques of Works Study

The definitions of work study specify two techniques of work study namely :

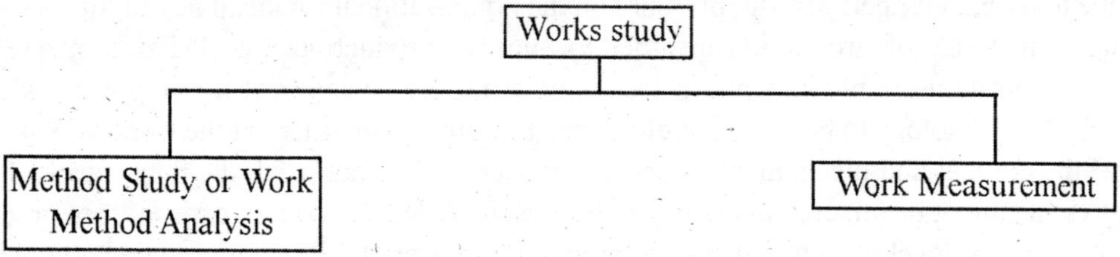

These techniques are interdependent and hence study results of one lead to the other *i.e.*, when **'best method'** has been devised (Method study) then only we carry out the work measurement in terms of time taken for the work through the steps of individual activities. The standardisation of work comes in only after work measurement.

Method Study : The technique involves finding out various activities to be performed to complete a job or work *i.e.*, study all its subactivities critically and rationalising these activities by eliminating any unneccessary or unwanted activity part from the total job content. Based on this critical study, a new method (better method) is developed for doing that work.

The method study, therefore, can be defined as ***"a critical examination of the existing way of doing a work with a view to develop and apply easier and more productive method of doing the same"***.

Work Measurement : After deciding the work content and sequence of operations through method study (Work Method Analysis) ***the technique used for establishing the time standards for a trained and qualified worker to perform the given work at a defined level of performance is called "Work Measurement"***.

Qualifications for the Works Study Team

In order to carry out systematic study, the qualifications of the works study team are highlighted to that the data collected and analysed are worth the effort. Some of the qualifications of the works study team are :

- Heterogeneous team
- Expertise in related fields
- Pleasant personality
- Open mind
- Good communicative skill
- No egos or preconceived ideas
- No vested interests in the study

Work Method Analysis

As we have amply discussed above, the machiness and materials are selected based on the requirement for production. It is upto the human beings as to how to use these resources to get optimum out of these. The worker productivity has been discussed above. How to improve the method to reach the stage of 'best method' is to be carefully studied and evaluated.

The first step for improving the work method is to ask workers suggestions only as they are in best position to do it due to their direct involvement day in and day-out. Their valuable suggestions can help tremendously. The job empowerment and job ownership discussed in earlier paragraphs are added tools to obtain excellent results in Method analysis and improvement.

The main aim of the method analysis is to improve productivity by improved production capacity (production efficiency), reducing the cost of production and achieving the best possible quality of the product. For any such analysis, we need answers to the following questions :

- What is being done ?
- Why is it being done ?
- Is every part of the job necessary ?
- Why is it being done this way ?
- Who could do it better ?

Thus it is seperating out the essentials from non-essentials. Better method of finding answers to these question is to walk over the existing method meticulously with a magnifying glass and analyse each and every part of a job to reach the level of "the best method". Value analysis helps in this process to a very large extent.

Areas of Application By Method Study

Improvement of work can be done for any activity. It is equally applicable for household jobs as for any production job. For production related work, few of the important areas for application of method study are :

- Improved flow of work
- Improved layout of facility
- Improved design of plant and equipment
- Improved method of material handling
- Improved utilisation of inputs
- Improved working conditions
- Improved output of men and machines
- Improved safety provisions
- Improved capital investment and cash flow
- Improved training of manpower.

Method Study Procedure

While carrying out Method Study, following steps are adopted :

- Select
- Record
- Examine
- Develop
- Install
- Maintain

Since Method Study is a systematic recording, analysis and critical examination of existing way of doing a work, above steps help in examination of the present and by eliminating unwanted tasks/activities, develop an improved method. The study does not finish simply be suggesting a new method, it includes suggesting new process of achieving results. Hence the newly developed method must be installed, opearted and maintained so as to prove its effectiveness and improvement over the old method.

Since it is step by step procedure, there is a necessity to develop the frame work of study *i.e.* data collection and study through a set of flow diagrams and process charts bringing out various activities associated. The 'walk-over' of the method can, then, be easily carried out by going through each and every activity very minutely for the purpose of discarding the non-essential activities.

Selection : For method study, the starting step is to select the area of application itself. The method study project should be such that the organisation can get worth-while benefit comensurate with the effort put in. The selection of the method study project is the responsibility of the top management but it is expected and desirable to invite suggestions from the floor level workers. They know where the shoe pinches and hence may be able to suggest something really useful. Work study consultants also can throw better ideas due to their day to day experience. But they can help only when the worth-while problem area has been identified by workers and the line managers. The selection of method for study, generally, should be done on three major considerations :

- Economic Consideration
- Technical Consideration
- Ergonomic Consideration

Economic consideration : While conducting business, cost and price are predominant discussion subjects. Sales coming down, customer asking for discounts or shying away due to higher price, material value going up or competitors market strategy forcing rethinking in terms of change of product or change in cost or price structure are few factors worth consideration during method study. For problem areas identification, following functions could be considered for method study :

- Wastages as scrap or rework
- Frequent accidents, hence layouts requiring improvements
- Enhanced handling costs, poor state of equipment or poor flow of materials.
- Any major bottleneck in process desiring change in procedure.
- Excessive overtime to keep up production.
- Excessives stress conditions in job performance.
- Bad tooling or inconsistent and poor product design.
- Poorly balanced operations between machines, workcentres or departments.
- Inconsistent quality or output volumes.

Technical considerations : Whenever inconsistency in flow of product/material resulting in excessive WIP or excessive rejects or reworks, (may be due to human, machine or infrustructure reasons) is noticed, method study should be carried out due to technical reasons for adequate and compatible equipment facilities and technical expertise. It may need the modification or improvement of product design or we may be looking at the design or vintage of machines, excessive cost of maintenance of facilities or material availability or substitution. The poor proficiency of the workforce due to turnover or poor training on machine may need special attention. Ventilation of or physical movement of WIP storage for scrap removal facility may be needing a relook.

Ergonomic Considerations : The physical and psychological impact of the work force may be posing serious problem in production. It may be either due to their resistance to change or any mental or emotional reaction due to society or religious beliefs. Unpleasant dirty or stressful job, uncongenial atmosphere of work place such as high temperature, fumes, dirt, or humidity could be the reasons for poor or inconsistant work. Jobs involving toxic, hazardness or accident prone activities need careful examination from safety safety of point.

In addition to the above, the jobs should be ergonomically designed *i.e.*, a human being should be able to perform it without undue stress. The seating chairs, the place of tools, the height of the machine or the overhead crane hook, proper left/right hand performance, sequences to the extent of arc of operations, should be part of the job design. Eye level observation for, say, inspection instruments or a high chair for a bank cashier are few ergonomic solution to satisfactory performance of the job.

Recording: After the project or job selection, the next step is to record observations regarding the existing method. This is to get proper relevant facts for thorough examination during investigation. These data are recorded either through flow diagrams or process charts.

The types of charts used would vary according to the method or job under study. The nature of data collection will indicate in what form it would be useful. If we streamline the method of collections of data in this useful form, it helps in its scrutiny by eliminating unncessary writing. At times the data needs to be converted to graphical representation for making it easier to grasp its resultant information and fact implications.

Depending on the scope of study, necessary information regarding human moments, machine operations, material handling and movements etc. are collected through any simple technique capable of containing all relevant and necessary data for analysis. The techniques such as charts or graphs etc. would reduce delays in eliminating certain obvious tasks or activities or the travel time.

Use of Symbols for recording

For displaying the flow of actions, some standard symbols act as universal code for easy understanding. These symbols are given in Table 13.1

Table 13.1 Recording symbols

Activity	Symbol	Usage
Operation	○	Work being done, main step in a process where material or product is changed during actual work.
Inspection	▭	Checking of operations, products, measurement of dimensions or performance, visual scruting for quality
Transport	⇨	Movement of materials, worker or any equipment.
Temporary delay	⊐ or D	Delay in the process, sequence of events have storage halts
Storage	▽	Storage of materials or WIP, controlled issue or receipt of material, components or product.

Through the use of these symbols, the recording of activities, involved in a method under study, is carried out for further examinations. The recordings are done in the form of following charts :

- Outline Process Chart

- Flow diagram or Flow Chart
- Left hand/Right hand process chart
- Multiple Activity Chart
- Simultaneous Motion Chart (SIMO Chart)
- Models and Templates
- Cyclographs or chrono-cyclegraph.

Outline Process Chart

On this chart, we record only two main activities *i.e.*, operations and inspection, when we need detailed analysis of these two activities as per deliberate decision such as operations and inspections etc., other activity just for support.

The chart for a certain work is drawn below :

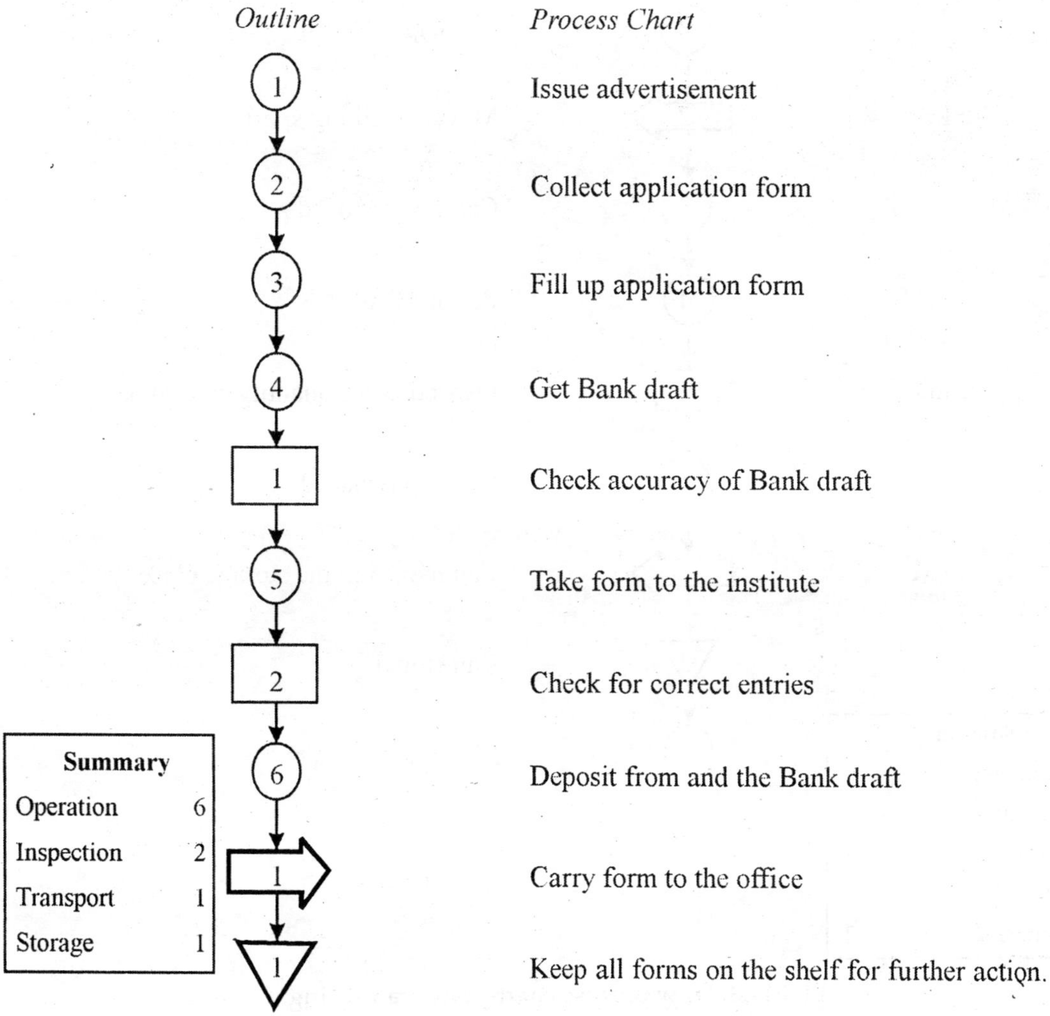

FIG. 13.2. Outline Process Chart for Admission forms

Flow Process Chart

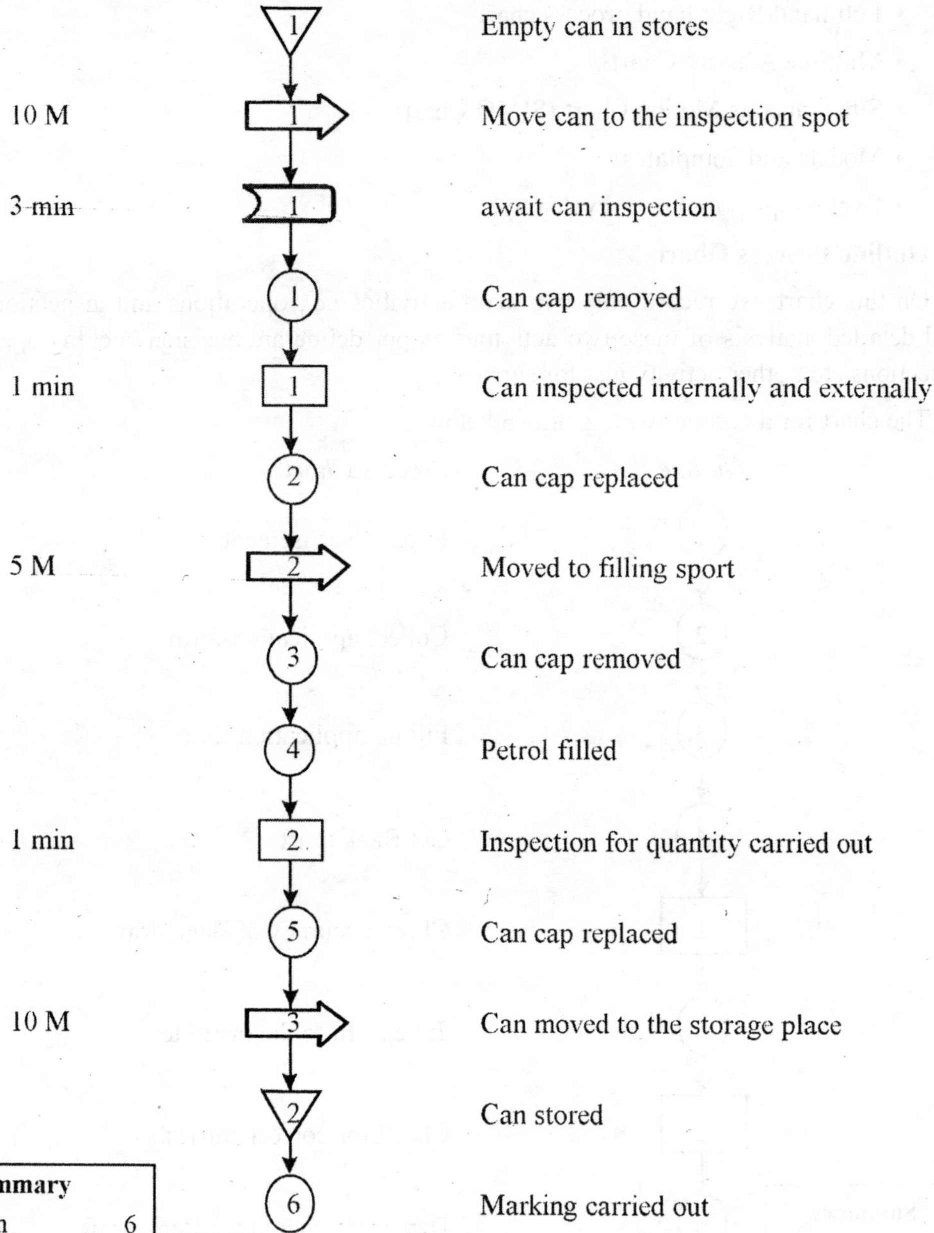

Summary	
Operation	6
Inspection	2
Transport	3
Delay	1
Storage	2

FIG 13.3. Flow process chart-petrol can filling.

These flow process charts are the flow representation of the sequence of all activities as can be seen in fig 13.3, bringing out all operations, inspection, transportations, delays and storages etc. During this recording, the time and distances should be recorded to make it easy for investigation and analysis.

These flow process charts are preferred for flow of the following activities:

(a) Material flow

(b) Product flow

(c) Manpower movement.

This information on the Flow Process chart can be recorded on the standard printed form as can be seen in Fig. 13.4.

Flow Process Chart	**Material/Product/Men type**		
Chart No. 1, Sheet 1	Summary		
Activities	Activity	Symbol	Present
	Operation	○	6
	Tranport	⇨	3
	Inspection	▭	2
	Delay	D	1
Method : Present	Storage	▽	2
Location :	Distance		
Operator :	Time		
Charted by :	Cost		

FIG 13.4. Printed form : Can filling

Left/Right hand Process Chart

These charts can be applied for various activities needing the use of both the hands such, as for assembly, machining or typing works. Paths or movements of arms may not be recorded. These charts are drawn to show synchronised jobs using both hands together for manual operations. It depicts the movements of hands/arms/feet for some operations whether in moving or static conditions. It can also indicate whether the hands are moving in opposite directions to one another. In such charts, operations, transport and delays are generally used, whereas inspections are rarely used. Pre-printed forms are also used when the volume of work can justify such an investment. One such printed form is given in Fig. 13.5 :

Method							Operator	
Part Name							Charted by	
Part Number							Date	
	Original			Improved			Saving	
	LH	RH	Both	LH	RH	Both	LH	RH
Operation Movement Delay Hold								
Total								

FIG 13.5. LH/RH Process Chart : Printed Form

Multiple Activity Chart

In this types of chart, the recording can be obtained for more than one activity or for more than one subject like men/machine chart. This recording is done on a common scale, but establishing the relationship between them. Through this chart, we can depict the activity interference or the ineffective utilisation of men/machine and due to interrelationship scale, we can rearrange the activities to reduce the ineffective time.

The activities of workers and machines are recorded in sequence in the form of bars, showing working and idle time. The times are recorded with the help of stop watches and duration of an activity can thus be recorded. The marking of the chart is done as under :

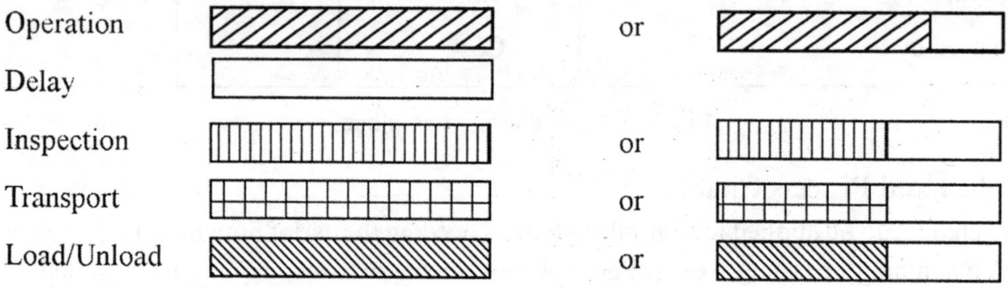

Whenever there is idle time, the bar is left blank, but the activity taking place is shaded in the bar. This chart can be used for team work activities either for opeartions or for maintenance. Analysis or work can be done when the operations are not balanced.

Multi-Activity chart can be shown as follows:

Activity :
Cycle begins :
Cycle ends :
Charted by :

Time	Man I			Man II			Machine		
	Activity	Time	Bar	Activity	Time	Bar	Activity	Time	Bar
0-5	Coming in	5	▨	Sitting	5	▨	Idle	5	
5-10	Wait	5		Asking for Requirement	5	▨	Idle	5	
10-20	Wait	10		Service being performed	10	▨	Idle	10	
20-22	Wait	2		Wait	2		Computer Works	2	▨

FIG 13.6. Multiple Activity Chart

The summary of the total work can be listed out as follows:

	Man I	*Man II*	*Machine*
Operation	x	y	z
Idle time	p	q	r
Total cycle times	x + p	y + q	z + r

Then the working efficiency or the utilisation time can be calculated. While analysing, we can plan avoiding an activity by amending it (combining). New method with better utilisation can, then, be planned out.

SIMO chart :

Since the name is Simulaneous Motion chart, we record the minute details of the simultaneous movement of different parts of the body of an individual during a certain operation cycle. It is really a two-handed chart (L/R hand chart) prepared on a common scale, to depict a job or cycle time of an activity. Even a camera can be used if the movement is very fast for naked eye. While recording, we make use of therblig's *i.e.*, certain motion symbols indicating balancing of both hands (to cover idle time of one hand against the other). It can give an indication of unnecessary motion, which can be eliminated and the activity smoothed out for better performance.

The recording can be done in terms of microseconds as can be seen in the chart (Fig. 13.6).

Therblig, actually is the name of the developer GILBRETH reversely pronounced and inter changing T and H. So instead of HTERBLIG, it is THERBLIG

In addition, we can record data with help of still photography, micromotion photography, memomotions photography, cyclography or chromo-cyclography.

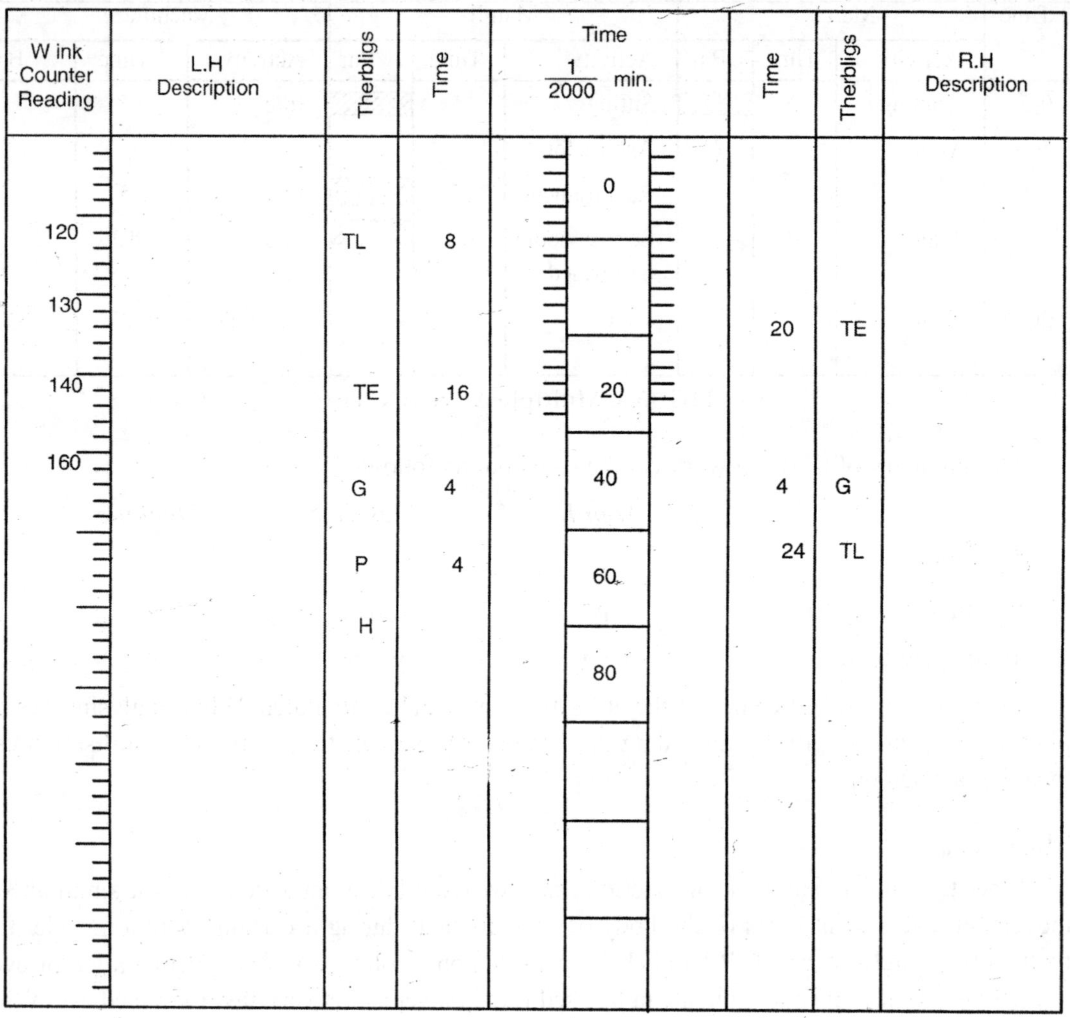

FIG. 13.6. SIMO chart

Examine : Having obtained all relevant data recorded on an appropriate chart we can proceed to carryout the critical study of all the facts produced by the record. The analyst has to think rationally, intelligently and dispassionately to approach the problem, identify critical stops and arrive at a plausible solution by divising new method of operation. The emphasis should be

to Elliminate
or
to Combine
or
to Simplify
or
to Rearrange } an activity in order to arrive at a better method

Each and every portion of operations, inspection, delay and storage etc must be questioned in the following manner :

- Why is it being done ?
- Where is it being done ?
- Who is doing it ?
- Is it necessary at this stage ?
- What is being achieved by this ?

We can find answers to these questions by examining these aspects critically through following questions :

- Can it be done differently ?
- Where should it be done ?
- When should it be done ?
- Who should do it ?
- How else can it be done ?

Develop : Having examined all the relevant data, and eliminating or simplifying various activities, we develop the detailed method in which the job can be done (with all unnecessary undesirable or non-essentials having been eliminated). We rework the new method in four stages.

- Draw up the plan and sequences of operations for essential activities.
- Fill up ancillary work, where required, to find the best possible and most efficient way to perform.
- Mock ups to be preferred and equipment accordingly arranged for trying out the new method.
- Improved method to be formulated in the process chart form.

Install : The plan of activities having been prepared as a result of analysis, method developed must be installed with all necessary changes as per the new scheme of things. Work force has to be taken into confidence while developing and installing it, so that its successful implementation can be achieved. Convenient locations and quantum of resources must be organised with specific responsibility of one person to oversee the installations. During this process, proper arrangement of tools, equipment and layouts must be made. All main and auxillary services are to be re-organised and if required selecting opearators and their training must be organised. Finally the plan should be rehearsed with the new team, so as to make them fully aware as to how the new method is being performed. Proper quality standards should be laid down, made transparent and explained to all related departments. Installation should have a time schedule and must be followed as best as can be.

Maintain : When new method has been installed and is operating satisfactorily, improvements must be recorded. If certain changes are required due to a strong ground suggestions (innovations thought out by the workers while working on the new method for a certain period of time), these must be included and tried out. These must be implemented after a deliberate attempt with careful scrutiny and thorough investigation.

13.7 Principles of Motion Economy

The ergonomical consideration in the method design is a must, when human beings or work force is involved in the performance of a job. A person sitting or standing can complete an opeation provided there is no hinderance to his work, while moving his arms and legs. When a person performs the job while seated, the elbow movement area is called Normal working area, whereas when he uses his full area *i.e.*, through shoulder movement, the area of movement is called Maximum Working Area.

This ergonomic concept is of full value when we consider the work operations through various motions of the body. While designing a new method or improving an old method, we should plan to reduce the motions of arms and legs to the minimum required. Otherwise it will unnecesserily fatique a person and his output would be reduced during working hours. Also smooth functioning of arms and legs need working area free of obstructions.

The optimum use of motions to reduce quantum of work is discussed below, being followed by industrial engineers or method designers :

Use of Human Body

- The two hands should be used at the same time, biginning and completing motions at the same time.
- Both hands should not be idle at the same time except while resting.
- Motions of the arms should be made in opposite and symmetrical directions and that too simultaneously.
- Momentum should be employed to assist the worker and should be reduced to minimum if it is required to be opposed by muscular effort.
- Hand motions should be restricted in the normal working area so that work can be performed satisfactionly without fatique.
- Hand motions should be smooth and continuous.
- Rhythm is essential for the smooth and automatic performance of an operation and work design should involve natural rhythem.

Work place layout

- There should be a definite and fixed work place for all the tools and materials.
- Tools, materials and controls should be close, directly in front of the operator in preferred area of eye movement.
- Gravity feed bins and containers should be used to deliver the materials close to the point of use.
- Tools and material location should facilitate the best sequence of motions.
- Good illumination should be provided for good visual perception.
- The height of the working platform and the chair should preferably be arranged that alternate posture of sitting and standing at work can easily be adopted.
- A chair of the types and height to persist good posture should be provided for the worker.
- Angle of vision of the worker should facilitate good hand movement.

Tools and Equipment Design

- The hands should be relieved of all work that can easily and economically be done through a jig, fixture or a tool operated device.
- Combine tools wherever possible
- Tools and materials should be prepositioned whenever required.
- Where each finger performs some specific movements, the load should be distributed.
- While using tools, the handles should be so designed so as permit a good hold. This will help more where there is large force to be applied.
- Good lever advantage should be made use of so that an operator can perform the job with ease.

Motions defined (Therbligs)

The Therbligs are given out in the succeeding table.

Sl.	*Therbling*	*Symbol*	*Colour*	*Definition*
1.	Assemble	A	Voilet	When part more together
2.	Avoidable Delay	AD	Lemon yellow	Begins when hard or body member deviates from standard method. Ends when member returns to standard routine.
3.	Unavoidable Delay	D	Yellow	Begins when today member is idle and when it starts working.
4.	Disassemble	DA	Light voilet	Begins when body number causes parts that were integral to begin to separate.
5.	Hold	E	Gold orange	Begins when movement of object ceases and ends with any movement.
6.	Find	F	Grey	Mental reaction at the end of search.
7.	Grasp	G	Red	Begins when body member touches an object. Ends when control is gained.
8.	Inspect	I	Burnt ochre	Begins when body member begins to feel or view an object. Ends when body number stop feeling or viewing.
9.	Plan	P	Brown	Begins when body member is idle. Ends when course of action is determined.
10.	Position	P	Blue	Begins when member causes part to locale. Ends when part line up.
11.	Preposition	PP	Pale blue	Same as position except it is used when line up is previous to use of part in another place.

Contd....

12.	Rest	R	Orange	Begins when body member is idle and ends when body member is able to work again.
13.	Release	RL	Carmine	Begins when body member begins to relax control of the object. End when body member has lost control with the object.
14.	Search	SE	Black	Begins when body member hunts for the part, ends when body member has found the object.
15.	Select	ST	Light Grey	Begins when body member touches several objects. Ends when body member has located the desired object.
16.	Transport Empty	TE	Olive	Begins when body member begins to move without load. Ends when body member touches part or stops moving.
17.	Transport Loaded	TL	Green	Begins when body member begins to move with an object. End when body member arrives at general destination or movement ceases.
18.	Use	U	Purple	Begins when body member actually begins to manipulate tools or control. End when tool control is lost.

Work Measurement

As scope of works study, we had identified two major techniques namely method study and work measurement. The work measurement is the operation of dividing the selected best method into smaller activities and observing the time required to perform these activities so as to arrive at the time required for a particular job. Hence work measurement is a follow up operation after the method study *i.e.*, first deciding how best a work can be done cost effectively and then setting the time element for each of its constituents to decide the production time for a job. It is required to be done for planning the production volumes, based on which the capacity planning can be doneto arrive at the number of machines and manpower necessary to meet the demand.

The work measurement can be and should be undertaken under two circumstances :

(a) Working out production time for a newly designed job.

(b) Working out revised production time for an old job under improved method necessitated for improved performance.

Proper work measurement generates useful data for planning, scheduling and controlling operations for labour and machine utilisation, job costing, budgeting and wage policy. While 'work measurement' can be defined as the application of the technique to observe and decide on the time taken by a well trained and qualified worker to carryout a specified work activity at a defined level of performance, it can be used for the purpose of planning, costing and work loading for workers.

It can help in creating congenial work atmosphere by technical approach to the work standard and satisfying unions about the healthy work estimates. Even incentive schemes can be worked out on this basis and a rational wage policy devised and implemented duly supported by the unions.

Important Definitions for Work Measurement

Standard Performance : The optimum rate of output achieved by a competant qualified worker on an average under standard working conditions for a certain definite period of time (including due allowances considered necessary during the time of operations).

Element of work : A distinct part of the total job which can be performed and measured independently.

Work cycle : The sequence of elements to be performed for producing certain units of production.

Qualified worker : Intelligent, healthy and duly trained person with necessary skill required to perform a work with satisfactory standard of volume, quality and safety.

Rating : The assessment of a workers output relative to the output of a qualified worker at the standard performance level.

Standard Rating : When a worker performs a work under given condition, at an output level considered to be the average output for a given period of time. Standard rating is either considered as 100 or 1. Ratings of workers, therefore, are related to this standard rating. If a worker complete the work at a rate slower than the standard rated worker, his rating will be proportionately reduced as 90, 95 etc or 0.9, 0.95 etc. Similarly, a faster worker will be rated higher than 1 or 100 related to the standard rating and will be rated on 1.05, 1.10 etc or 105, 110 etc.

Basic Performance Time (Normal Time) : It is the rate of a qualified worker on an average to complete a given specified job under specified working condition.

$$\text{Actual Working Time} = \frac{\text{Normal time}}{\text{Rating factor}}$$

or

$$\text{Element Normal Time} = \text{Average observed time} \times \text{Rating}$$

$$\text{Total Normal Time} = \text{Sum of all element times}$$

Standard Time : The time taken by a qualified standard worker (Rating 100) for completion of a specified job under specified conditions.

Allowances : While working for a certain period of time, a worker cannot be expected to perform at the same pace throughout. He needs some rest for fatique or needs time for water, or food etc. This time is called Allowance.

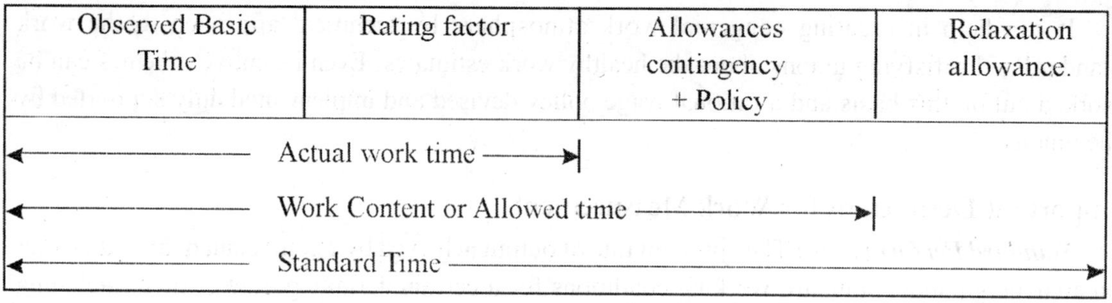

FIG. 13.7. Standard Time Contents

Standard Minute : The standard Minute (SM) expresses a unit of work in terms of the 100 BS scale. Standard performance is adopted as being 60 SM per hour. It is different from Standard Time (ST) wherein is added the infective and unoccupied time.

Techniques of Work Measurment

The main aim of work measurement is to obtain the time standard for a particular activity or work. Thus we normally observe the time of individual activities or elements of a work and after getting the Average Normal time, we add all permissible allowances to it to obtain standard time for the job or work. This acts as the company standard against which the individual performances of workers are measured.

For the purpose of obtaining the work measurment, following techniques are available (developed over a period of time).

- Direct Time Study on Job.
- Historical Data.
- Pre-determined Method Time System (PMTS)
  (a) Method Time Measurement (MTM)
  (b) Work Factor Method
  (c) Motion Time System (MTS)
- Work Sampling.

Direct Time Study on Job – It is the simplest technique used for measuring actual operation time of the workers by physically putting a number of workers on a specific job under specified conditions. The time taken by various workers is noted with the help of paper, pencil and a stop watch similar to the time observed for the athletic events. If we get these individual values from various workers as t_1, t_2, t_3-----t_n, then the average observed time is given by

$$t_{avg} = \frac{t_1 + t_2 + t_3 + \ldots + t_n}{n}$$

Though this method has wide applicability in the industry, it is not considered to be very good method due to its subjectiveness. But for an industry specific, this should form the basis of standardising time due to its compatibility and applicability to own work force of the organisation.

For completing timestudy, it is obvious that an activity is broken into its smaller elements, (after an accurate specification of the job have been laid down and it is possible to break it into smaller elements) for which resources such as materials, equipment and manpower can be specified. A convenient number of such cycles should be repeated.

In addition, as company policy, the element of allowances must be specified which generally varies between 10 to 15 per cent of the observed time. A typical time study sheet is given below :

<table>
<tr><td colspan="4">Operation
Plant/Machine
Tools and Wages</td><td colspan="4">Study Reference
Sheet Number
Time starting — Finishing — Total —
Operator</td></tr>
<tr><td colspan="4">Activity/Job Ref
Quality Material</td><td colspan="4">Studied by Date
Checked by Date</td></tr>
<tr><td>Element</td><td>Worker rating</td><td>Stop watch reading</td><td>Basic Time</td><td>Element</td><td>worker rating</td><td>Stop watch reading</td><td>Basic time</td></tr>
<tr><td>1</td><td></td><td></td><td></td><td>8</td><td></td><td></td><td></td></tr>
<tr><td>2</td><td></td><td></td><td></td><td>9</td><td></td><td></td><td></td></tr>
<tr><td>3</td><td></td><td></td><td></td><td>10</td><td></td><td></td><td></td></tr>
<tr><td>4</td><td></td><td></td><td></td><td>11</td><td></td><td></td><td></td></tr>
<tr><td>5</td><td></td><td></td><td></td><td>12</td><td></td><td></td><td></td></tr>
<tr><td>6</td><td></td><td></td><td></td><td>13</td><td></td><td></td><td></td></tr>
<tr><td>7</td><td></td><td></td><td></td><td>14</td><td></td><td></td><td></td></tr>
</table>

FIG 13.8. Typical Time Study Sheet.

From the above sheet, we obtain the individual time readings of the workers and then the Average Basic Time is calculated by the simple formula of Averages given above. This time (Average) *i.e.*, t_{avg} is then used as the standard time of the activity by adding number of t_{avg} or $\bar{t}$ for all elements.

$$\therefore \text{ Standard Time} = \sum_{1}^{n} \bar{t}_i + \text{allowances}$$

Where i = i^{th} element of activity

Standard Time = Basic or Normal time + allowance.

The statistical use of these observations is given below :

$$\text{The standard deviation } (\sigma) = \sqrt{\frac{\Sigma x^2}{N} - \left(\frac{\Sigma x}{N}\right)^2}$$

$$= \frac{1}{N}\sqrt{N\Sigma x^2 - (\Sigma x)^2}$$

$$\text{Standard error (SE)} = \frac{\sigma}{\sqrt{n}}$$

Where n = number of samples required

N = Number of readings taken

x = Individual time taken

(same as t_1, t_2 ---- etc)

From above, $$SE = \frac{1}{\sqrt{n}}\left[\frac{1}{N}\sqrt{\Sigma N\, \Sigma x^2 - (\Sigma x)^2}\right]$$

If we define accuracy level as 95%

Then Desired accuracy = $\pm$ 5%

Then $$SE = 0.05\left(\frac{\Sigma x}{N}\right)$$

and at 95% confidence level, std deviation = 2σ

$$\therefore \quad 0.05\left(\frac{\Sigma x}{N}\right) = \frac{2}{\sqrt{n}}\left[\frac{1}{N}\sqrt{\Sigma N\, \Sigma x^2 - (\Sigma x)^2}\right]$$

or $$\sqrt{n} = \frac{40\sqrt{N\,\Sigma x^2 - (\Sigma x)^2}}{\Sigma x}$$

$$n = \left(\frac{Z}{A}\right)^2\left[\frac{\sqrt{N\,\Sigma x^2 - (\Sigma x)^2}}{\Sigma x}\right]$$

Where Z = Number of Std. deviation for a given CL
and A = Desired Accuracy Level

Where Z = 1 for 68% CL
= 2 for 95% CL
= 3 for 99% CL

Thus for a desired accuracy level, the Z/A ratio can be used and the value of n, *i.e.*, the number of samples required for the time reading can be worked out and used.

Types of Allowances

When a human body works for a certain period of time during the day, it cannot be expected to show the same level output throughant the day. The man gets fatigued as the time passes. For being fair to him to work out standard time of operation, an allowance is specified to be added to his operation time so as to cover the sluggishness or the natural cause interruption or even accidental wastage of time.

Following allowances are generally added to the normal operation time :

Relaxation Allowance : To compensate for the fatigue, stress, general rest etc. It may be also due to delay by others if he is working on an unbalanced time.

Contingency Allowance : This is a special allowance permitted to be added to the working time to cater for any irregular occurances such as accidents or set up time etc. Some periodic activity allowances such as grinding tools, cleaning machines or removing scraps etc are part of this allowance. This is also called "Special Allowance".

Process Allowance : This allowance is added to compensate for enforced idleness not to workers account. It may be non-availablity of the product to him from the last opearation due to inbalanced time or when the worker is busy on some other machine in case of multiple machine control and he is unable to attend to a particular machine when he is busy elsewhere.

Policy Allowance : This is very special allowance permitted by the management to cater for some inherent features such as balancing the payments to workers or changing conditions of working. Say, if the normal standard time calculated by the organisation for an activity is 5.3 Standard Minutes (5.3SM) and the policy allowance permitted by the management is 0.3 SM. Then the applicable standard time would be (5.3 + 0.3) = 5.6 SM which is then the allowed time for completion of a given tesk at 100 rating.

To summerise, various allowance can be schematically shown as under :

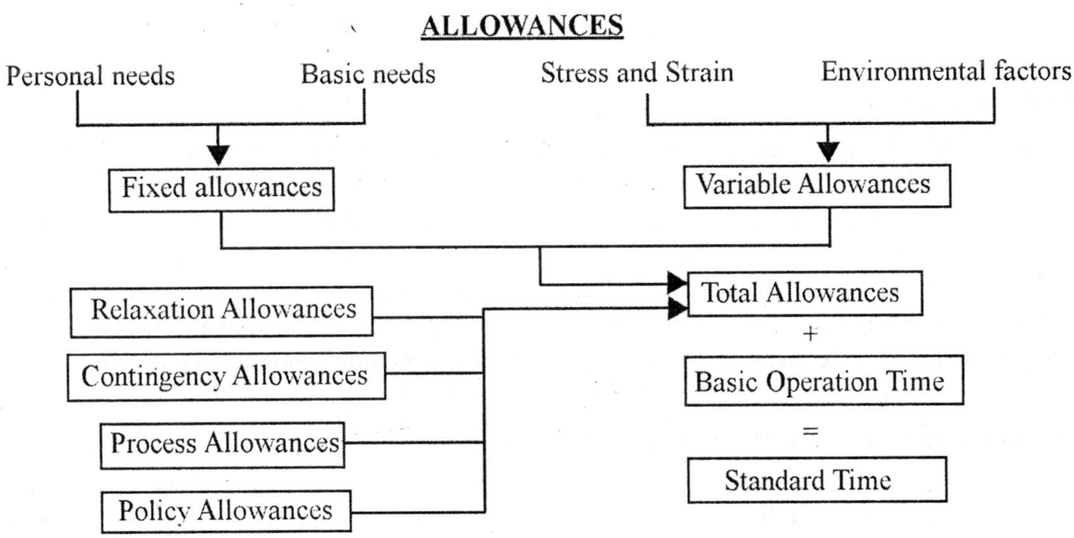

FIG. 13.8. Various Allowances

Based on the Direct Time Study and having decided on the allowances by the organisation the performace standards are set as follows

$$\text{Average Cycle Time} = \frac{\text{Sum of cycle times reorded}}{\text{number of cycles observed}}$$

$$\text{Normal Time} = \text{Average Cycle Time} \times \text{Worker Rating}$$

Available allowances fraction = Fraction time for all the allowances

$$\text{Standard time} = \frac{\text{Normal time}}{\text{Available fractions of time}}$$

$$= \frac{\text{Normal time}}{1 - \text{Allowance fraction}}$$

Problem 13.2

The recorded operating time of 5 worker is as under :

7.0, 6.8, 6.9, 7.1, 7.3 minutes. If the allowance fraction allowed is 15%, calculate the standard time, when the workers in question operate at a rating of 0.9.

Solution

$$\text{The average cycle time} = \frac{7.0 + 6.8 + 6.9 + 7.1 + 7.3}{5}$$

$$= 7.0 \text{ minutes}$$

$$\therefore \text{ Normal time} = 7.0 \times 0.9 = 6.3 \text{ minutes}$$

(When worker rating is 0.9)

$$\therefore \text{ Standard time} = \frac{6.3}{1 - 0.15} = 7.4 \text{ minutes}$$

(allowance fraction is taken as 0.15)

Historical Data

This is a techniques used for time study when either the work is repeatitive or such jobs have been performed earlier and their time estimates data are available with the organisation. By noting the elements of work used for a certain work, we can add all element times and obtain the Normal time for the total activity. Some standard date may be available, say, for preparatory work, setting up or reseting, removing, cleaning, tool changing or tightening etc. These are common elements performed for most of the jobs. Hence their operation time can be obtained by synthesis. Such data are specific for specific location under specific working conditions and must be used as such.

Pre-determined Motion Time System (PMTS)

The actual recording of observed time by stop watches have been questioned by the union representations as being subjective. To avoid such disputes and situation, we can use the method of PMTS where each job is taken as the combination of various motions (as described under Therebligs). There are standard time periods available from extensive studies and if all motions are recorded, these are to be treated as elements of the work and the Pre-determined Motion Time can be added for all the elements to obtain total operation time of the activity or job. Hence we follow the precedure as follows :

- Work to be broken down into elements of motions.
- Arrange these motions into sequence of operations

- Enter pre-determined rated time against each motion.

For example, an activity may involve the motions such as reach, grasp, move, release etc. Then we write the time values (pre-determined) against these motions and add their time together to obtain the total time to complete that operation.

There are three different methods for PMTS studies, namely :

- Methods Time Measurement (MTM)
- Work Factor (WF)
- Motion Time system (MTS)

Methods Time Measurement

This is the basic method for time measurement which is worked out for a job depending on the types of motions performed and then assigning a pre-determined time, which is made available from standard tables according to the type and nature of the motion. For carrying out this study, following major steps are performed.

1. Dividing the work into various relevant motions.
2. Establish the sequence of these motions
3. Assign the pre-determined time from standard tables giving the data for these motions

The MTM method is available for 8 manual movements, 9 pedal and trunk movements and 2 ocular movements. Therefore, there are standards time available for 19 motions with variations in the physical working conditions. The law govering the usage of these fundamental motions is called "Principle of limiting Motions". According to the principle of limiting Motions, we can seperate out the motion capable of being performed simultaneously by a trained operator from those which are not performed simultaneously.

In actual practice, this type of analysis is not easy to perform as it is cumbersome, time consuming and very costly. Various organisation use the data contained in the tables, developed over a period of experimentation by independent organisation hence based on laboratory data. The most widely used PMTS is Methods Time Measurement (MTM) developed by MTM Association of standards and Research.

The unit of measurement used in MTM technique is called a Time Measurement Unit (TMU), which is equivalent to 0.00001 hours. It is illustrated in Problem 13.3.

Problem 13.3

Following six activities are observed for the study (time given below).

Activity	**Standard (TMU)**
Reach	10.3
Grasp	3.3
Pressure	9.5
Move	12.6
Sub Total	**35.7**

Work out the Production rate, when the allowance fraction is given as 0.15.

Solution :

6 × Similar activity	6 × 35.7
Sub Total	**214.2**
Transfer	5.2
Move	10.6
Release	3.5
∴ Sub Total	= 233.5 TMU
Allowance fraction total	= 0.15
∴ Total time	= 233.5 × 1.15
	= 268.5 TMU

This time in TMU can now be converted into hours per cycle.

∴ 268.5 TMU = 0.00268 hrs/cycle

= 0.161 minutes/cycle

= 6.21 units per minute

= 373 units per hour.

The Pre-determined Motion Time Table are standard Industrial Engineering tables available for usage from any Industrial Engineering book and can be easily applied.

Work Factor Method

The name of the method comes from "Work Factor Company" which is an industrial consulting firm. For some time, it was called QSK system also (Quick-Shae-Kochler) *i.e.*, after the name of its authors.

Work Factor Company developed three types of work factors namely retailed work factor, Simplified work Factor and Abbreviated work factor systems

The WF time units in this method are :

- Detailed WF system – 0.0001 minute
- Simplified WF system – 0.0001 minute
- Abbreviated WF system – 0.005 minutes

There are tables used along with these work factor time units based on four major variables for the manual motions. These variable are as under :

- Body member used
- Distance moved
- Amount of control required
- Weight or resistance involved

Motion Time System

In this method there are five basic motions recognised :

- Finger
- Hand
- Arm
- Leg
- Body

Each further classified as Class A, B and C motions

The other factors affecting the motion time study are :

- Distance moved
- Weight moved
- Visual attention
- Simultaneously performed motions
- Precision required

The Data is tabulated as in MTM and WF methods.

Work Sampling Method

The above described methods of work measurement are based on jobs done repeatedly or certain tasks being performed frequently. But there are jobs which are different every time or most of the time they are performed differently. For such jobs, a new method has been developed, called "work sampling method".

'Work Sampling' can be defined as a work measurement technique, which involves only observations of the job being performed over a period of time and only determining the portion in which a worker is working. It is a statistical technique based on random sampling. Therefore, the observations are recording only for that proportion of work when the worker has been working or not-working and it is done picking up time randomtly and noticing how many time the worker at that point of observation has been working.

Thus, work sampling consists of sample observations of a workers activities say during 7 days. Randomly, if he has been seen working 25 times out of 30 times he was observed, his working time is $\frac{25}{30}$ *i.e.*, a portion of 0.833. This is written as p = 0.833

The observer obtains such proportions by observing the worker at different random occassions during that period and then a mean proportion of working time is calculated.

$$\therefore \quad \bar{p} = \left(\frac{p_1 + p_2 + \dots\dots\dots + p_n}{n}\right)$$

This proportion $\bar{p}$ is then used in the work measurement system to obtain number of observation based on occuracy level required *i.e.*, the confidence level in the accuracy of data. For 95% confidence level, we use z = 2, for 99% ct, z = 3 etc. These value are used statistically as follows:

Number of observation required = N

$$= \frac{\left[z^2\bar{p}\left(1-\bar{p}\right)\right]}{e^2}$$

Where $\bar{p}$ = average proportion of working time

z = normal variate

e = maximum absolute error desired

Since it is a statistical method, we have to follow a systematic approach to obtain the observation. The steps to be followed are :

- Define a working activity. Remaining activities will be treated as non-working.
- Observe the worker at randomly selected intervals, recording whether the activity being performed by the worker at that time falls under 'working' or 'non-working' category.
- Compute the proportion p of a time a worker is found working.

This being a statistical analysis, it will be more appropriate when the cycle time is kept very long so as to obtain large number of observations. In fact the same observer can observe more than one worker during this period and these results can be used for computing proportions p for the statistical inference.

This method of work sampling was tried out in UK Textile industry, after the textile industry was mechanised into power looms (soon after the industrial revolution, where in Europe, Textile industry benefitted by the revolution when factory system came into being). The study as a result of this method (introduced and tried out,) showed that the statistical concept of sampling could be used to advantage to achieve practical and fairly accurate inference for work measurement.

The technique soon found favour with the US industry and was introduced in various industries. The utilisation benefits and results showed that it was a very useful technique for production control with minimum cost. Formally it was given the name of work sampling or Ratio Delay or Activity Sampling.

British standards have, thus, defined Activity sampling (as they call it) as a ***"Technique in which a large number of instantaneous observations are made over a period of time of a group of machines, processes or workers. Each observation records what is happening at that instant and the percentage of observation recorded for a particular activity or delay is a measure of the percentage of time during which that activity or delay occurs"***

For useful inference in this a statistical sampling technique, sufficient number of observations should be obtained to get a known degree of accuracy. The sample size selection, therefore, is of importance for better result out of this technique.

We can use the Normal distribution curve which is a typical frequency distribution of importance for Activity Sampling. The confidence limit has to be decided in work sampling or Activity sampling based on the degree of accuracy required for the results. Normally the confidence level or confidence limit used in work sampling is 95% which means that these is a 95% probability that the random observation will show the facts accurately and 5% of the times it will not.

Various confidence levels, that can be adopted are :

CL 68.27%, $z = 1$

CL 95.45%, $z = 2$

CL 99.73%, $z = 3$

It means that if we follow confidence list of only 68.27%, the accuracy can be expected 68 times out of 100 observations and 32 times it will show error. This is approximation of the concept.

In actual practice, during work sampling, the recorder of the data will record observation at random intervals and hence the occurance generally will follow Binomial distribution. If we take p as the chance of working, we can use the following relationship :

$$\bar{x} = np \text{ and } \sigma = \sqrt{npq} \qquad [\text{Where } q = 1 - p]$$

At 3σ limit *i.e.*, 99.73%, confidence level, the amount of expected variation will be

$$np \pm 3\sqrt{npq}$$

If we take p and q as proportions of working and non-working,

the variation can be written as

$$\frac{np}{n} \pm \frac{3}{n}\sqrt{npq}$$

or $$p \pm 3\sqrt{\frac{pq}{n}}$$

Hence the standard error can be written as $SE = z\sqrt{\frac{pq}{n}}$ (Where z = normal variate).

Calculation of standard time.

If the total time taken for an activity is t, the proportionate working time = p . t

∴ Basic Operation Time = p . t

and Standard Time = p . t + Allowances

= pt (1 + 0.15)

= 1.15 pt

Where Allowance fraction is assumed as 0.15 of the operation time.

Problem 13.4

A random sample of 700 units from a large consignment showed that 200 units were demaged. Find (i) 95% (ii) 99% confidence limits for the proportion of the demaged units in the consignment.

[*Bombay University, (B.Com; April 1978)*]

Solution :

Using normal notations,

$$n = 100 \text{ and } p = \frac{200}{700} = \frac{2}{7} = 0.286$$

$$q = 1 - p = 1 - \frac{2}{7} = \frac{5}{7}$$

$$\text{Standard Error SE(p)} = \sqrt{\frac{pq}{n}}$$

$$= \sqrt{\frac{2}{7} \times \frac{5}{7} \times \frac{1}{200}}$$

$$= 0.017$$

(i) For 95% Confidence limits, we get (Where $p = \frac{2}{7} = 0.286$)

$$p \pm 1.96 \text{ SE(p)} = 0.286 \pm 1.96 \times 0.017 = 0.330$$

(ii) For 99% confidence limits for p, we get

$$p \pm 2.58 \text{ SE(p)} = 0.286 \pm 2.58 \times 0.017 = 0.242$$

∴ Proportion demage limits are 0.330 and 0.242

Problem 13.5

While conducting population survey of a city, the emunerator noticed that 40% of the male population were illiterate. If the trend continued, work out the probability that out of 2,00,000 males population, the number of illiterates will be

(i) Less than 75,000

(ii) More than 82,000

Solution :

We denote x as the random variable indicating the number of males in the city of population 2,00,000 (males)

By usual notations, n= 2,00,000

$$p = 40\% \text{ or } 0.4$$

$$q = 1 - 0.4 = 0.6$$

$$\text{Standard deviation of the population} = \sqrt{npq}$$

$$= \sqrt{0.4 \times 0.6 \times 2,00,000}$$

$$= 219$$

and Mean population $= np = 2,00,000 \times 0.4$

$= 80,000$

Hence the population is defined by the distribution (80,000, 219)

(i)When $x \leq 75,000$, then

$$Z_1 = \frac{75,000 - 80,000}{219}$$

$$= -22.8$$

(ii) When $x > 82,000$,

$$Z_2 = \frac{82,000 - 80,000}{219}$$

$$= 9.13$$

In either case, the value of Z is very high. Hence the probability of illiterates in the range of 75,000 to 82,000 will be negligibly small.

13.8 Production Standards

The objective of production is to produce product/Service at cost effective level *i.e.* effeciently and effectively from customers point of view for the organisational benefit. For ensuring that this is achieved, a manager has to specify what can be called a 'cost effective' production. The aim or the target, therefore, is required to be specified to evaluate the cost benefit for both the customer as well as that for the organisation. The target for the workers performance or output is, therefore, desired to be set at an appropriate level in term of quantity as well as quantity.

This aim or the target is termed as the **production standard**. In simple terms, the production standard is a qualified criterion for measuring or comparing the output. The target or standard can be set in an any of the following areas :

- Quantity
- Quality
- Cost
- Any other attribute of the output.

Based on the attributes and the production requirement, the standards are set at various levels such as :

- Individual standards or human output level
- Departmental standards
- Plant standards
- National standards
- International standards

Individual standards : These standards are set for the average performance of the worker that he is expected to produce under average conditions for a certain specified time period.

The output is the time an average worker is expected to consume for specific job performed by him. It is quantified as the number of units produced per hour or amount of work done her unit of time. A person can be expected to produce 10 products in an hour or digging 100 cubic feet of earth in an hour. This is set as a standard for every person of the organisation employed on a similiar job under average working conditions and permitted to work for a given period, say, a shift of eight hours.

The concept of working out "standard time" is applicable in this context. If the standard time for an activity is arrived at by taking the average time by a number of workers for an activity, observed over a period of time, it can be standardised for the whole organisation.

For example, if we experiment with 10 persons (heterogenous mix) for an activity and observe them for a period, say, one hour, their average time can be calculated as under :

$$\bar{t} = \frac{t_1 + t_2 + t_3 + \text{----} t_{10}}{10}$$

To make the average time more universal for the whole organisation, we can use 10 such experiments at different location plants and then averaging it out. This will be the average time under average working conditions. We obtain average time as

$$\bar{\bar{t}} = \frac{\bar{t}_1 + \bar{t}_2 + \bar{t}_3 + \text{----} \bar{t}_{10}}{10}$$

The $\bar{\bar{t}}$ time is more representative of the organisational set up and can be used as average Basic operation time.

Now, we can obtain standard time for the whole organisation as

ST = OT + Allowances

Where ST = Standard time

OT = Basic operation time.

This has already been discussed in the chapter during work measurement. The use of this standard is done in following ways :

- To set a target for production output.
- To utilise it as planning tool to design processes and production volumes.
- To use it as predicting and control tools for measuring efficiency of the individual workers for rating and incentive pay scheme.
- To prepare cost estimates, labour cost variance report and pricing of new product.

Department Standards : When the performance of a job is a team work *i.e.*, a number or group of individual workers is required to complete a job, say, an assembly operation, the individual outputs may be affected due to the delays or efficiency of other workers or due to unbalancing of the assambly line, it is unfair to judge the work performance of an individual worker. In this case we can work out the group output in term of, say, number of units assembled per hour or during a shift of eight hour. Setting of such group targets are called Departmental Standards. In fact, it is a combined affect of individuals as well as group output and hence a group standard in term of quantity, quality or the delivery schedule etc.

Generally in production, it is the departmental efficiency, which is more valid as standard, due to large variations, adjustments or reschedulings to achieve targets. Then the actual output is judged against the standards set. A department may be more efficient producing output higher than the Department Standards or it may have an output longer than the standard set. This may help in wage administration or job incentrives.

Plant Standards : The same logic follows when there are more than one department involved in the final output, such as service operations. The labour cost, maintenance cost and material utilisation in various departments may be different due to job variations or complexities or different accounting systems. Thus departmental managers may have multiple goods or a combination of departments might be used to achieve a longer goal of quality, quantity and cost. It is better to use plant standards for an effective goal achievement combining standards for marketing production, accounts, engineering and materials etc at different levels, but smoothing out at plant level.

National Standards : When a large number of units or organisations are involved for the measurement of efficiency, there is a necessity of setting a national goal say 8% industrial growth. The parameters in such cases have to be defined and measurement methods specified. Certain standards are set at the national level to standardise products/activities throughout the country. Indian standards are listed out in various IS codes issued by Institute of Indian Standards to denote quality standards of various products.

International Standards : In some cases, say, operating systems or environmental systems, there may be a necessity to lay down universal standard for the global operation. These are called International Standards. Examples are a standard length of "Meter" for the whole world. We also have Quality Management System (QMS) setting standards for global operation level in terms of ISO 9000 series of standards. Similarly in the environmental control system for global concern, there are Environment Management Systems (EMS) in terms of ISO 14000 series of standards.

The variations or updating of the output standards must be a continuous process due to the fact that "change is inevitable" and to cater for change "continuous Improvement" or kaizen must be adopted. Hence the industry should be in dynamic equilibrium and not sitting pretty on the production standards set once.

These are not contradictory concepts. We must set output norms for production and comparing these with the laid down standards. But with change in time, product/process design and the effect of learning curve, these standards must be revised at regular intervals. The time schedule should be decided by the organisation itself.

For example, even at the national level, we adopt changes in our 5 years plan. International standards ISO 9000 are updated every five years. In addition, ILO, IATA, FAO, IAOA, UNESCO and WHO etc are some international organisations setting their own standards but applicable in their area of jurisdiction across the globe. There are some voluntary standards which are generally followed in practice, but not mendatory.

13.9 Work Organisation

Discussion on work, so far, has been only on the physical and psychological angles.But another important aspect of work design is to take care of the work organisation. It is not enough how good the working conditions are, how well a job has been designed, how good the machines or the methods are, it is equally important that a worker is willing to work on the job duly involved and committed and that he feels very safe to operate in the work place.

It is equally important to understand the effect of the supporting organisation of work such as man-machine integration system and motivation provided through the incentive plans.

Job description, job enlargement job enrichment, job relation and job satisfaction are few of the methods to improve workers efficiency. But when we integrate his work well in compatibility of man-machine match, involve him in decision making and make him feel an important useful member of his team, the infrastrutural support in terms of his team helps him to perform better.

In some companies, an alternate work organisation concept has been utilised, called **"societal-technical approach"**. This means that we can induce better worker efficiency and a greater job satisfaction by virtue of creating campatibility between machines and men and creating team work concept by forming cohesive groups for results. There may be autonomous groups or self-motivated and self-directed teams of personnel for specific jobs. It has been observed that this leads to job emprovement, quality improvement and controls and ultimately cost reduction.

It is wrong to presume that all such good systems developed and utilised will always produce good results. The interests of workers, managers and that of the organisation may be at variance and in some cases change may not always be acceptable. Some very specially qualified people may not like the involvement of other persons and hence team concept may be resisted. Therefore, based on the detailed study of human behaviour and human psychology, the jobs design and system design must be upgraded continously and diligently.

13.10 Work Compensation and Incentives

The products produced should be worth the customer's satisfaction. The jobs and processes have to be designed to get the optimum output of the input resources. The impact of human motivation and involvement into the work is a large factor in this direction. But ultimate aim of any human worker remains as his bread earning capacity. His basic concern would be as to how much and on what basis he will be paid for the quantum of work done by him. Therefore, the work compensation system should be so designed that it promotes the level of human involvement the company would look for.

In general terms, this compensation is called the 'salary' or 'wages', which includes the basic salary, allowances, bonus and other benefits like children and family allowance, insurance, provident fund and any other specific amount considered by the company to be included in his regular salary. There are two general compensation systems :

- Piece rate or output based system or
- Time rate system

Piece rate or output based system : Under this system, a worker is paid accordingly to his performance of job or the amount of workdone, for which measurement system has to be agreed to initially. It may be the payment permitted on each piece of output produced. The element of quality achieved has to be related to this method as a pre-agreed arrangement.

Time rate system : In this case, workers are paid based on the time spent by them on work, regardless of quntity and quality of production. Workers may be paid on hourly, weekly or monthly basis. If worker is engaged for more than scheduled time, he is paid extra compensation. It may be again as on agreed basis. Overtime rate (generally double the normal rate) the is the compensation for extra hours. if he has worked for more than 40/48 hours a week.

Generally the fixed salary is paid on monthly basis. Extra hours compensations on agreed to basis are seperately included in the salry itself. It could be the combination of both the systems in general practice.

The workers generally have both the options available or a combination, but for managers, normally only the time-rate basis compensation system is preferred.

For 'agreed to' compensation, following list may be considered as a guide :

- Logical basis either piece rate or time bound system or a mix.
- Flexibility for any changes.
- Simple to understand and implement.
- Variations as per merit or improved performance.
- Jobs to be described fully.
- Motivation for enhanced productivity.
- Responsibility and accomtability based.
- Based on Uniform time standards across the organisation.

Based on these general principle, the amount paid would depend on the following aspects:

- Organisational capability to pay.
- Workers Capacity to work.
- Minimum wages as per Minimum Wages Act
- Minimum need of the employee
- Maximum worth of the employee
- Management Policy of graduation.
- Nature of work involved.
- General Standard of living
- Business Profitability
- Competitions strategy and market force.
- Government legislations.
- Union-Management relations.

When we compare the two compensation systems based on the factors described above, we find that time based system is easy to implement. It is preferred by the employee for the reason of regular security. When it is not easy to quantify the output such as a managers job or a supervisors work and the gradation is not easy to quantify, the agreed performance parameters should be the guide.

Wage Policy

Wage policy of an organisation is set of rules on which the payment of the company employees is based. Payment policy should include the quantum and the periodicity of payments. Wage includes gradewise basic salary, allowances, increments and any other fringe benefit offered by the company. For the purpose, job evaluation has to have a transparent and specified criteria and would include job description, job specification, job rating and job pricing etc.

• **Job description** : is a process of identifying various elements of the job to specify the duties a person is required to perform. It is to be based on working conditions, working outputs, equipment and tools, the place of operation and type and amount of supervision expected.

• **Job specification** : This identifies the requirement of the job such as technical and educational qualification, experience, age, his performance ability with reference to physical capability etc. Detailed check list of job elements would be advantageous.

• **Job Rating** : The level of operation a person is placed on *i.e.*, his grade or rank of working. This would include the classification and precedence such as a welder class 4 or senior supervisor or Production Manager. (This is setting the heirarchy).

• **Job Pricing** : It is to fix the wage payment level for the type and grade of the job. The method described as fixation of worker grades (ratings) as 105 or 110 and then wage fixation (as Minimum-wage structure of the company multiplied by the workers rating) is the job pricing for him. Some of the incentive schemes can be related to job pricing based on productivity of the individuals.

Hence for the jobs easily quantified, various incentive schemes have been designed and implemented. There are individual as well as group incentive schemes available.

Some of the group incentive schemes are listed below :

- Priestman plane (Minimum wage plan)
- Kaiser plan (gain sharing basis)
- Tonage plan (productivity based)
- Profit sharing (Bonus plan)
- Fringe Benefits (such as insurance, medical, entertainment, relocation allowance and Leave Travel Concessions etc.

Merit Evaluation : For the purpose of job rating, the merit evaluation criterion has to be evolved and announced in transparent way, so that every member of the organisation is aware as to what basis he would be judged on for this work performance for compensation. There are following methods available :

- Individual performance
- Paired rating
- Matrix for group comparison
- Key Result Areas (KRAs)
- Critical activity evaluation.

The scheme or the method followed depends on the adoption by a company.

Incentives : For motivating a worker, the company can work out the incentive schemes based on the importance of work, customer satisfaction level, quality desired and the capacity and willingness to pay.

There are financial as well as non-financial incentive schemes available, but selection of the incentive scheme is left to the discression between union or worker and the management. Over a period of time, a large number of schemes have been evolved but their usefulness varies from organisation to organisation.

Financial Incentives

In present scenerio, it is the innovation and ingenivity of thinking of the Human Resources Manager to work out the most favoured and useful incentive plan based on the culture of the organisation, attitude of workers and union and the type of work being performed by the ogranisation. Payment of Bonus on annual incentive basis or the grading of managers in term of additional increments are few good systems still operative to advantage in practically all the organisations. A well designed performance appraisal system helps in identifying the additional stengths of the employees on which the gradation of payments can be decided on tranparent basis.

In addition, another word catching the attention of workers and the management alike is gain sharing *i.e.*,better profit quantity and quality of product earned through, should be shared and the worker should be informed about the compensations on this aspect so as to increase his working proficiency and efficiency.

Non-Financial Incentives

These incentives can be put into the following categories :

- Promotions
- Job enrichment
- Job enlargement and rotation
- Participative management.
- Flexitime
- Societal interactions such as group picnics on company basis or celebrations of festivals together with sweet distribution and gifts on important occasions.
- Recognition of good workers though community recognition. Tee shirts or appreciation letters etc. are few incentives tried out for advantage.

13.11 Workers Unions

While dealing with workers to exhort them to produce their optimum, everything else discussed so far is possibly controllable, but the help or interference of the workers union. Hence any discussion on workers behaviour, their working capacity and willingness to participate in the product/process design and any motivation/incentives schemes will remain a question mark, if the workers unions are not taken into confidence. Though in the present environment of global competition, the workers have started realising that it is beneficial to the organisation to keep workers motivated and in good humours, it is also equally important for workers to offer all the commitment and involvement towards their work, if the benefits have to flow towards them. All the same, unions are still valid and are to be dealt with in right earnest. A negative attitude of the union representatives can lead to very difficult atmosphere to work in, whereas a positive union can be a real helping hand. To help in the process, well defined job is imperative so as to identify the method of compensation. Job enrichment and enlargement also must be effectively speltout. Unions may not be willing to adhere to these concepts but as unemployment increases, the workers would understand the way they have to work to protect their jobs. Ealier the worker realises that change will make their job interesting and challenging, earlier they would involve themselves in the jobs. Some unions may still show indifferent and interfering attitudes. By and large partnerships between unions and management are developing into healthy relationships. Generally if unions are treated as partners, they tend to co-operate. Hence they must be included in the process improvement.

Chapter 14

Resources Requirement Planning

Main issues:

1. Material Requirement Planning (MRP)
2. Manufacturing Resources Planning (MRPII)
3. Enterprise Resources Planning (ERP).

14.1 Procurement of Materials

Having discussed the strategies and facilities for production, the important issue for effective production is the availability of raw materials, subassemblies or assemblies, without which no production can take place.

It is not only the ordering or proçurement of materials that is important for production, much more valid is the materials management i.e., correct requirement planning, timely ordering, quality check at the time of its receipt and finally making it available at the place and time as on required basis. Little more effort will be required to plan work-in-process inventories and the final product schedule, which is, then, to be packaged, transported and delivered to the customers end as per demand and desired time schedule..

To plan materials of all kinds required for production or service, the start point is the detailed information about the customer's requirement i.e., the product, service and demand quantity. This requirement is now to be converted into production schedule known as the Master Production Schedule (MPS). The MPS gets translated into planning and provision of production facilities i.e., Capacity Requirement Planning (CRP) and according to the MPS and CRP, the materials are to be made available on each machine for a particular product at the appropriate scheduled time, when the manufacture is to start. This operation is termed as Materials Requirement Planning (MRP).

The system can be represented in the form :

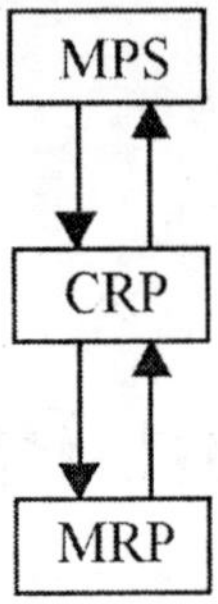

For all these areas of activities, following inputs are required :

MPS 1. Short range demand forecast.
2. Inventory Policy
3. Product design
4. Capacity limitation.
5. Manpower and machine availability.

CRP 1. Customer satisfaction policy.
2. Finances availability.
3. Types and number of machines available.
4. Shep floor plan/layout
5. Production/shift policy

MRP 1. MPS
2. Lot sizing and materials needed for each product.
3. Available stocks.
4. List of vendors.
5. Material budget and cash flow schedule.

From the above list, it is evident that though the Master Production Schedule (MPS) can be drawn based on the forecasted demand for a certain period of time, we have to ensure that enough production capacity is available and enough material can be procured. If there is any constraint either on the production capacity or on the material availability, the MPS will have to be revised and only optimum production can, therefore, be planned.

14.2 Material Requirement Planning (MRP)

Since materials are required to be made available to the production team as and when demanded, based on MPS, it is imperative for the purchase team to plan the quality and quantity of materials for each product for a certain period of time. In production system, there are large number of interruptions called "Random Fluctuations". due to which, there must be a constant vigil on procurement because the demand are generally irregular and dependent on the customer delivery schedule.

In case of fast food items, some products have good demand, but it is irregular depending on the arrival of the customer for a particular item. Some may be demanding pizzas, others burgers and some more only coffee at the same time. Thus demands, during the day, are totally dependent on the customer's schedule.

There can be yet another situation, where the demands may be large in quantity with varieties of items such as requirements of ornaments or sarees during festival or marriage season. For marriage functions, sarees may be in great demand, but the variation in types may be large. Also this demand comes down considerably soon after.

The demand also maybe fairly constant like any eatables. Consumption is also large due to the fact that customers need these all the time throughout the year. Yet another case arisess when a large product is required only once in a while, say, a large component for replacement in a machine, either as a policy decision or on random breakdown.

The variation in schedule and quantities for dependent demands can be taken care of by adopting a production schedule based on the quantities of each type of components. The time schedule of such requirements also may be varied. Such a variation for material planning and procurement can be handled through Material Requirement Planning (MRP). Through MRP, following aspects can be tackled.

- Changing and controlling the production lot schedules.
- Changing and controlling the purchase activity of materials.
- Scheduling and managing the maintenance operations.

MRP is a computer based information system (software) for ensuring scheduling of production as well as materials procurement with dependent demands. It uses the information of raw material inventory and work in process items having dependent demands. Even though there may be no product forecast in the long run, it is enough to know what product in what quantity is required to be produced, say, next week or next month, so that materials for such productions can be planned, procurred and product produced for customer's use at right time.

This process is called an **MRP explosion**, due to the reason of the conversion of product requirement into material requirement planning. Thus MRP takes MPS as the starting point for material planning. The procurement action is, then, taken accordingly. Since MRP controls production as well as the procurement of materials, its aim can be summerised as under:

- Customer satisfaction with product and service.
- Reduction in inventory/investment.
- Improving plant operation flexibility.

This is because the basic pholosophy of MRP is to obtain each raw material at the right time to produce the item as per the required schedule *i.e.*, MPS. Hence it can organise the end product as per customer's delivery schedule (better service through timely delivery), reduce inventory holding (only for requirement) and to support production as per the demand in the short term time span.

Elements of MRP

Various elements of MRP softwares are as under :

- Master Schedule File,
- BOM file,
- Stock status file,
- MRP analysis file and
- MRP report file.

The elements of MRP are drawn below as fig. 14.1

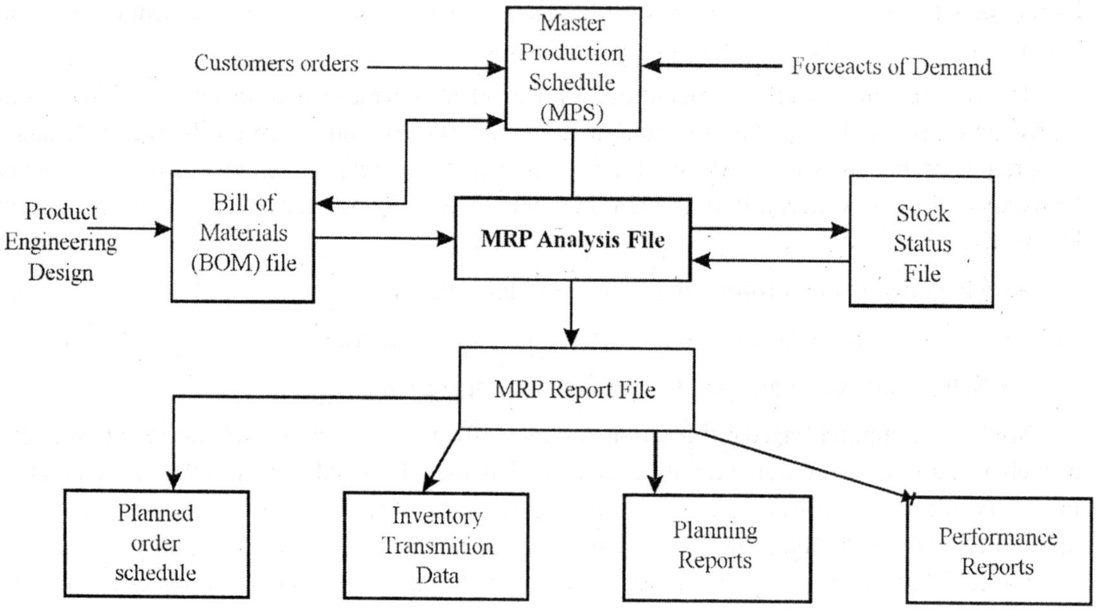

Fig. 14.1. MRP Configuration

As can be seen above, the main input source to MRP system is the Master Production Schedule (MPS) planning out the load of customer order and the forecast of demand for production. The other important input required are Bills of Materials (BOM) and the stock status. These three information sources help in the MRP analysis (computerised processing logic) to work out the Material planning for procurement of raw materials and components etc. It involves the release of orders for vendors, any rescheduling of orders due to change in requirement and also information about activities of procurement such as vendors status, budget position etc.

Objectives of Master Production Schedule

Master production schedule has the following objectives to be fulfilled :

- To schedule end products to be finished in time for their availability to the customer.
- To avoid any overloading or underloading of the production facilities for achieving low production cost results through effective utilisation of the production capacity.

Procedure for developing MPS

In the initial stage, there has to be a method of collecting all necessary inputs as follows :

- Customer orders
- Demand forecasts
- Inventory status reports
- Production capacity of man-machine combination and outputs
- Any specific prorities for schedule.

After collating the above information, the production scheduler starts assigning various work centres based on their requirements for products and their capacity for production. The schedule is then worked out for total demand product wise. Consolidated demand can be arrived at as shown in fig. 14.2 below :

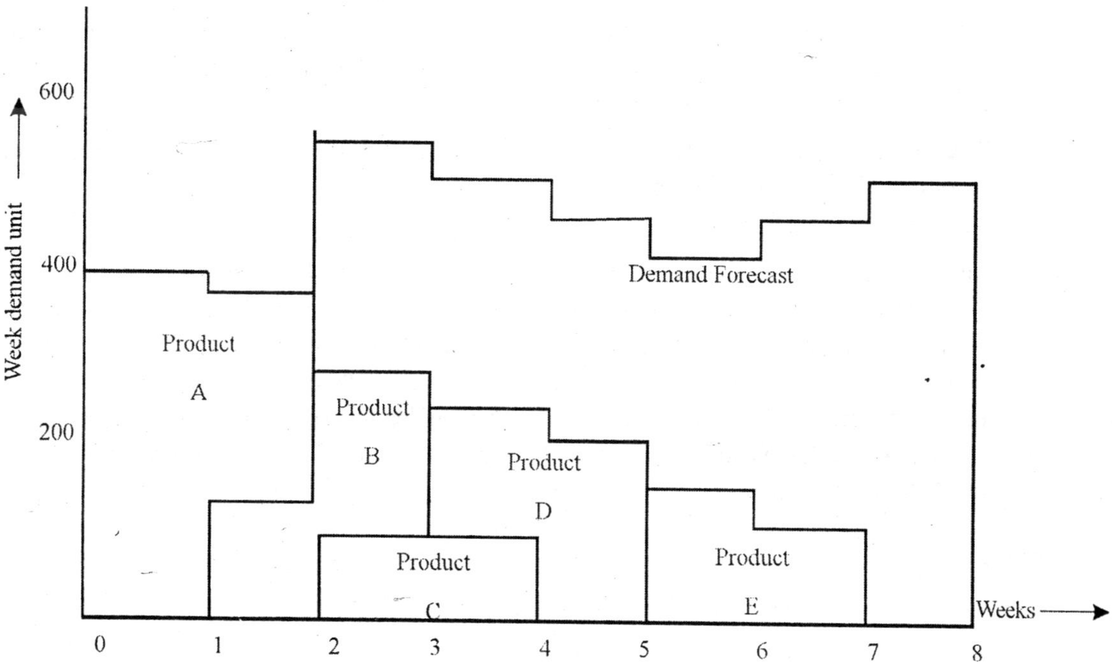

Fig. 14.2. Demand consolidation

These time-scheduled demands are then checked for capacity loading of the work centres and under-loading/over-loading adjusted, before work-centre are subjected to their scheduling. MPS for each product is drawn out first and then MPSs for all the products are superimposed for any adjustments of the machine loading slots.

Since the computerised MPS is possible now, the chances of any analmolies of scheduling can be easily located and modified. IBM's **Communications Oriented Production Information and Control System (COPICS)** is an example of the computerised scheduling system.

Developing Master Production Schedule (MPS) : The MPS requirement is a given schedule for the production of customers orders and the regular future demand of products. It draws out the schedule (start time and finish time of each product on each machine) for a particular period of time, say, a week or a month. It takes into account the schedule of orders and lot sizing of the end products as per the supply schedules. The capacity limitation is taken into account while drawing out the master production schedule. The division of the MPS into specified time intervals planned is called ***time buckets***. The material planning is done for these buckets, which may be a day, week or a month as decided by the management. It is based on volumes and supply schedules. Longer buckets are used for future planning. It may be based on product layout or process layout based on the advanced decision of the management as per product importance. Procurement lead time must be considered while deciding the time bucket, so that supplies are available when required.

While drawing out the Master Production Schedule (MPS) following aspects must be borne in mind:

- The product quantities must match with the sales requirement so that there is no unnecessary finished goods inventory build up. The schedule should also be based on the operations plan for actual production.
- The product mix and respective quantities must match the capacity of the production resources. Hence lot sizing must be deliberate.
- The capacity constraints must be built into the master schedule, so as to avoid any mismatch. Frequent changes in the MPS should be avoided, though these may become necessary for production control. The Sudden increase in MPS quantities may result in shortages of materials or disbalance in the machine schedules, leading to delayed deliveries. On the other hand, sudden decrease in MPS quantities can result in raw inventory buildup and reduced capacity utilisation, leading to additional cost of inventory holding as well as wastage of planned production capacity. Hence MPS must be frozen in near-term time schedule.

Problem 14.1.

Demands of two products A and B are as follows

Demand for product A

Weeks	1	2	3	4	5	6
Total demand	20	20	50	50	30	30

Demand for Product B

Weeks	1	2	3	4	5	6
Total demand	30	30	40	40	40	30.

The safety stock for product A is being planned as 30 units and for B, it is 40 units. The lot size for product A is 50 and for B, it is 60. It is also noticed that the initial inventory is 70 units for product A and 50 units for product B. Workout the appropriate production schedule.

Solution :

The MPS (Master Production Schedule) is as follows

Product A

Weeks	1	2	3	4	5	6
Total demand	20	20	50	50	30	30
Initial inventory	70	50	30	30	30	50
Production Need	—	—	50	50	50	50
End Inventory	50	30	30	30	50	70

Product B

Total demand	30	30	40	40	50	30
Initial inventory	50	80	50	70	90	50
Production need	60	–	60	60	–	60
End inventory	80	50	70	90	50	80

Bill of Materials File : Bill of Materials file, contains quantities of raw materials, assemblies, subassemblies and parts etc for a product. Hence this file is also called "Intended Bill of Materials" file or a Product structure file. Thus there will be as many BOMs as the number of products on the MPS. The quantity of each product is available from the MPS file, based on which the schedule of production has been worked out for capacity utilisation. The total material requirement for a time bucket is then calculated by multiplying the list of materials on the BOM by the quantity to be produced during this period. The help of product structure tree helps in working out the BOM correctly.

The materials so calculated are then resturctured to produce a material list, which is a combined list of quantitied for similar items for all the products to be manufactured during this time bucket under planning.

Problem 14.2.

Two products A and B are to be manufactured on a production facility. The BOM is given below:

Product A (Quantity 250)

Items	A/U	Quantity
1. Wood sal	Cft	25
2. Screws 1½"	Nos	300
3. Screews 2"	Nos	25
4. Polish	Lit	0.5

Product B (Quantity 250)

Items	*A/U*	*Quantity*
1. Wood chir	Cft	20
2. Screws 1½"	Nos	30
3. Screws 2"	Nos	50
4. Polish	Lit	0.5

Work out the materials required for both the products.

Solution :

Items		*A/U*	*Total materials requirement*
Product A			
1.	Wood Sal	Cft	$25 \times 250 = 6{,}250$
2.	Screws 1½"	Nos	$300 \times 250 = 75{,}000$
3.	Screws 2"	Nos	$25 \times 250 = 6{,}250$
4.	Polish	lit	$0.5 \times 250 = 125$
Product B			
1.	Wood chir	Cft	$20 \times 250 = 5{,}000$
2.	Screws 1½"	Nos.	$30 \times 250 = 7{,}500$
3.	Screws 2"	Nos	$50 \times 250 = 12{,}500$
4.	Polish	lit	$0.5 \times 250 = 125$

Hence the consolidated materials requirement works out as under :

Items	*A/U*	*Consolidated Materials Requirement*
1. Wood Sal	Cft	6,250

2. Wood chir	Cft	5,000
3. Screws 1½"	Nos	75,000 + 7,500 = 82,500
4. Screws 2"	Nos	6,250 + 12,500 = 18,750

This conversion to material list is done because the similar items are procured from one source only.

Stock status file : This file contains the availability of items/components in the stores, which can be made use of for the production.

These items may be lying unused either due to change in product design or change in manufacturing schedule. The inventory lying unused, therefore, must be taken into consideration to procure only what is needed during a particular time period. The safety stock inventory information is also available in this file. This safety inventory is not considered for updating the materials requrement.

This file would also have the data regarding outstanding production and purchase orders, which can be conveniently utilised for overall planning.

The fluctuation in production, for whatever reasons, can create a situation for this file suffering from inaccuracy, though accuracy status of materials has utmost importance. These inaccuries can arise due to physical movement of materials not recorded or the material ordered to move out but not physically lifted. The inaccurate material data or stock status can either result in inventory building or shortage of material stopping the production and hence delay in ordering the materials.

Very important feature of the BOM and stock status file is that the identification code for various materials must match. Otherwise information energing will be defective. An item lying under a different code may be useable, but it will not be picked up as inventory due to wrong identification. This stock status file also contains information about the procurement lead time for each item.

Interactions of these three input files will produce **Net requirement of materials** to be procured and their procurement lead times listed out.

MRP Analysis : MRP Analysis file has the processing logic built in to analyse the information obtained from the three input files i.e., **MPS**, **BOM** and **stock status** files. It accepts the master schedule, component quantities and the net materials requirement needing procurement. The Net quantity of procurement, then, gets segregated into the physical list of procurement vendor wise. All the venders cannot supply all the items on the list and are registered for specific supplies. The planned order release, therefore, get prepared and the orders are so printed out. The analysis and data processing will continue till the requirement for all the items for all the products on the MPS for a particular time bucket have been determined and processed for release orders.

MRP Reports File : The aim of MRP system is to work out material requirement plans for each product and also the master requirement plans aggregating all the requirement for all the products during specified time horizons.

Now, the following reports are generated out of the MRP Reports file:

- **Order and production release schedule :** Specifying the amount and lead time for all orders and production runs for each item.

- **Orders release :** Physical preparation of purchase orders to vendors specifying the items, quantity and lead time including all commercial terms of puchase.
- **Change reports :** These reports will spell out any modification to previously placed orders or production plans.
- **Load Reports :** It indicates the amount of each major resource to be utilised with this plan.
- **Future Planning Reports :** These reports can indicate the following :

  Vendors load Vs Capability

  Vendors supply behaviour i.e., quality or lead time adherance.

  Budget allocation Vs the procurement ordered.

  Other financial, production or delivery reports etc for any deviations or customisations.

A typical MRP report for an item is given below :

Item code no 751

Lead time 3 weeks

Report Date

Requirement	*Week*	*1*	*2*	*3*	*4*	*5*	*6*	*7*	*8*
Gross requirement				400					500
Available for next period	50	50	50						
Net requirement				350					500
Planned orders				350					500
Planned order release	350					500			

Fig. 14.3. MRP report item 751

Lot Sizing in MRP

In MRP, the lot to lot procurement can be built in if MPS is designed accordingly. By changing the quantity of end product (lot formation for a time bucket), the planning of material can automatically be modified. The total material ordered for procurement will be based on this specified quantity and production schedule accordingly adjusted. Whenever there is a change required in the production quantities or in the product itself, the modification in the MPS, (Reducing what is not required during the time bucket or adding quantity, if higher demand is anticipated). Schedule of any items that can not be produced due to some machine failure or repairs or otherwise), can also be modified in MPS.

By this method of modification in the MPS, we can control both the areas of operations:

- Change in the production by controlling product variety or quantity.
- Change in the material procurement for actual need only. On line release orders can be amended for change in supplies.

In case of specific customer's orders, the procurement is ordered based on the quantity of the order (as is can be assumed that there mauy not be another order from the customer in the near future for the same product). Similarly, if the product is standardised and is to be produced for stock, the lot sizing decision is the question of economics. EOQ can be the basis for such lot-size decision. Period Order Quantity (POQ) also can be selected as the basis for lot-size ordering.

Problem 14.3

The net requirement for the material from a given MPS is as follows:

Week	1	2	3	4	5	6
Quality	300	500	600	500	400	200

The annual demand for the product is assumed as 20,000 units for a 50 week period. Ordering cost is Rs. 200. The ordering is done when one unit of this product is carried in inventory from one week to another. The carrying cost per unit is Rs. 0.50.

(a) work out of the lot-for-lot production cost for it.

(b) Also work out the EOQ and the related cost of materials.

Solution :

Based on the data given, the inventory levels for lot-for-lot production are worked out in the following table.

Week	*Net requirement*	*Initial Inventory*	*Production lot*	*End Inventory*
1	300	0	300	0
2	500	0	500	0
3	600	0	600	0
4	500	0	500	0
5	400	0	400	0
6	200	0	200	0

Since there are 6 orders placed, the ordering cost = Rs. 6 × 200 = Rs. 1,200

(b) $$\text{EOQ} = \sqrt{\frac{2\,\text{DCo}}{\text{Ch}}}$$

$$= \sqrt{\frac{2 \times 20{,}000 \times 200}{50 \times 0.50}}$$

$$= 180 \text{ units}$$

∴ Ordering cost = 180 (2 + 3 + 4 + 3 + 3 + 2) = Rs. 3,060.

and Carrying cost = 0.50 × 400 = Rs. 200

The Calculations are as under:

Weeks	*1*	*2*	*3*	*4*	*5*	*6*
Requirement	300	500	600	500	400	200
Inventory	0	60	20	100	60	80
Production lot	360	540	720	540	540	360
	(2)	(3)	(4)	(3)	(3)	(2)
End inventory	60	20	100	60	80	80

Capacity Readjustments

Inspite of having the capacity constraint for working out the MPS, there is an inbuilt capability in the MRP system to identify potential bottlenecks and capacity problems in advance for effecting rescheduling.

In the discussion on lot size in MRP, we have brought out that any capacity constraint can be adjusted (even if it is temporary or short time problem), while drawing the MPS. Through the computer capability by changing the product mix or the product quantities, the MPS gets adjusted and rescheduled based on the information on man-machine output norms. A tentative schedule and corresponding material planning can be worked out. Material planning being an interactive process, can be changed by changing the input parameters or the quantities required. In case of over loading or underloading, the capacity balance is carried out and load reports smoothed out. Thus a firm schedule would emerge out of these adjustments.

Safety Stocks

Changes keep occuring. Uncertainty of operations is natural and the degree keeps varying. The uncertainty or randomness occurs due to following reasons:

- Manpower state and outputs.
- Machine ageing or maintenance levels changing.
- Availability of materials affected due to scarcity, substitutions or quality variation etc.
- Lead times change.
- Defects and scraps rate variation.
- Failure or delays in procurement.
- Financial problem of cash flow.
- Customers preferences varying.

These uncertainties lead to variations in production rates. The capacity and material constraints coupled with randomness in human behaviour, whether worker or the customer, have to be smoothed out by some appropriate measures. Safety stocks are one such solution. And this aspect can not be left to adhocism. These are regular deliberate decisions and hence must be incorporated into the system. Preparing a list of safety stock and the desired quantities must have a very logical approach because there is a large uncertainly in requirement. In constantly changing demand, one time list can be outdated in quick time. Products are also becoming short life cycle items. If the product is customer-specific, it has all the more reason not to use it as a yardstock for safety stocks planning as the product may not be required again at all and any unused item will become obsolete scrap very fast. Therefort it is essential to analyse the randomness of product and process and causes of variation. Then only we can develop a strategy to counter it. One solution to such a situation is just-in-time (JIT) concept. Utilisation of safety stocks should also clamped with the idea of Vendor Managed Inventory (VMI). Hence Captive Vendor Management is becoming popular in todays materials management system.

If variation is large and still persists, then the decision is to be based on the analysis of time or quantity variation. If variations are quantity based, safety study can help. But for time based variations, the philosophy of safety time in ordering the item earlier than required can be adopted. If materials are received earlier, these can be held in stock for short duration, incurring small carrying cost, rather than keeping the safety stock for a longer period or continously incurring large costs. As a deliberate risk, modified supplies should be resorted to, thus avoiding the safety stocks for longer period or in larger quantities.

Advantage and Disadvantages of MRP

From the description of MRP software, we can draw list of obvious advantages due to computer oriented (IT-enabled) system operation :

Advantages : Some of the obvious advantages are :

- Timely procurement
- Low inventories
- Effective Material Tracking
- Effective Production Scheduling
- Mass and batch production possible
- Production capacity variation easily controlled.
- Effective financial control on materials payments.
- Dynamics of the system taking care of changes in situations.

Disadvantages : There is a huge potential of cost-effective operations due to MRP implementation, but still the system suffers from the following limitations :

- Manpower failure i.e. records not being maintained well and updated. Hence poor data accuracy and data integrity.
- Training – Inspite of due care (it being a monotonous job), personnel would need the costant training for technical and motivational aspects.
- Inappropriate identification codes can fail the system any time.
- The software may not be appropriate for the type of its usage in a particular organisation.

Because of the above reasons, much simpler and user friendly systems are being developed and are in use in the industry. Infact, MRP usage in MRP II and ERP has undergone a tremendous change.

This has been necessitated due to the fact that in the simple system, MRP simply exploded the material requirement based on MPS. But in later years, a concept of closed–loop MRP System was developed, which meant that it is necessary to integrate the system with other functions of production and there should be a system for feedback of informatio, so that the production planning can remain valid for ever. This integration resulted in developing Manufacturing Resourcess Planning (MRP II) where- in the integration included the financial reports also, so that the budget plans, purchase effectiveness, shipping budgets as well as inventory cesting can be taken into account on the overall basis.

Later, the development of system was upgraded further from MRP II to Enterprise Resources Planning (ERP), which further included total integration of all business functions through the client server architecture and advancement in Software Engineering. These have been described in the chapter subsequently.

Dynamism in MRP usage.

We have already discussed how the MRP software helps in varying situation in practice. Hence it can be said that MRP is not static. It is responsive to be changes either in the customer order or due to internal production uncertainties. Updating with the current information will help in use of MRP under varying conditions. There are four aspects of MRP control of this dynamic environment, namely pegging, cycle counting, updating and time fences.

Pegging : As the name suggests, it is the process of running through the MRP records and product structure to identify how changes in one component will effect the records of the other components. MPS has to undergo the necessary updating and change.

Cycle Counting : To maintain the production schedules, updating MRP records are a must, otherwise the system will become inefficient and will not meet the delivery schedules. Cycle counting ensures that available inventories tally with the MRP records. Stock status file is required to take care of any defectives and hence not-available stock of items.

Updating : When any shop transactions take place, the MRP must be updated i.e., required change in the MPS. This will update the BOM and MRP analysis files for correct decision making.

Time Fence : It is a pre-decided length of time that must pass with out any change in the MPS. Then only the MRP system can stablise. Frequent change in the MPS will put pressure on the effective use of MRP system. This time fence can be reduced if the computer capability of speed is enhanced. This can avoid the erratic operations or system nervousness. This is called as "MPS frozen during the time fence".

14.3 Manufacturing Resource Planning (MRP II)

Material Requirement Planning (MRP) really cannot be operated in isolation without due effective inputs. This software has to interact with marketing and sales team for customer orders and forecast of demand. Bills of materials file information has to be in constant interaction with engineering and Research/development teams. The order releases and receipts have to be in touch with accounts and payment teams and inventory information is very useful input and usage for marketing and purchase department. Though the MRP software has been developed and can operate on its own, its integration with other organisational set ups is going to be much more useful for the company for cost benefit. Hence, it has been in use now as part of Manufacturing Resources Planning (MRP II) and Enterprise Resources Planning (ERP).

Manufacturing Resource Planning (MRP II), therefore, really means :

"A method for the effective planning of all resources of a manufacturing company". Ideally, it addresses operational planning in units, financial planning with a simulation capability to answer "what if" questions. It is made up of a variety of functions, each linked together to business planning, sales and operations planning, production planning, master production scheduling, material requirement planning and capacity requirement planning, used execution support systems for capacity and material. Output from these systems is integerated with financial reports such as business plan, purchase commitment report, shipping budget and inventory projections etc.

Manufacturing Resources Planning would require planning of the following inputs :

- Capacity Planning
- Material Planning
- Financial Planning
- Manpower Planning

Therefore, the MRP becomes only the subset of MRP II. Because MRP II is the next generation use of IT-enabled system for synchronising all the aspects of Manufacturing. It integrates engineering, marketing and sales, production, purchase and finance by using one unified data base to plan all the activities related to manufacturing. Like MRP, in MRP II also, the starting input resource is the Master Production Schedule (MPS), based on which the capacity planning is fine tuned. For capacity planning, it has to be a man-machine compatability at technical, administrative and psychological levels, so that product and process management matches the requirement. Hence manpower planning in terms of skill, number, attitude and aptitude has to correlate with the type, number and technical level of the machines.

Based on demand of products, MPS is finalised and MRP can be utilised to produce order releases. For execution of the production plans, the purchase schedules and the shop floor schedules are generated. Work centre loading, shop floor control and material procurement schedules and controls can be easily planned and implemented.

A general schematic diagram given in fig 14.4 can help in undertaking the MRP II planning.

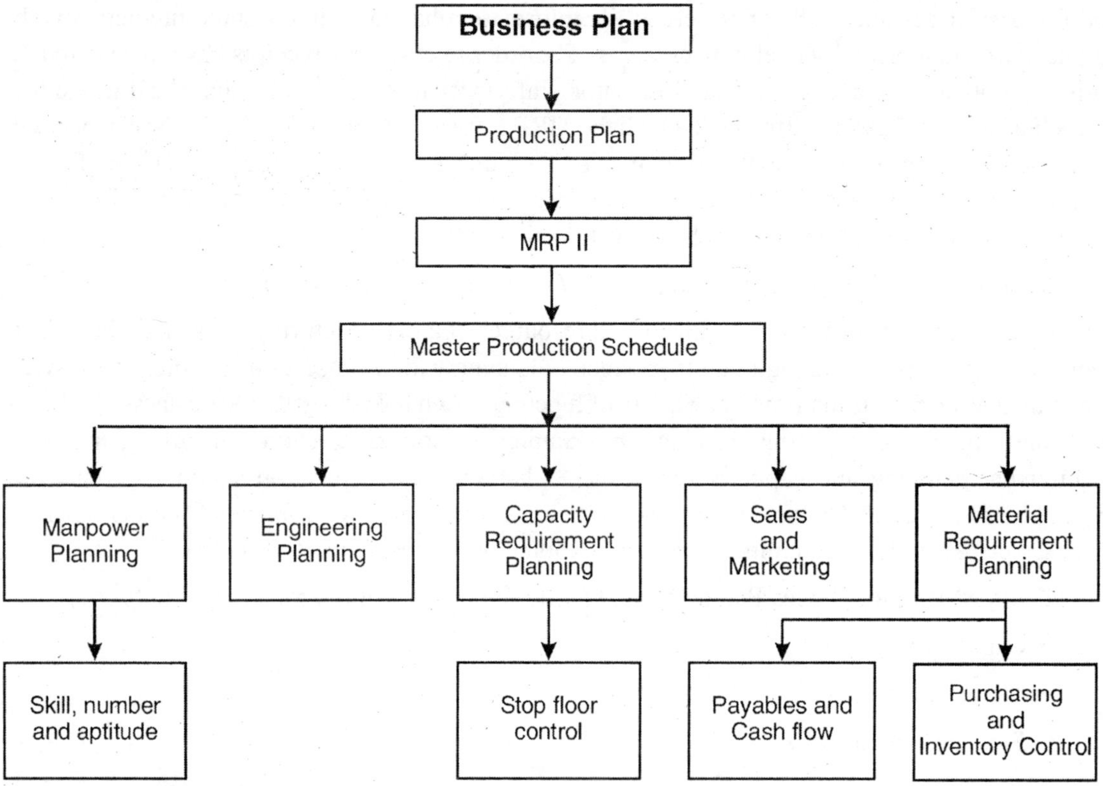

Fig. 14.4. MRP II Integrated System

As can be seen from Fig 14.4 given above, MRP II is a model of the organisation, which is being used for more than simply planning the production. The data availability and various internal interactions make it possible to evaluate the effects of decisions in a variety of different functional areas such as finances and cash flow, marketing and sales strategies as well as engineering aspects.

MRP II being essentially a computer based system, an appropriate model is to be selected for the use by the organisation after clearly evaluating the features and modules required. The major considerations for selection of an appropriate MRP II system are:

- technical capability
- data integrity
- education and Training of Employees and
- use of the system by the management and employees willingly.

14.4 Enterprise Resources Planning (ERP)

Today, the companies are operating under highly competitive environment and the very servival (not only growth) depends on how fast these units adapt themselves to the new demands, new markets, new cost atmosphere and new customer's behaviour. To survive under these fast changing situations, the use of Information Technology (IT) has become almost inescapable though the IT-enabled systems are not cheap to come by. The large advantage acrueing out of its use is when it balances out the cost. Thus the companies should have compatible mechanism to take full advantage of these systems. Since the usage of information system has become synomynous with growth and competitive advantage, there are large number of such systems available and are in use. We have already discussed MRP and MRP II in this category of resources planning systems.

More and more effective resources planning brings in cost advantage. MRP was upgraded to the close loop system which was built or developed not only for material planning, but also for additional requirements of sales and production planning, master production scheduling, purchase planning and capacity planning. When the execution of the plans was under way with control available in MRP structure, the control of production, use of capacity, variation in product mix for short life cycle products and detailed scheduling and distribution were available. In addition, various planning reports, future planning data, and control reports for vendors and quality assurance, were also possible.

While making MRP as part of a bigger system called MRP II, a method of effective resource planning for manufacturing was introduced, developed and used. It had the modules for manpower planning, capacity planning, product mix and man-machine compability, and even financial planning for the entire production system. It also have the capability of developing and managing alternatives. Thus this system is a combination of many functions such as business planning, production planning, master production scheduling, material requirement planing and capacity planning along with the financial planning and control.

In a quest to improve the information systems further, a system called Enterprise Resources Planning (ERP) has been developed, as a step forwards after MRP II. In this case, it is not only capable of planning for manufacturing but for planning of resources for all the business functions. This system integretes all business functions together for better cohension and control.

ERP Architecture

ERP is an accounting-oriented information system for indentifying and planning the resources for the entire organisation by intergrating all relevant functions through a common base called server. This system has now even improved to have a geographic user interface relational data base even for vendors, use of fourth generation langauage, computer-aided software Engineering tools, client server architecture and an open-system portability. From ERP, it has further improved to ERP II with customer and vendor interface added to it, thus extending its capability to integrated E-business.

ERP system application involves longer time as well as huge costs for implementation. But based on its utility in terms of large number of tangible and intangible benefits, the cost can be spread out through these benefits. ERP system consists of many software modules that can be seperately purchased and used for specific functional area.

The major large selling ERP system is by the vendor SAP (their software SAP R/3) which offers various modules such as Sales and Distribution, financial accounting, financial controlling. Human Resources, Work Flow, Industry Solutions, Production Planning, Materials Management, Quality management plant maintenance, Assets management and Project management etc.

Due to cost involved, the implementation needs a major commitment, will-power and patience of the management to see the results.

Today, the vendors are providing standard modules, modified to suit organisational specific requirements, thus making the software cost effective and cheaper. The major ERP vendors are:

- SAP
- BaaN
- IBM
- Oracle
- JD Edwards
- People soft
- Ramco
- CODA
- D & B
- Marcarn
- Platinum
- SMI
- Software 2000 etc.

Utility Area of ERP

Since ERP is an effective tool to integrate upstream and down stream functions of the organisational supply chain, it is helpful in planning all the resources of the organisation such as manpower, machines, materials, finances, production–(quantity and quality) and supply and distribution network by integrating all functions. It addresses the following concerns of the organisation:

- Developing infrasturcture to ensure quick response to customer's demands through resources and functions integration.
- Smoothing out the processes and procedures through IT-enabled system taking advantage of the logical application and integration of information through the client surver architecture.
- Improving response time for better customer satisfaction through service enhancement.
- Helping improvement in market share through variety of products and higher services levels.

Advnatages through ERP

The important concerns of the organisations are the customer stisfaction and market share through improved infrastructure and methods and procedures. It is evident that inspite of cost involved, following benefits can be obtained through ERP by integrating the information in horizontal as well as vertical directions for all the departments. Major benefits can be summerised as follows :

- Improved sales
- Improved capacity
- Improved productivity
- Improved departmental interactions
- Improved customer relationship
- Improved vendor management
- Improved inventory management
- Improved quality levels
- Reduction in the procurement cost
- Reduction in the production cost
- Reduction in manpower cost

Selection of ERP System

Though there are number of ERP systems available through various vendors, the utility objective remains the same. The general principle of ERP usage are as follows :

- Understand the business of the organisation and evaluate the functional fit of the system.
- Number of modules required and their integration for flexibility.
- Available business technology and client server capability of the firm.
- Amount of automation available and compatibility with upgrades possible.
- Customisation level required.
- Implementation schedule.
- Total cost involved i.e. cost of licensing, training, implementation, maintenance, customisation and cost of related hardwares.

With these principle of evaluation of an ERP package, the vendor selection must be deliberate and analytical. Each vendor should be able to understand the major criteria like functional capability, technical architecture, cost, service support, will power and the ability to implement.

Due emphasis on existing IT capability and technical capacity of the manpower are a must for successful implementation of ERP package.

Stages in ERP Project

Any ERP project passes through the following stages :

- Project Definition

- System study
- ERP modules design
- Implementation.

Typical ERP System

A typical ERP system is given below as representative of the resources planning technique for understanding how the ERP system operates. It works with the help of various modules interacting through the client server architecture.

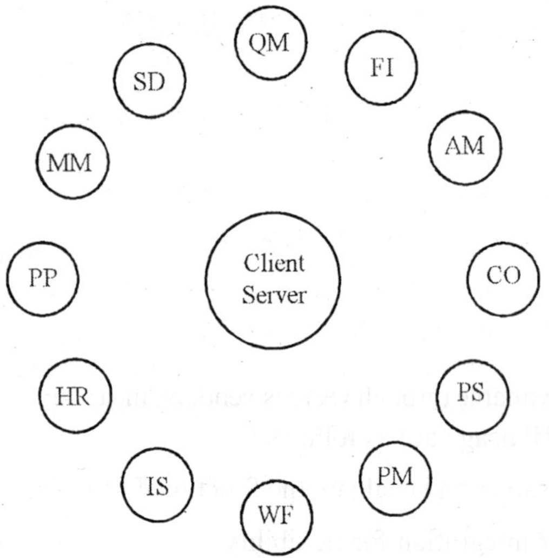

Where

WF = Work Flow
IS = Industry Solution
HR = Human Resources
PP = Production Planning
MM = Materials Management
SD = Sales and Distribution
QM = Quality Management
FI = Financial Accounting
PS = Project System
AM = Assets Management
CO = Controlling
PM = Plant Maintenance

Fig. 14.5 Typical ERP modules

All the modules indicated above have their individual database and information system to coordinate the integrated function of all related modules. Through the method of integration with client server architecture, the information in one module needing action by some other modules would automatically be available and would be acted upon without any formal reference and without wasting any time.

Various modules are developed under specific customised conditions and hence ERP software is costly. But vendors are now working on making it within reach of various clients through the process of standard modules and then fine-tuning these to the need of the organisation.

Selection of ERP vendors

Since there are number of ERP vendors operating in the market, there has to be the basis for selecting an appropriate package of ERP, thus identifying strength of each ERP package and its supplying vendor and requirement of the organisation at appropriate technical and economical level.

Some of the important factors for vendor selection of ERP are as follows :

- Cost
- Compatibility with requirement of the client
- Project implementation time
- Compatibility of the package with existing IT-system capability of the organisation
- Risk involved

Cost and Compatibility of Requirement : The cost of the software is large because the module development has to be customised for the type of the operations in the company and also the level of technology in use at present. Therefore the acquisition cost is high. In addition, the cost incurred for personnel and travel are also high for the study of the present systems, defining the key criteria, the development of the software, its validation and implementation. It is a long drawn process. To eastablish compatibility with clients requirement, the discussion takes longer as the companies donot have or supply enough data on their present operations and on their material supply vendors. The presentation on vendor responses or operational methods and efficiencies and the specification of their machines may not be very reliable. Thus it takes time to understand the present system in order to develop the modules compatible with companies intended requirements.

Projects Implementation Time : The uncertainty of above-described unvalidated data results in difficulty in working out project implementation schedule. The selection, development and physical implementation has to be worked out as the situation unfolds. Rough estimates and schedules, however, must be laid down to ensure that the project does not become unmanagable, uncontrollable and indefinite.

***Compatibility of package with existing IT* – enable sytems :** Fortunately most of the vendors have developed the ERP packages suitably competible with any operating system in companies but still the compatibility or upgradation has to be ensured, otherwise system developed may not bear full fruits due to data distortion or incomplete processing.

Hence during selection of the ERP package, following justifications must be deliberated upon :

Strategic justification : long term utility of the package.

Economic and financial justification : resulting from the cost benefit analysis of inputs and outputs. Hence consideration of time value of the money, net present value (NPV), the rates of return and the profitability index are to be taken into account.

Technological justifications : It depends on the level of technology that the company can afford to operate on and the level of technology available with the commercial systems. The state-of-art technology has to be understood for its efficency and compatibility before the price-tag is read.

Business justification : This is done through the type and level of business being done and intended to be operated at. The integration of all the core functions can bring in full fruits, but importance of the desired information and the effective use of MIS has to be efficient.

Hence the system has to match with the managerial thinking on the overall business system. Along with this, the organisation set up has to be co-ordinated with the ERP package to be operated on. Change Masters (psychologists and line managers justifying the change) may be required to make the need acceptable by all.

Risk Involved : The risk in the system results from integration efforts of personnel organisation, the nature of business, the external business environment as well as the technology. Hence change acceptance, study of environmental factors and time horizon for the technological obsolescence are to be dealt with at the highest level of management to reduce risk involved. An analytical framework, therefore, must be prepared and comprehensive justification worked out before embarking on adoption, selection and implementation of the ERP system.

Chapter 15

Procurement and Warehousing Management

Main issues:

1. Strategic Materials Management
2. Warehousing Management
3. Waste and Scrap Disposal.
4. Stock Verification and Valuations

15.1 Strategic Materials Management

Materials are the backbone of the production system and an important area of investment. Planning, procurement and control of materials, therefore, play very vital role in cost-effective production. On the average, almost 60 to 70 percent of the capital is tied up on materials, and a substantial amount is paid to its suppliers. In order to ensure effective utilisation of the capital, otherwise tied up in materials, a strategic view of materials management is desired at the top management level. A thorough market research of the local and domestic materials of all kinds i.e., basic raw materials, the manufactured products like assemblies, sub assemblies or even the full product like motors, air conditioning equipment and that of the materials needing import, must be resorted to. The facilities for such research are available either in the form of vendors, customers or the sales force. For materials/products not manufactured in India (NMI) or not available in the local market under quality or quantity heads, internet search can be adopted. Based the market intelligence so collected, a strategic plan for material procurement and control must be prepared in the form of Strategic Material Planning. The materials function can be broadly classfied under three heads:

- Material Planning – already discussed in chapter 14.
- Procurement

- Warehousing
- Inventory management

15.2 Procurement

Procurement of materials has become very challenging task for materials managers, because the quantity, quality, cost and its timely availability at a place required has to be co-ordinated. There is a large amount of uncertainly and variability in these areas. Hence a very close integrated approach is necessary. In the present context, several factors have increased the importance of procurement. These are :

- Large impact of materials cost on profits.
- Automated manufacturing operations and hence importance of material handling.
- Growth of business necessitating B-2B (Business to Business) internet transactions.
- Increased global competition demanding rigid cost and time control.

Japanese have been gaining tremendously from material cost savings due to controlled timely procurement (JIT) and that too with quality emphasis.

Automation has reduced the labour cost to a level of 10 to 15 percent in mass production systems. Therefore, the material cost is becoming major focus for control. Automation effectiveness also requires a very rigid control of design, delivery schedule and quality of input materials. Importance of a reliable vendor, therefore, increases. Internet transactions have enabled the purchase managers to look for a large number of alternatives and hence can opt for best quality of materials at most competitive prices. They can now even enter into online auctions. The online orders and quick amendments, when needed due to dynamic situations, are possible today. Global competition is bringing more and more cost-effective substitute materials, innovative designs and better technology to bring the cost further down. Effectiveness of total supply chain management will enhance with the purchase link becoming very strong.

We have to set, therefore, an eye on our competitive priorities for on-time deliveries, with high quality and flexibility built in. Purchase plans have to be flexible to be in tune with the operations strategies.

Responsibilities of a Purchase Manager

The objectives of the purchase functions are becoming major responsibilites of a purchase manager to obtain materials.

- in right quantity
- of right quality
- at the right place
- at right time
- from the right source
- at the right price

Before embarking on the purchase activity, the purchase manager must ensure that "make or buy" decision has been deliberated upon. Outsourcing decision for purchase is an important as that for supply distribution. Linear Programming Model (Simplex Method) can be used for optimum decision.

Keeping these objectives in view, a material manager shoulders this responsibilities in the following manner :

- Ensuring the materials requirement planning in a deliberate way.
- By maintaining a data base of reliable and available vendors.
- Make deliberate and effective decision on the selection of suppliers for specific supplies.
- Carryout tough, thread-bare and effective negotiations for entering into a supply contract with suppliers.
- Monitor the provisions of the contract and act as an interface between supplier and the company.

Procurement Activities

Base on the above-stated responsibilities of a purchase manager; important procurement activities are listed below :

- *Requisition for the demand* : document issued either by planning department or by the production department.
- *Scrutiny of the requisition indent* : for correct specifications, identification, standardisation, correctness of quantity or substitution of materials.
- *Selection of the source of supply and the vendor's source of supply* : to ensure quantity, quality, reliability, timeliness and the service level including help in market information.
- *Method of Procurement* : i.e., whether it is an EOQ system or project requirement system or strictly as per the MPS, whether on contract or on purchase orders.
- *Placing of purchase order* : after due negotiations on price, freight, terms of payment, mode of payment, time of delivery i.e., lead time etc.
- *Monitoring and Co-ordination* : Delivery schedules to be monitored closely for timely arrivals of materials. Project networks can be used for the purpose.
- *Quality Inspection* : either at the vendors end (if facilities exist) or at the warehouse at the time of physical delivery of materials. Very special attention and good sampling technique to be used to ensure good quality. Some materials could be accepted even on the basis of test certificates issued by government agencies during production at the suppliers end.

The quantities can be bulk, if a good discount or better prices are available and the materials donot deterirorate in warehousing. This method can be adopted, when there is anticipation of shortage of materials in the near future due to whatever reasons such as strikes, drop in market supply or even hoarding during budget season. This bulk purchase can also save tremendously on freight charges. But financial analysis needs to be done for such transactions working out discount benefit vis-a-vis cost of interest, holding, upkeep and accounting etc.

15.3 Vendor Evaluation

Selection of source of material depends on the type of supplier, material, the buyer and the suppliers. The selection of a supplier is done through vendor evaluation and rating system. Some of the important factors considered for vendor evaluations are as follows :

- Quality of supplies
- Right price
- Delivery and lead time adherance
- Emergent supply capability
- Suitable payment terms
- Reliability
- Financial stability
- Market information capability

Methods of Vendor evaluation

For Vendor Rating, different companies use different methods, but by and large, it is done on point basis. The weightages for various factors is to be decided as per the perception of the purchase department with reference the importance for their operations. These methods could be subjective, such as three categories named as favourable, unfavourable or excellent.

By granting the weightages for various factors, total superior weightage rating can be followed for selection. We can carryout this analysis and rate the vendors based on cost by allotting weightages to various cost elements, (such as cost of the item, cost of inspection, cost of rejection or replacement etc.) and rankings compared. Another important factor is knowledge of local tax laws by the vendor and the buyers. This can make a large difference during negotiations and may result in cost savings.

The vendor selection through AHP : A very systematic and logical approach called Analytic Hierarchy Process (AHP) is an easy and scientific method. This approach is special help to the decision maker because it depends on breaking the problem into smaller and finer activities so that each activity or factor can be easily analysed. Vendor selection by this method, therefore, can give avery logical results.

The Analytic Hierarchy Process (AHP) is a very robust and flexible multi-criteria decision analysis methology. The heirarchy should be constructed so that the attributes at the same level would be of the same order of magnitude and must be easily related to other attributes of the next higher level. Attributes are prioritised at each level by pairwise comparision with the importance of decision making. The various attributes can be compared out of the list such as technical competance, financial stability, prices, quality and delivery etc.

According to the present thinking, the companies adopt the principle of **'Captive Vendor Management'** by having loyal and dedicated vendors, fewer in number and treating them as part of the family. Even then, their selection needs a very careful analysis by adopting vendor rating method. As described above, we may be alloting due weightages to various factors and measure the performance on regular periodical bases. The process is not very easy and weightages can be subjective. Therefore AHP is used as a very strong tool to help decision maker inspite of a multi-criteria based problem.

Step 1. For usage of the method, pairwise comparison matrix is formed, say, for m objectives.

$$A = \begin{bmatrix} a_{11} & a_{12} & a_{13} & \cdots & a_{1m} \\ a_{21} & a_{22} & a_{23} & \cdots & a_{2m} \\ \vdots & & & & \\ a_{m1} & a_{m2} & \cdots & \cdots & a_{mm} \end{bmatrix}$$

where aij indicates the weightage of ith factor with reference to j^{th} factor. For appropriate vendor selection, it would be necessary that $a_{ij}.aji = 1$ and $aij = \frac{1}{aji}$

Step 2. As second step, divide each entry in column j by the sum of entries in the column j. The new matrix would be

$$B = \begin{bmatrix} \frac{a_{11}}{\Sigma a_i 1} & \frac{a_{12}}{\Sigma a_i 2} & \cdots & \frac{a_{1m}}{\Sigma a_i m} \\ \frac{a_{m1}}{\Sigma a_i 1} & \frac{a_{m2}}{\Sigma a_i 2} & \cdots & \frac{a_{mm}}{\Sigma a_{mm}} \end{bmatrix}$$

Step 3. Now compute column Vector C as the average of the entries of rows of B to yield column vector C.

$$\therefore C = \begin{bmatrix} C_1 \\ C_2 \\ \vdots \\ C_m \end{bmatrix} = \begin{bmatrix} \frac{\left(\frac{a_{11}}{\Sigma a_i 1}\right)}{m} & \frac{\left(\frac{a_{12}}{\Sigma a_i 2}\right)}{m} & \frac{\left(\frac{a_{1m}}{\Sigma a_i m}\right)}{m} \\ \vdots & & \\ \frac{\left(\frac{\Sigma a_{1m1}}{\Sigma a_i 1}\right)}{m} & & \frac{\left(\frac{a_{mm}}{\Sigma a_{mm}}\right)}{m} \end{bmatrix}$$

Where C_i would represent the relative degree of importance for the ith factor of vendor selection.

Step 4. Compute A.C,

$$\therefore \quad A.C = \begin{bmatrix} a_{11} & a_{12} & \dots & a_{1m} \\ \vdots & & & \\ a_{m1} & a_{m2} & \dots & a_{mm} \end{bmatrix} \begin{bmatrix} c_1 \\ c_2 \\ \vdots \\ c_m \end{bmatrix} = \begin{bmatrix} x_1 \\ x_2 \\ \vdots \\ x_m \end{bmatrix}$$

Step 5. Compute λmax, where

$$\lambda max = \frac{1}{m} \sum_{i=1}^{m} \left(\frac{x_i}{c_i} \right)$$

Step 6. Compare the consistency index (CI)

$$CI = \frac{\lambda max - m}{(m-1)}$$

Step 7. Compare CI with the Random Index for the approximate value of m to decide whether the degree of consistency has been satisfactory or not. If CI is sufficiently small the decision maker's comparison may be consistent with the usefulness of the weightages for various factors. If $CI/RI \leq 0.1$, the degree of consistency is satisfactory. But if $CI/RI > 0.1$, then AHP may not bring out useful results, meaning thereby that weightages have not be given due consideration. The values of RI for various value of m, are to be obtained from standard tables suggested by chuang (2001) as follows:

Random Index Table

m	2	3	4	5	6	7	8	9	10
RI	0	0.58	0.90	1.12	1.24	1.32	2.41	1.45	1.51

15.4 Make or Buy Decisions

It is not necessary to purchase all the materials listed out in the requisition received from the indenting department. When the indent is received, it is scrutinised to check as to which of these parts can be manufactured in own premises resulting in low cost high-quality product. It can also save time than that would be possible to buy from the market, on which quality control is difficult to exercise.

However all the manufacturers donot attempt to produce all the parts of the main equipment. It may not be economical if such an attempt is made, because the manufactures may not be having technologically advanced production facility, which could otherwise result in quick and quality production. In addition, it may not be physically possible due to production capacity constraint or it may not be economical to raise such spare capacity to take on such jobs (may be smaller volumes) and the capital investment may be disproportimate to the volume of production, even if the know-how and space are available, (when the quality is of prime consideration). If the facility is established, simultaneously a provision has to be made to sell spare manufactured parts/components (more than the own consumption requirement). The establishment of such a critical production capacity is called vertical integration. In case a definite capacity is spared for such manufacture, it is called "horizontal integration".

On the other hand, the suppliers or smaller manufacturers may be specialising in certain specific type of production with state-of-art production facilities and knowhow. It is then worthwhile to consider the buying option from these suppliers. Such a decision is called "outsourcing". In this case, a low cost high-quality procurement is possible from these 'outsources'. The detailed analysis on cost, quality and time has to indicate that it is advantageous to buy the parts/components from an outside source. Outsourcing vs vertical integration can be a delibrate strategic decision. Once it is decided to go for outsourcing, the other valid questions arising for careful consideration are:

- What all to buy ?
- How much to buy ?
- How to buy ?
- When to buy ?
- Where to buy from ?
- What price to buy at ?

For all these questions, a detailed cost-benefit analysis must be carried out to obtain a real benefit out of the purchases. Quantitative techniques like Decision Tree or Breakeven analysis are available. To make it worthwhile decision, forecasting techniques discussion in the book else where can be deployed with trend analysis and regression models. For answer to the first question as to what all to buy, a list can be prepared such as parts/components, assemblies and assemblies maintenance, production capacity, infrastructural capacity manpower availability or even after sales service.

15.5 Strategic Sourcing

As discussed in the preceding paragraphs, the procurement function has gone much beyond the conventional planning and placing orders. Due to high-technology involvement, the thrust on materials management has increased. The companies are adopting a concept called strategic sourcing. **Strategic sourcing** is *"a disciplined, systematic approach for reducing the total procurement costs of externally purchased materials, products and services while maintaining or improving the levels of quality, service and technology"*. Hence by following this sourcing method, companies have been able to achieve tremendous savings through application of techno-commercial, cost-effective measures, thereby making full use of their vendor's knowledge and capabilities. Today, the concept has changed to **Total Cost Ownership (TCO)**. For this purpose the professional and technical knowledge of the procurement team (which includes the vendor as an integral and effective member of the team) is made use of along with the integration of knowledge with cross functional management. Therefore it is a greater value addition because of the team work with team members from users, research and development, production, quality control, supply chain and finance departments. Through this process of deep analysis and systematic decision making process, following advantage acrue to the organisation:

- Reduced consumption and cost of materials on life-cycle costing basis
- Quality of product consistant
- Periodicity and continuity of supply of mateirals ensured
- Material substitution as per latest trend in the market can be affected along with reverse auction.

15.6 Dynamic Purchasing

For regular streamlined production, the MPS shows smoothened flow and for such production line, the material purchase can be done in batches depending upon the economic viability. The inventory can be planned to be restricted at minimum level (just enough to cater for lead time uncertainty) in order to reduce the holding cost. Such a purchasing strategy can be adopted only if either the purchase is multisourced for a single product or the company has reliable captive vendors identified. The local vendor will be a great help in provision of small batches and at lower transportation cost. Purchases can be done under Rate Contract system and then procurement is done on as required basis. This is called Dynamic Purchasing. Inspection of supplied material can be done at the vendors end only. The paper transactions are reduced drastically. If EDI or Internet ordering is resorted to, it becomes even simpler. The system is effective only in case of a devoted captive vendor or when there is more than one vendor, but reliable, and located near the purchaser.

15.7 Ethical Procurement

This is an ever-present problem in any purchase department. The selling party is all out to get order released in their names and they go to any extent to achieve this aim. Some of the method tried out are :

- Free lunches
- Free liquor
- Free evening-outs
- Free weekends at attractive places
- Free tickets for games
- Hard cash offerings

It is difficult to judge what is totally unethical from the point of view of the purchaser. Purchaser has wide powers to even make or mar the business of some suppliers. Hence it is very difficult to lay any real restrictions on such an issue.

To circumvent such situation, in the best interest of the company, some organisations donot allow any system of gifts and instead, an annual incentive is offered by the company. But more than this, an open discussion on ethical behaviour and good compensation to employees may be tried out, just to keep the channel of communication open and to develop a healthy working climate in the organisation. It is also worthwhile and very effective system to keep a strict vigil on purchases in terms of cost comparisons, the awards of purchase orders/contract to some specific suppliers i.e., keep the internal audit in place to ensure healthy path. Now with the internet operations and global buying, it is easy to keep internal audits effective.

15.8 Import Substitution

Imports can be affected for production plants, spare parts, components, important raw materials or special materials. Some products, not available in our country or available else where at cheaper rates can be imported such as crude petroleum from Middle east. But wherever possible, the alternatives for foreign goods must be searched so as to avoid dependence on other countries. The present state of liberalisation has made it easier to purchase such items from local sources, since many multinational companies are setting up joint ventures with Indian companies. For import substitution, following strategies are worth adopting:

- Source development under dedicated corporate policy
- Standardisation of designs and equipment
- Reverse engineering

Indigenous sources can be developed. It may be costlier initially, but in the long run, it will be quite helpful. Collaborations for obtaining drawings or technologies can be tried out. Similarly standardisation helps in mass production and by this process, local indigenous materials can be used. In case of standardisation, multi-sourcing can be helpful.

In some cases, reverse engineering can be tried out using following steps :

- Identify the item for the substitution
- Formulate multi disciplinary groups for identifying specification and functional requirements
- Redesign along with cost details and establish feasibility of local availability
- Produce the item locally and cost effectively.

15.9 Imports Procedure

Material/goods can be imported either directly or indirectly. For direct imports, the purchaser places an indent upon the manufacturer producing or supplying the required item or upon the dealer dealing with such an item. Necessary scanning on the websites can be very helpful in locating the right source. When the information available is not adequate, then indirect purchasing/ import can be resorted to. A locally known and reliable dealer can be trusted for obtaining such an import. The responsibility of placing order on the foreign supplier, and its shipping for the customer will lie on that dealer. However, the import procedure is listed below to make it easier to get the item imported:

• ***Obtaining the import licence :*** It is required depending on the restrictions for import in use at that time. If the item can be purchased under Open General Licence (OGL), then a formal licence is not required. Otherwise the appropriate licencing authority is to be approached. The items on the negative list of imports would need import licence to be obtained.

Placing an Indent : for the items/goods to be procured, the orders are placed either on the manufacturer or supplier in the foreign country or with the import agent. The indent should be clearly specifying the quantity, quality, method of payment, date of delivery, method of packing and marking, the illustrations regarding shipping and insurance along with complete specifications of the item.

The indent can either be a closed indent or an open indent. In closed indent, the importer clearly mentions the price at which or below which the goods are to be purchased for him or supplied to him. In case of open indent, the price is left to the agent to what price he pays for the goods purchased for the importer.

After placement of the indent, the importer will wait for the letter of advice from the agent, indicating the information about shipment and the method of procuring the import documents.

Procurement of Documents and Payment : Having received the advice letter from the agent, the importer will try to obtain the import documents like bill of lading and the shipping bill etc., so that the delivery can be taken on the arrival at the godowns of the customs/port.

The importer will make the payment and procure the documents from the agent. If the documents are against payment, cash payment is to be made, whereas if the documents are through the bank, the letter of credit (L/C) is to be operated to get the documents released from the bank.

Appointment of the Clearing Agent : Once the documents have been obtained, the importer has to get the delivery of the goods. For legal formalities of obtaining goods from port/customs, a clearing agent is usually appointed to save time on legal formalities. These experts can deal with the legal system in a concise and quicker manner for which they charge certain renumeration. Documents are handed over to the clearing agent, who will get the delivery of goods and despatch them to the importers destination. The clearing agent will present the Bill of lading to the shipping company and obtain endorsement in his favour. Freight, in case to be paid, will be paid by the clearing agent with necessary endorsement on the Bill of lading or otherwise, he will get a letter to the effect.

The clearing agent, then, will proceed to pay the custom duty, so as to obtain delivery of goods as soon as these arrive at the port. The Bill of Entry is filled in triplicate with full description of goods. Black forms are used for free goods, blue for the goods be sold within the country and violet for goods meant for re-export. He also pays the Dock dues by submitting two copies of the Application to Import, duly filled in to the landing and shipping Dues office. One copy of this document received back by him, along with three copies of the Bill of Entry, is submitted to the customs office. If no custom duty is to be levied, the goods are released. But in case any duty is to be paid, the agent has to pay to obtain delivery of goods. He then despatches the goods with advice to the importer.

Receipt of goods at Importers End : Against the documents of the clearing agent (despatch advice), the importer can take the delivery of goods from railway/road transport and have them shifted to his godown. The import procedure, thus, gets completed.

15.10 Warehousing Management

Warehousing Management is the function of receipt, storage and issue of materials. This must be done with utmost efficiency so that the costs incurred are kept at the minimum level. Storage is not desirable due to large blockage of money and cost incurred to keep the warehouse in good order. 'Inventory is a necessary evil'. Thus it must be resorted to only when must. When warehousing is essential, it must be managed very well so as to optimise the storage costs at all times i.e., receive stores when really due, have them inspected, keep them in good places in orderly manner and maintain proper accounting and its upkeep, so that loss of value is not increased due to deterioration while in stores. Overstocking and understocking, both are undesirable. Faulty accounting can result in poor planning or pilferage.

Warehousing functions

In warehousing, following activities are involved:

- Planning of the warehouse i.e., space required, layout and material handling equipment
- Planning the strategic and tactical of requirements for storage
- Planning for accounting and issue priorities
- Followup and receipt of materials
- Incoming quality inspections
- Safety planning for stocks and warehouse including fire, theft and obsolescence.
- Planning for maintenance and preservation of stored materials.
- Periodic stock verification and accounting
- Disposal of obsolete and non-usable stocks
- Planning for inventory reductions
- Co-ordination with concerned departments
- Good house keeping.
- Dispatching/delivery functions.

Organisation of Warehouse

Since there are large variety of materials stored in the warehouse, a good organisation can only help in efficient receipt, storage and retrieval of materials. The warehouses should be organised for all types of stocks such as :

- Raw materials stores (catagory wise)
- Components and sub-assemblies
- Finished goods
- Maintenance consumables and stores for spare parts

- Property stores such as furnitures, fittings, machinery
- Stationery stores
- Tools stores
- Chemical and explosive stores
- Scrap stores
- General stores such as uniforms, clothing etc.

Hence it is to be seen that a careful layout with due safety provisions built in for specific materials are worked out. Centralised structure or decentralised stores can be decided by the organisation with type of operations in view.

Location of Warehouses

Warehouse establishment is a strategic decision. If we consider only the present day requirement for selection of site and design the layout of the warehouse accordingly, it will become inadequate in no time due to dynamics of markets and other prevalent influencing factors. The environmental factors discussed in case of location of a factory, hold good here also. The changes such as technology, production methods, environmental factors, market conditions, governmental policies and even socialogical, economic and political developments are bound to influence the working. Future expansion for the capacity of the warehouse also needs to be considered, while making strategic decision on its location and size. Some of the important factors influencing the site are the potential market, volume and type of transport based on quality of roads. The accessibility to loading sidings are to be taken into consideration. An existing old building to be used as warehouse can save money, but it has the limitations of space and layout may be restricted to suit the requirement. But if there is a new building to be considered, then all the above mentioned factors should form the basis of design. Space requirement based on forecast and about 50% future expansion must be catered for. Infrastructal facilities such as lighting, aircondition, power, air supply etc. can be planned effectively. Special activities like spaces for vendors, inspectors, government officials, people from other industries etc are also to be planned for in the layout. For location of the warehouse, the 'Centre of Gravity Method' described under facilities location can be adopted. Transportation model is yet another technique for such analysis.

Layout of the Warehouse

The layout inside a ware-house has to have the relevance to the flow of materials, the incoming as well as outgoing. The volume and the weight are major considertions for layout planning. For planning the layout, the following information will be useful:

- Floor area and the volume available
- Floor design i.e., load capacity.
- Relative location with respect to other departments
- Type of construction i.e., beams, pillars etc.

- Quantity, size and weight of products
- Frequency and lot size
- Issue schedules
- Number of stores/departments to be planned and area of each
- Mode of transport
- Number of warehousing staff (to plan facilities for them)
- Special requirements like forced ventilation, air condition etc.
- Special material handling requirement such as conveyor belts or overhead cranes etc.

Based on the flow pattern, the layout can be developed as discussed under Microlayout System (Chapter 7) from flow point of view, (for smooth material flow and operations). There can be following flow patterns generally adopted:

Straight line

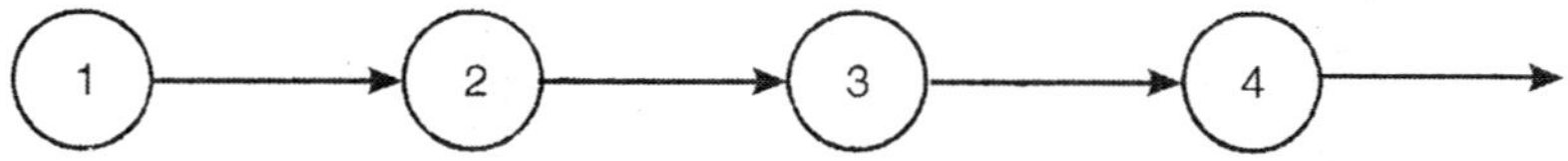

Zig Zag flow

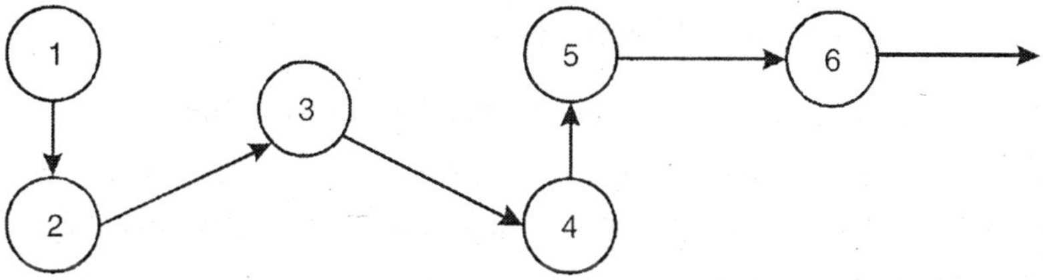

L-Shaped or U-Shaped flow

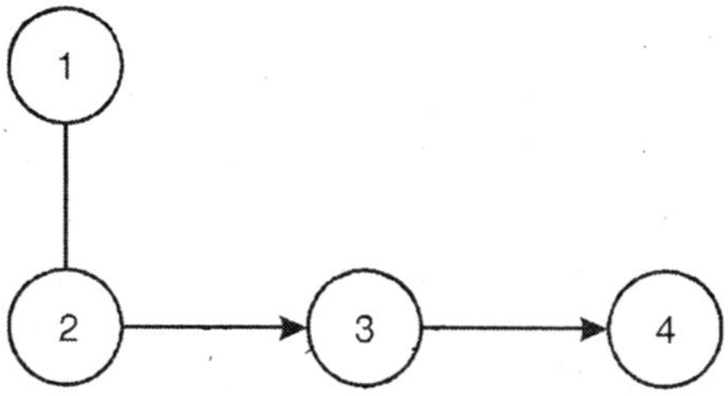

or

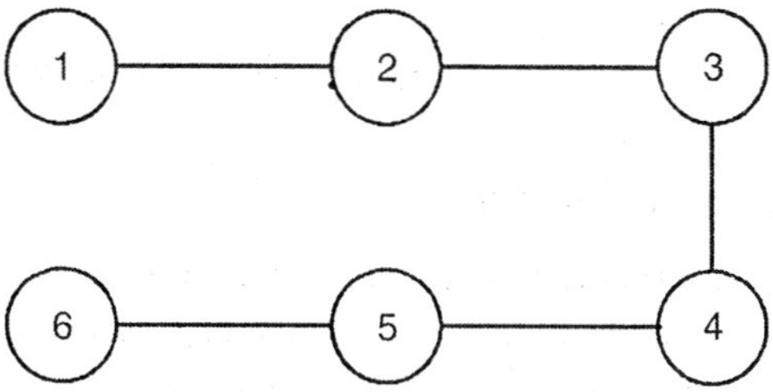

Circular flow

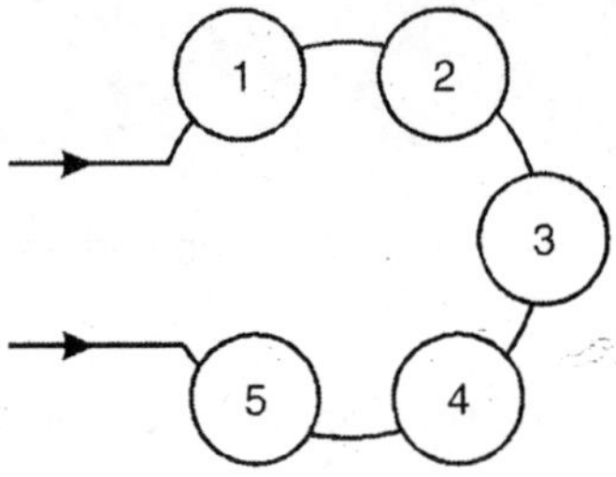

In addition to the material flow pattern, the stacking pattern of each store has to be planned specific to the requirement.

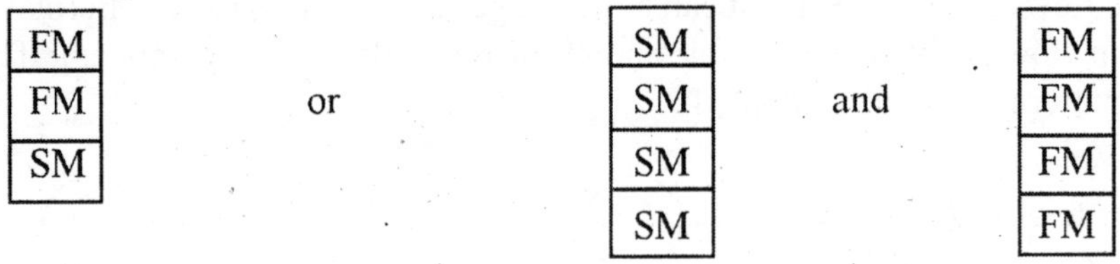

FM = Fast Moving items

SM = Slow Moving items

Increase in the speed of issue

Fig. 15.1 Flow pattern

While organising the stores layout, ABC analysis can come handy, as special care to be taken for A class stores, B needs more thought and planning whereas C class items can be planned on bin-system.

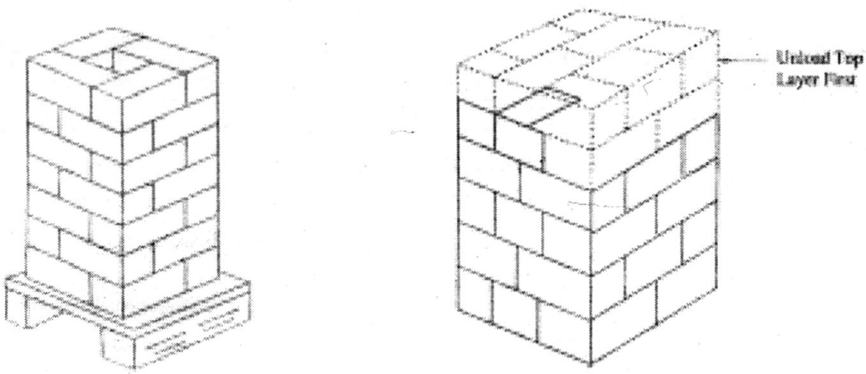

Fig. 15.2 Correct Stacking and Unloading

Identification Pattern

For correct positioning and retrieval of materials, the items have to have identification code. It could be colour code, alpha-numerical code or row-column code etc. There is nothing like a standard code. Hence the organisation has to develop its own codification for identifying their products in the warehouse. It will help in computerisation of the inventory and make the receipt, issues and accounting very easy. For example, all steel item can be coded as F_{23} etc., where as all chemical items can be code as C_{13} as so on.

We can use numerical code for identification of an item under the given category, say C_{13123} may mean, it is a chemical item, with stack place as 1st and 3rd column and the product is sulphuric acid identified as 23 etc.

The identification code helps in issues also so that the flow and transportation can be planned for the place identified by the code. Issues can be on First In First Out (FIFO) or Last In First Out (LIFO) basis.

Isles and corridors should be planned as per material handling equipment capability. Use of computers for layout planning should be used for systematic development of the space.

Automation and optimisation of Warehouses

In today's environment, it is good to have an automated warehouse, especially where there are large number of different products and the movement of materials is fast. In these automated warehouses, the operators are generally used only for computer setting and the pallets and materials move either through automated conveyors, cranes or AGVs (Automated Guided Vehicles). The placement, storage and the retrieval is controlled through programmable logic controllers. These systems are generally installed for cold storage warehouses, where specific temperature levels are maintained. The automated parking space for bicycles in Japan and automated car-parking in Delhi are good example of this catagory. though today it is very commonly used facility across the globle. For their successful operation, the space should be properly slotted, so that the slotting address can be easily picked from pullet rack or the product carton. Global retailing trends have neccessitated the development of tall, large, heavy duty industrial racks, duly integrated in the supply chain design. Implementation of Vendor-Managed Inventory (VMI) concept has led to the development of carefully crafted warehouse designs. Large exporters and manufactures use distribution warehouses fully automated.

15.11 Material Handling Equipment

Material handling equipment is to facilitate movement of materials from incoming trucks to the stores and then from stores to the production/use area. It is also required for effective movement of finished products to the issue area for loading into the distribution transport. In summary, these equipment increase mobility and speed, safety and efficiency adding to the value of material handling.

Few important factors for designing the Material handling system are listed below:

- Identification of the material
- Method of packaging
- Capacity of the equipment
- Size and weight of the load/container

- Nature of production process
- Building construction and layout
- Pathways, corridors-length and turns/radii

Types of Material Handling Systems

There are various types of material handling equipment in use (depending on space and load requirement)

Static type : Such as platforms, pellets, Rollers and Pipeline etc.

Fixed type :

- Horizontal movement – Such as chutes, belt conveyor, Roller conveyor, wheel and trolley conveyors etc.
- Vertical movement – such as lifts and elevators.
- Overhead Movement – such as Monorail, chain conveyor, overhead cranes, hoists or gantry cranes etc.

• *Mobile type :* Such as hand trolleys, pallet trucks, fork lift trucks or large industrial vehicles including specialised trucks say Milk, icecream carriers etc.

• *Automated Guided Vehicle Systems (AGVs) :* There are large innovations in the system of material handling management to make it very cost-effective such as move by containers, move of two trailors with one prime mover etc.

The material handling systems are required to cater for type of service expected by the customers. Three may be a large consignment of similar components/materials coming in or going out and hence a large container system can be used. But there is a different requirement for a piece-pick (or broken case pick) or split-pick system, where the products are picked and handled as individual units and placed in a container, possibly finding space for different individual units along. The catalogue companies predominantly use this system of pallet or case quantities or even one or two pieces of one or more items. In such cases, the Warehouse Management System (WMS), a database driven computer programme comes handy for material direction and tracking.

15.12 Waste and Scrap Disposal

Industrial waste is the resource rendered unusable. These resources can be anything from men, materials, machines, money or time. If resources are not utilised fully, it is a waste of energy. The wastes can be of following types:

- Avoidable and non-avoidable wastes may be due to poor planning or forced actions. Bad design creating operation waste or poor planning resulting in wastage of time.
- Types of resources such as manhours, machine hours or material wastages and idling of production capacity.

- Due to causes of waste – such as planning and design waste (product length 6 ft out of 8 ft rod), purchasing waste, conversion waste, usage waste or transportation waste etc.
- Output wastes – Such as unusable or Re-usable materials.

These wastages are to be avoided by proper planning and effective utilisation. Resources are generally scarce and waste add to the cost. The waste can be in the form of loss of production capacity, loss of sales, loss of revenue, loss of labour output, loss of opportunity cost or loss of goodwill etc.

Out of the wastes listed out above, the storage wastes and conversion wastes are of larger proportions, hence to be taken special care of. While storage wastes are due to deterioration in storage, pilferage, obsolescene or poor handling, these have to be controlled by keeping vigil on material lying in the stocks. If purchase man has committed a mistake of buying 100Nos. of 63 Amp Switches (a requirement of possibly 50 to 60 years) it is a total waste, but then, if it is allowed to lie in the stock without utilisation for a long time, it will obviously go bad, get rusted out. Hence vigilant warehousing manager must plan to dispose it off. Similarly a stock of 35 pumps bought but not used for whatever reasons must be used within a reasonable period, otherwise rusting and greese drying out will make them unuseable. If the stocks are small, it is easy to get pilferred. An item can become totally obsolecent and can be sold as scrap only, wasting a large amount of money. In order to keep inventory at a useful level, periodic check and review must be done and till these are utilised, these stocks are to be preserved and maintained well. Stock maintenance is very costly process, and hence long storages should be avoided.

In the same way, conversion wastes occuring due to inferior design, inefficient process and operations, poor performance of the workers resultings in high incidence of defectives, poor quality incoming materials or lack of managerial supervisions can be controlled by taking appropriate action against these reasons. The obvious solutions are proper technology selection, improved designs, carefully decided method of production, efficient plan maintenance, effective training of workers and defect analysis with quality control systems, proper supervision and close watch on incoming and wasted materials.

Along with these remedies, a tight control on manpower utilisation with proper output norms enforced (fixation of standard time), effective resource scheduling, proper design and use of jigs and fixtures etc must be exercised. Layout of the stores and design of isles and corridors can help saving wastage of time.

Salvage operations : Salvage means 'act of savings'. Since we have discussed wastes and waste control, we now restrict our discussion on waste control of materials only. This salvaging can be done in the form of reuse of the waste material. The reuse can be made effective either with rework or without rework. The reuse after rework means that by consuming manpower and material, the defective product, can be brought to the useable shape. The time and money involved in rework has now been useful. It is for consideration whether spending time and money on rework is worth the effort. Similarly reuse without rework means that an alternate use can be found and it saves additional rework efforts, such as used bottles, cans or package materials can be reused to advantage. Some defectives can be sold as 'Seconds' at least without incurring rework cost.

Scrap Disposal : A material can be termed as scrap when it is a wastage material out of production or surplus material lying which has no further use and therefore has to be disposed off. These scrap materials are generated due to following reasons :

- Poor purchase practice/not updated on requirements/not paying attention to usage.
- Technological oblescence/substitution advance material available.
- Change in the product design/mix.
- Poor sense of responsibility by purchase department, (non-involvement)

When scraps and surpluses are to be disposed off, the company must take preventive action by identifying the reason for scrap (it is loss) and ensuring its disposal and non-occurant procurement. It is a regular exercise as scrap keeps generating. If it is large, it needs investigation, if low, can be ignored and just disposed off (but recurrance should be controlled). Then we should identify the source and method of disposal. It may be done through tenders, auctions or simply by negotiations or destruction. If the company can recover some cost of it, it will be better and should be tried out. But there may be instances where scrap is offered free even offering money for its removal. The reason would be the utility value of the scrap.

The important issue to be paid attention in scrap disposal is its nuisance value for the society. There may be legal environmental issues involved, which must be taken care of. Throwing waste chemicals into waterways without any improvement treatment may cause loss of crop, fish or even death for people and will invite legal penalties. Treatment of affluents to bring them down to permitted BOD, will incur cost but is necessary in the larger interest of the society.

15.13 Stock Verification and Valuations

Inventory management is being discussed in the next chapter. A strategic view must be taken to buy, keep and control the materials with utmost care. Keeping the inventory results in high cost and in case the inventories are not accounted for meticulously, there is a strong chance that pilfrage, deterioration or obslescence can occur. This neccessitates the process of regular stock verification and valuation to be effective. This process is called stocktaking. The valuation helps in controlling the cost of marine insurance. In order to reduce the obstruction of material flow, generally, stock taking is done either during holidays or at the end of the month or else as per the company policy laid down by management. Stock verification and valuation, though involves extra cost, effort and time, but it is worth the effort to control inventory.

The stock verification can be adopted either on periodic cycle basis or on the residual inventory quantity basis. It can also be done through ERP, resulting in automatic on line valuation. In case of large inventory, acceptance sampling can be adopted.

Valuation : Though different methods are used by different companies for stock valuation, various options are given below:

- Bought out price on the date of purchase
- Average price for continuous replenishment

- Price at the latest stock purchase
- Based on cost of production if locally produced
- Based on the replacement cost

Since the insurance cost is paid based an inventory held in stock, generally on monthly basis, the valuation helps in saving this cost, if inventory control is done intelligently. This information of stock value is also entered as assets value in the book of accounts.

—•—

Chapter 16

Inventory Management

Main issues:

1. **Reasons for Inventory**
2. **Inventory Management**
3. **Inventory Models**
4. **Safety stock and Inventory control methods**
5. **Zero Inventory (ZIN)**

16.1 Introduction

Inventory may be defined as a stock of idle tangible resources of any kind having an economic value. The inventories can be in the form of raw material, semi-finished goods or finished products not delivered to the customer. These could even be the human resources idling or the financial resources such as working capital. The people or stocks in transit, till delivered at the place of use, are also inventories. For organisations, the inventories may be as much as 30 to 70% of their total assets. The lesser the inventories, the better the business due to the utilisation of released capital, otherwise tied up capital in the form of inventories.

Since inventory consumes a substantial portion of the working capital, it is not desirable to have a huge inventory. The inventories also require holding, maintenance, preservation and accounting functions. These can be lost due to thefts, spoilage, leakage or obsolescence. The cost of holding inventory may be very high depanding on the type of inventory and its maintenance requirements. Hence it is imperative to keep a very tight control over inventory. It is called "a Necessary Evil", a must to cater for uncertainty of supplies, when most needed, but to be kept at optimum level just to keep business going.

Controlling is a process by which the change in the system is modified to maintain it in healthy state at an optimum performance level. So is the case for inventory. The inventory control is absolutely essential to release working capital for something more useful. Various types of inventory in industry are as follows:

Factory	:	Raw materials, parts and components, semi-finished and finished goods.
Bank	:	Cash reserve tellers
Hospitals	:	Number of beds, specialised personnel and stock of drugs.
Airlines	:	Aircraft seat miles per route, parts for aircraft maintenance and repairs, stewards and other specialist persons for service, maintenance, testing and repairs etc.

16.2 Catagories of Inventory

Inventories are maintained for various purposes. Since the inventory consumes and blocks a substanted portion of the working capital, it is understandably imperative for all managers to understand the types and purposes of the inventory. Also, there has to be a system of knowing the existence of inventory, otherwise it may be lost sight of and easily forgotten, when required for taking a crucial decision. The inventories for different purposes are classified into various catagories, all of these may or may not exist at any one time. The major classifications are:

Movement or Process Inventory : These exist because their transportation takes time in reaching the point of consumption. These could be in the form of raw materials or finished goods in transit from the source to the destimation of utilisation.

Buffer Inventory : It is kept in the form of stocks to cater for the uncertainty of demand or supply. Future demands are normally forecasted, but these forecasts may not depict a changed situation or uncertain environment, resulting in sudden upsurge or decline in the demand without notice. Shortage costs are generally very high due to non-fulfilment of demand resulting in loss of good-will and credibility, in addition to loss of business. Buffer stocks act as cushion or safety against uncertain lead time, delays due to unforeseen natural calamities or quality problems in the supplied stocks.

Seasonal Invetories : Seasonal inventories are ketp to meet the higher than normal demand during a particular period of the year. Instead of increasing the production level (may not be possible always or may be quite capital intensive to provision additional facilities – inhouse or outsourced), it may be economical to manufacture some products during the lean or off season period, when demands are low. The production facilities, during low demand period for regular product, may be gainfully deployed for such production. It is also called 'Anticipation Inventory' such as airconditions and coolers for summers and heaters and geysers for the winter. Umbrellas for the monsson also from the same category.

Decoupling Inventory : These inventories are necessary to reduce the dependence of various steps of production over the previous operation. These may be raw materials or work in process (WIP) inventory, when the production process or production facility may not match with the system flow due to poor conditions of the machines, their breakdowns or even the working efficiency differentials of the workers on production lines. Some inventory is required for after-sales service, when demands donot follow a pattern.

16.3 Reasons for Carrying Inventory

Some of the important reasons for carrying inventory emerge out of environmental conditions and can be summerised as under :

- Variation in production
- Variable customer schedule such as quick customer response to demand in competitive service region.
- Uncertain vendor reliability in terms of lead time and quality of supply.
- Financial gains anticipated when prices are uncertain or fluctuate or when quantity discounts are attractive enough economically.
- Overhead of the procurement may be spread over larger quantity. Similarly, more units produced per run also balances the set up cost over larger number of units.
- Inventory can allow flexibility in scheduling and staffing, thus decoupling the production for any stoppages. WIP inventory can help in system retrieval process.
- Inventories can help uniform production over the entire year, even if there is demand fluctuation.

16.4 Costs Associated with Inventory

Various costs associated with inventory are as following :

Ordering Cost : Inventory, when necessary, requires to be created and in order to achieve this, the organisational set up (materials department) has to go through certain administrative functions while ordering the materials for procurement. The documentation, cost of ordering organisation, the communication costs like telephones, fax, postages or any other activity have to be considered. In addition, the tranportation cost, the inspection costs either at the vendors end or at the company stores, the cost or receiving and then cost of processing the payment are all part of this cost.

Purchase Cost : The cost of puchasing, after due negotiations, per unit item is called the purchase cost. Purchase cost can be controlled through tough negotiation in the form of discounts or price breaks secured during large scale ordering.

Carrying or Holding Cost : It is the cost incurred to keep the inventory in stocks and hence the quantity of items kept in the stock only is to be considered for working out the holding cost. Hence lesser the quantity held in stock, lesser is the holding cost. This cost includes the rental of the stores, the marine insurance, maintenance, depreciation, security and accounting of the stocks. It also includes the taxes paid and interest of the money tied up in inventories.

Shortage Cost : It is the cost incurred for not holding stocks when needed. It is the penalty of run out of stock, thereby disturbing the production/utilisation schedule as well as for not being in a position to supply products, when in demand. Hence this cost can be very high due to loss of goodwill and credibility of the organisation in addition to the loss of present and future business. This cost is difficult to quantify and not very apparent. Its effects are felt over a long period.

Buffer stock cost : It is the cost of keeping certain deliberate level of inventory to offset the shortage cost and is necessary to save good-will, credibility and the effect of turnaway customers. The stock so kept are also known as safety stocks, which involve not only cost of procurement/ordering, but also its cost of perpetual holding. Some critical items also can be kept as per strategic decision, when their availability at the time of need may be in doubt.

Salvage Cost : When demand for an item ceases to exist or the item may be deteriorating while in stock for a long time or it becoming obsolete, it is better to dispose off such an item. Such items are either sold on discount or even as scrap, so as to save at least the holding cost. The loss so incurred is called the salvage cost.

Hence it is important to dispationately decide as to when to buy and how much to buy. Inventory more than that absolutely necessary is a burden on business and hence should be avoided or controlled.

16.5 Important Terms of Inventory System

Demand : It is the customers requirement in terms of its size (i.e., quantity of items), the rate (how fast the product requirement arises) and the pattern (whether continuous or intermittent, increasing or decreasing and at what rate). Thus deterministic or probabilistic nature of the demands is to be collated and taken action on.

Order Cycle : It is the periodicity of two consecutive orders placed to meet the demand. The pattern of such demands is to be established to ensure timely procurement of materials for timely production. In some cases like large scale projects, environment or decision factors may take toll of the pattern and order cycle may be difficult to be ascertained. Such items are procured as and when required.

Time Horizon : It is the period over which the inveatory level is to be controlled. It can be finite or infinite depending on the nature of demand.

Lead Time : It is the period elapsed between the time of ordering to the time of actual receipt of materials at the company stores/place of requirement. The best situations could be just-in-Time (JIT) i.e., a case of zero lead time to avoid ordering and carrying costs. Otherwise a deterministic lead time is a good help for planning and cost effective execution.

Safety or Buffer Stock : It is the level of inventory deliberately procured and stocked when either the lead time is uncertain or the demand is critical or uncertain.

Re-order Quantity : It is the quantity of items ordered at a time to replenish the necessary inventory, either exhausted or as a result of a comprehensive inventory replacement policy. Generally it is Economic order Quantity (EOQ), which should be procured when required.

Re-order Level : It is the quantity of stock at which the fresh procurement action is taken so that the items are received just at a time required. The lead time is so adjusted that the remaining stock is just enough for consumption (reaching zero inventory level) during the lead time.

16.6 Inventory Replenishment Methods.

Inventory replenishment can be ordered through two methods:

(a) P-system (Period based procurement)

(b) Q-system (Quantity based procurement)

P-System : It is the system of inventory repleshment based on periodic reviews and placement of orders on a uniform period interval. This is applicable when demands are fairly constant, continuous and deterministic.

Q-System : It is placement of procurement orders based on quantity to cater for the demand for certain period of time. The period of procurement may be varied based on the consumption pattern, but the quantity of stock is generally kept as Economic Order Quantity (EOQ).

Inventory Replenishment Models

Various procurement models are discussed below under varied situations. These are quantitative methods of ordering materials in the cost effective manner. The models can be classified under two catagories :

(i) Deterministic Models

(ii) Stochastic Models

Deterministic Models : are mathematical relationship of variables when these variables are known with certainty.

Stochastic Models : are the models when the value or their variations are uncertain or probabilistic in nature.

However the steps followed in inventory modelling are as under :

- List out the characteristics and the assumptions for a given situation.
- Work out the annual cost equation for the inventory requirement.
- Transform or convert the annual cost system into an appropriate mathematical model, taking care of the variables and their inter-relationships along with the constraints of the system.
- Objective functions to be defined for optimisation of cost through how much to order and when to order.

Model I: EOQ with Uniform Demand

Assumptions :

- Annual demand, carrying cost and the ordering cost can be estimated.
- Average inventory level is treated as half the quantity of ordering, due to uniform demand pattern.
- No safety stocks are required to be consumed. The materials are planned to be received just as the previous inventory is exhausted.
- Stock-outs and customer's changing requirements are not considered important and ordered stocks are received all at once.
- Quantity discounts are not available.

For such a model, the variables considered are as follows

D = annual demand (deterministic and uniform during the year)

Q = The decision variable in terms of the quantity to be procured

Co = Unit ordering cost

Ch = Unit holding cost

Hence Average Inventory $= \frac{Q+0}{2} = \frac{Q}{2}$

Cost functions :

(i) ordering Cost $= \frac{D}{Q} Co$

(ii) Holding Cost $= \frac{Q}{2} Ch$

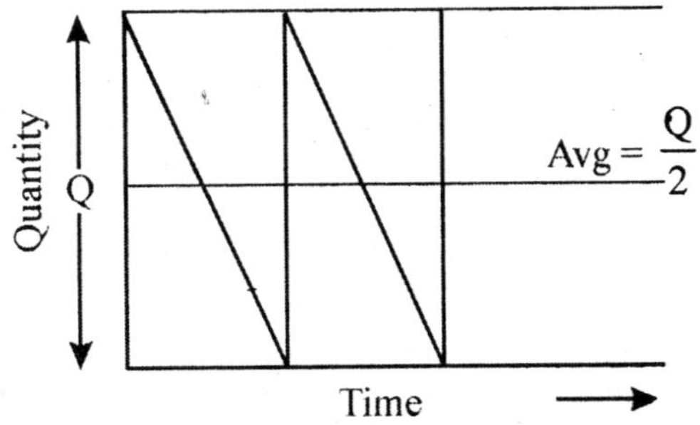

Fig. 16.1 Uniform Demand Time

$$\text{Total Inventory cost } (C) = \frac{D}{Q} . Co + \frac{Q}{2} Ch$$

Hence $$\frac{dC}{dQ} = \frac{-DC_0}{Q^2} + \frac{Ch}{2}$$

When lead time is constant, the cost derivative will be zero

$$\frac{D}{Q^2} Co = \frac{Ch}{2}$$

$$\therefore Q = \sqrt{\frac{2D\,Co}{Ch}}$$

This is called **Wilson's Lot Size Formula.**

Problem 16.1

X Y Z company buys in lots of 500 boxes which is a 3 month supply. The cost per box is Rs. 125 and the ordering cost is Rs. 150. The inventory cost is estimated at 20% of unit value.

(*i*) What is the total annual cost of the existing inventory policy?

(*ii*) How much money could be saved by employing the economic order quantity?

[*C.A. (Final), Nov., 1983*]

Solution :

$$\text{Ordering Cost (Co)} = \text{Rs. } 150$$

$$\text{Quantity of one order} = 500$$

$$\text{Annual demand} = 500 \times \frac{12}{3} = 2{,}000$$

$$\text{Carrying Cost} = \text{Rs. } 125 \times 20\% = \text{Rs. } 25$$

(*i*) Total annual Cost of existing inventory

$$= \frac{D}{Q} . Co + \frac{Q}{2} . Ch$$

$$= \frac{2{,}000}{500} \times 150 + \frac{500}{2} \times 25 = \text{Rs. } 6{,}850$$

(*ii*) Economic order quantity $= \sqrt{\frac{2D\,Co}{Ch}}$

or. $$Q\,(EOQ) = \sqrt{\frac{2 \times 2{,}000 \times 150}{25}} = 155$$

$$\text{Minimal Annual Cost} = \sqrt{2D\,Co\,Ch.} = \sqrt{2 \times 2{,}000 \times 150 \times 25} = 3{,}873$$

$$\text{Hence saving} = \text{Rs. } 6{,}850 - 3{,}873 = \text{Rs. } 2{,}977.$$

Model-II : EOQ with variable Demand

As different from the above model, the assumptions of demand undergoes a change i.e., instead of being uniform, the demand is variable and hence a time period for the demand is to be specified.

Let T = Time period for demand consideration with remaining assumptions as in Model I.

$$\text{Ordering Cost} = \frac{D}{Q}\,Co$$

$$\text{Carrying Cost} = \frac{Q}{2} . Ch. T.$$

$$\text{Total Cost} = \frac{D}{Q}\,Co + \frac{Q}{2}\,Ch. T$$

By the same method as above

$$Q = \sqrt{\frac{2D\,Co}{T.Ch.}}$$

and Total optimum Inventory

$$= \frac{D\,Co}{\sqrt{2\frac{D\,Co}{Ch.}}} + \frac{1}{2}\,TCh\sqrt{2\frac{D\,Co}{Ch.T}}$$

$$= \sqrt{\frac{2\,D\,CoCh}{T}}$$

Model III : EOQ with shortage permitted

Change in assumption from Model I.

"The cost of shortage is proportional to the shortage of units."

In this case, the total inventory Q = Qo + s

Where Qo = inventory with no shortage

s = demand during shortage.

Cs = Unit Shortage Cost.

Line ABC Shows the Consumption pattern

Here Total Cost = Co + Ch + Cs

Ordering Cost $= \frac{D}{Q} . Co$

Carrying Cost $= \frac{Qo}{2} . \frac{Qo}{Q} . t. Ch$

Shortage Cost $= \frac{s}{2} . t_1 C_s$

$= \frac{s^2}{2Q} . t. C_s$

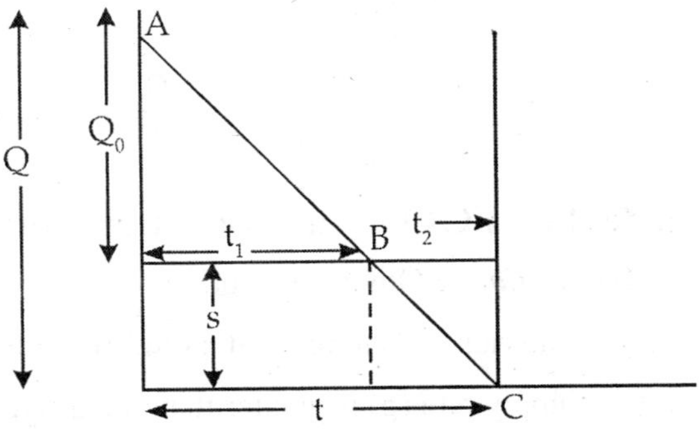

Fig. 16.2. Shortage Permitted

$$\text{Total Inventory Cost} = \frac{D}{Q} . Co + \frac{Qo^2}{2Q} t. Ch + \frac{s^2}{2Q} . t. C_s$$

$$Q \text{ (min EOQ)} = \sqrt{\frac{2DCo}{Ch} . \left(\frac{Ch + Cs}{Cs}\right)}$$

Problem 16.2

The demand of an item is uniform at a rate of 25 units per month. The fixed cost is Rs. 30 each time a production is made. The production cost is Rs. 2 per item and the inventory carrying cost is 50 paisa per unit per month. If the shortage cost is Rs. 3 per item per month, determine how often to make a production run and of what size? [*ICWA (Final), June 1981*]

Solution :

Given data indicates following values

D = 25 units

Ch = Re. 0.50 per item per month

$$Cs = \text{Rs. 3 per item per month}$$
$$\text{Production Cost} = \text{Rs. 2 per item}$$
$$\text{Production Set up Cost} = \text{Rs. 30 per set up.}$$

$$\text{Optimal (EOQ)} = \sqrt{\left(\frac{2DCo}{Ch}\,\frac{Ch+Cs}{Cs}\right)}$$

$$= \sqrt{\left(\frac{2\times25\times30}{0.5}\,\frac{0.50+3}{3}\right)}$$

$$= 60 \text{ units}$$

$$\text{Optimal time} = \frac{EOQ}{D}$$

$$= \frac{60}{25} = 2.4 \text{ months}$$

Model IV : EOQ with Production Lots

Assumptions : Other assumptions are the same as for Model I, except the following

(i) Materials are supplied at a uniform rate (p) and used at a uniform rate (d)

(ii) Supply rate (p) is greater than the usage rate (d).

Thus Maximum inventory level

$$= \text{(Inventory build up) (Period of delivery)} = (p-d)\left(\frac{Q}{p}\right)$$

Minimum inventory level = 0

$$\text{Hence Average Inventory Lever} = \frac{1}{2}\left[(p-d)\,\frac{Q}{p} + 0\right]$$

$$= \frac{Q}{2}\left[\frac{p-d}{p}\right]$$

$$\text{Annual carrying cost} = \frac{Q}{2}\left(\frac{p-d}{p}\right)Ch$$

$$\text{Annual ordering cost} = \left(\frac{D}{Q}.Co\right)$$

$$\therefore \text{Total annual cost} = \frac{Q}{2}\left[\left(\frac{p-d}{p}\right).\,Ch\right] + \left(\frac{D}{Q}\right)Co$$

$$Q\,(EOQ) = \sqrt{\frac{2D\,Co}{Ch}.\left(\frac{p}{p-d}\right)}$$

Diagramatically it is represented as under

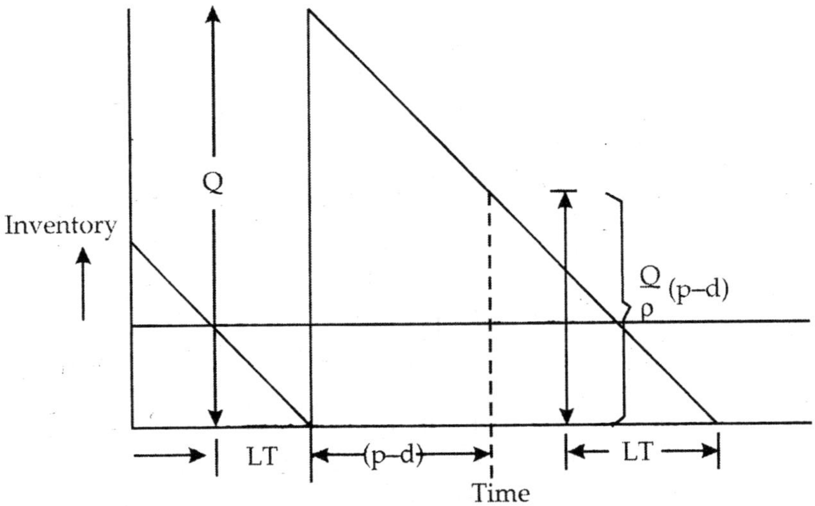

Fig. 16.3. EOQ with Production Lot

Problem 16.3

The annual demand of a product is 1,00,000 units. The rate of production is 2,00,000 units per year. The set up cost per production run is Rs. 500 and the variable production cost of each item is Rs. 10. The annual holding cost per unit is 20% of its value.

Find the optimum production lot size and the length of the production run.

[*Delhi University, M.Com., 1985*]

Solution :

Given data, D = 1,00,000; p = 2,00,000; Ch = 0.2; d = 1,00,000 and Co = 500.

Optimum production lot size is given by

$$Q\ (EOQ)^{*} = \sqrt{\frac{2DCo}{Ch}\left(\frac{p}{p-d}\right)}$$

$$= \sqrt{\frac{2 \times 1{,}00{,}000 \times 500}{0.2}\left(\frac{2{,}00{,}000}{2{,}00{,}000 - 1{,}00{,}000}\right)}$$

$$= 10{,}000 \text{ units}$$

$$\text{Length of the production run} = \frac{Q}{p} = \frac{10{,}000}{2{,}00{,}000}$$

$$= 0.05 \text{ year}$$

Problem 16.4

A Contractor has to supply 10,000 paper cones per day to a textile unit. He finds that when he starts a production run, he can produce 25,000 paper cones per day. The cost of holding a paper cone in stock for one year is 2 paisa and set up cost of production run is Rs. 18. How frequently should the production run be made?[*Delhi University, M.Com., 1970*]

Solution :

Let us assume that the production runs on 300 days in a year

$$\text{Given } D = 10{,}000 \times 300 = 30 \text{ Lakhs}$$

$$Co = \text{Rs. } 18$$

$$Ch = 0.02 \text{ per unit per year}$$

$$p = 25{,}000$$

$$d = 10{,}000$$

$$\therefore \quad Q\ (EOQ) = \sqrt{\frac{2DCo}{ch}\left(\frac{p}{p-d}\right)}$$

$$= \sqrt{\frac{2\times 30{,}00{,}000\times 18}{0.02}\left(\frac{25{,}000}{25{,}000-10{,}000}\right)}$$

$$= 95{,}000 \text{ units}$$

$$\therefore \text{Frequency of production} = \frac{95{,}000}{25{,}000} = 4 \text{ days}$$

Model V : EOQ with Quantity Discounts

- ***Changed Assumptions :*** Other assumptions as in case of Model – IV, except "Quantity Discounts are available".
- ***Additional Variable :*** Procurement Cost per unit of material. Hence Annual Procurement Cost = Annual demand × Unit procurement cost

$$= D.\ Cp.$$

Case (i) when materials are delivered at once,

$$EOQ = \sqrt{\frac{2D\,Co}{Ch}}$$

$$\text{and Total Annual Cost} = \frac{Q}{2}\,(Co) + \frac{D}{Q}\,.\,Ch + D.\,Cp$$

Case (ii) When deliveries are gradual replenishment

$$EOQ = \sqrt{\left(\frac{2D\,Co}{Ch}\right)\left(\frac{p}{p-d}\right)}$$

$$\text{and Total Annual Cost} = \frac{Q}{2}\left(\frac{p}{p-d}\right)Ch + \frac{D}{Q}\,.\,Co + D.\,Cp$$

Inventory Planning under uncertainty (Stochastic Models)

Stochastic Inventory Models

The dynamics of the inventory management has been discussed in paragraph 14.7 bringing out uncertainty of demand, lead time and randam fluctuation in the input resources. For dealing with inventory management for such situation, we use Stochastic Models.

These models deal with three types of situations:

- Variable demand
- Uncertain lead time
- Demand variation between lead time.

Variable Demand : It this situation, since demand keeps varying, the best method is to collect actual demand data over a period of time and allot probabilities to such demand levels. Then the forcasting of demand can be achieved. Let us take a case of variable demand data collected over last six months.

Range of actual daily demand	Frequency of Demand	Percentage Relative Frequrency
0 - 2500	55	30.5
2500 - 5000	75	41.7
5000 - 7500	40	22.2
7500 - 10000	10	5.6
	Total 180 days	Total 100%

Now we can calculate the mean and standard deviation of the data using the mid-point of demand range.

The average demand = 3809 say 4000.

The standard deviation = 2160 units.

Lead Time : When lead time is probabilistic, then we can correlate the lead time distribution through statistical methods. Let us illustrate this through an example:

Actual lead time (days)	*Frequency*	*Percentage Relative Frequency*
4	22	44
5	15	30
7	13	26
	50	100%

The Average Lead time from these data works out to 5 days

and standard deviation of lead time = 1.2 days.

Demand During Lead Time : The variation in the lead time itself can contribute to the variable demand and also the demand per unit period of lead time also is variable.

The demand during lead time can be calculated as 4000 × 5 = 20,000 (Average demand × Average lead time).

The lowest demand per day could be 4,000 for 4 days i.e., 16,000 units.

The maximum demand during higher of lead time i.e., 7 days = 4,750 × 7 = 33,250 units.

Thus we summerise that the demand during lead time can very from 16,000 units to 33.250 units. In between there can be large combinations, which can be worked out.

In lot size formula, average demand can be used for EOQ calculation in each case and the order point.

$$\bar{R} = \overline{dL} + 2\sigma_{\mu}$$

where $\overline{dL}$ = average demand during lead time.

In this case, we define some terms for probabilistic situations.

DDLT = Demand During Lead Time.

EDDLT = Expected Demand During Lead Time

σ = Mean Lead Time

σ_{DDLT} = Standard Deviation of Demand During Lead Time

σ_{LT} = Standard Deviation of Lead Time.

Optimal Safety Stock = Order Point – expected demand during lead time

= OP – EDDLT

It is represented in Fig 16.4 below

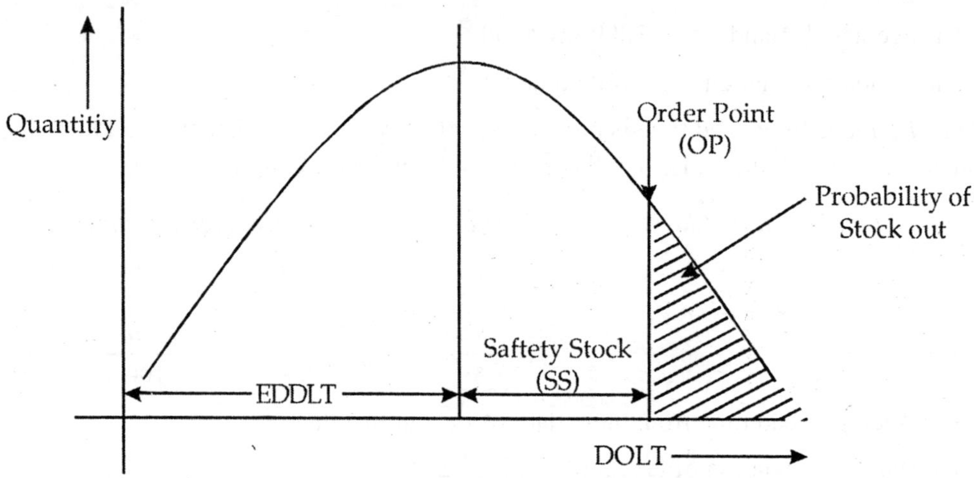

Fig. 16.4. Probability Distribution of Uncertain Demand.

16.7 Inventory Control Methods

In any organisation, variety of inventory is maintained depending on the type of business. To ensure the inventory levels to be at a reasonable level, it does become the concern of the management to have a proper control over its ordering, procurement, maintenance and consumption of this inventory. The control system must be designed to be effective. The control can be different for different type of inventory and can be divided under three heads :

- The order quantity
- The order frequency
- The time interval between successive reviews.

The widely used method of inventory control is knows as ABC analysis. It is abc called **Pareto analysis**. The procedure to adopt this technique is described below.

ABC Analysis

In this analysis, the classification of the existing inventory is based upon the annual consumption value of the items. Hence we obtain the quantity of inventory items consumed during the year and their procurement price, so as to obtain the annual consumption value and pattern of the inventory during the year under consideration. The horizon is generally kept as financial year. The categorisation of the items is done as follows:

Catagory	*Percentage of items*	*percentage of the annual consumption value*
A	0-20	70-80
B	20-30	10-15
C	60-70	5-15

Steps in ABC Analysis

As described above, we follow the procedure for ABC analysis through the undermentioned steps in that order:

Step 1 : Obtain the list of all materials consumed during last one year.

Step 2 : Note the unit purchase price against each item of consumed inventory along with their annual consumption quantity.

Step 3 : Obtain the Annual Consumption Value (ACV) for each item by multiplying the unit price with the quantities consumed.

Step 4 : Re-arrange the list of item according to their descending order of Annual Consumption Value (ACV), i.e., the first item appearing on the list with the highest value of ACV and then sequentially as these values decrease.

Step 5 : On the basis of this revised list as per step 4, work out the cummulative quantities and cummulative ACVs for all the items.

Step 6 : Having obtained cumulative quantities and cummulative ACVs, work out the relative percentages of quantities of inventory consumed. This will be cummulative percentage quantities and cummulative percentage ACVs.

Step 7 : From the information of step 6, plot these cummulative points by keeping the cummulative percentage quantities on the x-axis and cumulative percentage of ACVs on the y-axis. Draw a smooth curve through these points to obtain a relationship in the form of the curve given in fig 16.5 below.

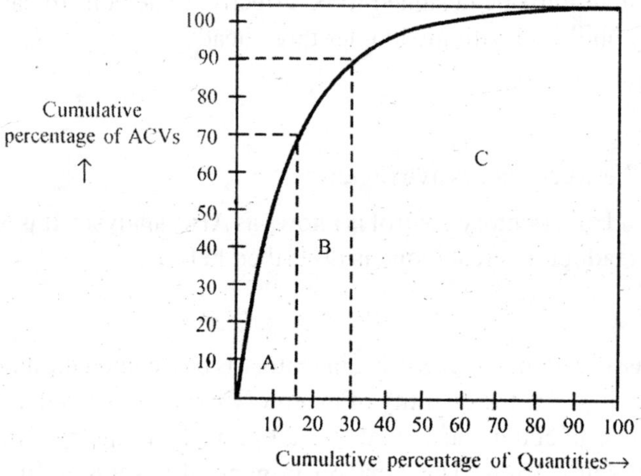

Fig. 16.5. ABC Analysis

Practial Issues : Though these methods of inventery control procurement and usage are elaborate and useful, due care must be taken for practical problems as follows :

Once ABC classification has been obtained the policy for control of these items can be formulated as under (duly marked in Fig. 16.5) :

A-items : Very tight control (items of high value). Generally exercised at a level of higher management.

B-items : Moderate Control to be exercised at the level of Materials Manager or middle level management.

C-items : Low value items. Control can be delegated to grass-root level either to the material supervisors or the departmental managers.

Problem 16.5

Carry out ABC analysis on the basis of the following data :

Items	*Units*	*Unit Price (₹)*	*Items*	*Units*	*Unit Price (₹)*
1	600	3.00	7	6,000	0.50
2	3,500	7.00	8	20	150.00
3	150	10.00	9	270	15.00
4	3,800	2.50	10	280	25.00
5	4,000	1.00	11	3,000	5.50
6	70	22.00	12	200	20.00

Solution :

Step 1 to 3. The annual consumption value is worked out as follows :

Item	*Units*	*Unit Price (Rs.)*	*Annual Consumption Value (Rs.)*
1	600	3.00	1,800
2	3,500	7.00	24,500
3	150	10.00	1,500
4	3,800	2.50	9,500
5	4,000	1.00	4,000
6	70	22.00	1,540
7	6,000	0.50	3,000
8	20	150.00	3,000
9	270	15.00	4,750
10	280	25.00	7,000
11	3,000	5.50	16,500
12	200	10.00	4,000

Step 4, 5 and 6. We arrange these annual consumption values in the descending order :

Items	*Consumption Value*	*Cumulative Consumption Value*	*Percentage Value (cumulative)*	*Units*	*Cumulative Number of Items*	*Percentage of Items (cumulative)*
2	24,500	24,500	30	3,500	3,500	15
11	16,500	41,000	50	3,000	6,500	30
4	9,500	50,500	62.2	3,800	10,300	47
10	7,000	57,500	71	280	10,580	48
9	4,750	62,250	76.7	270	10,850	49.6
12	4,000	66,250	81.7	200	11,050	50
5	4,000	70,250	86.6	4,000	15,050	69
7	3,000	73,250	90.3	6,000	21,050	96
8	3,000	76,250	94	20	21,070	96.2
1	1,800	78,050	96.2	600	21,670	99
6	1,540	79,590	98	70	21,740	99.3
3	1500	81,090	100	150	21,890	100

Now the graph can be drawn based on this information (Fig. 16.6)

Classification	Items A	– 15% in Number with 30% Consumption Value
	Items B	– 15% in Number with 20% Consumption Value
	Items C	– 70% in Number with 50% Consumption Value

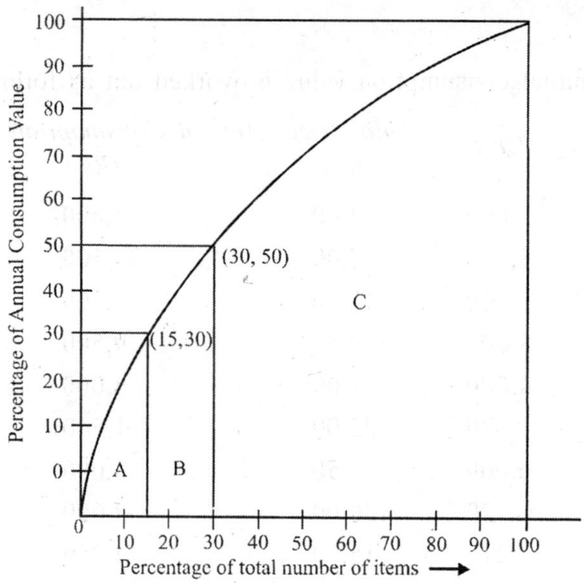

Fig. 16.6.

Other Inventory Control Methods.

- HML (Classification as per unit price of the items)

  H = High Price M = Medium Price L = Low Price
- VED (Classification based as importance or criticality)

  V = Vital few E = Essential D = Desirable
- FSN (Classification based on consumption pattern)

  F = Fast Moving S = Slow Moving N = Non-Moving
- SDE (Classification based on difficulty in procurement)

  S = Scare D = Difficult E = Easy
- SOS (Classification based on periodicity of demand)

  S = Seasonal OS = Off-Seasonal
- GOLF (Classification as per source of supply)

  G = Government Controlled, O = Ordinarily available

  L = Local availability F = Foreign Source of Supply.

16.8 Dynamics of Inventory Management

Inventory management is not an easy task for any Materials Manager. There are frequent and random changes in the production and procurement systems. There may be manpower problem like sickness, change of worker or absentism etc making productions highly probabilistic. Similarly there may be machine failures of shorter or longer durations, failure of maintenance staff of shortage or maintenance consumables or spares, poor control on lead time by suppliers or the part quantity rejected due to quality problem. There may also be a financial problem of cash flow. Similarly variations in demand occur due to wide fluctuations in sales quantities for various reasons resulting in frequent changes in the Master Production Schedule (MPS). All these eventualities pose serious constraints on the materials procurement policy and hence the total procurement system has to be kept highly dynamic changing the ordering quantities and schedule as per demand.

At times, even the warehousing capacity may become a big constraint. The concept of inventory at the vendors end i.e., Vendor Managed Inventory (VMI) comes handy in such cases. Quantity discounts may also be varying as per market forces and a large advantage can be obtained by buying more than required quantities. Similarly the benefit of stepped quantity discounts may be utilised. Hence the Materials Manager has to be highly dynamic in his approach towards the procurement and warehousing policy.

Inventory control can also be achieved though the cardexlite systems or through IBMs computerised method called **MAPICS (Manufacturing Accounting and Production Information Control System).** (Not described in this book).

16.9 RFID for Inventory Management

We have discussed Bar coding systems in chapter 11. Their utility for sales inventory control has been found to be of great value. A new technology called RFID has been evolved using the bar code systems to manage inventory of large proportions.

RFID is **Radio-Frequency Identification** and is a technology using radio waves to identify the inventory items. It stores the retrieving data through electro-magnetic transmission to an Radio Frequency compatible circuit. RFID tag (so called) is a single solid state memory chip with an antenna of same type. The system normally has three components i.e.,a tag, an antenna and a reader. The tag has a micro-chip and an antenna (either active, passive or semi-passive) available in two versions, read only or read/write. The reader can be like an PDA or a smell box that emits radio signals to activate the tag and to read and write the data on it. Readers are available in various shapes and sizes to control the data acquisation and communication of the system. These are built into a door. The electro-magnetic field produced by a reader can be captured constantly. This system is very useful when inventory items are in large numbers like US department of defence using it. Similarly the huge operation level of Walmart is using it effectively. This use results in a high workforce efficiency, improved configuration management, low inventories and low costs, increased safety and security, reduced machine downtime and an effective supply chain management. Another advantage is smaller bar code labels. Boeing and Airbus manufacturers are using it. This system can be used for tracking tools in tool crib to locate missed or misplaced tools. Reader can be configured either as a hand held or a fixed mount device. The reader emits radio waves in range of anywhere from one inch to 100 feet or more, depending upon its power output and the radio frequency used. When the RFID tag passes through the electromagnetic zone, the tag detects the readers activation signal and starts transmitting. The reader decodes the data from the tags integrated circuit and passes it to the host computer for further processing.

A schematic diagram, illustrating the RFID configuration is given in Fig. 16.7 below.

Fig. 16.7 A Simple RFID System

Section V
MANAGING THE VALUE CHAIN

Chapter 17

Supply Chain Management

Main issues:

1. Business Challenges in 21st Century
2. Structure of Supply Chain
3. Supply Chain Process
4. Improved Links and Lean Supply Chain
5. Operating Model of SCM
6. Logistics and outsourcing
7. Role of IT in SCM.

17.1 Introduction

Business philosophy can be obtained from a quote from Sir Edmund Hillary, a very tough Mountaineer. It says ***"The ladder to the top is long to climb. The climb is long and ordous. The obtacles are many. Only those who have grit and the stamina, those who are prepared to learn and re-learn from their mistakes and improve constantly and continue to grind can remain in the forefront and ultimately reach the top."***

The massage defines the rigours of the business in the present global environment. The grit and stamina has recently been shown by our steelman Laxmi Mittal in case of clinching the deal for the merger of Arcelor with his own large steel empire. He believed in the philosophy of "Keep on" and win the game "to reach the top".

The business is meant for customer, who is the sole aim and beneficiary of total business operations. Mahatma Gandhi has shown the path of total customer orientation in his famous statement, quoted below.

"A customer is the most important visitor on our premises. He is not dependent on us. We are dependent on him. He is not an interruption of our work. He is the purpose of it. He is not an outsider to our business. He is part of it. We are not doing him a favour by serving him. He is doing us a favour by giving us the opportunity to do so."

17.2 Dynamics of Customers Requirements

Today customer has become well informed and hence is becoming very demanding and aggressive. He wants to have his say in the following areas:

- Product specifications *i.e.,* feature
- Product Quality
- Product Price
- Place of delivery and delivery schedules
- Product variety and constant upgradation of product.

There is no short cut to business being totally customer-focused. To meet his demands, there is definite requirement of highest efficiency in all operations performed to make product/service available to him. Performance features for quality of the product/service are planned out, through being proactive and aggressive in marketing and production. Tahe strategic planning of resources such as trained work force, latest technology based machines and latest in materials with cost effective procurement becomes paramount to achieve this aim. Customer is ready to pay a reasonable price on the product, of better quality (customers perception).

The next focus has to be satisfaction of the customer by supplying the product practically at his door-steps and when he needs it, otherwise he takes no time to change his loyalty (He is very impatient). Hence the distribution network has to be planned and operated accordingly. Due to very large exposure, the customer also keeps changing his requirement. Product customisation and updation, both are becoming a big challenge for the supply chain managers, Flexible manufacturing system, variety production through employee participation for quality assurance are some of the areas needing attention of managers. In addition, the organisation needs to be constantly innovative at all times, not only to offer newer product, but even in terms of packaging design (so that the product looks different and new and should be so perceived by the customer).

The product variety demand is resulting in need for total customisation. If one is looking for a black colour car, it is to be provided with but may not be so for many customers. People wanting tooth pastes also can be divided into many categories such as a young child wanting to have the paste with dark red lines, or gel paste, a grown up boy may opt for grey line paste and the elderly people for their long tiame habit of purė white paste. Thus there is wide demand variability in practically every simple product. If we have some 400 odd car variants in the country today, for global supply, this number may be very large in terms of shapes, shades, engine capacity, seat comforts or the fuel consumption levels etc.

The change in customer preferences add to the woes of the supply chain manager. If, at a particular time, people in the age group of 18 to 25 prefer only coloured shirts, at another time, a white shirt may became a preferred product. These varieties are aranging large, when we go across the borders. As a culture of the country, a large number of people may prefer short-term use T-shirts at low costs, we have to modify our production and distribution accordingly. If cutomers need 'mixed fruit jams' in a particular area as a major demand, the product mix for that region has to be designed accordingly. Thus customer focus and demand variability are so closely inter-linked that there is no getting away from it and supply chain design and operation needs modification on constant update basis.

17.3 Business Challenges in 21st Century

Customer is supreme in total business strategy and with business shifting its focus from domestic to global, arena, the challenges to succeed in business have multiplied. The three major challenges for business managers for the 21st century can be listed as follows :

- Managing Customers
- Managing Uncertainty
- Managing Globalisation

Not that these challenges did not exist for businesses of yester-years, these have become very intense due to global competition and there is no respite from continuous increase in this direction. Either we perform (better than competitors) or we perish. The business, therefore, has to be done differently today keeping eyes and ears open to the global customers and global competitors.

Managing Customers. Business manager has to understand his customers in totality *i.e.* from technical, functional, aesthetical, psychological and societal angles. If he does not, his business would not prosper. The issue is very complicated. The customer of today is better exposed, better informed and hence more demanding. Due to the very exposure, he takes no time to shift his loyalty. This exposure can be half-baked truth. Most of the time, customer really does not understand what he wants. May be, he is clear (to a large extent) as to what performance to be expected from the product or service that he is looking for. How, when and at what quality and cost, are not easily answered questions. Business managers have to obtain it from the customers with due deliberation. For this purpose, a very detailed and elaborate market research, analysis, study, innovations and pro-active actions will be required.

This is only one angle of customer management. After the relevant (so believed complete) information is collected and transformed into the end result *i.e.* Product or service, this has to satisfy the need of the customer. The marketing and sales team have to be aggressive enough to place the item in the market in such a way that the customer understands it. accept it and can use it fearlessly. It must perform well over a period of time so that a perception of "good and suitable" is developed in the mind of the customer. This aspect is called "customer perception".

The third important parameter for customer management is the after-sales service *i.e.* the responsiveness and reliability to be established to develop faith of the customer in the organisational ability to match his requirement of product function. The contact, behaviour and preferably "one window or one person redressal" system are good methods to ensure this, A step further called "Proactive service" *i.e.* reach a customer before he needs you, can be very helpful. Psychologically it makes a large difference in customer management.

Managing Uncertainty. Uncertainty is a way of life. It is available to every living being at all points of time. The best part of uncertainty is that the past history or experience can help you very little to predict the future happening. The uncertainty in the customer's mind is, therefore, the most difficult aspect of business to be tackled. Even the best of psychologists find it difficult to reach the mind of his subjects. The socialists, social-scientists, behaviourialists and so many others have tried their minds, but very few can lay hands on the right nerve reaction.

As if this uncertainty was not enough, the addition of dimensions comes from the variations in cultures and national economies. Such matrices are difficult to obtain. Hence the requirements of one item (product/service) for an American customer are different from those of an English customer, also are different for a customer from Japan, Nigeria, China or Zimbabwe. We can not standardise even an item of food for their widely different cultures and economies. Other requirements multiply exponentially. It is not only, therefore, a very large challenge across the nations, but even in our own domestic consumption pattern. Therefore, for the similar requirement of product, say mode of transportation for self use, we have to offer either a bicycle or a bus or a car to a customer, based on his choice of time, quality, and the drain on his pocket. Similarly a cup of tea would need a variety of cups and varieties of tea leaves for different customers from different part of the country for different status of living.

The third level of uncertainty is felt in terms of a constant change in the customers requirement. This is due to change in social indicators, per capita income, exposure, or functional requirement itself. Changes due to natural forces or due to peers pressures also make the requirements uncertain. This change can be termed as "customers progressive preference", and can be quite telling on business strategy. Business managers, therefore, need to be proactive and innovative all the time to cater for this progression.

Managing Globalisation. To top the above-mentioned uncertainty, a change in the area of global business has altered the operational strategies totally during last two decades or so. This aspect has grown tremendously and all national boundaries have fallen apart due to global operations. Economic or Business Blocks such as European Union or North Atlantic Free Trade Association (NAFTA), ASEAN AND APEC or the global agreements in place like World Trade Organisation (WTO) have further enhanced the concept of business into "Global village" business administration. This has resulted in an intense competition. The effect is that the wheels of liberalisation has been set in motion and we can operate no more under 'closed economy' conditions. Imports and Exports have become almost a free business, with quota regime having vanished. Financial liberties, technology transfers. availability of unlimited quantity and variety of materials have thrown open a large number of opportunities with practically level ground for operations for all. To cater for this intense need, new technologies, new methods, capacity maximisation, efficiency increase and optimisation of resources have become a constant research area. Management has developed into an important area for research and study. Production and sales concepts have undergone drastic changes. Outsourcing for resource optimisation is becoming an effective tool in large number of areas. Globalisation has not only increased competition, it has also helped business in term of scale of economies. The products manufacture can be highly cost effective due to large volumes but challenge lies in the variety of the products. The major thrust of globalisation has been in expansion of business across the boundaries of the nations. Today, since we live in a global market place, it is virtually the sale of the same products around the world to varied customers. Another advantage of globalisation has been in the strategy of production in some advantageous location (country) with technology from another country, with raw materials or components from some other country, packaging in another place and distribution in and around the globe by a strategic partner (firm) in some other Country. This has resulted in the use of the best of cost effective resources of various kinds to put into the product. The quality of the products have improved (a definite gain for the customers) due to intense competition in markets when the companies strive hard for market share and profitability. Thus the ability to make products available to a constantly changing markets requirement on time, at desired locations to level of the customers paying capacity may make the difference to the graph of success, both, in terms of product acceptance, market share and the financial returns. This is where efficient production and timely distribution can help to a large extent for meeting delivery schedules.

17.4 Paradigm shift

Due to constantly changing environment of business, that too on a very fast pace, there has been a large change in thinking as to how the products reach the customers. This role has also undergone a major change called a paradign shift from logistics to Materials to Supply Chain Management. In summerised form, the thinking and role of material delivery has changed as follows :

1970's – Primary focus on integration of warehousing and internal transportation.

1980's – Focus on re-engineering of the cost structure of supplies.

1990's – Focus to improve customer service.

Present—customisation in product costs, quality and delivery schedules.

Reasons for shift in thinking

- Focus from manufacture to the customer.
- User friendly technology
- Stiff global competition
- Liberlisation and economic deregulation.

17.5 Definition and Scope of Supply Chain Management

Though supply chain has been defined by many people in their own thinking style, the most appropriate explanation, perhaps, has been offered by Orizona university as follows:

"A supply chain consists of all of the entities necessary to transform ideas into delivering products and services. Supply chain management directs and transforms a firms resources in order to design, purchase, produce and deliver high-quality goods and services. As goods and services flow from supplier to producers to customer to final user, supply chain management is thus the total integration of the interfaces among various elements of operations. One way to view supply chain management is as the management of linkages between organisations".

The competitive and global nature of today's business environment dictates that this direction and transformation take place in efficient and effective way. Continuing emphasis on time, cost and quality improvements have sharpened the need to co-ordinate and co-operate with trading partners around the world to achieve results that allow the customers to be happy. Thus supply chain Management focusses on the integration of activities across several companies to manage the flow of products, services, people, equipment, facilities and other resources. Supply Chain Management is also concerned with recycling, reuse and final disposal of products.

From this detailed explanation of supply chain and its management, the scope of Supply Chain Management (SCM) can be highlighted through Fig. 17.1 :

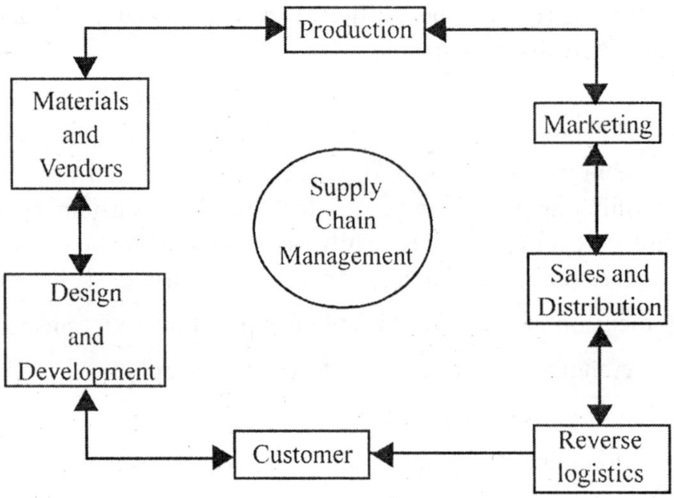

Fig 17.1 Scope of Supply Chain Management

Customer : Since the aim of supply chain management is customer satisfaction, the chain starts from customers requirement only and ends at him. Initial demand of product emerges from him through the interaction of the marketing team and any peridical changes based on his behaviour and preference are also to be taken into account for any further modications in designs, production and delivery of the products.

Product design and development : Develops products based on the requirement of the customers obtained through extensive market research. It includes the actual product design, production engineering and packaging. It should incorporate elements to facilitate production and distribution.

Materials and Vendors : It includes material specifications, planning and purchasing of raw materials or components for the end products. Vendors are part of this team to ensure supply of materials for every distinct phase of production even for assembly so as to ease its distribution. Quality of materials and cost effectiveness must be ensured.

Production : Production stage is where the materials are transformed into the finished product. Right material at right time and at right place is the responsibility of materials department.

Marketing : It is the area of product positioning in the market to create demand for the product. It involves controlling flow of orders to production, because production can start only after the demand has been established. Customers order and forecasted demand should be as realistic as possible. Continuous feedback to be in-built to update products.

Sales and Distribution : Distribution is the allocation and physical movement of products towards the markets where customers expect the delivery. It should match the product mix and delivery schedule of the customers. Sales team has to ensure right product supply to customers.

Reverse logistics : It is utilisation of the returning back of the logistics facilities such as trucks. The reverse logistics becomes effective when the packaging and products are designed in such a way that a re-use and re-cycling are possible. Materials can be seperated and re-used for subsequent productions and protective packaging. This material not only saves costs due to their reuse/recycling, the reverse transportation cost is also gainfully utilised, due to otherwise empty return of the distribution facilities. But reverse logistics creates problems when materials/products move between the countries unless there are agreements in place to facilitate such movements. Movement of products from some source to the factory such as raw material etc. is also useful.

These are important links of the supply chain and their management would mean keeping all the linkages equally strong. The weakest link of the chain determines its overall effectiveness and efficiency. It is from the efficiency point of view that the control of all links should be central so that their effective integration and level performance can be ensured.

While the goal of SCM is to reduce costs of producing and reaching the finished products to customers, inventory management is very crucial element of the chain.

17.6 Structure of the Supply Chain

Supply chains can be a very complex network involving many companies, many production lines and many materials. Raw materials can be the input to many products produced by many organisations. These materials can be supplied by many vendors and when transformed, can reach many destinations as numerous products to meet the requirements of million and millions of customers. To make this possible, a large coordination effort is needed. The communication and reverse logistics become further challenge to keep the supply chain moving. Thus the SCM involves all the management functions including marketing research, design, materials planning, process planning, production, purchases, warehousing, material handling, shipping and distribution.

The most complex supply chain that can explain the complexity of the system is that of the Defence forces, even in the normal peace time deployment, (it becomes very acute during the war), the millions and millions of products from arms, ammunitions, tanks and aeroplanes, food, clothing, guns and n number of commodities (n being very very large) are required. Further complication arises when very large product mix in terms of quantity, quality and diversity needing a very large quantity of materials for each product (almost infinite variety) is to be supplied to very large number of organisations to produce the required products (wide variety if the same item to be useful in different terrains (desert, cold region, jungles etc), and where the product required are so different. What is further challanging is that a correct product mix must reach a particular area of their deployment at the right time at the right place in right quantities. A minor failure can result in complete loss of face in terms of defeat (Even if there are 3000 snow boots deficiency for troops fighting at high altitudes and at temperature of – 40°c would mean very high reduction of 3000 troops efficiency and can become a major cause of defeat at times. Thus Supply Chain Management in such situations is very complex and has to be delibrately planned, otherwise a situation like German defeat in Russia will keep happening. In corporate world, these operations also can be very critical for very large and wide spread units.

In order to integrate various supply chain activities, we can summerise the structure of the supply chain as follows :

- Activities should be related both to each other and to the objectives of the supply chain.
- Activities (WBS) must be manageable as individual independently performable units, so that they can be allowed to operate independently within the overall frame work of the chain.
- Activities should be economically significant, adding values and using resources.
- Activities should have specific purpose which should not be duplicated within the overall value system for being cost effective.

Thus various activities performed under the supply chain are :

- **Plan :** working out operating strategy and performance targets.
- **Source :** decision on goods and vendors, inventory planning and material flow systems.
- **Produce :** commission of materials into end products as per Master Production Schedule (MPS).
- **Distribute :** making product available to the customer as and when required.
- **Return :** making it easier for the customer to return product if nor suitable. This is after sales service.

17.7 Factors influencing Supply Chain

Supply Chains can be operating domestically or across the country borders. But as a general rule, following factors dictate the design of supply chain :

- Geographic factors
- Economic factors

- Production factors
- Operating costs
- Trade Restrictions
- Time factor

Geographic Factors : There are lot many pecularities of locations affecting the customer in any particular region. The requirements of customers can be drastically different even in the neighbourhoods. Talking of India, a vast country, the attitudes, habits and culture of two states can be very different, such as people from Jammu and Kashmir are widely different from those from Uttar Pradesh, Himachal and Punjab. Thus planning for these areas have to be different. Different Product mix, and in varying quantities for even a part of a state can be very different. Hence industries need to be located close to the market in order to provide quick delivery to the customers and to respond quickly in case of demand change, say during festivals or change in climates.

Topography of the locations will pose different problems for movement of goods to these various regions. Distance also becomes important for materials that lose weight in transit or during production, such as coal or wood pulp. Type and mode of transport for distribution of goods and services in deserts are far different from those for hill states. When it comes to eastern regions of India, the water-ways change the method of distribution systems. When it is related to global operations, the mode, distance and cost matrix becomes much more pronounced and complicated. When manufacturing is done in one country, raw materials obtained from another country and distribution is done in yet other countries, the situation is not easily manageable. The tax structure, legal restrictions of various regions, community attitudes, the economic development of the region etc. come in the way of planning supply chain operations. Local competition in the geographic area may pose yet another challenge for business.

Economic Factors : The customers buy the products permitted by their pockets. This is true in any corner of the world. The disparity between developing and developed countries, therefore, is affecting the supply chain design due to product mix. The types of products will be varying to a large extent based on per capita income and economical differential pockets of the customer segments. On national and international level, the economic climate may result in deregulated industrial environment, availability of foreign funds for investment and resultant competitive atmosphere. This brings in the necessity of industrial alliances and partnership cashing on the strength of partners to achieve better results for winning the end user. Supply chain management, accordingly, undergoes a change to involve all partners in the chain, Horizontal and vertical integration of the supply systems make the chain cost-effective. The degree in automation in production and distribution also can be easily amalgamated based on the economic conditions. The ability of supply chain to serve several product markets through one network is economy of scope. But it is a challenge for logistics design.

Production Factors : In production, quality and availability of work force, materials and machines make the difference. The type and quality of the product will depend on the availability of work force (in terms of qualifications, experiences, attitudes and available quantity) to suit the type of production. Production process and quality standards have to be accordingly modified. To feed these products, compatible markets have to be located and hence supply chain linkages planned and implemented accordingly. The degree of automation for a suitable volume of production and the product quality can change the production scene.

Operating Costs : To ensure the end product within the reach of the customer, the entire chain has to be highly efficient and cost-effective. Hence cost consideration at each link needs a deeper look. If raw material are bulky, heavy and costly, this part of the chain has to be smaller *i.e.* shifting production facility near the raw material availability. Cost benefit analysis (Break Even Analysis) for the type of transportation should be very deliberate and only suitable process should be selected.

When we plan for the production, the design of the product takes a front seat. It may take a little longer to design (time can be contained by using IT-enabled system like CAD), but design suitable for manufacturing, assembly, quality and distribution must be finalised. Raw materials appropriate for these design parameters must be chosen and moved. Next important stage for operating cost reduction is selection of process. Break even analysis for the selection of process for cost and volume of production must be carried out. Variable costs are to be reduced to the best of ability and availability. Packaging, movement mode and type of transport specific for type of product should be selected at the optimum level.

Trade Restrictions : This aspect is closely connected with geographic factors as well as economic factors. Some countries or even states within the country have product movement restrictions. It is not only economic consideration in terms of various taxes involved, there are even physical movement restrictions. Excise duty, sales taxes, custom duties, restrictions on joint ventures/collabaration etc. are some important limitations. The domestic/international supply chains have to be planned taking all these into consideration.

Time Factor : With large number of options available to the customer today, his expectations have also grown high. Customisation is the result of this behaviour. Customer's preference of the product and its features, cost and quality has brought the manufactures to the flexible manufacturing system. Next priority is to catch the market share *i.e.* making product/service available to the customer when he needs it. Thus delivery schedules are becoming very important to obtain and maintain market share. To retain customer today is not easy. Due to various options of product and marketing strategies, loyalty change is a common phenomenon. The way this can be done, is beating the competition by variety being positioned ahead of expectations. When customer walks into the market, he picks up product, if available. To ensure this competitive edge over the competitors, therefore, the supply chain has to be designed, planned and implemented catering for the time schedule based on customers preference. IT-enabled chains make a difference in time scheduling of supply chain.

Another important factor for across the border movement is the communication facility and the level of technology convergence available in a particular region. Exchange of information is very crucial for designing the supply chain system from infrastructure as well as physical operation point of view. System incompatibilities, lack of infrastructure, local regulations such as freight restrictions and rates also need to be taken into account, while putting supply chain facilities on ground.

The solution lies in better and improved tele-communication facilities and WTO (World Trade Organisation) provisions in place, which make the operation of international of global supply chain easier.

Major Factors for Global Supply Chain

In addition to the above, some peculiar situations for global operations arise due to the following reasons :

- Segmentation, Production and Physical location of natural resources isa big challenge.
- Labour and experience - wider
- Production Technology - Latest could be available (use of JIT, CAM, FMS etc)
- Deregulation on transportation and use of EDI/IT.
- Local laws, regarding local material content, trade relation, labour use or joint ventures necessary.
- Political and financial risks.
- Competition from domestic suppliers.
- Trade blocks/tones, such as EU, Duty Free Trade zones etc.
- Environmental audits.
- Larger product variety
- Responsiveness/efficiency – different in different countries
- Timely supplies, inspite of long distances

GATT Regulations

Advantages

- Members consult over Trade problem.
- Better co-ordination Framework available for negotiations resulting in legal agreement.
- Domestic industry gets protection through tariffs.
- No discrimination among members
- Most favoured nation clause.

Disadvantages

- Greater complexity and risk.
- Response to macro-economic environment.
- Different culture, legal requirement and infrasturcture.

Though all these factors will indicate a different supply chain design, overall effect has to be the integration of all the factors together. Different products for different customers of different regions with different tastes, different time requirement, different costs and very different delivery sedules would need different production systems in different regions. To top it all, movement of goods from one region (place of manufacture) to another region (for distribution) may be needing different strategy due to some local trade restrictions.

These factors become much more pronounced when we consider International supply chains. Different countries have their different laws and hence crossing of borders will present variety of challenges and barriers such as general movement restructions, tariffs and non-tariff barriers, currency exchange rates and difficult payment policy and terms, large difference in product requirements, consumer tastes and business practices, difference in mode of transport or transport regulations, diverse policy on communications and warehousing etc. These are only few limitations. On ground, it is a very difficult and complex situation.

The effect on the supply chain could be higher inventories, higher investments and provision of currency exchange resulting in differential costing. It may need a local logistics partner with joint ventures formation as a price for market entry. Local competitions may give hick-ups to the international supply chain operators due to their local facility advantages.

Another important factor for international supplies across the border movement is the communication facilities and the level of technology convergence. Exchange of information is very crucial for designing the chain system from infrastructural as well as physical operation point of view. System incompatibilities, difference in infrastructure, local regulations and rates to be taken into account while putting supply chain facility on ground. Hence international supply chain is complex but is becoming easy to operate due to telecommunication facilities and WTO and GATT in place, which makes it easier to operate now across the borders.

17.8 Supply Chain Processes

With the emphasis on international or global environment operations (equally applicable for domestic operations with slight local regulation modifications), a brief insight over critical supply chain processes and issues, predominantly affecting the supply chain utility is imperative. Some of the issues are highlighted below :

Strategy: Supply chain is an essential part of the corporate business and hence the supply chain strategy has to fit into the corporate strategy of gaining competitive advantage resulting in greater market share. Hence the strategy adopted by the company must reflect in its supply chain operations i.e., efficiency through economy and scale, risk management, technology and flexibility in supply chain design to shift emphasis quickly as per market information.

Financial Management : It is important to understand the overall financial umbrella for supply chain management and data on different accounting systems with its comparability to arrive at sound supply chain decisions. Tax policies, custom duties and currency conversion rate etc are important areas to consider for risk reduction and sales enhancement. The regulations regarding counter-trading and import/export balance must be kept in mind for achieving success.

Organisation Capability : To operate a supply chain effectively, the environmental knowledge is imperative i.e., in addition to having domestic knowledge and skills, necessary skills and capability to operate global supply chain must be available. It is because, whereas the local political, economic, social and cultural variations are important to understand, the knowledge of cross – culture, political stability, socio-economic fibre of the country to deal with, helps in understanding foreign markets, logistics regulations and limitations, (such as Jordan has only one meter gange line which is used for Potash transfer and the rest of the country logistics depends on Road transport) foreign exchange rates, rules regarding repatriation of profits etc. In India also, cultural differences in J & K, Kerala, Bihar, West Bengal and Punjab are large. These variations are important to understand for employee motivation for reward/ recognition system.

Risk Management : Though enough Complexity exists in domestic SCM, but for global SCM, it is a bigger issue, adding the risk of dealing within the frame work of regulations by other countries. If it permits us to use flexibility of operations in another country, the risk management becomes easier. But if the economic and political environment are volatile and unstable, it is very risky to do business. Interest rates, wages rates and currency fluctuations may require changes in business strategy. Another area to guard against is legal framework and technical standards (Not different to compare technical standards for India, Japan, USA and UK). A detailed analysis on customs rules and taxation can be highly beneficial if full advantage is to be taken of the cost-saving provisions as per legal understanding. Having the flexibility to re-configure sourcing and production flows in response to the changes in taxations, it may be possible to minimise risk of global operations based on the modified SCM strategies and processes.Industry structure, where compititors behaviour is unpredictable, it is riskey to operate in. Environmental response is also important for risk in business.

Relationship Management : When competition is tough and conditions of business are not very conducive, full benefit should be planned by establishing good relationships with the customers and suppliers. It is important to balance out strategic objectives with the flexibility and risk management. Also the balancing act for social and cultural assymnetry also is imperative for advantages through negotiations or behavioural response of dealers and partners.

Information Technology Management : It is definitely a key issue in any supply chain design, be it small or large, local, domestic or global. Information transfer and that too in quick time influences the efficiency of the supply chain considerably. This is an effective and easy system to manage large complexity of environment and variations between the countries. The company has to look for a compatible IT-enabled system for information transfer in order to integrate and standardise global operations. Decision Support Systems (DSS) that can take care of global variables and enables 'what if' analysis is quick time helps the company to manage complexities in much better and faster way. It helps in correct documentation across the countries.

17.9 Prerequisities of Supply Chain Design

While we understand various issues connected with the domestic as well as global supply chain management, these have to culminate into an effective, efficient and lean supply chain. The results to be achieved out of an efficient supply chain are :

Right Product : The product has to suit the customers need, from all the angles, namely

- Technical
- Functional
- Psychological

- Physical and Aesthetical
- Social

Right Quality : This is what makes a customer happy and he is ready to pay for the quality he needs. Higher quality is costlier for him and lower quality products are no good to buy. Hence quality should be just right at the manufacturers end as well as at the retailers end. Quality is highly variable for customers and hence must be carefully balanced out for a segment of customers. From Raw material to distribution, the facility needs to be controlled to retain quality.

Right Quantity : This means a tight control over the product mix and demand quantity both. Exact information from sales to manufacture is desired i.e., identification of customers requirement and conveying to the producer is key to satisfy the customer. Some high value orders can be Build to order (BTO) (i.e., produce as per specific requirement) or better still ship to order (STO). Proper communication channels help a lot.

Right Time : Customer decides the delivery schedule or the right time as to when the produce is needed and it must be available at that time. If this does not happen, Customer either shifts to another equivalent product or may defer the purchase. Either way, unfulfitted demand is a loss, either temporarily or even strategically (may be due to loss of credibility of the company).

The timely availability of products, therefore, requires activation of all the links from design to materials planning and procurement, physical production, packaging and distribution. Suppliers are important to be co-operative and JIT operators. Good Warehousing and retailers enthusiasm plays an important role for timely deliveries.

Right Place : This is a distribution function. For the purpose of timely delivery at the desired right place depends on the design and operations of the distribution network. Mode of transportation, routes and documentation etc are to be taken care of. A superb quality product can be spoiled during transit, if mode of transport is inappropriate and hence the product may not be available for sale. So to reach a place in time, network planning has to be accurate i.e., whether the product is sent by railways or by road (in ordinary trucks or in containers) whether small trucks or in large trucks etc.

Right Person : It is 'man behind the gun' that can ensure effective supply. If person is not motivated or is not skillful enough, one mistake in documentations can hold up the supplies at any place of control. In case of global supplies, the entire consignment can be returned back if the packaging is not proper or if the documentation is not correct.

Hence, the supply chain design needs the following care :

- Proper customer feed back, through market research or through retailers or sales team communications.
- Proper Manufacturing through suitable MPS in terms of quantity and product mix. Information flow from the customer helps. JIT system can be effective tool in design.
- Use of Appropriate Transport mode either for raw materials, components or sub-assemblies or for the distribution of the finished products. This can ensure maintaining quality and availability of products in right place at right time.

- Strict vigil on Quality by the Quality Assurance team is also an important supply chain function ensuring the product to be of the level of customers requirement, neither high nor low. Total Quality Management (TQM) is an effective tool for the purpose.

17.10 Strategic Supply Chain Management

For supply chain strategy to be useful and effective, various components adding to the overall strategy are as under :

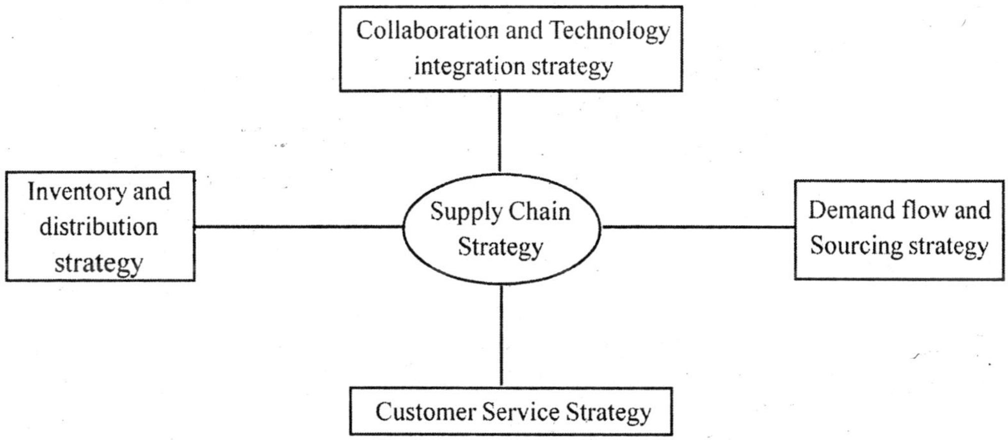

Fig 17.2. Strategic Supply Chain Components

Customer Service Strategy

Customer is the end user of the supply chain a well as the initiater of supply chain. Hence the customer service strategy has to start from method of collecting his requirements and ensuring its flow through the system to translate the requirement into end product to his liking, technically and psychologically. Therefore, the company has to evolve a strategy defining methods and means to respond to the customer needs and expectations. Care should be taken to ensure organisational objective of profit maximisation also. Intense competition, domestic as well as global, has made customer service as the differentiation in the marketing approach.

For the purpose of customer service, the company has to strategise on the following issues:

- Customer segmentation
- Service cost
- Revenue management

Customer segmentation : It is part of the information collection for identifying customers needs and is very crucial start up on the service strategy. The start up stage is market research. Customer, most of the time, does not really specify what he needs. He possibly, at best, can indicate the functional aspect of the product. For actual need, the market research expert has urge the customer to supply more and more information, the important parameters being the cost, time, performance and any other special information. Then only we can identify whether he is happy with a bicycle, a bus, a car or an aircraft for his functional requirement of moving from one place to another. Based on the cost or time, we can segment customers for different catagories of the product i.e., bicycles, bus, car and an aircraft as the case may be.

After the segmentation of customers, the company has to decide what segment of customer it wants to deal with. The customer satisfaction level and the quality requirements will specify the service strategy of the company. Hence we can summerise the steps for satisfactory service as follows :

(a) Market research for need identification.

(b) Segmentation of customers

(c) Identification of segment for the company

(d) Identification of service need in term of product price, quality and delivery schedule for different geographical regions.

Service Cost : Service has to be provided to the customer as an imperative. The level of service will indicate the cost associated with the service. The company has to evolve a strategy to provide optimum service to the customer and optimise company profitability at the same time. The issue of cost has to deal with the input cost, cost of provision and distribution and cost of service. The cost of the product has to be decided with reference to inputs involved along with the concept of Corporate Social Responsibility i.e., right price and service for the right product.

In addition, to keep a customer satisfied and loyal to the company, the organisation has to go a step forward by being proactive in providing something more than the competitors. Hence the concept of service cost in dynamic is nature, needing a constant watch and regular move forward to keep customers delighted.

Revenue Management : Business is done for earning profits and hence profitability and business growth go hand in hand. The proactive action for enhanced customer service has to keep this object in view all the time. The company has to determine appropriate response to customer needs and their fulfilment. Total customer service strategy has to aim at balancing act of customer satisfaction with appropriate level of service and corporate profitability. In fact, the deliberate strategy to achieve this could be either todrop out a particular segment and serve only a strategic segment or level or service to be diluted as a deliberate measure. Hence clear identification of potential income with detailed break up of costs to earn a reasonable revenue is the basis of customer service strategy. Some of the methods could be the involvement of regular designers, flexible manufacturing technologies and involvement of third party for distribution (3 PL to be discussed under logistics later) useful in deciding service levels.

Demand Flow and Sourcing Strategy

For demand fulfillment, there are various channels available i.e., dealers, retailers, stockists, wholesalers and distributors etc. Now we can use another channel through internet i.e., world wide web (www). For an appropriate channel, we have to consider the product service to be made available, the volume or the demand and the geographical area to which the demand pertains. The company has to make this choice so that through this demand flow, the customer service level can be decided.

Once the demand flow has been obtained, there has to be a concerted effort to plan how to meet this demand i.e., product mix with division of demand pattern for a particular area and then deciding how to produce and distribute the product.

Since supply chain has a number of elements involved such as source of supplies, storage or warehousing destinations and the type of distribution available for physical movement of stock, the actual supply chain configuration has to be planned i.e., where to get what and where to stock it till it is lifted for actual supply. Thus we have to decide on the number of supply points for the type of product mix and movement of these products to a central location, hence planning of inermediate warehousing stations and the mode of transport to distribute the supplies. This is what is termed as **supply chain configuration** listing out the role each facility has to play in moving the chain.

Another important consideration for the demand flow is **Vendor Managed Inventory (VMI)** under which, instead of collecting the supplies and locating it at the warehousing destination, the cost of holding can be saved by keeping the inventory at the vendors end and moving only when and where required .

Either way, the company has to decide whether it is inhouse production or it is collected from specific vendors. Reliable vendors can be developed as part of supply chain who can supply the products at competitive cost, provided quality can be ascertained and ensured. Make or buy decision is therfore, an important decision on outsourcing.

Thus we can summerise the demand and sourcing strategy under following elements :

- Channel design and selection
- Demand planning
- Supply chain configuration
- Vendor Managed Inventory (VMI)
- Production management
- Outsourcing decision
- Capacity management (in house as well as outsource facilities)

Collaboration and Technology Integration Strategy

For supply chain design, we have to plan what method of collaboration is to be maintained between the manufacturing and vendors or between manufacturing and customers. The chain has to be accordingly planned to keep these links infact and strong enough. Constant interaction through IT-enabled systems is helpful in producing very near to customers requirement. Also close collaboration with vendors can avoid unnecessary inventory. A large saving can be affected, provided this relationship is close, congenical and reliable. This is called **captive vendor management (CVM)**.

In addition, on the supply front, we can conveniently use outside sevice providers called 3-PL and 4-PL i.e., Third Party logistics Providers and Fourth Party logistics Providers. This is being discussed under Distribution. For making sure that our own and the outsourced facilities work in total tendom and smoothly, we have to provide the integration system i.e., the supplier and manufactures donot operate independently but based on technical and technological balance as per the information flow planned.

Thus, we have to work on the vertical integration system providing a common link of a chain between manufacturing, suppliers, distribution channels as well as customers to ensure development and delivery of the products all working as a cohesive integrated organisation. The amount of integration would depend on the level of technology available and amount of technological integration that can be affected as per volumes and costs involved.

To summerise the collaberation and Technological integration strategy, we can list out following elements :

- Manufacturing/Supplier integration.
- Manufacturing and customer relationship and information sharing.
- Distribution Outsourcing elements such as 3PL/4PL providers.
- Technology and Information integration for easy flow.
- Financial integration.

Inventory and Distribution Strategy

This is the core activity of the supply chain. The major cost incurred in the supply chain is due to the level of inventory kept at various locations to keep the chain moving smoothly. This is imperative and important for achieving higher level of customer satisfaction, so that a large number of customer can be served. By timely deliveries the loyalty of the customers can be ensured. This is great help in business growth. But these are conflicting requirements. The company has to offset cost of inventory for customer satisfaction or the other way round. Revenue level or profit margin has to be deliberated upon to keep the balance. Supply chain efficiency can be and has to be planned with minimum inventory, if all the links of the chain behave and work in cohesion.

For this purpose, an effective and efficient method of demand forecasting has to be designed and followed, working out volumes for each product mix element in near future. The inventory planning is to be carried out with distribution points requirement and accordingly the warehousing facilities designed, established, and operated.

Inventory policy on the basis of forecasted demand has to be evolved for safety stocks, minimum stocks, maximum stocks, reorder levels, lead times for procurement and reorder quantities etc for each stocking or warehousing destination. The company should obtain technological integration at the appropriate level for smooth flow of information to being down the inventory levels to just sufficient quantity. Warehousing facilities are to be established based on type and quantity of inventory, possibly at rail heads/road heads to minimise cost of transportation. The distribution channels are then designed according to movement pattern of supplies with mode of transport, time for movement and volume of inventory to be moved for distribution.

The final link in making the product available to the customer end is the Distribution Network. The distribution network will be developed on the basis of channel selection for distribution, the supply chain configuration available and the distribution planning method. This has to be a long term commitment for own resources or for engaging 3PL/4PL providers. Inventory and Distribution strategy can be summerised as follows :

- Demand forecasting
- Inventory planning
- Warehousing facilities planning
- Channel selection
- Distribution Network planning

17.11 Improved Supply Chain Links

There are various links in the supply chain system and it is imperature that these links operate at their highest level of efficiency without any major breakdown, so that integrated system is cost and time effective. Few suggestion are offered for maintaining these links in top operating conditions:

Human Link – To ensure the chain to be operated without loss of efficiency, it is necessary to follows the guiding principles as :

- Personnel selection and recritment must match the requirement. It is not only the technical qualification and performance level, but also their mental rebustness that is important for the type of job he is selected for.
- People Selected must be properly trained for their specific responsibilities. They also are to be trained to merge into the culture of working of the organisation, so that they become part of the team for smooth and efficient operation.
- Once trained and fully familiarised with the company operation, their motivation requirements must be identified and applied so that a person is committed and involved in the job fully.
- An unambiguous job description should be spelt out with defined measurable KPAs (Key Performance Areas) to build his confidence to perform. He should be brought to the level of 'JOB OWNERSHIP' through motivation, job description, job enrichment and job empowerment. When a person gets converted from human resource into an asset, the links operate most efficiently.

Market and Design link

For this link, following things should be kept in mind :

- Thorough market research for data collection for customer requirement.

• Effective marketing strategy for the type of product according to the environment where the product is to be positioned.

• Product design must match the customer requirement, but must be simple and produceable with reference to the resources available. Following principles can be adopted

- Minimum number of parts
- Reduced moving parts
- common components and standard modules
- Simplified design, say easy fasteners, Design for Manufacturing and Assembly (DFMA), easy for maintenance.
- Fool proof operation/Failsafe design
- Reasonable tolerances
- Rebust design for reliability
- Design for quality.

Processes and Production

Various aspects to be kept in views are as follows :

Machines

- Procurement as per production specifications
- Output as per demand conversion
- Easy maintainability
- Technology and automation as per actual requirement
- Suitable process selection
- Proper scheduling

Production

- Controlled Random fluctuation
- Quality oriented production
- Layouts and operation flexibility

Materials planning and procurement

- Effective forecast
- Detailed material planning – preferably through MRP
- Effective negotiations for cost and specifications
- Quality standards specified
- Lead times to be controlled
- substitution of materials taken advantage of
- Effective vendor analysis and control.

Distribution Network

- Proper Mode of distribution
- Packaging and transportation to match
- Routing to be cost-effective
- Create intermediate stocking points if necessary, to act as buffer
- Delivery schedules to be worked out and controlled.
- IT-enabled system to track movement of goods.

Service innovation

- Proactive offerings
- Work on customers psychology.
- Customer participation.
- Quality standards as per demand.

17.12 Lean Supply Chain for Competitive Advantage

The system of lean operations has been tried out successfully by Toyota Productions. Lean supply chain, like lean Manufacturing, means that all wastages must be eliminated by reducing inventory at all stages. Lean supply chain, therefore, would mean proper intergration and synchronising all the links through proper planning and control.

Following are few areas needing attention to effect lean Supply Chain Management :

- Elimination of waste.
- Simple and co-ordinated design.
- Optimisation of inventory.
- JIT Sourcing with Captive Vendor Management (CVM) technique.
- Vendor Managed Inventory (VMI).
- Efficient warehousing management.
- Continuous improvement.
- Simple and safe design with quality manufacturing.

In order to achieve the lean supply chain, following principle can be adopted :

- Flexibility of operations.
- IT-enabled communication systems.
- Use project management technique to plan and operate supply chain. It is called Activity Based Management (ABM).
- Clearly defining the efficiency measuring parameters and standards.
- Policy on Benchmarking.

17.13 Operating Model for SCM

For operating a supply chain effectively, there are three important major constituents to be controlled :

• Supply chain partner or links such or design, source, suppliers, production, distribution and market spread.

• Supply chain Enabltees have two distinct sources:

  • Tools and Techniques

  • Information and Measures

• Resources that make the chain work smoothly

  • Information systems

  • Human Resources competencies.

Tools and Techniques that are helpful in design and implementation of a supply chain are :

  • Measuring and Benchmarking performance.

  • Activity-Based Management (ABM)

  • Network Modelling

  • Inventory analysis.

The Network Modeling based activity analysis is being discussed in the chapter on "Project Planning and Control'. Inventory analysis has already been dealt with under Inventory Management. Benchmarking will be discussed under the chapter on "Quantity Planning and Assurance".

SCM operating Model is depicted in Fig. 17.3

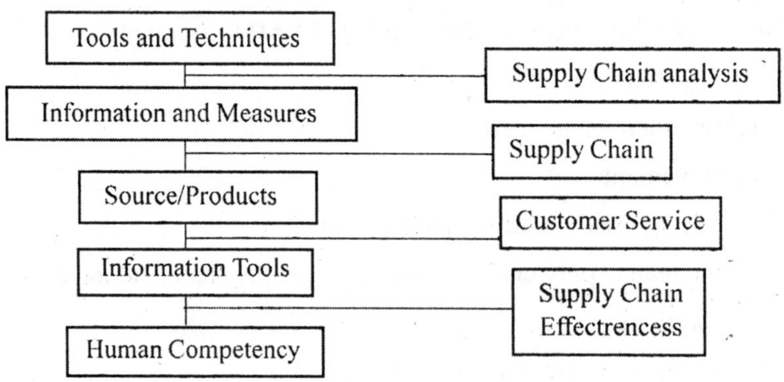

Fig 17.3. SCM Operating Model.

17.14 E-Procurement

Traditional purchasing system, in today's environment, should tranform into the electronic procurement (E-Procurement), because of fast development of IT-enabled systems with their obvious advantages of cost. Purchasing costs are coming down considerably due to this E-procurement revolution. E-procurement has two dimensions :

- E-purchasing
- E-sourcing

E-purchasing

It is a web-centric requisioning system, which operates with on-line catelogue and paper less purchase system. Use of EDI is now going out of circulation. With web centric system, it is possible to issue electronic approvals and release orders. It is so fast a process that with due authentication, it is instant information to the vendors (Better to use captive vendors, who are few, loyal and reliable). It has in-built capability of offering significant operational and financial incentive to the vendors as well as to the internal customers like production and accounts/finance. With huge saving due to tremendous time saving capability and reduction of cost of physical operations, the system is in vogue practically in every company. The company either lags behind or perishes on cost benefit alone as they cannot remain competitive without this advantage. In addition to EDI, three more important approaches to E-purchasing are catualogue hubs, exchanges and auctions, all so very useful in todays global competition environment.

Catalogue hubs : These are used for reducing costs of placing the orders, thereby reducing the cost of the goods. The suppliers lists and costs are available on live (on the hub) and can be used by the buyers as per their requirement of purchase electronically. The negotiations on the prices can be done easily. The employers can use their computer for selection of items needed and the system, then, generates purchase orders on the negotiated price.

Exchanges : It is an electronic market place where the buyers and sellers come together to transact their businesses. The business is transacted without the contract negotiations and hence "spot – purchases" can be resorted to.

Auctions : It is a step further to the "Exchanges", where competitive bidding concept is resorted to. The sale is offered to the highest bidder to dispose off the excess materials. A similar concept called "The Reverse Auction" is also in use where in the suppliers bid for the contract with the buyes. This is also very popular these days. Internet is the help for all these facilities.

E-Sourcing

E-purchase decisions are faster today due to large information available regarding products and costs with specification and quality standards. E-Sourcing means the availability of the information about electronic catalogue and online data about large source of products across the globe. It provides real-time information to offer full visibility on the terms and conditions of procurement and competitive analysis of products. This additional on-line information makes buyers and vendors more open and informed about the way negotiation can take place. This develops a collaborative attitude and creates large value-addition to buyer and supplier both. We can easily have B2B (Business to Business) transactions with much reduced costs.

E-procurement, hence, is an imprtant link of our Supply Chain System. SAP defines E-procurement as the B-2-B sales and purchasing products and services on the global level.

17.15 Logistics Management

Logistics, broadly, refers to the management of the movement of materials, within the factory and outside either out going product to the customer or the incoming materials from the suppliers.

It is the development of the concept of **integrated logistics management** that has now resulted into its new name as supply Chain Management (with logistics still being a part of it). Integrated logistics management had transportation, production planning, demand management, distribution network, location of plants and warehouses and inventory management as its constituents.

Logistics Activities can be diagramatically shown as under :

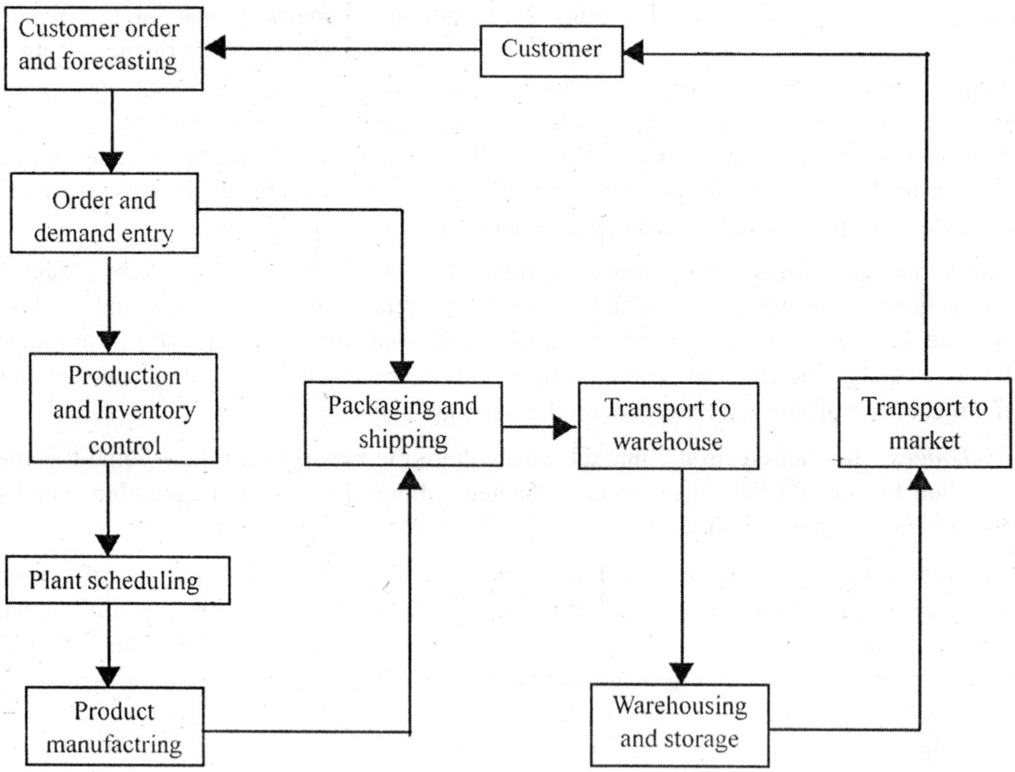

Fig. 17.4 Logistics Activities Flow

As can be seen from above, major elements of logistics are as follows :

- Demand forecasting
- Order processing Management
- Inventory planning and control

- Warehousing and storage management.
- Packaging and shipping
- Transportation
- Waste management
- Customer Service
- Parts and Service Support
- Distribution Communications

Logistics Cost Structure

From the above list, it can be seen that the total logistics cost comes from the following areas

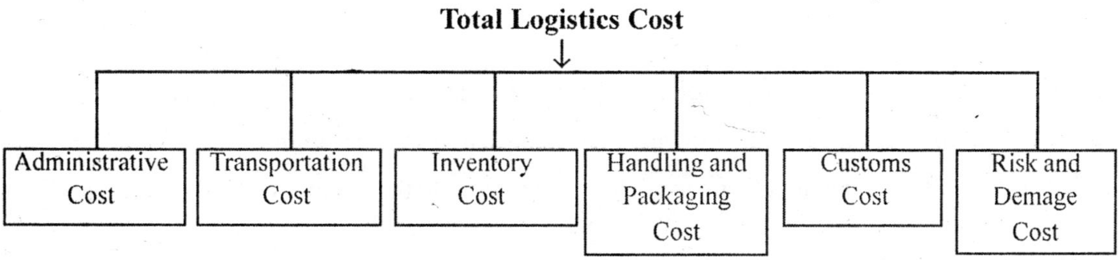

Fig. 17.5 Logistics cost areas

Though each area needs a careful examination, planning and control, transportation and inventory holding costs require a very special look, due to their higher contribution to the logistics cost. The impact of "lean operation" concept on the logistics should be studied so that various forms of wastes in logistics can be eliminated. The "Lean Six-Sigma", therefore, would need identification of unnecessary inventories and the availability of source at the nearest market to reduce variation in cost, while enhancing the speed and flow of logistics chain. Its impact on selection of retailers, wholesalers, Distributors, Manufactures and Suppliers has to be studied with a 'convex lens' in hand at all times.

Due to the movement of materials within and outside the firm, logistics can be divided into two major areas :

- Micro logistics (inside the firm)
- Macro logistics (outside the firm)

Micro level logistics : The transportation of all forms of materials within the company (internal network) is a linkage process in logistics for the internal distribution of the goods. The design of Micro level logistics involves the following aspects :

Operational : the product characterstics, the environmental aspect, and the company policy.

Mode Selection : the load size, density value, the competitive necessity and the cost analysis.

Channel Strategy : identification of available channels and their interactions.

These aspects decide what type of internal transportation can be planned. In fact, for internal use, the requirement is totally different from that needed for external use due to limited space. The lot size/load size are as per work centre requirement in terms of production materials and assembly components. Hence the material handling has to be carefully planned in terms of fork lift trucks, conveyor belts or overhead cranes etc. The equipment scheduling and control is imperative for any cost benefit usage.

Some of the activities in movement of materials within the factory are as follows :

- Removing materials from incoming vehicles and placing these inside stores.
- Moving materials for inspection.
- Removing inspected materials to the warehouses.
- Delivering material from warehouse to the production facility.
- Movement of materials through the operations.
- Removing finished goods to stores.
- Moving finished products for packaging at the packaging and shipping bay.
- Loading packaged loads into vehicles for moving to the shipping place.

At the levels of movement from one plant to another or to the company warehouses, a different planning is required. It will depend on the product size, lot/load size, frequency and urgency of movement for production control etc.

Macro level logistics

There are large number of modes available for Macro level logistics. The physical movement modes are as follows :

- Air ways
- Inland water ways
- Ports
- Railways and
- Roads

Air and Inland water movement : While the air and inland water movements are specific for certain companies involved in small air freighted products or movement by barrages when there is no other provision. Hence these can be used to advantage under those conditions.

Ports : India has 11 major ports and 139 minor operational ports being operated under the central and state governments respectively. Major ports under Ports Trust of India are at Haldia, Mumbai, Nhava Sheva, Madras, Cochin, Vishakhapatnam, Kandla, Mormugoa, Paradip, New Mangalore and Tuticorin to handle major cargo load of the country from and to other countries. These handle heavy cargo including containerised cargo. There are special dedicated coal ports at Pradip and Ennore, handling coal movement only. Total material handling capacity of these ports is around 250 million tonnes.

Railways : India has the worlds largest railway network. Its cargo handling capacity is plantiful. Indian Railways handle about 50% of the freight traffic of the country. The actual load requirement is much more and we find present freight capacity very inadequate and poorly co-ordinated. There is insufficient investment for capacity augmentation. It needs integration with other modes of transport for movement from Railheads to the place of actual usage. Still it is very cost effective mode of material movement.

Roads : India has a vast road network (about 3 million km). The motor vehicle population is expanding at phenominal speed. In addition to the personal vehicles on the road, there is large freight volume moving every day using this the road network. Freight traffic has crossed over 1000 billion tons Km (BTK). It is not only the development of national highways and express ways etc. much more is needed to connect smaller sectors, interior roads (about 50% of the villages still to be connected). We are moving fast in road development with the control of development and maintenance being put under National Highway Authority of India. Even private sector participation has been brought into. This speed has to be maintained for sustained national growth to a level of 8 to 10%. Road network is the life line of the economy and hence the network has to be spread and well-managed.

For freight movement, Road transport has a pivotal role to play. This is very large industry needing co-ordinated and integrated management. Quality of roads through newer and newer technology is also a must for sustained maintenance and usage. Integration of this sector for an effective supply chain success is required among many sector players, such as transporters of various catagories, marketing, aggregating, storing and delivery function players in the form of various agents and brokers. Automanufactuers have to play their role in making innovative auto transport systems like volvo designed two containers platform being handled by one prime mover.

Special Aspects of Freight Movement

Some of the other new developments taking place continiouslly in the field of logistics are piggy-back rail shipments, truck trailors on ships, light weight containers, unitised loads, drop shipping and consolidated shipments. Improvements are being thought of everyday as the cost of transportation is going upwards due to fuel cost rising.

Legislation such as Motor Vehicle Act 1988 and rules and regulations for various taxes are in place so as to control the operation of goods carried. Drivers training and efficiency updating provisions will ensure smooth operations.

Similarly finance sector has to play its role in lending money to truck owners, i.e., banks and hire/purchase companies. These facilities also need regulation for a healthy development of the sector.

Removal of inter-state barriers also needs to be thought of, so that the movement of goods across the country is smoothed out. Highway management in terms of garaging, maintenance and repair facilities are to be developed in a coordinated manner to ensure professional touch in these facilities, so vital for smooth flow of distributions network.

17.16 Transportation Cost Models

Various OR/MS approaches and models are available and are being developed to affect savings of large proportions in this sector.

Large number of transportation problems are encountered in physical distribution of goods. Source of supply, availability of materials or commodity for distribution, the requirement of demand at a particular location or at number of destinctions are some of the parameters involved in such problems. The aim is to effect distribution with minimal cost associated with transportation of supply from the source to the destination within the constraints of availability and demand.

Transportation Model :

The alogorithm involved in transportation model is as follows :

Step 1. Formulate the problem and establish the cost matrix i.e., unit cost involved in transporting material from a particular source to a specific demand destination. The matrices can be prepared even for time. profit or distance based information.

Step 2. Obtain the initial basic feasible solution using either the least cost method or the Vogel's Approximation Method (VAM). The initial basic solution should satisfy the following conditions.

• It should satisfy all demand/supply conditions.

• The number of positive allocations from supply source to the destinations should be equal to **m + n – 1**, where m is the number of rows and n the number of columns of the transportation matrix. Under this condition only the solution is treated as feasible. Otherwise the solution is treated as degenerate.

Step 3. Test the initial basic solution for its optimality using either the stepping stone method or Modified Distribution (MODI) method, only if feasibility condition is satisfied.

Step 4. Iterate the solution till such time optimal feasible solution is arrived at.

Least Cost Method

This method can be used to obtain initial basic solution of the matrix, if the matrix is of minimisation type. Otherwise it has to be converted into one by subtracting all elements of the matrix from the highest element of the matrix.

The method has the following steps.

Step 1. Select the least cost cell in the whole matrix i.e., all rows/columns. In case of a tie, select the least element arbitrarrily.

Step 2. Allocate maximum possible supply units subject to the constraint of demand requirement for that supply/demand contribution combination.

Step 3. Eliminate row/columns fully satisfied with the allocation.

Step 4. Adjust the supply and demand requirements out of unallocated supply/demand.

Step 5. Repeat step 1 to 4 to allocate all the supplies to all the destinations.

Step 6. Check the feasibility condition for the solution i.e., number of allocations should be equal to m + n – 1.

Step 7. Proceed to test the optimality of the solution so obtained only if feasibility condition is satisfied.

Vogel's Approximation Method (VAM)

This is a preferred method over the least cost method, as the solutions obtained through this method are likely to be more efficient, thereby reducing the time for optimality test. The steps involved in this method are as under :

Step 1. Consider each row of the cost matrix individually and find the difference between two least values (i.e., lowest and the next higher). This difference is called the Row penalty for each row and is written against the relevant row.

The same procedure is adopted to get column penalty by subtracting the minimum element of the column from its next higher value and write these accordingly against each column.

Step 2. Locate the maximum of these penalty values (row and column) and allocate maximum supply/demand requirement to the least value cell in that row/column.

Step 3. Delete the row/column satisfying the allocation i.e., where no demand/supply remains to be considered.

Step 4. Repeat step 1 to 3 to allocate the maximum supply/demand requirement till all the allocations have been attained.

Step 5. Test the feasibility of the solution (allocations = m + n – 1)

Step 6. Proceed to test optimality of the so obtained initial basic feasible solution.

Testing the optimality of basic feasible solution

Stepping Stone Method : The following procedure is adopted under this method for the optimality check:

Step 1. Calculate the opportunity cost of each empty cell (cell with no allocation). It is obtained by formulating the loop of unoccupied cell with minimum of 3 occupied cells along the horizontal/ vertical lines of these cell elements and alloting at least one unit to the unoccupied cell.

Step 2. If the total opportunity cost of the loop cells is positive, the loop cell allocation cannot be improved : In case of negative total opportunity cost, the solution can be improved.

Step 3. In case of non-optimal solution (negative total opportunity cost for a particular empty cell), the allocation of units to this empty cell should be made from any appropriate occupied cell of the loop involved in opportunity cost calculation.

Step 4. The steps 1 to 3 are repeated till the overall cost of allocation is minimised (i.e., when the opportunity costs for all unoccupied cells are positive).

Step 5. The total cost of transportation is calculated based on optimal level allocations so obtained.

MODI Method : This is also called U-V method. By this method, the initial basic solution is gradually improved through iterative process. Following steps are involved in MODI method:

Step 1. Calculate the values of auxiliary variables Uis and Vjs for all rows and columns of the basic solution matrix using the relationship.

$$C_{ij} = U_i + V_j \text{ for all occupied cells}$$

Where Cij = Cost element at the occupied cell ij.

Ui = auxiliary value of row for occupied cells.

and Vj = auxiliary value of column for the occupied cells.

To start any value Ui or Vj can be selected as zero.

Step 2. For all unoccupied cells, calculate the incremental value of auxiliary variables, with the help of following relationship :

$\Delta ij = Cij - (Ui + Vj)$

The value Δij is called cell evaluation index or opportunity index.

Step 3. (i) If all $\Delta ij > 0$, then solution is optimal.

(ii) If all $\Delta ij = 0$, the solution is unchanged and an alternate solution is feasible.

(iii) If some $\Delta ij < 0$, there can be an improved solution by introducing cell (ij) in the basis.

Step 4. Formulate a closed loop for the unoccupied cell (ij), brought into the solution as per step 3. Start with the maximum negative opportunity cost cell.

Step 5. Allocate the largest number of units to the (ij) cell with respect to supply/demand constraint and readjust the supply/demand position as a result of this allocation.

Step 6. Calculate the cost of the allocations from this modified allocation matrix and repeat step 1 to 5 till we react all $\Delta ij \geq 0$. This is optimal solution to the problem.

Step 7. Calculate the cost of tranportation as per the optimal allocations.

Problem 17.1

There are four production factories in an organisation named F_1, F_2, F_3 and F_4. At these factories, the costs of production per product unit are Rs. 2, 3,1 and 5 respectively. The number of units each factory can produce in a day are 50, 70 30 and 50 respectively. While receiving demand from market, the supply chain manager noticed that locations 1, 2, 3 and 4 needed 25, 35, 105 and 20 units respectively, on daily basis. The transportation costs per unit from a factory to a market location are as follows.

Market locations

		M_1	M_2	M_3	M_4
	F_1	2	4	6	11
Factories	F_2	10	8	7	5
	F_3	13	3	9	12
	F_4	4	6	8	3

Suggest, how the supply chain manager should schedule his logistics to meet the demands of the markets at minimum cost.

Solution:

Transportation costs and production costs are given separately. Combining these two together, we formulate the total cost matrix as follows:

Market locations

Factories	M_1	M_2	M_3	M_4
F_1	2 + 2 = 4	4 + 2 = 6	6 + 2 = 8	11 + 2 = 13
F_2	10 + 3 = 13	8 + 3 = 11	7 + 3 = 10	5 + 3 = 8
F_3	13 + 1 = 14	3 + 1 = 4	9 + 1 = 10	12 + 1 = 13
F_4	4 + 5 = 9	6 + 5 = 11	8 + 5 = 13	3 + 5 = 8

The demand/supply position can now be super imposed on the matrix to get the transportation table as under.

Factories	M_1	M_2	M_3	M_4	*Supply*
F_1	4	6	8	13	50
F_2	13	11	10	8	70
F_3	14	4	10	13	30
F_4	9	11	13	8	50
Demand	25	35	105	20	185\200

It can be seen from the table (cost matrix) that the supply units 200 are in excess of demand of the market. *i.e.* 185. Thus 200-185 = 15 units will remain in inventory. For solving the problem, a dummy market demand of 15 units (not shipping *i.e.* the shipping cost is zero) is created with all cost elements as zero. Thus the modified matrix will be

Factories	M_1	M_2	M_3	M_4	*Dummy* M_5	*Supply*
F_1	4	6	8	13	0	50
F_2	13	11	10	8	0	70
F_3	14	4	10	13	0	30
F_4	9	11	13	8	0	50
Demand	25	35	105	20	15	

Using Vogel's Approximation Method (VAM), we proceed to work out the optimal feasible distribution schedule for this balanced situation :

							R_1	R_2	R_3	R_4	R_5	R_6
	$4_{(25)}$	$6_{(5)}$	$8_{(20)}$	13	0	50	4–0=4	6–4=2	2	2	⑤	—
	13	11	$10_{(10)}$	8	0	70	8–0=8	10–8=2	2	2	2	2
	14	$4_{(30)}$	10	13	0	30	4–0=4	10–4=6	–	–	–	–
	9	11	$13_{(15)}$	$8_{(20)}$	0 ⑮	50	8–0= ⑧	9–8=1	1	3	5	⑤
	25	35	105	20	15	200						
C_1	9–4 =5	6–4 =2	10–8=2	8–8=0	0–0=0							
C_2	5	2	2	0	–							
C_3	⑤	5	2	0	–							
C_4	–	⑤	2	0								
C_5	–	–	2	0								
C_6	–	–	3	0								

Having done the penalty calculation (Next min-min) and alloting units at maximum penalty row/column, we obtain the feasible solution as follows :

4(25)	6(5)	8(20)	13(0)	0(0)
13(0)	11(0)	10(70)	8(0)	0(0)
14(0)	4(30)	10(0)	13(0)	0(0)
9(0)	11(0)	13(15)	8(20)	0(15)

And the transportation cost $= 4 \times 25 + 6 \times 5 + 8 \times 20 + 10 \times 70 + 4 \times 30 + 13 \times 15 + 8 \times 20$

$= 100 + 30 + 160 + 700 + 120 + 195 + 160$

$=$ Rs. 1465

Problem 17.2

The matrix for unit costs of movement from sources of supply P, Q and R to the distributions points K, L and M are given below. The position of supplies and demands is also given in the matrix.

Sources of Supply	*Destinations*			*Supply*
	K	L	M	
P	4	8	8	76
Q	16	24	16	82
R	8	16	24	77
Demand	72	102	41	215 / 235

Obtain minimum cost distribution schedule.

Solution :

Initial Check

- It is a minimisation problem ? – Yes (a case of cost minimisation)
- It a balanced supply/demand situation – No

Then we have to prepare a balanced matrix by adjusting additional demand [(76 + 82 + 77)] – (72 + 104 +41) = 20] of 20 units to a imaginary destination N. The modified matrix is as under :

	K	*L*	*M*	*N*	*Supply*
P	4	8	8	0	76
Q	16	24	16	0	82
R	8	16	24	0	77
demand	72	102	41	20	235

Initial basic solution :

(a) Using least cost method.

Step 1. The least cost element of the matrix is at the cell say, PN i.e., zero.

Step 2. Allocate maximum units with supply/demand constraint i.e., 20 (demand 20 only against supply possibility of 76)

Step 3. Since the demand from the column N has been satisfied, we eliminate column N, adjusting remaining supply for now P as 56 (i.e., 76 – 20).

Step 4. Now we repeat step 1 to 3 and get the following allocations.

	K	*L*	*M*	*N*
P	4 (56)	8	8	0 (20)
Q	16	24 (41)	16 (41)	0
R	8 (16)	16 (61)	24	0

∴ The transportation cost = $4 \times 56 + 24 \times 41 + 16 \times 41 + 8 \times 16 + 16 \times 61 = 2968$

There are 6 allocations. Since $m + n - 1 = 3 + 4 - 1 = 6$, it is a feasible solution. Hence optimality test can be conducted.

Optimality test by Stepping Stone Method

Step 1. Formulating loops for unoccupied cells

For PL ⇒ PL — RL — RK — PK — PL

For PM ⇒ QM — QL — RL — RK — PK — PM

For QK ⇒ QK — QL — RL — RK — QK

For RM ⇒ RM — QM — QL — RL — RM

Net cost change for cell PL = 8 – 16 + 8 – 4 = – 4
Net cost change for cell PM = 8 – 16 + 24 – 16 + 8 – 4 = – 4
Net cost change for cell QK = 16 – 24 + 16 – 8 = 0
Net cost change for cell RM = 24 – 16 + 24 – 16 = 0

taking values for cells as positive and negative alternately.

Step 2. There are two negative cost cells, both at – 4. Hence any one can be considered for allocation.

Step 3. Taking PL as the improvement cell, we can allocate units to it either from its vertical/ or horizontal loop cell i.e. minimum of 56 and 61 i.e., allocate 56 and readjust the supply/demand position as follows:

Supply from P remaining as 20 i.e., (76 – 56 = 20) and Demand at reducing to 46 i.e., (102 – 56 = 46)

Step 4. Repeating step 1 to 3 for the revised allocations, we get the optimal solution as under (since cost change for all the unoccupied cells are either zero or positive, it is optimality of the solution)

4	8 (56)	8	0 (20)
16	24 (41)	16 (41)	0
8 (16)	16 (5)	24	0

And optimal cost = 8 × 56 + 24 × 41 + 16 × 41 + 8 × 16 + 16 × 5 = 2136

Problem 17.3

The distribution of commodity from warehouses A, B, C and D is planned to three markets P, Q and R. The level of surpluses and requirements at various location are given in the following matrix with the related units costs of transportation. Work out the optimal distribution of commodity units.

	P	Q	R	Surplus
A	2	7	4	5
B	3	3	1	8
C	5	4	7	7
D	1	6	2	14
Requirement	7	9	18	34

Solution :

Initial check

(a) Is it a case of minimisation ? – Yes

(b) Is it a balanced matrix ? – Yes

Now, we proceed to obtain the initial basic solution of the problem, using Vogel's Approximation Method (VAM).

Step 1. Obtain the row/column penalty by subtracting the minima of row/column from corresponding next higher element of the same row/column. The values are written as under:

	P	Q	R	R_1
A	2	7	4	4 – 2 = 2
B	3	3	1	3 – 1 = 2
C	5	4	7	5 – 4 = 1
D	1	6	2	2 – 1 = 1
C_1	2 – 1 = 1	4– 3 = 1	2 – 1 = 1	

The maximum of these penalties is 2 (tie between A and B)

Step 2. Taking row A to be a row of allocations (selected A out of tie) and allotting at the minimum element in row A, the position emerges as follows:

	P	**Q**	**R**	**Surplus**
A	2 (5)	7	4	5 – 5 = 0
B	3	3	1	8
C	5	4	7	7
D	1	6	2	14
Requirement	7 – 5 = 2	9	18	

Minimum element in row A is 2 and as per surplus/requirement balance, only 5 units can be allocated at this cell as shown above.

Step 3. Since row A has exhausted its supplies, it is eliminated.

Step 4. The remaining requirement of P has been adjusted to (7 – 5) = 2

Step 5. Repeating step 1; we locate row/column penalties and selecting the maximum of these penalties, we get :

	P	**Q**	**R**	**Surplus**	**R_2**
B	3	3	1	8	2
C	5	4	7	7	1
D	1	6	2	14	1
Requirement	2	9	(18)		
C_2	2	1	1		

The maximum penalty is 2 (tie between row B and column P). Repeating step 2, selecting column P for allocation, we allocate maximum of supply/requirement in column P, but at minimum element as 1. The allocation is as under.

	P	Q	R	Surplus	R_3
B	3	3	1	8	2
C	5	4	7	7	1
D	1(2)	6	2	14 – 2 = 12	(4)
Requirement	2 – 2 = 0	9	18		
C_3		1	1		

Step 3. Column P, having met its full requirement of 2 units, is eliminated. Similarly for D:

	Q	R	Surplus	R_4	R_5
B	3 (2)	1 (6)	8	2	2
C	4 (7)	7	7	3	3
D	6	2 (12)	12	(4)	
Requirement	9	6			
C_4	1	1			
C_5	1	(6)			

Having repeated step 1 to 3 again, we get the initial basic solution as under :

	P	Q	R
A	2 (5)	7	4
B	3	3 (2)	1 (6)
C	5	4 (7)	7
D	1 (2)	6	2 (12)

It has m + n – 1 = 4 + 3 – 1 = 6 allocations

Hence it is a feasible solution and can be tested for optimality.

The cost of tranportation = 2 × 5 + 3 × 2 + 1 × 6 + 4 × 7 + 1 × 2 + 2 × 12 = 76

We can now proceed for its optimality test under MODI method,

Optimality Test (MODI method).

Step 1. To start with, we put $U_A = 0$

The remaining value of Ui and Vj are as under (Cij = Ui + Vj for all occupied cells)

	P	Q	R	Ui
A	2 (5)	7	4	0
B	3	3 (2)	1 (6)	–2
C	5	4 (7)	7	3
D	1 (2)	6	2 (12)	– 1
Vj	2	1	3	

Step 2. Working out Δijs for all unoccupied cells.

$$\Delta AQ = Cij - (Ui + Vj)$$
$$= 7 - (0 + 1) = +6$$

Similarly $\Delta AR = 5 - (0 + 3) = +2$

$$\Delta BP = 3 - (2 + 2) = -1$$
$$\Delta CP = 5 - (3 + 2) = 0$$
$$\Delta CR = 7 - (3 + 3) = +1$$
$$\Delta DQ = 6 - (-1 + 1) = +6$$

Step 3. Since cell BP has a negative value, it qualifies for modified allocation.

Step 4. Now we bring call BP into basis and formulate a loop for it, having at least 3 occupied cells enroute.

loop for BP ⇒ BP → BR → DR → DP → BP

Step 5. We allocate 2 units to cell BP (being balance of occupied cells on the loop i.e., 6 units of BR and 2 units of DP). Adjusting this allocation, we get

	P	Q	R	Ui
A	2 (5)	7	4	–1
B	3 (2)	3 (2)	1 (4)	0
C	5	4 (7)	7	1
D	1	6	2 (12)	1
Vj	3	3	1	

Step 6. Repeating steps 1 to 5, we get the next solution (Uis are –1, 0, 1 and 1) as written and (Vjs as 3, 3 and 1).

Calculating $\Delta AQ = 7 - (-1 + 3) = +5$

$$\Delta AR = 4 - (-1 + 1) = +4$$
$$\Delta CP = 5 - (1 + 3) = +1$$
$$\Delta CR = 7 - (1 + 1) = +5$$
$$\Delta DP = 1 - (1 + 3) = -3$$
$$\Delta DQ = 6 - (1 + 3) = +2$$

The only negative value of Δij is – 3 for cell DP and hence we bring DP into basis and make allocations. By loop formation, we get :

	P	Q	R	Ui
A	2 (5)	7	4	2
B	3	3(2)	1(0)	0
C	5	4(7)	7	1
D	1(2)	6	2(2)	1
Vj	0	3	1	

Step 6. Repeating (Uis are 2, 0, 1, 1 and Vjs as 0, 3, 1)

$$\Delta AQ = 7 - (2 + 3) = +2$$
$$\Delta AR = 4 - (2 + 1) = +1$$
$$\Delta BP = 3 - (0 + 0) = +3$$
$$\Delta CP = 5 - (1 + 0) = +4$$
$$\Delta CR = 7 - (1 + 1) = +5$$
$$\Delta DQ = 6 - (1 + 3) = +2$$

Since all Δ ijs are positive, it is the optimal solution.

Thus the optimal allocation for distribution is as follows :

	P	Q	R
A	2(5)	7	4
B	3	3(2)	1(6)
C	5	4(7)	7
D	1(2)	6	2(12)

The optimal cost of transportation $= 2 \times 5 + 3 \times 2 + 1 \times 6 + 4 \times 7 + 1 \times 2 + 2 \times 12$

$= 10 + 6 + 6 + 28 + 2 + 24$

$= 76$

Problem 17.4

Transport Corporation is maintaining a contract from the manufacturer to supply its products from two plants to three customers. The contract rate of supply per tonne of load from each plant to each customer (in rupees) is given in the following matrix :

Plant	Customer		
	A	B	C
1	15	30	20
2	20	25	15

Plant 1 had the monthly capacity of 1000 tonnes whereas plant 2 has the monthly capacity of 2000 tonnes. The monthly demands from customer is given as under :

Customer A 500 tonnes

Customer B 1500 tonnes

Customer C 1000 tonnes

Work out the optimum cost transhipment schedule from each plant to each customer per month.

Solution :

This problem can be solved using Linear Programming through simplex method or by using Microsoft Exel Sheet. Let us first formulate the mathematical model for the problem.

Objective function Min (Cost) $= 15x_1 + 30x_2 + 20x_3 + 20x_4 + 25x_5 + 15x_6$

Where x_1 = tonnes of load sent from Plant 1 to customer A

x_2 = tonnes of load sent from Plant 1 to customer B

x_3 = tonnes of load sent from Plant 1 to customer C

x_4 = tonnes of load sent from Plant 2 to customer A

x_5 = tonnes of load sent from Plant 2 to customer B

x_6 = tonnes of load sent from Plant 2 to customer C

Constraints :

$x_1 + x_2 + x_3$ ≤ 1000 (Capicity of Plant 1)

$x_4 + x_5 + x_6$ ≤ 2000 (Capicity of Plant 2)

$x_1 + x_4$ ≥ 500 (Demand of Customer A)

$x_2 + x_5$ ≥ 1500 (Demand of Customer B)

$x_3 + x_6$ ≥ 500 (Demand of Customer C)

The Microsoft Exc\el Sheet can be written as

Decision Variables

Variables	x_1	x_2	x_3	x_4	x_5	x_6	and Z = 0
Values	15	30	20	20	25	15	

Constraints

x_1	x_2	x_3	x_4	x_5	x_6	RHs
1	1	1	0	0	0	1000
			1	1	1	2000
1			1			500
	1			1		1500
		1			1	1000

The spread sheet can be used by choosing linear option, writing the constraints and obtaining the value of x_1 to x_6, then optimising the transportation cost.

17.17 OutSourcing Logistics

Outsourcing with its inherent advantages has been accepted as an important management function for increasing performance of non-core supply chain activities. The main advantage of the outsourcing is the benefit of the organisation to concentrate on their core-competency and use of the core-competencies of some other organisation in the logistics field. Though the concept has its inherent risks (may be loss of control) yet care can be taken to reduce the risks by placing proper management barriers to avoid any failure, mismatch or frauds of any nature. The logistics services can be sub-contracted to specialised companies so that their fleet and its maintenance at optimum level can be taken benefit of.

There are risks of outsourcing such as a party failing in its operations, going bankrupt, changing their field of operations or offering merger or acquisitions to some other firm.

These risks can be covered by short term contracts (Say one year) and penalty clauses being really tough.

Reasons for Outsourcing

There can be several reasons for outsourcing the logistics function to outsiders. These could be either financial constraints or service enhancement. Some companies adopt outsourcing as a strategic decision.

Financial constraint can be a large reason to use outsourcing when the company does not have enough capital to invest and the logistics requirements are very high. It can also be done to release a large capital (by sourcing out of facilities) for other important core function projects. Cost reduction could be another reason for outsourcing on financial grounds.

In service enhancement area, the company may be able to have a greater flexibility (due to area segmentation of the outsoured company operations) or it could be cashing on the service forcused capability (due to speciality based operations).

Strategically, the company may be using the services of the best in logistics industry with large professional expertise and hence a firm grip on supply chain management. Due to this availablility of service at the outsourced company, the ability to use diversified manufacturing will be enhanced, gaining the advantage of flexibility available.

Logistics Outsourcing

There are number of options available for outsourcing in logistics :

(a) Third Party Logistics (3PL) providers

(b) Fourth Party Logistics (4PL) providers

(c) Fifth Party Logistics (5PL) providers

(d) Seventh Party Logistics (7PL) providers

Third Party Logistics Providers

A Third Party Logistics (3PL) provider is the organisation providing services to the main company as part of its logistics channel that specialises in large number of the logistics services. This 3PL provider may have a long term formal-informal relationship, through contract for a given period of time. They provide many services like transportation, warehousing, custom services, freight financing, product support service or specialised consulting for distribution network design and operation and re-engineering of the supply chain. A very recent development known as RFID technology (described in the book elsewhere) for tracking and control of goods is in use by 3PL providers for tracking their consignments.

The scope for 3PL (also called TPL some times) is increasing day by day as the complexity of operations are growing due to intense competition in the market place. Every field of working is becoming specialised and hence both the users as well as the service providers are becoming dependent on each other. Obvious benefits of better operating perfomance, cost management and scheduled service delivery are being reaped by the users, with providers getting richer through their long term association and sustained growth.

The 3PL providers are relying more and more on information technology to optimise warehousing and physical movement of the inventory on a turnkey basis. The 3PL industry has come under intense cost pressure due to large capital costs of technology and also due to intense competition in their respective fields of operations. Infact 3PL providers are also getting fragmented into specialised units in tranporting and warehousing etc. This enables them to expand their services world wide. This has become feasible due to more and more dependence on IT-enabled system controlling the operation on real time basis.

Today, we observe many companies entering into outsourcing contracts i.e., logistics function being handed over to outside firms. One such example is that of TVS logistics, which offers services as JIT agents i.e., they provide distribution services for automobiles of Premier Automobiles and tractors of Mahindra and Mahindra. They are providing the expert advice and operation on physical transportation, warehousing, inventory control, customer services, sales and distribution, after sales services, logistics information networks and spare parts distribution for all their models. Similarly, two large companies of the allied fields, UPS and GATI have collaborated with Dynamic Logistics to provide courier and parcel services within the country by setting up collection and distribution centres to ensure efficient handling and assured timely delivery to the customers. These strategic alliances are paying rich dividends to the collaborating partners.

Fourth Party Logistics (4PL) Providers

It is a new concept in supply chain outsourcing system. It is the outsourcing with a step forward to 3PL providers. In this case, a 4PL provider forms an alliances among 3PL providers, the technology providers and the management consultants. Hence they are supercordinaters of best services providers in their respecitye fields.

The 4PL provider, therefore, is an integrator of the supply chain elements due to their strengths of assembly and management of resources, capabilities and technologies of the service providers and their own resources. Thus 4PL provider is a management facility provider for ensuring an effective synchronisation and collaborative benefits together.

These risks can be covered by short term contracts (Say one year) and penalty clauses being really tough.

Fifth Party Logistics (5PL) providers

This is the concepts in use for outsourcing, where in the utility of 4PL providers is enhanced through E-hubs.

Seven Party Logistics (7PL) Providers

This concept of outsourcing has been advocated and is being used by Accenture, the American consulting firm (large focus on Outsourcing). The 7PL concept combines the strengths of 3PL and 4PL providers together (7PL = 3PL + 4PL), thereby creating the co-ordinated effect at optimum level of that of the third party logistics (actual service providers) with that of the fourth party logistics (as expert management and technology providers) ensuring the utility and co-ordination together. It saves costs further, by optimising the efforts under the same roof as integrated logistic solution.

17.18 Warehousing Management

Warehousing needs special attention because materials, when lying in storage, have to be cared for. Warehouse may be the place for stocking either the raw materials or finished goods, before these are utilised. Depending upon the stock levels (inventory is recommended to be at obsolute minimum level to save unncessary cost), these may be small stores, large warehouses or even mechanised and automated stores.

The design and the space required for warehouse is a policy decision based on the level of inventory planned to be accomodated. Along with the space, the designed provision of material handling equipment also has to match. Conveyor belts, small trucks, forklift trucks or cranes etc could be provisioned as per the materials movement requirement. Inventory may be kept itemwise or in pallets, in low stocking or in high stocking system. Accordingly the handling is to be planned. Stock requisition is prepared by production control, whereas the purchasing is ordered by the purchase department. When stores start arriving, it becomes the responsibility of the warehousing personnel to receive, inspect, account for stock and maintain them till the stores are moved out where required.

Stock record is an important function of warehousing as it is required to be updated at all points of time. Necessary accounting or record entries are to be affected as soon as the materials movement takes place either brought in or sent out. Periodic physical checking of stock is also necessery to keep the materials under control. This is most important for high value, fast moving items, where stock taking must be frequent. These days, inventory accounting is maintained on line. Constant interaction of the warehousing staff with the purchase department is also necessary to coordinate timely arrival of materials, otherwise expediting has to become aggressive. There may still be some delays in materials receipts as per the lead time specified. Hence proper co-ordination between warehousing and purchase is imperative.

Packaging Innovations

For effective and integrated Supply Chain, the packaging plays an important role. The most commonly used material for packaging is corrugated sheets, which is about 80 percent recyclable. The carton design is based on the product size and weight. Even package protective materials are used to avoid any demage to the sensitive products. Generally styrofoam peanuts or sealed air type of protective materials are in use. Today, with the development of new materials and better technology, quite a few innovations have been brought in for packaging. Orem, Utah-based table and chair manufacturer Mity-lite and Columbus use specially designed packaging. UPS has been operating a package engineering group for more than 30 years, visiting and working with customers, it observes different processes tests prototypes and helps with design. Designing and arranging the type of packages with product fixing arrangement in container system of conveyors (trucks or automatic convey or belts etc.) can be a great help in storage, retrieval and transporting the products or material containers from a warehouse, bringing in large cost saving in the warehouse design and layouts.

17.19 E-Business and Supply Chain Management

The importance of effective use of internet for efficient and integrated supply chain is already been emphasised. For getting enhanced benefit of EDI, E-procurement and E-sourcing, more and more companies have become involved in E-business. E-business means use of internet (on-line transactions) to improve business operations such as design, purchase, inventory management, communications, customer service, online orders and purchase control. The word B-2-B (Business to Business) is being used for e-transactions between companies and is also called E-commerce. EDI is being fast replaced by internet based E-commerce. This is because, it enables instantaneous availability of information to all concerned.

Electronic Commerce (E-commerce) has, thus, drastically changed the way of conducting business by the companies. It helps in redesigning the customer-relationship process, marketing and the order-placement process. Whereas B2B systems permit commerce between companies. Business to Consumer (B2C) system allows customers to transact business over internet.

The utility of IT-enabled system is not only for inventory or operations. It is applicable over the entire supply chain and hence it can be said that the Supply Chain Management is becoming effecient due to E-business transactions. Addition in the system are ERP softwares helping in revolutioning the designs and space requirements of warehouses and the distributions network systems. Hence some package carriers such as FEDEX and UPS have gained tremendous growth and profits in their operations due to the E-business usage.

Though individual softwares in respective areas are available like MRP, ERP etc, there is a need to develop a concise and exhaustive software for Supply Chain Management, so that it can be standardised and universally applied at optimum cost.

For better supply chain planning, the extensive use of Microsoft EXCEL is being made, keeping integration between Plants and warehouses and between warehouses and customer markets. This works for supply chain simulation, so that effectiveness of the system can be judged from planning if the system is going to be workable. With Internet use, it becomes an Intelligent Supply Chain with Intelligent Information Centre.

A very effective supply chain software is in use with Boeing company for coordinating their operations for "Dreamliner" air craft. Being have outsourced about 70% of their operations and they co-ordinate these tier I, II, III vendors through this software. Also to integrate all internal and external links, companies use Interanet and Extranet, so as to connect their customer and vendors with internal operations. The KMG International toothpaste company operates 250 chains across the world with 50 suppliers. American DELL computers use SCM in PC business through suppliers in Taiwan, assembly shop in Singapore, couriers on extranet and internal transactions on intranet.

Benchmarking Performance for Supply Chain Managers

Supply chain managers have to be vigilant about the working efficiency of their supply chains and hence an effective integration system is a must for competitive advantage in domestic as well as global market.

Performance measuring permeters suggested are the Benchmarks for the managers to prove their efficient skill. The measuring system is given below :

- Qualitative : Customers satisfaction level
- Quantitative :
  - Product quality (defects and wastage rates)
  - Delivery lead time
  - Change response time *i.e.* responsiveness.
  - System flexibility and cost ratio
  - Resource utilisation percentage
  - Inventory turnover ratios etc.

Qualitative Parameters : Customer satisfaction is measured on the basis of complaints received by the organisation. This is, in large number of cases, subjectively determined. Quite a large proportion of customer satisfaction depends on the sales and after sales service. Hence the development of any specific model for this parameter is not always easy, due to large number of intangible ingredients. (which cannot be easily quantified). Also those are variations in these intangible ingredients, which make it further difficult to systematise. Generally the customer satisfaction level depends on three important parameters

- Quality
- Cost
- Delivery schedule

While the quality and cost of the product/service is related to the segment of clients, it is meant for, the delivery schedules common to all customers. There is a need to measure quality of input and production facilities and their efficiency. The cost would depend on the type of materials and production process, along with the distribution cost. Both these parameters can be controlled through avoidance of wastes at all levels. Thus a measure can be developed on these subsystem efficiencies. For delivery schedule, the measure is developed in the logistics efficiency and distribution pattern selected.

Quantitative Parameters : The list of few parameters listed above are common to qualitative measurement also. We can select important parameters on a common base, which can be used to quantify the effectiveness and efficiency of the supply chain.

Measuring Procedure

For the performance measurement of supply chains, we need to identify :

- What to measure ?
- How to measure ?
- How to use the information for performance improvement ?

Important Areas for Performance Measurement are as follows :

- Input measure — Human out put, supplier selection and efficiency measure.
- Internal processes — Machine utilisation and inventory management
- Out Put measure — Defects rate, rejections etc.
- Logistics and distributions — Product mix and time Schedule.

In addition, integration efficiency helps in time scheduling of supply chain.

Human Output : Important issue in production is Man-Machine compatibility, and there has to be an optimisation established based on the man output vs machine put. Human output is controlled through the concept of (*a*) Standard time (*b*) Learning curve and (*c*) Meantime between Failures (MTBF).

Standard time is laid down by the organisation for various activities and keeping quality as datum, the grading/rating of workers is decided. The volume of production and quality is then measured on the basis of standard time. Improvement in human performance can be decided on the learning curve basis. MTBF is a measure of maintenance team efficiency.

Supplier Selection and Efficiency Measure : For the supply of materials (raw materials, components or sub assemblies), the selection of supplier is an important area for efficient operation of supply chain. Various parameters adopted for supplier selection are as under :

- Loading of the suppliers (*i.e.* quantum of materials supplied)
- Adherence to quality (*i.e.*, minimum rejections based on AQL and limits of tolerance)
- Adherence to lead time (*i.e.* timely supplies, contract compliance)
- Continuous improvement (*i.e.* help in efficiency increase)
- Information sharing (*i.e.*, marketing intelligence and technical support).

- Joint value Analysis (*i.e.,* effective mutual cost reduction)
- Location of the supplier (*i.e.,* flexibility in suppliers time)
- Financial standing (*i.e.* Price terms and supplies assurance)

These measures are used for selection of the supplier for supply chain effectiveness. Better graded suppliers will help in maintaining smooth flow of inputs to ensure smooth production and timely out put. Higher level of supplier relationship leads to efficient supply chain.

Machine utilisation :

Capacity utilisation : For cost reduction, machine utilisation ratio is an important parameter to be measured and improved. The Master Production Schedule (MPS) is to be planned out to produce the required product mix in time for deliveries. The parameter for measure is the ratio of idle time to total available time of the machine.

Machine availability. This is maintenance efficiency. To ensure optimum machine availability for production purpose, effective maintenance should be specified. The measure adopted is MTBF *i.e.* (Mean Time Between Failures). Better the MTBF, better would be the machine availability.

Inventory Management : For efficient production, the requirement is optimum level of inventory of raw materials. Buffer stock and lead time for inventory replenishment are important decisions. The measure parameters are minimum period of stock levels *i.e.*, days inventory in stock.

Output Measure : The product mix and volume of output is fixed at the optimum level with MPS accordingly planned. The important parameter of output from customers point of view is the quality of product. This is measured in term of defect rate of production. How to measure defects rate is also important, because it is a flexible parameter. The method followed is deciding on Acceptance Quality level (AQL) or Accepted outgoing Quality level (AO QL), which is the highest percentage of defective products accepted as per the satisfaction level for the customer segment. For high customer satisfaction level, the AQL should be low (Say 2% or so) and it may vary with reference to the segment of the customer deciding the quality level expectations. Thus anything beyoned AQL level has to be controlled. The measuring methodology is the control chart procedure, which can indicate whether the process is under control or not.

Logistics and Distribution : Efficiency of the supply will defend on the availability of product mix as per the market requirement. Thus the logistics has to be planned out the basis of these supplies. The efficiency of logistics will be based on minimum cost of supply at desired place of supply with correct mode and type of transportation.

In the distribution area, the decision on stock points or type of distribution *i.e.* wholesalers, retailers or direct supply will be decided based on the specific product.

The measure of efficiency of logistics and distribution is the delivery time responsiveness to meet the flexible market demand.

Supply chains have multiple objectives to satisfy and hence would need different measures to ascertain the level of their desired performance. The efforts are being made to develop compresive measures to describe overall performance, rather than in a particular area of importance.

Supply Chain Monitoring Effects

Monitoring the supply chain is a herculean task for any supply chain manager due to large area of operation and a large number of uncertainties at each stage. In order to help a monitoring manager, a number of new technology solutions are emerging. Information Technology tools are now available in various area of operation and even for effective integration of various subsystems. Some of these tools are described further in brief :

- Material Planning
- Manufacturing
- Logistics

Material Planning : MRP and MRP II are strong softwares for flexible material resources planning and control.

Manufacturing : MRP II is the resource planning software. In addition, Data sweep has created an advanced sophisticated system for manufacturing tracking, in the areas of capacity, the output, the work in process and machine availability status. This information is capable of transmission through the internet to various concerned parties so that effective manufacturing process monitoring is available to plan supply chain logistics accordingly. For quality measurement, various companies are using six sigma concept to ensure higher and higher leval of customer satisfaction due to reduced defect levels (3.4 defects per million products, very high level of quality). The method DMAIC has been discussed under "Important Benchmarks for Competitiveness" under this chapter only.

Logistics : The use of RFID (described in the previous chapter) is very useful technology to track and control individual products, containers, pallets and various transport vehicles as these pass through various check posts along the entire route of the supply chain (These posts may be either a workhouse, or a port or an airport). This information is also available through internet to all concerned parties and it provides total visibility of physical movements of products supplies. **Smartseal** is a tool available to secure monitoring of products against tempering, pilferage or thefts etc. It also enables effortless customs clearance.

Other Monitoring Technologies :

- *The Food Service market exchange Instill :* It provides the service for the customers, to ensure uniform quality at uniform rates to the entire chain of similar customers. It has a uniform contract compliance assurance built in, also a purchase tracking service for multi-unit food service operators to enhance purchase reuse space activity control. **Dicarta** also provides an internet based software solution to help companies construct and monitor compliance of contractual agreements.
- *E-Hubs* : as monitoring system enable companies to detect problems for quick solutions.
- *A cross-chain Monitoring supply chain integration* : is also available to help sharing of information and monitoring across companies. Now companies can share demand information, collaborate in planning and exchange decisions for supply chain integration (strategic collaboration or partnership). Another software **"Sea Chain Suite"**, from Sea commerce implemented by Mopar Parts Group has helped in monitoring multiple part performance.

In addition, there are some supply chain metric such as Inventory turns, cycle time, DPMO and Fill Rate used to track supply chain performance covering the areas of procurement, production, distribution, warehouses, inventory, transportation and customer service *i.e.*, practically a measure of all key areas of supply chain. SCM demands an intensive, inter-disciplinary and cross-company software for operation under mutual trust of all the partners.

Benefits of Performance Measurements

As described in the proceeding paragraphs, the progress or improvement in any field of work can be known only if there is a method of measurement of performance. Then only comparison with the previous performance levels can be done and improvements established. In this age of high uncertainty, demanding customers and continuous flow of information through the IT-enabled systems, such measurements are becoming possible and useful for corporate profitability. In summary, the benefits of performance measurement of supply chain can be listed out as follows :

(*a*) Performance measurement identifies the long term goal and the strategic orientation of the organisation for customer satisfaction and corporate profitability.

(*b*) It creates transparency for the stake holders though the information provided

(*c*) It, therefore, makes decision making process of the organisation, well structured and well-defined.

(*d*) It establishes standard method of operational performance across the departments, thereby improving internal accountability.

(*e*) The comparison of performance through established measures and methods enables the decision makers to move ahead in a specified direction to achieve better results. Better operational integration is adopted as a result.

—●—

Section VI
QUALITY ENGINEERING

Chapter 18

Criticality of Quality Control

Main issues:

1. Quality perception and dimensions
2. Costs of Quality
3. Quality Conformance and SQC
4. Quality Improvement Approaches
5. Dynamics of Quality Assurance
6. Reliability
7. Quality in Services

18.1 Quality and Customer Satisfaction Level

What is quality ? This questioon often asked, with no definite answer. Actually the so defined quality of products and services is not what the producing organisation decides, but is determined by the end user i.e., the customer.

Quality is what customer likes it to be. Quality is the perception of the customer about the product/service specifications he expects against the money he pays for it. Hence the quality can not be defined in absolute standard terms. Similarly the quality is not decided by the provider as per his wish or requirement. It has to be commensurate with the market demand. When a cusomer buys a low priced product (this is as per his requirement) and he is satisfied, it is good quality for him. On the other hand, a customer buying a high priced item supposely of high quality, may not be satisfied if the product doesnot satisfy all his requirements. The customer satisfaction level, therefore, depends on the value of the product/service for a customer. In order to create desirable value for the customer, the provider must create the outward focus to match the customer requirements.

Customer satisfaction can be defined as "the degree of happiness experienced by a customer with the product/service provided". The definition is equally applicable for internal as well as external customers. A satisfied employee will act as "The Man behind the Gun" to achieve the best of quality with his utmost involvement and commitment and this goodwill is easily reflected in quality/customer satisfaction achievement. This responsibility of producing right value for the external customer, therefore, lies with the organisation. Same is important for the internal customer when provision is made for high employee satisfaction.

The customer value mainly depends on his expectation. Hence due to vast variation in customer expectation, the quality for customer satisfaction cannot be standardised, and not so easily achieved. Total customer satisfaction, therefore, is a myth and cannot be ensured. The quality provider caters for a particular segment of customer and should create value to ensure development of a right perception for that segment (product features and price go together). Since services are intangible, the quality and the resultant customer preception is more subjectively determined.

To illustrate the concept of "fitness for use" and the customer's perception variation, let us consider a case of the service being offered by a restaurant serving tea/coffee. The customer walks in and asks for a cup of coffee. Very promptly, a cup is served with coffee spilling over its edges. If it is accepted, the customer has defined the acceptable level of his quality. If this cup is refused and the waiter is asked to serve coffee in a neat cup, he understand the quality standard and brings coffee in a well washed, clean cup. At another occasion, a customer may want a large cup of coffee at enhanced price, bringing home the point that for a demanded bigher level of service, customer can willingly pay a higher price.

Companies have to obtain these requirement through market research and incorporate it in design specifications. It should, then, assure its adherance through proper process selection. The output quality should match the customer need. There may be minor variations in quality specifications, called limits of Tolerance', but by and large, the quantity should be as desired by the user.

Hence we can sum up the requirements of quality as under :

1. Quality is "fitness for use". – says Dr. JURAN
2. Do the right thing right the first time and every time. – Dr Deming states
3. Quality is meant for customers satisfaction
4. Customer should be provided with the product/service at a price and quality desired by him.
5. Customer gets what he pays for or customer pays for his level of quality.

"The fitness for use" is achieved through two components namely product features and defects elimination. Whereas product features include performance, reliability durability, serviceability and aestheties, etc, the comformance to these requirements is assured through defect elimination by proper quality control techniques. The service features cover accuracy, timeliness, friendliness courtsey, reputation and anticipation of customer needs.

18.2 Dynamics of Quality Requirement

The above discussion brings out the dynamics of quality perception. Customers requirements are not the same at all times. These keep changing as per his exposure and economic or mental growth. We must be alive to this dynamics. "Do the right thing right first time and every time" indicates that companies should produce consistant quality with the aim in view for continuous improvement. It also means that quality should match the changed requirement with time. This would need "constant innovation" to be part of business plan. Concept of 'Everytime' includes this aspect.

Business Managers know that customer (most of the time) does not specify exactly what he wants. Atleast, he can define the requirement in terms of performance or value. We have to understand his quality perception. After understanding this, the technology, design process and human capability limitations must be explained to him at that stage if his expectation is very high, rather than getting the product rejected by him when all the efforts have gone into. The requirement of one segment of customers may not be the some that for another segment of customers. A product may be of very good quality for an Asian customer, but may not be useful for an American or European customer, due to their culture or climatic variations. This dynamics is becoming acute with global market operations.

These dynamic situations have been addressed by various Quality Gurus like Joseph Juran, Edwards Deming, Philip, Crossby, Genichi Taguchi, Shigeo Shingo and Ishikawa etc. through developing and demonstrating their philosophies and concepts for quality improvement.

18.3 Areas of Quality

The quality improvement and adherance is possible only, if the following areas of operations are paid attention to :

Quality of Working Culture : The involvement of the whole organisation is required to ensure quality implementation in all its operations, be it in line system or in the support systems. For quality production and service, the company has to standardise the working culture for utmost integration of internal as well as external customers.

Quality of Design : All attributes of customers expectation to be included.

Quality of Production Facilities : The man-machine compatibility with right specifications to be ensured.

Quality of Processes : Right selection of technology and the production process, capable producing the demanded quality.

Quality of Conformance : The physical operation of the production facilities must ensure that product or service adheres to the design and performance parameters.

Quality of Customer Service : Service is where customer perceives the quality level of the products. Hence prompt attention to his needs therefore, becomes top priority for involved.

Quality of Working Culture : The involvement of the whole organisation is required to ensure high standard of quality and its implementation in all its operations, be it in line system or in the supporting functions. For quality production and service, the company has to standardise the working culture for utmost integration of internal as well as external customers.

18.4 Dimensions of Quality

Some of the parametres on which a customer relies on his quality evaluation are :

- Performance level as per customer use
- Features of the product and the service operations
- Appearance of product and the service personnel
- Serviceability and promptness in service after sales.
- Reliability of product quality and workers competance
- Durability – long lasting usage
- Safety is product features and operations
- Sensory characteristics-well cooked food should be tasty also.

18.5 Survey for Customer Requirement

It is of utmost importance to obtain the requirement of the needs and wants of the customers through a sample survey, so that these can, then, be structured into various segments of the customers. The sampling survey also needs careful throught before it is embarked upton.

Various steps suggested are highlighted below :

Step in Sampling Survey : Since sampling method can be made reliable and useful through scientific structuring, appropriate sample design and reliably large sample size, we can adopt following steps for sample survey :

- Specify objectives and the scope of the survey
- Define the population to be studied
- Selection of specific, unbiguous, stable and appropriate sample units as a representative part of the population
- Data collection – relevant and complete
- Decide on a structured schedule for the study
- Structured questionaire and selection of sample design and size
- Appropriate ground work to be properly designed, organised and monitored so as to avoid sampling errors.
- Try pre-run or pilot survey for validation of the sample design and size. Appropriate training of the data collection staff can, then, be organised.
- Summary and analysis of the sample data as tabulation, statistical analysis and report writing with conclusions and recommendations

For the purpose of unbiased survey, a simple random sampling or at best stepped or stratified sampling is better method. This has to be a deliberate decision based on the objective of the survey. Tables of Random Numbers can be used to advantage for randomness of the data collection.

Sampling is, therefore, used to get the survey done faster and analysis results can be used as fairly reliable. Sampling involves the study of a small group of the target population sector or unit. Sampling method is most desired under the following situations :

- The population (generally) is very large (almost infinite) and 100% survey is either practically impossible to conduct or is undesirable from the cost-effecitiveness angle of such a survey.
- When information or analysis is required at short notice for a quick decision making process, it is better to obtain quick results by sample survey.
- When we are trying to carry out destruction testing of a group of units', it is preferred to rely on sample testing rather than study of all the units.
- When cost of conducting total population survey is prohibitive, we can rely on sample survey.
- The reliability of the census of population survey also cannot be guaranteed due to vastness of the data and its defective structure. In such cases, sample reliability can be used with same degree of usefulness.

Since the data volume in a sample survey is limited, it is possible to pay attention to all relevent elements and more authentic results can be expected and that too at limited cost and effort level.

18.6 Quality Achievement Costs

In order to achieve quality within the design specifications and permitted tolerance, following costs are to be taken care of :

- *External failure costs*
  - (a) Complaint investigation and analysis
  - (b) Replacement/repair cost
  - (c) Legal Liablities
  - (d) Loss of good will & credibility
- *Internal failure cost*
  - (a) Scrap and rework
  - (b) Retesting
  - (c) Machine downtime cost
  - (d) Buffer stock cost
- *Appraisal Cost*
  - (a) Incoming and outgoing material inspection
  - (b) In-process inspections
  - (c) Manufacturing testing teams and instruments maintenance
- *Prevention Costs*
  - (a) Good quality planning

(b) Product/process review and updation

(c) Training cost

(d) Data analysis and result implementation.

18.7 Quality Planning in Manufacturing

To maintain good quality during manufacturing, detailed quality planning can save the cost to a very large extent. The quality parameters are decided in advance and to achieve quality in manufacturing, the action plans are worked out in details. Through these timely actions, internal as well as external failure cost can be reduced. Some actions, which can help in cost reduction during manufacturing are as follows:

- Plant location and layout – can reduce capital investment and material flow cost.
- Selection of Machines and Processes – Cost effective production due to appropriate technology and machine utilisation.
- Product design – Easy design for manufacturing for assembly, quality and fail-safing is a good help.
- Quality Assurance – Reasonable tolerances will help in defect prevention. The measuring instruments should be kept in good shape. Sampling methods and inspection criteria to be specified and announced for transparency
- Process control – use of statistical approach for process control and due corrections adopted when necessitated.
- Selection and Training – Appropriate technical training for production and inspection staff. Specific training needs must be identified.
- Feed-back mechanism – To be utilised to advantage, so that errors can be identified and corrected. A vigilant quality team required.

18.8 Quality Conformance and SQC

The product and Process Design have been discussed in Chapter 2, 3 and 5. The product/service must have all the desired characterstics as per customers requirements. A proudct may be good for one set of customers, may not be so for another group, depending on the culture and behaviour at any point of time. Also a product may be good in quality but not confortable in use or vice versa. Hence there has to be a balance of various dimensions of quality in the product/service.

Quality control, therefore, becomes important to ensure inclusion of various characterstics desired in a product and their adherance in actual practice. Quality control in produced items is required at the manufacture's end and at the material vendors end (to check quality of inputs). Due to inherent variability, the concept of Acceptance limits is to be applied through proper design and performance variations permissable.

For the purpose of quality control and certification, every country has established professional bodies. In India, The Indian Association of Quality and Reliability (IAQR) is one such organisation. Other prominant institutions such as Indian Standards Institution (ISI),

Institution of Engineers and Aeronautical Society etc are also promoting quality in the products in their respective areas of responsibility.

The normal traditional thinking on quality control is to ensure enough and rigorous system of inspection under the belief that through inspections, we can assure the customer that the defective products are not reaching them. The Japanese thinking advocated by Dr. Deming is a step ahead under which the system ensures non-production of defective products. Hence the basic difference of quality control between Japanase and Americans was the defect prevention rather than defect elimination. Input quality control starts the process of defect prevention.

Input Quality Control : The quality conformance should start at the input end to avoid any defective material, poorly maintained machine or less skillful worker contributing to the level of poor quality. On the input side, proper training of the workmen, proper selection of machine and process and good maintenance along with good quality material must be ensured. The basic concept of quality conformance should be "prevention of defects", rather than controlling these. The concept of 'zero defect', therefore, is the method of quality control through the inputs. The rigid control of the input assumes greatest importance for defect prevention.

Output quality Control : When the system ensures good quality of inputs, there is every likelihood that product coming out of the production system will be of good quality. But product quality on the output side is important due to random fluctuations occuring during production. Feed-back system with effective inspections, therefore, will ensure defectives elimination. Production model caters for such a pracantion.

Statistical Quality Control

While the input resources need quality-check, the variation in process in still noticed due to random fluctuations (either natural or system effect). The random fluctuations occur in the form of variation in temperatures, workers mental state or absentism or machine state and these cause variations in the quality of the product. Some variability can be controlled, when it is due to assignable reasons and is noticed. Some variations can be arising due to random mistakes at various levels such as wrong setting of the machine, aged machines or tools going out of alignment or even defective raw material not noticed during inspections. Thus we need establishing systems to control these variations in the products/services, so as to ensure that the defects donot reach the customer to the best of our ability. Statistical Quality control is such a technique to ensure the quality of the product/service.

The method used is the concept of quality control charts, which were suggested by Schewhart. These follow the priniciple of allowable variations (as per the functional suitability of the product specification/service efficiency). A typical control chart is drawn as Fig. 18.1 below

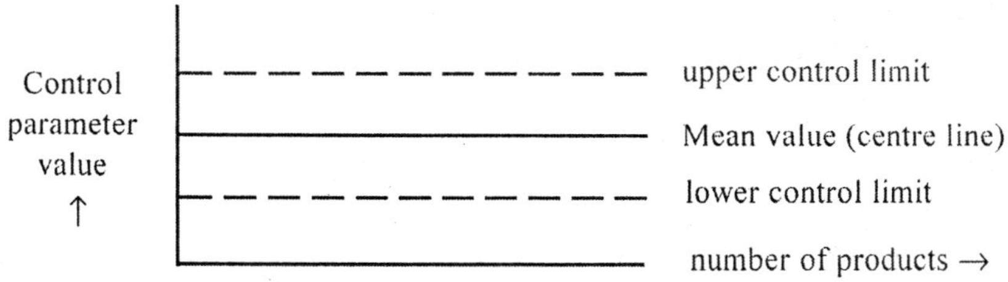

Fig. 18.1 Control Chart

These limits emerge from the permissible variability as Limits of Tolerance, which take care of functional acceptability of the characterstic. If the measure of the characteristic in various product samples remain within this range of Upper Control Limit (UCL) and Lower Control Limit (LCL) around the mean value (expected specification), the products are said to be acceptable. The variations, generally, should be distributed on either side of the Centre Line (CL) to indicate balanced production. If the observation shift towards one side, it shows the presence of assignable cause and must be corrected after due analysis.

Techniques of Statistical Quality Control (SQC)

There are two techniques adopted for Statistical Quality Control

- Acceptance Sampling
- Statistical Process Control (SPC)

Acceptance Sampling : It is an important statistical technique used for quality control. The concept is based on sampling the output and comparing the results of the samples based on Acceptable Quality laid down as per the limits of tolerance for a product. The technique is adopted to decide whether to a accept or reject a lot or a shipment of input or output. Generally, it is perceived to be "after-the-fact" procedure i.e., quality control applied after the production has ended. But the technique is equally applicable and must be applied even to, or possibly, more rigidly, to the input level quality control. Thus quality control through 'acceptance sampling' applies to each stage of operation so as to ensure defect free product, It is applicable to the acceptance of raw materials and components (through sampling inspection) conforming to the desired specifications as well as to the outputs of production.

In order to optimise time for inspections, and still ensuring effective quality control, we adopt random sampling method (appropriate sample size selection) unless the product/material is of critical nature, where 100% inspection may be a must or desirable or justifiable. In general case, we adopt a reasonable sample plan and acceptable level, as described below.

Sampling Plans : Three types of sampling plans are adopted in Acceptance Sampling.

Simple Sampling Plan : A randomly selected sample of size n is taken from the total supplies under inspection and the quality of each unit of the sample is determined on a pre-decided specified parameter for testing. For acceptance of the lot (from where random sample has been chosen), a value of defectives (c) known as **Acceptance number** is pre-specified and it is expected that the number of defectives (c) must be below the level acceptable/specified. If the value of c is higher than specified, the lot is rejected or else accepted.

Double Sampling Plan : It is a two stage plan. In the first stage, we select a sample of small size (say n_1) and check if a clear decision for acceptance of a lot emerges out of the observed value (say c_1), (within the acceptable region).

If the result is not conclusive (border case), then a second stage sample of size (n_2) is tested and corresponding defective number (c_2) is obtained. The decision is now taken (for acceptance of lot or otherwise) based on the cummulative evidence i.e., $c_1 + c_2$ out of $n_1 + n_2$ samples ($n_2 > n_1$).

Multistage Sampling Plan : It is based on a number of small sized samples (say n_1, n_2, n_3 etc) obtaining defect result as c_1, c_2, c_3 etc. The final decision of acceptance or rejection of the lots is taken base on the cummulative result as

$$n = n_1 + n_2 + n_3 + \dots\dots\dots$$

and
$$c = c_1 + c_2 + c_3 + \dots\dots\dots$$

Operating Characterstic Curve (OC Curve)

It is a concept of working out the reasonable acceptance number for accepting the lot of a large shipment. The sample size is selected on the statistical relationship of

$$z = \frac{x - \bar{x}}{\sigma/\sqrt{n}}$$

Where z = normal variate *i.e.*, the value of acceptable level of variation from the mean

x = Value of the parameter tested

$\bar{x}$ = mean value of the specification

σ = standard deviation of the population

n = sample size adopted

Since selection of c out of a value n must be most judicious, we can draw a curve of operations based on a certain value of n and c. The OC curve, as it is known, is drawn in Fig. 18.2, given below

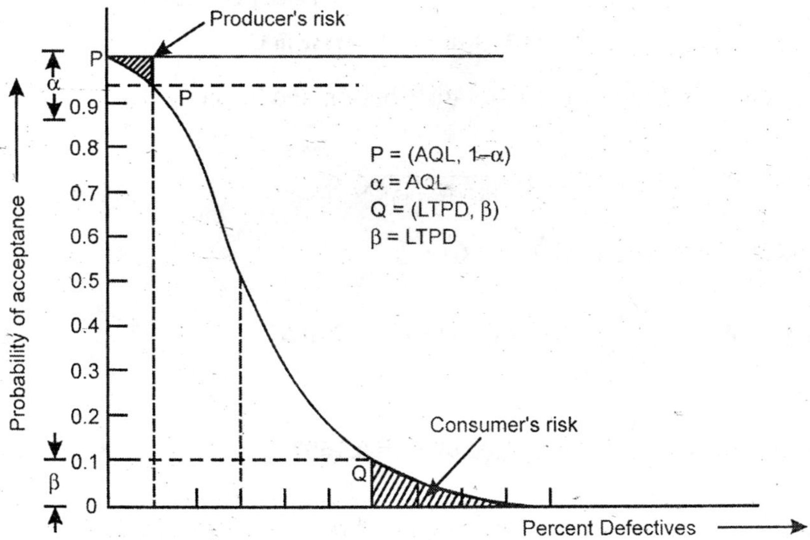

Fig. 18.2 OC Curve for a Sampling Plan

From the curve, we obtain the following information.

AQL = Acceptance Quality Level

LTPD = Lot Tolerance Percentage Defective

α = Producer's risk

β = Consumer's risk

A unique curve emerges on the basis of a given value of n and c. (i.e., n_1, c_1, and the other for n_2, c_2). Fig. 18.3 indicate the effect

The curve is drawn for a particular n and c. If there is variation in n and c, the shape of the curve can be drawn as follows :

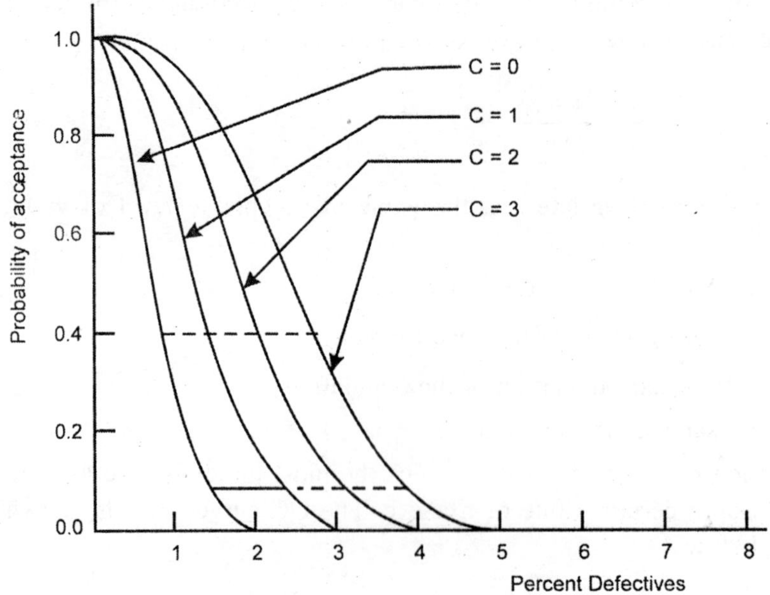

Fig. 18.3 : Effect of Increase in C

The curve generally follows binomial distribution and hence

$$p\ (r = \text{number of defect}) = \frac{n!}{r!(n-r)!}\, p^r\, q^{n-r}$$

In we consider n = 100 and AQL = 0.01

$$p\ (r = 0) = \frac{100!}{0!(100)!}\,(0.01)^0\,(0.99)^{100} = \mathbf{0.366}$$

$$\text{and } p\ (r = 1) = \frac{100!}{1!(99)!}\,(0.01)^1\,(0.99)^{99} = \mathbf{0.2697}$$

Thus the probability of a lot being rejected will be (1 – 0.3660 – 0.2697) = 0.306. This is called the producers risk (α) and is called type I error. On the other hand, if we select 5 per cent LTPD, a similar calculation can be performed to establish Type II error (β) or the consumer's risk.

Problem 18.1

In a manufacturing organisation, the sub assembly produced from an out source (supplier). has an AQL of 2 per cent defectives. The supplier is willing to run a 5 per cent risk of having lots of this or lower level rejected. The manufacturing firm has laid down a level of eight per cent or more defectives as LTPD and wants to ensure that the acceptance level of such poor quality will not be more than 10 per cent. For sample testing for acceptance of a large lot supplied by the supplier, suggest the sample size (n) and acceptable defectives (c).

Solution :

From the given data,

$$\text{AQL} = 0.02, \ \lambda = 0.05$$

$$\text{LTPD} = 0.08 \text{ and } \beta = 0.10$$

Hence $$\frac{\text{LTPD}}{\text{AQL}} = \frac{0.08}{0.02} = 4$$

From the Standard Acceptance Sampling Table, we can now work out the sampling plan. (Refer table 7 at the end of this book)

From the table, rated equal or just highert than 4 is 4.057. This value indicate the value of acceptance number c as 4.

Now, following the value (c) as 4, we obtain

$$\text{n. AQL} = 1.96 \qquad \text{(at 5\% risk)}$$

$$\therefore \qquad n = \frac{1.96}{0.02} = 98.5$$

Thus the appropriate sampling plan is n = 99 and c = 4

When we consider the sampling without replacement, we can follow hyper-geometric distribution, instead of Binomial Distribution.

Statistical Process Control (SPC)

This is a quality control technique for detecting and eliminating non-random variations, arising during production process. When the variation are random, the process is said to be in control and when these variations become non-random, the process is termed as 'out of control'. The process will have to be monitored by examining the sampling units of production periodically. The limits of tolerance i.e., the control limits of variations are laid down as described below and actual sample units measurements are then compared for 'in-control' or 'out-of-control' process. For this purpose, quality control charts are utilised (These have been developed by Dr. Walter Schewhart of the Bell Telephone Laboratories. There are two type of control charts in use:

- Control Charts for Variables
- Control Charts for Attributes

Control Charts for Variables

The Variables measured for quality control are quantitative measures, such as lengths, width, elasticity, humidity or temperatures etc. The sample size n is the number of units selected from the products and the mean and standard deviation of the measurements are obtained. There are control charts for two variables

- Mean chart (called $\overline{x}$ – chart)
- Range chart (called R – chart)

Control charts when standards are known :

Mean Chart : For mean chart, the quantitative parameters are used. When standards are given, with μ and σ as mean and standard deviation of the product population,

The UCL and LCL are defined as follows

$$UCL/LCL\ (\overline{x}) = \mu \pm \frac{3\sigma}{\sqrt{n}} \text{ for 99\% confidence level}$$

or $$UCL/LCL\ (\overline{x}) = \mu \pm \frac{1.96\sigma}{\sqrt{n}} \text{ for 95\% confidence level}$$

The limits based on 95% confidence level are generally called the warning limits. The expression on $\pm$ 3σ limits are as per chebyshev's theorem.

Control charts when standards are not known :

Mean chart : When μ and σ are not known, we obtain these values from the observations only and the values of the control limits are modified as under :

$$CL = \overline{\overline{x}} = \frac{\Sigma \overline{xi}}{k}$$

where $\overline{x_i}$ = mean of the ith sample μ (estimates)

k = number of samples

$\overline{\overline{x}}$ = Mean of the means of samples

Range chart : The range is the difference in the extreme value of the characterstic observations in a sample.

Thus $R = x_{max} - x_{min}$

Where x_{max} = Maximum Value of Variable

and x_{min} = Minimum value of the variable

and R = Range of observations (Variation).

(i) Since $\overline{R} = \frac{\Sigma R_i}{k}$ (Ri = range of Sample i, k = number of samples)

and value of σ can be taken as $\sigma = \frac{\overline{R}}{d_1}$

The control limits, obtained are as under :

$$\therefore \qquad \text{UCL/LCL}\,(\bar{\bar{x}}) = \bar{\bar{x}} \pm \frac{3\bar{R}}{d_1\sqrt{n}} \qquad \text{(i)}$$

These limits can also be written as

$$\text{UCL/LCL} = \bar{\bar{x}} \pm A_2\bar{R}\ (A_2 \text{ from the table}) \qquad \text{(ii)}$$

The values of d_1 and A_2 are to be obtained from the standard tables appended at the end of this book. (Refer table 6 at the and of the book)

Where $A_2 = \frac{3\sigma}{\sqrt{n}}$ Where σ = standard deviation

and K = Number of samples

(ii) We use the following relationships for the control limits for R-chart

$$\text{UCL (R)} = \bar{R}\ D_4$$

and

$$\text{LCL (R)} = \bar{R}\ D_3$$

The value of D_3 and D_4 can be read from Quality Control table. (Refer table 6)

(iii) When s value is available, thus relationship can be used.

Since $\sigma_{\bar{x}} = \frac{\sigma}{\sqrt{n}}$

in case of range, $\sigma_{\bar{R}} = d_2\sigma$

Hence when $\text{CL} = \bar{R} = d_1\sigma$

$$\therefore \qquad \text{UCL (R)} = \bar{R} + 3\left(\frac{d_2}{d_1}\right)\bar{R} \text{ (Value of } d_2 \text{ from the book table)}$$

$$= \bar{R}\left(1 + \frac{3d_2}{d_1}\right)$$

$$\text{and LCL (R)} = \bar{R}\left(1 - \frac{3d_2}{d_1}\right)$$

Where values of d_1 and d_2 can be substituted from table given at the end of the book.

Control Charts for Attributes :

For attributes, we can draw the quality control charts based on the following :

- based on defectives (p and np charts)
- based on defects. (c - chart)

Defective based-chart :

(i) **p-chart :** We draw the proportion (p) chart: which is based on the number of defective in a lot or a sample.

Centre line = mean p = $\bar{p}$

where $\bar{p} = \frac{\Sigma p}{n}$

$$\therefore \text{UCL/LCL}(\bar{p}) = \bar{p} \pm 3\sqrt{\frac{\bar{p}(1-\bar{p})}{n}}$$

This is given on 3σ concept.

(ii) **np-chart :** It is similar to p-chart, but is based on defectives in different samples. When p is the proportion of defectives in samples of size n

then $\text{UCL/LCL} = n\bar{p} \pm 3\sqrt{n\bar{p}(1-\bar{p})}$

Defect based chart (C-chart) :

It is called c-chart as c is the number of defects in different products. The average number of defects can be written as $\bar{c} = \frac{\Sigma c}{n}$

$$\therefore \text{UCL/LCL} = \bar{c} + 3\sqrt{\bar{c}}$$

Control of process:

When all measured observations are not within the limits of UCL and LCL, the process can suggest the corrections in the production process.

If the observations are generally concentrated on one side of the centre of the mean line, though the process may be in control, but would need correction in the following ways :

(i) Training/Retraining of the operators

(ii) Resetting/maintenance of the machine.

Hence it is necessary to examine the cause of variations and introduce corrective measures.

Problem 18.2

For a production process, the given parameter i.e., the mean diameter of the workpiece is 10 cm, while the standard deviation is 0.7 cm. While checking the quality of the outgoing products, the inspector draws the sample of size 16. Indicate the warning and the control limits on the mean control chart.

Solution :

Since μ and σ are given,

$\mu = 10$ cm $\sigma = 0.7$ cm

$n = 16$

we can use the relationships as

$$UCL/LCL\ (\overline{X}) = \mu \pm \frac{3\sigma}{\sqrt{n}}$$

$$= 10 \pm \frac{3 \times 0.7}{\sqrt{16}}$$

$$= 10.52 \text{ cm and } 9.48 \text{ cm.} \qquad \text{(control limits)}$$

$$UWL/LWL\ (\overline{X}) = \mu \pm \frac{1.96\sigma}{\sqrt{n}}$$

$$= 10 \pm \frac{1.96 \times 0.7}{\sqrt{16}}$$

$$= 10.343 \text{ and } 9.657 \text{ cm} \qquad \text{(warning limits)}$$

The control chart for mean is drawn as under (Fig. 18.4)

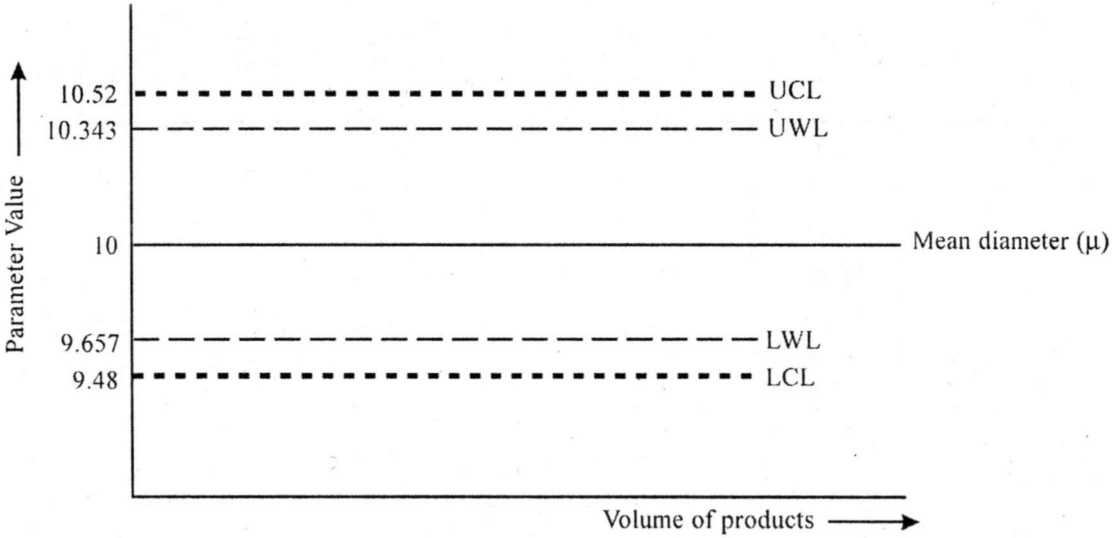

Fig 18.4 Mean Chart

Problem 18.3

When the mean diameter in the previous problem is not specified, but σ is given as 0.7 cm, work out the control limits for R-chart.

Solution :

Since μ value is not given, we estimate it as

Mean diameter $= d_1\sigma = 3.532 \times 0.7$ (value of $d_1 = 3.532$ for n = 16 from book table)

$= 2.4724$

$\therefore$ UCL/LCL (R) $= d_1\sigma \pm 3d_2\sigma$

$= (3.532 \times 0.7) \pm 3\ (0.749 \times 0.7)$

$= 4.044$ cm and 0.9 cm

(Value of d_2 for n = 16, obtained from book table)

The Range-control chart is drawn as under :

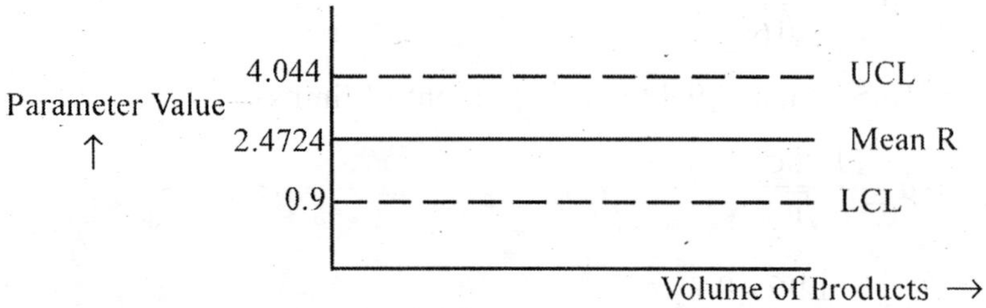

Fig. 18.5 Range chart

Problem 18.4

An inspection team has collected the following data during quality inspections in a cabinet manufacturing unit.

Samples	Observed Dimensions (in Cms)					
	1	**2**	**3**	**4**	**5**	**6**
1	3.56	3.49	3.48	3.51	3.50	3.53
2	3.50	3.50	3.52	3.53	3.49	3.47
3	3.49	3.54	3.55	3.54	3.49	3.48
4	3.55	3.52	3.52	3.50	3.51	3.52
5	3.49	3.48	3.49	3.49	3.53	3.54
6	3.48	3.47	3.53	3.54	3.55	3.53

Draw a control chart for the observations so obtained.

Solution :

From the given data,

$$\bar{x}_1 = \frac{3.56 + 3.49 + 3.48 + 3.51 + 3.50 + 3.53}{6}$$

= 3.51 cm (Mean dimension of sample 1)

Similarly $\bar{x}_2 = 3.50$ cm,

$\bar{X}_3 = 3.51$ cm

$\bar{x}_4 = 3.52$ cm,

$\bar{X}_5 = 3.40$ cm

and $\bar{x}_6 = 3.51$ cm

For the purpose of these calculations, we prepare the table as under :

Samples	Σx_i	$\bar{x}$	R
1	21.07	3.51	0.08
2	21.01	3.50	0.06
3	21.09	3.51	0.07
4	21.12	3.52	0.05
5	20.82	3.40	0.06
6	21.10	3.51	0.08

$$\therefore \quad \bar{\bar{X}} = \frac{\Sigma \bar{X}_i}{R}$$

$$= \frac{3.51 + 3.50 + 3.51 + 3.52 + 3.40 + 3.51}{6}$$

$$= 3.51 \text{ cm}$$

$$\therefore \quad \bar{R} = \frac{\Sigma R_i}{K}$$

$$= \frac{0.08 + 0.06 + 0.07 + 0.05 + 0.06 + 0.08}{6}$$

$$= 0.06$$

Mean Chart

$$\text{UCL/LCL}\,(\bar{x}) = \bar{\bar{x}} \pm \frac{3\bar{R}}{d_1\sqrt{n}}$$

$$= 3.51 \pm \frac{3 \times 0.066}{2.53 \times \sqrt{6}} \qquad \text{(Value } d_1 = 2.53 \text{ from book table)}$$

$$= 3.54 \text{ cm and } 3.48 \text{ cm}$$

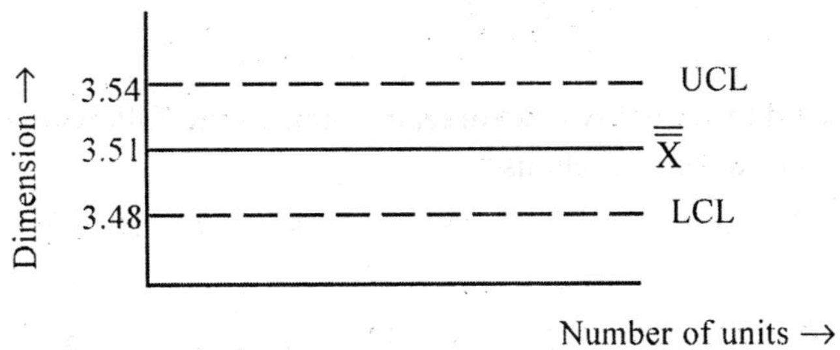

Fig. 18.6 Mean Chart

Individual values of observed dimensions can be compared with these UCL and LCL Values.

Range Chart

For n = 6, d_2 = 0.848 (from the table)

(a) $$UCL/LCL\ (R) = \bar{R} \pm 3\frac{d_2}{d_1}\ \bar{R}$$

$$= 0.66 \pm 3\left(\frac{8.48}{2.53}\right)0.66$$

$$= 0.132 \text{ cm and zero}$$

(b) $$UCL\ (R) = \bar{R}\ D_4$$

$$= 0.066 \times 2.004 \qquad \text{(Value of } D_4 \text{ from table)}$$

$$= 0.132 \text{ cm}$$

and $$LCL\ (R) = \bar{R}\ D_3$$

$$= 0.066 \times 0 \text{ (Value of } D_3 \text{ from table)}$$

$$= \text{zero}$$

Thus we see that values of UCL and LCL obtained from both the relationships are the same. These have been drawn on the Range control chart below :

Individual value of Ranges should now be superimposed on this chart for comparison.

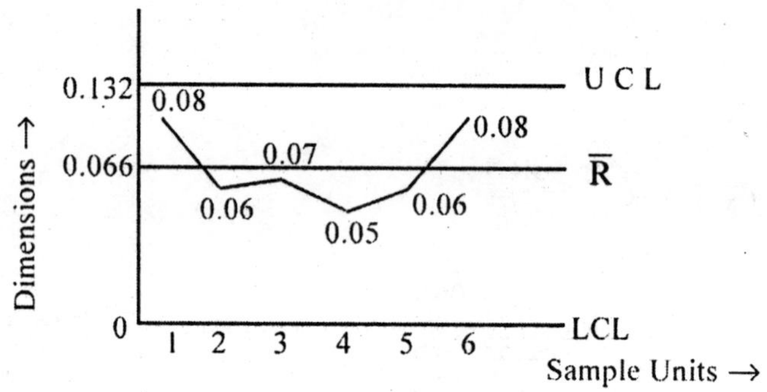

Fig. 18.7 Range Control Chart

Problem 18.5

A consignment inspected by a quality control team obtained the following results through inspection of material brought to the warehouse:

Lot Number	1	2	3	4	5	6	7	8	9	10	11	12
Number of defectives	10	12	15	10	12	11	12	11	12	13	14	20

The samples were of 100 items each. Draw the p-chart and np-chart for the same.

Solution :

Given $\quad n = 100$

$\therefore$ Total number of items inspected $= 12 \times 100$

$= 1,200$

$\therefore$ Total number of defectives $= 10 + 12 + 15 + \ldots\ldots\ldots$

$= 160$

$$\therefore \quad \bar{p} = \frac{160}{1200} = 0.134$$

(i) Hence for p-chart,

$$CL = \bar{p} = 0.134$$

$$UCL/LCL = \bar{p} \pm 3\sqrt{\frac{\bar{p}(1-\bar{p})}{n}}$$

$$= 0.134 \pm 3\sqrt{\frac{0.134 \times 0.866}{100}}$$

$$= 0.236 \text{ and } 0.032$$

The p-chart is given in the fig 18.8 below

Individual values of p_1, p_2 etc. can now be loaded and compared.

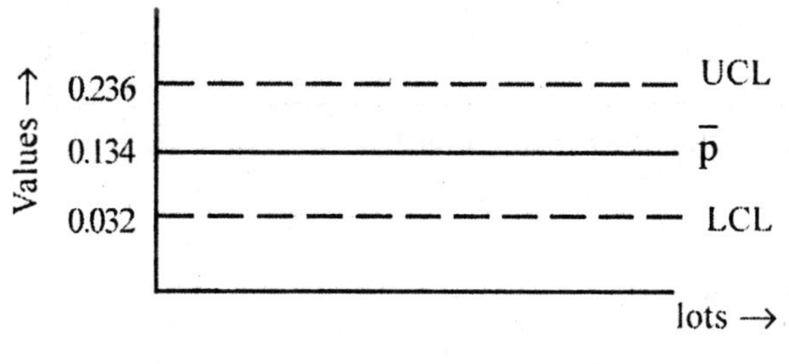

Fig. 18.8 (p-chart)

(ii) For np-chart

$n\bar{p} = 100 \times 0.134$

$= 13.4$

and $UCL/LCL = n\bar{p} \pm 3\sqrt{n\bar{p}(1-\bar{p})}$

$= 13.4 \pm 3\sqrt{100 \times 0.134 \times 0.866}$

$= 23.6 \text{ and } 3.2$

The np chart is drawn below :

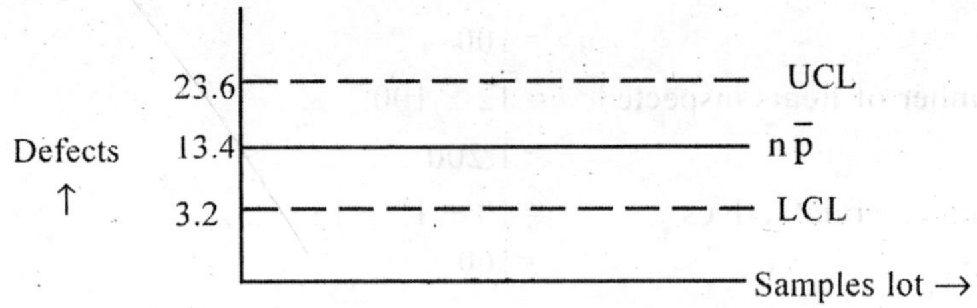

Fig. 18.9 np Chart

Problem 18.6

The following table indicates the results obtained from an inspections of equipment (product line).

Product Number	Number of defects
1	5
2	3
3	6
4	3
5	3
6	4
7	3
8	5
9	4
10	4

Work out the control limits and draw the c-chart.

Solution:

For C-chart, the given data is

Total number of products $= 10$

Total number of defects $= 5 + 3 + 6 + 3 + \ldots\ldots\ldots$

$= 40$

$\therefore$ Average number of defects $(\bar{c}) = \frac{40}{10}$

$= 4$

Hence for control chart

$$CL = \bar{c} = 4$$

$$UCL(c) = \bar{c} + 3\sqrt{\bar{c}}$$

$$= 4 + 6 = 10$$

$$\text{LCL (c)} = \sqrt{\bar{c}} - 3\sqrt{\bar{c}}$$

$$= 4 - 3 \times 2 = -2$$

Since limit cannot be negative (number of defects has to be a positive number), it is to be treated as **zero**. Hence the control chart is drawn as under:

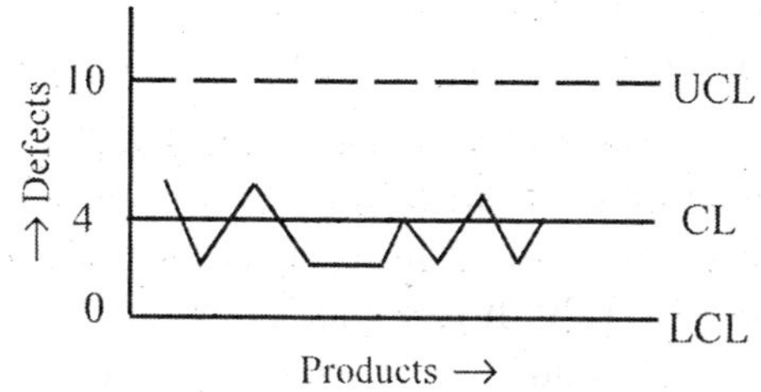

Fig. 18.10 C-chart

Problem 18.6

In a manufacturing organisation, the sub assembly produced from an outsource (supplier) has an AQL of 2 per cent defectives. The supplier is willing to run at 5 per cent risk of having lots of this or lower level reject. The manufacturing firm has laid down a level of eight per cent or more defectives as (LTPD) and wants to ensure that the acceptance level of such poor quality will not be more than 10 per cent. For sample testing for acceptance of a large lot supplied by the supplier, suggest the sample size (n) and acceptable defectives (c).

Solution:

From the given data,

$$\text{AQL} = 0.02,\ \alpha = 0.05$$

$$\text{LTPD} = 0.08,\ \beta = 0.10$$

Hence $$\frac{\text{LTPD}}{\text{AQL}} = \frac{00.08}{0.02} = 4$$

From the Standard Acceptance Sampling Table, we can now work out the sampling plan. (Refer table 7 at the end of this book)

From the table, rated equal or just higher than 4 is 4.057. This value indicate the value of acceptance number c as 4.

Now, following the value (c) as 4, we obtain

$$n \,.\, \text{AQL} = 1.96$$

$$\therefore \quad n = \frac{1.96}{0.02} = 98.5$$

Thus the appropriate sampling plan is n = 99, c = 4

18.9 Quality Control through i-theory

During initial production, we carry out 100% test on successive products and establish the value of *i*, i.e., the general standard of quality expected out of the man-machine combination. Let us say this value against AQL = 2.0, is obtained as 4. Going upward in the row of 2.0 and column 4, we get the inspection frequency as 1/10. The sample testing frequency being 1/10 would mean that inspector picks up (at random) any one product out of every 10 products for the quality inspection and continues to do so for the whole lot of production on that day.

After a little later date, when the production manager feels that there seem to be a variation in the quality, he orders *i*-testing once again following 100% test on few succesive products and get the value of *i*. If this value is different from earlier value of 4, say 5, then the inspection frequency for AQL = 2.0 will be 1/20. It is obvious that now more number of successive units are passing 100% test and hence the quality has improved, and have a reduced level of inspection at 1/20 i.e., testing only one product out of every 20 can now be resorted to. The inspection effort has considerably reduced due to production effort inprovement. If the quality goes down (*i* value coming lower) the inspection should, by logic, become more stingy and hence larger number of products used for inspection to ensure AQL for the customer. The variation in sample size, therefore, can be adopted for quantity control of production.

Having obtained the `value of *i* and the inspection frequency, it is now the easy to got the sample size.

Calculation of Sample Size:

The sample size, qualifying for a reasounally good results for quality, can be obtained either by statistical method or by actual system study. The method of *"i-test"*, desciabed in this chapter is related to actual production quality because the i-value is determined from the sample drawn from actual production line.

The values of i are given in the table against the inspection frequency say 1/5 or 1/10 etc, which means that either one unit is to be inspected out of every five or one unit out of every ten products coming out of the production line. (Refer Table 18.1 given below).

Table 18.1 Table of i-values.

AQL	Values of i for inspection frequencies				
	1/5	1/10	1/20	1/50	1/100
0.0					
1.0					
2.0	3	4	5	6	7
3.0					
4.0					

In this method, following parameters are used:

i = number of successive products passing one hundred percent inspection.

AQL = Acceptance Quality Level in percentage defectives.

Value of i has to be obtained from physical inspection of products to judge the outgoing quality of production.

For example,

If i = 3, it means that product No 1, 2, and 3 successively have passed 100% inspection test and 4th has failed.

Similarly if i = 4, it implies that first four units out of production line have passed 100% test and 5th unit has failed.

When we analyse this statement, it means that as the value of *i* increases, more and more units of production are passing the test, when chosen successively. It implies that the quality of production is improving if *i* values are higher. In table 18.1 we can see that these *i* values are increasing to the right against a particular AQL value.

The inspection frequency is decreasing as we go from left to the right of the table, which implies that as the value of *i* increases, the inspection frequency comes down say from 1/5 to 1/10 to 1/20 and so on, thus as the quality for the product is found to be better, the requirement of inspection goes down, because with improved quality, the inspection efforts can be reduced.

The AQL level has to be fixed by the top management based on the level of customer satisfaction planned for the customer segment aimed at.

Now, for an AQL of say 2.0, (meaning thereby that 2.0% defectives can be accepted by the customer as good quality product) we plan out the inspection effort.

Probelm 18.8

A manufacturing unit has planned production of 400 units over a period of a shift of 8 hours. If the inspection frequency has been arrived at is 1/20, decide on the sample size of the unit.

Solution :

Sample frequency 1/20

Production units = 400

$$\therefore \text{ n (sample size)} = \frac{400}{20} = 20 \text{ units}$$

Hence the inspector will select 20 units randomly during the day and subject them to the quality inspection.

Reasons for the change in quality of production :

- Change in the worker.
- Learning experience of the worker.
- Ageing of the machine.
- Poor maintenance, resulting in breakedown of the machine.
- Change in the working conditions i.e., temperatures or voltage fluctuations etc.

• Changes in the input material quality

The system of working out AOQL (Acceptable Outgoing Quality Level) can be adopted by deciding the value of type II errors and the number of defectives found an actual inspections.

Problem 18.9

If we choose a value of (type II error or consumers risk at 10 percent) and LTPD at 5%, and Process Average Value of defectives acceptable π = 2 to 2.3%. Find the value of AOQL (Acceptable outgoing Quality Level).

Solution :

Let us prepare a simple table with AOQL = π (p)/100.

Lot Size	*Sample Size*	*number of defectives*	*AOQL* π *p/100*
101-300	60	2	0.64
301-500	100	4	0.99
501-700	150	4	1.30
701-900	175	5	1.40
901-1100	200	7	1.50

18.10 Use of Computers for Quality Control

Computers can be used for quality control as number of softwares are available in the market. The information required for the operation of the software would be the lot number of raw materials so that potential defect area can be located.

The softwares can help the manager to get timely information on the quantity of products. With automation, the use of software is still easier. One such software known is **Business snapshot 17.1** used for Statistical Process Control. With the advancement of computer technology, there are effective softwares available for quality control. Though the work on acceptance sampling was available way back in 1920s (Dodge and Roming Sampling Instpectors tables), the 1963 version of MIL STD 105D is available for three types of sampling, single, double and multiple samplings. Again in 1978, schilling developed a table for LOT sensitive sampling plan for compliance testing and acceptance inspections. These methods have reduced design flexibility and hence, now new methods have been developed using **Artificial Neural Network (ANN)**. One ANN is used for the relationship function between one input attribute lot size and output attribute sample size approximted and generalised. Another ANN establishes the relationship function between two discrete input attributes (lot size and AQL) and output attribute acceptance number approximated and generalised. We, then, can obtain the sampling plans with the help of these ANNs for any given values of lot size and AQL. The method is quite versatile and more user-friendly to obtain a straight forward solution without involving any excess computation.

18.11 Process Capability

Process Capability is the ability of the process to ensure the design specifications, which means that the mean value of the specification should be possible to be attained with the help of the process selected for production. Then only the tolerance limits i.e., UCL and LCL can be maintained as per permitted variation. This would mean the compatibility of the machine and operator working at the desired level of operations. The process within the ambit of UCL and LCL may be in control, but still the mean value may be shifted higher or lower if the machine is faulty or its setting defective or else the operator not fully skilled for the type of tolerance level production. The difference is brought about in the comparitive figure given below:

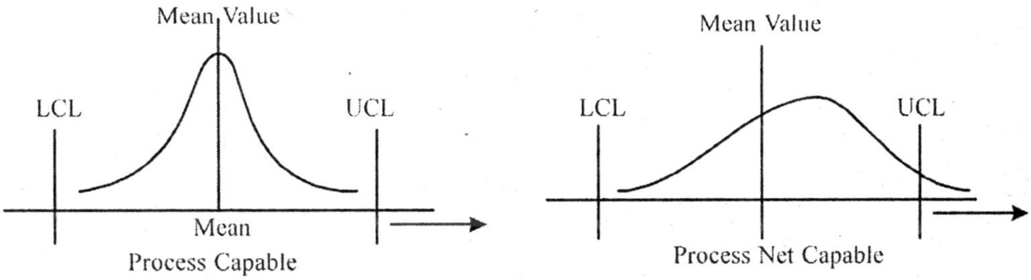

Fig. 18.12 Process Capability

If the variation in the process capability is desired, the effect can be highlighted with the help of Fig. 18.13 given below :

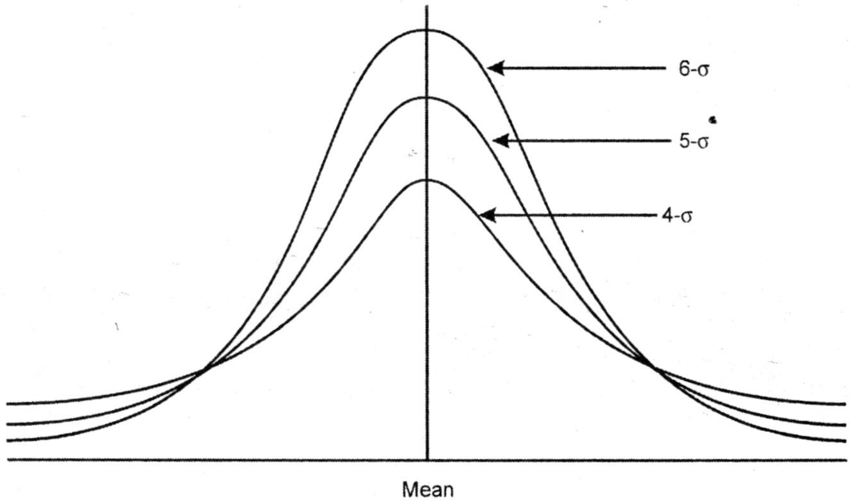

Fig. 18.13. Effect of Variability in Process Capability

In order to clarify this further, an approach has been evolved called Capability Ratio, which is defined as follows :

$$\text{Capability Ratio} = Cp = \frac{UCL - LCL}{6\sigma}$$

The Cp can have any positive value. If $Cp \geq 1.0$, it indicates that the process is capable of producing products as per customer requirement. If $Cp \leq 1.0$, the process does not have this capability of production.

The process is said to be capable, if the Capability Ratio is greater than the critical value and the process distribution is centred on the Mean value of the design specification. But if the output mean is closer to the UCL, lengthy results can be achieved and for mean value to be closer to LCL, quick results can be generated.

In this case, we compute the Process Capability Index (PCI) denoted as C_{PK}, from the following relationship :

$$C_{PK} = \text{Min of}\left(\frac{\bar{\bar{x}} - LCL}{3\sigma} \text{ and } \frac{UCL - \bar{\bar{x}}}{3\sigma}\right)$$

This index will always be lower than the capability Ratio, due to the critically of the process results.

Thus if $\bar{\bar{x}}$ = UCL = 510, LCL = 300 and $\sigma = 20$

$$\text{Then } C_{PK} = \text{Min of}\left(\frac{420 - 300}{3 \times 20}, \frac{500 - 420}{3 \times 20}\right) = 1.33$$

18.12 Quality Improvement Approaches

Various Quality Gurus have advocated improvement approaches for quality. But the basic emphasis remains as "Total Quality Control (TQC)". Few important concepts are given below:

Deming's statistical approach : Dr. Denning has been instrumental in philosophising developing and helping implementation of quality improvement programmes for the Japanese. His philosophy has been to achieve quality improvement through statistical methods. He has laid emphasis on working on the system, noticing and measuring operation variations and analysing the manufacturing problem with the help of process control charts.

Juran's management process improvement approach : Dr. Juran emphasised necessity of improving managerial inputs for quality adherance. He used the theory of rationally, analysis and management process to get to the problem. He was recommended a deep involvement of the top management in quality improvement through the "habit of Annual improvement". He, therefore, believed in total involvement of the organisation in quality improvement, training and utilisation of manpower.

Crosby's Approach : Philip crosby has advocated a concept of "Quality is free". He ws the person advocating the concept of 'zero defects and "Quality without Tears". He suggested an approach that "the quality, what the customer demands, is to be available in any case. But what costs additional money is the unquality thing – all the actions that involve not doing jobs right the first time. Quality is not only free, it is an honest-to-everything profit maker. Every penny you donot spend on doing things wrong, over or instead becomes half a penny right on the bottom line". Thus crosby's approach of quality control is an attitude and awareness of those involved in production.

The Shingo Approach : Shigeo shingo was the co-developer of the Toyota's just-in-time system. He advocated a concept of 'Fail-Safe' design approach. He introduced the system for drastic cut in the equipment set up time, called **Single Minute Exchange of Die (SMED)** procedure. The second improvement suggested by him was the use of source – inspection and fail-safe Design procedure (Poke yoke) to achieve high quality leading to ZERO – Defects.

The necessity of this approach was the fact that SQC methods donot reduce or prevent defects. In order to minimise the defects in products and services, the detailed inspection of inputs (source inspection) and a deliberate fail-safe design comes handy.

The concept of Failsafe design depends on the procedure (checklist) developed for the purpose of :

(a) Preventing the worker from making an error leading to a defect in the system.

(b) Obtaining quick feedback on any abnormalities in the process, so as to correct it in time.

Kaoru Ishikawa Approach : Ishikawa has advocated the concept of "Quality Circles" in his book" Guide to Quality Control". This has helped Japanese Industry in a big way in the process of quality improvement through employee empowerment. He has also suggested the use of ***Fishbone Diagram*** for highlighting the Customer's Complaints, thereby locating the production problems. A typical fishbone diagram is given below to suggest the usefulness of such an approach. (Arrows indicate various reasons for the problem).

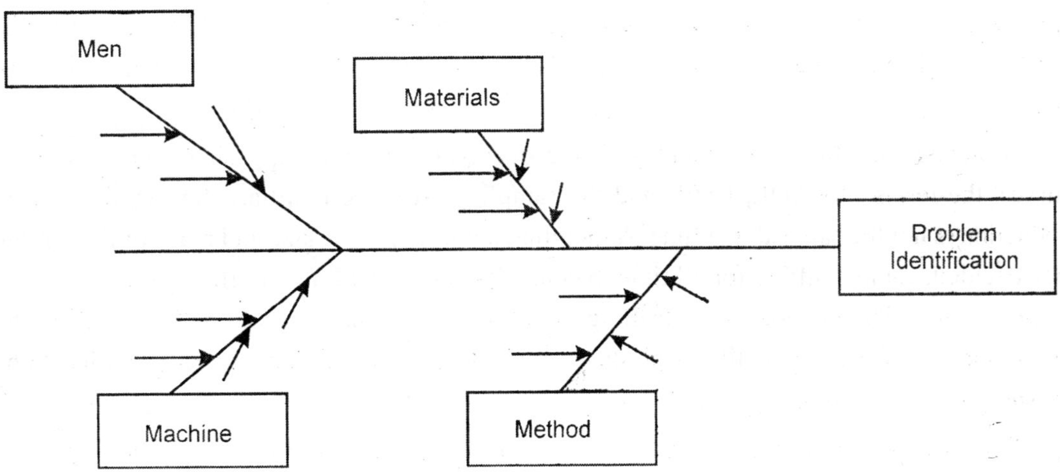

Fig. 18.11. Fishbone Diagram

The process of **Failure Mode and Effect Analysis (FMEA)** at the initial stage of design and material selection is helpful in defect prevention procedure.

By following the basic ideas of these approaches, many world top order companies have benefitted immensely, such as Toyota Motors, who have been the leaders in automobile quality, achieving low-cost but high quality products. They believe in stockless production with high inventory turnover. They also believe in total work force participation in quality, quality control at the production plants and use of statistical methods for ensuring quality of their products. The same approach has been adopted by NISSAN and have proved successful.

Similary FORD Motors, after involving Dr. Deming in their operations, actively followed his theories, became world leaders in quality using trusted and tried techniques. For Japanese, quality improvement is treated at their top business priority.

XEROX corporation has also achieved very high quality results with low cost. This corporation used competitive benchmaking, Employee Involvement (EI) and leadership through Quantity as effective tools for quality improvements Continuous Improvement (CI) has been their motto and they have succeded tremendously by taking advantage of their employees support. XEROX is the quality award winning firm in USA.

18.13 Dynamics of Quality Assurance

According to the requirement of sample testing, it is to be decided by the producer what level of customer satisfaction can be provided, considering the capability of his resources. This becomes the datum of quality standard of the company and keeping the customer preference in mind, the place and level of inspections are decided. These inspection are carried out at the input level (receipt of raw materials and components/assemblies), at WIP stage and at the Finished goods end. The strength and capability of the inspection teams vary and so do their places.

From the sampling theory and with the discussion on operating characteristics curve (curve), the terms like AQL, LTPD and the sampling sizes are familiar. But the situation in production is not the same all the time. A sampling method, sample size and place of inspection, once decided, cannot suffice for all time to come. Reason is the Random fluctuations effect on the production. The method of controlling type I and type II error has to be dynamic. As the production proceeds, the quality of product/service keeps changing and hence there has to be a system dynamic enough to cater for quality assurance at different intervals.

This dynamics of inspections is taken care of by using i-tables (standard quality inspection tables). The usage has already been explained to understand how these tables are useful in dynamic solution of quality (refer paragraph 18.9 above).

18.14 Quality in Services

With the measurable parameters identified in services, the use of control charts can be very effective in knowing quality of services. But the data is time-consuming and Quality being subjectively determined by the customer, it is not easy to identify (always) as to why a particular service operation has been rated high or low.

However, few selected parameters on the basis of which services quality can be judged are as follows :

Quantitative Standards :

- Defects rate
- Repair time
- Mean time to provide service
- Turnover rates
- Arrival and departure times or punctuality
- Waiting time

Qualitative Standards

- Responsiveness
- Nature of contact
- Empathy
- Conformance to customers requirements and values
- Acceptable manner or courtsey
- Honesty and safety
- Conformance to organisation goals
- Professionalism.

18.15 Reliability

Reliability can be said to be the quality maintained over a period of time. In short, it can be defined as the probability that an equipment or product performs satisfactorily for a specified period of time under specified operating conditions.

Therefore, relaibility can be said to be controlled by performance parameters, design parameters, failure occurance time and the operating conditions. When we say that the product or equipment is reliable to the extent of 95%, it means that its chancees of failure under specified usage are only 5% over a given period. These operating conditions are, therefore, to be listed out such as climatic and other environmental condition, specific operating specifications and instructions and maintenance schedules etc. and these conditions are not to be violated.

Reliability helps in creating the 'Perception of Quality' in the mind of the customer and when he develops faith that the product/equipment is reliable, he has eastablished perception of better quality performance of the product for a longer period.

In this regard, how and when failure occurs needs to be related to the equipment and to its components. Since reliability is compounding quality performance of all the product components individually, it works as a chain and the reliability of any one member of the chain would effect the reliability of the product.

Thus reliability is a measure of satisfactory operation at any point of time or over a period of time. Hence we can decide overall reliability both ways.

(a) Reliability at a point of time : We can have system components either in series or in parallel. The reliability at any time can be given by the relationships:

(i) Series components

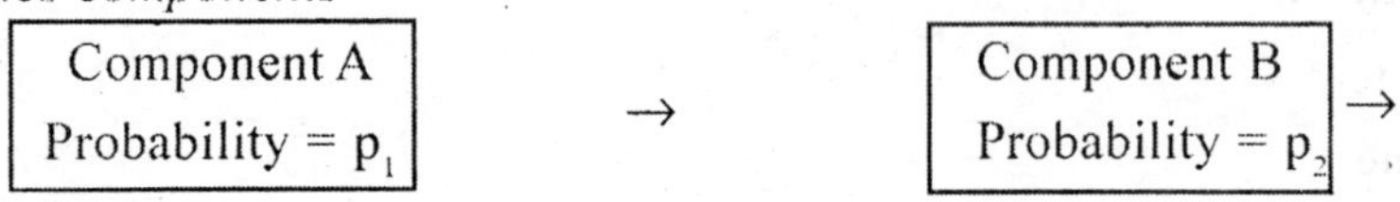

∴ reliability $R = p_1 \times p_2$

Where p_1, p_2 are probabilities of reliability of components A and B respectively.

If $p_1 = 0.7$ and $p_2 = 0.8$

∴ System reliability $R = 0.7 \times 0.8$

$= 0.56$

Thus the system reliability has reduced.

(ii) Parallel components

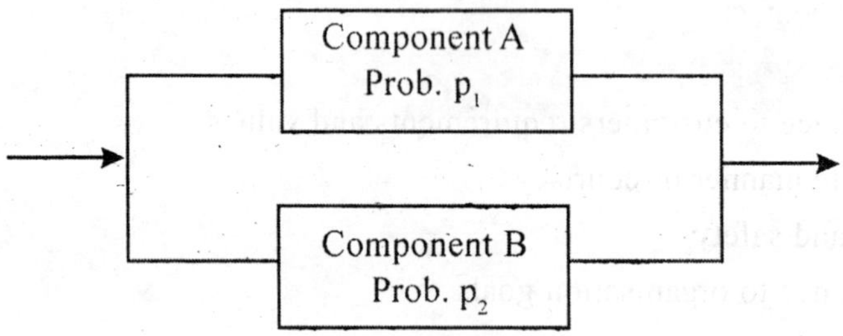

Hence if $p_1 = 0.8$ and $p_2 = 0.8$

Total system reliability $= 0.8 + (0.2 \times 0.8)$

$= 0.96$

Which is higher than the individual components reliability.

Reliability relationship to time can be expressed as

$$R = e^{-T/m}$$

Where R = System reliability

T = Length of service before failure

m = Mean Time Between Failures (MTBF)

Have failure rate $\lambda = \frac{1}{m}$

$$\text{or } \lambda = \frac{1}{\text{MTBF}}$$

$$R = e^{-\lambda T}.$$

(iii) *Utilisation Factor* : Based on MTBF, we can write the utilisation Factor (U) as follows :

$$U = \frac{\text{MTBF}}{\text{MTBF} + \text{MTTR} + \text{MTIBR}}$$

Where MTBF = Mean Time Between Failures

MTTR = Mean Time To Repair

and MTIBR = Mean Time In Between Repair.

Problem 18.10

Determine the system reliability, if the individual component reliability probability is as marked in the diagram :

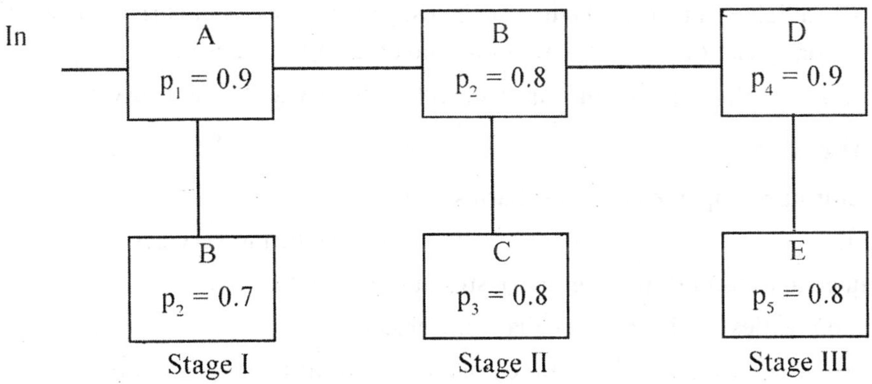

Solution :

Reliability of Stage I	$= 0.9 + (0.1 \times 0.7)$	$= 0.97$
Reliability of Stage II	$= 0.8 + (0.2 \times 0.8)$	$= 0.96$
Reliability of Stage III	$= 0.9 + (0.1 \times 0.8)$	$= 0.98$
System reliability	$= 0.97 \times 0.96 \times 0.98$	= **0.9715**

18.16 International Quality Awards

Quality was not on high priority with the American, European and Canadian companies some years back and hence the business was being lost to japanese, who had gained tremendous grounds in this area due to active participation of most of the Japanese companies under the able guidance of Quality GURU Dr. W. Edwards Deming after World War II. This opened the eyes of these companies and quality deficiencies have since been made up. The realisation that quality management and quality control were vital elements in Japanese economic success,

Americans started focussing on quality management. Few notable names in the improvement list are Motorola and Xerox. National and international efforts by the professional organisations involved the government and to recognise efforts in product quality, a quality improvement award under the name of the former American Secretary of Commerce, Malcolm Baldrige, was instituted in 1987.

Malcolm Baldrige Award

The aim of the award was to recognise the outstanding achievements in the field of product quality and its wide publicity to encourage others to follow suit in America. This award is given annually and it covers all manufacturing, service and small businesses. In 1996, even no-profit educational and healthcare services were included. Some of the well-known companies having won this award are Westinghouse, XEROX, ERO and cadilac.

As per the award notification, Malcolm Baldrige National Quality award seeks to improve the following :

- Stimulate American Companies to improve quality and productivity
- Establish guidelines and criteria that can be used by business, industrial, governmental and other organisations in evaluating their quality improvement efforts.
- Recognise the achievements of improvement in quality goods and services.

Eligibility for the Award

- Manufacturing Companies or Subsidiaries that
  (i) produce and sell manufactured products or manufacturing services.
  (ii) produce agricultural, mining or construction products.
- Service companies or subsidiaries that sell service.
- Small businesses with less than 500 employees operating independently.

The award has been the incentive to quite a few American companies and they have shown remarkable improvement in their quality areas. Based on the dynamics of economy and the resultant business transformations, there has been a change in the award criteria weightages. As per the latest information, the present Baldrige award structure is as under:

1. Leadership	110 points
2. Strategic Planning	80 points
3. Customer and market focus	80 points
4. Information and Analysis	80 points
5. HRD and management	100 points
6. Process management	100 points
7. Business Results	450 points
(a) Customer Satisfaction	130 points
(b) Financial and Marketing	130 points

(c) HR Results	35 points
(d) Supplier and Partner	35 points
(e) Company specific	130 points
Total	1000 Points

The Deming Prize for Quality

As we know, Dr. W. Edwards Deming was the man instrumental in quality education and improvement in Japan right after the World War II. He tought statistical process as a quality improvement methodology to Japanese and in recognition of his untiring efforts and contribution to the Japanese industry, a quality award was instituted in his name, so rightly called "The Deming Prize for Quality". This prize has been awarded every year since 1951 by the union of Japnese Scientists and Engineers to Companies that have shown success in their quality improvement efforts. Very few companies outside Japan apply for this prize, but in 1991, an American Company "Florida Power and Light (FPL)" was the only one to win this prize. The other notable names of the prize winners are Toyota Motors, NECIC/Micro Computer Systems and Kansai Electric Power. There is also an indian name in the list that of sundram Fasteners.

The programmes of quality improvement generally have following main activities :

- Senior management activity
- Customer satisfaction activity
- Employee involvement activity
- Training activity

—•—

Chapter 19

Total Quality Management

Main issues:

1. **Total Quality Management as a concept - Evolution**
2. **Principles of TQM and Concept**
3. **Implementation, Success and Failures of TQM programmes**
4. **International Management System - ISO 9000/ISO 14000 Standards**
5. **Benchmarking and Six Sigma.**

19.1 Definition of TQM and its frame work

In the previous chapter, we have highlighted the meaning of quality from the customer's point of view and its various dimensions along with certain methods. The teachings of various Quality Gurus notably Dr JURAN. Dr. Deming and Crosby were also highlighted.

Dr. Deming had philosophised various quality concepts and taught Japanese how to use these techniques to become world leaders. Quality Circles (QC), JIT, TQC, and may more such ground concepts were developed and made to succeed, when floor level workers were involved and empowered for operational efficiency.

On the other hand, Dr. Juran emphasised the quality importance as the function of management. He believed in customers perception as quality standard. He insisted that good product quality was the result of good organisational approach and management involvement. This was essential to 'keep up' the quality, meaning thereby, a road for Continuous Improvement (CI).

Total Quality Management was the term that emerged out of the thinking of these two Quality Gurus. It was advocated that for management of quality, the whole (Total) involvement of the whole organisation (including top management-an essential link) was required.

Thus we can define Total Quality Management (TQM) as follows:

"A management philosophy that seeks to integrate all organisational functions (marketing, design, engineering, production, finance and customer service etc) to focus on meeting customer needs and organisational objectives".

The aim or the objective of TQM, therefore, is "Do the right thing right, the first time and every time". This has already been discussed in the previous chapter. The meaning of all the three words of TQM is

Total – Made of the whole (all)

Quality – Degree of excellence, a product or service provides

Management – Act, art or manner of handling, controlling and directing etc.

Modified approach to TQM

A step forward in defining TQM is suggested by this author as under :

"Thrust and Quest to Marvel" (TQM)

This indicates not only the responsibility of all towards quality, but total thrust with full energy focussed and internal urge of the whole organisation to achieve excellence. This is bringing out the best of everyone towards excellence to raise its degree to the optimum limits. This new meaning of TQM highlights a total commitment, involvement and internal urge of all components of the company to bring the best in each product/service.

19.2 Objectives of TQM

Customer satisfaction is the primary concern in business. Dr. Deming wrote functions for quality improvement as under :

$$Q = f(C, P)$$

where Q = Quality Level

C = Cost

P = Productivity

He explained the concept that the upgradation of quality will result in cost reduction and increased productivity.

$$\text{Hence } Q\uparrow = f(C\downarrow P\uparrow)$$

He went on to add that every one knows it, but few people will accept it on the face value.

Hence we can summerise the objectives of TQM as follows :

- Improvement of quality of product/service
- Reduction in wastages of all kinds
- Increase in productivity
- Reduction in cost and time
- Improvement in the customer's quality perception about the product/service.
- Long term improvement in market share and competitive advantage
- Workforce motivation due to larger acceptance of the product and the resultant gain sharing.

19.3 Quality Achievement Stages

Various stages for quality achievement can be listed out as under :

- Excellence as attitude.
- Standards/specifications reasonable.
- Methods/Processes designed for quality.
- Procedures drills and failsafing.
- Measurement, evaluation and Periodical Audits

Excellence as Attitude

Whatever you do in life must be well done. This is an attitude to perform. The results are achieved only when the job has the total involvement of the doer i.e. he wants to do it well. The excellence attitude is partially inbuilt in people and partially to be created. Through the process of training and motivation, the attitude of a person can be changed. If it is also superimposed by the gain sharing philosophy, it is easy to achieve. Change in the mindset of workers is a must to achieve by setting standards and specifications. The quality has to be a measurable item, but the measurement parameters and their values differ from use to use. There are some standards set either by an individual, his team, company, nation or even globally to follow these as benchmarks. For example, "No drink" can be a standard for a community, standard time is to be set by an organisation for operation across the company. Similarly a 'meter' length is a universal standard. The performance of an individual or a product/equipment is judged against these standards. The standards set for achievement have to be reasonable to attain, not necessarily easily, but compatible with available resources.

Specifications come from the design, but the limits of tolerance must be reasonably set to serve the purpose of use. Overdoing or underdoing, both, can be bad, for a specific type of fit. For a horticulture/agricultural instrument, the tolerance may not necessarily be the same as that for computer components assembly.

Methods/Processes designed for Quality :

When we work out how the production of a designed product is to be achieved, it must be kept in mind that the quality should be possible to be achieved with the method or process selected. The Design for quality, design for manufacturing and assembly and design for simplicity have already been discussed in the chapter on "Product Design".

Procedure drills and failsafing : Once the process is identified and the flow chart has been prepared as to what method can be used for the product (designed quality), the drill (step wise operations) must be listed out as a 'check list' like a heuristic algorithm, to ensure that worker does not make a mistake in operations. It is also important that design and production should be fail-safe, i.e., checklist and its amplification should be easy to attain and that too with such sequence that even by chance, a worker is not allowed to make mistake. If a devotee wants to reach the gate of the deity, he should the shown the way duly prominantly marked in such a way that even with a 'short cut' on his mind, it does not allow him to deviate from the laid down path. This is called fail-safing for a service.

Measurement, Evaluation and Periodic Audits : Nothing can be improved, if it is not properly measurable. Hence for quality, a measurement standard has to be set, like a dimension to be 10cm. The person measuring it has to know how to do it. A tolerance shown as 10 ± 0.1 means the measured dimension can very between 9.9 to 10.1 cm. If it is not within this range, the quality achieved is poor and hence the product is likely to be rejected. If we want to find whether a person is healthy or not, one parameter selected could be 'Hb' test and its value should be, say between 10 and 16. If the test results show a value as 9.0, the person is considered not healthy, whereas if it is 14.5, the person is reasonably healthy. The quality of health, hence, can be evaluated with measurement done and compared with the standard set.

The most important question still remains to be answered. The question is as to what should be measured ? Here is a short list of areas for measurement

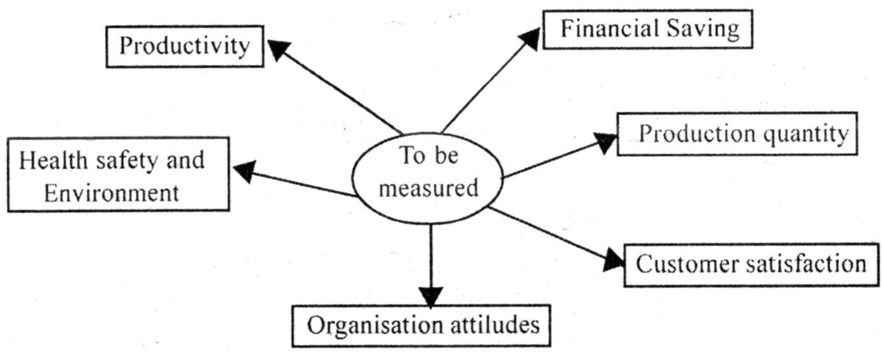

Fig 19.1. Areas of Quality

In production model, when we allow feedback mechanism to operate, error can be detected and measured. Then it can be corrected to get quality product out of production. The evaluation of the product quality, therefore, has to be based on measurement value of actual parameter and its comparision with the laid down permissible value. This process is called audit, i.e., measuring the performance against the expected. The audit for quality has to be done off and on either randomly or under a laid down policy as quality keeps varying and a constant watch can be kept only through periodical audits.

19.4 Principles of TQM

From the above discussion, it is now worthwhile to prepare a check list for the principles on which TQM should be based, so that everybody involved in it knows as to what is expected of him :

- Top Management driven project.
- Customer focussed product design and evaluation as per his standards.
- Design for quality conformance.
- Quality is everybody's baby

- Emphasis on "Do it right the first time and every time".
- Monitoring for quality problems and control system in place.
- Aimed as 'Continuous Improvement'.

19.5 Quality Philosophy

"The greatest waste in America is the failure to use the abilities of people" – said Dr. Deming E.W. He, therefore, advised the following 14 points for quality.

Dr. Deming's 14 point programe

1. Constancy of purpose i.e., creating and publishing the aim and purpose of the organisation. A long term plan.

2. Learn the new philosophy for new economic age i.e., seeking continuous improvement and non-acceptance of non-conformance.

3. Understand the purpose of inspection and try to reduce and then eliminate acceptance sampling. Defect prevention is key to TQM.

4. End awarding business on Price alone : i.e., lowest bid should not be the criterion. It should be associated with quality levels. Loyalty and trust of suppliers to be created by explaining expected quality, method of measurement and feedback to supplier.

5. Improve constantly the system of production and service, so that the focus remains on preventing problem before they happen. Variations should be constantly reduced.

6. Institute training on the job and resources should be made available for it. Training on statistical methods for quality evaluation helps.

7. Teach and Institute leadership : Supervision must be effective and so should be suprevisors. Instead of fault-finding attitude, supervisors should create a positive, supportive atmosphere with worker's pride flourishing.

8. Drive out fear, create trust and create a climate for innovation. For the purpose, managers should encourage open and effective communication and team work. Fear of being powerless, of being rediculed, lack of job security, that of physical harm or even not knowing the job create uncertainty in the mind of the worker and his performance suffers.

9. Optimise the efforts of Teams, Groups and staff areas. Internal barriers to be rumoved and better co-ordination and integration of efforts must be ensured. Develop healthy competition and not negative attitudes.

10. Eliminate numerical goals, posters and slogans, which ask for new levels of productivity without providing improved methods.

11. Eliminate Exhortations for the work force. Let people work in the atmosphere of job improvement and job ownership. Goals should be achieveable, not very easy, but not very tough also, but definetly compatible with the availability of resources. "Eliminate Numerical Quotas for Work Force. Instead of alloting numerical quotas, the management should institute methods for improvement. Work standards should focus on quality rather than on quantity. The management by objectives (MBO) should be eliminated. Instead, it should be process capability based.

12. Remove Barriers that rob People of Pride of Workmanship : People should have full faith in their capabilities. The loss of pride occurs due to following reasons:

(a) Inadequate training

(b) Punitive Supervision

(c) Poor design, leading to defective work

(d) Ineffective equipment

(e) Not aware of organisation goals

(f) Being blamed for system problems

It, therefore, needs full job description and proper resources for the work performance.

13. Encourage Education and Self-Improvement for Everyone : It is a long-term commitment of the organisation to continuously train and educate people based on their deficient areas and training should match the changing requirements.

14. Take Action to Accomplish Transformation.

Continuous Improvement (Kaizen)

Continuous Improvement should be the primary responsibility of the top management and a necessary atmosphere and corporate culture must be created, constantly modifying the product and process with changing times. Full commitment, involvement and accessability should be available with the top echlon.

Deming's Quality Wheel

Based on the 14 principle of Dr. Deming's Teachings, a valuable technique to promote Continuous Improvement (CI) or kaizen was suggested. This is called Demings wheel or shewhart cycle or a Quality wheel or Simply 'plan-do-check-Act cycle. It covers the follows steps :

Plan : The first step is to study the process for collection of information for issues as per objectives, then brainstorm the problem within the teams and use analysis to arrive at the working solutions.

Do : Implement the plan on trial basis. We collect data on the performance of the action plan drawn.

Check : The data obtained is to be evaluated through measurement of the progress made into the project implementation, whether the plan has really improved the system or not. The extensive use of statistical tools including control charts will help in evaluation (checking).

Act : It purpose of system improvement has been served i.e., goals met and issues resolved, then the system in the improved form is communicated to the workers to make them feel proud and confident of their success. The system, then, gets implemented effectively. If not, we have to restart the cycle to prepare alternate action plan. In case of improvement plan being successful, next level of improvement is to be planned.

In simple form, the PDCA-cycle is down as fig 19.2.

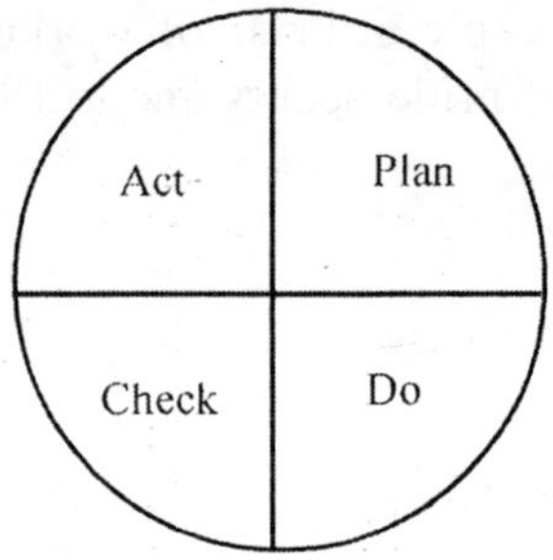

Fig. 19.2. PDCA Cycle

Diagramatically, the detailed action plan at each stage is represented in Fig, 19.3.

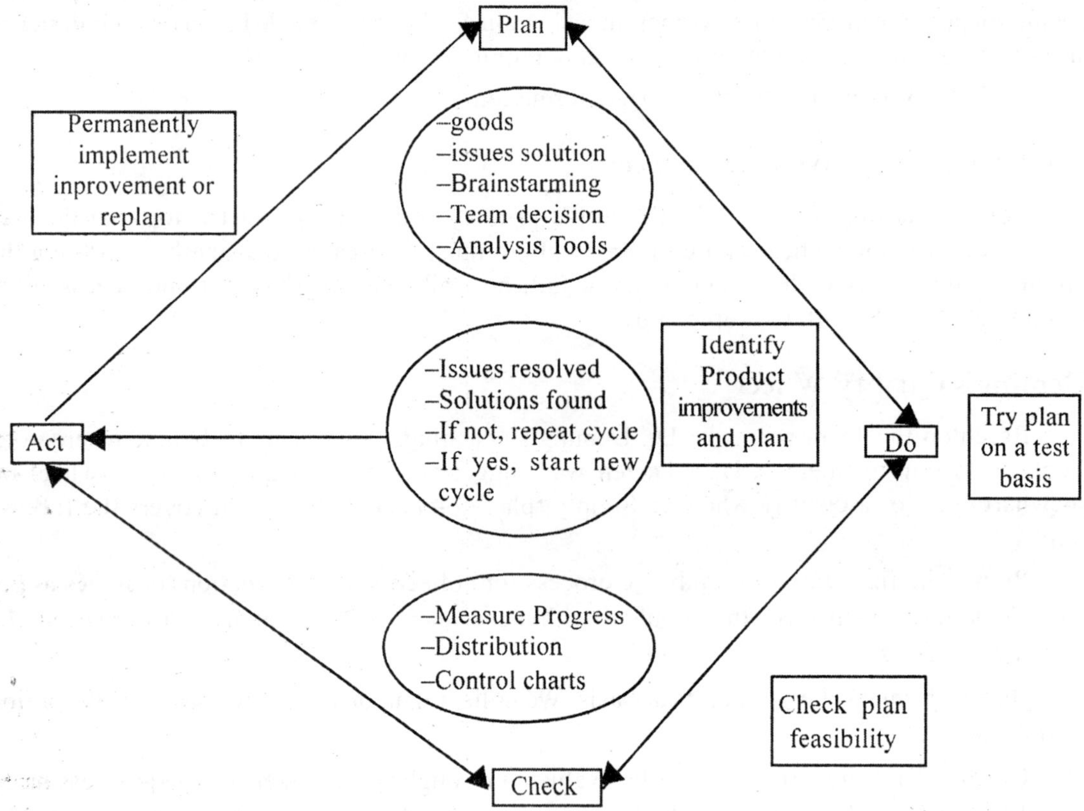

Fig. 19.3 Deming's Quality Wheel

Kaizen Culture : For effective implementation of kaizen or continuous Improvement, the involvement of the whole organisation is a must. The culture developed at various levels is as follows :

Management oriented : Improvement Projects and allocation of resources.

Group oriented : Method and Process Design and monitoring techniques.

Individual oriented : Job description, empowerment and job ownership.

19.6 Elements of TQM :

Various elements essentially as the basis of TQM are given below (Refer Fig. 19.4).

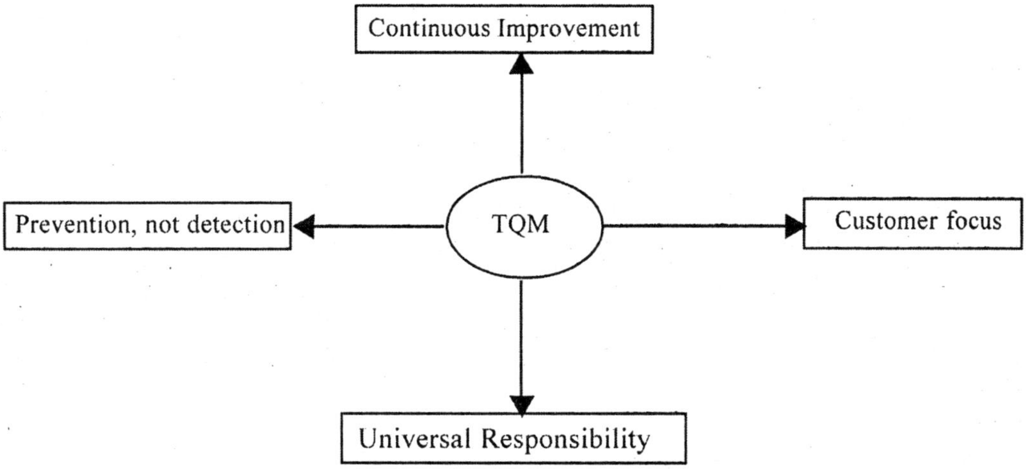

Fig. 19.4. Elements of TQM

19.7 Concepts in Total Quality Mangement

Based on these elements, Various TQM sconcept are enumerated below :

- TQM a top management responsibility.
- Quality as per customer's perception and standards.
- Process design selection as a help to quality conformance.
- Prevention of defects, not detection.
- Everyone of the organisation is involved.
- Continuous Improvement (CI).
- Vendor team relationships.
- Quality measurement.
- Benchmarking.
- Value improvement.
- Root cause correction.
- Employee Involvement (EI).

19.8 TQM Implementation

TQM implementation would involve the following stages :

Business Planing

- Planning framework
- Technology

- Infrastructure
- Product/Process design and flexibility
- Financial planning

Focus and Support

- Top management commitment
- Employee Involvement
- Customer Interaction
- Integration and resources compatibility
- Recognition and reward system.

Strategic Assessment

- Risk management
- Competitive strategy
- Vendors Policy
- Evaluation Policy

Participation

- Communication
- Team approach
- Change management

Diagrammatically, implementation plan is depicted in Fig. 19.5,below.

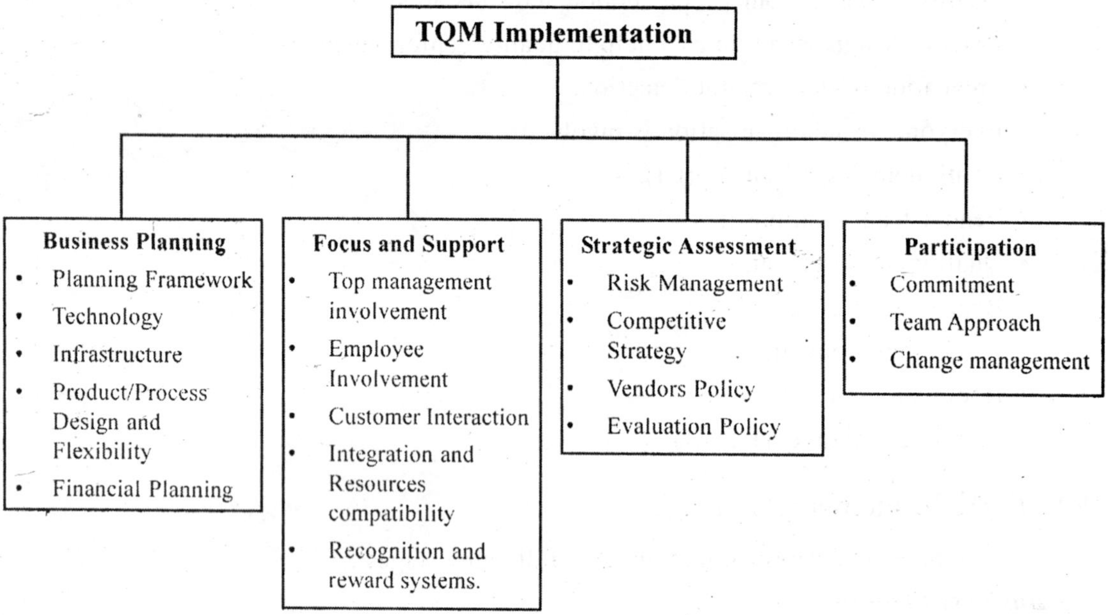

Fig 19.5 TQM implementation.

Action Plan for Top Management involvement

Top Management should be spending some useful time to understand the tools and technique of TQM and continuous improvement. The technical, psychological and financial gain must be highlighted so that TQM is adopted as the Chief Executives Personal Mission (CEPM). The suggestions and plans obtained through "Bottoms up" approach should be serutinised at various levels from workers to linemanagers to the top echlon. The effort to discuss these improvements or suggestions in staff meetings will help a great lot. The discussion with the customers and suppliers through organised meet also will produce better commitment from CEO and when the TQM project plan gets initiated by top management as a party to the above action plan. It is bound to be having his blessings along with the allocated resources for various quality projects. This will ensure their affiliation for involvement and message to the organisation for effective implementation.

Blueprint for Continuous Improvement

With top management issuing out plans for the TQM and continuous improvement projects, the implementation plans are to be drawn out based on the suggestions submitted by the organisational heirarchy. Since 'bottomsup' exercise is over, now it is the turn of 'top down' work. The mission statement and the strategic goals are to be fine-tuned with inputs from the employees, customers and the vendors. The strategic goal is to be divided into phased improvement projects, because it is a concept of continuous improvement. It should not be tried out in one go, like BPR, but slowly and gradually working upwards. Initially top management decides smaller projects in each department on the basis of resources that can be spared to complete these projects. It is to instill initial confidence in employees mind that improvement is possible and that they can achieve it. It is for the same reason that the strategy should be shared with the employees to convert it into 'their' work. Plan Document should also contain the transparent measuring methodology so as to judge the efficacy and level of improvement achieved .

TQM Projects

Very specific phased projects must be identified and developed with the inputs and knowledge gained from assessment of the business environment. The gaps to be covered (lag between industry and own organisation) must be divided into phases to ensure its completion with available resources. Projects should be fine-tuned at each stage for various departments. The prioritisation of projects in the right sequence will achieve better results.

TQM Teams

For each project for continuous improvement, specific teams must be formulated with specific responsibilities listed out i.e., the project vision, aim and time schedule. These teams should involve 'change masters' helping psychological upliftment of the department personnel (so that the change is not resisted at any stage). The team should be left to work out their own action strategy by focusing specific problems and issues being faced. 'What if' analysis by the teams will result in alternative plans, from where the most preferred solutions can be adopted,implemented and results audited. Suggestions in staff meetings will help a great lot. The discussion with the customers and suppliers through organised meets also will produce better commitment from the CEO in the form of the allocated resources for these improvement project.

A successful team must

- use participative approach to get the best results from all the members
- Motivate all personnel through transparent measurement approach to obtain their utmost involvement
- allow open communication for bright ideas
- provide for individual and team reward and recognition system.

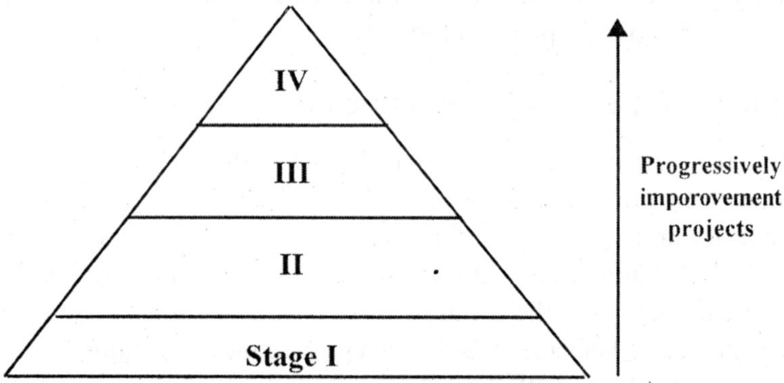

Figure 19.6 Stages for TQM Projects

Education and Training of Employees

To be an effective member of the team of the continuous improvement project, nobody should feel inadequacy to contribute. Hence based on the project selected, appropriate education and training should be imparted to the employees. To ensure the training effectiveness, the present level must be evaluated with care and then the training content and schedule should be prepared on need-based system. It should be ensured that all the members are coversant with the required tools and techniques used during the project implementation.

Benchmarking (BM) and Auditing

The continuous improvement teams have their own evaluation strategy and system developed for their specific projects. But there should be a central impartial team to audit the project result to suggest follow up actions. For the purpose, an effective, easily operatable information system must be installed for horizontal as well as vertical dissemination of information to avoid repetition of efforts among the teams. Bechmarking helps in deciding gap coverage from the contents of the projects. The Benchmarking analysis produces the following information:

- Quantitative data for performance measurement
- Qualitative data on key success parameters

Recognition and Rewards

It is also important for the management to keep the good employees in 'good humour' by providing real time recognition and gainsharing strategy. In addition cash awards, best employee award, bonus, promotion etc. can be tried out. The actual schemes very from company to company based on the policy decided by the top management.

19.9 Adoption of TQM Globally

TQM is a philosophy receiving world wide acceptance. More and more companies are utilising the concept in their day to day work. Some companies using these tools and techniques for the name-sake suffer in the long run. In global competitive arena, they cannot survive for long. The lack of management commitment and ineffective leadership to improve operations speak poorly on the organisational strategies for global survival. While the Japanese have embraced the quality concepts in very large proportion, USA is in the process of adopting the system slowly, realising that there is no way out now, in order to offset the Japanese dominance. Japanese achieve this dominance through their emphasis on training and education, Quality Circles and Commitment of top management with lot of patience. Europe has changed its focus and attitude towards quality management and the results are favourable.

In developing nations, the situation is still far from satisfactory. There are some genuine concerns for quality implementation, such as economic levels, lack of leadership and political will, lack of commitment and lack of education and training. The major issues for poor quality performance in developing countries can be summerised as under :

- Lack of training and employee involvement
- lack of management commitment due to cultural heritage
- Belief that "quality costs money".
- Lack of trust between suppliers and management
- Lack of established standards and inadequete implementation
- Obsolete technologies and economic limitations
- Quality of life poor and social indicators low
- Social abressions such as terrorism, religious fundamentalism and voilence etc.

19.10 Success and Failures of TQM Programmes

After having discussed as to what care must be taken to formulate TQM plan and the resultant projects, it is the implementation that can still mar or make a project. The important issue is continuous support of the top management followed by the role of workers and managers. If these people are committed, the success is easy to come by. There may be few exceptions due to wrong strategy or poor perception. But failures can be minimised, if the basic principles of TQM are fully followed. Few reasons for failures of TQM projects can be highlighted as under :

- Lack of commitment and support of the Top Management, initially or in between.
- Focus on specific techniques and not system as a whole.
- Lack of employee commitment and participation.
- Improper or inadequate training.
- Expectations of quick results and hence loss of tempo, if faster results are not visible.

19.11 Benchmarking – An Effective Tool

Benchmarking means identifying and measuring the best practice processes that work efficiently elsewhere and then emulating them. The aim is to reduce duplication by learning from others who have already found a better solution.

Benchmarking also can be said to be the practice of establishing certain internal work standards of performance comparing with some world leaders.

Benchmarking can be adopted in a particular specific area of work. Hence the decision on the parameter to be selected for Benchmark is important. Benchmarking may be down on product defectives level or at the customer service level. It is also important to realise by all the companies that continuous improvement at all times is possible and hence the "so called best" should also be striving hard to improve the performance further. Hence the Benchmarking can be adopted at a certain point of time and own standards set to cover the 'gap' with reference to what can be achieved with our resources available. It is also true that what is best today may not be so tomorrow and what is best for some, may not be so for others. Hence the decision of Benchmarking has to be very deliberate with the sole objectives of "customer satisfaction" in mind. Benchmarking, therefore, is an important tool to practice TQM.

Types of Benchmarking

Benchmarking can be applied in a variety of ways and hence various terms used for the purpose of Benchmarking are as follows :

- Strategic Benchmarking
- Performance Benchmarking
- Process Benchmarking

Strategic Benchmarking : This term is used by the organisation, which want to improve their overall performance through change in their long-terms strategy of operation. This is adopted with a view to achieve high performance success by concentrating on their core-competencies or developing a new innovative product with new process and service to jump to the front ranks of the industry. The organisation has to, therefore, improve their capability for a sudden change matching the business environment or else offer strategically new concept to the market.

Performance Benchmarking : It is the collection of performance of data (generally numerical) and then making comparison with other compatible organisations (underlined word is compatible). Therefore, we decide as to what are the most important performance yardsticks and where do we rank ourselves, compared with others in our industry and other analogous industries. Hence this comparison could be either internal or external.

Process Bechmarking : It is the comparison of practices, procedures and the performance, with specially selected benchmarking partners, studying one business process at a time (keyword is one business process).

For getting the data on performance or process, internally or externally, we have to work very hard, with a mental approach as to why others should be telling you what they do or more importantly, how they do it. Hence we have to follow a very 'tight rope' path to get the worthwhile infermation for benchmarking. And even when you have been successful in your endevour, can you really apply it to your aqanisation. Is it as easy to comply with it, with reference to your culture, competancy and resources? In America, there is an organisation called **"The International Benchmarking Clearinghouse (IBC),"** operating from Houston, which has a long database of best practices. This database available on an electronic bulletin board can be accessed only by I BC members. This is a system of 'information sharing' and can be adopted for Benchmarking. Similar methods can be adopted by some companies forming a strategic Alliance for the purpose of sharing informations and gaining with each other's experience. Collaboration can come handy for the purpose. It helps in competiting under global performance pressure. As the information is available from whatever source either through a "strategic Alliance" or "Collaboration" or "Industrial Espionage", it is a matter of deliberation to what part of this information and how it can be used in your own organisation with respect to your implementation capability.

To summerise, Benchmarking is a system through which we locate the organisation which does the business processes really well and which of these can be adapted to own organisation. Hence benchmarking creates value by

- focussing on key performance gaps
- identifying better ideas from other companies
- creating a consensus to move forward
- making better decisions from a larger base of facts.

Therefore, successful Benchmarking can-be achleved through :

- A consistent commitment from top management
- Understanding your own processes and them deciding upto what level these can be improved and when.
- There must be a willingness to change and adapt.
- Recognise leading edges within or outside your organisation.

Steps for successful benchmarking

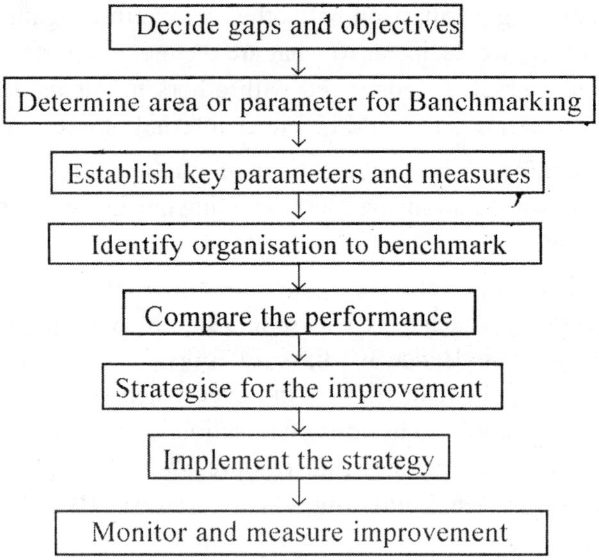

Fig. 19.7. Benchmarking implementation

Global or International Benchmarking

For competives edge in the global market, a company has to decide its strategic goal in benchmarking itself with reference to others in the industry, outside the industry, within the country and at the global level. For global competition, benchmarking standards have to match with those best in the world. But it is important to decide on the strategic parameter on which to excel in the global competition. Few of the relevant benchmarking parameters (globally) are as under :

- Cost of capital including foreign exchange variable
- New product development cycle with reference to the newest technology available worldwide.
- Advertising cost on internet and other global media.
- Human expertise with reference to the global technology
- Purchase order cycle time and volumes as per scale of economies.

In the new century, a manager faces lot of challanges due to liberalisation, privatisation and Globalisation (LPG), Sophistication in customisation and shrinking margins due to intense global competition,. Tomorrow is not a return of today or yesterday. It is always a new Critical Path for Tomorrow. Adaptive mindset, new learning ability, creativity and hence constant upgradation of skill are few attitudes to be developed and practiced everyday. Environmental demand along with social systems variability are to be in company thinking circuit for future success. Hence global benchmarking is locating the best you can adopt, then adapt or perish, either change or be left behind. It is, therefore, a strategic partnership with own people, own organisational subsystem and strategic alliances with those who are head of you, will bring in the new culture to operate better. Then only the company can sustain the world class capabilities. TIME IS THE ESSENCE OF SUCCESS.

Code of Conduct for Benchmarking

Having benchmarked the process, parameter and the organisation for study, the study team should ensure the following :

- Benchmarking agreement with the alliance partner
- Data collection plan and method of obtaining it
- Measurement system of present and benchmarked parameter
- Absorbing and systematising the information collected

During the process of information collection from the benchmarked partner, the team must follow ethics of partnership.

19.12 Six-Sigma – Measure of Quality Excellence

This is a method for measuring the performance of the organisation through a statistical tool. Since some companies are claiming to be operating at six - sigma level, they can be benchmarked against in specific areas of operations and performance gradually improved. It is the result that is benchmarked under TQM atmosphere.

Six-Sigma is a measuring tool for quality improvement. The significance of six - sigma is in its statistical meaning that specifies only 3.4 defects per million opportunities. The defect is any mistake or error, not acceptable to a customer either in a product or in service. In the quality language, it is non-conformance to the customer's specification or expectation. These defects are measured for opportunity, which means the possibility of non-conformance. Therefore, when we talk of implementing or operating a six-sigma concept, we mean not permitting more than 3.4 defects out of one million such opportunities or else it is 3.4 chances of a defective product reaching a customer out of one million product supplied to the market.

Statistically, the concept of six-sigma can be shown by a graph as under :

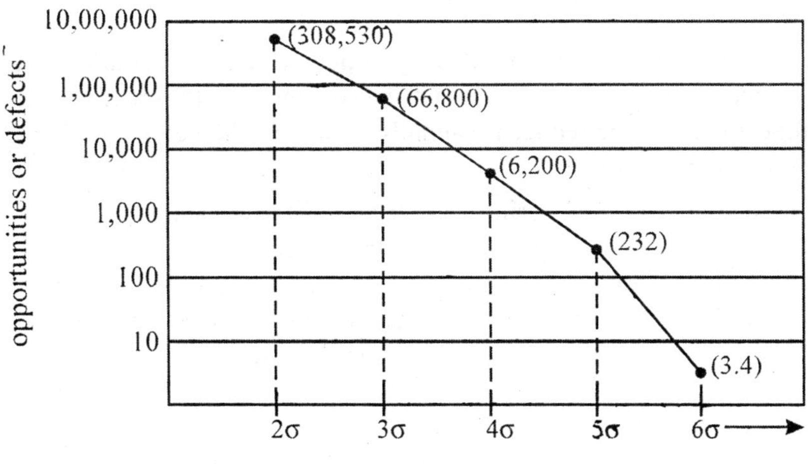

Fig. 19.7 Number of defects as per Sigma-deviation

The same can be depicted in the form of a table given below (Table 19.1)

Table 19.1 Defects Levels

Number of parts	$\pm 3\sigma$ defects per million	$\pm 4\sigma$ defects per million	$\pm 5\sigma$ defects per million	$\pm 6\sigma$ defects per million
1	66,800	6,210	232	3.4
10	4,99,200	60,400	2,320	34
100	9,99,000	4,63,600	23,000	3,40
1000	10,00,000	9,98,000	2,07,600	3,390

For almost 100% customer satisfaction, the requirement is almost 100% non-defective products. The effort to achieve it is very very large, but a sustained one. Six Sigma will encourage the whole organisation i.e., marketing, product design, process design, production and material planning, quality control, distribution, accounting landing up finally at after-sales service. Each area is as significant a contributor as any other.

We have been stressing a great deal on the use of human beings as human assets. There is absolutely no short cut to this concept, if Six-Sigma has to susceed. Constant upgradation training and education is the key factor for success for this achievement. Thus the most important resource needed is "knowledgeable person".

As per the statement of six-sigma, such a high level of quality achievement is very difficult and would need constant and deliberate all-time effort by every single person of the organisation, where this is planned to be achieved. SIx-sigma is a statistical measure, called standard deviation, it which means how much your quality parameter is deviating from the expected average quality. Six-Sigma provides an opportunity to be systematic, disciplined and deliberate to organise your process in such a way that a carefully crafted fail-safe design is not allowed to go haywire. Since this level cannot be achieved in a day or by an abrupt method, it is a continuous improvement approach operating TQM projects and keep improving through the levels of 3σ, 4σ, 5σ, reaching towards 6σ. As we keep reducing number of defects in our products through product/process compatibility we head towards 6σ improvement. All form of wastes, operating costs and cycle time etc. are to be reduced gradually, so as to achieve higher profitability and a far-greater customer satisfaction.

As we discussed under TQM blueprint, there has to be the emphasis on carefully selected worthwhile continuous improvement project in all the spheres of the organisation. Strategic selection of projects, team composition, strategy for project completion and transparent measurement system (for monitoring the progress) are in focus at all times. Since at the organisational level, all the departments have to contribute towards six-sigma achievement (integration of all is a must), this concept is to be treated as organisational philosophy and totalily of business strategy for customer satisfaction.

Due to the process dynamics, the variability has to have its defined upper specification limit (USL) and Lower Specification Limit (LSL). Next important question is what to measure.

The answer to this question has to come from the segment of customers being served. Their main concern has to become a measurable parameter, so as to satisfy them in their crucial area of concern.

Implementation of Six-Sigma

The main approaches in vogue for six-sigma implementation are as under :

- DMAIC approach
- DMADV approach
- BPR-DFSS approach

DMAIC Approach for Six-Segma

Define 1. What does the customer want ? Identify specific problem.
2. Specific defect as per the customer's perception.

Measure 1. Collect authentic, reliable data for analysis.
2. Method of defects measurement to be utilised effectively.

Analyse 1. What are the main influencing factors ?
2. Identify resultant improvement areas.

Improve 1. Specify the improvement and its implication on design and process.
2. Is improvement tangible and optimal ?

Control 1. How are we going to maintain the improvement forever ?
2. Does the process need the reallocation of resources ?
3. How to cascade feedback to system ?

DMADV Approach

This is yet another approach for Six-Sigma implementation where the improvement is achieved for new products through re-design effort. The stages, in this case, are :

D = Define the parameter for improvement

M = Measurable system to show improvement

A = Analyse the design for improvement

D = Design the product based on this analysis

V = Verify the improved design through simmulation and actual operation.

From the above discussion, it emerges clearly that it is a continuous improvement methodology that heads towards the result of six-sigma. When the defects level (due to ongoing continuous improvement) reduce to 3.4 per million parts, it is said that the organisation has reached success in their six-sigma implementation. Thus the concept of Design for Six-Sigma (DFSS) should be aimed at to achieve worthwhile improvement.

BPR-DFSS Approach

Generally it is perceived that achieving six-sigma level of performance is a gradual process, when improvement in defect elimination (reduction) is obtained through 3σ to 4σ to 5σ to 6σ

stages, because it may not be possible to design the overall system for a complete six-sigma capability. However, if the organisation wants to aim at it right in the beginning of operations or at one go, then BPR approach is very helpful. The method adopted then, has to be

- Total innovative design (complete fail-safing approach).
- R and D to back up the innovative approach through deliberate invention and new process technology.
- Develop the product and conduct pilot sample testing.
- Optimise the process to ensure six-sigma result
- Implement the production and Monitor for consistent result through proper training of manpower and maintenance of tools.

TQM has been used as an effective tool by Ashok leyland in the area of Manpower, not for manpower reductions but for cost cutting through 4 days a week. Working Internal restructuring was adopted, JIT brought in and then TQM applied. They worked on five main Pillars (5Ps) i.e., Programme, Probe, Prioritisation, Plan and Position. Success story is known.

Various areas, where six-sigma can be applied are

- Manufacturing
- Purchase
- Engineering
- Design
- Service
- Administration
- Quality Assurance
- Maintenance Services.

A Case Study – (Six-Sigma)

Mumbai "dabbawalas" have achieved a level of service to which any business should aspire. "Efficient organisation" with the profit motive can achieve the results as done by these Dabbawalas.

These are the men, who deliver 1,75,000 lunches (or "Tiffins") each day to offices and schools throughout Mumbai, the business capital of India. Lunch is in a tin container consisting of a number of bowls, each containing a separate dish, held together in a frame. The meals are prepared in the homes of the people who commute into Mumbai each morning and the tiffins are delivered in their own Tiffin carriers. After lunch, the process is reversed. And what a process? Forbes have found out that inspite of all the complexity, the 5,000 tiffinwallahs make a mistake only about once every two months i.e., one error in every 8 million deliveries, or 16 million if you include the return trip. "If we made 10 mistakes a month, no one would use our service," says the president of their association. Thus the achievement is through compulsion, a driving force for six sigma achievement. How do they do it? The meals are picked up from commuter's homes in suburbs around central Mumbai long after the commuters have left for work, delivered to them on time, then tiffins picked up and delivered home before the commuters return.

This system developed by this group is an under :

Each tiffin carrier has, painted on its top, a number of symbols which identify where the carrier is picked up, the originating and destination stations and the address to which it is to be delivered. After the Tiffin carriers are picked up, they are taken to the nearest railway station, where they are sorted according to the destination station. Betweem 10:15 a.m. and 10:45 a.m. they are loaded in creates onto the baggage cars of trains. At the destination station, they are unloaded by other Tiffinwallas and re-sorted, this time according to street address and floor.

The crates are about 100-kilogram each. This crate is carried on tiffinwallah's head-wagons and cycles and are delivered by 12:30 p.m., to the person concerned. Tiffins a picked up at 1:30 p.m., and returned where they came from.

The charge for this extraordinary service is just about 150 rupees per month, enough for the tiffinwallahs, who are mostly self-employed. After paying ₹ 60 per crate and ₹ 120 per man per month to the Western Railway for transport, the average Tiffinwallas gets about ₹ 3,250. Each person pays ₹ 10 to their Association. After minimal expenses, a sum of about ₹ 50,000 a month go to a charitable trust that feeds the poor. (This is social offering of the Tiffinwallas Association).

It is thus a combination of superb service and charity which is so remarkable.

What is wonderful about this system is that it extends the design and uses the Tiffinwallas, the end user and their cognitive and memory structure as well. Since one Tiffinwalla is not going to pick more than 10-20 Tiffins, he can easily sort, recognize at the originating station and deliver it to the owner. Also within a building, the Tiffinwala knows which floor to deliver. Within a floor a owner can recognize his Tiffin amongst others. Thus these Tiffins carry only a symbol (not name) of the originating station, a symbol for the destination and a symbol for the building of the addressee.

The most surprising and remarkable part is that most of these workmen are illiterate, self-employed, self-motivated and so committed.

19.13 International Quality Management Systems

Yet another method to improve product quality in the organisation has been introduced through improving the working systems. For designing such method, ISO (International Organisation for Standardisation) was established in Geneva in 1947. India has been a founder number of this organisation. A committee (ISO/TC 176) has worked on international standards for Quality Management System (QMS). ISO 9000 series is referred to as QMS, which are guidelines related to design, development, production, testing and servicing of products. ISO 9004 specially addresses the application of TQM systems.

The standards under QMS are

ISO 8402 : Definitions of the concepts

ISO 9000 : 2000 Selection and use of Standards

ISO 9001 : 2000 Quality Assurance Models

ISO 9004 : 2000 Quality System Elements performance improvement

ISO 19011 : Guidelines on quality and environmental auditing.

ISO 9000 series was first formulated in 1987, amended in 1994 and further amended in the year 2000, when the standards had undergone a major change, focussing on customer satisfaction.

ISO 9001, 9002, 9003 for 1994 series have been merged into ISO 9001 : 2000 and now has to be designated as such. Old certifications under 1994 version are no more valid. These standards have a life of 5 years, unless extended or amended.

ISO 9000 : 2000 Series standard series have been further amended as **ISO 9000 : 2008** Series standards.

The standards can be followed by any organisation, large or small and that too in any field of activity.

Major changes of ISO 9001 : 2000 standards (from 1994 version) were as under :

- Process orientation for quality management system is recommended.
- Continuous Improvement of products, processes and the quality managment system shall be the main objective of the top management.
- The management shall control regularly main process outputs for quality.
- Objectives shall refer to functional levels and be controlled regularly by the management.

The greatest value can be achieved by using all the standards in an integrated manner and hence ISO 9001 : 2000 and ISO 9004 : 2000 have been formated as a consistent pair of standards to reap full benefit. These have been harmonised in structure and terminology in such way as to move smoothly from one to the other. The ISO 9000 series standards are generic in nature and hence can be used by any organisation. Few of the other characterstics are :

- These are international standards for global application.
- These are neither legal nor binding.
- These are voluntary standards to be adopted, if needed, for system application. These are not a standards for any specific product.
- The certification is valid only for a period of three years, after which it has to be renewed.
- Certificate can be revoked if working standard falls below desired level.
- These are not the only ISO standards. There are many more for different purposes, like ISO 10006 : 1997 and ISO 10007 : 1995 for Project Management, ISO 10013 : 1995 for Bank documentation, QS 9000 for automobile sector and TL 9000 for telephone industry and AS 9000 for the Aerospace industry etc.
- For global operations, the company and vendors at ISO 9001 level can be great help for proper integration and smooth trust – worthy operations.

Principles of ISO 9000 : 2000

According to ISO, the new ISO 9000 : 2000 standards are based on eight quality management principles. ISO chose these principles because they can be used to improve organizational performance and achieve success.

The standardised descriptions of these principles as they appear in ISO 9000 : 2000 are listed below :

1. ***Focus on your customer :*** Organizations rely on customers. Therefore:
   - Organizations must understand customer needs.
   - Organizations must meet customer requirements.
   - Organizations must exceed customer expectations.
2. ***Provide leadership :*** Organizations rely on leaders. Therefore:
   - Leaders must establish a unity of purpose and set the direction the organization should take.
   - Leaders must create an environment that encourages people to achieve the organization's objectives.
3. ***Involve your people Organizations :*** rely on people. Therefore:
   - Organizations must encourage the involvement of people at all levels.
   - Organizations must help people to develop and use their abilities.
4. ***Use a process approach :*** Organizations are more efficient and effective when they use a process approach. Therefore:
   - Organizations must use a process approach to manage activities and related resources.
5. ***Take a systems approach :*** Organizations are more efficient and effective when they use a systems approach. Therefore:
   - Organizations must identity interrelated processes and treat them as a system.
   - Organization must use a systems approach to manage their interrelated processes.
6. ***Encourage continual improvement :*** Organizations are more efficient and effective when they continually try to improve. Therefore:
   - Organizations must make a permanent commitment to continually improve their overall performance.
7. ***Get the facts before you decide :*** Organizations perform better when their decisions are based on facts. Therefore:
   - Organizations must base decisions on the analysis of factual information and data.
8. ***Work with your suppliers :*** Organizations depend on their suppliers to help them create value. Therefore:
   - Organizations must maintain a mutually beneficial relationship with their suppliers.

ISO 9000 and Small Businesses

Though ISO 9000 standards can be equally applied by any organisation, for small business, there may be certain clarifications or slightly variable methodology. Hence ISO has published a hand book ISO 9000 for Small Businesses **(ISBN 92–67–10238–9)** which clarifies that these standards are not meant for big companies only. This booklet aims at explaining to managers the quality system standards in simple language so as to clear the intention and market access within the reach of any manufacturing or service organisation regardless of size, through implementation of an ISO 9000 quality standards.

Certification Procedure for ISO 9000 Standards

Any company interested in adopting ISO 9000 series standards in their working must decide firmly why they want to do it. Once the intention of global competition sinks in, the system would need a methodical change and hence we strive hard to obtain ISO 9000 certificate. Following procedure is to be adopted for the purpose :

- Ensure the organisation is aware and understand the contents and intentions of ISO 9000 standards.
- Top management to decide the implication and resources for implementation.
- Depute a management representative from the organisation to drive and monitor the implementation schedule.
- Identify the gap of quality system present and to be achieved through ISO 9000 implementation.
- Train the key personnel (TQM implementation team) for standards implementation.
- Write down the company Quality Manual, specifying the work instructions and Standard Operating Procedures (SOPs) to comply with the standards.
- Train a group of employees as internal quality auditors and the workers for following instructions.
- Follow the system as per standard operating procedure (SOPs) duly monitored by the internal quality auditor and take corrective action, wherever required.
- Select an outside certifying Agency or Body for external audit and certifications.
- Compliance of third party audit by the Certification Agency and Grant of the ISO 9000 certificate.
- Certification followed by peridical surveillance visits to ensure compliance and maintenance of procedures and systems.

Authorities for Certification

ISO certification is done under the Authority of International organisation for Standardisation (ISO), with its head office at Geneva (Switzerland). Each country had its own National Standards organisation (NSO), affiliated with the ISO. The certifying agencies work under the guidence of NSO. There are number of such Certification Agencies in India. The choice of the agency is left to the company needing this external audit and certification for ISO 9000 standards.

19.14 International Environmental Management Systems

Similar of ISO 9000 series standards as Quality Management Systems (QMS), there are ISO 14000 series standards as Environmental Management Systems (EMS). Similar to ISO 9001 : 2000 the standard for Method Certification, there is ISO 14001 for environmental certification.

ISO 14001 is an internationally recognised standard for environmental management systems, with the following characterstics :

1. Conformance to this standard can help a company remain competitive in the market place. For many companies, both their competitors are seeking registration and their customers are beginning to demand conformance to ISO 14001 guidelines, similar to that with ISO 9001 standard, the continuous improvement requirement of the standards lead to registered companies eventually needing to require that their suppliers also comply with ISO 14001 standards.

2. In addition, by establishing and maintaining an Environmental Management System (EMS), that meets the standards established by 14001, companies will be implementing a strong and effective environmental management programme.

Benefits of EMS Implementation

Few of the obvious benefits of implementing an EMS in accordance with the ISO 14000 standards, are

1. Identifying areas for reduction in energy and other resources consumption.
2. Reducing environmental liability and risk, helping to maintain consistent compliance with legislative and regulatory requirements.
3. Benefitting from regulatory incentives that reward companies showing environmental leadership through certified compliance with an internationally recognised EMS standard.
4. Preventing pollution and reducing wastes, responding to pressure from customers and shareholders, improving community goodwill, profitting in the market for 'green' products, respond to insurance companies pressure for better environmental atmosphere.

Requirements for ISO 14001

The five major elements of ISO 14001 are environmental policy, planning, implementation and operation, checking and corrective action and finally the Management Review.

As with ISO9001, the key to a successful ISO14001, (EMS) is having documented procedures that are implemented and maintained in such a way that successful achievement of environmental goals commensurate with the nature and scale of our activities is promoted. In addition, the EMS must include appropriate monitoring and review to ensure effective functioning of the EMS and to identity and implement corrective measures in a timely manner.

ISO14001 standards include the need for sites to document and make available to the public and Environmental auditing agencies.

In addition, procedures must be established for ongoing review of the environmental aspects & impacts on product, activities & services.

Based on these environmental aspects & impacts, environmental goals and objectives must be established that are consistent with the environmental policy. Programs must, then, be set in place to implement these activities. As with the QMS, internal Audits of the EMS must be conducted routinely to ensure that non-conformances to the system are identified and addressed. In addition, the management review process must ensure top management involvement in the assessment of the EMS, and as necessary, addressing need for changes.

The Enrionmental Management System (EMS) document is the central document that describes the interaction of the core element of the system and provides a third-party auditor with the key information necessary to understand the environmental management systems in-place at the company. Consistent with the principles of ISO14001, the Environmental Policy and Environmental Aspects/impacts analysis, including legal & other requirements, shape the program by influencing the selection of specific measurable environmental goals, objectives, & targets. Specific programs and/or projects must then be developed to achieve these environmental goals, objectives & tergets (in ISO14001 terms, this would be referred to as "Implementation & Operation"). The checking & corrective action elements of the system help to ensure continuous improvement by addressing root causes on non-conformances. The ongoing management review of the EMS and its elements help to ensure continuing suitability, adequacy, & effectiveness of the program.

General Comments on EMS

- ISO 14000 Series standard are also generic standards and their adoption for local concerns need slight modification to make them environmentally mendatory provisions. In India, we have adopted ISO 14000 standards verbitum as IS 14000 standards and these are legal and binding on all Indian Companies.
- ISO 14000 standards are a continuation of the ISO 9000 quality standards, it is expected that ISO 14001 may eventially became a pre-requirement for attainting ISO 9001 re-certification.
- For many companies having ISO 9001 certifications and to follow TQM path, ISO 14001 registration is next logical step to follows.
- Green products and green atmosphere is becoming requirement of the day to large environmental concern like global warming.
- ISO 14001 is a part of the family of international environmental standards i.e. ISO 14000 series. The other relevant standards of the series are

  (i) ISO 14010 environmental auditing

  (ii) ISO 14020 environmental labelling

  (iii) ISO 14060 environmental aspects of products.

These standards are in the stage of finalisation.

Green Purchasing

Through ISO 14001, the companies identify environmental aspects of their products and services and upgrade the environmental behaviour of their suppliers, having a significant impact on the environment by following Green Puchase policies. A larger number of environmental issues are associated with the purchasing decisions of the companies. Few of these are :

- Is the product durable and use few polluting constitiuents ?
- Is the company producing products in compliance with environmental laws and regulations ?
- Is the product designed to minimise waste ?
- Is the product re-usable and technically recyclable ?
- Is the product energy efficient ? Can it be run on renewable energy ?
- Is the product free of any banned substance ?
- Can be packaging be designed as recyclable ?

19.15 Integrating Quality, Environmental and safety standards

The quality standards (QMS) and the environmental standards (EMS) described above have worldwide applications and the success of using these standards have given rise to some other useful international standards as follows :

QS 9000	for automotive industry
TL 9000	for telecommunication industry
Tick IT	for software industry
HACCP	for food industry
AS 9000	for Aerospace industry
OHSAS 18001	for occupational health and safety management
SA 8000	for social accountablility

These standards are available for use worldwide. Some companies may like to use these standards for addressing their issues in many fields together and adopt very comprehensive management systems. There is a need to integrate these standards to avoid any overlapping confusion, and avoid to diverse interpretation or preferences. The basic goal of customer focus, market leadership and total involvement of employees/customers should be kept in mind, while integrating all the standards together.

This would result in the approach of focus on total business rather than just quality or costs. Various advantages accrued through environmental management as well as safety management have been possible only because of adoption of open–ended approach to suit the specific industry or organisational set up.

—●—

Section VII
MANAGING OPERATIONS THROUGH PROJECT MANAGEMENT

Chapter 20

Project Planning & Scheduling

Main issues:

1. Production as a Project
2. Project Planning and Scheduling
3. Project Feasibility Report
4. CPM/PERT Models
5. Resources Planning and Allocation
6. Crashing of project activities.

20.1 Introduction to Project Management

Any management system revolves around utilisation of human as well as non-human resources. It is generally observed that for carrying out management function, the resources are at premium. Hence an efficient manager is one who optimises his inputs to achieve the best and gets maximum out of his resources under most trying conditions. While motivation of human resources plays a very major role in accomplishing the tasks by a given schedule, the optimisation of the non-human assets for varied and large number of activities, therefore, needs certain tried out techniques to be applied.

Project is a mission with pre-determined performance objectives. The mission is accomplished within complex project environments by putting together human and non-human resources into a temporary organisation, headed by the Project Manager.

Project Management has two district levels of control, firstly at the conceptual or planning level, it is working out details of what is to be accomplished, how it is to be achieved and therefore, what all resources would be required for the purpose. Secondly at the execution level, it is the effective response of the project co-ordination including the Project Manager, to the problems arising, delays occurring and changes necessitated either due to technical, administrative reasons or due to clients requirements. All possible opportunities coming in way during actual execution should be grabbed by the project controllers in order to make project cost-effective. This would require constant vigilance and utter dedication of all concerned.

20.2 Unique Project Operations

Generally the operations one repetitive and routine in nature. Even with the variety production, basic operations are repetitive. But when the product to be manufactured is unique, possibly one of its type, then a project specific for the product has to be prepared involving design, process selection, production schedule and accordingly the design and operation of the specific software for the purpose.

Thus any production planning becomes project planning.

In such cases, the scheduling of activities becomes very important. The few important charactersties of such a work are :

(a) There are distinct smaller activities, which can be performed independently, leading to the total sum of the project.

(b) The variety of tasks to be performed have a definite sequence of operation, some tasks are possible to be performed simultaneously or concurrently, while other can only follow some tasks as per sequence.

(c) There is usually a tight schedule of time and

(d) Resources are flexible so as to be reallocated cost when some activitity is over

20.3 Responsibilities of the Project Manager

The Project Manager is the hub of all the activities of any project. His responsibilities are enormous and spread over all the possible fields of operations. In fact, he can, safely, be called a Magician, because he has to perform so many functions all at a time.

To summarise the role and responsibility of the Project Manager, we can look at the pyramid as given below :

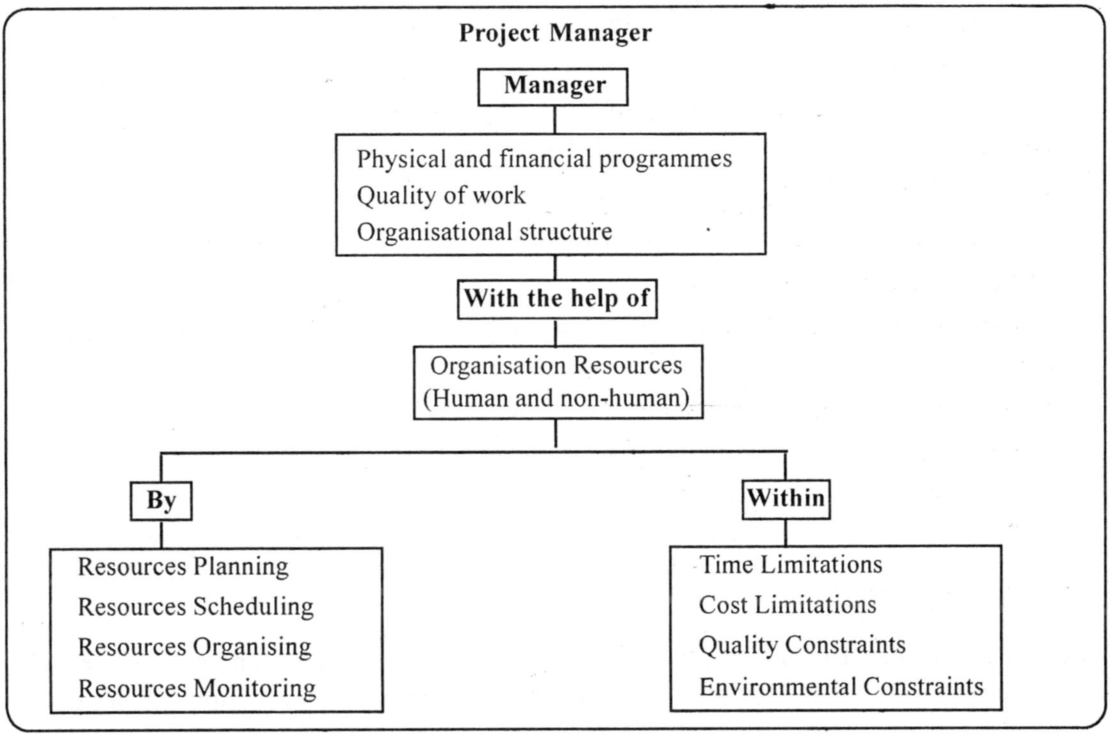

Fig. 20.1 Responsibility of Project Manager

20.4 Project Feasibility Report

To ensure that a project serves the purpose for which the work is being undertaken, a detailed analysis of inputs, outputs and opportunities is carried out. This report establishes the soundness of the project from the following angles:

Economic aspect - the report indicates the economic justification of the investment for the project. The costing of various inputs and their effective utilisation for achieving the desired financial gain is listed out in the economic feasibility of the project. It includes financial inputs into human resources as well as materials and machines requirements and their market analysis.

Technical aspects - This portion is based on the analysis of the technology use, type of equipment needed and their usage and availability including the sources of supply.

Social aspect - In order to establish special benefit of the project, this aspect is analysed for cost benefit against improvement in social indicators for the society.

Production aspect - It contains the detailed specifications and description of the product selected for manufacture. It analyses its utility, demand, profitability and reason for its selection. Export potential of the product must also be established including design and quality concerns.

Managerial aspect - The Qualitative Requirements (QRs) for the project personnel must be listed out in this part of the report to include qualifications and experiences of the managers at various levels.

Major contents of the feasibility report layout should be as follows:

- Objective and scope of the report
- Project Background and Description
- Product Characteristics
- Market Demand and Facilities Required
- Sales forecast, production details and plant capacity.
- Raw materials and other inputs.
- Manufacture details including site location, process of manufacture and production schedules.
- Plant organisation and machinery requirements.
- Manpower planning and implementation schedules.
- Financial and economic feasibility including profitability, payback period etc.
- Various clearances required from central and state governments, wherever needed,

20.5 Project Life Cycle

A project passes through a life cycle. The various phases would depend on the size and the complexity of the project, but generally a project can be divided into following phases:

- Concept phase
- Engineering and production phase
- Planning and organisation phase
- Implementation phase
- Project winding up and handing over phase.

The Concept Phase : During this phase, necessity of the project is established through the following activities:

- Formulation of the scope
- Synthesising the architecture, *i.e.*, product identification and its analysis.
- Planning and preparing a business ease for zeroing on to a product and its social utility.

Engineering and Production Phase : To carryout technical feasibility and technological assessment. It is also called definition phase. Working out raw materials, plants and equipment, technology, manpower and financial aspects are done in this phase.

Planning and Organising Phase : Major issues tackled in this phase are total planning of the project. It includes engineering design, project infrastructure, organisations, schedules, licences, system and procedures for the project. More time spent on this phase would facilitate its smooth completion. It is here we work out "What If Analysis", so that possible bottlenecks can he visualised and alternate courses of action suggested in case such an eventuality arises.

Implementation Phase : This is actual execution phase of the project based on detailed planning carried out during the earlier phase. CPM/PERT networks are to be effectively used for planning and execution of the project. The use of these techniques has been illustrated in this chapter at a later stage.

Project Winding Up and Handing Over Phase : This is a stage when work gets completed and is handed over for actual usage. Production can start soon after or the usage of software in a software project can commence. The disposal of project staff and other resources is a big challenge during this phase.

20.6 Project Environment and Conflicts

All projects are unique in nature and hence planning and execution create its own peculiarities. All projects operate under many uncertain conditions such as follows.

- The same work under the same conditions will be estimated differently by ten different estimators or by one estimators of ten different times.
- The more ridiculous the deadline, the more it costs to try to meet it.
- You can freeze the clients specification's but he won't stop expecting.
- The conditions attached to a promise are forgotten.and the promise is remembered.
- A user will tell you anything you ask about, nothing more.
- No major project is ever installed on time, within budget with the same staff that started it.

Hence, we take care of socioeconomic, technological, legal and behavioural environments into consideration, while planning a project.

In any project, conflicts are inevitable and arise mainly due to following conditions prevailing :

- Diversity of experts on the project team for diverse responsibilities.
- Degree of authority of the project manager and his reward and punishment powers.
- Objective of the project not clearly defined.
- Role ambiguity among various personnel of project team. These conflicts can generally be resolved by following methods :
- Leadership of the project manager with due authority.

❒ Withdrawal ❒ Smoothing

❒ Compromising ❒ Forcing

❒ Confrontation.

Hence, the following strategies can help in resolving conflicts:

- Treat people as adults and mature.
- Keep communication channels open and clear.
- Vary management style as per situation.
- Social interaction and mutual self-respect.
- Train people in human relation and encourage team building.

20.7 Organisation Structure

Project organisations are required to ensure smooth planning and execution of any project. For all day-to-day activities, small or large groups are formed based on the activity requirement. A variety of organisational structures are used to facilitate completion of various activities leading to project completion. Few suggested forms of organisations are given below :

Project Organisation - It is a self-contained unit with its own technical and administrative staff such as financial, personnel, materials and commercial manpower. A major project freedom can then be exercised with due accountability attached. It can be illustrated as follows.

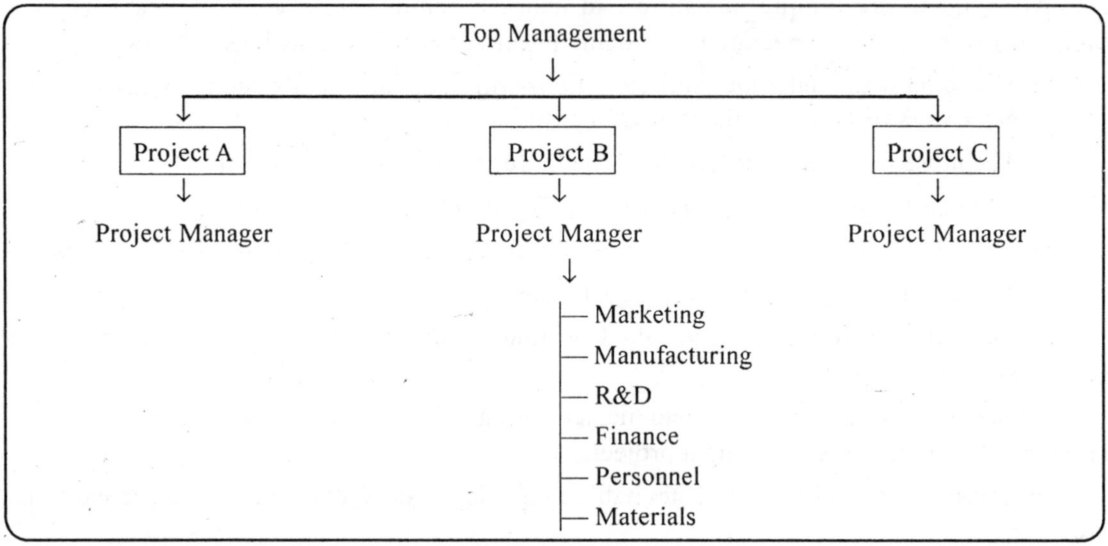

Fig. 20.2 Project Organisation

Functional Organisation - In this type of setup, functional departments are separate entities for their specialised type of work such as marketing, materials, sales etc. These departments are broken into smaller units so that these subunits can provide support to a particular project of their specialised function, but still under their parent department for technical and administrative control. It can be represented in a diagrammatic form as follows.

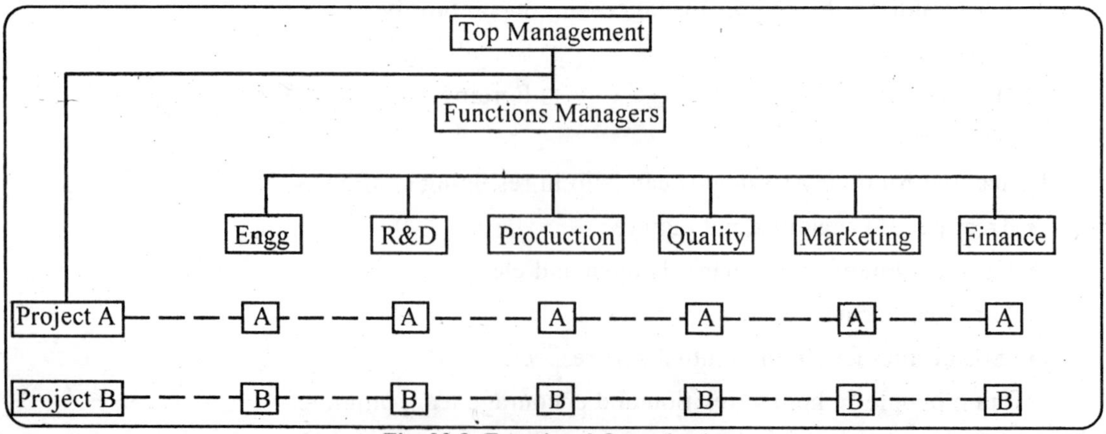

Fig. 20.3. Functional Organisation

These sub-team may be earmarked, but have no real separate identity. Each person for functional department work under his own manager and any changes can be made at any time depending of requirement and availability of departmental personnel.

Matrix Organisation – The difference between the functional and matrix organisation rests in the approach. In matrix organisation, the top management and the functional manager dedicate a team of departmental personnel to a project for total support, but the technical control remains with the functional manager.

20.8 Project Planning and Control

Completion of any project by a certain definite time schedule is the essence of any management challenge. The organisation has to decide the goal or the mission of the project in very clear terms and then plan the work by working out resources for its completion. The scheduling of the activities will be based on three important constraints:

- Time schedule.
- Money constraint.
- Manpower and equipment constraints.

Within the above constraints, the detailed planning of the project must be carried out based on the following:

- Mission of the project/objective of the management.
- Extent of control desired/critically of the project.
- Resources and techniques available for control.

Network techniques are the pictorial representation of the activities and their interrelationship to help in the planning, scheduling and controlling the project. In simple and small level project, there may not be a requirement of use of very sophisticated techniques, but when project is very large and there are very complex activity relationship with resources being very limited, network techniques come to the help of the project manager in a big way.

Though there are quite a few such techniques available today along with effective software packages like MS-project and Primavera, we shall restrict our discussion to the basic technique of CPM (Critical Path Control) and PERT (Programme Evaluation and Review Technique). Though most commonly used and most easily understood techniques of Bar-Chart and Gantt-chart are still in use for small projects, large projects need detailed planning and control, thereby needing the use of CPM and PERT with newer and latest softwares mentioned above.

CPM and PERT were developed in late 1950's, though quite independently, but with the same purpose and using the same terminology. The minor variation is that PERT was used for dealing with uncertainties in activity completion time. The major strength of CPM was its ability to take care of the trade-off facility in terms of time and cost variations i.e., it caters for additional resources for counteracting time over-run and vice-versa. In the present context, the difference between CPM and PERT has largely vanished.

Widely diverse projects are amenable to analysis by PERT and CPM. Few of them are listed below:

- Research and development programme
- Construction of a plant
- Building a mega project of irrigation
- Launching of a space-ship
- Over-haul of an organisation
- Training of manpower
- Starting an Adult Literacy programme
- Arranging a dinner/Cocktail party
- Product Development, manufacture and distribution operations

20.9 Objectives of the Network Analysis

The use of Network analysis is made in achieving following objectives:

- Minimisation of total project cost.
- Minimisation of total project time.
- Trade-off between the time and cost of the project.
- Optimisation of human and non-human resources.
- Minimisation of conflicts, delays and interruptions.

Advantages of Network Analysis

Network Techniques are handy tools for a project manager to achieve the following advantages :

Planning Stage : listing out activities and then sequencing, resources planning and estimation of cost and time for various activities. This helps in defining the total project.

Scheduling Stage : working out inter-relationships amongst various activities, their inter-dependence and possible improvements, scheduling of flow path of activities and associated resources. This would indicate the largest schedule called critical path of the project. This helps in getting the quantum of optimal resources.

Controlling Stage : Having used Network techniques extensively for planning and scheduling of the project, these become effective tools for monitoring and controlling the time and cost schedules. Constant review, bringing status report into focus, can help in reallocation of resources wherever bottlenecks are noticed. Trade-off between time, cost and environmental conditions can be achieved effectively.

20.10 Basic Rules of Network Analysis

Basically CPM or PERT use a graphical presentation depicting the project in its entirety. Networks can be drawn for different levels of project such as project level, sub-project level, tasks and activities levels etc. While drawing out these graphical forms of Network, some conventions or basic rules have to be followed. The rules for establishing the Network system are enumerated below :

• There should be one starting node and one finishing node for a project/work to indicate beginning and end of the work.

• A decision-maker prepares the list of activities and their inter-dependence and inter-relationships. Each activity is represented by a circle called node or event and an arrow, i.e., one activity should have only one arrow representing it as given in Fig. 20.4 below :

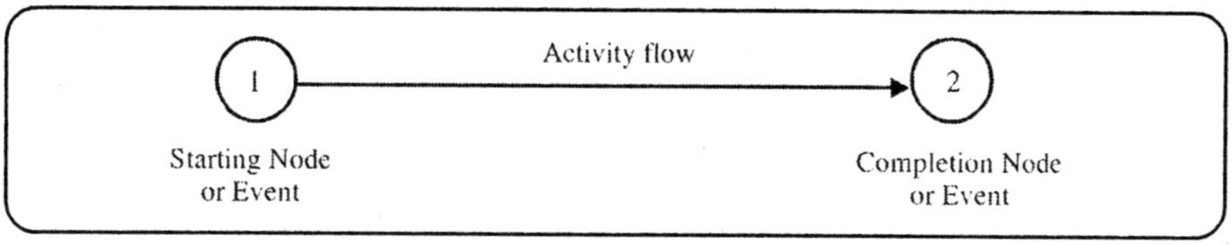

Fig. 20.4. Activity representation

It assures that time flows in the forward direction, but the length of an arrow has no significance as to decide proportionality of time.

• Each activity must have a preceding and a succeeding event. Hence an activity is designated by a pair of preceding and succeeding events so numerically numbered. The head-events always should have a number higher than that of the tail event. Starting event is the preceding event and completion event is the succeeding event, as 1 and 2 above (Fig. 20.4).

• There should be no loops in the project network. The network as given below is NOT permissible. (Fig. 20.5 refers)

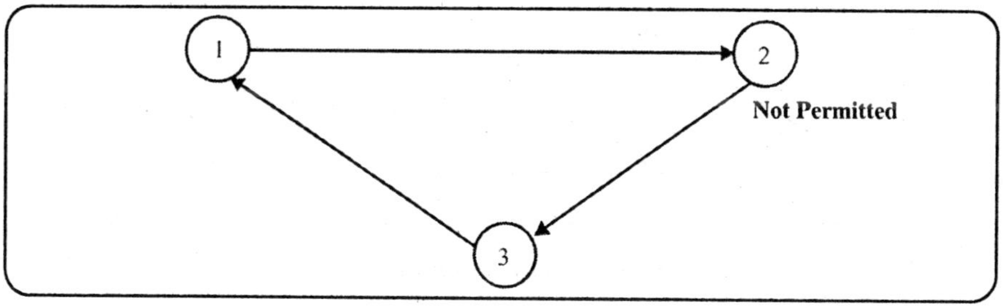

Fig. 20.5. Loop Formation

• There can not be more than one activity having the same preceding and succeeding events. The following is NOT permitted. (Fig. 20.6 indicates)

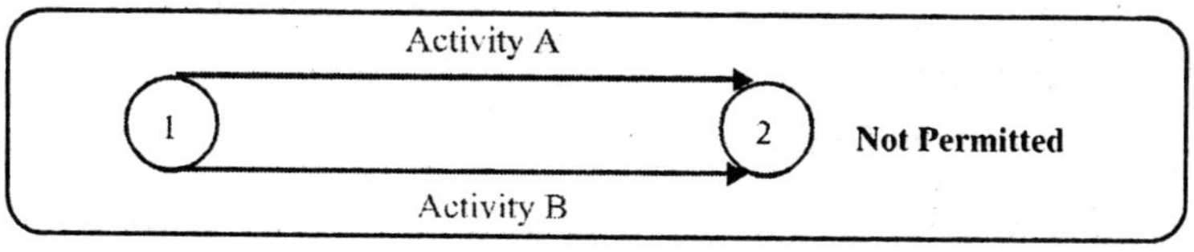

Fig. 20.6.Misuse of Arrow

• The same event can be a preceding or a succeeding activity to more than one activity of the network. This shows the precedence of operations of the project. Numbering of events should be in the order of happening i.e., succeeding event should be numbered only when all the preceding events have been numbered. Generally beginning of the project should be denoted by starting node (single) and end by a single completion node. A situation can be illustrated like this. Numbering of events have been suggested by **Fulkerson's Rule** as given below : (Fig. 20.7 refers)

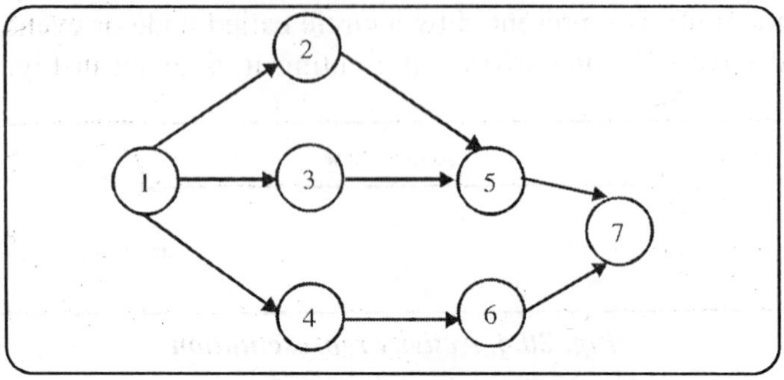

Fig. 20.7. Fulkerson's Rule

• There can be some activities happening simultaneously or concurrently and these are called concurrent activities. In order to establish proper relationship, we use the concept of dummy activity. Dummy activity does not consume time or any other input resources. In Fig. 20.8, activity 1-2 and 3-4 are concurrent activities, but dummy activity (2-4) means that before we undertake activity (4-5) activity 1-2 and 3-4 both must get completed, whereas (2-5) can be undertaken without any reference to (4-5).

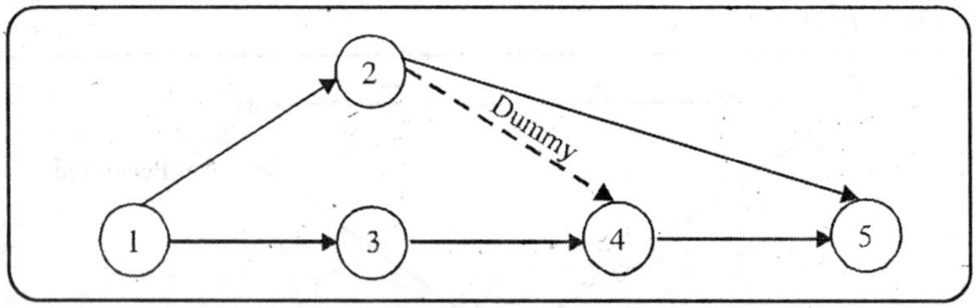

Fig. 20.8. Concurrent and Dummy Activity

20.11 Time Estimation for NetWork

For any job to be performed, it has to be broken down into activities and then time estimation for each activity needs be worked out. For this purpose, we estimate the activity time in the following manner:

t_o = optimistic time

t_m = most likely time

t_p = pessimistic time

t_e = weighted average time or expected time for completion

Optimistic time : It is the shortest time that may be required for completion of an activity, when all resources are available and no bottleneck is expected.

Most likely time : It is the amount of time required to complete an activity under real-life situation where there may be some bottlenecks experienced but quickly resolved without losing time.

Pessimistic time : It is the longest time required for completion of an activity when unforeseen or unexpected interruptions occur during its completion.

Then expected time = Weighted average time

$$\therefore \quad t_e = \frac{t_o + 4\,t_m + t_p}{6}$$

To obtain time estimates, following aspects are to be borne in mind:

- Time estimates should be obtained for each activity independently on the network, but not along a specific path.
- The time estimates t_o, t_m, t_p should be obtained independently of each other. but total time required for the project should not cloud up time estimation of related activities.
- Time estimates t_o, t_m and t_p to be treated as estimates only for planning the work and not as committed schedule.
- Estimates should include permissible allowances and environmental occurrences.

Problem 20.1

All activities of a project are given below along with their inter-relationships. Draw the network for the same

Activity	*Description of the Activity*	*Predecessor Activity*
A	Mobilisation of resources	—
B	Erection of cam site	A
C	Excavation	B
D	Lay foundation	C
E	Erect form work	D
F	Erect columns/Walls	E
G	Draw electric wiring	F
H	Install plumbing	F
I	Plaster walls	F
J	Erect interior work	G, H, I
K	Plaster outside	H

Solution :

This network can be drawn as Fig. 20.9 below

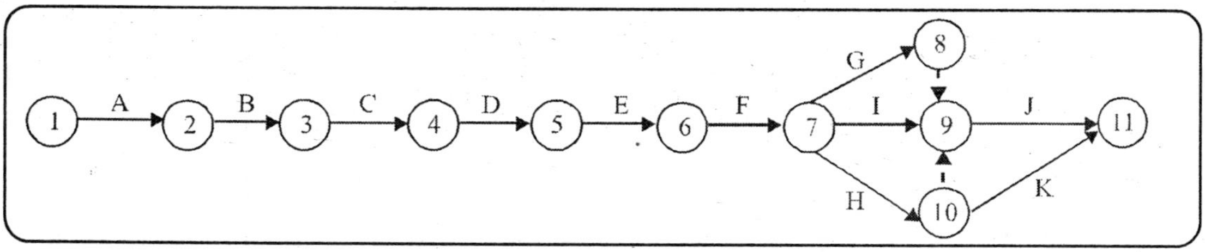

Fig. 20.9 Precedence Diagram

Problem 20.2

For the network given below, work out the expected time of completion of various activities, with the given tabulated data.

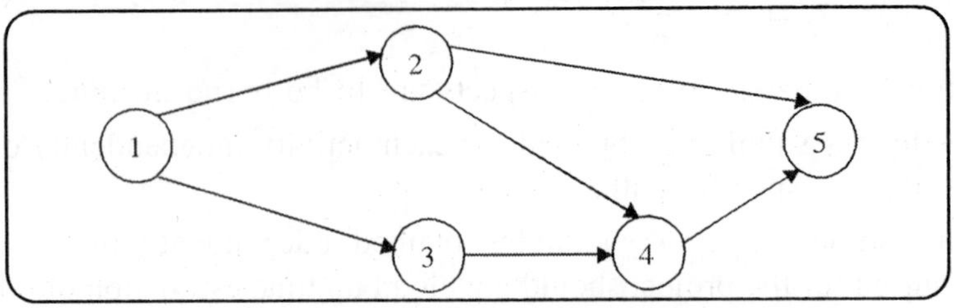

Fig. 20.10 Activity Relationships

Tabulated Data.

Activity	*Optimistic Time*	*Pessimistic Time*	*Most Likely Time*
1 - 2	5	12	7
1 - 3	12	17	13
2 - 4	15	21	18
3 - 4	2	5	3
2 - 5	8	14	10
4 - 5	21	35	26

Solution :

For working out the expected estimated average time for all the activities, the table can be organised as follows:

Acitvity	t_o	t_p	t_m	t_e
1 - 2	5	12	7	7.5 say 8
1 - 3	12	17	13	13.5 say 14
2 - 4	15	21	18	18
3 - 4	2	5	3	3.1 say 4
2 - 5	8	14	10	10.1 say 11
4 - 5	21	35	26	26.7 say 27

This is to be written on the network as follows (Normally t_e is rounded off to the next higher integer value).

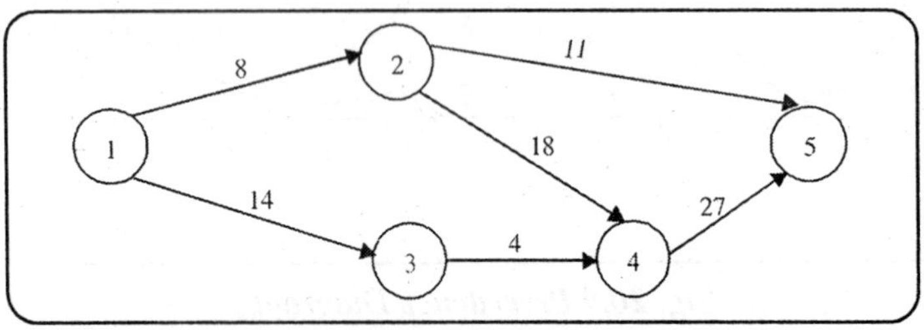

Fig. 20.11 Estimated time Indication

20.12 Calculations for EOT and LOT

From the activities durations marked on the network, the Earliest Occurrence Time (EOT) and Latest Occurrence Time (LOT) for various events is to be arrived at. For the purpose, the event nodal circle is divided into 3 parts. Top half indicates the event serial, whereas the lower half is divided into 2 parts, the left indicating the EOT and the right one mentioning the LOT. Network in Fig. 20.12 is used for the calculations of EOT and LOT.

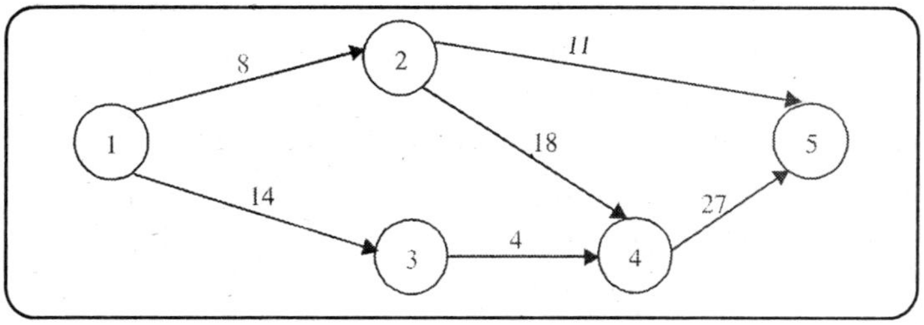

Fig. 20.12 Activity Network

Determination of the Earliest Occurrence Time (EOT) : We consider an event to occur, when all activities leading to it have been accomplished. Thus from the given network diagram, event 4 will occur only when activities (1-2), (1-3), (2-4) and (3-4) have been completed. Since activity (2-4) cannot start unless event 2 has occurred, the EOT for event 2 is 8 units. Likewise activity (3-4) can not begin unless event 3 has occurred. This activity (1-3) takes 14 units of time for completion. Hence event 4 would occur only when both the paths 1-2-4 and 1-3-4 have been completed. The Earliest Occurrence Time (EOT) of an event is the time when this event can occur the earliest.

Path 1-2-4 takes 26 units (8 + 18) of time whereas Path 1-3-4 takes only 18 units (14 + 3) of time. Thus EOT for event 4 will be 26 units (8 + 18) of time, considering beginning of the event 1 as zero.

The EOTs so calculated can be represented on the network as follows :

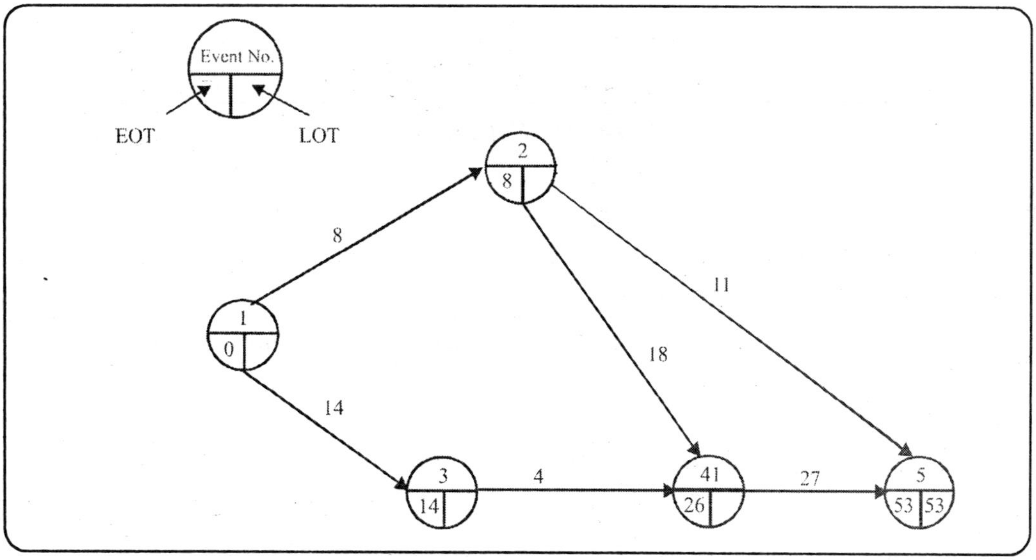

Fig. 20.13 EOT Calculations

It can be seen that the EOT of the end event (event 5 in this case) would represent the minimum time required for completion of the project. With the assumption that the next activity would start soon after the occurrence of the event preceding it, these times would also mean the earliest starting time (EST) of the next activity or succeeding activity. This is called Forward pass in CPM.

Determination of Latest Occurrence Time (LOT) : The latest occurrence time for any event represents the latest time by which time the event can occur, based on the time permitted for the project by a definite period. Hence calculation of the latest occurrence time (LOT) starts from the end event, whose EOT and LOT are set at the same level. In the configuration given above, the LOT for event 5 will be 53 units of time.

Working backwards (called backward pass) LOT for event 5 will, therefore, be 53 units and for event 4, it will be LOT of end event minus the duration of activity (4-5). LOT for event 4 works out to 26. Similarly LOT for event 2 will be 53 – 10 = 43 units working on path 2-5, but it is connected with 5 through (2-4) and (4-5). Since event 4 is connected with event 2 also, event 4 can finish latest by 43 – 18 = 25 units also, but it is earlier than 26 units calculated from activity (4-5). Hence LOT for event 4 will be 26 units only. Similarly we calculate LOT for other events also and these are indicated in bottom right half of the event node, as follows:

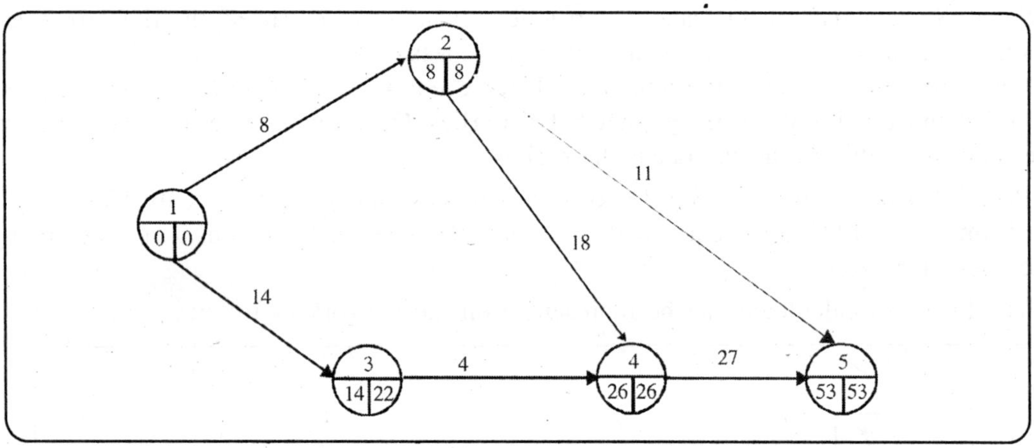

Fig. 20.14 LOT Calculations

Slacks

It is the time available as cushion on a node and is the difference of LOT and EOT. Slacks for the above network diagram are given below:

Event	*LOT*	*EOT*	*Slack = LOT – EOT*
5	53	53	0
4	26	26	0
3	22	14	8
2	8	8	0
1	0	0	0

From the above description and values of EOT and LOT marked on the network diagram, we find that events 1, 2, 4, 5 have the same EOT and LOT. Thus there is no slack on these events. Such a path i.e., 1-2-4-5 is called critical path, since there is no cushion available for activity starting and completion. Wherever these figures are different, the cushion available between EOT and LOT is called the slack for the event. Path 1-2-4-5 will also be the longest path of the network.

20.13 Determination of the Critical Path

After having obtained the estimated expected time of each activity, we can now work out the time schedule for reaching a particular event or the total time required for the project. From the concept of the total elapsed time for a particular event to occur, it is then easy to determine the critical path on the network based on the longest time schedule for all activities.

Thus two conditions must be satisfied for critical path :

- It is the path joining nodes of zero slacks.
- It is also the largest path of the network.

Problem 20.3

Obtain the critical path and project duration for the following PERT network :

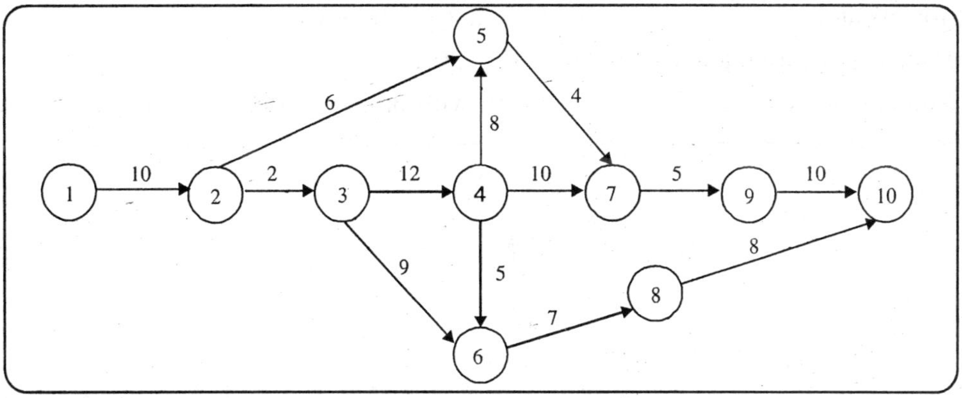

Fig. 20.15 Network for CPM

Solution :

Starting from event 1 on forward pass, we get the EOTs for various events as follows:

EOT for event 1 = 0 (Start event)

EOT for event 2 = 10 (activity 1-2 takes 10 units of time)

EOT for event 3 = 10 + 2 = 12

EOT for event 4 = 12 + 12 = 24

EOT for event 5 = Max [10 + 6, 24 + 8] = 32

EOT for event 6 = Max [12 + 9, 24 + 5] = 29

EOT for event 7 = Max [24 + 10, 32 + 4] = 36

EOT for event 8 = 29 + 7 = 36

EOT for event 9 = 36 + 5 = 41

EOT for event 10 = Max [36 + 8, 41 + 10] = 51

Similarly, going on the backward pass, we can calculate LOT for various events, starting from event 10 where EOT = LOT = 51.

LOT for event 10 = 51

LOT for event 9 = 51 – 10 = 41

LOT for event 8 = 51 – 8 = 43

LOT for event 7 = 41 – 5 = 36

LOT for event 6 = 43 – 7 = 36

LOT for event 5 = 36 – 4 = 32

LOT for event 4 = Min [36 – 5, 36 – 10, 32 – 8]
= 24

LOT for event 3 = Min [24 – 12, 36 – 9]
= 12

LOT for event 2 = Min [12 – 2, 32 – 6]
= 10

LOT for event 1 = 10 – 10 = 0

The graphical representation is given in Fig. 20.16.

The critical path is 1 - 2 - 3 - 4 - 5 - 7 - 10 with project duration of 51 units of time.

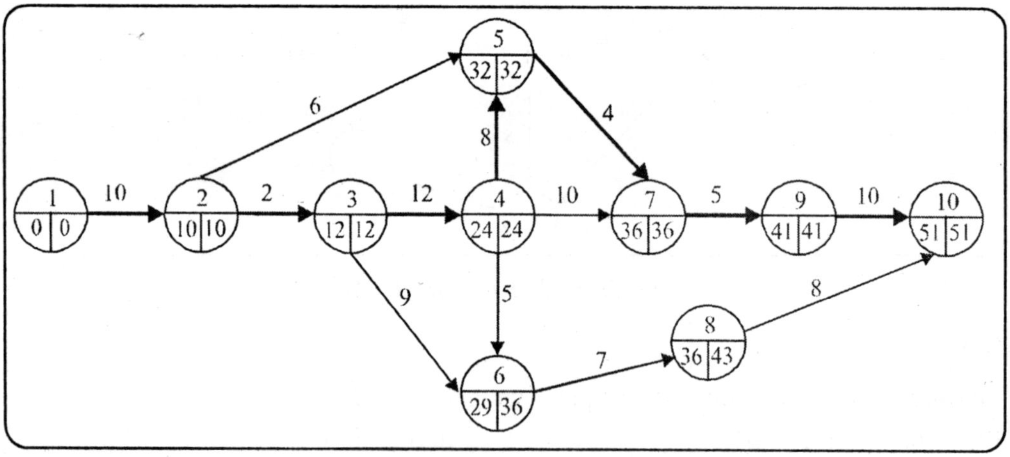

Fig. 20.16 **Critical Path Determination**

20.14 Computation of activity floats

There are three measures of float : (*a*) total float (*b*) free float and (*c*) independent float. From the given estimates of activity time and event slacks, these measures can be worked out as follows :

Total Float : Of an activity is the extra period available for completion of the activity, if the activity is started as early as possible. Total float of an activity is equal to

Latest occurrence time for succeeding activity – Earliest occurrence time for the activity – Duration of the activity.

or, $$\text{Total Float} = \text{LOT}_{(S)} - \text{EOT}_{(A)} - \text{T}_{A}$$

Free Float : Of an activity is the extra time available to complete the activity when activity start on LOT of the preceding event and is completed by the EOT of succeeding event.

$$\text{Free Float} = \text{EOT}_{(S)} - \text{EOT}_{(A)} - \text{T}_{A}$$

Independent Float : Of an activity is the extra time available to complete the activity when activity starts at EOT of the preceding event and completed by EOT of its succeeding event.

∴ $$\text{Independent Float} = \text{EOT}_{(S)} - \text{LOT}_{(A)} - \text{T}_{A}$$

This can be indicated for activity (i, j) as follows

$$\text{Total Float} = \text{TF}(i, j) = \text{LOT}(j) - \text{EOT}(i) - \text{d}(ij)$$
$$\text{Free Float} = \text{FF}(i, j) = \text{EOT}(j) - \text{EOT}(i) - \text{d}(ij)$$
$$\text{Independent float} = \text{IF}(ij) = \text{EOT}(j) - \text{LOT}(i) - \text{d}(ij)$$

Where $\text{d}(ij)$ is the duration of activity (i, j).

A table given below will illustrate the working out of floats :

Activity	*Duration*	*EST (i)*	*EFT (j)*	*LST (i)*	*LFT (j)*	*TF*	*FF*	*IF*
1-2	13	0	13	0	13	0	0	0
1-3	12	0	12	6	18	6	0	0
2-4	2	13	15	24	26	11	5	5
3-4	8	12	20	18	26	6	0	(6)
2-5	15	13	28	13	28	0	0	0
4-5	2	20	22	26	28	6	6	0

It can be seen that activities, which do not have a float even under most favourable conditions, are critical for the project and hence would form a part of critical path. Here activities (1-2) and (2-5) are critical activities.

20.15 PERT Model

For drawing networks, so far we have used the concept of expected mean duration estimates of activities. This was obtained based on optimistic (t_o), pessimistic (t_p) and the most likely time (t_m). In real life situation, there are bound to be variabilities in the project duration and this is considered in formulating the PERT model.

In case the time estimates are not deterministic in nature, the uncertainty is taken care of by calculating standard deviation (SD or σ) or the variance (V) of the duration t_e. This is expressed and denoted in a PERT network, where it is assured that such activity time follows Beta Distribution with the following characteristics:

- It is a uni-nodal distribution.

- It has finite non-negative end points.
- It is not necessarily symmetrical about nodal value.

The relationships for estimated mean time, standard deviation and variance are given below :

$$t_e = \frac{t_o + 4\,t_m + t_p}{6}$$

$$\sigma_{te} = \left(\frac{t_p - t_o}{6}\right)$$

and $$V_{te} = \sigma_{te}^{\,2}$$

The variability in the PERT method can be measured either by variance or by its square root, the standard deviation.

Problem 20.4 :

The time estimates for a network is indicated in the table as follows :

Activity	t_o	t_p	t_m
1 - 2	5	12	7
1 - 3	12	17	13
2 - 4	15	21	18
3 - 4	2	5	3
2 - 5	8	14	10
4 - 5	21	35	26

Work out the standard deviations and the variances for various activities.

Solution :

The table for the problem is utilised for working out the standard deviations and variances of various activities as under :

Activity	t_o	t_p	$\sigma = \frac{t_p - t_o}{6}$	$V = \sigma^2$
1-2	5	12	1.16	1.45
1-3	12	17	0.83	0.69
2-4	15	21	0.67	0.43
3-4	2	5	0.5	0.25
2-5	8	14	1.0	1.00
4-5	21	35	2.33	5.32

Project Variance

Taking the activity time calculations from the example of Problem 20.2, the critical activities are found to be only (1-2) and (2-5). Hence the project variance will depend only on these two activities (other activities donot affect the project duration). Hence

Activity	t_p	t_o	$\sigma = \frac{t_p - t_o}{6}$	$V = \sigma^2$
1 - 2	20	8	2	4
2 - 5	12	4	1.67	2.8

Variance of the project (critical path duration) = Sum of activity variances

and standard deviation of the critical path duration = $\sqrt{\Sigma V}$

In the above example, SD of the critical path = $\sqrt{4+2.8}$ 2

= 2.6

Since for a long project, there will be a large number of activities on the critical path, critical path duration can be assumed to be following a normal distribution and hence the probabilities of values lying within a certain range will be

Mean ± σ, Mean ± 2σ, Mean ± 3σ with respective probabilities as 0.682, 0.954 and 0.998, which are obtained by calculating the areas under the curve for these variation limits.

With the mean time T, the probability of the completion of the project by certain specified date (D) can be calculated as

$$Z = \frac{D-T}{\sigma}$$

Then cumulative probabilities upto Z can be obtained from the probability distribution table for normal distribution. (Refer Table 2 at the end of the book).

By this method, probability of completion of the project by a certain time schedule can be estimated. These probabilities of each individual activity can be written along with mean time duration to depict the PERT network (say activity can have duration probability marked on arrow such as 5(0.8)).

Problem 20.5

Consider the following schedule of activities and related information for the construction of a new plant :

Activity	*Expected Time*		*Expected Cost (Rs. 00,000's)*
	Months	*Variance*	
1 - 2	4	1	5
2 - 3	2	1	3
3 - 6	3	1	4
2 - 4	6	2	9
1 - 5	2	1	2
5 - 6	5	1	12
4 - 6	9	5	20
5 - 7	7	8	7
7 - 8	10	16	14
6 - 8	1	1	4

You should assume that the cost and time required for one activity are not dependent upon the cost and time of any other activity and variations are expected to follow a normal distribution. You are required to calculate :

(*a*) the critical path
(*b*) expected cost of construction of the plant
(*c*) expected time required to build the plant
(*d*) the standard deviation of the expected time. [*ICWA (Final), Dec., 1982*]

Solution :

The network diagram of the project activities is drawn as follows. It reflects EOT, LOT, Critical path and the project duration.

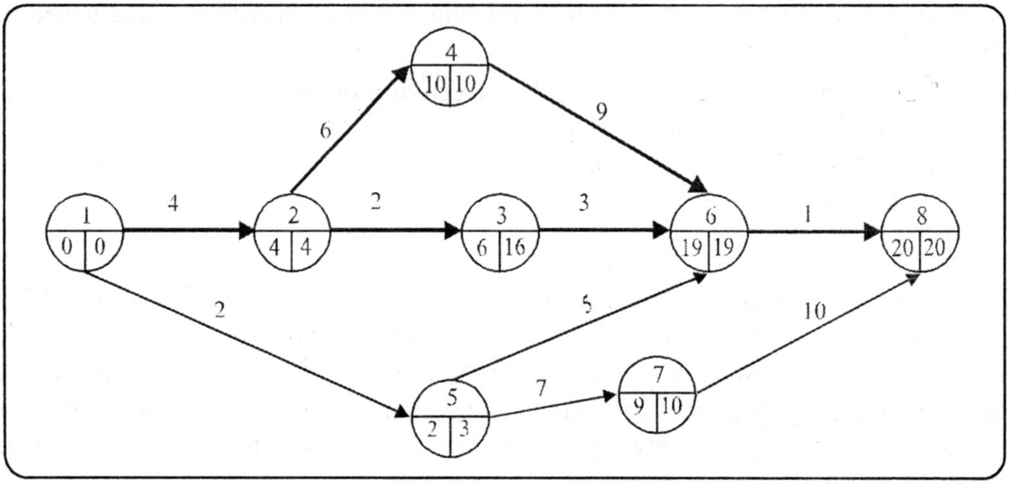

Fig. 20.17 Network Diagram for the Plant

(*a*) Critical path drawn in thick line is 1 – 2 – 4 – 6 – 8. Since there are no slacks on these activities and it is the longest path.

(*b*) Expected cost of construction= 5 + 3 + 4 + 9 + 2 + 12 + 20 + 7 + 14 + 4 = Rs. 80,00,000.

(*c*) Expected time of completion= EOT or LOT of the end event.

= 20 months

(*d*) Standard deviation of the expected time obtained as 20 months is

Activity	*Variance*
1 - 2	1
2 - 4	2
4 - 6	5
6 - 8	1
Total	**9 months**

Standard deviation of the expected time $= \sqrt{9} = 3$ months

20.16 Crashing of Activities

Whereas PERT model was primarily developed for project with uncertainty of events and time, CPM was developed for deterministic approach, following assumptions are made while dealing with CPM analysis:

- Project costs have two distinct sub-components; the direct costs consisting of direct labour and material costs and the indirect costs involving items like indirect supplies, rent, taxes, insurance and overhead services etc.
- Certain activities of the project can be expedited by crashing the time schedule with the help of additional resources.
- Crashing of time i.e., time reduction enhances direct costs like overtime, extra wages and emergency costs of services etc. Based on these assumptions, let us consider crashing the time schedule of the project. The procedure followed is as under :
  - Obtain critical path in the network by normal estimated mean times.
  - Examine the cost-time slope of the activities on the critical path and start crashing of activity with the least slope.
  - Construct the new critical path after crashing of an activity has been completed and revised schedule and costs obtained.
  - Repeat steps (*ii*) and (*iii*) till crashing of all the activities on such revised critical path at each iteration has been obtained.

Problem 20.6

The activities, duration and direct activity costs are given below. The indirect cost is Rs. 3,000 per week. Obtain the crash cost and duration of the project.

Activity	*Time in Weeks*		*Cost*		*Cost to Expedite per week (cost slope)*
	Normal	*Crash*	*Normal*	*Crash*	
1 - 2	2	2	3000	3000	—
2 - 3	4	3	4000	5000	1000
2 - 6	8	8	6000	6000	—
3 - 4	3	2	2000	3500	1500
3 - 5	2	2	2000	2000	—
4 - 6	4	3	4000	5000	1000
5 - 6	3	3	4000	4000	—
6 - 7	8	5	8000	12000	1333

Solution :

Step 1 : Drawing the network, the critical path has been obtained (EOT, LOT marked).

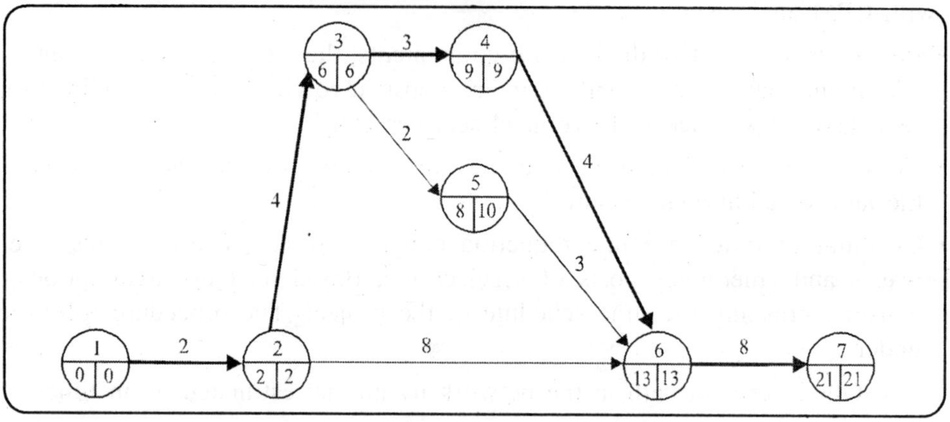

Fig. 20.18 Network and Critical Path

Hence Critical Path is 1-2-3-4-6-7 (Fig. 20.18).

Step 2 : The least cost-time slope of activities on the critical path is 1,000 on activity 2-3 an well as 4-6. Hence any of the two activities can be taken up for crashing. Selecting 4-6 we get the network as follows: (Refer Fig. 20.19)

Thus the Critical Path remains as 1-2-3-4-6-7 with crashing of activity 4-6 from 4 weeks to 3 weeks and project duration reducing from 21 to 20 weeks.

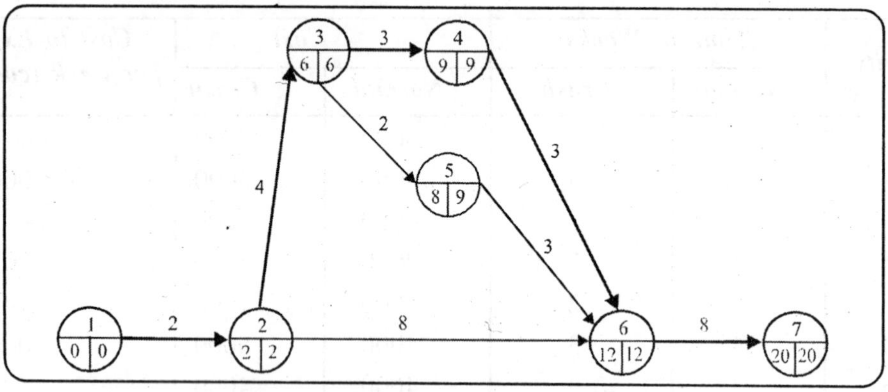

Fig. 20.19 Revised Critical Path

Step 3 : Since critical path remains the same, we can now select activity 2-3 for crashing, which can be crashed from 4 to 3 weeks.

New network can be drawn as follows :

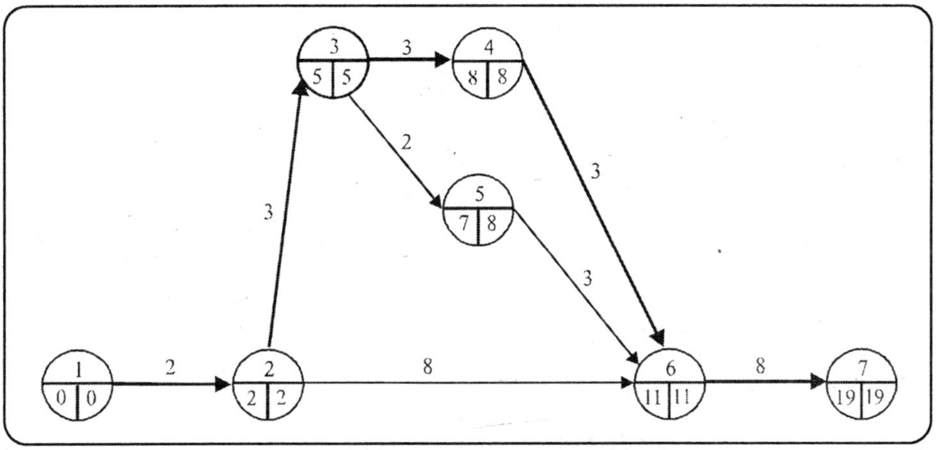

Fig. 20.20 Revised Critical Path

Revised Critical Path is 1-2-3-4-6-7 which is same as above with total duration reducing from 20 to 19 weeks (Refer Fig. 20.20).

Step 4 : Now we can take up activity 6-7 (next least slope i.e., 1,333) for crashing from 8 weeks to 5 weeks giving network as follows : (Fig. 20.21 refers)

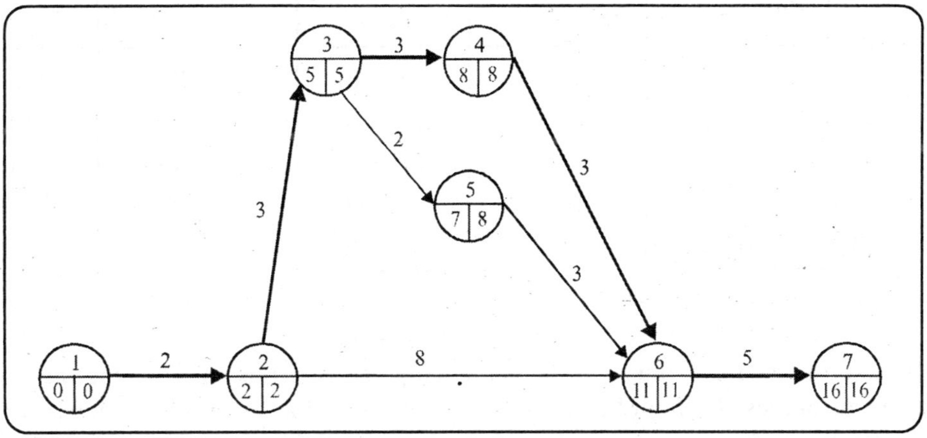

Fig. 20.21 Revised Critical Path

Step 5 : Critical Path still remains 1-2-3-4-6-7 with revised duration of 16 weeks. Next activity qualified for crashing on Critical Path is 3-4 with next slope level of 1,500. This activity is to be crashed from 3 to 2 weeks and revised network can be drawn as follows :

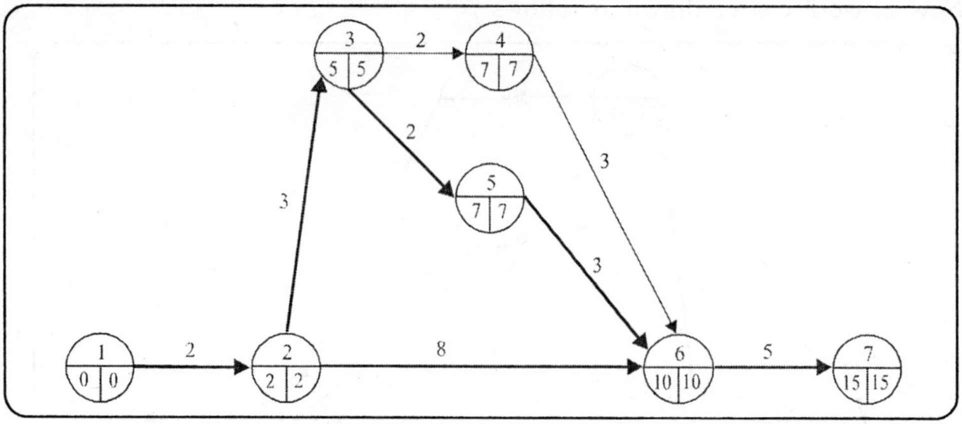

Fig. 20.22 Final CP after all crashings

Now we find the all activities have come to the level of being critical with total project duration changing from 16 to 15 weeks and now no other activity can be crashed (Fig. 20.22 refers).

We can now draw the matrix of project duration and total cost of the project.

Activity Crashing	*Project Duration*	*Direct Cost*	*Indirect Cost*	*Total Cost*
None	21	33,000	63,000	96,000
(4-6)	20	34,000	60,000	94,000
(4-6), (2-3)	19	35,000	57,000	92,000
(4, 6), (2, 3), (6-7)	16	39,000	48,000	87,000
(4-6), (2-3), (6-7), (3-4)	15	40,500	45,000	85,500

It can thus be seen that the cost and time considerations on crashing the project duration from 21 to 15 weeks brings out the optimal solution in this form.

The time-cost trade-off, thus, can be achieved when it is possible to expedite the work by increasing resources. It should also be technically feasible to crash the activities. Then only trade-off is effective.

Updating the network based on actual progress of work is required to help in periodic review. CP thus may change on reviews. When there is a time or cost-over-run, the trade-off analysis is an important managerial tool to set-off certain relevant decisions for control function of the project.

20.17 Resources Allocation

While discussing the scheduling issues as per CPM/PERT techniques, the resources levels were not considered. The activity-relationship were the only considerations in that discussion. However, the schedule undergoes a change as soon as the resources constraints are taken into account. Following situations are dealt with :

Allotment of resources to various activities - For any activity, the level of resources is calculated based on the quantum of work, output norm for various categories and the time schedule available for each activity. The relationships of men and machines outputs are established and it is better system to indicate resources only in terms of manhours or mandays etc. (even for machine output, with equivalents worked out) so that shortage of one resource can be compensated by the other with given equivalence. For example, if output of a man is 50 cubic metres for a day and it is 500 cubic metres for a machine, the equivalent of a machine would be 10 mandays. Thus, for every machine used, 10 mandays can be added as resource allocation for an activity. It is presented on the network as follows.

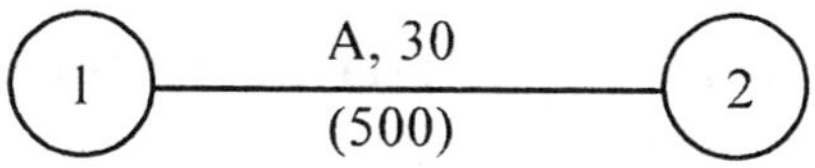

Where A is the name of the activity, 30 days is the duration and 500 mandays are resources required.

Resources Modification (Time Resources Trade Off) - As can be seen from para 20.16, modifications to the resources levels have to be carried out, if the project is to be speeded up or slowed down. Crashing of activities can be made possible under following assumptions :

- Additional appropriate resources are available to the extent required.
- Utilisation of additional resources is technically and administratively feasible.

Resources Constraints. Generally, all project managers face the difficulty of inadequate resources for the project. Since the work also can be changing in its quantum (depending on changes suggested by the client from time to time), a constraint updation of network is necessary. Even without changes, the resources inadequacy forces a project manager towards innovation and he has to do his best to organise his work in such a way so that the completion date and total budget does not bust beyond limits. Certain modification to the time schedule is, however, imperative when resources are in short supply and project manager is forced to adopt rescheduling of work. This is necessitated due to following reasons:

Time limitations: When project has to be completed by certain date. Here time is critical and crashing may be a solution to the problem.

Resources limitations: When resources as per requirement are not available. Rescheduling of activities, therefore, has to be resorted to.

There are two approaches to the constrained allocation situations namely, heuristics and mathematical optimisation models. We are restricting ourselves to the heuristic approach as it is practical to adopt under most situations. As per present software capabilities, the resource levelling can be easily accomplished. On a practical level, heuristics can be applied when problems are large, complex and non-linear. The use of bar chart can be adopted even for small problems as follows :

- Draw the network diagram as per activity relationship and convert it to the bar chart form (on time scale basis as most softwares do).

- The resources required for ail the activities as per time schedule indicated are marked.
- Total resources availability is then distributed to various concurrent activities, keeping in mind that critical activities on the network are not deprived of their full quota of resources.
- Wherever there is shortage of resources on non-critical activities, the rescheduling is adopted with reference to old schedule required for any activity with available resources.
- All related and affected activities are then rescheduled on the network and accordingly fresh schedule of the project is finalised.

With the reference to the inadequacy of manpower or financial allocations (budget the rescheduling has been shown in problem 20.7.

Problem 20.7

For the network given in Fig. 20.23, workout the project completion time and reschedule the same with the following resources constraints :

Total manpower available 50 persons

Total budget allocations

(a) First year	Rs. 50 lacs
(b) Second year	Rs. 89 lacs
(c) Third year	Rs. 55 lacs

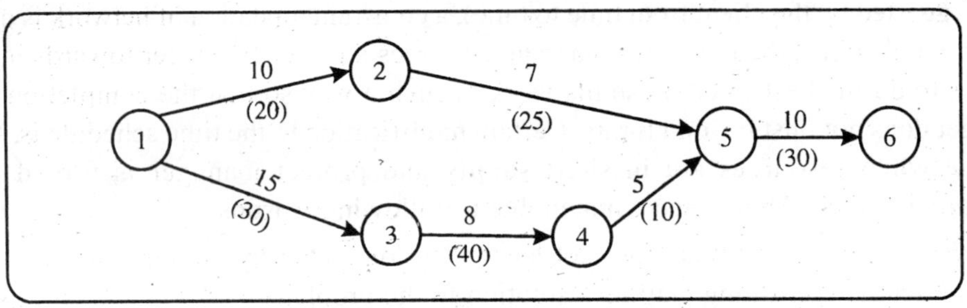

Fig. 20.23 **Time-Resource Presentation**

The figures given above the arrows for various activities indicate the duration in months whereas the figures given below the arrow (in brackets) indicate total number of men required on daily basis.

Solution:

For the given network, we proceed to obtain the EOT and LOT for each node and then identify the critical path.

Having worked out EOT and LOT for the forward pass and backward pass, the critical path is identified as 1-3-4-5-6. This can be seem from the network given in Fig 20.24.

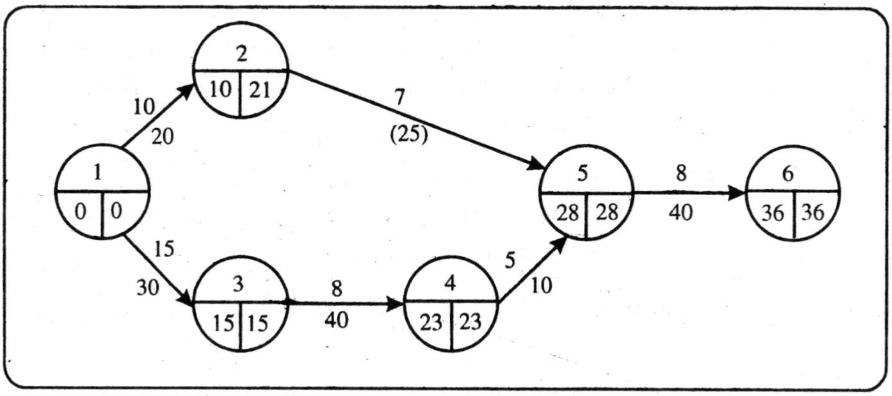

Fig. 20.24 **Network with EOT/LOT**

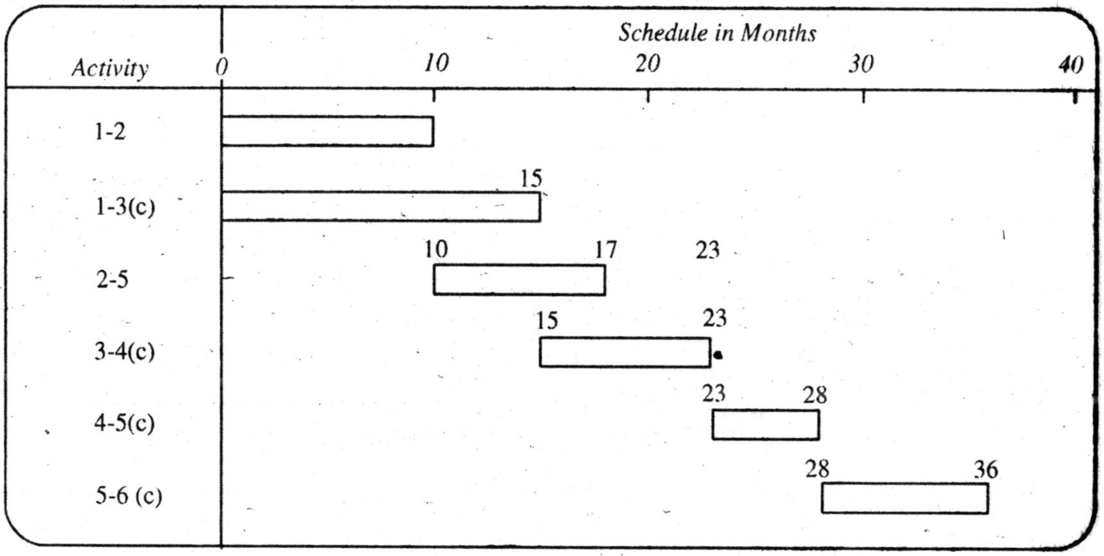

Fig. 20.25 **Bar Chart Scheduling**

Manpower Constraint Scheduling. Since there are 50 people available the work on activity 1-2 and 1-3 can start simultaneously with sufficient and required manpower. Activity 1-2 is over in 10 months and it will release 20 people. Activity 1-3 is a critical activity and hence its resources (i.e., 30 people) can not be touched. Activity 2-5 is a non-critical activity and hence reduced manpower (50-30 busy on activity 1-3) i.e., only 20 as against the requirement of 25. This work 2-5 can therefore be completed in 9 months (instead of 7 originally planned) with this reduced manpower. Next critical activity 3-4 can be started soon after 1-3 is over in 15 months and all the 30 people are now free for activity 3-4. The requirements of 40 people from 3-4 cannot be made available as 20 are busy on activity 2-5. It is suggested to employ 40 people on critical activity 3-4 and only 10 to be employed on non-critical activity 2-5, which can be completed by 23rd month, (with 20 people for 5 months and 10 people for next 8 months), which is well within the limit of 28 months (EOT/LOT for node 5).

After completing activity 2-5 and 3-4 by 23rd month, activity 4-5 can start from 24th month with all 30 people available. Similarly activity 5-6 can be completed as scheduled from 29th to 36th months. We observe that 20 people can be dispensed with at the end of 23rd month (as they are no more required).

The revised schedule of the project, therefore, can be drawn in the bar chart form as follows (Critical activities have since been suffixed with (C) on the bar chart). The bar charts are also called GANTT charts with slight modifications.

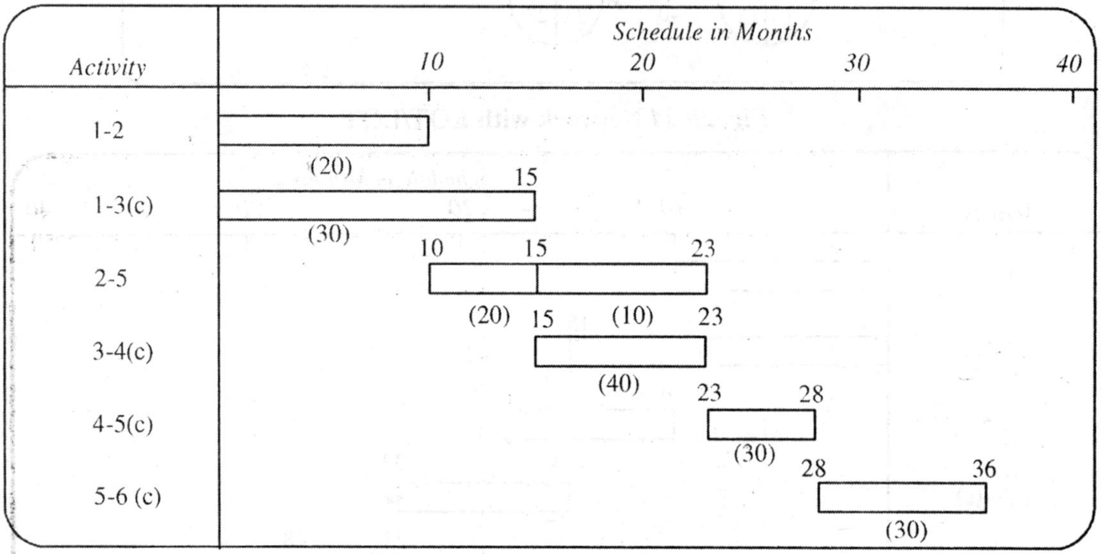

Fig. 20.26 **Bar Chart Scheduling**

Financial Constraint. Before we discuss the financial constraint, we laydown the assumption that for drawing the reschedule, we treat the activities to be consuming all the money uniformly over the entire period of its completion.

The cost of various activities are as under.

Activity 1-2	20 lacs	Rs. 2 lacs per month
Activity 1-3	45 lacs	Rs. 3 lacs per month
Activity 2-5	35 lacs	Rs. 5 lacs per month
Activity 3-4	40 lacs	Rs. 5 lacs per month
Activity 4-5	30 lacs	Rs. 6 lacs per month
Activity 5-6	24 lacs	Rs. 3 lacs per month

We now mark the funds requirements for these activities based on earliest start.

Total funds requirement for first year	= 66 lacs
Total funds requirement for second year	= 80 lacs
and funds requirement for third year	= 48 lacs
Total project cost	= 194 lacs

The revised scheduling according to the financial constraint is drawn in Fig 20.26 where the funds availability shown as under :

First Year	50 lacs
Second Year	89 lacs
Third Year	55 lacs

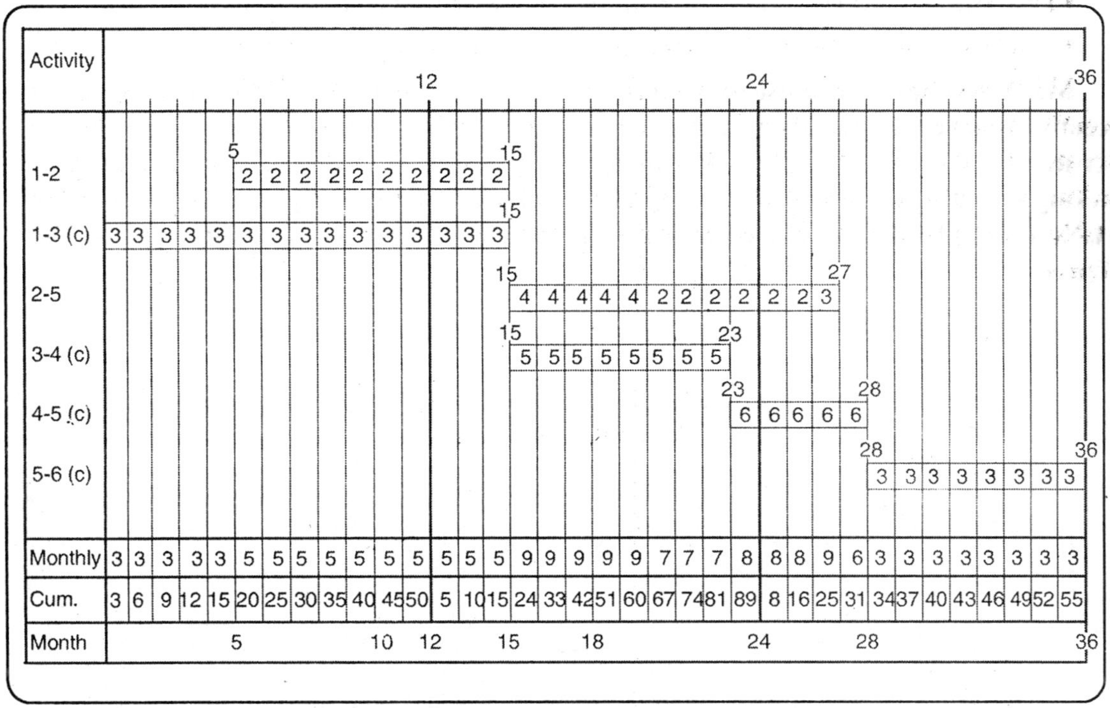

Fig. 20.26 **Financially Constrained Schedule**

20.18 Computer Softwares for Project Management

Due to large number of applications and need for quick results for complex projects in all areas of life, the use of computer for planning, execution and monitoring of projects has become almost imperative. Most project management applications, therefore, are operated through computer softwares extensively.

There are quite a few softwares available in the market. With the due input on activity time estimates, procedence relationships and any special over-riders, the softwares are capable of developing the network (CPM/PERT), calculating the slack for each activity, developing critical path along with the duration and variance of activities as well as for the whole project. A selective list of PM softwares for Project Management are appended below :

- Microsoft Project : Microsoft corporation (www.microsoft.com)
- Primevera Project Planner : Primavera Systems Inc. (www.primavera.com)
- Oracle Projects : Oracle Corporation (www.oracle.com)
- Power Projects : ASTA Development Inc. (www.astaus.com)

- Globalogic Projects : Globalogic Inc. (www.globalogicinc.com)
- Turboprojects : IMSI (www.imsisoft.com)
- AMS Realtime Projects : Advanced Management Solutions (www.amsrealtime.com)
- Fast Track Schedule : AEC Software Inc. (www.aecsoft.com)
- Artemis Views : Artemis Management System. (www.artemispm.com)

MS Project has been in use for majority of projects across the world for a long time. But recently Primavera Project Planner has become very popular, as it is considered to be highly user-friendly and easy to implement. The activity planning, resources information, material tracking and number of useful physical and financial reports for the project are easily available in table and graphical forms. Project Management Institute (PMI) (www.pmi.org) can be usefully referred.

—●—

Annexures A

Discussion Points

1. Define production Management and operation Management.
2. What was Industrial Revolution ? What advantages acrued out of it for production system?
3. Briefly explain "Scientific Management" and its implications for production management.
4. How did the techniques "Operations Research" emerge and to what extent these techniques are useful in todays business ?
5. Explain the Random Fluctuations and the utility of Feedback mechanism in a Production Model.
6. Briefly describe the effect of globalisation on business operations.
7. How is the operations strategy related to the business strategy ?
8. How has the computer Revolution Changed the method of operations in present Business Scenerio ?
9. How do you see the Indian Productions Industry developing in near future and how does it address the global competition ?
10. How is the customer changing the thinking of today's managers ? What important areas are getting affected due to dynamic nature of the customer's requirements ?
11. How do you find the corporate transformation related to the global competition ?
12. Describe various stages of product design and various design approaches.
13. How would you use various product and process design principles to ensure closeness of product to the customer requirements ?
14. How does value engineering concept help in making a product cost effective ?
15. Describe CAD, QFD and DFMA as useful tools for product design.
16. How is the service design different from product design and how would you take care of the environmental concerns for product as well as service design ?

17. List out and describe various environmental factors affecting the product demand.
18. What are the judgemental (Qualitative) methods and quantitative methods of forecasting the product demand ? Describe them briefly.
19. "Regression Model of forecasting is a long term method". Justify the statement. How would you relate it with the correlation coefficient ?
20. What is the utility of computers in Demand Forecasting ?
21. What are the major factors considered for process design ? How would you relate degree of automation with qualtiy requirement of the product ?
22. What is Group or Cellular Manufacturing and how does it help in variety production ?
23. What are the methods used for the economic evaluation of the process ?
24. Describe Break Even Method for selecting an appropriate process for manufacturing ?
25. What are various important steps for service design ? Explain these briefly with suitable examples.
26. Why is it important to design a product for quality and for ease of production and assembly ?
27. What is mean by 'Concurrent Engineering' ? What is its significance for design of a product ?
28. Define the terms - economies of scale, input rate capacity and capacity utilisation percentage.
29. Describe how managers may simultaneously consider both quantitative and qualitative factors in facility location analysis ?
30. What are the important factors based on which a layout can be considered good ?
31. Describe use of computers for layout planning and explain ALDEP software for layout planning, briging out improvements incorporated in CORELAP software.
32. Why balancing of production and assembly lines is required ? Describe general procedure and at least one method of affecting it.
33. What benefits should be expected from automation in production and service lines ?
34. Describe the following in brief :
    (a) Automatic attachments
    (b) Robots
    (c) Automated process control
    (d) Automated flow lines
    (e) Automated storage system
    (f) CNC and DNC machines
35. Describe the necessity, scope and usage of Flexible Manufacturing System (FMS).
36. Define and briefly explain : CAD/CAM and CIM.

37. What are various types of Production Planning Control systems ? Explain with the aid of a diagram.
38. What is Master Production Scheduling ? How it is useful in MRP Software ?
39. Describe various sequencing rules. How are these helpful in scheduling jobs on a shop floor ?
40. Write down various steps of Johnson's rule for job sequencing. Explain it with the help of an example.
41. What are major challenges being faced by service managers in their job scheduling ? How much help should be taken from a customer for service design ?
42. How do you achieve customer satisfaction under various service strategies adopted ?
43. How do managers make their workers and lower managers committed and involved in their works, so that they prove to be assets for the organisation ?
44. Define Productivity and explain the method of measuring it. Write the effect of learning curve on productivity.
45. Write various steps in job design. What important factors are considered in this process ? What is the importance of job description, job empowerment, job rotation and job ownership ?
46. Do managers really have to take care of the health and safety of the workers ? Are they themselves not responsible for it ? Under what legistation, the workers are protected for safety ?
47. Describe various steps for works study and list out important factors considered for a works study to be effective.
48. Briefly describe various principles of motion economy and their utility in method design and work measurement.
49. Why production standards are important for an organisation ? What types of standards are available for their effective utilisation ?
50. Relate work compensation and incentive methods to the role of workers unions in any large organisation.
51. How is demand forecasting different in small businesses than that in large business ?
52. For better customer satisfaction, product design, process design and inventory management has to be carefully integrated – comment.
53. For control of production volumes, the output norms for the men and those for machines are to be matched after due consideration of actual condition. How is this to be achieved and why is derating of the men and machine capability important ?
54. What is inventory and why is it called "a necessary evil" ? What methods can be adopted to keep the inventory at the optimum level ?

55. What are various costs associated with inventory and how can these be minimised ?
56. Describe 'WILSONS' LOT SIZE formula for inventory management. Is the method called Economic Order Quantity (EOQ), the best policy for cost effective procurement ?
57. Explain the relevance and importance of safety or Buffer stocks for the production system.
58. Describe various steps of ABC method of inventory control. Why are the inventories classified as A, B or C and what control measures are taken on this basis ?
59. Define the terms : produce to order, produce to stock, lot size, Reorder level, Reorder point and vendor managed inventory.
60. Define resource requirement planning ? Identify the major elements of resource requirement planning.
61. Describe MRP software capabilities and method of interaction of its various files. How are MPS, CRP and MRP related ?
62. Describe two bin system of inventory control. Also explain the pull-system of Kanban controlled production with the help of a diagram.
63. How is MRP II different from MRP ? Do you know any specific softwares for MRPII ?
64. How do you relate ERP to MRP ? How is ERP designed for an organisation ?
65. Show a typical ERP system with some important modules and explain the integration system achieved for all the modules. What is the importance of client server architectiure in this system ?
66. Write important stages of implementing an ERP system for an organisation. How can the cost of the ERP package be reduced for small organisations ?
67. How did JIT come into being and how is it relevant even today for cost effective manufacturing ?
68. What are various JIT production systems in use in the manufacturing and service industry ?
69. "JIT implementation is a methodical process". How do you visualise the support from purchasing and maintenance departments being vital in its implementation ? Is JIT practiced in inventory only ?
70. Describe the necessity of synchronous production and its implementation requirements.
71. Explain Goldratt's Theory of Constraints. Why did Goldratt think about it and how did he use it to relate it to the production ground reality ?
72. What is Optimised Production Technology (OPT) and how is it useful tool in todays business context ?
73. What is Business Process Re-engineering ? How is it related to business improvement ? write steps to implement BPR in practice.
74. What is Supply Chain Management ? Describe the objectives and the scope of Supply Chain. How its it such an important concept in global business scenerio ?

75. Explain various supply chain processes with reference to domestic as well as global business point of view.
76. What is strategic supply chain and how is it implemented by various organisations today ?
77. By listing out factors for achieving competitive advantage in the business, explain the importance of lean supply chain. Also describe briefly the operating model for SCM.
78. Show the importance of E-purchasing and E-sourcing in effective functioning of supply chain. Also relate the concept of 'Capture Vendor Management' to increase the effectiveness of supply chain operations.
79. How do you define logistics Management ? How is different from Distribution Management ?
80. Explain the concept of outsourcing in logistics and write the functions of the Third Party Logistics (3PL) providers and the Fourth Party Logistics (4PL) providers.
81. Define Quality and show the level of quality as per the customer perception. Explain this with the help of various dimensions of quality.
82. What are various costs incurred to maintain quality ? What is Quality conformance and how is it related to the dynamics of quality requirements ?
83. Describe the meaning and methods for Statistical Process Control. Briefly mention the importance of acceptance sampling for process control.
84. Draw a neat Operating Characterstics Curve (OC Curve) for a certain value of n and c (sample size and number of defects) and explain the concepts of AQL, LTPD, Type I, II errors and producer's and customers risks in production.
85. What methods are used for uniting product specifications and tolerances for deciding process control ? What methods do you adopt for selecting the 'Sample Size' for testing ?
86. How is quality perception different in service as compared to the production ? What parameters can be selected for product quality and service quality measurements ?
87. Define TQM (Total Quality Management) and write its objectives as emerged from this definition. Write various stages through which quality can be ensured.
88. What are various principles and elements of TQM ? Describe Dr. Demings Quantity wheel to indicate importance of various elements of TQM.
89. List out and briefly explain various concepts in TQM and describe methods to implement these.
90. Write a short note on ISO 9000 standards as regards their utility to the industry worldwide. How is its use different for small businesses ?
91. Environmental Management System (EMS) is gaining importance globally and hence ISO 14000 standards are almost becoming a prelude to get ISO 9000 certification. Why ? What are major benefits of implements ISO 14000 standards ?

92. Explain "negotiation skill" for procurement and its utility in ethical buying.
93. 'Warehousing' should be treated as profit centre these days. Why ? Explain the costs controlled through effective warehousing.
94. Write short notes on 'scrap and waste disposal' bringing out their importance inside and outside the factory.
95. Define Maintenance Management. What all do we maintain and why ? Also explain how the maintenance is to be carried out.
96. Explain various maintenance and replacement policies defined by various organisations.
97. How do you relate project planning concept to the production system ? How would you use project feasibility report to advantage in your production decisions ?
98. For various organisations and at various locations working under different conditions, the working methods would need modifications. Describe general environmental conditions and conflicts arising on various projects.
99. Taking the rules of network analysis, explain how various activities are co-ordinated with the help of a CPM network. How do you relate PERT to actual working environment ?
100. How would you carryout reduction in time schedules in activities, if the project needs to be completed earlier ?
101. Define the total productivity for a manufacturing sector vis-a-vis a service sector. How can an organisation improve productivity by considering both the people and the production variables ?
102. What are the sources of variability that forces an organisation to adopt flexible manufacturing ?
103. The goal of CIM may be to increase profitability, quality, flexibility and customer satisfaction. Explain.
104. What are the performance objectives of the supply chain ?
105. How is SCM different from ERP ?
106. Quality and Productivity are closely inter-related. Explain the linking parameters.
107. Discuss various concepts of TQM. How do you write a success story of an organisation through TQM implementations ?
108. List out critical factors for making JIT successful.
109. What are the goals of TPM ? How do you minimise waste through TPM methodology ?
110. Does ERP implementation requires BPR ? Discuss both sides of the coin i.e., arguments for and against.
111. Do you think TQM and BPR are the same philosophy ? Discuss.
112. Do operations strategies take into account the uncertainty of the market or is it the other way around ? Discuss.

113. Explain how the Delphi technique forecasting results are better than those obtained through Group technique.
114. How is the product mix related to the capacity utilisation decision ?
115. Aggregate plans and master production schedules are developed on the basis of demand forecasts. How the aggregate plans accomodate the actual demand variation ?
116. What are the priority sequencing rules ? Why does an operations manager need them and how does he select the appropriate rule for working ?
117. Discuss the advantages and disadvantages of the periodic inventory system compared with the quantity order system (i.e., P and Q systems).
118. Show the relationship of the Master Production Schedule (MPS) with other modules of the MRP system. How is the variability of demand catered for through the MRP operation ?
119. Explain shigeo shingos seven wastes. How these wastes are minimised through JIT and FMS production systems ?
120. For increase in output quality, the quantity of output suffers. Is it true ? Explain.

Annexures B

Decision Analysis

1. In a bank there are five cashiers dealing with clients loan disbursements. The number of clients serviced during four weeks of the month are as under :

Week	*Average Number of cashiers*	*Clients served*
1	4	1250
2	5	1560
3	5	1600
4	4	1320

Compute the service productivity of cashiers for each week. What do these figures indicate ?

2. A company is trying out an investment plan under which an initial outlay required having a six year useful product life is ₹2,00,000. This is expected to have a solvage value of ₹25,000 at the end of six year. Annual increment revenue is expected at ₹30,000 and annual increment operating expense as ₹21,000. What is the internal rate of return (IRR) for this investment ?

3. The XYZ Company during the festival season combines two product A and B to form a gift pack, which must weigh 5 Kgs. At least 3 Kgs of A and not more than 4 Kgs of B should be used. The net profit contribution to the company is ₹5 per Kg for A and ₹6 per Kg for B. Use any method to find the optimal product mix.

4. A manufacturecr produces electric hand saws and electric drills, for which the demand exceeds his capacity. The production cost of a saw is ₹6 and the production cost of a drill is ₹4. The shipping cost is 20 paise for a saw and 30 paise for a drill. A saw sells for ₹9 and a drill sells for ₹5.50. The budget allows a maximum of ₹2,400 for production cost and ₹120 for shipping cost. Determine the number of saws and drills that should be produced in order to maximise the excess of sales over production and shipping cost.

[*Poona University, MBA., 1982*]

5. A company manufacturing two products A and B has three major production departments with capacities as detailed under :

Department	*Production Capacity*	
	Product A	*Product B*
1	3,000	2,000
2	3,500	7,000
3	5,000	3,000

Solve the problem by graphical method for the optimal production if the input costs are ₹20 and ₹40 respectively, whereas the products are sold at a price of ₹60.

6. GJ Breweries Ltd. have two bottling plants, one located at G and the other at J. Each plant produces three drinks – whiskey, beer and brandy, named A, B and C respectively. The number of bottles produced per day are as follows :

Drink	*Bottles at plants per day*	
	G	*J*
Whiskey A	1,500	1,500
Beer B	3,000	1,000
Brandy C	2,000	5,000

A market survey indicates that during the month of july, there will be a demand of 20,000 bottles of whiskey, 40,000 bottles of beer and 44,000 bottles of brandy. The operating costs per day for plant at G and J are 600 and 400 monetary units. For how many days should each plant be run in july so as to minimise the production cost, while meeting all the market demand ? Solve graphically.

[*ICWA., June 1984, Mysore University, BE 1984*]

7. A firm makes products X and Y and has a total production capacity of 9 tonnes per day, X and Y requiring the same production capacity. The firm has a permanent contract to supply atleast 2 tonnes of X and 3 tonnes of Y per day to another company. Each tonne of X requires 20 machine hours of production time and each tonne of Y requires 50 machine hours production time. The daily maximum possible number of machine-hours is 360. All the firms output can be sold and the profit made is ₹80 per tonne of X and ₹120 per tonne of Y. It is required to determine the production schedule for maximum profit and the calculate this profit.

[*Delhi University, M.B.A., April, 1983*]

8. The ABC manufacuring company can make two product P1 and P2. Each of the products requires time on a cutting machine and a finishing machine. Relevant data are :

Details	*Products*	
	P_1	P_2
Cutting hours (per unit)	2	1
Finishing hours (per unit)	2	3
Profit (₹per unit)	6	4
Maximum Sales (per week)	150	200

The number of cutting hours available per week is 390 and the number of finishing hours available for week is 810. How much of each product must be produced in order to achieve maximum profit for the company ?

[*C.A. (Final), May, 1983*]

9. In a certain television factory, two types of television sets are produced with a profit of 6 units from each television of type I and 4 units from each television of type II. In addition, 2 and 3 units of raw material are needed to produce television of type I and II respectively and 4 and 2 units of time are required to produce one television of type I and II respectively. If 100 units of raw materials and 120 units of time are available, how many units of each type of television should be produced to maximise profit meeting all the constraints on the problem. First of all, you should write the mathematical model concerning the given problem and then solve the same applying simplex method of linear programming.

10. A company makes three products X, Y and Z which flow through three departments : Drill, Lathe and Assembly. The hours of department time required by each of the products, the hours available in each department and the profit contribution of each of the products are given in the following table :

Product	*Time Required*			*Profit contribution*
	Drill	*Lathe*	*Assembly*	*per unit* (₹)
X	3	3	8	9
Y	6	5	10	15
Z	7	4	12	20
hours Available	210	240	260	

The marketing department of the company indicates that the sales potential for products X and Y are unlimited, but for product Z, it is only 30 units. Determine the optimum production schedule.

11. A company has factories at F_1, F_2 and F_3 which supply warehouses at W_1, W_2 and W_3. Weekly factory capacities are 200, 160 and 90 units respectively. Weekly warehouse demands are 180, 120 and 150 units respectively. Unit shipping costs (in rupees) are as follows.

Factories		*Warehouse*		*Supply*
	W_1	W_2	W_3	
F_1	16	20	12	200
F_2	14	8	18	160
F_3	26	24	16	90
Demand	180	120	150	

Determine the optimal distribution for this company to minimise the shipping costs.

[Madras University, M.Com., Nov., 1982]

12. A company is spending ₹1,200 on transportation of its units from three plants to four distribution centres. The supply and demand of units with unit cost of transportation are given as :

Plants		*Distribution Centres*			*Supply*
	D_1	D_2	D_3	D_4	
P_1	20	30	50	15	7
P_2	70	35	40	60	10
P_3	40	12	60	25	18
Demand	5	8	7	15	

What can be the maximum saving by optimal scheduling ?

13. A motor manufacturer has two plants and three distribution centres. The supply and demand position of motors and unit cost of distribution are given in the following matrix :

		Distribution Centres	
	D_1	D_2	D_3
Requirement	60	65	75
Unit cost of transport :			
Plant A	30	50	20
Plant B	20	10	60

Capacity of Plant A = 200 motors

Capacity of Plant B = 250 motors

Presently the firm is spending ₹6,500 per month on distribution. What maximum savings can be obtained by optimal distribution scheduling.

14. A wholesaler has three retail stores at Saharanpur, Meerut and Dehradun. The maximum demand of these stores for the product are 2,000; 5,000; and 3,000 respectively. The shipping costs from retail stores to small towns are given in the table.

	Small Towns (Sale Centres)				
Retail Stores	*A*	*B*	*C*	*D*	*E*
Saharanpur	45	40	60	50	25
Meerut	20	35	40	60	20
Dehradun	60	50	60	50	40

If Sales Centres need 3,500, 2,000, 1,500, 1,000 and 2,000 units of products, what should be the optimal shipping schedule at minimum cost ?

15. A company has four factories F1, F2, F3 and F4 from which it ships its products to four warehouses W1, W2, W3 and W4 which are the distribution centes. Transportation costs per unit between various combination of factories and warehouses are as given below :

Factories	*Warehouses*				*Availability*
	W1	*W2*	*W3*	*W4*	
F_1	48	60	56	58	140
F_2	45	55	53	60	260
F_3	50	65	60	62	360
F_4	52	64	55	61	
Requirement	200	320	250	210	

Find the transportation schedule, which minimises the distribution cost.

[*C.A., (Final), May, 1982*]

16. ABC manufacturing company wishes to develop a monthly production schedule for the next three months. Depending upon the sales commitments, the company can either keep the production costant, allowing fluctuations in inventory or the inventories can be maintained at a constant level, with flactuating production. Fluctuating production necessitates in working overtime, the cost of which is estimated to be double the normal production cost of ₹12 per unit. Fluctuating inventories result in inventory carrying cost of ₹2 per unit. If the company fails to fulfill its sales commitment, it incurs a shortage costs of ₹4 per unit per month. The production capacity for the next three months are shown below :

	Production Capacity		
Months	*Regular*	*Overtime*	*Sales*
1	50	30	60
2	50	0	120
3	60	50	40

Determine the optimum production schedule.

[*Poona University, M.B.A 1983*]

17. A company has four manufacturing plants and five warehouses. Each plant manufactures the same product, which is sold at different prices at each warehouse area. The cost of manufacturing and cost of raw materials are different in each plant due to various factors. The production capacities of the plants are different. The data are given in the following table:

Items	*Plants*			
	1	*2*	*3*	*4*
Manufacturing cost per unit	12	10	8	8
Raw material cost per unit	8	7	7	5
Capacity	100	200	120	80

The sales price, transportation costs and demands are given below:

Warehouses	*Transportation cost per unit*				*Sales price per unit*	*Demand*
	1	*2*	*3*	*4*		
A	4	7	4	3	30	80
B	8	9	7	8	32	120
C	2	7	6	10	28	150
D	10	7	5	8	34	70
E	2	5	8	9	30	90

(i) Formulate it as a transportation problem to maximise profits.

(ii) Find the solution using VAM method.

(iii) Test the optimality and find the optimal solution.

[*ICWA; June, 1990*]

18. There are five work centres in a production shop and there are four workmen, who can be deployed on these work centres. The study carried out shows that time taken by various workmen on these workcentres are much at variance and therefore a judicious selection and allocation of workmen is needed to get optimum production. The table showing time taken by workmen is given as follows :

Work Centres	*Workmen*			
	W1	*W2*	*W3*	*W4*
C_1	10	9	8	12
C_2	3	5	4	2
C_3	25	20	14	16
C_4	7	9	10	9
C_5	18	14	16	25

Workout the optimum allocation for various work centres.

19. A compnay is faced with the problem of assigning six different machines to five different jobs. The costs are estimated as follows (hundreds of rupees)

Machines	Jobs (Cost in hundred of rupees)				
	1	*2*	*3*	*4*	*5*
1	2.5	5	1	6	1
2	2	5	1.5	7	3
3	3	6.5	2	8	3
4	3.5	7	2	9	4.5
5	4	7	3	9	6
6	6	9	5	10	6

Solve the problem assuming that the objective is to minimise total cost.

20. Six jobs go first over machine I and then over II. The order of completion of the jobs has no significant. The following table gives the machine time in hours for six jobs and the two machines:

Jobs	1	2	3	4	5	6
Machine I	5	9	4	7	8	6
Machine II	7	4	8	3	9	5

Find the sequence of the jobs that minimises the total elapsed time to complete the jobs. Find the minimum time by using Gantt chart or any other method.

[*Meerut University, M.Com., 1979*]

21. In a machine shop, eight different products are being manufactured, each requiring time on two machines A and B as given below :

Products	*Time (in minute) on machine A*	*Time (in minutes) on machine B*
I	30	20
II	45	30
III	15	50
IV	20	35
V	80	36
VI	120	40
VII	65	50
VIII	10	20

Decide the optimum sequence of processing of different products in order to minimise the total manufacturing time for all the products. Name and discuss the scheduling model used.

22. Six jobs have to be processed at three machines A, B and C in the order ACB. The time taken by each job on each machine is indicated below. Each machine can process only one job at a time.

Jobs	J_1	J_2	J_3	J_4	J_5	J_6
Processing time in hours on machine						
A	12	8	7	11	10	5
B	7	1	9	6	10	4
C	3	4	2	5	1.5	4

Determine the sequence for the jobs so as to minimise the total processing time.

[Delhi University, M.Com., 1982, 1985]

23. An assembly line has the following tasks to be performed :

Task	*Immediate Predecessor*	*Task Time in minutes*
A	—	2.0
B	A	1.5
C	A	0.8
D	C	1.0
E	B, C	2.5
F	E	2.0
G	F	1.3
H	F	2.1
I	F	0.9
J	H, I	0.8

Using Moodie and Young's heuristic method, balance the line for a cycle time of 3.0 minutes. Workout minimum idle time.

24. For the given precedence, work out the number of workstations and the delays on each workstation for a production rate of 4 units per hour. The unit time element for each activity is indicated with the activity circle itself.

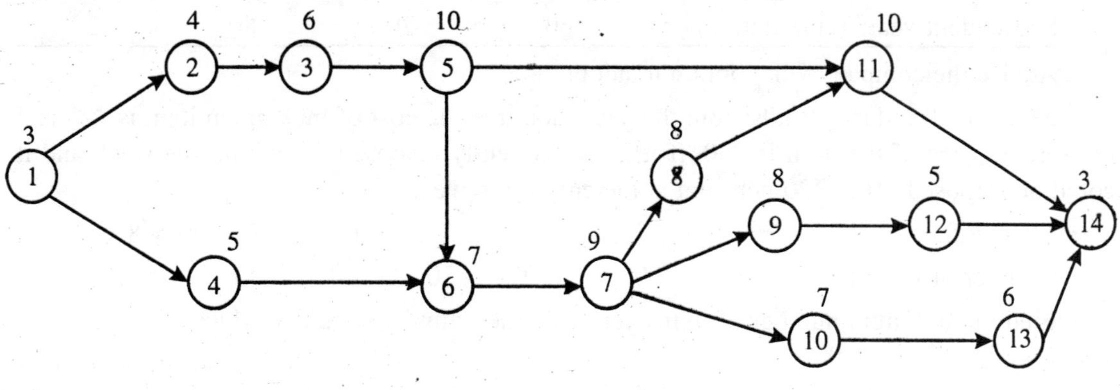

25. Machine A costs₹45,000 and the operating costs are estimated at ₹1,000 for the first year, increasing by ₹10,000 per year in the second and subsequent years. Machine B costs ₹50,000 and the operating costs are ₹2,000 for the first year increasing ₹4,000 per year in the second and subsequent years. If you now have a machine of type A, should you replace it with B ? If so, when ? Assume that both the machines have no resale value and that the future costs are not discounted.

26. A machine-owner finds from his past experience that the cost per year of maintenance of a machine, whose purchase price is ₹6,000 is as given below:

Year	*1*	*2*	*3*	*4*	*5*	*6*	*7*	*8*
Maint cost	1,000	1,200	1,400	1,800	2,300	2,800	3,400	4,000
Resale price	3,000	1,500	750	375	200	200	200	200

At what stage is replacement due ?

27. A person has two independent investments A and B available to him, but he can undertake only one at a time due to certain constraints. He can choose A first and then stop, or if A is successful, then take B or vice versa. The probability of success of A is 0.6 while for B, it is 0.4. Both investments require an initial capital outlay of ₹10,000 and both return nothing if the venture is unsuccessful. Successful completion of A will return ₹20,000 (over cost) and successful completion of B will return ₹24,000 (over cost). Draw decision tree and determine the best strategy.

28. A company has two options : either invest in a large plant (investment ₹50 lakhs) or in a small plant (outlay ₹25 lakhs). In the later option, after one year, depending on the market response, it can expand by investing ₹30 lakhs further. The market survey puts response into two categories-good and bad. The chances of good response initially are 0.6 and bad response 0.4. However, if the initial response is good, subsequent response will be good with probability of 0.9. Similarly, if the initial response is bad, subsequent response is lively to be bad with probability 0.9. The estimated pay-offs are :

Period	*Small plant*		*Large plant*	
	good	*bad*	*good*	*bad*
Initial year	15	5	20	5
Subsequent years (cumulative)	60	20	80	20

Advise the company what option to adopt.

29. A small industry finds from the past data, that the cost of making an item is ₹25 and the selling price of the item is ₹30, if it is subsequently disposed off within the week and it could be disposed off at ₹20 per item at the end of the week.

Weekly Sales	:	< 3	4	5	6	7	≥ 8
Number of weeks	:	0	10	20	40	30	0

Find the optimum number of items per week the industry should produce.

[*C.A., May 1986*]

30. Matrix company is planning to launch a new product, which can be introduced initially in Western India or in the entire country. If the product is used only in western India, the investment outlay will be ₹12 million. After two years, Matrix can evaluate the project to determine whether it should cover the entire country. For such an expansion, it will have to incur an additional investment of ₹10 million. To introduce the product, in the entire country right in the beginning would involve an outlay of ₹20 million. The product, in any case, will have a life of 5 years, after which the plant will have zero value. If the product is introduced only in Western India, demand will be high or low with probabilities of 0.8 and 0.2 respectively and annual cash flow of ₹4 million and ₹2 million respectively. If the product is introduced in the entire country right in the beginning, the demand would be high or low with probabilities of 0.6 and 0.4 respectively and the annual cash inflows of ₹8 million and ₹5 million respectively. Based on the observed demand in Western India, if the product is introduced in the entire country, the following probabilities would exist for high and low demand on all India basis.

Western India	***Whole country***	
	High demand	***Low demand***
High demand	0.9	0.1
Low demand	0.4	0.6

The handle rate applicable to the project is 12 percent :

(a) Set up a decision tree for the investment situation.

(b) Advise matrix company on the investment policy it should follow.

[*I.C.W.A., June 1990*]

31. A manufacturer produces and stocks three items which are produced in lots. The demand rate for each item may be considered constant and deterministic. Back orders are not permitted. The inventory holding cost is 20 per cent and the policy is not to have an investment in inventory above ₹20,000. Given the following additional data, find the optimal lot size for each item :

Item	1	2	3
Demand rate (units per year)	1,200	600	2,000
Cost per unit (₹)	25	125	60
Set up case per lot (₹)	60	90	120

What is the opportunity cost of capital tied up in inventory ?

32. For a certain item, the demand rate is 1,000 units per year. The unit ordering cost is ₹10, unit cost of the item ₹0.50 and the inventory charges are 30 percent per year. The lead time can be assumed as two years. Determine (i) optimal order quantity, (ii) re-order point and (iii) minimum average cost.

[*I.A.S. (ME), 1982*]

33. Data for a typical engineering firm reads as per table given below. Using ABC technique, show graphically which of the below given items you would classify as A, B or C ?

Part Number	*Annual Consumption (units)*	*Unit Price (₹)*
1866	24,000	0.06
2429	22,000	0.10
4805	32,000	0.03
11,240	14,000	0.08
38,383	8,000	0.25
1,47,901	6,000	0.25
4,00,361	6,000	0.30
4,00,535	4,000	0.40
4,00,694	2,000	1.60
7,55,435	2,000	35.00
7,74,845	6,000	2.00
7,85,369	4,000	0.30
8,14,061	2,000	0.60
9,13,170	2,000	11.00
9,13,517	16,000	0.40

34. The annual demand for a product is 1,00,000 units. The rate of production is 2,00,000 units per year. The set up cost per production run is ₹5,000 and the variable production cost of each item is ₹10. The annual holding cost per unit is 20 percent of its value. Find the optimum production lot size and the length of the production run.

[*Delhi University, M.Com., 1985*]

35. In a bank, cheques are encashed at a single teller counter. Customers arrive at the counter in a poisson manner at an average rate of 30 customers per hour. The teller takes at an average a minute and a half to cash the cheque. The service time has been shown to be exponentially distributed.

(a) Calculate the percentage of time the teller is busy.

(b) Calculate the average time a customer is expected to wait.

36. Customer arrive at a sales counter manned by a single person according to a poisson process with a mean rate of 20 per hour. The time required to serve a customer has an exponential distribution with a mean of 100 seconds. Find the average waiting time of a customer.

[*C.A., May, 1987*]

37. A car servicing station has two bays, where service can be offered simultaneously. Due to space limitation, only 4 cars are accepted for servicing. The arrival pattern is poisson with 12 cars per day, the service time in both the bays is exponentially distributed with $\mu = 8$ cars per day per bay.

Find the average number of cars in the service station, the average number of cars waiting to be serviced and the average time a car spends in the system.

[*I.A.S. (Maths), 1988*]

38. Past data about the requirement of a material for manufacturing shop are given as under :

Months	***Requirement (Numbers)***
July 09	784
Aug. 09	863
Sep. 09	940
Oct. 09	960
Nov. 09	1030
Dec. 09	1150

(a) Using 3 months average, forecast the demands for January, February, March and April 10.

(b) Compute the weighted 3 month average for January 2010, assuming the weights as 0.4 for the latest previous month, and 0.35 and 0.25 for just previous months respectively.

39. From the data given in problem 38 above, compute the exponential smoothing forecast for the month of January 10, using smoothing constant value as 0.7.

40. In an office, the demand of work varies with the amount of business documentation centre.

The number of typists required to meet the workload for the last 14 days is given in the following table :

Days :	1	2	3	4	5	6	7	8	9	10	11	12	13	14
Typists :	10	11	12	12	13	13	14	10	12	11	14	15	16	16

Using the simple exponential smoothing technique for forecasting future demands, comment on the forecasts against the actual demand, if the smoothing constant used by the consultant are 0.3, 0.4 or 0.5.

41. How far does the time series help in forecasting ?

If the average production level in a mill is given as under :

Years :	1991	1992	1993	1994	1995	1996	1997	1998	1999
Production :	435	415	450	463	470	482	475	490	500

Fit a straight live trend and establish the forecast of the production for the following years 2000 and 2001.

42. The consumption of milk in a new colony is going up every quarter for the last four years. The consumption pattern is tabulated below :

Years	*Demand of milk in litres*			
	Iqr	*IIqr*	*IIIqr*	*IVqr*
2007	1,250	1,260,	1,270	1,280
2008	1,310	1,335	1,350	1,350
2009	1,370	1,395	1,415	1,500
2010	1,670	1,730	1,780	1,830

Can you forecast demand for the four quarters of the year 2011 ?

43. The weekly demand of a product, which is presented to be normally distributed, has an average level of 100 and the standard deviation as 10. How low the stock level be accepted so that we can be sure 95% of the time that the product will be supplied to the market well before the stock out situation ?

44. Following table indicates the result of inspection of 15 lots of 100 items each.

Lot number :	1	2	3	4	5	6	7	8	9	10	11	12	13	14	15
Number of defectives :	5	3	2	7	8	10	5	6	2	3	4	9	8	10	7

Draw a suitable control chart to ascertain if the process is in control.

45. In a manufacturing unit, a sample of 5 sheets is taken every one hour. The data collected from the measurement of thickness of these sheets is tabulated below:

Sample Number	*Thickness of Sheets in mm.*				
	I	*II*	*III*	*IV*	*V*
1	25	31	22	26	24
2	32	31	30	34	33
3	35	34	33	32	32
4	26	25	29	30	25
5	33	34	30	29	33
6	34	32	31	28	27

Draw control chart for mean and range and establish whether the process is under control.

46. The material manager of a company is interested in determining the re-order point for an item, the pattern of demand for which is as given in the following table :

Number of Units per day	*Number of days on which the demand occured*
0	5
1	9
2	16
3	38
4	23
5	9

Past experience indicates that there are fluctuations in the lead time for procurement of the item. The following data are available from the records for the last 30 orders :

Lead Time (weeks)	*Number of times the lead time occured*
1	18
2	7
3	5

The management policy is to ensure that the proportion of stockouts should not exceed 5 percent. Illustrate how the simulation approach can be used to determine the re-order point. (Analysis for 20 orders is adequate).

[*Delhi University, M.B.A., Dec., 1983*]

47. A firm has a single channel service station with following arrival and service time pattern :

Arrivals (Minutes)	*Probability*	*Service Time (Minutes)*	*Probability*
1	0.2	—	—
2	0.15	1	0.25
3	0.15	1.5	0.3
4	0.2	2	0.15
5	0.22	2.5	0.15
6	0.08	3	0.15

The arival at the service station is of random pattern and queue starts developing at 9 A.M. and proceeds only for 2 hours. The queue discipline is first-cum-first served basis. If the attendant's wages are ₹10 per hour and customer waiting time costs ₹12 per hour, workout the service pattern on Monte Carlo simulation method and justify if you need to engage a second attendant.

48. For overhandling of vehicles, following time table is followed in the repair workshops.

Jobs	*Immediate Prodecessor*	*Expected time (days)*
A	—	3
B	A	2
C	B	2
D	B	3
E	C	4
F	C and D	2
G	D	3
H	C	2
I	D	1

J	D	4
K	D	3
L	F	2
M	G	3
N	D, E, I	2
O	N	1
P	I, J, M, N	3
Q	G	2

Draw the network and identity the critical path.

49. Consider the following schedule of activities and relate information for the construction of a new plant :

Activity	*Expected Time*		*Expected Cost*
	Months	*Variance*	*(000's ₹)*
1-2	4	1	5
2-3	2	1	3
3-6	3	1	4
2-4	6	2	9
1-5	2	1	2
5-6	5	1	12
4-6	9	5	20
5-7	7	3	7
7-8	10	2	14
6-8	1	1	4

You should assume that the cost and time required for one activity are not dependent upon the cost and time of any other activity and variations are expected to follow a normal distribution.

You are required to calculate :

(a) The critical path

(b) expected cost of construction to build the plant

(c) expected time required to build the plant

(d) The standard deviation of the expected time.

[*I.C.W.A., Dec., 1987; I.C.M.A., (London), May 1977*]

50. M/s Voltas Ltd gives the following information relating to Sales of refrigerators for the last ten years :

Years :	1988	1989	1990	1991	1992	1993	1994	1995	1996	1997
Sales (000's) :	8	10	11	11	18	15	19	19	22	24

Find the trend line by least square method and compute trend values. Estimate sales for the year 2002.

[*Osmania University, M.B.A., Sept., 1998*]

51. A production unit is producing two items A and B. Item A fetches a profit of ₹30 per unit, whereas B gets only ₹20 per unit. The unit has two machines, both capable of producing item A and B. On machine P, item A takes 10 hours and the item B needs 12 hours. The maximum working hours available on machine P are 500 machine hours. For machine Q, the production time for A is 15 hours and for item B, it is 20 hours. Available machine hours on machine Q are 700. Calculate the product mix for getting maximum profit.

52. Following data have been obtained for a unit :

Year	*Sales*	*Fixed Cost* (₹)	*Variable Cost* (₹)
2004	10,000	80,000	45,000
2005	20,000	60,000	60,000

Work out the P/V ratio and the Breakeven point with the help of P/V ratio.

53. An inspection team, during work sampling, found that an operator was seen idling on 400 occassions and found working on 1600 occassions. Examine whether the data is accurate within ± 5% at 95% confidence level. Estimate the range of his working time.

54. A machine part has been found to have the mean wearout time of 6 years with standard deviation of 1 year. Workout the reliability of the machine part that it will last for 7 years and also its life with 95% reliability.

55. The present layout of a shop is given below

← 80 ft →

A	B	C	60 ft
D	E	F	

The length and width of department (A, B, C, D, E, F) is 80ft × 60 ft as shown above. The daily movement of loads between the department are as under.

	Department					
	A	***B***	***C***	***D***	***E***	***F***
A	—	40	30	10	30	20
B	—	—	20	20	20	10
C	—	—	—	40	40	80
D	—	—	—	—	40	60
E	—	—	—	—	—	90
F	—	—	—	—	—	—

Assuming all flows have same unit costs, use CRAFT method of working out the total daily flow cost. (only horizontal and vertical movement take place).

Also use steepest pairwise interchange method (CRAFT) to workout any improvement in the layout. (Show the initial and improved layout flow cost).

56. A job was broken down into three activities and a total run of 10 cycles was observed by the work measurement team. The allowances permitted were 10% of the operation time. The observations of the team are tabulated in the following table :

Activities	*Observed time (minutes)*										
	1	*2*	*3*	*4*	*5*	*6*	*7*	*8*	*9*	*10*	*Ratings*
1	3.53	3.13	3.25	3.47	3.47	3.8	3.61	3.47	3.37	3.43	110%
2	2.47	2.42	2.15	2.53	2.54	2.67	2.13	2.43	3.27	2.48	105%
3	3.10	3.33	3.47	2.97	3.40	3.34	3.07	3.43	2.98	3.15	100%

(*a*) Workout the average time to perform each activity.

(*b*) Workout the normal time required to perform each activity.

(*c*) Compute the standard time for each activity and that for the job.

57. An assembly is made up of two A parts, one B part and one C part. Complete the MRP schedule for the assembly and all its components.

	Assembly	A part	B part	C part
Lot size	900	1500	1500	2000
Lead time	1 week	1 week	1 week	2 week
Inventory	500	400	800	800
Safety stock	200	—	—	500
Allocated	500	—	600	500

	week				
Component	1	2	3	4	5
Gross Requirement		1000	700	900	800
Receipts due assembly	1000				
A receipts due	700				
B receipts due	1000				
C receipts due	2000				

58. A company has the following data for their production decision :

Manufacture	*Process A*	*Process B*	*Buy*
Annual volume	10,000	10,000	10,000
Fixed cost per year	₹1,00,000	₹8,00,000	—
Variable cost Per unit	₹75	₹70	₹80

Decide (a) whether use Process A for manufacture or process B?

(b) should the company buy the product ?

(c) when should they start manufacture through process A instead of buying?

59. An Inspection team produced the following results from their work:

Sample No	1	2	3	4	5	6	7	8	9	10
Percent Defectives	4	3	3	6	1	9	5	12	4	3

They have taken samples of 100 units. Compute 3σ limits for the process through p-chart and establish the process in control condition.

60. It costs ₹4000 for a group of 5 machines to maintain. When one machine malfunctions between maintence cycle, it costs ₹6,000. The breakdown history of the machines is as follows:

Weeks between maintenance	***Probility that a machine will malfunction***
1	0.1
2	0.2
3	0.3
4	0.4

It only costs are the basis of preventive maintence, how often should the preventive maintenance be performed to maintain the expected cost of malfuction and the cost of maintenance ?

61. A project is represented by the network shown below and has the following data.

Task	A	B	C	D	E	F	G	H	I
Optimistic time :	5	18	26	16	15	6	7	7	3
Pessimistic time:	10	22	40	20	25	12	12	9	5
Most likely time:	8	20	33	18	20	9	10	8	4

Determine the following:

(a) Expected task times and their variance.

(Marathwada University, M.Sc. (App. Maths.), 1982)

(b) the earliest and latest expected times to reach each event.

(Delhi University, M.Sc. (Maths). 1983)

(c) The critical path.

(d) The probability of an event occurring at the proposed completion date, if the original contract time of completing the project is 41.5 weeks.

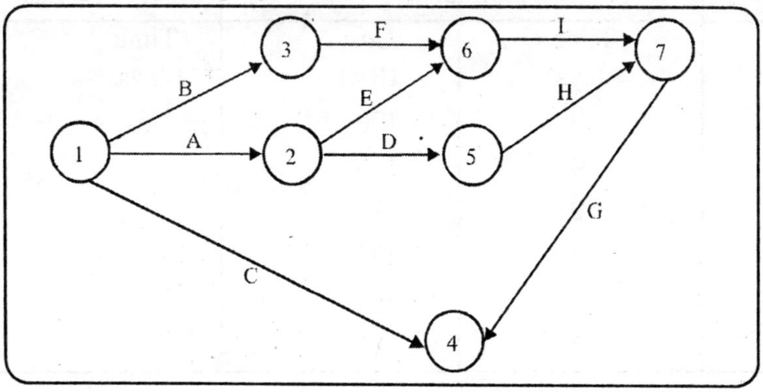

[Andhra Uiniversity, (Prod. Council), 1983]

62. Consider the following schedule of activities and related information for the construction of a new plant.

Activity	Expected time		Expected Cost
	Months	Variance	(Rs. in Thousands)
1–2	4	1	5
2–3	2	1	3
3–6	3	1	4
2–4	6	2	9
1–5	2	1	2
5–6	5	1	12
4–6	9	5	20
5–7	7	8	7
7–8	10	16	14
6–8	1	1	4

You should assume that the cost and time required for one activity are not dependent upon the cost and time of any other activity and variations are expected to follow a normal distribution.

You are required to calculate.

(a) the critical path

(b) expected cost of construction to build the plant

(c) expected time required to build the plant

(d) the standard deviation of the expected time.

[*ICWA, Dec., 1987; ICMA (London), May 1977*]

63. For the data given in the table below, draw the network. Crash systematically the activities and determine the optimal project duration and cost, given the project in direct cost as Rs. 70 per day.

Activity	Normal		Crash	
	Time (days)	Cost (Rs.)	Time (days)	Cost (Rs.)
1–2	8	100	6	200
1–3	4	150	2	350
2–4	2	50	1	90
2–5	10	100	5	400
3–4	5	100	1	200
4–5	3	80	1	100

64. The President of ABC Manufacturing company has an opportunity to participate in a project that has a sales price of Rs. 90,000 but it must be completed within 8 weeks. Since the President at 8.30 am on Monday (start of the 8 week) has to determine the profitability of the project on an 8 week basis, so that the firm can start the production order at 10 am in order to stay within 8 weeks demanded by the customer whereas the time/cost is based on 10 week basis. A table of times and cost is given below. Did the President accept the project?

Event	Preceding Event	Normal Time (*weeks*)	Cost (Rs.)	Time (weeks)	Crash Cost (Rs.)]
4	1	2	8,000	1	13,000
2	1	2	17,000	1	19,000
3	1	6	11,000	5	13,000
4	2	4	6,000	3	10,000
3	2	2	9,000	1	11,000
5	2	7	8,500	6	12,000
5	4	4	10,000	3	16,000
5	3	3	5,000	2	7,000

65. Following are the man-power requirements for each activity in a project.

Activity	Normal	Crash
1–2	10	2
1–3	11	3
2–4	13	4
2–6	14	3
3–4	10	1
4–5	7	3
4–6	17	3
5–7	13	5
6–7	9	8
7–8	1	11

(a) Draw the network and find out the total float and fee float for each activity.

(b) The customer stipulates that during the first 26 days, only 4 to 5 men and during remaining days 8 to 11 men only can be made available. Rearrange the activities suitably for levelling the manpower resources, satisfying the above condition.

Toyota Production System

INTRODUCTION

Toyota production system is one of best examples of production technique, treated as a model for many manufactures the world over. Inspite of the fact that this production system has been perfected after about two decades of hard work of its managers and workers alike, it came under fire during of the year 2010, because of their crushing series of safety-related recalls of automobiles. The firm's boss Akio Toyoda, along with senior executives of the firm, had to face the American Congress due to this great concern. The other car-manufacturers were equally worried that they, also, are likely to face the same situation because there is not a single car manufacturer, that has not followed the TPS model for its manufacture.

Toyota's "lean Production", basically, is known to be an example of excellence in automobile manufacturing, but it has taken about 20 years to reach this level. Hence it is inconceivable that other manufacturers can copy and follow it is just about 4-5 years. It takes time to set the tone right in all the operations. Seeing this system only as a set of tools and procedures does not speak the full extent of the system in practice. The key to the success of the system is the untiring efforts of the whole Toyota organisation in the application of the concept of "Kaizen" or Continuous Improvement which has been possible only through the learning and application of the concept due to their quest in "Quality product",

SYSTEM DEVELOPMENT

Toyota production system is developed through the following rules:

1. The Philosophy of complete elimination of waste, imbibing all aspects of the problem to achieve the most efficient output
2. It is an integrated socio-technical system wherein the human and non-human resources are allocated same priority and importance
3. It is based on the concept of
   - Jodoka : *ie.*, automation with a human touch
   - Just-in-Time *ie.,* production as per demand.

4. Application of the above concept under the key operation called Kaizen, which is achieved through
    - Social System — through employees learning and training.
    - Technical system — through process Improvement

It can be easily understood that.

"Quality is never by accident.

It is always the result of an intelligent effort" ***—by John Ruskin***

or

"Quality is the result of attitudes and values. It is achieved by viewing quality as a way of life" ***—The Book Author***

To achieve the quality results, Toyota follows following rules as an organisation philosophy :

1. How people work i.e. specifications, documentation of all work processes including content, sequence, timing and outcome.
2. How work connects i.e. following clear yes/no signals directly linking customer and suppliers.
3. How the system flows i.e., every product and service travels a prescribed simple, single and direct flow path.
4. How to Improve *i.e.,* lowest level workers guided and involved in the improvement process through job description, Job-empowerment and job-ownership concept.
5. How to detect problem i.e., Integrated failure tests automatically signal deviations for every activity, connection and flow fath. This is achieved through effective feedback mechanism for all operational paths.

THE JOURNEY

The TPS was developed by Toyota founders along with the Shigeo Shingo, working in close association with Henry ford and Deming setting the following yardsticks based on the above-mentined five "rules":

- Reduced lead time and cost with improvement in quality.
- Diversification and risk-reduction strategy
- Emphasis on human strength and ergonomics rathers than process automation
- Continuous experimentation and measurement strategy
- Long term philosophy (Ford and Shingo)
- Right process to produce right results with involvement of everyone.
- Value-addition by developing people and partners (organisational commitment)
- Continuously solving root problems through education, training and job empowerment.

Each and every yardstick is not easy to follow and certainly not in a day. It takes time to run through each operation and then improve it slowly and gradually. Hence Kaizen is treated by Toyota as "a way of doing business". These principles are, though deceptively simple, may be difficult but not impossible to replicate.

Few important tools described in thus book are effectively in use by Toyota and quite a few other companies to ensure lean and defect free production, which is so vital in the global competitive environment of the day. These are as follows :

- *5-S approach* : describes house keeping and orderly work with commitment and involvement of workers.
- *SMED approach* : indicates as to how to reduce set up time, in between products taken up for production.
- *Poka-Yoke :* It is a design technique to ensure foot-proof system in method and operation, so as to avoid mistakes creating defective parts. Defect-free product with defect-free delivery of product and service is ensured through this technique.
- *Kanban :* A manufacturing and inventory management tool used to pull product from one workstation to the next, used to reduce reaction time of workers as well as set up time between change over of the products.
- *TPM approach :* Ensures management of physical assets by involving workers and the maintenance staff for upkeep of the equipment and assets.
- *Standardisation of work* : Preparing a checklist or documenting guidelines for each job in bring in and improving consistency across operators.
- *Takt-Time approach :* A method of working out the production rate to cater for the customer demand schedule.
- *Creating teams/Cells :* Reduces cycle time to enhance productivity through the concept of 'team work' organising the equipment and personnel for a specific job.

Due to the large emphasis by Toyota on consistent quality, they have been able to outsell their competitors while being priced higher. It is also worth a notice that the highly successful 'Just-in-time' production system was developed by Toyota without using computers, yet having an effective information flow. Improvement has been possible due to use of latest technology. It is also known that by designing and using common components, Toyota Motors reported savings of about 660 million US dollars. Though automation has been increasingly used by Toyota for many product and service operations, their emphasis still remains on the human aspects for Kaizen.

THE WOES

Inspite of having developed and practiced a well-designed waste-free lean production system, the Company Toyota Motors suffered its reputation due to global recalls of their automobiles in 2010, which Toyoda acknowledged that it was due to the outstretching of their lean philosophy in the pursuit of high growth, for increasing their global market share from 11% to 15%. This increase was said to be driven by "ego" and not by market demand.

The problem arose due to their association with some unfamiliar suppliers, who did not have deep understanding of the Toyota culture. As Toyota went past General Motor in their production level in 2008, the problems started mounting. Toyota identified as a tier-two supplier CTS corp, which was the maker of "throttle-pedal assemblies."

A consequence of Toyota's rapid expansion was its dependence on the suppliers outside Japan, with whom it did not have a long working-experience. Though Toyota's single-supplier philosophy worked well in the past, the expansion did not work well in this context. Now the entire auto-industry is deliberating whether sole-sourcing concept has gone too far. Today the thinking is changing to have (may be) three suppliers for major components with benchmarking technique for quality supplies. Close-monitoring and captive vendor Management (CVM) is, therefore, gaining momentum.

GENERAL COMMENTS

1. Manpower (all levels) duly trained and committed is the back bone of any organisation to beat any competition.
2. Methods, Procedures and detailed planning must have "what if" analysis inbuilt to provide quick flexibility to the operating system.
3. Patience with due diligence and keen eye on the innovation helps in meeting customer's changing requirements.
4. Captive Vendor Management (CVM) should be applied intelligently based on the complexity and magnitude of the operations. Sole-sourcing, single sourcing or outsourcing should be commensurate with the level of requirements.
5. Effective use of technology helps in integrating customer's needs to production, distribution and after sales service. It helps in quick reactions to concept of defect prevention and defect elimination in all fields of operations.
6. "Doing it right the first time and every time" can take the company to the top. Reaching top is important, but remaining there is more important. Hence "Kaizen" should never be lost sight of.

—●—

Appendix B
(Service Management)

Southwest Airlines Corporation

HISTORY

Like few Indian low cost airlines, South West Airlines Corporation is one of the best American low cost airline. The model of operation of this airline is something very different from other airlines. It started its operations in June 1971 with just three Boeing 737 aircrafts. Initially its was serving only three Texas Cities, namely Dallas, Houston and San Antonio. It later grew into the fourth largest airline (in terms of domestic customer carried) in 2002. It had, by now, a pleet of 366 Boeing 737 aircrafts. It was the only major short haul, high frequency, point-to-point carrier with lowest fare offer.

For twentynine Consecutive years, it showed year end profitability results till 2001. In 2001, it had 35,000 employees with a total operating revenue of 5.6 Billion US Dollars generated out of a passenger load factor of 68.1. From 1997 till 2001, it ranked the top as the most admired airline world-wide with top rank also in Customer service satisfaction.

THE PRODUCT DIFFERENTIATION

South West Airline operated from Dallas "love field" domestic airport and has "LUV" as the theme of its employees and Customer relationship. The same "LUV" was its Stock Exchange symbol. It operated on totally different concept and hence had the distinction of "A complete Product Differentiation" concept to ensure the loyalty of its customers. Following points indicate as to how differently the airline operated to earn the above-mentioned distinction :

1. It operated on point-to-point destinations ensuring quick turn-around.

2. It operated on Boeing 737 aircraft only reducing its maintenance cost with streamlined spare inventory.

3. It operated to low density airfields/less congested airports, in order to reduce "wasted time".

4. It operated only on short-haul sectors with average flight time of about 55 minutes.

5. It operated on a 20 - minute turn-around time (from the time a plane landed until it was ready for take - off), as against 35 minutes for United Airlines or about 45 minutes for other Competitors.

6. It operated only one class of seats, hence had simple pricing scheme Ticket processing, therefore, was simple and quick. The tickets could be available through vending machines at some airports. Number of Seats fitted, in the aircroyt were more, leading to more passenger - strength.

7. It has no fixed seats. It operated on the basis of "as available" concept. The customer could just walk in, collect a token (to be handed over while boarding) and get into any available seat.

8. High Frequency Service really did not need any flight booking. Even otherwise its booking cost was just one US dollar in 2002 as compared to an average of 6 to 8 US dollars for booking through a travel agent.

9. The luggage booking/loading problem was non-existant because of high-frequency short-haul journeys. It served no meals but only peanuts, beverages or cookies.

10. Because of the above provisious, it required only 4 ground crew with 2 at the gate.

11. The airline operated "Kanban" system for passenger strength through issue of numbered plastic token (no boarding passes). The last token issued automatically indicated full capacity. (The same tokens collected at aircraft entry and re-used.)

12. The staff recruitment system was unique in that the employees themselves screened the candidates. Thus the pilots hired pilots and ground crew hired ground crew. This ensured deep involvement of all the employees, treating the airline as their own.

13. The aircraft crew was minimal, say just 2, because it did not need people for any substantial work. With no food served, the two members would willingly operate for any activity needed during the flight operation.

14. The airline preferred Couple-employment, instead of just males or females. This went far for employee satisfaction.

15. The CEO, himself, at times was available on the aircraft (not for checking, but for actual help), bringing the whole employee strength closer to each other.

16. The CEO's philosophy for the airline was "putting people first". If they are happy, satisfied, dedicated, Committed and energetic, they will take real good care of the customers.

17. Due to the operating model, the airline attracted "loyal" customers, who preferred the flights to match their quick trun - around schedule with normally familiar faces, who knew their habits and would get better service.

18. The working culture of the organisation as hard work, high energy, fun, local autonomy and creativity was reinforced through regular training at its Universty of People. The employees were further encouraged through in-flight contests and recognition of personal initiative.

19. To enhance the commitment futher, the airline had the policy of "gain-sharing", on year to year basis right from 1974 onwards. The employees owned about ten percent of company's stock. For example, the employees of this airline earned an additional 14.1 percentage of each employees annual salary in the year 2000 (tax deferred compensation).

20. It paid its employees on the trip-basis.

21. It was the only airline whose pilots did not belong to any national union, thereby selecting/deciding themselves the number of hours they would fly.

22. The other employees of the airline belonged to the nationalised union, with flexible contracts to allow them to come in and go out regardless of task at hand. This did not create any work problem as employee would keenly take on any work at any time and perform it with total dedication.

23. The average age of the airline employees was 34 years and by and large they were among the highest paid in the industry.

24. The airline office had its walls filled with the photographys of its employees. At one time, there were about 1000 married couples (2000 employees) working for the airline.

25. The employees were hired for their attitudes as much as aptitude, so that people would work with "laughter and grace".

26. The Airline now operates to about 707 destinations across USA and has added facility for bookings and advance check in etc.

COMMENTS:

1. Employees treated as assets and hence worked diligently, willingly and loyally.

2. Job Empowerment and job-enlargement were practiced on large scale.

3. The operating model ensured low operating cost and low maintenance cost with higher passenger density and less turn - around time.

4. The "gain-sharing" policy ensured the deep commitment of the workers for quality operations.

5. Customer-loyalty and retention were ensured through the "product differentiation".

—•—

Appendi1x C
(Supply Chain Management)

Boeing 787, The Dreamliner

THE PROBLEM

For an aircraft of the size of Boeing 787, the Dreamliner, the number of components, assemblies and subassemblies required is very large. The challenge lies in the design, manufacture, supplies and assembly at many places. The integration and co-ordination of all these operations is really enormous. For an effective scheduling of all the supplies to arrive at the assembly station, a very strong, deliberate and efficient software, there, becomes the utmost necessity.

THE SET UP

Being has four main faclities in the US. Three of these are assembly facilities for different models of the aircraft, as indicated below :

(a) Renton, Washington – for the assembly of Boeing 737 and 757 aircrafts.

(b) long Beach, California – for the assembly of Boeing 717 aircrafts

(c) Everett, Washington (near Seatle) – for the assembly of Boeings 747, 767 and 777 aircrafts.

(d) The fourth main set up is based at Wichita, Kansas. This facility is the manufacturing base for parts and components for all types of aircraft's, but 717.

THE CUSTOMERS

The customers for Boeing Company are various Airlines and the leasing companies. The order line is large with about 500 airlines, buying about 200 new aircrafts. The leasing companies are also few dozens in number — large and small. The famous leasing companies are ILFC, CIT, GECAS and Ansett.

The airlines order the aircrafts with their financing arrangements having been finalised. Few small airlines prefer the financing from their leasors. In fact they also obtain aircrafts on lease from these leasing companies.

THE ORDERING CHANNEL

It is imperative to arrive at the reasonalty accurate forecast for demand of aircrafts, because such a product needs heavy investment in design, manufacture, assembly and distribution. The orders for Boeing are received through their sales teams being in constant touch with various airlines and leasing companies. The order channel has to have a long-term strategy due to constant technology upgrades and other environmental factors running the fate of the aerospace industry.

Large airlines keep updating their fleet planning as per the market demand, normally for two to 10 years horizon. The order channel for the smaller airlines have different systems interms of sizes, price, delivery schedules as well as (very important) maintenance agreements. The lessors normally order larger number of variety aircrafts based on their clients requirements.

THE PARTS/COMPONENTS SUPPLIERS

For Boeing company, the suppliers are chosen in three main areas

(a) Aero structures

(b) Engines

(c) Avionics

Supplies for Aero structures: Aero structures are the structural assemblies required for the frame of aircraft. These structures are the fuselages, wings and the landing gears. Various components of these systems are as follows:

(i) Fuselages – Barrel sections, Nose, Fin, Tail, Rudder, Tailplane and elevators

(ii) Wings – Control surfaces and winglets

(iii) Landing Gear – the structure for landing tyres.

Because of the expertise required for all different areas, the Boeing company contracts out their structures requirements to the specialist suppliers, having adequate capital, the design capability, manufacturing expertise along with adequately trained skilled work force and government approval for production of these parts or sub assemblies. These tier I suppliers further are supported by their lower tier suppliers. Recent trend emerging for these supplies is more delegation of responsibility to the tier I and II supplier for more complex Components. The aircraft manufactures, therefore, have simpler and faster assembly processes. There is a necessity of pre-integrated Aero structure components to reach the final assembly location.

Presently Boeing has 14 Aero structure manufacturers in USA, the major players being Aero structures Crop, Vought Aircraft Industries and Goodrich corporation. Because of a growing demand for more value –added components for reducing manufacturing and assembly costs and lead-times, there is a trend now for consolidation. The possibility of mergers, therefore, becomes larger, so far, aero structures manufactures have been supplying in their region only, but now due to deregulation and consolidation, the suppliers to Boeings have diversified for Airbus also, in addition to extending their help to Defense as well as commercial aircraft production.

Boeing has also been outsourcing their Aero structures from Asia. Boeing outsources majority of aero structures from thirteen major suppliers in US and eleven in Canada. They have 5 suppliers in Japan, 3 in Korea and 4 in China with Japanese handling more complex assemblies.

Suppliers for Engines : There are four suppliers of engines for Boeing. These are Rolls-Royce, Prat and Whitney, CFMI and General Electric. There is a stiff competition among these four, due to the selection process of the regulatory bodies. There are logics problems encountered during certification process, which is time-consuming and costly.

Supplies for Avionics: Boeing has sufficient Avionics manufacturing capability with their suppliers such as Honeywell, Rockwell Collins and Thales SA. At present Boeing supplies about fifty percent of the avionics for their commercial aircraft, the remaining being supplied by customer selected suppliers.

The supply chain: The supply chain of Boeing 787 is complicated and requires a heavy integration of all it links. Boeing retains not more than 35 percent of the total 787 work share, thus about 65 percent of the activity has to be coordinated through this suppliy chain, which is very challenging task.

Various components, assemblies and sub-assemblies are designed, manufactured, tested and distributed to various locations for timely assembly at the level of tier II and tier I suppliers and then finally at the final assembly point of the Everett plant of Boeing. The scheduling of these activities has to be very fine-tuned so that required component/parts are available at the right place just in time. The inventories at various locations have to be well defined and made available as per the requirement. If there is any delay/anticipated delay in any one activity, the whole chain has to re-adjust to its schedule.

The logistics also poses a serious problem as modes of transportation varies widely, may be a ship from China or Japan or road delivery between various suppliers within USA or Canada. These have different lead times and still requires perfect matching.

SUPPLIERS RELATIONSHIPS

For the purpose of Boeings supplier relationships on the Dreamliner 787, the following few point need be highlighted;

• Major partnering suppliers with "large work content'' can make design trades within each work package and across companies to find optimal system solutions.

• Boeing only provides high-level interface definition, the tier I suppliers are responsible for the detailed interface definitions and designs.

• Boeing has contracted with all its suppliers with the proviso of carrying all the non-recurring costs-with the trade off as risk-sharing partnership of proporty rights. If the aircraft does well, these risk-sharing partners derive direct benefits of revenue sharing based on the initially-agreed-up expected unit sales volume.

• Suppliers work together with Boeing acting only as referee in case of conflicts.

BOEING'S SUPPLY CHAIN SOLUTION

Boeing has used Exostar's Supply Chain Management solution for the above-described multi-tier visibility and control of Demand Forecast, Order life cycle and the Inventory Management for their aircraft Boeing 787, the Dreamlinear. It is a very powerful network solution under the name of E2 open software, used to manage the complete order life cycle and returns process. It has helped in tracking planning schedules, consumption and replenishment details under the scheme of "Boeing Partner Managed Inventory Programme." Boeing utilises Exostar for its design collaboration, sourcing and procurement solutions controlling thousands of suppliers.

Boeing leverage its extended supply chain and partner manufacturing resources effectively for cost effective operations. Since Boeing is only the final assembler of the aircraft, effective integration and control of their structural and systems partners located all over the world is of utmost importance for their successful delivery of the aircraft. It is all the more important because the final assembly time is only three days and hence inventory arrival schedule has to be rigid with reference to the design, manufacture and logistics success for the items to arrive Just on time at Everett, USA.

The E_2 open system also monitors process exceptions frequently occurring between partners providing notification and the evaluation of the potential impact against schedules. In addition, it helps in ensuring a coordinated effect with all the partners of real time supply chain performance reducing the risks, and improving cycle time. Exostar's Sas (software-as-a-service) delivery model and existing network of connectivity into the A&D supply Base allows Boeing to go-live with the solution in less than 90 days from the start of the project.

THE DIFFICULTY LEVEL

(a) The vertical models fail at times. For example, the wing-joints on both sides of the aircraft failed to perform as predicted by the model. For this reason, the solution established is "we do testing for a reason. And that's because model aren't perfect", in the **words** of Scott Fancher, Boeing 787 programme General Manager. **Patrick Shanahou,** Vice-president and General Manager, Airplain Programmes adds, "we'll go back and look at where the model failed to predict this situation (wing stress) and (then) tune them up".

(b) It was also noticed that the Italian subcontractor was asked to stop production due to the failure of composite skin on the fuselage. The remedy required a patch, adding some weight to the design.

The latest update

(i) The Dream Liner has been produced in two versions namely 787-8 and 787-9. The version 787-8 will carry 210 to 250 passengers with haulage of 7680 to 8220 nautical miles whereas 787-9 can carry 250 to 290 passengers with haulage capacity of 8000 to 8500 miles

(ii) 50% of the aircraft aerostructiure including Fuselage and wings has been built from composite metal.

(iii) The innovative self-health monitoring system has been installed to give information about its maintenance requirement to the base computer.

(iv) Very fuel efficient, new design Engines are being used for the aircraft provided by Rolls-Royce and General Electric. These engines are about 20% more fuel efficient comparing to the similarly placed aircrafts

(v) Having been launched in April 2004, Being received its first order from All-Nippon Airways. A total of 821 aircrafts is very healthy order book for Boeing.

(vi) First flight having been taken on 15 Dec. 2009, Boeing (Source-Internal) has received its FAA and EASA certification during August 2011 arid the aircraft is now flying in various sectors.

(vii) Barring few 'hicups', the aircraft is oerating successfully.

—•—

Glossary of Terms

Batch production : A process suitable for production of a variety of products in varying volumes.

Behavioral management : A theory of management dealing with human relations and the behavioral sciences.

Behavioral science : A science that explores how human behavior is affected by variables such as leadership, motivation, communication, interpersonal relationships, and attitude change.

Bench marking : Practice of establishing standards of performance to run business competitively.

Bias : A forecast error measure that is the average of forecast error with regard to direction and shows any tendency consistently to over or underforecast.

Bill of materials : A document describing the detail of materials including all components the quantity needed for producing one unit of a product.

Bottleneck station : The station on an assembly line that requires the longest task time.

Break-even analysis : A graphical and algebric representation of the relatiionship among volume of output, costs and revenues.

Break-even point : The level of output volume for which total costs equal total revenues.

Breakthrough : A solution to a chronic problem; a dramatic change for the better in quality, stimulated by concentrated, analytic, company-wide quality improvement programmes.

Bucket unit of time : Measurement of time in MRP system.

Buffer stock : Inventories of product against the effects of unusual product demand and uncertain lead time.

Business plan : A statement of an organisation's overall level of business activity for a specified period of time.

Business Process Re-engineering (BPR) : Drastically re-designing a process to achieve substantial improvements.

Capacity : A facility's maximum productive capability usually expressed as volume of output per period of time.

Captive Vendor Management (CVM) : The control of vendors when only few dedicated vendors are associated with the company's supplies.

Cardex file system : A manually operated inventory control system in which an inventory card represents each stock item with transactions kept on the card.

Carrying (holding) costs : Costs of maintaining the inventory warehouse and protecting the inventoried items.

Causal forecasting models : Statistical forecasting models based on historical demand data as well as on variables believed to influence demand. These are also called associative forecasting models.

Cellular layout : The arrangement of a facility so that equipment used to make similar parts or families of parts is grouped together. It is also called a Group layout.

Central limit theorem : A statistical hypothesis that the sampling distribution approaches normality as the size of the samples increases, regardless of the distribution of the measurements of individual sample units.

Chance event : An event leading potentially to several different outcomes, only one of which will definitely occur; the decision maker has no control over which outcome will occur.

Change master : The facilator of change; the role of the production/operations manager in bringing about behavioral changes in other people.

Chronic problem : A long-term problem that causes continually poor quality, usually addressed through breakthrough measures.

Classical management : A theory of management, emphasizing efficiency at the production core, the separation of planning and doing work, and management principles and functions.

Computer search : A set of direction that systematically guides a computer in evaluating alternative aggregate plans.

Computer aided manufacturing (CAM) : Manufacturing systems utilising computer software programmes controlling the machine on the shop floor.

Computer-aided design (CAD) : Computer software programes that allow a designer to carry out design transformations repidly.

Computer-integrated manufacturing (CIM) : Computer information systems utilising a shared manufacturing database for engineering design, manufacturing and information management.

Consumer's risk (type II error) (β) : The risk or prohability of incorrectly concluding that the conversion process is in control.

Continuous operations : Operations characterised by standardized, high-volume, capital-intensive products made to store in inventory; by small product mix; and by continuous product flow.

Control chart : A chart of sampling data used to make inferences about the control status of a conversion process.

Control limits (CL) : Upper (UCL) and lower (LCL) boundaries defining the range of variation permit in a product characteristic such that the conversion process is in control.

Controlling : Activities that assure that actual performance is in accordance with planned performance.

Conversion process : The process of tranforming inputs of labor, capital and materials into outputs of goods and services.

Crashing; Accelarating, Speeding : up an activity by enhancing resources, to reduce the time required for an activity or a project.

Deming Prize : Established in 1951 for innovation in quality management to be awarded annually to a company distinguishing in quality management programmes.

Critical path : In a project network, a path whose activities are expected to consume the most time.

Critical ratio : The ratio of inspection costs to percent defective.

Cycle counting : Counting on hand inventories at regular intervals to verify inventory quantities shown in the MRP.

Cycle time : Time elapsing between completed units coming off an assembly line.

Decision tree : A diagram used to structure and analyse a decision problem through a systematic, sequential decision points, alternatives and chance events.

Decision variable : A numerical, controllable parameter that, if modified, yields a variety of results.

Decoupling : Using inventories to break apart operations so that the supply of one operation is independent of the supply of another.

Degeneracy : A quality of a linear transportation programming problem such that there are too few occupied cells to enable evaluation of the empty cells.

Delphi technique : A qualitative forecasting technique in which a panel of experts working separately and not meeting, arrive at a consensus through the summarzing of ideas by a skilled coordinator.

Demand pattern : General shape of a time series; usually constant, trend, seasonal or some combination of these shapes.

Demand stability : Tendency of a time series to retain the same general pattern over time.

Demand-based forecasting models : A statistical forecasting model based solely on historical demand data.

Deming's 14 points for quality : Guidelines for improving quality, proposed by Dr. W. Edwards Demings, as part of total quality control.

Dependent demand : Demand for an item that can be linked to the demand for another item.

Depreciation : An accounting procedure to recover expenditures for an asset over its lifetime.

Design specifications : The important, desired characteristics of a product or service specified in detail during the design phase.

Detailed capacity planning : An iterative process of modifying the MPS or planned resources to make capacity consistent with the production schedule.

Detailed scheduling : Determining start times, finish times, and resources assignments for all jobs at each work center.

Deterministic model : A model in which variable values are known with certainty.

Development : Technical activities concerned with translating basic applied research results into products or processes.

Direct time study : A work measurement technique that involves observing the job, determining the job cycle, stop-watch-timing the job cycle, and calculating a performance standard.

Distribution Network : Organisation to distribute products to customers.

Double sampling : Acceptance sampling based on a first, small sample and, if results are inconclusive, a second, larger sample.

Dummy activity : In a project network a fictitious activity consuming no time, symbolized by a broken line, showing a definite activity sequence relationship.

Drum : The bottleneck process that sets the pace of the entire production system. Term used in Goldratt's Theory of Constraints (TOC).

Earliest-due-date rule (EDD) : Priority rule that gives top priority to the waiting job whose due date is earliest. It is also called earliest date of delivery.

E-Business : use of internet to conduct business transactions.

Economic life : Length of time through which an asset is useful.

Economic order quantity (EOQ) : The optimal order quantity, fixed by a Q inventory control method.

Efficiency : A measure (ratio) of actual outputs to the desired outputs.

Electronic Data Interchange (EDI) : A computer system allowing two companies to conduct business electronically with each other.

Event : In a project network the beginning or ending of an activity, symbolized by a node.

Expected beginning time (T_B) : In the amount of time expected to be consumed before an activity can begin.

Expected completion time (T_c) : In a network the amount of time an activity is expected to consume.

Expediting : Tracking a job's progress and taking special actions to move it through the facility as planned.

Exponential smoothing : An averaging method that exponentially decreases the weighting of old demands.

External failure costs : Costs attributable to the failure of products at the customers end.

Factor ratings : A decision procedure in which each alternative is rated according to a factor relevant to the decision, and each factor is weighted according to importance.

Feasible (infeasible) solutions : Solutions that satisfy (do not satisfy) the restrictions of a linear programming problem.

Feedback : Information in the control process that allows management to decide whteher Organisational activities need adjustment.

Finite loading : A scheduling procedure that assigns jobs to work centers and determines their starting and completion dates by considering the work center's capacities.

Firm planned order : A planned order release scheduled within the MRP time fence.

First-come-first served rule (FCFS) : Priority rule that gives top priority to the waiting job that arrived earliest in the production system.

Fishbone (cause and effect) diagram : A schematic model of quality problem and their causes; used to diagnose and solve these problems.

Fixed-position layout : The arrangement of a facility so that the product stays in one location; tools, equipment, and workers are brought to it as needed.

Flexibility : The capability of a manufacturing system to adapt successfully to changing environmental conditions and process requirements.

Flexible manufacturing system (FMS) : A computer controlled process technology suitable for producing a moderate variety of products in moderate volumes.

Flow process chart : A graphic tool to analyse and categorise interstation activities so that the flow of the product throughout the overall production process in represented.

Flow time : The total time that a job is in the system (the sum of waiting time and processing time).

Forecast : Use of past data to determine future events.

Forecast error : The numeric difference of forecasted demand and actual demand.

Forward scheduling : Determining the start and finish times for waiting jobs by assigning them to the earliest available time slots at the work center.

Fraction defective : The ratio of defective units to total number of units produced.

Gantt chart : A bar chart showing the relationship of project activities in time.

Gantt load chart : A graph showing work loads on a time scale.

Gantt scheduling chart : A graph showing the time requirements of waiting jobs scheduled for production at machines and work centers.

Goods : Tangible : Products produced through manufacturing.

Gradual replacement model : A deterministic inventory model characterized by constant and known demand and lead time demand being met as the production is underways.

Graphical planning procedure : Two dimensional model relating cumulative demand to cumulative output capacity.

Group technology : A way of organising and using data for components that have similar properties and manufacturing requirements.

Heuristic : A procedure in which a set of rules is systematically applied; an algorithm

Histogram : A bar graph of frequency distributions.

Homogeneous resources : Resources for which units supplied by one source are qualitatively equivalent to units supplied by any other source.

Human relations : Phenomenon recognized by behavioral scientists that people are complex and have multiple varied needs and that the subordinate-supervisor relationship directly affects productivity.

Hybrid Layout : Layout using a combination of layouts as an assembly line combined with process layout.

Implementation : Activities concerned with designing and building pilot models, equipment, and facilities for and with initiating the marketing channels for products or services emerging from research and development.

In-control process : A process for which all variations are random and within permissible quality tolerances.

Independent demand : Demand for an item that occurs separately of demand for any other item.

Individual risk-taking propensity : The degree to which an individual tends to take or avoid risks.

Infinite loading : Assigning jobs to work centers without considering the work center's capacity (as if the capacity were unlimited).

Initial solution : The feasible solution tested first using the simplex method in solving a linear programming problem.

Input/output control : Activities to monitor actual versus planned utilization of a work center's capacity.

Inputs : Men, materials, machines and capital resources required for a conversion process into goods or services.

Inspection : The observation and measurement of inputs and outputs.

Intermittent operations : Operations characterized by made-to-order, low-volume, labor-intense products; by interrupted product flow; and by frequent schedule changes.

Internal failure costs : Costs attributable to errors and defects in production at the manufacturing facility.

Internal rate of return : Interest rate at which the present value of outflows equals the present value of inflows.

Intuitive forecasts : Forecasts that essentially are a manager's guesses and judgements concerning future events; qualitative forecasting methods also called judgemental forecasts.

Inventory : Stores of goods and stocks, including raw materials, work-in-process, finished products or supplies when not in use.

Inventory control : Activities that maintain stockkeeping items at desird levels.

Inventory modeling : A quantitative method for deriving a minimum cost operating system.

Inventory status file : The complete documentation of the inventory status of each item in the product structure including item identification, on-hand quantity, safety stock level, quantity allocated and lead time (also called stock status file).

Job : A group of related tasks or activities that needs to be performed to meet Organizational objectives.

Job design : Activities that specify the content of each job and determine how work is distributed within the Organization.

Job enlargement : Redesigning jobs to provide greater variety, autonomy, task identity, and feed back for the employee.

Job enrichment : Redesigning jobs to give more meaning and enjoyment to the job by involving employees in planning, organising and controlling their work.

Job rotation : Moving employees into a job for a short period of time and then out again.

Job satisfaction : Employee perceptions of the extent to which their work fulfills or satisfies their needs.

Job shop technology : A process technology suitable for a variety of custom-designed products in small volumes.

Just-in-time (JIT) : A manufacturing system whose goal it is to optimize processes and procedures through waste reduction continuously.

Kaizen : The Japanese concept of continuous improvement in all activities.

Kanban : a "visual record;" a method of controlling materials flow through a JIT manufacturing system by using cards to authorize a work station to transfer or produce materials.

Labor efficiency : The ratio of outputs to labor input, the labor actually worked to achieve their output.

Labor standard : A quantitative criterion reflecting the output expected from an average worker under average conditions for a given time period.

Labor turnover : A measure of the stability or change in an Organisation's work force; the employee terminations and entrances levels.

Layout : Physical location or configuration of departments, work centers and equipment in the conversion process for production.

Lead time : The time passing between ordering and receiving goods.

Lead-time demand : Units of stock demanded during lead time; can be described by a probability distribution in stochastic situations.

Lean Manufacturing : Production system with minimum of resources used.

Level output rate plan : An aggregate plan for a constant rate of output for all time periods of production.

Line balancing problem : Assigning tasks among workers at assembly line stations so that performances time are made as equal as possible.

Delivery schedule : Line of Balancing (LOB) : Method of scheduling and controlling production stages to maintain.

Linear decision rules (LDRs) : A set of equations for calculating optimal work force, aggregate output rate, and inventory level.

Linear programming : Mathematical model for selecting the optimal allocation of rsources to maximize profits or minimise costs.

Linear Regression Analysis : A model establishing a relationship between a dependent variable and one or more independent variables; all variables being linear in nature.

Load : The cumulative amount of work currently assigned to a work centre for future processing.

Load-distance model : An algorithm for laying out work centers to minimise product flow, based on the number of loads moved and the distance between each pair of work centers.

Longest-operation-time (LOT) rule : A line-balancing heuristic that gives top assignment priority to the task that has the longest operation time.

Lot : Group of products produced under the same conditions.

Lot splitting : Processing only part of a job at one time, then the rest of the job at a later time.

Lot-for-lot ordering : A lot sizing policy in which order quantity equals net requirements for the period.

Lot Tolerance Percent Defective (LTPD) : The percentage of defective products in a lot considered as bad lots.

Machine Attachments : Add on to the machines to reduce the involvement of human efforts and time required for an operation.

Machine life : An average length of time an asset is capable of functioning.

Manufacturing resource planning (MRPII) : An integrated information system that shares data among and synchronizes the activities of production and the other functional areas of the business.

Manufacturing Accounting and Production Information Control System (MAPICS) : IBM's computerised common data based system for manufacturing information and control.

Mass service technology : A process technology suitable for labor intensive, low customer contact services.

Master production scheduling (MPS) : A schedule showing week by week how many of each product must be produced according to customer orders and demand forecasts.

Material requirements planning (MRP) : A system of planning and scheduling the time-phased materials requirements for production operations.

Materials management : Activities relating to managing the flow of materials into and through an organisation.

Mathematical modeling : Creating and using mathematical representations of management problem to predict outcomes of proposed courses of action.

Maximum allowable cycle time : Maximum time allowed to elapse between completed units coming off an assembly line, if a given capacity is to be achieved.

Mean absolute deviation (MAD) : A forecast error measure that is the average forecast error without regard to direction; calculated as the sum of the absolute value of forecast error for all periods divided by the total number of periods evaluated.

Method time measurement : A widely accepted form of predetermined time study.

Ministry of International Trade and Industry (MITI) : The unit of Japanese government responsible for industrial planning for the activities that formulate industrial policy and determine the patterns of future growth and decline among the various industries comprising the Japanese economy.

Modeling management : A theory of management, emphasizing decision-making systems, and mathematical modeling .

Modular design : The creation of products from some combination of basic preexisting subsystems.

Monte Carlo Similation : A similation technique for generating random numbers (Values) from discrete distributions.

Most likely time (t_m) : In activity network the single best guess of the amount of time an activity is expected to consume.

Multiechelon inventories : Products stocked at various levels–factory, warehouse, retailer, customer–in a distribution system.

Multiple sampling : Acceptance sampling based on many small samples.

Multistage inventories : Parts stocked at more that one point of the sequential production process.

Natural limits : Three standards deviations above and below the average of sample unit measurements.

Net change method : Method for updating the MRP system in which only those portions of the previous plan directly impacted by informational changes are reprocessed.

Net present value : The result of discounting all cash flows of an investment back to their present values and netting out the inflows against the outflows

Net requirements : The net quantity of an item that is acquired to meet the scheduled output for the period. Calculated as gross requirements minus scheduled receipts for the period minus amounts available from the previous period.

Network : The sequence of all activities, symbolized by nodes connected by arrows.

Network modeling : Analysing the precedence relationships of project activities and depicting from graphically.

Next-best rule (NB) : A priority rule that gives top priority to the waiting job whose setup cost is least.

Node: In network modeling, a circle at one end of a line; the symbol for the beginning or ending of a project activity.

Nominal group technique : A qualitative forecasting technique in which a panel of experts working together arrive at a consensus through discussion and ranking of ideas.

Normal time : The average cycle time for a job, adjusted by a worker rating to account for variations in "normal" performance.

Numerically controlled (NC) machines : Machines programmed through computers to perform a cycle of operations repeatedly.

Objective function : A mathematical equation that measures the value of all proposed decision alternatives; (a linear programming equation).

Occupational Safety and Health Administration (OSHA) : A division of the U.S. government created by the Williams-Steiger Occupational Safety and Health Act of 1970 to develop and enforce standards for job-related safety and health.

Office automation (OA) : Computer-based systems for managing information resources.

Open order : A customer order (job) that has been launched into production and is in process.

Operating characteristic (OC) curve : Given a sampling plan, the graph of the probability of accepting a product lot as a function of the quality of the lot.

Operating system : Inventory control policies concerning when and how much stock to recorder.

Operation chart : A graphic tool to analyse and time elementary motions of the right and left hand in performing a routine repetitive task.

Operations management : Management of the conversion process, which converts all relevant inputs into desired outputs of good and services; Process of planning, designing and operating production systems.

Operations splitting : Processing part of a job at one work center and the rest at another.

Operations strategy : A long term plan for the production of products, services setup a roadmap to achieve the business goals.

Operations system : The part of an Organisation that produces the Organisation's physical goods or services.

Opportunity costs : Returns that are lost or forgone as a result of selecting one alternative over another.

Optimistic time (t_0) : In activity network the least amount of time an activity is expected to consume.

Optimized production technology (OPT) : A production planning system that emphasises identifying bottleneck work centers and careful management of materials and resources related to those bottlenecks in order to maximise output and reduce inventories.

Order quantity : As part of the operating system the amount of stock that should be reordered.

Ordering cost : Average cost of each inventory repleshment for materials (excluding material cost). It includes cost of processing of requisition, purchase order, portage, telephone calls, quality inspections and receiving.

Organisation development (OD) : Managing organizational change by applying knowledge from psychology, sociology, and other behavioral sciences.

Organising : Activities that establish a structure of tasks and authority.

Out-of-control process : A process for which some variations are non-random (variations outside quality tolerances).

Outputs : Good or services produced by a conversion process out of given input resources

Outsourcing : Hiring out or subcontracting some of the work that a company cannot do by itself.

***p*-chart :** A control chart using sample fractions defective.

PERT language : The terms and symbols specific to PERT.

Pareto analysis : Frequency distributions of quality cost sources.

Part-period method : A lot sizing policy in which order quantity varies according to a comparison of holding versus ordering costs.

Path : A portion of the network, including the first and last activities for which each activity has a single immediate successor.

Path time : The amount of time expected to be consumed by activities on a path. It is also called activity duration.

Payback period : Length of time required to recover the investment (the ratio of net income to net annual income from investment).

Pegging : The process of tracing through the MRP records and all levels in the product structure to identify how changes in the records of one component will affect the records of other components.

Percent defective : The percent of total units to these found defective only of a lot inspected.

Periodic inventory system : An operating doctrine for which reorder points and order quantities vary; stocks are replenished up to a fixed base stock level after a fixed time period has passed. It is called P-system.

Pessimistic time (t_p) : In activity network the greatest amount of time an activity is expected to consume.

Physical distribution : Activities relating to materials management as well as storing and transporting finished products through the distribution system to customers.

Plan-Do-check Act (PDCA) : cycle. A concept of continuous improvement as an endless cycle.

Planned order : A customer order (job) that is on the books and planned for production but that has not yet been launched into production.

Planned order receipts : The quantity of an item that is planned to be ordered so that it will be received at the beginning of the time period to meet net requirements for the period. The order has not yet been placed.

Planned order release : The quantity of an item that is planned to be ordered and the planned period for releasing this order that will result in the order being received when needed. It is the planned order receipt offset in time by the item's lead time.

Planning : Activities that establish a course of action with associated resources requirements.

Planning for operations : Establishing a program of action for converting resources into goods or services.

Planning the conversion system : Establishing a program of action for acquiring the necessary physical facilities to be used in the conversion process.

Poke-yoke : Total quality control technique for a foolproof production free from defects. It is also called fail-safing or fool-proofing.

Pond Draining Approach : A production planning and control system that uses a large amount of raw materials, WIP and finished goods inventories.

Preautomation : An analysis that is performed before automating a production process to reveal unnecessary equipment and activities so that they can be eliminated rather than automated.

Predecessor task : A task that must be performed before performing another (successor) task.

Predetermined time motion study (PTMS) : A work measurement technique that involves observing a job, recording job elements, with preestablished motion units, and calculating a performance standard.

Prediction : Subjective estimates of the future.

Prevention costs : Costs of planning, designing and equipping a quality control programme.

Preventive maintenance (PM) : JIT philosophy of daily extensive checkups and repairs for production equipment, lengthening their useful life well beyon the traditional time frame.

Principles of motion economy : A broad set of guidelines focusing on work arrangements, the use of human hands and body and the use of tools.

Priority sequencing rule : A systematic procedure for assigning priorities to waiting jobs, thereby determining the sequence in which jobs will be processed.

Process (oriented) layout : The arrangement of a facility so that work centers or departments are grouped together according to their functional type.

Process capability : The ability of a conversion process to produce a product that conforms to design specifications; a range of variation from the design specifications under normal working conditions.

Process management : One of several theories of classical management, emphasizing management as a continuous process of planning, organising and controlling to influence the others actions.

Process technology : Equipment, people and systems used to produce a firm's products and services.

Procurement costs : Costs of placing an order, or setup costs if ordered items are manufactured by the firm.

Producer's risk (type I error) (α) : The risk or probability of incorrectly concluding that the conversion process is out of control or rejecting a good lot.

Product (oriented) layout : The arrangement of a facility so that work centers or equipment are in a line to afford a specialized sequence of tasks for a specific product.

Product group (family) : A set of individual products that share or consume common blocks of capacity in the manufacturing process.

Product life cycle : Pattern of demand throughout the product's life; similar patterns and stages can be identified for the useful life of a proces.

Product mix problem : A decision situation involving limited resources that can be used to produce any of several combinations of products. (A linear programming technique).

Product reliability : The probability that a product will perform as intended for a prescribed lifetime under specified operating conditions.

Product structure : The levels of components to produce an end product.

Production sharing : It is design and financing of a product by one country, rawmaterials provision and manufacturing by another country, assembly by yet another country and selling by another country world wide. Hence it is utilisation of the best facilities across the globe.

Production smoothing : Production planning the reduces drastic period-to-period changes in levels of output or work force.

Productivity : A ratio of outputs to inputs. Total factor productivity is the ratio of outputs to the total inputs of labor, capital, materials and energy; partial factor productivity is the ratio of outputs to one, two or three of these inputs.

Productivity gain sharing : Rewarding employees for increases in organisation-wide group performance.

Program Evaluation and Review Technique (PERT) : An application of network modeling originally designed for planning and controlling the U.S. Navy's Polaris nuclear submarine project.

Progress reporting : Monitoring the time and cost variances during the progress of a project and depicting them graphically, including actual costs of work completed (ACWC), budgeted costs of work completed (BCWC) and budgeted costs of work scheduled (BCWS).

Project : A one-time-only set of activities that has a definite beginning and ending point in time.

Project planning : Activities that establish a course of action for a project.

Project scheduling : Activities that establish the times and the sequence of project tasks.

Project technology : A process technology suitable for producing one-of-a-kind products.

Pull manufacturing system : A system of production in which product are produced only as they are ordered by (customers).

Purchasing : Activities relating to procuring materials and supplies consumed during production.

Push manufacturing system : A system of production in which products are produced according to a schedule derived from anticipated product demand. An MRP-based or EOQ based system.

Q–inventory system : An inventory operating system for which an optimal reorder point and an optimal order quantity *Q*–the economic order quantity are fixed.

Quality : The degree to which the design specifications for a product or service are appropriate to its function and use, and the degree to which a product or service conforms to its design specifications.

Quality circle (QC) : A small group of employees who meet frequently to resolve company problems.

Quality Function Deployment (QFD) : A formal system for identifying customer wants and eliminating wasteful product features and activities that do not contribute to product value.

Quality motivation : Programmes to motivate workers to improve quality; includs incentive and merit pay systems.

Quantity discount : A policy of allowing item cost to vary with the volume ordered; usually the item cost decreases as volume increases due to economics of scale in production and distribution.

Queue : A waiting line.

Queue discipline : priority to sequence arrivals through service system.

Queuing theory : Concepts and models to describe and measure patterns of job arrivals and patterns of servicing customers and to evaluate the effectiveness of serving customers who wait in lines (queues) to be served.

***R* chart :** A control chart using sample ranges.

Random fluctuations : Unplanned or uncontrollable environmental influences (strikes, floods absentism or non-receipt of materials as per lead time etc.) that cause planned and actual output to differ.

Random Sample : Sample of a product in which each unit of a lot has equal chance of inclusion.

Receiving inspection : The inspection of inputs.

Regenerative method : A procedure, used at regular intervals, to update the MRP by completely reprocessing entire set of information and recreating the entire MRP.

Regression analysis : A causal forecasting model in which a functional relationship is established between variables from historical data, and then used to forecast dependent variable values.

Re-manufacturing : Re-use of used durable products, i.e., reusing some parts of old products, if they meet the quality standards, adding new components to the product making it fully useable again.

Reorder point : As part of the operating system, the inventory level at which stock should be reordered.

Research and development (R&D) : Organizational efforts directed toward product and progress innovation; implementation. Includes stages of basic research, applied research, development and implication.

Restrictions : Restraints on the value of the decision variables of a linear programming problem. Also called limitations or constraints.

Robot : A programmable machine capable of moving materials and performing routine, repetitive tasks.

Robotics : The science of selecting robots for various applications.

Robust product : A product that can perform under a wide range of environmental conditions without failing.

Rope : A communication system to work stations to ensure synchronisation with the bottleneck machine.

Rough-cut capacity planning : The process of testing the feasibility of master production schedules in terms of capacity.

Route sheet : A document that shows the routing of a component, including the work centres and operation times, through its production processes.

Routing : The processing steps or stages needed to create a product or to do a job.

Safety stock : Quantity of material held as inventory to be used when demand is greater than expected or when ordered materials are not supplied for regular production.

Salvage value : Income from selling an asset.

Sample : A set of representative units of output selected and measured as part of sampling.

Sample range : The arithmetic difference of the highest and lowest measurement for a sample.

Sample unit : A representative unit of output selected and measured as part of sampling.

Sampling : The process of selecting and measuring representative units of output.

Sampling plan : A plan for acceptance sampling specifying the number of units to sample and the number of sample units that must conform to specifications if the production lot is to be accepted.

Scheduled receipts : The quantity of an item that will be received from suppliers as a result of orders that have been placed (open orders).

Scientific management : One of several theories of classical management, emphasizing economic efficiency at the production core through management rationality, the economic motivation of workers and the separation of planning and doing work.

Service level : A treatment policy for customers when there are stockouts; commonly established either as a ratio of customers served to customers demanding or as a ratio of units supplied to units demanded.

Services : Intangible products to satisfy customer demand.

Setup cost : The cost of revising and preparing a work centre for processing a job.

Setup dependence rule : A priority rule in which the jobs needing minimum set up time for change over to another job are taken up for production.

Shingo's seven wastes : Seven sources of manufacturing wastes identified by Shigeo Shingo as targets for reduction through continuous improvement in the production process.

Shop floor control : Activities that execute and control shop operations; includes loading, sequencing, detailed scheduling, and expediting jobs in production.

Shortest-processing-time rule (SPT) : A priority rule that gives top priority to the waiting job whose operation time at a work center is shortest.

Simple average : Average of demands occuring in all previous periods; the demands of all periods are equally weighted.

Simple lot size formula (Wilson formula) : A deterministic inventory model characterized by one stock point, no stockouts, and constant and known demand, lead time and unit cost.

Simple median model : A quantitative method for choosing an optimal facility location, minimizing costs of transportation and based on the median load.

Simple moving average : Average of demands occuring in several of the most recent periods; most recent periods are added and older ones dropped to keep calculations current.

Simplex method : An algorithm for solving a linear programming problem by successively choosing feasible solutions and testing them for optimality.

Single sampling : Acceptance sampling based on a single sample.

Slack time (T_S) : In network model, the amount of leeway time an activity can consume and still allow the product to be completed on time.

Slack variable : A variable in a linear programming problem representing the unused quantity of a resource.

Smoothing coefficient : A numerical parameter that determines the weightage of old demands in exponential smoothing.

Specialization of labor : Breaking apart jobs into tasks and assigning tasks to different workers according to their special skills, talents, and tools.

Specification limits (SL) : Upper and lower (LSL) boundaries defining the limits of variation in a product characteristic such that the product is fit for use.

Standard : A quantitative criterion established as a basis for comparison in measuring or judging output.

Standard time : The ratio of normal time to the available fraction of time.

Statistical forecasting models : Casting forward past data in some systematic method used in time series analysis and projection.

Statistical process control (SPC) : The use of sample statistics to detect and eliminate non-random variations in the conversion process.

Stepping stone method : An alogrithm of the transportation method of linear programming that uses a set of occupied cells to evaluate the effect on costs if an empty cell was to become occupied.

Stochastic model : A model in which variable values are probabilistic.

Stock (storage) point : A location of inventory.

Stockkeeping item : An item of inventory.

Stockless production system : A system of production that allows no (or as small as possible) inventories of raw materials, work-in-process, or finished goods; the JIT philosophy.

Stockout costs : Costs associated with demand when stocks have been depleted; generally lost sales or backorder costs.

Strategic Alliance : The joint ventures among companies to explore larger business opportunities.

Strategic planning : A process of thinking through the organization's current mission and environment and then setting forth a guide for tomorrow's decision and results.

Strategic outsourcing : Subcontracting a particular process for quick reaction to change in customer demand, competitors actions or change in technology.

Synchronous Manufacturing : System of production, planning and control in which the entire organisation works together to achieve the organisational goals.

Taguchi method of quality control : A method of controlling quality developed by Dr. Genichi Taguchi, that emphasizes robust product design and the quality loss function.

Task : The smallest group of work that can be assigned to a work station.

Task sharing : Assigning one task each to two workers and assigning a third task to be shared between the two, thereby reducing idle time.

Technology : The level of scientific sophistication in plant, equipment and skills in the conversion process.

Templates : Two-dimensional cutouts of equipment drawn to scale for planning the facility layout.

Theory of constraints : The philosophy and production control approach of managing inevitable bottlenecks or operational constraints. Theory advanced by Eliyahu Goldratt.

Total Quality Management (TQM) : system of producing high quality products and services rather than through defects detection.

Thrust and Quest to Marvel (TQM) : The system of producing quality work through deep involvement and optimal internal energy by all concerned.

Throughputs : Items going through the conversion process contrasted with outputs coming out of the conversion process.

Time fence : A designated length of time that must pass without changing the MPS, to stabilize the MRP system.

Time measurement unit (TMU) : A unit of time, equivalent to 0.00001 hours used as a basis for methods time measurement (MTM), a widely accepted form of predetermined time study.

Time series analysis : In forecasting problems, analysis of demand data plotted on a time scale to reveal patterns of demand.

Total quality control (TQC) : The Japanese approach to quality control, stressing continuous improvement through attention to manufacturing detail rather than attainment of a fixed quantitative quality standard.

Transportation model : A special linear programming formulation for determining how sources should ship resources to destinations so that total shipping costs are minimized.

Turnover : The ratio of sales to assets.

Two Bin System : Fixed order quantity inventory Control System using two bins to hold a material in inventory; ordering done when one bin is empty and both filled when inventory is replenished.

Uniform load scheduling (level scheduling) : A method of scheduling in which small quantities of each product are produced each day, throughout the day.

Value-added : When blending inputs into a product or service, the increased value of output compared to the sum of the value of inputs.

Value-added manufacturing : A method of manufacturing that seeks to eliminate wastes in processing, adhering to the principle that a stage of value addition to the product for the customer should be eliminated.

Variable output rate (chase) plan : An aggregate plan that changes period-to-period output to correspond with the demand fluctuations.

Vendor Managed Inventory (VMI) : A supplier monitors and replenishes the inventory items at the customer's facility as and when required.

Vertical Integration : Amount of production and distribution chain brought under the control of the company.

Warehousing : Management of materials while these are in storage.

Work breakdown structure (WBS) : A methodology for the level-by-level breakdown of a project into successively more detailed subcomponent activities and tasks.

Work center : A facility, set of machines, or work station that provides a service or transformation needed by a job (order).

Work measurement : The determination of the degree and quantity of labor in performing tasks.

Work sampling : A work measurement technique that volves in defining the state of "working" observing the job over time, and computing the portion of time the worker is "working."

Worker rating : In determining normal time, a factor of adjustment to account for variations in "normal" worker performance.

Work-in-process inspection : The inspection of a product at one or more stages of production.

$\overline{X}$ **-chart :** A control chart using sample averages.

Zero defects : A programme to change workers' attitudes about quality by stressing error-free performance. It means products within the tolerance limits of specifications.

Subject Index

J

N

O

P

Q

R

TABLES

TABLE 1. RANDOM DIGITS

Row	Random Numbers of 4-digits									
1	0695	7741	8254	4297	0000	5277	6563	9265	1023	5925
2	0437	5434	8503	3928	6979	9393	8936	9088	5744	4790
3	6242	2998	0205	5469	3365	7950	7256	3716	8385	0253
4	7090	4074	1257	7175	3310-	0712	4748	4226	0604	3804
5	0683	6999	4828	7888	0087	9288	7855	2678	3315	6718
6	7013	4300	3768	2572	6473	2411	6285	0069	5422	6175
7	8808	2786	5369	9571	3412	2465	6419	3990	0294	0896
8	9876	3602	5812	0124	1997	6445	3176	2682	1259	1728
9	1873	1065	8976	1295	9434	3178	0602	0732	6616	7972
10	2581	3075	4622	2974	7069	5605	0420	2949	4387	7679
11	3785	6401	0540	5077	7132	4135	4646	3834	6753	1593
12	8626	4017	1544	4202	8986	1432	2810	2418	8052	2710
13	6253	0726	9483	6753	4732	2284	0421	3010	7885	8436
14	0113	4546	2212	9829	2351	1370	2707	3329	6574	7002
15	4646	6474	9983	8738	1603	8671	0489	9588	3309	5860
16	7873	7343	4432	2866	7973	3765	2888	5154	2250	4339
17	3756	9204	2590	6577	2409	8234	8656	2336	7948	7478
18	2673	7115	5526	0747	3952	6804	3671	7486	3024	9858
19	0187	7045	2711	0349	7734	4396	0988	4887	7682	8990
20	7976	3862	8323	5997	6904	4977	1056	6638	6398	4552
21	5605	1819	8926	9557	2905	0802	7749	0845	1710	4125
22	2225	5556	2545	7480	8804	4161	0084	0787	2561	5113
23	2549	4166	1609	7570	4223	0032	4236	0169	4673	8034
24	6113	1312	5777	7058	2413	3932	5144	5998	7183	5210
25	2028	2537	9819	9215	9327	6640	5986	7935	2750	2981
26	7818	3655	5771	4026	5757	3171	6435	2990	1860	1796
27	9629	3383	1931	2631	5903	9372	1307	4061	5443	8663
28	6657	5967	3277	7141	3628	2588	9320	1972	7683	7544
29	4344	7388	2978	3945	0471	4882	1619	0093	2282	7024
30	3145	8720	2131	1614	1575	5239	0766	0404	4873	7986
31	1848	4094	9168	0903	6451	2823	7566	6644	1157	8889
32	0915	5578	0822	5887	5354	3632	4617	6016	8989	9482
33	1430	4755	7551	9019	8233	9625	6361	2589	2496	7268
34	3473	7966	7249	0555	6307	9524	4888	4939	1641	1573
35	3312	0773	6296	1348	5483	5824	3353	4587	1019	9677
36	6255	4204	5890	9273	0634	9992	3834	2283	1202	4849
37	0562	2546	8559	0480	9379	9282	8257	3054	4272	9311
38	1957	6783	4105	8976	8035	0883	8971	0017	6476	2895
39	7333	1083	0398	8841	0017	4135	4043	8157	4672	2424
40	4601	8908	1781	4287	2681	6223	0814	4477	3798	4437

TABLE 1. Continued

Row	Random Numbers of 4-digits									
41	2628	2233	0708	0900	1698	2818	3931	6930	9273	6749
42	5318	8865	6057	8422	6992	9697	0508	3370	5522	9250
43	6335	0852	8657	8374	0311	6012	9477	0112	8976	3312
44	0301	8333	0327	0467	6186	1770	4099	9588	5382	8958
45	1719	9775	1566	7020	4535	2850	0207	4792	6405	1472
46	8907	8226	4249	6340	9062	3572	7655	6707	3685	1282
47	6129	5927	3731	1125	0081	1241	2772	6458	9157	4543
48	7376	3150	8985	8318	8003	6106	4952	8492	2804	3867
49	9093	3407	4127	9258	3687	5631	5102	1546	2659	0831
50	1133	3086	9380	5431	8647	0910	6948	2257	0946	1245
51	4567	0910	8495	2410	1088	7067	8505	9083	4339	2440
52	6141	8380	2302	4608	7209	5738	9765	3435	9657	6061
53	1514	8309	8743	3096	0682	7902	8204	7508	8330	1681
54	7277	1634	7866	9883	0916	6363	5391	6184	8040	3135
55	4568	4758	0166	1509	2105	0976	0269	0278	7443	2431
56	9200	7599	7754	4534	4532	3102	6831	2387	4147	2455
57	3971	8149	4431	2345	6436	0627	0410	1348	6599	1296
58	2672	9661	2359	8477	3425	8150	6918	8883	1518	4708
59	1524	3268	3798	3360	2255	0371	7610	9114	9466	0901
60	6817	9007	5959	0767	1166	7317	7502	0274	6340	0427
61	6762	3502	9559	4279	9271	9595	3053	4918	7503	5169
62	5264	0075	6655	4563	7112	7264	3240	2150	8180	1361
63	5070	8428	5149	2137	8728	9110	2334	9709	8134	3925
64	1664	3379	5273	9367	6950	6828	1711	7082	4783	0147
65	6962	7141	1904	6648	7328	2901	6396	9949	6274	1672
66	7541	4289	4970	2922	6670	8540	9053	3219	8881	1897
67	5244	4651	2934	6700	8869	0926	4191	1364	0926	2874
68	2939	3890	0745	2577	7931	3913	7877	2837	2500	8774
69	4266	6207	8083	6564	5336	5303	7503	6627	6055	3606
70	7848	5477	5588	3490	0294	3609	1632	5684	1719	6162
71	3009	1879	0440	7916	6643	9723	5933	0574	2480	6893
72	9865	7813	7468	8493	3293	1071	7183	9462	2363	6529
73	1196	1251	2368	1262	5769	9450	7485	4039	4985	6612
74	1067	3716	8897	1970	8799	5718	4792	7292	4589	4554
75	5160	5563	6527	7861	3477	6735	7748	4913	6370	2258
76	4560	0094	8284	7604	1667	9286	2228	9507	1838	4646
77	7697	2151	4860	0739	4370	3992	8121	2502	7670	4470
78	8675	2997	9783	7306	4116	6432	7233	4611	7121	9412
79	3597	3520	5995	0892	3470	4581	1068	8801	1254	8607
80	4281	8802	5880	6212	6818	8162	0052	1755	7107	5197

TABLE 2. AREAS UNDER THE NORMAL CURVE

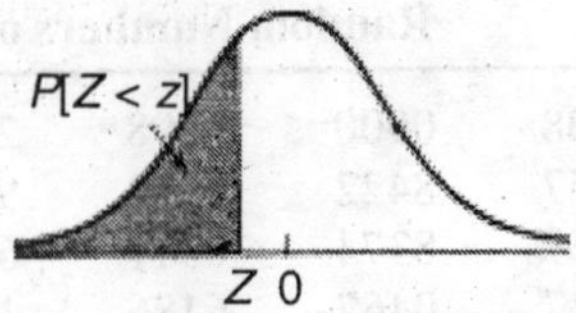

Standard Normal Probabilities

z	.00	.01	.02	.03	.04	.05	.06	.07	.08	.09
–3.5	.0002	.0002	.0002	.0002	.0002	.0002	.0002	.0002	.0002	.0002
–3.4	.0003	.0003	.0003	.0003	.0003	.0003	.0003	.0003	.0003	.0002
–3.3	.0005	.0005	.0005	.0004	.0004	.0004	.0004	.0004	.0004	.0003
–3.2	.0007	.0007	.0006	.0006	.0006	.0006	.0006	.0005	.0005	.0005
–3.1	.0010	.0009	.0009	.0009	.0008	.0008	.0008	.0008	.0007	.0007
–3.0	.0013	.0013	.0013	.0012	.0012	.0011	.0011	.0011	.0010	.0010
–2.9	.0019	.0018	.0018	.0017	.0016	.0016	.0015	.0015	.0014	.0014
–2.8	.0026	.0025	.0024	.0023	.0023	.0022	.0021	.0021	.0020	.0019
–2.7	.0035	.0034	.0033	.0032	.0031	.0030	.0029	.0028	.0027	.0026
–2.6	.0047	.0045	.0044	.0043	.0041	.0040	.0039	.0038	.0037	.0036
–2.5	.0062	.0060	.0059	.0057	.0055	.0054	.0052	.0051	.0049	.0048
–2.4	.0082	.0080	.0078	.0075	.0073	.0071	.0069	.0068	.0066	.0064
–2.3	.0107	.0104	.0102	.0099	.0096	.0094	.0091	.0089	.0087	.0084
–2.2	.0139	.0136	.0132	.0129	.0125	.0122	.0119	.0116	.0113	.0110
–2.1	.0179	.0174	.0170	.0166	.0162	.0158	.0154	.0150	.0146	.0143
–2.0	.0228	.0222	.0217	.0212	.0207	.0202	.0197	.0192	.0188	.0183
–1.9	.0287	.0281	.0274	.0268	.0262	.0256	.0250	.0244	.0239	.0233
–1.8	.0359	.0351	.0344	.0336	.0329	.0322	.0314	.0307	.0301	.0294
–1.7	.0446	.0436	.0427	.0418	.0409	.0401	.0392	.0384	.0375	.0367
–1.6	.0548	.0537	.0526	.0516	.0505	.0495	.0485	.0475	.0465	.0455
–15	.0668	.0655	.0643	.0630	.0618	.0606	.0594	.0582	.0571	.0559
–1.4	.0808	.0793	.0778	.0764	.0749	.0735	.0721	.0708	.0694	.0681
–1.3	.0968	.0951	.0934	.0918	.0901	.0885	.0869	.0853	.0838	.0823
–1.2	.1151	.1131	.1112	.1093	.1075	.1056	.1038	.1020	.1003	.0985
–1.1	.1357	.1335	.1314	.1292	.1271	.1251	.1230	.1210	.1190	.1170
–1.0	.1587	.1562	.1539	.1515	.1492	.1469	.1446	.1423	.1401	.1379
–.9	.1841	.1814	.1788	.1762	.1736	.1711	.1685	.1660	.1635	.1611
–.8	.2119	.2090	.2061	.2033	.2005	.1977	.1949	.1922	.1894	.1867
–.7	.2420	.2389	.2358	.2327	.2297	.2266	.2236	.2206	.2177	.2148
–.6	.2743	.2709	.2676	.2643	.2611	.2578	.2546	.2514	.2483	.2451
–.5	.3085	.3050	.3015	.2981	.2946	.2912	.2877	.2843	.2810	.2776
–.4	.3446	.3409	.3372	.3336	.3300	.3264	.3228	.3192	.3156	.3121
–.3	.3821	.3783	.3745	.3707	.3669	.3632	.3594	.3557	.3520	.3483
–.2	.4207	.4168	.4129	.4090	.4052	.4013	.3974	.3936	.3897	.3859
–.1	.4602	.4562	.4522	.4483	.4443	.4404	.4364	.4325	.4286	.4247
–.0	.5000	.4960	.4920	.4880	.4840	.4801	.4761	.4721	.4681	.4641

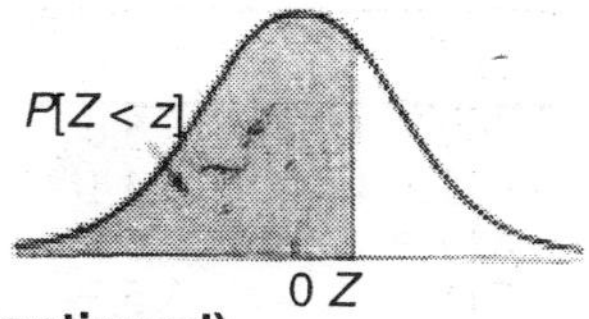

Standard Normal Probabilities (Continued)

z	.00	.01	.02	.03	.04	.05	.06	.07	.08	.09
.0	.5000	.5040	.5080	.5120	.5160	.5199	.5239	.5279	.5319	.5359
.1	.5398	.5438	.5478	.5517	.5557	.5596	.5636	.5675	.5714	.5753
.2	.5793	.5832	.5871	.5910	.5948	.5987	.6026	.6064	.6103	.6141
.3	.6179	.6217	.6255	.6293	.6331	.636S	.6406	.6443	.6480	.6517
.4	.6554	.6591	.6628	.6664	.6700	.6736	.6772	.6808	.6844	.6879
.5	.6915	.6950	.6985	.7019	.7054	.7088	.7123	.7157	.7190	.7224
.6	.7257	.7291	.7324	.7357	.7389	.7422	.7454	.7486	.7517	.7549
.7	.7580	.7611	.7642	.7673	.7703	.7734	.7764	.7794	.7823	.7852
.8	.7881	.7910	.7939	.7967	.7995	.8023	.8051	.8078	.8106	.8133
.9	.8159	.8186	.8212	.8238	.8264	.8289	.8315	.8340	.8365	.8389
1.0	.8413	.8438	.8461	.8485	.8508	.8531	.8554	.8577	.8599	.8621
1.1	.8643	.8665	.8686	.8708	.8729	.8749	.8770	.8790	.8810	.8830
1.2	.8849	.8869	.8888	.8907	.8925	.8944	.8962	.8980	.8997	.9015
1.3	.9032	.9049	.9066	.9082	.9099	.9115	.9131	.9147	.9162	.9177
1.4	.9192	.9207	.9222	.9236	.9251	.9265	.9279	.9292	.9306	.9319
1.5	.9332	.9345	.9357	.9370	.9382	.9394	.9406	.9418	.9429	.9341
1.6	.9452	.9463	.9474	.9484	.9495	.9505	.9515	.9525	.9535	.9545
1.7	.9554	.9564	.9573	.9582	.9591	.9599	.9608	.9616	.9625	.9633
1.8	.9641	.9649	.9656	.9664	.9671	.9678	.9686	.9693	.9699	.9706
1.9	.9713	.9719	.9726	.9732	.9738	.9744	.9750	.9756	.9761	.9767
2.0	.9772	.9778	.9783	.9788	.9793	.9798	.9803	.9808	.9812	.9817
2.1	.9821	.9826	.9830	.9834	.9838	.9842	.9846	.9850	.9854	.9857
2.2	.9861	.9864	.9868	.9871	.9875	.9878	.9881	.9884	.9887	.9890
2.3	.9893	.9896	.9898	.9901	.9904	.9906	.9909	.9911	.9913	.9916
2.4	.9918	.9920	.9922	.9925	.9927	.9929	.9931	.9932	.9934	.9936
2.5	.9938	.9940	.9941	.9943	.9945	.9946	.9948	.9949	.9951	.9952
2.6	.9953	.9955	.9956	.9957	.9959	.9960	.9961	.9962	.9963	.9964
2.7	.9965	.9966	.9967	.9968	.9969	.9970	.9971	.9972	.9973	.9974
2.8	.9974	.9975	.9976	.9977	.9977	.9978	.9979	.9979	.9980	.9981
2.9	.9981	.9982	.9982	.9983	.9984	.9984	.9985	.9985	.9986	.9986
3.0	.9987	.9987	.9987	.9988	.9988	.9989	.9989	.9989	.9990	.9990
3.1	.9990	.9991	.9991	.9991	.9992	.9992	.9992	.9992	.9993	.9993
3.2	.9993	.9993	.9994	.9994	.9994	.9994	.9994	.9995	.9995	.9995
3.3	.9995	.9995	.9995	.9996	.9996	.9996	.9996	.9996	.9996	.9997
3.4	.9997	.9997	.9997	.9997	.9997	.9997	.9997	.9997	.9997	.9998
3.5	.9998	.9998	.9998	.9998	.9998	.9998	.9998	.9998	.9998	.9998

TABLE 3 : VALUES OF EXPONENTIAL FUNCTIONS

x	e^x	e^{-x}	x	e^x	e^{-x}
0.0	1.000	1.000	5.0	1.48.4	0.0067
0.1	1.105	0.905	5.1	164.0	0.0061
0.2	1.221	0.819	5.2	181.3	0.0055
0.3	1.350	0.741	5.3	200. 3	0.0050
0.4	1.492	0.670	5.4	221.4	0.0045
0.5	1.649	0.607	5.5	244.7	0.0041
0.6	1.822	0.549	5.6	270.4	0.0037
0.7	2.014	0.497	5.7	298.9	0.0033
0.8	2.226	0.449	5.8	330.3	0.0030
0.9	2.460	0.407	5.9	365.0	0.0027
1.0	2.718	0.368	6.0	403.4	0.0025
1.1	3.004	0.333	6.1	445.9	0.0022
1.2	3.320	0.301	6.2	492.8	0.0020
1.3	3.669	0.273	6.3	544.6	0.0018
1.4	4.055	0.247	6.4	601.8	0.0017
1.5	4.482	0.223	6.5	665.1	0.0015
1.6	4.953	0.202	6.6	735.1	0.0014
1.7	5.474	0.183	6.7	812.4	0.0012
1.8	6.050	0.165	6.8	897.8	0.0011
1.9	6.686	0.150	6.9	992.3	0.0010
2.0	7.389	0.135	7.0	1,096.6	0.0009
2.1	8.166	0.122	7.1	1,212.0	0.0008
2.2	9.025	0.111	7.2	1,339.4	0.0007
2.3	9.974	0.100	7.3	1,480.3	0.0007
2.4	11.023	0.091	7.4	1,636.0	0.0006
2.5	12.18	0.082	7.5	1,808.0	0.00055
2.6	13.46	0.074	7.6	1,998.2	0.00050
2.7	14.88	0.067	7.7	2,208.3	0.00045
2.8	16.44	0.061	7.8	2,440.6	0.00041
2.9	18.17	0.055	7.9	2,697.3	0.00037
3.0	20.09	0.050	8.0	2,981.0	0.00034
3.1	22.20	0.045	8.1	3,294.5	0.00030
3.2	24.53	0.041	8.2	3,641.0	0.00027
3.3	27.11	0.037	8.3	4,023.9	0.00025
3.4	29.69	0.033	8.4	4,447.1	0.00022
3.5	33.12	0.030	8.5	4,914.8	0.00020
3.6	36.60	0.027	8.6	5,431.7	0.00018
3.7	40.45	0.025	8.7	6,002.9	0.00017
3.8	44.70	0.022	8.8	6,634.2	0.00015
3.9	49.40	0.020	8.9	7,332.0	0.00014
4.0	54.60	0.018	9.0	8,103.1	0.00012
4.1	60.34	0.017	9.1	8,955.3	0.00011
4.2	66.69	0.015	9.2	9,897.1	0.00010
4.3	73.70	0.014	9.3	10,938	0.00009
4.4	81.45	0.012	9.4	12,088	0.00008
4.5	90.02	0.011	9.5	13,360	0.00007
4.6	99.48	0.010	9.6	14,765	0.00007
4.7	109.95	0.009	9.7	16,318	0.00006
4.8	121.51	0.008	9.8	18,034	0.00006
4.9	134.29	0.007	9.9	19,930	0.00005

TABLE 4. BINOMIAL COEFFICIENTS

$$P(X < c) = \sum_{x=0}^{c} \binom{n}{x} p^x (1-p)^{n-x}$$

		P										
		.05	.10	.20	.30	.40	.50	.60	.70	.80	.90	.95
	c											
n - 1 0	0	.950	.900	.800	.700	.600	.500	.400	.300	.200	.100	.050
	1	1.000	1.000	1.000	1.000	1.000	1.000	1.000	1.000	1.000	1.000	1.000
$n = 2$	0	.902	.810	.640	.490	.360	.250	.160	.090	.040	.010	.002
	1	.997	.990	.960	.910	.840	.750	.640	.510	.360	.190	.097
	2	1.000	1.000	1.000	1.000	1.000	1.000	1.000	1.000	1.000	1.000	1.000
$n = 3$	0	.857	.729	.512	.343	.216	.125	.064	.027	.008	.001	.000
	1	.993	.972	.896	.784	.648	.500	.352	.216	.104	.028	.007
	2	1.000	.999	.992	.973	.936	.875	.784	.657	,488	.271	.143
	3	1.000	1.000	1.000	1.000	1.000	1.000	1.000	1.000	1.000	1.000	1.000
n - 4	0	.815	.656	.410	.240	.130	.063	.026	.008	.002	.000	.000
	1	.986	.948	.819	.652	.475	.313	.179	.064	.027	.004	.000
	2	1.000	.996	.973	.916	.821	.688	.525	.348	.181	.052	.014
	3	1.000	1.000	.998	.992	.974	.938	.870	.760	.590	.344	.185
	4	1.000	1.000	1.000	1.000	1.000	1.000	1.000	1.000	1.000	1.000	1.000
n- 5	0	.774	.590	.328	.168	.078	.031	.010	.002	.000	.000	.000
	1	.977	.919	.737	.528	.337	.188	.087	.031	.007	.000	.000
	2	999	.991	.942	.837	.683	.500	.317	.163	.058	.009	.001
	3	1.000	1.000	.993	.969	.913	.813	.663	.472	.263	.081	.023
	4	1.000	1.000	1.000	.998	.990	.969	.922	.832	.672	.410	.226
	5	1.000	1.000	1.000	1.000	1.000	1.000	1.000	1.000	1.000	1.000	1.000
$n = 6$	0	.735	.531	.262	.118	.047	.016	.004	.001	.000	.000	.000
	1	.967	.886	.655	.420	.233	.109	.041	.011	.002	.000	.000
	2	.998	.984	.901	.744	.544	.344	.179	.070	.017	.001	.000
	3	1.000	.999	.983	.930	.821	.656	.456	.256	.099	.016	.002
	4	1.000	1.000	.998	.989	.959	.891	.767	.580	.345	.114	.033
	5	1.000	1.000	1.000	.999	.996	.984	.953	.882	.738	.469	.265
	6	1.000	1.000	1.000	1.000	1.000	1.000	1.000	1.000	1.000	1.000	1.000
$n = 7$	0	.698	.478	.210	.082	.028	.008	.002	.000	.000	.000	.000
	1	.956	.850	.577	.329	.159	.063	.019	.004	.000	.000	.000
	2	.996	.974	.852	.647	.420	.227	.096	.029	.005	.000	.000
	3	1.000	.997	.967	.874	.710	.500	.290	.126	.033	.003	.000
	4	1.000	1.000	.995	.971	.904	.773	.580	.353	.148	.026	.004
	5	1.000	1.000	1.000	.996	.981	.938	.841	.671	.423	.150	.044
	6	1.000	1.000	1.000	1.000	.998	.992	.972	.918	.790	.522	.302
	7	1.000	1.000	1.000	1.000	1.000	1.000	1.000	1.000	1.000	1.000	1.000

TABLE 4. (Continued)

	c	P .05	.10	.20	.30	.40	.50	.60	.70	.80	.90	.95
$n = 8$	0	.663	.430	.168	.058	.017	.004	.001	.000	.000	.000	.000
	1	.943	.813	.503	.255	.106	.035	.009	.001	.000	.000	.000
	2	.994	.962	.797	.552	.315	.145	.050	.011	.001	.000	.000
	3	1.000	.995	.944	.806	.594	.363	.174	.058	.010	.000	.000
	4	1.000	1.000	.990	.942	.826	.637	.406	.194	.056	.005	.000
	5	1.000	1.000	.999	.989	.950	.855	.685	.448	.203	.038	.006
	6	1.000	1.000	1.000	.999	.991	.965	.894	.745	.497	.187	.057
	7	1.000	1.000	1.000	1.000	.999	.996	.983	.942	.832	.570	.337
	8	1.000	1.000	1.000	1.000	1.000	1.000	1.000	1.000	1.000	1.000	1.000
$n = 9$	0	.630	.387	.134	.040	.010.	.002	.000	.000	.000	.000	.000
	1	.929	.775	.436	.196	.071	.020	.004	.000	.000	.000	.000
	2	.992	.947	.738	.463	.232	.090	.025	.004	.000	.000	.000
	3	.999	.992	.914	.730	.483	.254	.099	.025	.003	.000	.000
	4	1.000	.999	.980	.901	.733	.500	.267	.099	.020	.001	.000
	5	1.000	1.000	.997	.975	.901	.746	.517	.270	.086	.008	.001
	6	1.000	1.000	1.000	.996	.975	.910	.768	.537	.262	.053	.008
	7	1.000	1.000	1.000	1.000	.996	.980	.929	.804	.564	.225	.071
	8	1.000	1.000	1.000	1.000	1.000	.998	.990	.960	.866	.613	.370
	9	1.000	1.000	1.000	1.000	1.000	1.000	1.000	1.000	1.000	1.000	1.000
$n = 10$	0	.599	.349	.107	.028	.006	.001	.000	.000	.000	.000	.000
	1	.914	.736	.376	.149	.046	.011	.002	.000	.000	.000	.000
	2	.988	.930	.678	.383	.167	.055	.0.12	.002	.000	.000	.000
	3	.999	.987	.879	.650	.382	.172	.055	.011	.001	.000	.000
	4	1.000	.998	.967	.850	.633	.377	.166	.047	.006	.000	.000
	5	1.000	1.000	.994	.953	.834	.623	.367	.150	.033	.002	.000
	6	1.000	1.000	.999	.989	.945	.828	.618	.350	.121	.013	.001
	7	1.000	1.000	1.000	.998	.988	.945	.833	.617	.322	.070	.012
	8	1.000	1.000	1.000	1.000	.998	.989	.954	.851	.624	.264	.086
	9	1.000	1.000	1.000	1.000	1.000	.999	.994	.972	.893	.651	.401
	10	1.000	1.000	1.000	1.000	1.000	1.000	1.000	1.000	1.000	1.000	1.000
$n = 11$	0	.569	.314	.086	.020	.004	.000	.000	.000	.000	.000	.000
	1	.898	.697	.322	.113	.030	.006	.001	.000	.000	.000	.000
	2	.985	.910	.617	.313	.119	.033	.006	.001	.000	.000	.000
	3	.998	.981	.839	.570	.296	.113	.029	.004	.000	.000	.000
	4	1.000	.997	.950	.790	.533	.274	.099	.022	.002	.000	.000
	5	1.000	1.000	.988	.922	.753	.500	.247	.078	.012	.000	.000
	6	1.000	1.000	.998	.978	.901	.726	.467	.210	.050	.003	.000
	7	1.000	1.000	1.000	.996	.971	.887	.704	.430	.161	.019	.002
	8	1.000	1.000	1.000	.999	.994	.967	.881	.687	.383	.090	.015
	9	1.000	1.000	1.000	1.000	.999	.994	.970	.887	.678	.303	.102
	10	1.000	1.000	1.000	1.000	1.000	1.000	.996	.980	.914	.686	.431
	11	1.000	1.000	1.000	1.000	1.000	1.000	1.000	1.000	1.000	1.000	1.000

TABLE 4. (Continued)

		P										
	c	.05	.10	.20	.30	.40	.50	.60	.70	.80	.90	.95
$n = 12$	0	.540	.282	.069	.014	.002	.000	.000	.000	.000	.000	.000
	1	.882	.659	.275	.085	.020	.003	.000	.000	.000	.000	.000
	2	.980	.889	.558	.253	.083	.019	.003	.000	.000	.000	.000
	3	.998	.974	.795	.493	.225	.073	.015	.002	.000	.000	.000
	4	1.000	.996	.927	.724	.438	.194	.057	.009	.001	.000	.000
	5	1.000	.999	.981	.882	.665	.387	.158	.039	.004	.000	.000
	6	.000	1.000	.996	.961	.842	.613	.335	.118	.019	.001	.000
	7	.000	1.000	.999	.991	.943	.806	.562	.276	.073	.004	.000
	8	.000	1.000	1.000	.998	.985	.927	.775	.507	.205	.026	.002
	9	.000	1.000	1.000	1.000	.997	.981	.917	.747	.442	.111	.020
	10	.000	1.000	1.000	1.000	1.000	.997	.980	.915	.725	.341	.118
	11	.000	1.000	1.000	1.000	1.000	1.000	.998	.986	.931	.718	.460
	12	1.000	1.000	1.000	1.000	1.000	1.000	1.000	1.000	1.000	1.000	1.000
$n = 13$	0	.513	.254	.055	.010	.001	.000	.000	.000	.000	.000	.000
	1	.865	.621	.234	.064	.013	.002	.000	.000	.000	.000	.000
	2	.975	.866	.502	.202	.058	.011	.001	.000	.000	.000	.000
	3	.997	.966	.747	.421	.169	.046	.008	.001	.000	.000	.000
	4	1.000	.994	.901	.654	.353	.133	.032	.004	.000	.000	.000
	5	1.000	.999	.970	.835	.574	.291	.098	.018	.001	.000	.000
	6	1.000	1.000	.993	.938	.771	.500	.229	.062	.007	.000	.000
	7	1.000	1.000	.999	.982	.902	.709	.426	.165	.030	.001	.000
	8	1.000	1.000	1.000	.996	.968	.867	.647	.346	.099	.006	.000
	9	1.000	1.000	1.000	.999	.992	.954	.831	.579	.253	.034	.003
	10	1.000	1.000	1.000	1.000	.999	.989	.942	.798	.498	.134	.025
	11	1.000	1.000	1.000	1.000	1.000	.998	.987	.936	.766	.379	.135
	12	1.000	1.000	1.000	1.000	1.000	1.000	.999	.990	.945	.746	.487
	13	1.000	1.000	1.000	1.000	1.000	1.000	1.000	1.000	1.000	1.000	1.000
$n = 14$	0	.488	.229	.044	.007	.001	.000	.000	.000	.000	.000	.000
	1	.847	.585	.198	.047	.008	.001	.000	.000	.000	.000	.000
	2	.970	.842	.448	.161	.040	.006	.001	.000	.000	.000	.000
	3	.996	.956	.698	.355	.124	.029	.004	.000	.000	.000	.000
	4	1.000	.991	.870	.584	.279	.090	.018	.002	.000	.000	.000
	5	1.000	.999	.956	.781	.486	.212	.058	.008	.000	.000	.000
	6	1.000	1.000	.988	.907	.692	.395	.150	.031	.002	.000	.000
	7	1.000	1.000	.998	.969	.850	.605	.308	.093	.012	.000	.000
	8	1.000	1.000	1.000	.992	.942	.788	.514	.219	.044	.001	.000
	9	1.000	1.000	1.000	.998	.982	.910	.721	.416	.130	.009	.000
	10	1.000	1.000	1.000	1.000	.996	.971	.876	.645	.302	.044	.004
	11	1.000	1.000	1.000	1.000	.999	.994	.960	.839	.552	.158	.030
	12	1.000	1.000	1.000	1.000	1.000	.999	.992	.953	.802	.415	.153
	13	1.000	1.000	1.000	1.000	1.000	1.000	.999	.993	.956	.771	.512
	14	1.000	1.000	1.000	1.000	1.000	1.000	1.000	1.000	1.000	1.000	1.000

TABLE 4. (Continued)

		P										
		.05	.10	.20	.30	.40	.50	.60	.70	.80	.90	.95
	c											
n = 15	0	.463	.206	.035	.005	.000	.000	.000	.000	.000	.000	.000
	1	.829	.549	.167	.035	.005	.000	.000	.000	.000	.000	.000
	2	.964	.816	.398	.127	.027	.004	.000	.000	.000	.000	.000
	3	.995	.944	.648	.297	.091	.018	.002	.000	.000	.000	.000
	4	.999	.987	.836	.515	.217	.059	.009	.001	.000	.000	.000
	5	1.000	.998	.939	.722	.403	.151	.034	.004	.000	.000	.000
	6	1.000	1.000	.982	.869	.610	.304	.095	.015	.001	.000	.000
	7	1.000	1.000	.996	.850	.787	.500	.213	.050	.004	.000	.000
	8	1.000	1.000	.999	.985	.905	.696	.390	.131	.018	.000	.000
	9	1.000	1.000	1.000	.996	.966	.849	.597	.278	.061	.002	.000
	10	1.000	1.000	1.000	.999	.991	.941	.783	.485	.164	.013	.001
	11	1.000	1.000	1.000	1.000	.998	.982	.909	.703	.352	.056	.005
	12	1.000	1.000	1.000	1.000	1.000	.996	.973	.873	.602	.184	.036
	13	1.000	1.000	1.000	1.000	1.000	1.000	.995	.965	.833	.451	.171
	14	1.000	1.000	1.000	1.000	1.000	1.000	1.000	.995	.965	.794	.537
	15	1.000	1.000	1.000	1.000	1.000	1.000	1.000	1.000	1.000	1.000	1.000
n = 16	0	.440	.185	.028	.003	.000	.000	.000	.000	.000	.000	.000
	1	.811	.515	.141	.026	.003	.000	.000	.000	.000	.000	.000
	2	.957	.789	.352	.099	.018	.002	.000	.000	.000	.000	.000
	3	.993	.932	.598	.246	.065	.011	.001	.000	.000	.000	.000
	4	.999	.983	.798	.450	.167	.038	.005	.000	.000	.000	.000
	5	1.000	.997	.918	.660	.329	.105	.019	.002	.000	.000	.000
	6	1.000	.999	.973	.825	.527	.227	.058	.007	.000	.000	.000
	7	1.000	1.000	.993	.926	.716	.402	.142	.026	.001	.000	.000
	8	1.000	1.000	.999	.974	.858	.598	.284	.074	.007	.000	.000
	9	1.000	1.000	1.000	.993	.942	.773.	.473	.175	.027	.001	.000
	10	1.000	1.000	1.000	.998	.981	.895	.671	.340	.082	.003	.000
	11	1.000	1.000	1.000	1.000	.995	.962	.833	.550	.202	.017	.001
	12	1.000	1.000	1.000	1.000	.999	.989	.935	.754	.402	.068	.007
	13	1.000	1.000	1.000	1.000	1.000.	.998	.982	.901	.648	.211	.043
	14	1.000	1.000	1.000	1.000	1.000	1.000	.997	.974	.859	.485	.189
	15	1.000	1.000	1.000	1.000	1.000	1.000	1.000	.997	.972	.815	.560
	16	1.000	1.000	1.000	1.000	1.000	1.000	1.000	1.000	1.000	1.000	1.000

TABLE 4. (Continued)

		P										
		.05	.10	.20	.30	.40	.50	.60	.70	.80	.90	.95
	c											
$n = 17$	0	.418	.167	.023	.002	.000	.000	.000	.000	.000	.000	.000
	1	.792	.482	.118	.019	.002	.000	.000	.000	.000	.000	.000
	2	.950	.762	.310	.077	.012	.001	.000	.000	.000	.000	.000
	3	.991	.917	.549	.202	.046	.006	.000	.000	.000	.000	.000
	4	.999	.978	.758	.389	.126	.025	.003	.000	.000	.000	.000
	5	1.000	.995	.894	.597	.264	.072	.011	.001	.000	.000	.000
	6	1.000	.999	.962	.775	.448	.166	.035	.003	.000	.000	.000
	7	1.000	1.000	.989	.895	.641	.315	.092	.013	.000	.000	.000
	8	1.000	1.000	.997	.960	.801	.500	.199	.040	.003	.000	.000
	9	1.000	1.000	1.000	.987	.908	.685	.359	.105	.011	.000	.000
	10	1.000	1.000	1.000	.997	.965	.834	.552	.225	.038	.001	.000
	11	1.000	1.000	1.000	.999	.989	.928	.736	.403	.106	.005	.000
	12	1.000	1.000	1.000	1.000	.997	.975	.874	.611	.242	.022	.001
	13	1.000	1.000	1.000	1.000	1.000	.994	.954	.798	.451	.083	.009
	14	1.000	1.000	1.000	1.000	1.000	.999	.988	.923	.690	.238	.050
	15	1.000	1.000	1.000	1.000	1.000	1.000	.998	.981	.882	.518	.208
	16	1.000	1.000	1.000	1.000	1.000	1.000	1.000	.998	.977	.833	.582
	17	1.000	1.000	1.000	1.000	1.000	1.000	1.000	1.000	1.000	1.000	1.000
$n = 18$	0	.397	.150	.018	.002	.000	.000	.000	.000	.000	.000	.000
	1	.774	.450	.099	.014	.001	.000	.000	.000	.000	.000	.000
	2	.942	.734	.271	.060	.008	.001	.000	.000	.000	.000	.000
	3	.989	.902	.501	.165	.033	.004	.000	.000	.000	.000	.000
	4	.998	.972	.716	.333	.094	.015	.001	.000	.000	.000	.000
	5	1.000	.994	.867	.534	.209	.048	.006	.000	.000	.000	.000
	6	1.000	.999	.949	.722	.374	.119	.020	.001	.000	.000	.000
	7	1.000	1.000	.984	.859	.563	.240	.058	.006	.000	.000	.000
	8	1.000	1.000	.996	.940	.737	.407	.135	.021	.001	.000	.000
	9	1.000	1.000	.999	.979	.865	.593	.263	.060	.004	.000	.000
	10	1.000	1.000	1.000	.994	.942	.760	.437	.141	.016	.000	.000
	11	1.000	1.000	1.000	.999	.980	.881	.626	.278	.051	.001	.000
	12	1.000	1.000	1.000	1.000	.994	.952	.791	.466	.133	.006	.000
	13	1.000	1.000	1.000	1.000	.999	.985	.906	.667	.284	.028	.002
	14	1.000	1.000	1.000	1.000	1.000	.996	.967	.835	.499	.098	.011
	15	1.000	1.000	1.000	1.000	1.000	.999	.992	.940	.729	.266	.058
	16	1.000	1.000	1.000	1.000	1.000	1.000	.999	.986	.901	.550	.226
	17	1.000	1.000	1.000	1.000	1.000	1.000	1.000	.998	.982	.850	.603
	18	1.000	1.000	1.000	1.000	1.000	1.000	1.000	1.000	1.000	1.000	1.000

TABLE 4. (Continued)

		P										
	c	.05	.10	.20	.30	.40	.50	.60	.70	.80	.90	.95
n = 19	0	.377	.135	.014	.001	.000	.000	.000	.000	.000	.090	.000
	1	.755	.420	.083	.010	.001	.000	.000	.000	.000	.000	.000
	2	.933	.705	.237	.046	.005	.000	.000	.000	.000	.000	.000
	3	.987	.885	.455	.133	.023	.002	.000	.000	.000	.000	.000
	4	.998	.965	.673	.282	.070	.010	.001	.000	.000	.000	.000
	5	1.000	.991	.837	.474	.163	.032	.003	.000	.000	.000	.000
	6	1.000	.998	.932	.666	.308	.084	.012	.001	.000	.000	.000
	7	1.000	1.000	.977	.818	.488	.180	.035	.003	.000	.000	.000
	8	1.000	1.000	.993	.916	.667	.324	.088	.011	.000	.000	.000
	9	1.000	1.000	.998	.967	.814	.500	.186	.033	.002	.000	.000
	10	1.000	1.000	1.000	.989	.912	.676	.333	.084	.007	.000	.000
	11	1.000	1.000	1.000	.997	.965	.820	.512	.182	.023	.000	.000
	12	1.000	1.000	1.000	.999	.988	.916	.692	.334	.068	.002	.000
	13	1.000	1.000	1.000	1.000	.997	.968	.837	.526	.163	.009	.000
	14	1.000	1.000	1.000	1.000	.999	.990	.930	.718	.327	.035	.002
	15	1.000	1.000	1.000	1.000	1.000	.998	.977	.867	.545	.115	.013
	16	1.000	1.000	1.000	1.000	1.000	1.000	.995	.954	.763	.295	.067
	17	1.000	1.000	1.000	1.000	1.000	1.000	.999	.990	.917	.580	.245
	18	1.000	1.000	1.000	1.000	1.000	1.000	1.000	.999	.986	.865	.623
	19	1.000	1.000	1.000	1.000	1.000	1.000	1.000	1.000	1.000	1.000	1.000
n = 20	0	.358	.122	.012	.001	.000	.000	.000	.000	.000	.000	.000
	1	.736	.392	.069	.008	.001	.000	.000	.000	.000	.000	.000
	2	.925	.677	.206	.035	.004	.004	.000	.000	.000	.000	.000
	3	.984	.867	.411	.107	.016	.001	.000	.000	.000	.000	.000
	4	.997	.957	.630	.238	.051	.006	.000	.000	.000	.000	.000
	5	1.000	.989	.804	.416	.126	.021	.002	.000	.000	.000	.000
	6	1.000	.998	.913	.608	.250	.058	.006	.000	.000	.000	.000
	7	1.000	1.000	.968	.772	.416	.132	.021	.001	.000	.000	.000
	8	1.000	1.000	.990	.887	.596	.252	.057	.005	.000	.000	.000
	9	1.000	1.000	.997	.952	.755	.412	.128	.017	.001	.000	.000
	10	1.000	1.000	.999	.983	.872	.588	.245	.048	.003	.000	.000
	11	1.000	1.000	1.000	.995	.943	.748	.404	.113	.010	.000	.000
	12	1.000	1.000	1.000	.999	.979	.868	.584	.228	.032	.000	.000
	13	1.000	1.000	1.000	1.000	.994	.942	.750	.392	.087	.002	.000
	14	1.000	1.000	1.000	1.000	.998	.979	.874	.584	.196	.011	.000
	15	1.000	1.000	1.000	1.000	1.000	.994	.949	.762	.370	.043	.003
	16	1.000	1.000	1.000	1.000	1.000	.999	.984	.893	.589	.133	.016
	17	1.000	1.000	1.000	1.000	1.000	1.000	.996	.965	.794	.323	.075
	18	1.000	1.000	1.000	1.000	1.000	1.000	.999	.992	.931	.608	.264
	19	1.000	1.000	1.000	1.000	1.000	1.000	1.000	.999	.988	.878	.642
	20	1.000	1.000	1.000	1.000	1.000	1.000	1.000	1.000	1.000	1.000	1.000

TABLE 4. (Continued)

		p										
		.05	.10	.20	.30	.40	.50	.60	.70	.80	.90	.95
	c											
n = 25	0	.277	.072	.004	.000	.000	.000	.000	.000	.000	.000	.000
	1	.642	.271	.027	.002	.000	.000	.000	.000	.000	.000	.000
	2	.873	.537	.098	.009	.000	.000	.000	.000	.000	.000	.000
	3	.966	.764	.234	.033	.002	.000	.000	.000	.000	.000	.000
	4	.993	.902	.421	.090	.009	.000	.000	.000	.000	.000	.000
	5	.999	.967	.617	.193	.029	.002	.000	.000	.000	.000	.000
	6	1.000	.991	.780	.341	.074	.007	.000	.000	.000	.000	.000
	7	1.000	.998	.891	.512	.154	.022	.001	.000	.000	.000	.000
	8	1.000	1.000	.953	.677	.274	.054	.004	.000	.000	.000	.000
	9	1.000	1.000	.983	.811	.425	.115	.013	.000	.000	.000	.000
	10	1.000	1.000	.994	.902	.586	.212	.034	.002	.000	.000	.000
	11	1.000	1.000	.998	.956	.732	.345	.078	.006	.000	.000	.000
	12	1.000	1.000	1.000	.983	.846	.500	.154	.017	.000	.000	.000
	13	1.000	1.000	1.000	.994	.922	.655	.268	.044	.002	.000	.000
	14	1.000	1.000	1.006	.998	.966	.788	.414	.096	.006	.000	.000
	15	1.000	1.000	1.000	1.000	.987	.885	.575	.189	.017	.000	.000
	16	1.000	1.000	1.000	1.000	.996	.946	.726	.323	.047	.000	.000
	17	1.000	1.000	1.000	1.000	.999	.978	.846	.488	.109	.002	.000
	18	1.000	1.000	1.000	1.000	1.000	.993	.926	.659	.220	.009	.000
	19	1.000	1.000	1.000	1.000	1,000	.998	.971	.807	.383	.033	.001
	20	1.000	1.000	1.000	1.000	1.000	1.000	.991	.910	.579	.098	.007
	21	1.000	1.000	1.000	1.000	1.000	1.000	.998	.967	.766	.236	.034
	22	1.000	1.000	1.000	1.000	1.000	1.000	1.000	.991	.902	.463	.127
	23	1.000	1.000	1.000	1.000	1.000	1.000	1.000	.998	.973	.729	.358
	24	1.000	1.000	1.000	1.000	1.000	1.000	1.000	1.000	.996	.928	.723
	25	1.000	1.000	1.000	1.000	1.000	1.000	1.000	1.000	1.000	1.000	1.000

TABLE 5. VALUES FOR POISSON DISTRIBUTION

x\λ	0.1	0.2	0.3	0.4	0.5	0.6	0.7	0.8	0.9	1.0
0	0.9048	0.8187	0.7408	0.6703	0.6065	0.5488	0.4966	0.4493	0.4066	0.3679
1	0.0905	0.1637	0.2222	0.2681	0.3033	0.3293	0.3476	0.3595	0.3639	0.3679
2	0.0045	0.0164	0.0333	0.0536	0.0758	0.0988	0.1217	0.1438	0.1647	0.1839
3	0.0002	0.0011	0.0033	0.0072	0.0126	0.0198	0.0284	0.0383	0.0494	0.0613
4	0.0000	0.0001	0.0003	0.0007	0.0016	0.0030	0.0050	0.0077	0.0111	0.0153
5	0.0000	0.0000	0.0000	0.0001	0.0002	0.0004	0.0007	0.0012	0.0020	0.0031
6	0.0000	0.0000	0.0000	0.0000	0.0000	0.0000	0.0001	0.0002	0.0003	0.0005
7	0.0000	0.0000	0.0000	0.0000	0.0000	0.0000	0.0000	0.0000	0.0000	0.0001

x\λ	1.1	1.2	1.3	1.4	1.5	1.6	1.7	1.8	1.9	2.0
0	0.3329	0.3012	0.2725	0.2466	0.2231	0.2019	0.1827	0.1653	0.1496	0.1353
1	0.3662	0.3614	0.3543	0.3452	0.3347	0.3230	0.3106	0.2975	0.2842	0.2707
2	0.2014	0.2169	0.2303	0.2417	0.2510	0.2584	0.2640	0.2678	0.2700	0.2707
3	0.0738	0.0867	0.0998	0.1128	0.1255	0.1378	0.1496	0.1607	0.1710	0.1804
4	0.0203	0.0260	0.0324	0.0395	0.0471	0.0551	0.0636	0.0723	0.0812	0.0902
5	0.0045	0.0062	0.0084	0.0111	0.0141	0.0176	0.0216	0.0260	0.0309	0.0361
6	0.0008	0.0012	0.0018	0.0026	0.0035	0.0047	0.0061	0.0078	0.0098	0.0120
7	0.0001	0.0002	0.0003	0.0005	0.0008	0.0011	0.0015	0.0020	0.0027	0.0034
8	0.0000	0.0000	0.0001	0.0001	0.0001	0.0002	0.0003	0.0005	0.0006	0.0009
9	0.0000	0.0000	0.0000	0.0000	0.0000	0.0000	0.0001	0.0001	0.0001	0.0002

x\λ	2.1	2.2	2.3	2.4	2.5	2.6	2.7	2.8	2.9	3.0
0	0.1225	0.1108	0.1003	0.0907	0.0821	0.0743	0.0672	0.0608	0.0550	0.0498
1	0.2572	0.2438	0.2306	0.2177	0.2052	0.1931	0.1815	0.1703	0.1596	0.1494
2	0.2700	0.2681	0.2652	0.2613	0.2565	0.2510	0.2450	0.2384	0.2314	0.2240
3	0.1890	0.1966	0.2033	0.2090	0.2138	0.2176	0.2205	0.2225	0.2237	0.2240
4	0.0992	0.1082	0.1169	0.1254	0.1336	0.1414	0.1488	0.1557	0.1622	0.1680
5	0.0417	0.0476	0.0538	0.0602	0.0668	0.0735	0.0804	0.0872	0.0940	0.1008
6	0.0146	0.0174	0.0206	0.0241	0.0278	0.0319	0.0362	0.0407	0.0455	0.0504
7	0.0044	0.0055	0.0068	0.0083	0.0099	0.0118	0.0139	0.0163	0.0088	0.0216
8	0.0011	0.0015	0.0019	0.0025	0.0031	0.0038	0.0047	0.0057	0.0068	0.0081
9	0.0003	0.0004	0.0005	0.0007	0.0009	0.0010	0.0014	0.0018	0.0022	0.0027
10	0.0001	0.0001	0.0001	0.0002	0.0002	0.0003	0.0004	0.0005	0.0006	0.0008
11	0.0000	0.0000	0.0000	0.0000	0.0000	0.0001	0.0001	0.0001	0.0002	0.0002
12	0.0000	0.0000	0.0000	0.0000	0.0000	0.0000	0.0000	0.0000	0.0000	0.0001

TABLE 5. (Continued)

x \ λ	3.1	3.2	3.3	3.4	3.5	3.6	3.7	3.8	3.9	4.0
0	0.0450	0.0408	0.0379	0.0334	0.0302	0.0273	0.0247	0.0224	0.0202	0.0183
1	0.1397	0.1304	0.1217	0.1135	0.1057	0.0984	0.0915	0.0850	0.0789	0.0733
2	0.2165	0.2087	0.2008	0.1929	0.1850	0.1771	0.1692	0.1615	0.1539	0.1465
3	0.2237	0.2226	0.2209	0.2186	0.2158	0.2125	0.2087	0.2046	0.2001	0.1954
4	0.1734	0.1781	0.1823	0.1858	0.1888	0.1912	0.1931	0.1944	0.1951	0.1954
5	0.1075	0.1140	0.1203	0.1264	0.1322	0.1377	0.1429	0.1477	0.1522	0.1563
6	0.0555	0.0608	0.0662	0.0716	0.0771	0.0826	0.0881	0.0936	0.0989	0.1042
7	0.0246	0.0278	0.0312	0.0348	0.0385	0.0425	0.0466	0.0508	0.0551	0.0595
8	0.0095	0.0111	0.0129	0.0148	0.0169	0.0191	0.0215	0.0241	0.0269	0.0298
9	0.0033	0.0040	0.0047	0.0056	0.0066	0.0076	0.0089	0.0102	0.0116	0.0132
10	0.0010	0.0013	0.0016	0.0019	0.0023	0.0028	0.0033	0.0039	0.0045	0.0053
11	0.0003	0.0004	0.0005	0.0006	0.0007	0.0009	0.0011	0.0013	0.0016	0.0019
12	0.0001	0.0001	0.0001	0.0002	0.0002	0.0003	0.0003	0.0004	0.0005	0.0006
13	0.0000	0.0000	0.0000	0.0000	0.0001	0.0001	0.0001	0.0001	0.0002	0.0002
14	0.0000	0.0000	0.0000	0.0000	0.0000	0.0000	0.0000	0.0000	0.0000	0.0001

For a given value of λ, entry indicates the proability of obtaining a specified value of x.

TABLE 6 : CONTROL CHART FACTORS

Sample Size, n	Factors for $\bar{x}$ Charts			Factors for R Charts	
	$d_2 = \frac{R}{\sigma}$	$A_2 = \frac{3}{d_2\sqrt{n}}$	$d_3 = \frac{\sigma_R}{\sigma}$	$D_3 = 1 - \frac{3d_3}{d_2}$	$D_4 = 1 + \frac{3d_3}{d_2}$
2	1.128	1.881	0.853	0	3.269
3	1.693	1.023	0.883	0	2.574
4	2.059	0.729	0.880	0	2.282
5	2.326	0.577	0.864	0	2.114
6	2.534	0.483	0.848	0	2.004
7	2.704	0.419	0.833	0.076	1.924
8	2.847	0.373	0.820	0.136	1.864
9	2.970	0.337	0.808	0.184	1.816
10	3.078	0.308	0.797	0.223	1.777
11	3.173	0.285	0.787	0.256	1.744
12	3.258	0.266	0.779	0.283	1.717
13	3.336	0.249	0.770	0.308	1.692
14	3.407	0.235	0.763	0.328	1.672
15	3.472	0.223	0.756	0.347	1.653
16	3.532	0.212	0.750	0.363	1.637
17	3.588	0.203	0.744	0.378	1.622
18	3.640	0.194	0.739	0.391	1.609
19	3.689	0.187	0.734	0.403	1.597
20	3.735	0.180	0.729	0.414	1.586
21	3.778	0.173	0.724	0.425	1.575
22	3.819	0.167	0.720	0.434	1.566
23	3.858	0.162	0.716	0.443	1.567
24	3.895	0.157	0.712	0.452	1.548
25	3.931	0.153	0.708	0.460	1.540

Note : If $1 - 3d_3/d_2 < 0$, then $D_3 = 0$

TABLE 7 : ACCEPTANCE SAMPLING PLAN

Serial	LTPD÷AQL	n.AQL
0	44.89	0.052
1	10.946	0.355
2	6.509	0.818
3	4.890	1.366
4	4.057	1.970
5	3.549	2.613
6	3.206	3.286
7	2.957	3.981
8	2.768	4.695
9	2.618	5.426

TABLE 8 : INTEREST RATE FACTORS (SPPWF)

Present Value of Re 1

Year Hence	1%	2%	4%	6%	8%	10%	12%	14%	15%	16%	18%	20%	22%	24%	25%	26%	28%	30%	35%	40%	45%	50%
1	0.990	0.980	0.962	0.943	0.926	0.909	0.893	0.877	0.870	0.862	0.847	0.833	0.820	0.806	0.800	0.794	0.781	0.769	0.741	0.714	0.690	0.667
2	0.980	0.961	0.925	0.890	0.857	0.826	0.797	0.769	0.765	0.743	0.718	0.694	0.672	0.650	0.640	0.630	0.610	0.592	0.549	0.510	0.476	0.444
3	0.971	0.942	0.889	0.840	0.794	0.751	0.712	0.675	0.658	0.641	0.609	0.579	0.551	0.524	0.512	0.500	0.477	0.455	0.406	0.364	0.328	0.296
4	0.961	0.924	0.855	0.792	0.732	0.683	0.636	0.592	0.572	0.552	0.516	0.482	0.451	0.423	0.410	0.397	0.373	0.350	0.301	0.260	0.226	0.198
5	0.951	0.906	0.822	0.747	0.681	0.621	0.567	0.519	0.497	0.476	0.437	0.402	0.370	0.341	0.328	0.315	0.291	0.269	0.223	0.186	0.156	0.132
6	0.942	0.888	0.790	0.705	0.630	0.564	0.507	0.456	0.432	0.410	0.370	0.335	0.303	0.275	0.262	0.250	0.227	0.207	0.165	0.133	0.108	0.088
7	0.933	0.871	0.760	0.665	0.583	0.513	0.452	0.400	0.376	0.354	0.314	0.279	0.249	0.222	0.210	0.198	0.178	0.159	0.122	0.095	0.074	0.059
8	0.923	0.853	0.731	0.627	0.540	0.467	0.404	0.351	0.327	0.305	0.266	0.233	0.204	0.179	0.168	0.157	0.139	0.123	0.091	0.068	0.051	0.039
9	0.914	0.837	0.703	0.592	0.500	0.424	0.361	0.308	0.284	0.263	0.225	0.194	0.167	0.144	0.134	0.125	0.108	0.094	0.067	0.048	0.035	0.026
10	0.905	0.820	0.676	0.558	0.463	0.386	0.322	0.270	0.247	0.227	0.191	0.162	0.137	0.116	0.107	0.099	0.085	0.073	0.050	0.035	0.024	0.017
11	0.896	0.804	0.650	0.527	0.429	0.350	0.287	0.237	0.215	0.195	0.162	0.135	0.112	0.094	0.086	0.079	0.066	0.056	0.037	0.025	0.017	0.012
12	0.887	0.788	0.625	0.497	0.397	0.319	0.257	0.208	0.187	0.168	0.137	0.112	0.092	0.076	0.069	0.062	0.052	0.043	0.027	0.018	0.012	0.008
13	0.879	0.773	0.601	0.469	0.368	0.290	0.229	0.182	0.163	0.145	0.116	0.093	0.075	0.061	0.055	0.050	0.040	0.033	0.020	0.013	0.008	0.005
14	0.870	0.758	0.577	0.442	0.340	0.263	0.205	0.160	0.141	0.125	0.099	0.078	0.062	0.049	0.044	0.039	0.032	0.025	0.015	0.009	0.006	0.003
15	0.861	0.743	0.555	0.417	0.315	0.239	0.183	0.140	0.123	0.108	0.084	0.065	0.051	0.040	0.035	0.031	0.025	0.020	0.011	0.006	0.004	0.002
16	0.583	0.728	0.534	0.394	0.292	0.218	0.163	0.123	0.107	0.093	0.071	0.054	0.042	0.032	0.028	0.025	0.019	0.015	0.008	0.005	0.003	0.002
17	0.844	0.714	0.513	0.371	0.270	0.198	0.146	0.180	0.093	0.080	0.060	0.045	0.034	0.026	0.023	0.020	0.015	0.012	0.006	0.003	0.002	0.001
18	0.836	0.700	0.494	0.350	0.250	0.198	0.146	0.108	0.093	0.080	0.060	0.045	0.034	0.026	0.023	0.020	0.015	0.012	0.006	0.003	0.002	0.001
19	0.828	0.686	0.475	0.331	0.232	0.164	0.116	0.083	0.070	0.060	0.043	0.031	0.023	0.017	0.014	0.012	0.009	0.007	0.003	0.002	0.001	
20	0.820	0.673	0.456	0.312	0.215	0.149	0.104	0.073	0.061	0.051	0.037	0.026	0.019	0.014	0.012	0.010	0.007	0.005	0.002	0.001	0.001	
21	0.811	0.660	0.439	0.294	0.199	0.135	0.093	0.064	0.053	0.044	0.031	0.022	0.015	0.011	0.009	0.008	0.006	0.004	0.002	0.001		

Year Hence	1%	2%	4%	6%	8%	10%	12%	14%	15%	16%	18%	20%	22%	24%	25%	26%	28%	30%	35%	40%	45%	50%
22	0.803	0.647	0.422	0.278	0.184	0.123	0.083	0.056	0.046	0.038	0.026	0.018	0.013	0.009	0.007	0.006	0.004	0.003	0.001	0.001		
23	0.795	0.634	0.406	0.262	0.170	0.112	0.074	0.049	0.040	0.033	0.022	0.015	0.010	0.007	0.006	0.005	0.003	0.002	0.001			
24	0.788	0.622	0.390	0.247	0.158	0.102	0.066	0.043	0.035	0.028	0.019	0.013	0.008	0.006	0.005	0.004	0.003	0.002	0.001			
25	0.780	0.610	0.375	0.233	0.146	0.092	0.059	0.038	0.030	0.024	0.016	0.010	0.007	0.005	0.004	0.003	0.002	0.001	0.001			
26	0.772	0.598	0.361	0.220	0.135	0.084	0.053	0.033	0.026	0.021	0.014	0.009	0.006	0.004	0.003	0.002	0.002	0.001				
27	0.764	0.586	0.347	0.207	0.125	0.076	0.047	0.029	0.023	0.018	0.011	0.007	0.005	0.003	0.002	0.002	0.001	0.001				
28	0.757	0.574	0.333	0.196	0.116	0.069	0.042	0.026	0.020	0.016	0.010	0.006	0.004	0.002	0.002	0.002	0.001	0.001				
29	0.749	0.563	0.321	0.185	0.107	0.063	0.037	0.022	0.017	0.014	0.008	0.005	0.003	0.002	0.002	0.001	0.001	0.001				
30	0.742	0.552	0.308	0.174	0.099	0.057	0.033	0.020	0.015	0.012	0.007	0.004	0.003	0.002	0.001	0.001	0.001					
40	0.672	0.453	0.208	0.097	0.046	0.022	0.011	0.005	0.004	0.003	0.001	0.001										
50	0.608	0.372	0.141	0.054	0.021	0.009	0.003	0.001	0.001	0.001												

TABLE 9 : INTEREST RATE FACTORS (USPWF)

Present Value of Re 1

Year Hence	1%	2%	4%	6%	8%	10%	12%	14%	15%	16%	18%	20%	22%	24%	25%	26%	28%	30%	35%	40%	45%	50%
1	0.990	0.980	0.962	0.943	0.926	0.909	0.893	0.877	0.870	0.862	0.847	0.833	0.820	0.806	0.800	0.794	0.781	0.769	0.741	0.714	0.690	0.667
2	1.970	1.942	1.886	1.833	1.783	1.736	1.690	1.647	1.646	1.605	1.566	1.528	1.492	1.457	1.440	1.424	1.392	1.361	1.289	1.224	1.165	1.111
3	2.941	2.884	2.775	2.673	2.577	2.487	2.402	2.322	2.283	2.246	2.174	2.106	2.042	1.981	1.952	1.923	1.868	1.816	1.696	1.589	1.493	1.407
4	3.902	3.808	3.630	3.465	3.312	3.170	3.037	2.914	2.855	2.798	2.690	2.589	2.494	2.404	2.362	2.320	2.241	2.166	1.997	1.849	1.720	1.605
5	4.853	4.713	4.452	4.212	3.993	3.791	3.605	3.433	3.352	3.274	3.127	2.991	2.864	2.745	2.689	2.635	2.532	2.436	2.220	2.035	1.876	1.737
6	5.795	5.601	5.242	4.917	4.623	4.355	4.111	3.889	3.784	3.685	3.498	3.326	3.167	3.020	2.951	2.885	2.759	2.643	2.385	2.168	1.983	1.824
7	6.728	6.472	6.002	5.582	5.206	4.868	4.564	4.288	4.160	4.039	3.812	3.605	3.416	3.242	3.161	3.083	2.937	2.802	2.508	2.263	2.057	1.883
8	7.652	7.325	6.733	6.210	5.747	5.335	4.968	4.639	4.487	4.344	4.078	3.837	3.619	3.421	3.329	3.241	3.076	2.925	2.598	2.331	2.108	1.922
9	8.566	8.162	7.435	6.802	6.247	5.759	5.328	4.946	4.772	4.607	4.303	4.031	3.786	3.566	3.463	3.366	3.184	3.019	2.665	2.379	2.144	1.948
10	9.471	8.983	8.111	7.360	6.710	6.145	5.650	5.216	5.019	4.833	4.494	4.192	3.923	3.682	3.571	3.465	3.269	3.092	2.715	2.414	2.168	1.965
11	10.368	9.787	8.760	7.887	7.139	6.495	5.937	5.435	5.234	5.029	4.656	4.327	4.035	3.776	3.656	3.544	3.335	3.147	2.752	2.438	2.185	1.977
12	11.255	10.575	9.385	8.384	7.536	6.814	6.194	5.660	5.421	5.197	4.793	4.439	4.127	3.851	3.725	3.606	3.387	3.190	2.779	2.465	2.196	1.985
13	12.134	11.343	9.986	8.853	7.904	7.103	6.424	5.842	5.583	5.342	4.910	4.533	4.203	3.912	3.780	3.656	3.427	3.223	2.799	2.468	2.204	1.990
14	13.004	12.106	10.563	9.295	8.244	7.367	6.628	6.002	5.724	5.468	5.008	4.611	4.265	3.962	3.824	3.695	3.459	3.249	2.814	2.477	2.210	1.993
15	13.865	12.849	11.118	9.712	8.559	7.606	6.811	6.142	5.847	5.575	5.092	4.675	4.315	4.001	3.859	3.726	3.483	3.268	2.825	2.484	2.214	1.995
16	14.718	13.578	11.652	10.106	8.851	7.824	6.974	6.265	5.954	5.669	5.162	4.730	4.357	4.033	3.887	3.751	3.503	3.283	2.834	2.489	2.216	1.997
17	15.562	14.292	12.166	10.477	9.122	8.022	7.120	6.373	6.047	5.749	5.222	4.775	4.391	4.059	3.910	3.771	3.518	3.295	2.840	2.492	2.218	1.998
18	16.398	14.992	12.659	10.828	9.372	8.201	7.250	6.467	6.128	5.818	5.273	4.812	4.419	4.080	3.928	3.786	3.529	3.304	2.844	2.494	2.219	1.999
19	17.226	15.678	13.134	11.158	9.604	8.365	7.366	6.550	6.198	5.877	5.316	4.844	4.442	4.097	3.942	3.799	3.539	3.311	2.848	2.496	2.220	1.999
20	18.046	16.351	13.590	11.470	9.818	8.514	7.469	6.623	6.259	5.929	5.353	4.870	4.460	4.110	3.954	3.808	3.546	3.316	2.850	2.497	2.221	1.999
21	18.857	17.011	14.029	11.764	10.017	8.649	7.562	6.687	6.312	5.973	5.384	4.891	4.476	4.121	3.963	3.816	3.551	3.320	2.852	2.498	2.221	2.000

N Year Hence	1%	2%	4%	6%	8%	10%	12%	14%	15%	16%	18%	20%	22%	24%	25%	26%	28%	30%	35%	40%	45%	50%
22	19.660	17.658	14.451	12.042	10.201	8.772	7.645	6.743	6.359	6.011	5.410	4.909	4.488	4.130	3.970	3.822	3.556	3.323	2.853	2.498	2.222	2.000
23	20.456	18.292	14.857	12.303	10.371	8.883	7.718	6.792	6.399	6.044	5.432	4.925	4.499	4.137	3.976	3.827	3.559	3.325	2.854	2.499	2.222	2.000
24	21.243	18.914	15.247	12.550	10.529	8.985	7.784	6.835	6.434	6.073	5.451	4.937	4.507	4.143	3.981	3.831	3.562	3.327	2.855	2.499	2.222	2.000
25	22.023	19.523	15.622	12.783	10.675	9.077	7.843	6.873	6.464	6.097	5.467	4.948	4.514	4.147	3.985	3.834	3.564	3.329	2.856	2.499	2.222	2.000
26	22.795	20.121	15.983	13.003	10.810	9.161	7.896	6.906	6.491	6.118	5.480	4.956	4.520	4.151	3.988	3.837	3.566	3.330	2.856	2.500	2.222	2.000
27	23.560	20.707	16.330	13.211	10.935	9.237	7.943	6.935	6.514	6.136	5.492	4.964	4.524	4.154	3.990	3.839	3.567	3.331	2.856	2.500	2.222	2.000
28	24.316	21.281	16.663	13.406	11.051	9.307	7.984	6.961	6.534	6.152	5.502	4.970	4.528	4.157	3.992	3.840	3.568	3.331	2.857	2.500	2.222	2^000
29	25.066	21.844	16.984	13.591	11.158	9.370	8.022	6.983	6.551	6.166	5.510	4.975	4.531	4.159	3.994	3.841	3.569	3.332	2.857	2.500	2.222	2.000
30	25.808	22.396	17.292	13.765	11.258	9.427	8.055	7.003	6.566	6.177	5.517	4.979	4.534	4.160	3.995	3.842	3.569	3.332	2.857	2.500	2.222	2.000
40	32.835	27.355	19.793	15.046	11.925	9.779	8.244	7.105	6.642	6.234	5.548	4.997	4.544	4.166	3.999	3.846	3.571	3.333	2.857	2.500	2.222	2.000
50	39.196	31.424	21.482	15.762	12.234	9.915	8.304	7.133	6.661	6.246	5.554	4.999	4.545	4.167	4.000	3.846	3.571	3.333	2.857	2.500	2.222	2.000

TABLE 10 : LEARNING CURVES: TABLE OF UNIT VALUES

Unit	60%	65%	70%	75%	80%	85%	90%	95%
1	1.0000	1 0000	10000	1.0000	1.0000	1.0000	1.0000	1.0000
2	.6000	.6500	.7000	.7500	.8000	.8500	.9000	.9500
3	4450	.5052	.5682	.6338	.7021	.7729	.8462	9219
4	3600	.4225	.4900	.5625	.6400	.7225	.8100	9025
5	.3054	.3678	.4368	.5127	5956	.6857	.7830	.8877
6	2670	.3284	.3977	.4754	.5617	.6570	.7616	.8758
7	2383	.2984	.3674	.4459	.5345	.6337	.7439	8659
8	2160	.2746	.3430	.4219	.5120	.6141	.7290	.8574
9	.1980	.2.552	.3228	.4017	.4930	.5974	7161	.8499
10	1832	.2391	.3058	.3846	.4765	.5828	.7047	.8433
12	.1602	.2135	.2784	.3565	.4493	.5584	.6854	.8320
14	.1430	.1940	.2572	.3344	.4276	.5386	.6696	.8226
16	.1290	.1785	.2401	.3164	.4096	.5220	.6561	.8145
18	1188	.1659	.2260	.3013	.3944	.5078	.6445	.8074
20	.1099	.1554	2141	.2884	.3812	.4954	6342	.8012
22	.1025	.1465	,2038	.2772	.3697	.4844	.6251	.7955
24	.0961	.1387	.1949	.2674	.3595	.4747	.6169	.7904
25	.0933	.1353	.1908	2629	.3548	.4701	.6131	.7880
30	.0815	.1208	.1737	.2437	.3346	.4505	.5963	.7775
35	.0728	.1097	.1605	.2286	.3184	.4345	.5825	.7687
40	.0660	.1010	.1498	.2163	.3050	.4211	.5708	.7611
45	0605	.0939	.1410	.2060	2936	.4096	.5607	.7545
50	.0560	0879	.1336	.1972	.2838	.3996	.5518	.7486
60	.0489	.0785	.1216	.1828	.2676	.3829	5367	.7386
70	.0437	.0713	.1123	.1715	.2547	.3693	.5243	7302
SO	.0396	,0657	.1049	.1622	.2440	.3579	5137	.7231
90	.0363	.0610	.0987	.1545	.2349	.3482	.5046	.7168
100	.0336	.0572	.0935	.1479	.2271	.3397	.4966	.7112
120	.0294	.0510	.0851	.1371	.2141	.3255	.4830	.7017
140	.0262	.0464	.0786	.1287	,2038	3139	.4718	.6937
160	.0237	.0427	.0734	.1217	.1952	.3042	.4623	6869
180	.0218	.0397	.0691	.1159	.1879	.2959	.4541	.6809
200	.0201	.0371	.0655	.1109	.1816	.2887	.4469	.6757

Unit	60%	65%	70%	75%	80%	85%	90%	95%
250	.0171	.0323	.0584	.1011	.1691	.2740	.4320	.6646
300	.0149	.0289	.0531	.0937	.1594	.2625	.4202	.6557
350	.0133	.0262	.0491	.0879	.1517	.2532	.4105	.6482
400	.0121	.0241	.0458	.0832	.1453	.2454	.4022	.6419
450	.0111	.0224	.0431	.0792	.1399	.2387	.3951	.6363
500	.0103	.0210	.0408	.0758	.1352	.2329	.3888	.6314
600	.0090	.0188	.0372	.0703	.1275	.2232	.3782	6229
700	.0080	.0171	.0344	.0659	.1214	.2152	.3694	.6158
800	.0073	.0157	.0321	.0624	.1163	.2086	.3620	.6098
900	.0067	.0146	.0302	.0594	.1119	.2029	.3556	.6045
1,000	.0062	.0137	.0286	.0569	.1082	.1980	.3499	.5998
1,200	.0054	.0122	.0260	.0527	.1020	.1897	.3404	.5918
1,400	.0048	.0111	.0240	.0495	.0971	.1830	.3325	.5850
1,600	.0044	.0102	.0225	.0468	.0930	.1773	.3258	.5793
1,800	.0040	.0095	.0211	.0446	.0895	.1725	.3200	.5743
2,000	.0037	.0089	.0200	.0427	.0866	.1683	.3149	.5698
2,500	.0031	.0077	.0178	.0389	.0806	.1597	.3044	.5605
3,000	.0027	.0069	.0162	.0360	.0760	.1530	.2961	.5530

Bibliography

Adams E.C. and R.J. Ebert, Production and operation Management, Prentice Hall, NJ 2002.

Agrawal S.C., Maintenance Management, Prabhu Book Service 1968.

Baçkman M., Location Theory, Random House, N.Y. 1968.

Buffa E.S., Operation Management, John Wiley, N.Y. 1976.

Buffa E.S. and Sarin, John Wiley, N.Y. 2004.

Buffa E.S. and W.H. Taubert, Production, Inventory System, Planning and Control, Homewood Illinois, Richord Inc. 1972.

Francis R.L., Facilities layout and location, Prentice Hall W.J., 1974.

Chary S.N., Theory and Problems in Production and Operations Management, Tata Mc Graw-Hill Publishing Co. New Delhi 1997.

Churchman, C.W., R. Achoff and E.L. Arnoff, Introduction to operations Research, John wiley and Sons 1957.

Deming, W.E., Theory of Sampling, John Wiley and Sons, N.Y.

Gopal I, Anand G. and M.K. Starr Supply Chain Management for Global Competitiveness – 1998.

Gopal Krishnan P. and R.G. Shandilya; Management of Quality and Inspections, Tata McGraw-Hill New Delhi 1979.

Grant B. and R.S. Leaves Worth, Statistical Quality Control, Mc Graw Hill N.Y. 1972.

Gupta S.P. and M.P. Gupta, Business Statistics, Sultan Chand & Sons, 1972.

Hall, W.R., Zero Inventories, Dow Jones Irwin, 1983.

I.L.O. Introduction to workstudy, ILO Geneva 1979.

I.L.O. Wages and Working conditions in Multinational Enterprises I.L.O. Geneva 1978.

James L. Riggs; Production System, John niley and Sons, Singapore 1987.

Joseph S. Martinich, Production and Operations Management, John wiley & Sons 1997.

Juran J.M., F.M. Gryna and R.S. Bingham, Quality Control Handbook, Mc Graw-Hill, N.Y. 1978.

Miles L.D., Techniques of Value Analysis and Engineering, Mc Graw Hill, N.Y. 1962.

Muddel M.C. Motion and Time Study, Prentice Hall N.J. 1978.

N.G. Nair, Production and Operations Management, Tata McGraw Hill N.D., 1997.

Norman Gaither, Greg Frazier Operations Management, Thomson-South Western 2002.

Peter Drucker, F. The Practice of Management, Harper and Row N.Y. 1954.

Riggs J.L., Production System – Planning, Analysis and Control, John Willey – N.Y. 1970.

Starr M.K., Operations Management, Prentice Hall, N.J. 1978.

Sunil Chopra, Peter Meindal; Supply Chain Management, Strategy Planning and Operations – Prentice Hall College D.U. 2004.

Vohra N.D., Quantitative Techniques in Management, Macmillan N.D. 1990.